"Showing clarity and theological awareness, Craig Bartholomew and Heath Thomas open up these important books. With close attention to the text, they demonstrate the abiding significance of their message. This book deserves to be read widely and should have a place on any reading list on the Minor Prophets. Highly commended!"
David Firth, tutor in Old Testament at Trinity College, Bristol,
and author of *Including the Stranger: Foreigners in the Former Prophets*

"This timely theological reading of the Twelve attends to the long impact they have had: in their original context; as practiced by Jesus of Nazareth; as read by New Testament authors; and in light of the concerns of our own time. It is an accessible introduction to the Twelve that adds more—highlighting key texts and themes arising in individual books and pointing out the connections that hint at their preservation as an anthology. Authors Bartholomew and Thomas, like prophets of old, listen for the voice of God. This volume is no mere academic exercise but will shape faithful action in its readers."
Jeanette Mathews, author of *Performing Habakkuk* and *Prophets as Performers*

"Bartholomew and Thomas have produced an impressive major resource for the study of the book of the Twelve. Concerned above all to bring the prophets' powerful message to today's church, they write with urgency and empathy about the contemporary world, convinced that this is what motivated the prophets in their own times. Firmly grounded in scholarship on the ancient Hebrew and Greek texts, and their interpretation in the church from the earliest Christian centuries, Bartholomew and Thomas offer sensitive, close readings of each book. At the same time, they attend to complex hermeneutical issues, notably the theological relationship of each book to the Twelve considered as a corpus, and also to the New Testament. This book should become indispensable for serious study of the Prophets."
Gordon McConville, professor emeritus of Old Testament at the University of Gloucestershire

"Bartholomew and Thomas have produced an accessible yet consummate guide to reading the minor prophetic books theologically, ranging from ancient Near Eastern background considerations to New Testament and early Christian interpretation. They help novices and experts alike navigate this collection of small and significant texts with helpful tables (who doesn't appreciate a good table?), thoughtful reflection, and pastoral hearts."
Brittany N. Melton, associate professor of Old Testament at Regent College

"Craig Bartholomew and Heath Thomas have written an accessible, thoroughly researched, and theologically insightful introduction to the Minor Prophets. Christians of every stripe will find this volume invaluable as an entry point to these undervalued prophetic books. The authors have provided historical and contextual analysis with contemporary theological application, and they strike a balance between exacting scholarship and accessible writing."
Colin Toffelmire, associate professor of Old Testament at Ambrose University

"This new primer on the Minor Prophets provides the kind of orientation that is needed to engage with and embrace the message of these timely Old Testament books. This work is historically accurate and rhetorically sensitive, and yet builds the necessary theological framework for listening anew to these prophetic words in their inscripturated form for our present generation. Prepare to be challenged!"

Mark J. Boda, professor of Old Testament at McMaster Divinity College in Hamilton, Ontario

The Minor Prophets

A THEOLOGICAL INTRODUCTION

CRAIG G. BARTHOLOMEW
& HEATH A. THOMAS

An imprint of InterVarsity Press
Downers Grove, Illinois

InterVarsity Press
P.O. Box 1400 | Downers Grove, IL 60515-1426
ivpress.com | email@ivpress.com

©2023 by Craig G. Bartholomew and Heath A. Thomas

All rights reserved. No part of this book may be reproduced in any form without written permission from InterVarsity Press.

InterVarsity Press® is the publishing division of InterVarsity Christian Fellowship/USA®. For more information, visit intervarsity.org.

Scripture quotations, unless otherwise noted, are translated by the author.

The publisher cannot verify the accuracy or functionality of website URLs used in this book beyond the date of publication.

Cover design: David Fassett
Interior design: Daniel van Loon

ISBN 978-1-5140-0168-4 (print) | ISBN 978-1-5140-0169-1 (digital)

Printed in the United States of America ∞

Library of Congress Cataloging-in-Publication Data
A catalog record for this book is available from the Library of Congress.

30 29 28 27 26 25 24 23 | 13 12 11 10 9 8 7 6 5 4 3 2 1

Dedicated to Senator David Coltart of Zimbabwe

who over his lifetime has embodied so much of the spirit

of the Minor Prophets.

Dedicated to Claude and Janice Thomas.

True lovers of justice and people of faith.

Contents

Preface ix

Introduction 1

Abbreviations 5

1 Reading the Minor Prophets with the Church
   and in the Academy 7

2 The Ancient World of Prophecy 27

3 Hosea 40
   Yahweh: Lover and Lion

4 A Tale of Two Futures 57
   Hosea 2:16-25 [2:14-23]

5 Joel 69
   The Valley of Decision

6 The Day of the Lord 85

7 Amos 94
   Yahweh, the "Master of Geopolitics," and the Affliction of Joseph

8 Amos and Creation 116
   The Hymn Fragments

9 Obadiah 130
   Edom's Fall and Yahweh's Kingdom

10 Jonah 142
   The Patient God

11 Spiritual Formation 161
   Jonah and His Canticle: Jonah 2:3-10 [2:2-9]

12 Micah 172
   Divine Forgiveness and the Remnant

13 He Has Told You What Is Good 189
   Micah 6:6-8

14	Nahum and Zephaniah	202
	God, the Nations, and Israel	
15	Habakkuk	223
	A Protesting and Patient Faith	
16	Faith in the Faithful God	237
	Habakkuk 2:2-4	
17	Zechariah	249
	Prisoners of Hope	
18	The King Receives His Kingdom	282
	Zechariah 9:9-10	
19	Haggai and Malachi	292
	Restoration and Remembrance	
20	The Theology of the Minor Prophets	312
21	The Minor Prophets and Jesus	333
22	The Theology of the Minor Prophets for Today	355
General Index		373
Scripture Index		378

Preface

THE MINOR PROPHETS ARE RICH BEYOND MEASURE. To a person they bring us before Yahweh, who speaks to his people in times of crisis. We have finalized this book during the pandemic, in so many ways just such a time. Without for a moment detracting from the death and pain of this time, *the good news from the Minor Prophets is that in such dire times God speaks.* There is much sustenance and comfort to be found in these books for such a time as ours.

The bad news is that in such dire times God speaks. Our hunch is that when, God willing, we look back on the pandemic, we will see that even as it stripped us bare in so many ways, it foregrounded the best and worst behavior. It has also exposed the idols of our time, the cracks in our cultures, and in the process often triggered terrible behavior. At all levels—individual, social, economic, and political—the Minor Prophets proclaim both judgment and hope.

We are glad to acknowledge the vast amount of excellent work on these books: historical, literary, redactional, and so on. However, this is less so in terms of their message and theology for today. While engaging the full gamut of research on the Minor Prophets, our hope is that this work will help students, laity, academics, and pastors to hear the message of the Minor Prophets and to preach and convey it to our world today. God knows, we need it.

We note for the reader that there are points of considerable difference between Hebrew versification reflected in the Masoretic Text and English versification of the Minor Prophets. For ease of reading, we have followed convention to list the Hebrew first, followed by the English numbering in square brackets. It will help readers to have a full listing of differences at the outset.

Table P.1. Hebrew and English versification

BOOK	HEBREW	ENGLISH
Hosea	2:1-2	[1:10-11]
	2:3-25	[2:1-23]
	12:1	[11:12]
	12:2-15	[12:1-14]
	14:1	[13:16]
	14:2-9	[14:1-8]
Joel	3:1-5	[2:28-32]
	4:1-21	[3:1-21]
Jonah	2:1	[1:17]
	2:2-11	[2:1-10]
Micah	4:14	[5:1]
	5:1-14	[5:2-15]
Nahum	2:1	[1:15]
	2:2-14	[2:1-13]
Zechariah	2:1-4	[1:18-21]
	2:5-17	[2:1-13]
Malachi	3:19-24	[4:1-6]

This volume is the second in a series with IVP Academic. It follows on from Craig Bartholomew and Ryan O'Dowd's *Old Testament Wisdom: A Theological Introduction*. Since it was commissioned, a great deal has happened in Heath's life and Craig's life. Heath became president of Oklahoma Baptist University, and Craig moved back to Cambridge, UK, where he is the director of the Kirby Laing Centre for Public Theology. Patience, is, as we see in Jonah, an attribute of God, and we are grateful to IVP Academic and Anna Gissing in particular for their patience in waiting for us to complete this work. We are grateful to Jon Boyd and Rachel Hastings for their editorial help in the latter stages of the project. The good news is that the next volume, *The Pentateuch: A Theological Introduction*, coauthored by Craig Bartholomew and A. J. Culp, is already under commission.

Introduction

*The riches of the Word of God to be found
in the Minor Prophets' writings are almost inexhaustible.*

ELIZABETH ACHTEMEIER

T HE NEW AMERICAN BIBLE has a fascinating translation of Psalm 89:20 [89:19], namely, "To *your friends the prophets* you said . . ." "Your friends the prophets" is a creative translation of the Hebrew *laḥăsîdêkā*, which is more literally translated as "to your faithful ones." Nevertheless, the NAB translation is helpfully evocative of the close relationship the prophets shared with Yahweh as the ones who received his word and bore it to his people (see Jn 15:15).

Craig lives in the United Kingdom, where the queen was a figure of fascination, respect, and admiration. Wisely, and necessarily as queen, she kept her private life to herself. Imagine if you were fortunate enough to have become friends with the close friends of the queen. They would provide you with an endlessly fascinating window into the mind of the queen herself. So it is with God's friends the prophets. They are uniquely given access to God's mind, but precisely not in order to keep it to themselves but so that they can convey it to God's people and thus to us. When we come to the Minor Prophets, then, we are standing on holy ground. They grant us the extraordinary privilege of listening in to what God had to say to his Old Testament people at different times in their journey with him, and as such they keep calling us back into his presence and to live *today* as his people. They usher us into the presence of the God who lays claim to every aspect of our lives and has a great deal to say to his people and thus to us today.

Among royalty and nobility, a distinction is made between major nobility and minor nobility. It is the major ones, such as the king and the queen, who really count. However, it would be a mistake to approach the Minor Prophets as comparably less significant than the Major Prophets Isaiah, Jeremiah, and Ezekiel. The word *minor* relates only to the lengths of the books associated with these prophets and says nothing about their relative importance. We do well to remember that the greatest prophet of all, Jesus of Nazareth, never wrote a single book, and yet we would never downplay his role as the prophet par excellence, the Word of God. Nor should we downplay the Minor Prophets. They have an explosive message that we urgently need to retrieve for today. The title of Daniel Berrigan's delightful work—*Minor Prophets, Major Themes*—alerts us to the fact that *minor* is a relative term.[1]

OF NO EARTHLY GOOD?

A criticism often made against Christianity is that it is otherworldly and entirely concerned with heaven and thus of no earthly good. While it is true that Christians have at times fallen into the trap of so attending to heaven that they have little to say about the visceral realities of earthly life, the old religious message of the Minor Prophets demonstrates unequivocally that it is untrue of biblical Christianity, with the prophets' searing attention to social, political, religious, and cosmic issues.

Amid the crisis of modernity, the limits and shadow side of the Enlightenment tradition—amid its many gifts—are increasingly recognized, but where is a solution to be found? Sociologists such as the late John Carroll are penetrating in their analysis of the crisis but see little hope for a solution in the church and its doctrines.[2] Christians who are obsessively focused on heaven may indeed have little to say to contemporary issues of injustice. Not so the Minor Prophets. For example, on acting with justice to our fellow humans, the prophet Amos declares, "Let justice roll down like waters, and mercy like an ever-flowing stream" (Amos 5:24). On what is essential for the life of faith, Micah instructs, "He has told you, O human, what is good; and what the LORD requires of you but to do justice, to love mercy, and to walk humbly with your God" (Mic 6:8). On the coming of the Spirit of God and the ability for all God's people to speak prophetically,

---

[1] Daniel Berrigan, *Minor Prophets, Major Themes* (Eugene, OR: Wipf & Stock, 2009).
[2] John Carroll, *The Existential Jesus* (Berkeley: Counterpoint, 2007).

Joel exclaims, "And it shall come to pass afterward, that I will pour out my Spirit on all flesh" (Joel 2:28).

Life *Coram Deo*

Composed of poetry and prose, the Minor Prophets are masterful works of literature that address the range of human life and the ultimate realities of life and death with unblinking honesty and uncompromising hope. More than dusty artifacts from the ancient past, these texts speak with extraordinary power to the present world. They do so because they disclose the overwhelming reality of Israel's God, the Maker of heaven and earth, and the covenant God of his people Israel. God is the great one with whom Israel and the nations must deal, ever before humanity as the Creator and Redeemer of all life, including "many animals" (Jon 4:11). Everything human existence comprises—politics, economics, family life, religion—is placed in necessary relation to *this God*. *Coram Deo* is a wonderful Latin expression that captures this vision perfectly, life lived before the face of God. In this way, the Minor Prophets can in no way be described as insignificant.

The Minor Prophets also frame the Jewish and later Christian concepts of a future hope. We witness this in the Minor Prophets' anticipation of an end to all war (Mic 4:1-5), of comprehensive peace and justice (Amos 5:24; Mic 6:8), of the fate of the wicked (Hab 2:6-20), and the glorious reign of God (Obad 21). If we catch a glimpse of this eschatological vision cast on the canvas of the Minor Prophets, then we will begin to see that the Christian hope is far from inadequate or otherworldly but a meaningful response to the fragility of human experience amid the challenges of history. In these and so many other ways, these texts provide hidden treasure in Scripture, if only we will begin to plumb them for their inexhaustible riches.

An Uncomfortable Presence

As Israel discovered again and again, having a prophet around can be downright uncomfortable. Prophets have an uncanny ability to point out those areas of our lives where we are comfortable in our sin, and the Minor Prophets are no exception in this respect. Of course, it is no fun having such areas identified, and we, like the Israelites, easily become uneasy and resistant. However, the good news is that the prophets never make us uncomfortable simply in order to be difficult. They identify such areas of our lives in order to get us firmly back on track in God's ways, and these are the ways to a fully human existence. Even as they say no to our sin, the prophets stand as signposts to life as God intends it, to personal and societal flourishing for all, including animals. Irenaeus famously said, "The glory of God is the human person fully alive," and it is to such life that the Minor Prophets beckon us. How can we not follow?

Abbreviations

AB	Anchor Bible Commentary
AOTC	Apollos Old Testament Commentary
BDB	Brown, Francis, S. R. Driver, and Charles A. Briggs. *A Hebrew and English Lexicon of the Old Testament*
BEATAJ	Beiträge zur Erforschung des Alten Testaments und des antiken Judentums
BET	Beiträge zur biblischen Exegese und Theologie
BIS	Biblical Interpretation Series
BZAW	Beihefte zur Zeitschrift für die alttetestamentliche Wissenschaft
CBQ	*Catholic Biblical Quarterly*
CD	Barth, Karl. *Church Dogmatics*. Edited and translated by Thomas S. Torrance and Geoffrey Bromiley. Edinburgh: T&T Clark, 1936–1969
CHANE	Culture and History of the Ancient Near East
COS	*The Context of Scripture*. Edited by William. W. Hallo and K. Lawson Younger. 3 vols. Leiden: Brill, 2002
HBM	Hebrew Bible Monographs
HBS	Herders biblische Studien
HCOT	Historical Commentary on the Old Testament
HSM	Harvard Semitic Monographs
HThKAT	Herders theologischer Kommentar zum Alten Testament
IECOT	International Exegetical Commentary on the Old Testament
ITC	International Theological Commentary
JBL	*Journal of Biblical Literature*
JHS	*Journal of Hebrew Scriptures*
JSJSup	Journal of the Study of Judaism Supplement Series
JSOT	*Journal for the Study of the Old Testament*
JSOTSup	Journal for the Study of the Old Testament Supplement Series
JSS	*Journal of Semitic Studies*
JTI	*Journal of Theological Interpretation*

LHBOTS	Library of Hebrew Bible/Old Testament Studies
LNTS	Library of New Testament Studies
LSTS	Library of Second Temple Studies
LXX	Septuagint
MT	Masoretic Text
NA[28]	*Novum Testamentum Graece*, Nestle-Aland, 28th ed.
NICOT	New International Commentary on the Old Testament
NT	New Testament
OBO	Orbis Biblicus et Orientalis
OT	Old Testament
OTL	Old Testament Library
ROT	Reading the Old Testament
SBLDS	Society of Biblical Literature Dissertation Series
SHBC	Smyth & Helwys Bible Commentary
SSBT	Studies in Scripture and Biblical Theology
STI	Studies in Theological Interpretation
STR	*Southeastern Theological Review*
SubBib	Subsidia Biblica
THOTC	Two Horizons Old Testament Commentary
VT	*Vetus Testamentum*
VTSup	Supplements to Vetus Testamentum
WBC	Word Biblical Commentary
ZAW	*Zeitschrift für die alttestamentliche Wissenschaft*

1

Reading the Minor Prophets with the Church and in the Academy

FROM ITS INCEPTION, the church received the Old Testament as Holy Scripture. The result is that we never read the Minor Prophets de novo but always in the company of that one, holy, catholic, and apostolic church. In this chapter we will explore how the church has read the Minor Prophets and then attend to modern study of them in the academy, much of which has operated apart from Christian faith.[1]

It is important to be aware that the early church had access to Hebrew and Greek versions of the Minor Prophets. Jews were scattered across the Mediterranean, and once Alexander the Great conquered Persia, Greek became the lingua franca of his empire, and thus a demand for the Old Testament in Greek grew. Between the third century BC and the first century AD, the entire Old Testament was translated into Greek, and not surprisingly it became the form of the Old Testament used by many Jews and was inherited as such by most Christians. In terms of the mission of the early church, what thereby became the Septuagint was of vital importance.[2] After Pentecost, the Old Testament was already available throughout the Roman Empire in Greek, and it provided a vocabulary and language for speaking about Christian faith, thereby laying a foundation for the rapid spread of the gospel.

However, that there were Greek and Hebrew versions of the Old Testament available complicates matters today for textual critics who seek to establish the original version of the text, since the Septuagint is far older than the Hebrew

---

[1] For a helpful, recent introduction to the Minor Prophets, see Julia M. O'Brien, ed., *The Oxford Handbook of the Minor Prophets* (Oxford: Oxford University Press, 2021).
[2] See Ellis R. Brotzman and Eric R. Tully, *Old Testament Textual Criticism: A Practical Introduction* (Grand Rapids, MI: Baker Academic, 2016), chap. 4.

Masoretic Text. In recent decades Old Testament textual criticism has become exceedingly complex, and readers are referred to Ellis Brotzman and Eric Tully's *Old Testament Textual Criticism* for an up-to-date and accessible orientation to the subject. With some Old Testament books there are significant differences between the Septuagint and the MT, but fortunately divergence between Greek and Hebrew traditions in the Minor Prophets is not as severe as, say, one finds in Jeremiah.[3] As we will see below, a major issue in contemporary studies of the Minor Prophets is whether they are twelve individual books or a collection, namely, the Book of the Twelve. This is a key site of difference in the Greek and Hebrew text traditions.[4] In this respect it is worth noting that their order differs in the MT and the LXX, as evident in table 1.1.

Table 1.1. Order of Minor Prophets in MT and LXX

MASORETIC TEXT	SEPTUAGINT
Hosea	Hosea
Joel	**Amos**
Amos	**Micah**
Obadiah	**Joel**
Jonah	**Obadiah**
Micah	**Jonah**
Nahum	Nahum
Habakkuk	Habakkuk
Zephaniah	Zephaniah
Haggai	Haggai
Zechariah	Zechariah
Malachi	Malachi

THE EARLY CHURCH AND THE MINOR PROPHETS

The Bible "formed Christians into a people and gave them a language," Robert Wilken writes. Early, educated Christians knew the great books of the Greek and Roman traditions. "Yet when they took the Bible in hand they were overwhelmed. It came upon them like a torrent leaping down the side of a mountain."[5] These early Christians thus received the Minor Prophets as Scripture, mostly in the Greek manuscript tradition. As an inner-Jewish

---

[3]On these differences see Emmanuel Tov, *Textual Criticism of the Hebrew Bible*, 3rd ed. (Minneapolis: Fortress, 2012), 286-326.
[4]See the still-helpful discussion of Russell Fuller, "The Form and Formation of the Book of the Twelve: The Evidence from the Judean Desert," in *Forming Prophetic Literature: Essays on Isaiah and the Twelve in Honor of John D. W. Watts*, ed. James W. Watts and Paul R. House, JSOTSup 235 (Sheffield: Sheffield Academic Press, 1995), 86-101; see also the more recent explorations of Greek and Hebrew manuscript traditions of the Twelve in Jakob Wöhrle and Lena-Sophia Tiemeyer, eds., *The Book of the Twelve: Composition, Reception and Interpretation*, VTSup 184 (Leiden: Brill, 2020), 271-304.
[5]Robert L. Wilken, *The Spirit of Early Christian Thought* (New Haven, CT: Yale University Press, 2004), 52-53.

movement, Christianity was founded on the Old Testament. The Scriptures of Israel "provided the terms and the images, the context, within which the apostles made sense of what happened [in Jesus of Nazareth], and with which they explained it and preached it, justifying the claim that Christ died and rose 'according to the Scriptures' [1 Cor 15:3-5]."[6] In the early centuries of the Christian church (AD 100–400), the Old Testament became the foundation for presenting Jesus in the economy of God.

> For early Christians, the *hypothesis* [unitive plot of the text] that held together the unwieldy bulk of Scripture was the rule of faith, while Scripture's *skopos* [the key purpose of the text] was to convey Christ. When Christians used this rationale, it was because they believed Scripture ultimately derived from a single author, God the Father, through his Son (the Logos) and the Spirit.[7]

Amid this ecology, the Old Testament provided a prophetic foundation to the reality of God's salvation in Jesus the Messiah. "There was no Christian understanding of Jesus of Nazareth without a dependence on the Hebrew prophets."[8]

Ignatius of Antioch (ca. AD 35–110) asserts,

> But as for myself, the archives are Jesus Christ, the sacred archives are his crucifixion, his death, his burial and his resurrection, and the faith which is through him: in these I wish to be justified by your prayers.... But something special comes with the Gospel: the coming of the Savior, our Lord Jesus Christ, his passion, and his resurrection. *For the beloved prophets proclaimed him*, but the gospel is the completion of immortality. (*To the Philadelphians* 8.2–9.2)[9]

In this way, the Old Testament is seen as prophetic of the work of Jesus and his gospel, and it was read as a series of prooftexts or prophecies about Jesus' messiahship.[10] In no small part the Minor Prophets fund that vision. "A good

---

[6] John Behr, *The Way to Nicea*, Formation of Christian Theology 1 (Crestwood, NY: St. Vladimir's Seminary Press, 2001), 27.

[7] Lisa D. Maugans Driver, *Christ at the Center: The Early Christian Era* (Louisville, KY: Westminster John Knox, 2009), 110. See Wilken, *Spirit of Early Christian Thought*, 61-69, on the Bible as "a single story." Wilken notes, "The rule of faith, which, of course, was drawn from the Bible, reverberated back on the Bible as a key to its interpretation" (66).

[8] Ronald E. Heine, "Early Christian Reception of the Prophets," in *The Oxford Handbook of the Prophets*, ed. Carolyn J. Sharp (Oxford: Oxford University Press, 2016), 407.

[9] Except where otherwise noted, all translations of ancient and modern languages derive from the authors.

[10] Eugen J. Pentiuc, *The Old Testament in Eastern Orthodox Tradition* (Oxford: Oxford University Press, 2014), 18-19.

number of the twelve prophets were given prominence in key places of the New Testament, but among the church fathers *they were accorded an even more significant role* in scriptural exegesis of prophecies pointing to Jesus Christ as the promised Messiah."[11]

In the second to the fourth centuries AD, key texts emerged from the Old Testament to demonstrate truths about Jesus. These "proofs from prophecy" were developed among others in Justin Martyr (ca. AD 100–165) and Eusebius (ca. AD 260–340). Ronald Heine identifies six proofs of prophecy from the early days of the church.[12] Two proofs derive from the Minor Prophets: Zechariah 6:12, demonstrating the preexistence of Christ, and Micah 5:1 [5:2], demonstrating the prophets foretold the incarnation by revealing the birthplace of Jesus.

Based on Zechariah LXX, the early church read Zechariah 6:12 as a prophecy about Jesus' preexistence: "Behold! A man, 'East' [*anatolē*] is his name, and from beneath him he will rise up [*anatelei*] and build the house of the LORD" (Zech 6:12 LXX). The man's name in the Greek is linked to the notion of rising, the east, or the eastern sky. The Greek translator reads something other than the Hebrew, which is not "east" but "Branch" or "Sprout" (*ṣemaḥ*). The Hebrew term offers a horticultural image; the Greek presents a celestial image. For early Christian interpreters with little Hebrew, the celestial image cast a vision of a heavenly figure who built the house of the Lord; the referent could be understood as the preexistent Christ. This understanding appears in Justin Martyr, Origen, Gregory of Nyssa, Eusebius, and Ambrose.[13] By contrast, the Hebrew tradition of reading *ṣemaḥ* is messianic, but not in terms of the preexistence of Jesus. Rather, the term indicates the "Branch" of the Davidic house that will be anointed and appointed by God for his redemptive purpose. This can be applied typologically to Jesus, as the messianic priest-king who builds the house of the Lord.[14]

The second key prophetic proof of Jesus' ministry comes in Micah 5:1 [5:2], which speaks of Bethlehem as the birthplace of the Davidic king. Micah 5:1 [5:2] was important for the Christian church precisely because of

---

[11] Alberto Ferreiro, "Introduction to the Minor Prophets," in *The Twelve Prophets*, ed. Alberto Ferreiro, Ancient Christian Commentary on Scripture: Old Testament 14 (Downers Grove, IL: IVP Academic, 2003), xxxviii, emphasis added.

[12] Ronald E. Heine, *Reading the Old Testament with the Ancient Church: Exploring the Formation of Early Christian Thought*, Evangelical Ressourcement (Grand Rapids, MI: Baker Academic, 2007), 97-141.

[13] See Heine, *Reading the Old Testament*, 105-7.

[14] Al Wolters, *Zechariah*, HCOT 19 (Leuven: Peeters, 2014), 193-96.

Reading the Minor Prophets with the Church and in the Academy 11

its geographic specificity. Tertullian, Origen, and Eusebius each use the specificity of Bethlehem to argue that the Messiah could only be born in this place, not in any other; moreover, no one in Jewish history was born there that could fit the leadership role of the anointed king of Israel ("messiah") *except* Jesus (not even David!). Thus, this text demonstrates the incarnation of Jesus in this place (Bethlehem) at this unique time in history.[15]

The major patristic and medieval works on the Minor Prophets are listed in table 1.2.

Table 1.2. Influential Patristic and Medieval commentaries on the Twelve Prophets

AUTHOR	SCOPE OF COMMENTARY
Origen (ca. AD 184–253)	all Twelve Prophets (known to Eusebius but lost)
Didymus the Blind (ca. AD 313–398)	Zechariah
Jerome (AD 340–420)	all Twelve Prophets
Theodore of Mopsuestia (AD 350–428)	all Twelve Prophets
Cyril of Alexandria (AD 378–444)	all Twelve Prophets
Theodoret of Cyrus (AD 393–458)	all Twelve Prophets
Venerable Bede (672–735 AD)	all Twelve Prophets (written but lost)
Išoʿdad of Merv (ca. AD 850)	all Twelve Prophets
Monks of the Abbey of St. Germain, authorship unclear: Haimo of Halberstadt (died ca. AD 855) or Remegius of Auxerre (AD 841–908)	all Twelve Prophets
Theophylact of Ochrid (AD 1088–1120)	Hosea, Jonah, Nahum, Habakkuk, Micah
Rupert of Deutz (AD 1075–1129)	all Twelve Prophets
Andrew of St. Victor (AD 1110–1175)	all Twelve Prophets
Glossa Ordinaria (twelfth century AD onwards), authorship unclear: Gilbert of Auxerre (d. 1134) or Ralph of Laon (d. 1133)	all Twelve Prophets
Albertus Magnus (AD 1200–1280)	all Twelve Prophets
Nicholas of Lyra (AD 1270–1349)	all Twelve Prophets

While the church fathers are agreed in seeing the Minor Prophets as a major source for the disclosure of Christ, the difference between Alexandrian and Antiochene readings must be noted, as seen, for example, in the contrast between Theodore of Mopsuestia and Cyril of Alexandria. Wilken speaks of allegorical interpretation as inevitable, but this inevitability is

---

[15]Heine, *Reading the Old Testament*, 120-21.

placed in question by the far more historical interpretation of the Antiochene fathers, such as Theodore of Mopsuestia.[16] In his work on Theodore, Rowan Greer notes of allegorical exegesis, "The exegesis by means of fulfilment of prophecy . . . tends so to see all events in terms of their fulfilment, that the events themselves become unimportant and meaningless. Prophecy then becomes not a speaking to the contemporary scene, but purely prediction of events to come in the distant future."[17] The Antiochenes disagreed with the Alexandrians on *how* to determine what the Old Testament is saying. Whereas Origen followed Philo in resorting to allegory, "The Antiochenes, beginning at least with Lucian, Eusebius of Emesa, and Eustathius of Antioch, strongly opposed Origen, believing that an interpreter should always stay with what the text actually states. Theodore became the leading spokesperson for this critical viewpoint, being especially concerned about what is the right standard for interpreting the Christian Scriptures."[18]

THE MINOR PROPHETS AND MODERN BIBLICAL INTERPRETATION

The Renaissance in Europe prioritized the original languages in biblical interpretation as well as in classical resources. The priority of going back "to the sources" (*ad fontes*) resonates in the work of Reformers Martin Luther and John Calvin.[19] These Christian leaders exhibit pastoral sensibilities in their interpretation of the Minor Prophets, always and ever engaging the biblical text from the reality of God's salvific work in Jesus of Nazareth, the Messiah, and the community of the Christian church that Jesus instantiates. In this way, it is appropriate to argue that Luther and Calvin read the Minor Prophets as participants within the divine drama of redemption in Christ

---

[16]Wilken, *Spirit of Early Christian Thought*, 69-77.
[17]Rowan A. Greer, *Theodore of Mopsuestia: Exegete and Theologian* (London: Faith Press, 1961), 95. See also Frederick G. McLeod, *Theodore of Mopsuestia* (Oxford: Routledge, 2009), chaps. 3-4.
[18]McLeod, *Theodore of Mopsuestia*, 18.
[19]For Luther, see his commentaries on the Minor Prophets and the recent work of Andrew J. Niggemann, *Martin Luther's Hebrew in Mid-career: The Minor Prophets Translation*, Spätmittelalter, Humanismus, Reformation 108 (Tübingen: Mohr Siebeck, 2019). For Calvin, see his commentaries and Jon Balserak, *Establishing the Remnant Church in France: Calvin's Lectures on the Minor Prophets, 1556-1559*, Brill Series in Church History 50 (Leiden: Brill, 2011); Frederik A. V. Harms, *In God's Custody: The Church, A History of Divine Protection, A Study of John Calvin's Ecclesiology Based on His Commentary on the Minor Prophets* (Göttingen: Vandenhoeck & Ruprecht, 2010); G. Sujin Pak, "Luther and Calvin on the Nature and Function of Prophecy: The Case of the Minor Prophets," in *Calvin and Luther: The Continuing Relationship*, ed. R. Ward Holder (Göttingen: Vandenhoeck & Ruprecht, 2013), 13-37.

rather than on the outside of it. They sit firmly within the scope of traditional Christian interpretation.[20]

Yet, Luther and Calvin nonetheless represent transitional figures in the history of interpretation of the Minor Prophets on the way toward modern biblical interpretation. On the one hand, they were interested in interpretation in the original languages (especially Hebrew exegesis of the prophetic books) and were interested in the historical situations of the prophetic books. On this front, they can be marshaled as exemplars of modern biblical interpretation. On the other hand, they remained radically committed to each of the Minor Prophets as testifying distinctively within the unified testimony of Scripture to proclaim Christ, albeit with different emphases: Luther with his law-gospel dialectic, and Calvin with a covenantal structure to the Old Testament leading to Jesus Christ. In this they represent the best of what we find in premodern biblical interpretation. And they cannot be marshaled as exemplars of modern biblical interpretation in the historical turn, if one means by this historical events disconnected from the economy of divine providence.

Regarding Christian interpretation, one should note that, on the whole, they align with the Antiochene tradition rather than the Alexandrian. This is immediately apparent when one reads Calvin on the Minor Prophets. David Puckett notes, "Calvin was uncomfortable with traditional Christian exegesis of the Old Testament promises because he believed interpreters were wrong to ignore the historical circumstances in which the promises were originally given."[21]

The great strength in the history of interpretation is the indelible link forged between the Minor Prophets and Jesus of Nazareth. A weakness—albeit one addressed by the Antiochenes, the Reformers, and their followers—is a potential failure to hear the witness of the Minor Prophets first on their own terms. In many ways historical criticism helpfully retrieves this historical dimension; alas, it overcorrects and easily ends up losing the link with Jesus and the New Testament.

---

[20] Thomas Renz, "Luther's Lectures on Habakkuk as an Example of Participatory Exegesis," in *Reading the Book of the Twelve Minor Prophets*, ed. David G. Firth and Brittany N. Melton, SSBT (Bellingham, WA: Lexham Academic, 2022), 64-87.

[21] David L. Puckett, *John Calvin's Exegesis of the Old Testament*, Columbia Series in Reformed Theology (Louisville, KY: Westminster John Knox, 1995), 125. Puckett suggests that Calvin's concern to interpret according to the intention of the author is most clearly seen in his exegesis of Hosea (34).

When modernity took hold in the West, it manifested itself in every discipline, including biblical studies. Amid the diversity in modernity, the radical Enlightenment came to dominate, and it was extremely wary of the role of religion in the great public spheres of life, including the university.[22] Whereas in Marxism and the Soviet Empire religion was clearly identified as the enemy, in the West religion was tolerated but privatized. In the public spheres of life and in academic studies, autonomous reason should reign supreme as the royal route to truth.

Christian scholars responded to this challenge in different ways. Some accepted the epistemic foundation(s) provided by the Enlightenment and were comfortable leaving their faith at the door of their studies and lecture rooms.[23] Others were more critical. A perennial temptation of believers was to withdraw into Pietism, a temptation that evangelicalism fell afoul of for the first half of the twentieth century.

For those who remained committed to rigorous academic study of the Bible, the new developments could not be ignored. The historical turn in biblical studies, with its method of historical criticism(s), dominated all major universities by the start of the twentieth century. As we will see below, historical criticism brought immense gains to study of the Minor Prophets. However, it had a shadow side, which believing scholars struggled to come to grips with.

The historical turn: Historical criticism and the Minor Prophets. With the historical turn in biblical studies in the eighteenth and nineteenth centuries, scholars probed the words and the experiences of prophets to get *behind the text* to their authentic core and genius. Heinrich Ewald's influential account of prophets appeared in the 1830s. He believed the prophet received a vision from God for his time, and his inner spirit was captivated by the divine vision so that he could do nothing but communicate the message to the people of his day.[24] Those influenced by Ewald (e.g., Bernard Duhm) saw the historical-critical work of profiling the prophet as essential to discerning between authentic, early prophecy and the later, inauthentic tradition that grew from the early prophet.

---

[22]Jonathan Israel, *A Revolution of the Mind: Radical Enlightenment and the Intellectual Origins of Modern Democracy* (Princeton, NJ: Princeton University Press, 2010).

[23]See Michael J. Buckley, *At the Origins of Modern Atheism* (New Haven, CT: Yale University Press, 1990), for the view that accepting the epistemic foundation(s) provided by the Enlightenment was a mistake.

[24]Heinrich Ewald, *Die Propheten des Alten Bundes* (Stuttgart: Adoph Krabbe, 1840).

Duhm's *The Theology of the Prophets* (1875) established modern study of the prophets in the academy and is our starting point for how the Minor Prophets have been read since then.[25] Duhm saw the prophets as geniuses whose spiritual insight came from their direct encounters with God. Prophets were unique and specially gifted to communicate their spontaneous vision to contemporaries. Religious ritual, legal material, and a theocratic state were later innovations developed in the Persian period but did not represent the high point of prophecy.[26] For Duhm, the purest forms of prophetic speech emerged early in Israel's history, and they were then incrementally encumbered by innovations and tradition. Duhm applied his insights to the Minor Prophets both in his *The Theology of the Prophets* and a later translation of the Twelve.[27] Duhm's scholarly program launched source-critical analysis of the prophetic books, including the Minor Prophets. Scholars became interested in which early sources informed later sources and how these sources were brought together into the form of the text in which we now find them.

Sigmund Mowinckel built on Duhm's research, but he was interested in tradition and in the social contexts, especially the cult, which he argued provided the matrix for prophetic speech.[28] Mowinckel adapted his tradition-historical method from his doctoral supervisor, Hermann Gunkel. In Mowinckel's understanding, the Minor Prophets did not begin as a book but as short, individual sayings infused with tradition. These sayings were spoken orally and then later inscribed as written sayings. Scribes or other prophets spliced together these sayings with other material to form prophetic passages and then individual books. Later scribes or prophets spliced these into the corpus of the Twelve Prophets. For Mowinckel, the goal of interpreting the Minor Prophets was to explore the entire process so as to determine the growth and development of the tradition.

A focus on individual, orally delivered and then (later) written sayings within the growth of a tradition comprises the work of form criticism on the Prophets. A central figure in this respect is Claus Westermann, whose *Basic Forms of Prophetic Speech* (1964) was foundational and continues to influence research. Westermann contended that the most basic genre of

---

[25]Bernard Duhm, *Die Theologie der Propheten als Grundlage fur die innere Entwicklungsgeschichte der israelitischen Religion* (Bonn: Adoph Marcus, 1875).
[26]Duhm, *Die Theologie der Propheten*, 264-76.
[27]Bernard Duhm, *Die Zwölf Propheten in den Bersmassen Urschrift* (Tübingen: Mohr, 1910).
[28]Sigmund Mowinckel, *Prophecy and Tradition: The Prophetic Books in the Light of the Study of the Growth and History of Tradition* (Oslo: J. Dybwad, 1946).

prophetic speech is one in which a divinely appointed prophet of Yahweh pronounced judgment against an individual or nation. The phrase "thus says the LORD" indicates the "messenger formula," and it has an analog in the ancient Near East, particularly Mari texts (see chap. 2).[29] The oral forms Westermann recognized are listed in table 1.3.

Table 1.3. Forms of prophetic messages

PROPHETIC GENRES	KEY FEATURES	EXAMPLES FROM THE MINOR PROPHETS
Prophetic utterance	Hebrew: *nĕ'ūm* YHWH, "utterance of Yahweh." The most basic genre in prophetic speech. This phrase can occur at the beginning, middle, or end of a prophetic word from God to a person or group.	Hos 2:15 [2:13], 18 [16], 23 [21]; 11:11; Joel 2:12; Amos 2:11, 16; 3:10, 15; 4:3, 6, 8, 9-11; 9:7-8, 13; Obad 4, 8; Mic 4:6; 5:9 [5:10]; Zeph 1:2-3, 10; 3:8; Hag 1:13; 2:4, 14, 17, 23; Zech 1:4; 2:9 [2:6], 14 [10]; 8:17; 10:12; 11:6; 12:4; 13:8; Mal 1:2
Messenger speech	Hebrew: *kōh 'āmar YHWH*, "thus says the LORD" or *'āmar YHWH*, "says the LORD." Used in prophetic books, it indicates God's speech to the prophet as well as the prophet's self-identification as the spokesperson and messenger for God. The messenger speech suggests a word-for-word disclosure of God's message to the audience through the prophet.	Amos 1:3, 5-6, 8-9, 11, 13, 15; 2:1, 3-4, 6; 3:11-12; 5:3-4, 16-17, 27; 7:17; 9:15; Obad 1; Mic 2:3; 3:5; Nahum 1:12; Hag 1:2, 5, 7; 2:6, 11; Zech 1:3-4, 14, 16-17; 2:12 [2:8]; 3:7; 6:12; 8:2-4, 6-9, 14, 19-20, 23; 11:4; Mal 1:4
Oracle/ pronouncement	Hebrew: *maśśā'*, "oracle." The *maśśā'* oracle in prophetic superscriptions especially is a generic term for a divine revelation given to a prophet. Such oracles achieve two things: (1) they identify and reveal God's intentions in human affairs, and (2) they provide direction for human response in the light of God's revelation.	Nahum 1:1; Hab 1:1; Zech 9:1; 12:1; Mal 1:1
Judgment oracle	Announcement of judgment or disaster on individuals, groups, or nations. This genre contains four basic aspects: (1) introduction to the judgment, (2) statement of the reasons for judgment (the accusation), (3) a logical connector (often Hebrew *lākēn* or *'al-kēn*, "therefore") linking the statement of disaster and the rationale for the announcement of judgment/punishment that will follow, and (4) the judgment/punishment that will be meted out.	Hos 2:7-9 [2:5-7]; Amos 1-2; 4:1-2; 7:14-17; Mic 1:2-7; 2:1-4, 9-12; 3:1-4; 6:9-16; Zeph 2:8-11; Hag 1:1-11; Zech 7:8-14
Oracle against nations	A kind of judgment oracle, but this form is directed against foreign nations who threaten Israel or Judah, or those nations that do not meet the standard of Yahweh's justice and righteousness.	Amos 1-2; Joel 4:4-8 [3:4-8]; Obadiah; Nahum
Disputation text	Hebrew: *rîb*. The disputation takes on the characteristics of a trial in which Yahweh is the prosecutor and judge. Clearly, the offending party is the defendant. No set pattern emerges, but God brings a disputation against the defendant, and God is the arbiter of the complaint.	Hos 4; Mic 6

---

[29]Claus Westermann, *Basic Forms of Prophetic Speech*, trans. Hugh C. White (Louisville, KY: Westminster John Knox, 1991), 90-128.

PROPHETIC GENRES	KEY FEATURES	EXAMPLES FROM THE MINOR PROPHETS
Woe oracle	Hebrew: *hôy*. This is a critique of a specific action of an offending party. Two basic elements emerge in the oracle: (1) an introductory exclamation using *hôy*, "woe!" followed by a participle or noun describing the actions/attitude in question; and (2) additional elements that give further specificity to the situation of the critique.	Hos 7:13; Amos 6:1-7; Mic 2:1; Nahum 1; Hab 2:6-20; Zeph 3:1; Zech 11:17
Prophetic instruction	This prophetic instruction is a didactic form used to provide guidance to individuals and groups. Often it is associated with priestly instruction in the light of a specific question and emerges with characteristics of wisdom instruction.	Hag 2:11-13; Mic 6:6-8; (Hab 2:1?)
Prophetic liturgy	These liturgies encompass prayers, complaints, and hymns and use cultic language and terminology as well as theophanic elements, suggesting that these liturgies were developed and perhaps performed.	Joel 1–2; Nahum 1; Hab 3
Salvation oracle	A counterpart to the judgment oracle, this is a message of restoration or salvation by the hand of Yahweh. It is composed of three elements: (1) notice of the situation that will lead to a change, often including the Hebrew particle *ya 'an kî*, "because"; (2) an announcement of salvation or blessing, often including the Hebrew *lākēn*, "therefore," followed by a statement of disaster that will *not* occur; and (3) Yahweh's act of salvation and/or blessing. In some cases, the reassurance *'al tîrā'*, "do not fear," appears as well.	Hos 1:10–2:1; Joel 2:21-22; Obad 17-21; Mic 2:12-13; 4:1-5; Nahum 1:12-15; Zeph 3:14-20; Hag 2:4-8, 20-23; Zech 8:20-23; 9:9-17
Messianic oracle	A variation on the salvation oracle, this is a specific message of future hope that depicts a future messianic king anointed and appointed by Yahweh for his task of just rule and deliverance.	Hos 3:5; Mic 2:13; 5:1-8; Zeph 3:15; Hab 3:13; Zech 9:9; 14:9, 17; Mal 1:14

Toward the literary turn. James Muilenburg praised the achievements of form criticism, but he supplemented it with rhetorical criticism.[30] Because form criticism tended to fixate on conventions, to separate form from content, and to isolate small units from the broader literary context, it neglects the "individual, personal, unique, particular, distinctive, precise, versatile, and fluid features of the text." Form criticism was unable to assess the *intentionality* of Hebrew composition, the "structural patterns, verbal sequences, and stylistic devices that make a coherent whole."[31]

Muilenberg's goal was to address these limitations with rhetorical criticism. Rhetorical criticism (1) defines "the limits or scope of a literary unit, to recognize precisely where and how it begins and ends." One recognizes textual limits by assessing form and content. (2) Rhetorical criticism then discerns

---

[30] James Muilenburg, "Form Criticism and Beyond," In *Beyond Form Criticism*, ed. Paul R. House (Winona Lake, IN: Eisenbrauns, 1992), 49-69, esp. 50-52.

[31] Phyllis Trible, *Rhetorical Criticism: Context, Method, and the Book of Jonah* (Minneapolis: Fortress, 1994), 26.

structure in the text by exploring component parts within it and delineating rhetorical devices "employed for marking, on the one hand, the sequence and movements of the pericope, and on the other, the shifts or breaks in the development of the writer's thought." Rhetorical devices are identified by assessing, inter alia, particles, adverbs, interjections, and conjunctions. Stylistic and narrative analysis are important as well (including intertextuality): "The narrators and poets of ancient Israel and her Near Eastern neighbors were dominated not only by the formal and traditional modes of speech of the literary genres or types, but also by the techniques of narrative and poetic composition."[32]

Sometimes dubbed *new* form criticism, rhetorical criticism in the Minor Prophets is extraordinarily fertile, emerging in the late 1960s and persisting to the present day.[33] In rhetorical criticism, one notes a *literary* turn toward the Minor Prophets away from purely *historical* study of these texts. A recent collection of essays devoted to the written-ness of prophetic texts and their compositional design speaks to the stability of this approach in assessing the Minor Prophets.[34]

Rhetorical criticism thus signals a move toward an analysis of the Minor Prophets as literature. Literary studies analyze the Minor Prophets as artifacts: they are literary art and should be read and interpreted in relation to their aesthetics.[35] Literary studies of the prophets explore the vitality of poetics, parallelism, metaphor, imagery, sound and sense, and other features common to close reading of biblical prophets. One witnesses this kind of application to the Minor Prophets in, for example, the landmark Zephaniah commentary of Adele Berlin, Herbert Mark's literary analysis of the Twelve Prophets, Francis Landy's literary reading of Hosea, and works devoted to poetics in both individual prophetic books and the Minor Prophets as a whole (e.g., plot development, characterization, narrative techniques, metaphor, poetry and parallelism, imagery, intertextuality, and thematic explorations).[36]

---

[32] Muilenburg, "Form Criticism and Beyond," 57, 59.

[33] See the bibliography of rhetorical approaches to the Minor Prophets in Duane F. Watson and Alan Hauser, *Rhetorical Criticism of the Bible: A Comprehensive Bibliography with Notes on History and Method*, BIS 4 (Leiden: Brill, 1994), 92-97.

[34] Mark J. Boda, Michael H. Floyd, and Colin M. Toffelmire, eds., *The Book of the Twelve and the New Form Criticism*, Ancient Near East Monographs 10 (Atlanta: SBL Press, 2015); see also John Robert Barker, *Disputed Temple: A Rhetorical Analysis of the Book of Haggai* (Minneapolis: Fortress, 2017).

[35] For an excellent introduction to literary studies, see David J. H. Beldman, "Literary Approaches and Old Testament Interpretation," in *Hearing the Old Testament: Listening for God's Address*, ed. Craig G. Bartholomew and David J. H. Beldman (Grand Rapids, MI: Eerdmans, 2012), 67-95.

[36] Adele Berlin, *Zephaniah*, AB 25A (New York: Doubleday, 1994); Herbert Marks, "The Twelve Prophets," in *The Literary Guide to the Bible*, ed. Robert Alter and Frank Kermode (Cambridge,

Comparably, some scholars explore unifying themes and concepts in a literary/synchronic reading of the Minor Prophets, rather than purely diachronic explorations offered in historical criticism. Paul House and Edgar Conrad execute literary readings of the corpus of the Minor Prophets thematically (House) and the Twelve within the Latter Prophets (Conrad).[37] House's work is thematic, while Conrad focuses on the role of the reader in a synthetic analysis of the text.

Raymond Van Leeuwen and Ruth Scoralick assess how, in diverse ways, the self-disclosure of Yahweh emerges in the Minor Prophets through the thematic repetition of Exodus 34:6-7 in Hosea 1:6; Joel 2:13; Jonah 3:9; Micah 7:18-20; and Nahum 1:2-3. These and other texts that allude to Yahweh's attributes lend to the Twelve a thematic unity.[38]

In separate studies, Rolf Rendtorff and Paul-Gerhard Schwesig assess the significance of the day of Yahweh as a significant theme in most of the Minor Prophets.[39] One finds mention of it in Hosea 9:5; Joel 3:4 [2:31]; Amos 5:18-20; Obadiah 15; Micah 2:4; Habakkuk 3:16; Zephaniah 1:7-16; Haggai 2:23; Zechariah 14:1; Malachi 4:1 [3:19]. At this point, it suffices to note that in its presentation in the Book of the Twelve, the day of Yahweh is an event of the revelation of Yahweh where he enacts judgment and/or salvation for Israel and/or the nations. We shall say more about the day of Yahweh in chapter six.

Finally, Jason T. LeCureaux argues that the theme of return and restoration is a unifying theme in the Minor Prophets.[40] The language of *šûb*

MA: Belknap, 1987), 207-33; Francis Landy, *Hosea*, Readings (Sheffield: Sheffield Academic Press, 1995); Brad E. Kelle, *Hosea 2: Metaphor and Rhetoric in Historical Perspective* (Leiden: Brill, 2005); Stuart Lasine, *Jonah and the Human Condition: Life and Death in Yahweh's World*, LHBOTS 688 (London: T&T Clark, 2019).

[37]Paul R. House, *The Unity of the Twelve*, JSOTSup 97 (Sheffield: Almond, 1990); Edgar W. Conrad, "Reading Isaiah and the Twelve as Prophetic Books," in *Writing and Reading the Scroll of Isaiah: Studies of an Interpretive Tradition*, ed. C. C. Broyles and C. A. Evans, VTSup 70 (Leiden: Brill, 1997), 3-17; Conrad, *Reading the Latter Prophets: Toward a New Canonical Criticism*, JSOTSup 376 (London: T&T Clark, 2003).

[38]Raymond C. van Leeuwen, "Scribal Wisdom and Theodicy in the Book of the Twelve," in *In Search of Wisdom: Essays in Memory of John G. Gammie*, ed. L. Perdue, B. B. Scott, and W. J. Wiseman (Louisville, KY: Westminster John Knox, 1993), 31-49. For a different exploration on this theme, see Ruth Scoralick, *Gottes Güte und Gottes Zorn. Die Gottesprädikationen in Exodus 34,6f und ihre intertextuellen Beziehungen zum Zwölfprophetenbuch*, HBS 33 (Freiburg im Breisgau: Herder, 2002).

[39]For major studies on the theme, see Rolf Rendtorff, "Alas for the Day! The 'Day of the LORD' in the Book of the Twelve," in *God in the Fray: A Tribute to Walter Brueggemann*, ed. Tod Linafelt and Timothy K. Beal (Minneapolis: Fortress, 1998), 186-97; Paul-Gerhard Schwesig, *Die Rolle der Tag-JHWHs-Dichtungen im Dodekapropheton*, BZAW 366 (Berlin: de Gruyter, 2006).

[40]For a full study, see Jason T. LeCureaux, *The Thematic Unity of the Book of the Twelve*, HBM 41 (Sheffield: Sheffield Phoenix, 2012).

as "restore/return" emerges as prominently as the day of Yahweh. See, for example, Hosea 11; Joel 4:1, 4, 7 [3:1, 4, 7]; Amos 9:11; Obadiah 1:15; Micah 4:8; 5:3 [5:4]; Nahum 2:3 [2:2]; Zephaniah 2:7, 10; 3:20; Zechariah 9:12; 10:6, 9; Malachi 3:7.

The literary turn did not mean historical criticism ceased, and in redaction criticism of the Minor Prophets the literary and historical came together.[41] Redaction criticism attends not to the original prophet who uttered the words of prophecy but rather (akin to tradition history) how scribes received, interpreted, and reinterpreted earlier prophecy for their day, editing earlier texts to compose a new prophetic text for new generations. In the twentieth century especially, redaction criticism assessed how individual prophetic books in the Minor Prophets developed and were edited together. Marvin Sweeney provides a helpful overview of redaction criticism of each book in the corpus, as does the recent edited volume by Jakob Wöhrle and Lena-Sophia Tiemeyer.[42]

In the late twentieth century, however, redaction criticism attended to the editing and growth of the entirety of the Minor Prophets as a unified, composite book. As early as 1921, Karl Budde argued that the editing of the Minor Prophets leaves us unable to see the form and nature ("Gestalt und Persönlichkeit") of each individual prophet in his own time.[43] He argues that the prophetic books in the Minor Prophets tend to strip away biographical details (he explores Hosea, Amos, and Micah), leaving the prophets sitting loose to history. When we read the book of Amos or Hosea, for example, we do not read the words of an originating prophet or his biographical experiences, but rather we read the perspectives of later editors that refract the former words of Amos or Hosea and incorporate them into a final scribal composition that comprises the *book* called Amos or Hosea within a corpus called the Minor Prophets ("the Twelve"). For Budde, the scribal activity was completed in the third or fourth centuries BC, and the scribes deleted the biographical profiles of the prophets so that Yahweh's voice predominated. Budde argues that

---

[41]For an excellent introduction to redaction criticism of the Minor Prophets, see Marvin A. Sweeney, "The Prophets and Prophetic Books, Prophetic Circles and Traditions," in *Hebrew Bible/Old Testament: The History of Its Interpretation*, vol. 3/2, *The Twentieth Century*, ed. Magne Saebo (Göttingen: Vandenhoeck & Ruprecht, 2015), 500-530; Wöhrle and Tiemeyer, *Book of the Twelve*.
[42]Sweeney, "Prophets and Prophetic Books," 525-29.
[43]Karl Budde, "Eine Folgenschwere Redaktion des Zwölfprophetenbuch," *ZAW* 39 (1921): 218-29; see esp. 218.

the theological focus in the editorial process made the Twelve a more sacred book.⁴⁴

Scholars respond in various ways to Budde's basic hypothesis of the editing of the entire corpus.⁴⁵ If the individual books are edited, and if the edited books are brought together into *one* Book of the Twelve, then perhaps the edited volume should be read as a whole instead of one by one. In fact, the ancients may have viewed the Minor Prophets as a unified book. Among Jewish interpreters, these prophetic books were read in some way as a collection. Jewish rabbis identified the Minor Prophets simply with the moniker *terê ʿāśār*, "The Twelve," indicating the collection of these twelve smallish prophetic books ought to be understood in some way together. The Jewish text of Sirach (ca. 200 BC) reflects this disposition in Sirach 49:10. In this text, the "bones of the Twelve prophets" comfort Jacob with words of hope. The prophets in view are the Minor Prophets or "the Twelve," providing a message of hope for God's people.

Indeed, some explore the Minor Prophets not only as twelve individual prophetic books but also as an anthology that can be read as *one* book. James Nogalski offers a comprehensive redaction-critical exploration of the Minor Prophets.⁴⁶ He argues for an early "Book of the Four," namely, portions of Hosea, Amos, Micah, and Zephaniah as well as a collection of Haggai–Zechariah 1–8. Scribes united the twelve prophets together through intentionally repeated terms ("catchword chains") that tie the corpus together. For example: Hosea 14:2 [14:1] // Joel 2:12; 4:16 [3:16] // Amos 1:2; 9:12 // Obadiah 19, 1 // Jonah (messenger to nations); Jonah 4:2 // Micah 7:18-19 // Nahum 1:2-3; 1:1 // Habakkuk 1:1; 2:20 // Zephaniah 1:7.⁴⁷ The book of Joel is key to Nogalski's argument. In his estimation, the entire corpus gains significant shape with the addition of Joel and the editorial activity to the other

---

⁴⁴Budde, "Eine Folgenschwere Redaktion," 225-26. Budde's conclusion remains untenable, and most have rejected or ignored it even while recognizing the genuine insight of the edited nature of the twelve prophetic books.

⁴⁵See James D. Nogalski, "Where *Are* the Prophets in the Book of the Twelve?," in Boda, Floyd, and Toffelmire, *Book of the Twelve*, 163-82. Nogalski agrees with Budde that the Book of the Twelve does not focus on the profile of the prophet in the same way as does, say, Isaiah, Jeremiah, or Ezekiel. "The character of the core material collected does *not* focus upon the prophet as person. There are no large scale prophetic narrative collections; in fact, there are no prophetic narratives apart from Jonah, Amos 7:10-17, and Hos 1 and 3" (182).

⁴⁶James D. Nogalski, *Literary Precursors to the Book of the Twelve*, BZAW 217 (Berlin: de Gruyter, 1993); Nogalski, *Redactional Processes in the Book of the Twelve*, BZAW 218 (Berlin: de Gruyter, 1993).

⁴⁷For a full listing of how the Minor Prophets allude to one another, see Nogalski, *Redactional Processes*, 290-91.

books that went along with the Joel layer. It serves as the literary anchor to the remainder of the Minor Prophets.[48]

Others nuance Nogalski's approach. Christopher Seitz recognizes the fertility of redactional models but presses beyond them to read the Twelve Prophets canonically, taking the edited nature of the Twelve as foundational for a canonical and theological reading. In so doing, Seitz builds on the impetus of Brevard Childs.[49] For Seitz, a canonical reading of the Twelve (indeed, of the prophets) opens up theological associations between texts, framing divine agency and human response. Thus the Twelve Prophets becomes an index to identify divine, rather than merely human, intentions for Israel and the nations. History is not about excavating the lives of the prophets or the history of Israel in the Twelve, but rather the Twelve is understood as projecting an economy of divine action in past, present, and future.

Returning to redaction criticism, Aaron Schart agrees with Nogalski on many points, but for him the touchstone book is Amos rather than Joel. He argues for a six-step model of editorial development by which the final form of the Twelve gained its shape.[50] Amos and Hosea were combined, then a Deuteronomistic editor added Micah and Zephaniah to compose the Book of the Four prophets. Nahum and Habakkuk then were added, followed by the Haggai–Zechariah corpus. Joel and Obadiah were then brought into the corpus, with Jonah and Malachi finalizing the process.

Dissatisfied with previous models because they neglect the redactional development of the individual books in concert with the redaction of the Minor Prophets as a whole, Wöhrle explores each individual book's redactional history (except Hosea) and relates these to the development of the Twelve in its entirety. He confirms a Book of the Four and the Haggai–Zechariah 1–8 corpus. However, his model proceeds along an eight-step process of editorial growth to arrive at the final shape of the Twelve.[51] This

---

[48] Nogalski, *Redactional Processes*, 274-80.
[49] Christopher R. Seitz, *Prophecy and Hermeneutics: Toward a New Introduction to the Prophets*, STI (Grand Rapids, MI: Baker Academic, 2007), 93-246; Seitz, *The Goodly Fellowship of the Prophets: The Achievement of Association in Canon Formation* (Grand Rapids, MI: Baker Academic, 2009), 77-104.
[50] Aaron Schart, *Die Entstehung Des Zwölfprophetenbuchs: Neubearbeitungen von Amos Im Rahmen schriftenübergreifender Redaktionsprozesse*, BZAW 260 (Berlin: de Gruyter, 1997).
[51] Jakob Wöhrle, *Die frühen Sammlungen des Zwölfprophetenbuches: Entstehung und Komposition*, BZAW 360 (Berlin: de Gruyter, 2006); Wöhrle, *Der Abschluss des Zwölfprophetenbuches: Buchübergreifende Redaktionsprozesse in den späten Sammlungen*, BZAW 389 (Berlin: de Gruyter, 2008).

brief overview barely scratches the surface, as German-speaking scholarship (especially) continues to explore redactional models for the Twelve.

However, some are not as convinced by redactional models for a unified Book of the Twelve. Tchavdar Hadjiev asserts, "The 'Book of the Twelve' was not rediscovered but (re)invented by modern scholarship."[52] Similarly, Ehud Ben Zvi thinks that the Twelve ought to be read as a compilation, or anthology, of twelve individual prophetic books, without reference to redactional models.[53] Ben Zvi argues that even if individual books in the Twelve occur on a single scroll (*a* Book of the Twelve), as evidenced by some Dead Sea Scrolls, a unitary scroll does not necessitate a unified internal reading logic, demonstrated by catchword chains or the like.[54] The Twelve is a collection of *individual* prophetic books with distinctive contributions. Peterson, too, remains unconvinced that the diversity of models described above provide a clear picture of the redactional development of the Twelve along a unified theme. In his view, the Twelve is an anthology devoted to the theme of the day of the Lord, without committing one to the redactional models described above.[55]

In this volume, we focus on the individual messages of the Minor Prophets and then secondarily correlate these messages within the corpus of the Twelve. In this way, we read these prophetic books as a kind of anthology. We recognize redactional models as we go along, even giving preference to one or another redactional model within the volume at certain points. However, we believe that the anthology model makes best sense of the material. Secondarily, we correlate these individual prophetic books as productive co-texts that can and should be read alongside one another. We

---

[52] Tchavdar S. Hadjiev, "A Prophetic Anthology Rather than a Book of the Twelve," in Wöhrle and Tiemeyer, *Book of the Twelve,* 90-108, here 103.
[53] Ehud Ben Zvi, *Social Memory Among the Literati of Yehud,* BZAW 509 (Berlin: de Gruyter, 2019). This volume comprises substantial contributions Ben Zvi has made in memory studies and the Hebrew Bible over a period of years. For memory and the prophets, see especially his "Remembering the Prophets Through the Reading and Rereading of a Collection of Prophetic Books in Yehud: Methodological Considerations and Explorations," in *Social Memory Among the Literati,* 80-108.
[54] Ehud Ben Zvi, "Twelve Prophetic Books or 'The Twelve': A Few Preliminary Considerations," in Watts and House, *Forming Prophetic Literature,* 125-57, esp. 131. See also his contribution in Ehud Ben Zvi and James D. Nogalski, *Two Sides of a Coin: Juxtaposing Views on Interpreting the Book of the Twelve/The Twelve Prophetic Books,* Analecta Gorgiana 201 (intro. Thomas Römer; Piscataway: Gorgias Press, 2009), 47-86.
[55] David L. Peterson, "A Book of the Twelve?," in *Reading and Hearing the Book of the Twelve,* ed. James D. Nogalski and Marvin A. Sweeney, Symposium Series 15 (Atlanta: Society of Biblical Literature, 2000), 1-10; Ronald L. Troxel, *Prophetic Literature: From Oracles to Books* (Chichester, UK: Wiley-Blackwell, 2012), 82-83.

also explore what happens when these books are read corporately rather than only individually.[56]

The theological turn. The literary turn in biblical studies was followed by the postmodern turn, with its wild pluralism and smorgasbord of methods. Insofar as the literary turn attended to the books of the Minor Prophets as coherent literary wholes, it presented a major change to historical criticism. However, before the literary turn could be fully appropriated, the postmodern turn was upon us. It yielded a bewildering variety of readings of the Minor Prophets, including deconstructionist, ideological of many sorts, psychoanalytic, and so on.[57] While too many of these have been examples of eisegesis rather than exegesis, they have provided fresh insights, and we will refer to these where relevant in the chapters that follow. Postmodernism challenged the hegemony of historical criticism but retained its basic presuppositions so that even as postmodernism has waned, historical criticism remains the default mode of much study of the Minor Prophets.

With its diversity, postmodern interpretation opened the door again to religion in biblical studies. Not surprisingly, therefore, a minority approach called theological interpretation developed, building on the seminal theological interpretation of Karl Barth, and Brevard Childs's canonical criticism. This theological turn, in our view, introduces the possibility of fresh readings of the Minor Prophets that draw on all the insights of historical criticism and the literary turn, but it makes the goal of its work listening for God's address through the Minor Prophets today. Theological interpretation is a broad movement but at its best is read *from faith*—thus rejecting the epistemic foundations of the Enlightenment—*to faith*—thus leveraging all our academic resources toward attending to God's address.

Each of the approaches offered in the academy demonstrates some gains. However, our approach in this volume will be to integrate literary, historical, and kerygmatic aspects in the service of theological interpretation. Although we note some historical development of biblical books within and across the Twelve, our main goal is to ascertain the theology of the Twelve not by excavating the world behind the text or the historical development

---

[56]Note the excellent discussions in Heiko Wenzel, ed., *The Book of the Twelve: An Anthology of Prophetic Books or the Result of Complex Redactional Processes?*, Osnabrücker Studien zur Jüdischen und Christlichen Bibel 4 (Göttingen: Vandenhoeck & Ruprecht, 2018).

[57]See, e.g., Yvonne Sherwood, *A Biblical Text and Its Afterlives: The Survival of Jonah in Western Culture* (Cambridge: Cambridge University Press, 2000).

of the Twelve (whether as a unified corpus or as individual books). Our entry into understanding the theological presentation of the Minor Prophets is through a close reading of the biblical texts, their communication strategies, and the world they project and invite us to indwell. Where intertextuality between texts, shared themes, and motifs appears throughout the Twelve, we will explore it to understand more fully how these texts present the God disclosed in these books.

To this end, we must embrace the fact that the Minor Prophets/the Book of the Twelve takes the reader on a journey from the eighth century BC through Assyrian, Neo-Babylonian, and Persian dominance in the ancient Near East. It is a journey of delight, horror, and hope. These texts display the vagaries of the kingdoms of Israel in the north and Judah in the south, the exile of the northern kingdom and southern kingdom, and finally the restoration period after the exile.

The Minor Prophets thereby present a microcosm of Israel's history, and these texts depict Yahweh governing history, calling Israel and the nations to account. Those who are "wise" (Hos 14:10 [14:9]) are invited to trust in Yahweh's plans because of his justice. God orchestrates history as a movement of judgment and redemption, from the monarchy in the eighth century BC to the Persian period in the fifth century BC. In this movement, God works toward redemption for Israel and the nations. As he is king over his creation (Amos 4), the Twelve present Yahweh's comprehensive attentiveness to *all* of life: humanity, nations (Zeph 3; Mal 1), land (Hos 2:20-25 [2:18-23]), and beasts (Joel 1:18). The Twelve instill hope within its readers that Yahweh will restore creation in the future through his reign. This future emerges through metaphors, images, and distinctive language in the Twelve.[58] In the meantime, the Minor Prophets expects their readers to be formed and transformed by his word so that they might live well and rightly before God, by faith.

The New Testament provides a fuller context to hear the Twelve as Christian Scripture and reveals the cohesion of the biblical witness. For this reason, each of our chapters on the Minor Prophets will draw attention to New Testament reception and adaptation of the Twelve Prophets as they disclose Jesus of Nazareth, who is the focus of the revelation of God.[59]

---

[58] Note the careful study of Simon J. De Vries, "Futurism in the Preexilic Minor Prophets Compared with That of the Postexilic Minor Prophets," in *Thematic Threads in the Book of the Twelve*, ed. Paul L. Redditt and Aaron Schart, BZAW 325 (Berlin: de Gruyter, 2003), 252-72.

[59] Heath A. Thomas, "Hearing the Minor Prophets: The Book of the Twelve and God's Address," in Bartholomew and Beldman, *Hearing the Old Testament*, 372-73.

Recommended Reading

Firth, David G., and Brittany N. Melton, eds. *Reading the Book of the Twelve Minor Prophets*. SSBT. Bellingham, WA: Lexham Academic, 2022.

O'Brien, Julia M., ed. *The Oxford Handbook on the Minor Prophets*. Oxford: Oxford University Press, 2021.

Seitz, Christopher R. *Prophecy and Hermeneutics: Toward a New Introduction to the Prophets*. STI. Grand Rapids, MI: Baker Academic, 2007.

Thomas, Heath A. "Hearing the Minor Prophets: The Book of the Twelve and God's Address." In *Hearing the Old Testament: Listening for God's Address*, ed. Craig G. Bartholomew and David J. H. Beldman, 356-79. Grand Rapids, MI: Eerdmans, 2012.*

Wenzel, Heiko, ed. *The Book of the Twelve: An Anthology of Prophetic Books or the Result of Complex Redactional Processes?* Osnabrücker Studien zur Jüdischen und Christlichen Bibel 4. Göttingen: Vandenhoeck & Ruprecht, 2018.

Wöhrle, Jakob, and Lena-Sophia Tiemeyer, eds. *The Book of the Twelve: Composition, Reception and Interpretation*. VTSup 184. Leiden: Brill, 2020.*

Recommended reading marked with a "" indicates introductory works.*

2

The Ancient World of Prophecy

ISRAEL WAS AN ANCIENT NEAR EASTERN NATION, and the Old Testament comes to us through Yahweh's immersion in its life. The result is that the literature of the Old Testament is similar to *and* dissimilar from that of the ancient Near East. The Minor Prophets thus emerge from the world of prophecy within the ancient Near East. Israel came onto the historical scene relatively late in the history of the ancient world, and prophetic material from it spans the second millennium BC to the Persian period (roughly 2000–400 BC). Thus, if we want to understand the Minor Prophets more fully, it is helpful to understand prophecy in the ancient world and the empires in which it emerged.

CONCEPTUALIZING PROPHETS AND PROPHECY IN THE ANCIENT WORLD

Biblical prophets, like their ancient Near Eastern analogs, speak for deities and relate intimately to the divine. Israel's prophets proclaimed the word of Yahweh, and ancient Near Eastern prophets spoke for the myriad of deities in the ancient world. The earliest sources for prophecy derive from the middle of the third millennium BC to the end of the fifth century BC.[1] These regions include upper and lower Mesopotamia to the land of Canaan.

Jonathan Stökl relates the role of prophet to a broader group he calls "diviners." This broader designation enables one to divide prophetic actions into discrete categories. In the ancient Near East one finds "technical diviners," or those who are trained in specific skills—whether interpreting

---

[1] This timeframe differs from the otherwise excellent work of Jonathan Stökl, *Prophecy in the Ancient Near East: A Philological and Sociological Comparison*, CHANE 56 (Leiden: Brill, 2012), 1. We believe prophecy extends beyond the lower limit of the Persian period before the rise of Hellenism in the fourth century BC. Some prophetic texts in the Minor Prophets appear to be quite late (Joel and Malachi) but do not readily display Greek influence.

dreams (dream divination) or examining entrails or livers of animals (haruspicy and extispicy), celestial movements (astrology), or the like to discern divine will, fortune, or ill. These technical diviners are complemented by "intuitive diviners." These are diviners who need not be trained with a technical skill such as astrology or haruspicy, but they receive a divine message for an individual or group. Stökl provides a taxonomy of diviners, adapted in figure 2.1.[2]

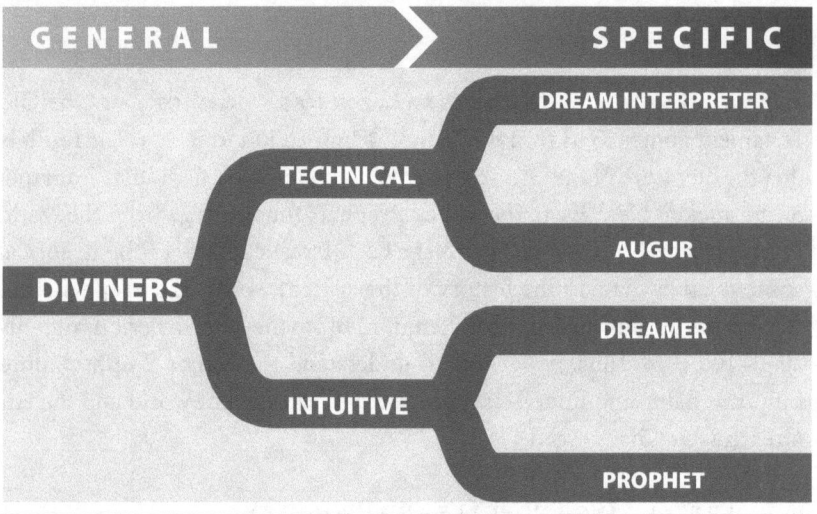

Figure 2.1. A taxonomy of diviners in the ancient world

In this framework, prophets of Israel and Judah should be classified as intuitive diviners. Some of Israel's prophets exhibit characteristics of dreamers (e.g., the prophet Zechariah, who experiences dream-visions), but overwhelmingly Israel's prophetic heritage exhibits those who hear from God and deliver God's messages to individuals or groups (such as Amos, Hosea, Habakkuk, Jonah, etc.).

---

[2]Stökl, *Prophecy in the Ancient Near East*, 10. Martti Nissinen uses the terminology "inductive" and "non-inductive" divination in *Prophets and Prophecy in the Ancient Near East*, with contributions by C. L. Seow and Robert K. Ritner, Writings from the Ancient World 12 (Atlanta: Society of Biblical Literature, 2003), 1. John H. Walton distinguishes between the two types of divination as "inspired" (= intuitive diviner) and "deductive" (= technical diviner) in *Ancient Near Eastern Thought and the Old Testament: Introducing the Conceptual World of the Hebrew Bible* (Grand Rapids, MI: Baker Academic, 2006), 240-41. He borrows these designators from Jean Bottéro, *Religion in Ancient Mesopotamia* (Chicago: University of Chicago Press, 2001), 170-71.

What was the communication structure(s) of divination? Thomas Schneider clarifies this question for ancient divination, and we adapt his work in table 2.1.[3]

Table 2.1. Schneider's Communication Structures for Prophecy

I	II	III	IV
explicit message	implicit message	explicit message	explicit message
external addressee	external addressee	external addressee	internal addressee
h » H » G » H » h	H » g » H » h	G » H » h	G » h
4 communication acts	3 communication acts	2 communication acts	1 communication act
oracles	divination	prophecy	dreaming

Note: *h* stands for passive human receiver of the divine message; *H* stands for the active human diviner; *G* stands for the active deity/god who speaks; *g* stands for the passive divine will as is interpretable from omens.

Note that the complexity of interaction between human(s) and divine interchange decreases as one moves from the left of the table to the right. In the most complex divination act (situation I), the human goes to a priest to receive an oracle about a query. The priest then goes to the deity to request direction or an answer and then relays this back to the petitioner. In situation II, the diviner engages astrology or extispicy (or some other means) to determine the will of the gods.[4] Once known, the diviner communicates that to the interested party, often a royal figure. In situation III, the deity addresses the prophet with a message that the prophet must then in turn relay to an individual or group. Finally, in situation IV, the deity engages an individual (a prophet or another individual) through a dream, which may or may not be interpreted by the dreamer.[5]

Despite marginal evidence of situations I, II, and IV, without doubt most prophetic communication in the Minor Prophets presents situation III: God speaks to the prophet, who in turn addresses the message to an individual or group (or both). The prophets of Israel and Judah speak the messages of God to the people of God and to outsiders, as in Jonah, captured by formulaic phrases that reinforce the prevalence of situation III in the Minor

---

[3]Thomas Schneider, "A Land Without Prophets? Examining the Presumed Lack of Prophecy in Ancient Egypt," in *Enemies and Friends of the State: Ancient Prophecy in Context*, ed. Christopher A. Rollston (University Park, PA: Eisenbrauns, 2018), 62.
[4]Extispicy and haruspicy are forms of divination that examine the entrails of animals (often sacrificial) to determine the will of the gods or one's fate.
[5]Schneider, "Land Without Prophets?," 62-63.

Prophets: "word of the Lord" (*dəbar YHWH*: 40x); "thus says the Lord" (*kōh 'āmar YHWH*: 43x); "utterance of Yahweh" (*nə'ūm YHWH*: 40x).[6]

The Gods of the Prophets

How did the ancient peoples *view* their deities? The prophets of Mesopotamia and the Transjordan spoke on behalf of multiple deities in their polytheistic pantheons. So too with the Canaanites, Israel's most immediate neighbors. These deities exerted authority over elements in the natural world, human skills and culture, and life and death. High deities (El and Asherah) copulated and procreated various sons and daughters who were also divine beings. Far from secular/sacred distinctions we see in the modern world, the totality of existence for the ancients was awash with the divine.

This list of Canaanite deities pales in comparison with Mesopotamian religion. The University of Pennsylvania worked with an international team to catalog the gods and goddesses of ancient Mesopotamia.[7] Due to limitations of time and funding, the project only cataloged the *fifty* most significant deities in the pantheon. But the earliest accounting of the Mesopotamian pantheon (2600 BC) lists no less than 560 deities.[8]

The Mesopotamian pantheon reveals how the ancients viewed their world as infused with gods. Each element in the material world was a part and an extension of the divine order of things. Deities could battle one another and contest one another's will, even taking on the characteristics of one another. If the high god Enlil gave a decree of judgment against a city, no deity could thwart it. As a result, the Mesopotamian patron deities were known to lament the downfalls of their cities.[9]

Patron (or national) deities were thought to protect and provide for the city-state in which they were worshiped: Chemosh was the patron deity of Moab, Marduk was the patron deity of Babylon, Hadad was the patron deity of Damascus, Aššur was the patron deity of Nineveh, and so on.[10]

---

[6]On our counting.
[7]Based on data prepared by the UK Higher Education Academy–funded Ancient Mesopotamian Gods and Goddesses project. The data is accessible via http://oracc.museum.upenn.edu/amgg/index.html.
[8]Glenn S. Holland, *Gods in the Desert: Religions of the Ancient Near East* (Lanham, MD: Rowman & Littlefield, 2010), 114.
[9]Piotr Michalowski, *The Lamentation over the Destruction of Sumer and Ur*, Mesopotamian Civilizations 1 (Winona Lake, IN: Eisenbrauns, 1989).
[10]Holland, *Gods in the Desert*, 83, 114-18, 171, 219-21.

Patron deities conspired with the royal house, authorizing the king's authority. For instance, in Babylon this close connection between king and patron god was renewed and invigorated each year at the New Year's festival (the Akitu festival).

Patron gods could be defeated in battle by another deity, leading to the desecration and sacking of the patron god's shrine in their own city. One finds evidence of these kinds of defeats in the city-lament tradition of Mesopotamia.[11] While patron deities were thought to protect their cities and people, from the evidence of the city-lament tradition, patron deities could be stripped of their authority by the power of the high god in the pantheon.

How does this map onto the conceptual world of Israel's prophets? Zephaniah's initial prophetic word is suggestive. Yahweh is the Creator God of the universe and the covenant God of Israel. Distinct from their ancient Near Eastern neighbors, Israel's prophets collapsed both the decree of destruction and the activity of the foe onto Yahweh rather than differentiating it to two deities. This was an outcome of Israel's view of Yahweh, the supreme God of creation and covenant, the high god and the patron God of Israel. Unlike the patron deities in the Mesopotamian city laments, in prophetic texts (and in the biblical book of Lamentations) Yahweh is never overpowered or coerced to abandon his sanctuary by another, more powerful deity. Rather than differentiating the loss of Jerusalem and its decree for destruction as two deities—a high god and a patron deity—monotheistic orthodoxy understood Yahweh as the agent of destruction *as well as* the one who suffered the loss of his sanctuary (in the place of the patron deities).[12] In light of the devastation of the city and cult, there remained therefore an implicit hope in the deity.

---

[11] For Mesopotamian city laments, see "Sumerian Canonical Compositions. A. Divine Focus. 4. Lamentations: Lamentation over the Destruction of Sumer and Ur," trans. Jacob Klein, *COS* 1.166:535-39; Samuel N. Kramer, "A Sumerian Lamentation," and "Sumerian Lamentation," trans. Samuel N. Kramer, in *Ancient Near Eastern Texts Relating to the Old Testament*, 3rd ed., ed. J. B. Pritchard (Princeton, NJ: Princeton University Press, 1969), 455-63, 611-19. For the Curse of Agade, see Jerrold S. Cooper, *The Curse of Agade* (Baltimore: Johns Hopkins University Press, 1983); Michalowski, *Lamentation over the Destruction*. For *balag* and *eršemma* see Paul Wayne Ferris, Jr., *The Genre of Communal Lament in the Bible and the Ancient Near East*, SBLDS 127 (Atlanta: Scholars Press, 1992), 38-53. Much of the discussion that follows on city laments derives from Heath A. Thomas, *Poetry and Theology in the Book of Lamentations: The Aesthetics of an Open Text*, HBM 47 (Sheffield: Sheffield Phoenix, 2013), 144-47.

[12] For a positive assessment of exclusive monotheism in the Judahite state in the eighth and seventh centuries BC, see N. Avigad, "The Contribution of Hebrew Seals to an Understanding of Israelite Religion and Society," in *Ancient Israelite Religion: Essays in Honor of Frank Moore*, ed. Patrick D. Miller Jr., Paul D. Hanson, and S. D. McBride (Philadelphia: Fortress, 1987), 195-208.

If this is how gods are viewed in the ancient world, how then does prophecy relate to ancient peoples' views of the divine? What did prophecy look like, and who could prophesy? To these questions we now turn.[13]

Prophecy in Egypt

Prophecy of the situation III sort described above was not present among the Egyptians.[14] Some forms of prophetic activity like situation III were possible prior to the Hellenistic age in Egypt, but any evidence of it has been lost.[15] Thus there would not appear to be much value in comparing Israel's prophetic literature and Egyptian texts, because they do not share a common heritage.[16] However, it is worth remembering that in the Old Testament, Moses is the prophet par excellence, and if we take his historicity seriously, as we do, then Moses' prophetic ministry stands in sharp contrast to the religion of Egypt.

Prophecy in Mesopotamia

With a close connection between temple, palace, and prophecy, prophets in Mesopotamia served as royal advisers. They accessed the heavenly realms via ecstatic utterances, augury, extispicy, haruspicy, or astrology in order to legitimize the crown (ensure proper succession, etc.), to warn the court of unforeseen outcomes or the fallout of a decision (war, tariff, etc.), or to justify royal action.[17]

In our survey of prophecy in Mesopotamia, we will start from the earliest evidence in Old Babylonia, including the vast material from the ancient location of Mari. The city-state of Mari lay on the west bank of the Euphrates River, and it was significant in northern Mesopotamia until Hammurabi of Babylon destroyed the city between 1760 and 1757 BC. For twelve hundred years, Mari existed as a major cultural site, evidenced by the roughly fifteen thousand tablets unearthed by archaeologists in the 1930s, affording a vivid picture of ancient Mesopotamian prophecy.[18]

---

[13]For ancient Near Eastern prophetic texts, see Martti Nissinen, *Ancient Prophecy: Near Eastern, Biblical, and Greek Perspectives* (Oxford: Oxford University Press, 2017), esp. "Appendix 2: Catalogue of Ancient Near Eastern Documents of Prophecy," 361-66.

[14]Some have cataloged as prophetic the Egyptian prophecies of Neferti, the admonitions of Ipu-Wer, the Instruction of Amen-Em-Het and the Wenamun travelogue. But these should not be counted as prophetic, if by that we intend a deity speaking to a human recipient.

[15]Schneider, "Land Without Prophets," 78-79.

[16]See Schneider, "Land Without Prophets," 69-73.

[17]Walton, *Ancient Near Eastern Thought*, 267-69.

[18]For English translations, see Nissinen, *Prophets and Prophecy*, 13-92.

Prophets in ancient Mesopotamia performed specific functions related to temple and palace, and they can be categorized into professional and occasional roles (see table 2.2).

Table 2.2. Prophets in Old Babylonia

PROFESSIONAL PROPHETS IN OLD BABYLONIAN TEXTS	
āpilum	function in the royal court as spokespersons for the gods
(bārû)	(technically trained in various forms of divination, such as extispicy)[a]
(tupšarru)	(technically trained as scribes, but the term is used to describe celestial diviners)[b]
nabû	possible technical diviner and precursor to the Israelite nabî
LAY PROPHETS IN OLD BABYLONIAN TEXTS	
muḫḫûm and qammatum	cultic personnel, likely linked to a specific shrine, who give a spontaneous message from a deity through ecstatic performance and is often linked to lament
assinnu kurgarrû	cultic personnel, likely linked to a specific shrine, who give a spontaneous message from a deity through ecstatic performance, perhaps linked with music and dancing

[a] With Stökl, we do not include this figure in our study, as we are exploring (primarily) intuitive divination (prophecy) rather than technical divination.
[b] John H. Walton, *Ancient Near Eastern Thought and the Old Testament: Introducing the Conceptual World of the Hebrew Bible* (Grand Rapids, MI: Baker Academic, 2006), 264.

We place the *bārû* and *tupšarru* in parentheses in table 2.2 because of their fit with "technical divination" rather than intuitive divination, or prophecy proper. Therefore, these two kinds of diviners do not mirror prophecy found in Israel or Judah.

The *āpilum*, by contrast, represent professional spokespeople for deities (situation III). They emerge in the Mari texts and performed specialized functions. In the Mari texts, these were the only figures able to send correspondence to the king. Stökl characterizes the *āpilum* as agents in a "royal advisory service" whose primary function was to give the king and other leaders divine information that would help them make decisions.[19] They lived in and around the royal court and were able to go to other regions, cities, and temples to communicate to diverse parties on behalf of the crown and their representative deity. In terms of royal succession, military advance, or significant state decisions, the crown would consult

---

[19] Stökl, *Prophecy in the Ancient Near East*, 47-50; Jonathan Stökl, "A Royal Advisory Service: Prophecy and the State in Mesopotamia," in Rollston, *Enemies and Friends*, 87-88.

the *āpilum* to receive divine guidance as they deliberated. Sometimes the *āpilum* were sent out on military excursions.

Unlike the *āpilum*, lay prophets in Old Babylonia enjoyed careers other than prophecy. The *muḫḫûm* were cultic personnel related to specific shrines (probably the deity Ištar). They did engage in strange behavior; one text describes a *muḫḫûm* consuming a living lamb.[20] *Muḫḫûm* may have enacted their utterances in an altered state of mind (which may explain consuming a living lamb), but that is unclear.[21] Mari texts indicate that *muḫḫûm* experienced spontaneous and ecstatic experiences; the *muḫḫûm* appear in texts that relate to lament as well, which may signify that they had a special role in Mesopotamian laments. They do interact with the king, especially in texts related to the monthly ritual of Ištar, and likely they served the deity Ištar. The *qammaum* may have been a distinctive kind of female *muḫḫûm*.[22]

The *assinnu*, like the *muḫḫûm*, were cultic personnel and prophesied only occasionally. In the Mari texts, *assinnu* often appear with the *kurgarrû* (likely cultic personnel as well). Some argue these groups were homosexual or transgendered persons and because of this could traverse planes of existence (physical-spiritual, heaven-earth, etc.). However, this suggestion is uncertain. It is best to see these groups as belonging to the broad category of lay prophets, likely serving at the temple of Ištar and engaged in ecstatic prophecy. Because they are associated with Ištar, some of their activity was related to the warlike tendencies of the deity they revered.[23]

Neo-Assyrian archives provide ample evidence for prophecy during the seventh century BC.[24] The material derives from the royal archive of Nineveh, and their oracles are addressed primarily to the kings Esarhaddon (681–669) or Assurbanipal (668–627), sometimes to the queen mother. As a result, prophetic activity is *primarily* presented as giving advice to the royal court, often encouraging the court to "fear not" or to go forward with a decision (battle, war, or the like). The goddess Ištar features prominently in these letters. Prophets designated in this material are noted in table 2.3.

---

[20]Stökl, *Prophecy in the Ancient Near East*, 54.
[21]Walton, *Ancient Near Eastern Thought*, 264.
[22]Stökl, *Prophecy in the Ancient Near East*, 53–57, 62.
[23]Stökl, *Prophecy in the Ancient Near East*, 61.
[24]For English translations, see Nissinen, *Prophets and Prophecy*, 97–178.

The Ancient World of Prophecy

Table 2.3. Prophets in Neo-Assyrian Texts

raggimu/raggintu	male and female spokespersons for Assyrian deities that function (apparently) similarly to *āpilum*
maḫḫû	cultic personnel, likely linked to a specific shrine, who give a spontaneous message from a deity through ecstatic performance and is often linked to lament; analogue to the Old Babylonian *muḫḫûm*

Raggimu are analogs to the *āpilum*, but it is not clear whether they were linked primarily to the temple or royal palace. However, like the *āpilum*, they spoke to the royal court in letters and give oracles to the king. This leads us to believe that they were associated with the palace and functioned as royal advisers who inquired of the deity for guidance to deliver to the court.[25] The *maḫḫû* carry an analogous role to the Old Babylonian *muḫḫûm*, lay prophets primarily associated with the temple and cult and only occasionally prophesying through ecstatic utterance.

Old Babylonian and Neo-Assyrian sources show Mesopotamian prophecy functioned primarily to legitimize and advance the interests of the kingdom. The will of the deity (Bel, Ishtar, Nabu, El, Shamas, Sin, Marduk, or another god) was subsumed into the action of the royal court. In this way, Mesopotamian prophecy did little to critique royal designs or the aspirations of the crown. John Walton rightly claims, "Divination in the ancient Near East was focused on the *legitimation* of the king and the current regime."[26]

Prophecy in the Transjordan

Prophets emerged among other nations and people groups surrounding Israel and Judah. North and east of Israel, the Zakkur stela celebrates the victory of King Zakkur over King Ben-Hadad III of Damascus and his coalition forces in the eighth century BC. Zakkur was the king of the Syrian cities of Hamath and Luash. In the text, the coalition armies gather against Zakkur, and he asks Baalshamayn ("the Lord of Heaven") for help. Baalshamayn responds to Zakkur through "seers and through visionaries," encouraging him to "fear not" and proceed with victory in battle.[27] Like the Old Babylonian predecessors, seers and visionaries informed royal action: he should not fear because divinity has given the battle into his hands.[28]

---

[25]Stökl, "Royal Advisory Service," 99-106.
[26]Walton, *Ancient Near Eastern Thought*, 268.
[27]Nissinen, *Prophets and Prophecy*, 204-7.
[28]See Hélène Sader, "Prophecy in Syria: Zakkur of Hamath and Lu'ash," in Rollston, *Enemies and Friends*, 115-34.

Moving south toward Israel and Judah, we see evidence of the most significant Iron Age II prophet, Balaam, son of Beor. Balaam is known in archaeological evidence from the site of Deir ʿAlla, where an eighth century BC inscription depicts the actions of Balaam, son of Beor, a "seer" (*ḥzh*).[29] In this inscription, Balaam undergoes a vision in the night in which the gods come to him, and he sees a divine being like El, the Canaanite high god of the pantheon. The vision speaks of impending doom. After receiving the vision, Balaam wept, fasted (mourning actions associated with prophecy), and proclaimed to the people the vision he received.[30]

Balaam's message of doom is presented in terms of ominous ecological signs (clouds without light, birds of prey circling overhead, and mangled baby birds) and horrible reversals (hyenas receive instruction, adolescent foxes laugh at wise men, a poor woman mixes expensive myrrh). Balaam's message presents a dark and topsy-turvy world of doom. The gods have decreed, in their power, an inversion of the natural order of things, and Balaam must communicate this dire news. There is mention of action against the king ("I have punished the king"), but the identity of the king or his people remains unclear. This dark and ominous word of doom comes to Balaam unsolicited. The text reads, "The gods came to him during the night," and he must face their word of doom. In the night vision, El sits as the high god of the pantheon of gods, and the text indicates that Balaam responds to the entire weight of their message.

Balaam's oracle is a message against a king, and therefore it is possible that his words were designed to *counteract* a king's authority rather than purely legitimate it. Balaam is known as a prophet for hire who was supposed to pronounce doom against Israel but eventually spoke a word of blessing from Israel's God.

Prophets and Prophecy in Israel

In the light of what we have seen in the ancient world, how does prophecy in Israel compare? First, prophets in Israel, as in the ancient world, were understood as spokespeople for the divine. Israel's prophets stand within the

---

[29] For the text and translation, see Nissinen, *Prophets and Prophecy*, 207-12. For full discussion of the text, see Joel S. Burnett, "Prophecy in Transjordan: Balaam Son of Beor," in Rollston, *Enemies and Friends*, 135-204.

[30] Émile Puech, "Balaam and Deir ʿAlla," in *The Prestige of the Pagan Prophet Balaam in Judaism, Early Christianity and Islam*, ed. George H. van Kooten and Jacques van Ruiten, Themes in Biblical Narrative 11 (Leiden: Brill, 2008), 25-47.

stream of tradition of intuitive diviners who mediate between gods and humans. Through dreams and experiences with the gods, prophets in both the ancient world and in Israel share a common heritage.[31] This fact is unsurprising, as the cultural world of Israel did not drop, as it were, from the sky. Still, despite the similarities, Israel's prophets and prophecy are distinct from their ancient Near East neighbors in significant ways.

Terminology for prophets. Prophets are known in the biblical material by a variety of terms: "prophet" (*nby'*), "seer" (*r'h*), and "visionary" (*ḥzh*).[32] We get a glimpse of at least two of these terms in a brief aside by the narrator of 1 Samuel 9:9: "Formerly in Israel, when one went to inquire of God, he said, 'Come, let us go to the seer' [*r'h*], for the prophet [*nby'*] was formerly called a seer [*r'h*]." These terms may have something to do with different functions: the "seer" (*r'h*) may been an intuitive diviner rather than a technical diviner. It may be that the "seer" (*r'h*) was an independent prophet who had links with other prophetic groups or guilds called the "sons of the prophets" but not with the royal court; the "visionary" (*ḥzh*) was a diviner of the royal court (especially in Judah); the "prophet" (*nby'*) was a catchall term that encompassed the work of both "seer" (*r'h*) and "visionary" (*ḥzh*) as well as other activity.[33]

Alongside this terminology, prophetic activity has a story in Israel. In the early days, various figures are identified as prophets, though these figures *never* identify themselves as such: Abraham (Gen 20:7), Moses (Deut 34:10), Aaron (Ex 7:1), Miriam (Ex 15:20), Deborah (Judg 4:4), Samuel (1 Sam 3:20), and Gad (1 Sam 22:5). These figures intercede on behalf of others (Gen 20:7), receive visions or dreams from the deity (Num 12:6; see also Deut 13:1-5), speak God's word with dancing and music (Ex 15:20), inquire of God through technical means (1 Sam 28:6), and (most prevalent) receive a word from God (Ex 7:1; see also Deut 18:15-22).

The words from Amos 3:7 are instructive: "Indeed, the LORD Yahweh does nothing unless he reveals his counsel to his servants, the prophets." The word of God has been given, and the prophet is to speak the word: "A lion has roared: Who will not fear? The LORD Yahweh has spoken: Who will not prophesy?" (Amos 3:8). The prophets of Israel speak the word of Yahweh.

---

[31]See, e.g., 1 Sam 28:6, 15, where prophecy is correlated to technical divination through the Urim (and Thummim) and possibly dream interpretation.
[32]See Stökl, *Prophecy in the Ancient Near East*, 156-200.
[33]Stökl, *Prophecy in the Ancient Near East*, 196-200.

Social location of the prophets. Prophets remained tethered to the life and times in which they lived and the diverse conditions for which they contended. As reflected in the Twelve, prophets could be rich, poor, city or rural folk, priests and everyday people. Amos was a shepherd from Tekoa. Habakkuk may have been an urban priest. Haggai lived in Judah under a Persian occupation force, as did Zechariah. Biblical prophets came from diverse backgrounds, were not restricted to a specific social class, and may have been called by God to prophesy at any time. Although they could be from the north or south, most of the prophets we find in the Minor Prophets are associated with the south.

Actions of the prophets. Prophets spoke the word of Yahweh to encourage or denounce priests, leaders, king, the populace writ large, or even other nations. This fact radically distinguishes Israel's prophets from Mesopotamian ones. Rather than being instruments of the throne, prophets were instruments of Yahweh's will, and whenever God's people were tempted to turn from action that pleases Yahweh, Yahweh raised a prophet to denounce such waywardness. It mattered little whether that person or group was in leadership or not.

Gender of the prophets. Prophets could be male or female. The twelve prophets of our study are male, but male prophets were not universal in ancient Israel. Female prophets appear in texts that belong to nearly every age in the biblical testimony. Moses and Aaron's sister Miriam is described as a prophetess in Exodus 15:20-21. In the days of the judges, prior to the monarchy, Deborah is called a prophetess (Judg 4:4). A prophetess emerges in Isaiah 8, where the prophet Isaiah conceives a son with his wife, the "prophetess" (Is 8:3). Isaiah's wife was a prophetess during the reign of Ahaz, king of Judah. Apparently female prophets persisted to the late monarchy in Judah, as the prophetess Huldah appears at the discovery of the law scroll in the reign of Josiah (2 Kings 22:14). In Joel, the salvation oracle of Joel envisions a day when *all* will prophesy with the power of the Spirit of God: "Then afterward I will pour out my spirit on all flesh; your sons and your daughters shall prophesy, your old men shall dream dreams, and your young men shall see visions. Even on the male and female slaves, in those days, I will pour out my spirit" (Joel 2:28-29 NRSV [MT 3:1-2]).

The collection of the prophets. However the lives of Israel's prophets unfolded, aspects of the prophetic experiences were inscribed in texts, compiled in scrolls, and arranged into collections. This is especially true for the Minor Prophets. The Minor Prophets are a book of books; each individual work is theologically meaningful on its own but theologically enriched through intertextual and thematic interchange with the rest of the books in the Twelve. Thus, both the individual and corporate messages of the Minor Prophets are taken into account in the following chapters.

Recommended Reading

Bottéro, Jean. *Religion in Ancient Mesopotamia*. Chicago: University of Chicago Press, 2001.

Nissinen, Martti. *Ancient Prophecy: Near Eastern, Biblical, and Greek Perspectives*. Oxford: Oxford University Press, 2017.*

Rollston, Christopher A., ed. *Enemies and Friends of the State: Ancient Prophecy in Context*. University Park, PA: Eisenbrauns, 2018.

Stökl, Jonathan. *Prophecy in the Ancient Near East: A Philological and Sociological Comparison*. CHANE 56. Leiden: Brill, 2012.

Walton, John H. *Ancient Near Eastern Thought and the Old Testament: Introducing the Conceptual World of the Hebrew Bible*. Grand Rapids, MI: Baker Academic, 2006.*

Recommended reading marked with a "" indicates introductory works.*

3

Hosea

YAHWEH: LOVER AND LION

Marriage is that most intimate relationship that Genesis 2:24 evocatively describes as becoming "one flesh." Nowadays divorce is often seen as a necessary stepping stone in one's personal growth. However, as divorcées know only too well, divorce is never a celebration, even when necessitated by the ongoing unfaithfulness of one of the partners. Particularly when triggered by unfaithfulness, divorce opens up an unprecedented range of agonized emotions as the one flesh is ripped apart. Hosea, the opening book in the larger Book of the Twelve, uses the metaphors of marriage and divorce to evoke the seriousness of Israel's unfaithfulness, its dire consequences, and the Lord's pathos as Israel's God, as her lover.[1]

Hosea and His Context

The word order is unusual in Hosea 1:1, opening as it does with "The word of Yahweh."[2] This is the "proper title of the book," and what follows is grammatically subordinate to it.[3] As in Joel, Micah, and Zephaniah, the collective singular refers to the whole book and locates its origin in Yahweh. This title reminds us that in Hosea we are dealing with the word of the living God. However, the prophetic word was always spoken in and to a particular context, and to understand Hosea it is essential to take the details of Hosea 1:1 seriously. Such superscriptions are common in the prophetic books (see Is 1:1; Jer 1:1; Amos 1:1; Mic 1:1; Zeph 1:1), although not all the Minor Prophets contain them. "The word of the Lord that came to Hosea son of Beeri

---

[1]See Nicholas R. Werse, *Reconsidering the Book of the Four: The Shaping of Hosea, Amos, Micah and Zephaniah as an Early Prophetic Collection*, BZAW 517 (Berlin: de Gruyter, 2019).
[2]The normal word order is verb, subject, object.
[3]Hans W. Wolff, *Hosea*, Hermeneia (Minneapolis: Augsburg Fortress, 1974), 3.

during the reigns of Uzziah, Jotham, Ahaz and Hezekiah, kings of Judah, and during the reign of Jeroboam son of Joash king of Israel" (Hos 1:1 NIV).

Knowing what we do about these kings, we know that Hosea prophesied around the middle of the eighth century BC. He began his public ministry during or soon after that of Amos and was a contemporary of Isaiah and Micah. Most but not all of Hosea's prophecies are directed toward the northern kingdom as it headed down the tumultuous slope toward the punishment of exile at the hand of Assyria in 722/1 BC. Judging from the list of southern kings in Hosea 1:1, the "kings of Judah," Hosea must have prophesied for some thirty-eight years, although nothing is known about him apart from this book. He exercised his ministry during the tragic final days of the northern kingdom, during which the six kings following Jeroboam II (Zechariah, Shallum, Menahem, Pekahiah, Pekah, Hoshea) reigned within twenty-five years (see 2 Kings 14:23-27).[4]

Silence can be deafening, and already in the superscription we have a sense of God's anger with the northern kingdom in the omission of the names of the kings following Jeroboam II. Micah similarly omits them in his superscription: "Like the other prophets of the eighth century BC, Isaiah and Hosea, he omits their names because they usurped *I AM's* throne through assassinations; they set themselves up but not by *I AM's* prophetic designation (Hos 8:4)."[5]

Assyria was the great and brutal power of the day,[6] and Menahem notoriously accepted it as overlord and paid tribute to it. Soon after this, Israel was dismembered by Assyria as a result of the intrigue of Pekah, who succeeded to the throne by murdering Menahem's son, Pekahiah. Only the territories of Ephraim and western Manasseh remained under the Israelite king's jurisdiction, and then, as a result of Hoshea's disloyalty, Samaria was captured and its people exiled in 722/1. Thus the northern kingdom came to an end. There is no indication in Hosea that he lived to see the demise of the northern kingdom, and it would thus appear that his ministry lasted at least until shortly before the northern kingdom went into exile.

Hosea means "He has helped," formed from the perfect hiphil of *yš'* ("to help or deliver"). As we will see from his book, there is some irony to this

---

[4]Jeroboam II is indicated as such by his being "the son of Joash."
[5]Bruce K. Waltke, *A Commentary on Micah* (Grand Rapids, MI: Eerdmans, 2007), 40. Note that Waltke mistakenly speaks of "seventh century prophets."
[6]See Craig G. Bartholomew, *The Old Testament and God*. Old Testament Origins and the Question of God 1. (Grand Rapids, MI: Baker Academic, 2022), chapter 8.

name, since his main concern is Israel's apostasy and the coming judgment. Hosea's father's name was Beeri, but apart from what we learn about Hosea in this book, we know nothing else about him. It has generally been assumed that Hosea was a northern prophet who was born and lived in the northern kingdom. He certainly is well acquainted with what is going on in the north, and because he repeatedly refers to the northern kingdom as "Ephraim," it is suggested that he came from this tribe. However, Judah—the southern kingdom—is included in his prophecies, and unless we take such references to be later additions, Hosea clearly had the whole of Israel in mind even as he focused in particular on the north. We are told what we need to know, and that, it turns out, is quite remarkable enough. In order for Hosea to function as a prophet to Israel, he had to experience something of God's own pain.

THE BOOK OF HOSEA

While we gain access to the historical ministry of Hosea in his times as we explore his words in their historical context, it is important to remember that in the final form of the book a—at least—double trajectory is in view.[7] The story of Hosea's marriage—described in the third person in Hosea 1 and thus not by Hosea himself—and the record of his prophecies were brought together into a single book *after* the conclusion of his ministry and are preserved in this way for later generations, the second trajectory. The title of the book, "The word of Yahweh," alerts us to the fact that what God did and spoke through Hosea has ongoing relevance for future generations. Undoubtedly, the first audience after the north would have been the southern kingdom, which was itself taken into exile in 587/6. As we will see, the substantial use of Hosea in the New Testament alerts us to the continuing validity of the book as God's word for his people.

OUTLINE

As noted above, Hosea has a superscription or title (Hos 1:1) introducing the prophet and his context. Hosea 14:10 [14:9] functions as an epilogue or conclusion. Between these two, the book has two major sections. Hosea 1–3 deals with Hosea's marriage and children as metaphors for understanding Israel's relationship with Yahweh. Hosea 4–14 contains prophetic speeches in which Hosea brings Yahweh's case against Israel and Judah. As Andrew

---

[7]See James Trotter, *Reading Hosea in Achaemenid Yehuda*, JSOTSup 328 (Sheffield: Sheffield Academic Press, 2001).

Dearman notes, "A theme for chs. 4–14 comes in the court case (*rîb*) announced by Yahweh against Israel in 4:1-3. Most of what follows in 4:4–11:11 is a variation on the theme of Israel and Judah's culpability and coming judgment."[8] Hosea 11 and Hosea 14 in particular sound notes of hope. In this way Hosea 4–14 provides a recapitulation of the themes of sin-judgment-renewal in Hosea 1–3.[9]

Hosea has a small number of introductory and concluding markers, so it is hard to be sure of the literary structure. Our proposed structure is as follows.[10]

Hosea 1:1	Title
Hosea 1:2–3:5	Hosea's marriage and children, and Yahweh's marriage to Israel
Hosea 4:1–14:9 [4:1–14:8]	Yahweh's case against Israel
Hosea 14:10 [14:9]	Conclusion

Hosea 1–3: Hosea's and the Lord's Marriages

Hosea 1–3 brings Israel's unfaithfulness to dramatic expression. Hosea 1:2-9 is a third-person prose account of Hosea's marriage and children. Hosea 2 extends this to Yahweh's relationship with Israel in a prophetic speech in which Yahweh addresses Israel directly in the second person.[11] Hosea 3 is first-person narrative in which Hosea recounts how he was instructed to love his wife, Gomer, again even though she had moved in with another man. The move from third person to second person to first person creates a growing dramatic intensity until in Hosea 3 we receive a powerful sense of what loving his unfaithful wife, Gomer, meant in practice for Hosea. As the reader reflects on Hosea's pain, we are meant to be aware of how we are often unfaithful to one greater than Hosea.

"When Yahweh began to speak": Hosea 1:2-11. Literally, the Hebrew of Hosea 1:2a is, "The beginning of the word of Yahweh through Hosea." "That

---

[8] J. Andrew Dearman, *The Book of Hosea*, NICOT (Grand Rapids, MI: Eerdmans, 2010), 18.
[9] Dearman, *Book of Hosea*, 18.
[10] For detailed analyses of the structure, see the commentaries, e.g., Francis I. Anderson and David N. Freedman, *Hosea*, AB 24 (New York: Doubleday, 1980), 3-7.
[11] See Eleonore Stump, *Wandering in Darkness: Narrative and the Problem of Suffering* (New York: Oxford University Press, 2010), on the significance of second-person accounts of suffering. On metaphor and rhetoric in Hos 2, see Brad E. Kelle, *Hosea 2: Rhetoric and Metaphor in Historical Perspective* (Leiden: Brill, 2005).

came to" in Hosea 1:1 is typical vocabulary in the Old Testament for authentic divine revelation. "To speak through Hosea" alerts us to the fact that, like Jeremiah, Ezekiel, and Jonah, it is the totality of Hosea's experience and ministry that is revelatory. But, as with the shock of God's command to Jonah to "Go to Nineveh," nothing prepares us for the command God gives to Hosea as he sets his prophetic ministry in motion: "Go marry a promiscuous woman and have children with her."

Not surprisingly, commentators have struggled with this verse. Historically, many have interpreted the account of Hosea's marriage allegorically, primarily in an attempt to escape the implication that God calls on his prophet to marry a prostitute. God's command does not specify a particular woman, and it seems that Hosea is free to choose among many. But the fact that the woman is named as Gomer, daughter of Diblaim, subverts an allegorical reading.[12]

A more helpful question is that of the precise meaning of $’ēšet\ zənûnîm$ ("a promiscuous woman"). Multiple suggestions have been proposed:

- A young woman given to prostitution.
- A woman inclined toward adultery: $zənûnîm$ could be an abstract plural indicating a trait or spirit but not necessarily one acted on.
- A metaphorical-ritual interpretation according to which Gomer had received the marks of one who had participated in the Canaanite bridal rite of initiation. As part of the Canaanite cult of fertility, virgins were required to have intercourse with a stranger in the temple precincts. Symptomatic of Israel's idolatry, such practice was widespread, and in this respect Gomer would not have been exceptional but an average, modern, young Israelite woman.[13]

Among Hosea's hearers and readers, the twist in the tale is that any shock in relation to Yahweh's command and its morality is that Israel is guilty of far worse. Yahweh's covenant relationship with her is an exclusive one like marriage, and "this land is guilty of unfaithfulness to Yahweh" (Hos 1:2).

Hosea 1:4-8 deals with the three children born to Hosea and Gomer, namely, a son called Jezreel, a daughter called Lo-Ruhamah, and a second son called Lo-Ammi. Strange names, even in Hebrew, but pregnant with

---

[12]Douglas Stuart notes of Gomer, "Much ultimately useless effort has been expended seeking some sort of symbolic value for her name, of the name Diblaim. The symbolism is in Gomer's title, 'prostituting woman,' rather than in her name." Stuart, *Hosea-Jonah*, WBC 31 (Nashville: Nelson, 1987), 27.

[13]Wolff (*Hosea*, 14-15) advocates for this view.

symbolic significance. Jezreel, literally "God sows," was the name of the fruitful plane between the highlands of Samaria and Galilee. "With such a provocative riddle Hosea's prophetic ministry began, which was in the year 750 at the latest."[14]

In Hosea 1:4-5 Jezreel functions in two place-related ways: God will visit the blood of Jezreel—a reference to Jehu's massacre of the idolatrous pro-Ahab forces there—on the house of Jehu, and it is there that he will break Israel's military power, her "bow." Jehu was anointed by Elisha to become king of the north and to execute vengeance on the Baalism there.

Most translations and commentaries interpret Hosea 1:4 as God asserting that he will punish the northern kingdom for the massacres by Jehu. This is strange since Jehu was anointed by Elisha's messenger to wipe out the Baalism in the north and is commended in 2 Kings for doing so. Thus, according to Hans Wolff, in Hosea's period there was no connection to the Elisha narratives, and Hosea interprets Jehu's revolution *differently* from that of the circle around Elijah and Elisha (2 Kings 10:30). However, if Wolff's interpretation is right, this is not a new word on the attacks on Baalism but a contrary one. It would be strange indeed for God to relate his coming judgment on the northern kingdom to Jehu's actions against the Baalists in this way, when the northern kingdom has succumbed to the very idolatry that Hosea will prophesy against.

Literally, Hosea 1:4 reads, "and I will visit/avenge the blood of Jezreel on the house of Jehu and I will destroy the kingship of the house of Israel." A clue lies in that the visiting of the blood of Jezreel on the house of Jehu is linked to the destruction of the northern kingdom. The one and only northern king mentioned in Hosea 1:1 is Jeroboam son of Joash. "Son of Joash" links Jeroboam to Jehu's line, Jeroboam being the last king of Israel recognized by Yahweh. But as we learn from 2 Kings, Jeroboam II intensified the idolatrous behavior already tolerated by Jehu. There is irony at work here—the northern kingdom, ironically in Jehu's line, has become like the house of Ahab, and just as it was destroyed, so too will the northern kingdom be destroyed.[15] Unlike the names of the following two children, "Jezreel" is somewhat ambiguous, and as the child grew his name must have caused the Israelites to reflect on their past and what happened at Jezreel. In this sense

---

[14]Wolff, *Hosea*, 17.
[15]This reading is already found in Theodore of Mopsuestia, *Commentary on the Minor Prophets*, 42-43. He notes that "all those who ruled later over Israel imitated Ahab's attitude" (42).

it is akin to many of Jesus' parables: Let those who have ears to hear, hear! Jehu is a symbol of God's *no* to idolatry, and as the names of the next two children reveal, Yahweh is about to say no again in no uncertain terms.

Hosea's daughter is named Lo-Ruhamah, meaning "not loved" or "no-mercy," because God intends to cease acting in love toward the northern kingdom. Somewhat later Hosea has another son, and his name is even more disturbing: Lo-Ammi means "not my people" and amounts to a declaration of divorce from Yahweh.[16] One can only imagine the effect on Hosea and the Israelites of observing these children growing up. Wolff writes, "In the marriage from which the children came, the guilt of faithless Israel lived before his [Hosea's] very eyes. The children with these peculiar names forced the people to hear the word of Yahweh, since they raised questions that elicited from the prophet again and again . . . those words which had been divinely entrusted to him."[17]

Remarkably, amid this strong declaration of judgment and divorce, we find in Hosea 1:7, 2:1-2 [1:10-11]; 2:16-25 [2:14-23] declarations of hope for Israel. In Hosea 1:7 God will show love to Israel and save it. The strong statement of divorce in Hosea 1:8-9 is followed by a declaration that yet the Israelites will be like the sand on the seashore, and in the place where "Not my people" was pronounced they will be called children of the living God. Hosea 1:11 and Hosea 2:16 [2:14] evoke the idea of a new exodus, with God bringing his people up out of the land again (Egypt) and alluring her in the desert. Hosea also concludes with a vision of hope (Hos 14:4-8).

How are we to understand this strange juxtaposition of judgment and hope? Among modern scholars, it has been common practice to separate the hope element from the judgment one and discern different sources or redactional layers underlying them. However, this is highly speculative, and this pattern, strange as it may appear to us, is common throughout the prophets. There are two answers to this issue. The first is that until the judgment falls there is always hope of repentance from Israel and grace from God. Hence the exhortations in Hosea 2:4 [2:2] to the Israelites to rebuke their mother (Israel) for her adultery. The very fact that Hosea warns of coming judgment holds within it the possibility of change and repentance before it is too late. Using the image of Israel as Yahweh's promiscuous, adulterous wife, Hosea 2 goes out of its way to stress God's repeated efforts

---

[16]Wolff argues for three years later.
[17]Wolff, *Hosea*, 22.

to constrain his wife and to restore her to a right relationship with him. Indeed, a noteworthy characteristic of Hosea is the relative absence of introductions to Yahweh's speeches, so that he is portrayed as speaking directly to his adulterous wife, Israel.[18] Hosea is also called to embody this patient persistence of Yahweh by buying Gomer back again from prostitution and adultery (Hos 3).

Second, the reference to great numbers—"like the sand on the seashore"—is a reference to the promise to Abraham and the patriarchs (Gen 22:17). In the next chapter we will exegete Hosea 2:4-23 in detail. Suffice it here to note that this promise will not fail, and just as God now sows judgment (Jezreel), so the day will come when he sows grace. This eschatological dimension looks beyond the punishment of exile that is to come.

The Charge Against Israel: Hosea 4–13

Hosea 4–13 is made up of typical prophetic speeches in which Hosea repeatedly sets out the Lord's charge—Hosea 4:1 uses the Hebrew term for a legal case (*rîb*)—against Israel. The Hebrew is difficult at points, but the overall message is crystal clear: Israel has been unfaithful, and judgment is coming. Today's reader finds the repetitive nature of these chapters somewhat tedious. Theologically, however, this very repetitiveness is instructive, indeed *performative*.[19] Again and again . . . and again God warns his people, but to no avail. It is not possible after reading these summaries or extracts from Hosea's long, thankless, and painful ministry to argue that God was rash in his judgment of the northern kingdom.

We will not review Hosea 4–13 in detail but rather identify the major themes that emerge in these chapters. Throughout the book, the powerful metaphor of adultery casts its shadow. Literally, Israel is promiscuous in its pursuit and worship of other gods (see Hos 4:12, 13, 17; 5:11; 7:14; 8:5, 6; 9:10; 10:5, 8; 13:1, 2). Unlike today, Israelites were not in danger of becoming atheists but were highly religious. The problem was their idolatry and syncretism (Hos 11:7) and consequent "lack of inwardness," as Wolff describes it. They did not follow Yahweh and his ways faithfully. Baal worship is identified as the major problem (Hos 2:11 [2:8], 13 [16], etc.), and the high places

---

[18]Adrio König, *Here Am I!* (Grand Rapids, MI: Eerdmans, 1982), 72.
[19]Time and again the Bible performs its message in the way it is written. See Jeanette Mathews, *Prophets as Performers: Biblical Performance Criticism and Israel's Prophets* (Eugene, OR: Cascade, 2020), and volumes in the Biblical Performance Criticism series published by Cascade.

(Hos 4:13) as well as the shrines of Gilgal and Beth Aven (Hos 4:15; 9:15) are singled out as places of idolatry. Beth Aven means "house of wickedness" and is a play on the name Bethel, which means "house of God." Hosea 4:13 is particularly evocative of the Israelites' promiscuity: they sacrifice to Baal wherever possible.

In Hosea *Baal* has become a collective name for the Canaanite deities. Hosea stresses that contrary to wayward Israel's belief, worship of Baal will not secure a fertile land and will not produce the new wine and food that she loves so much. Israel has forgotten that the grain, the new wine, and the oil come from Yahweh and not from Baal (Hos 2:8). Part of the punishment will be that the resources of the land will wither and dry up, with drastic implications for animal life as well (Hos 4:3). Hosea 4:3 refers intertextually to Genesis 1 with its three places of land, skies, and sea. In a judgment motif of uncreation, the inhabitants of all three places will be swept away. There is terrible collateral damage to the judgment of evil. The Baal cult also involved literal prostitution as a means of promoting the fertility of the land (Hos 4:14).

In the twentieth century there was much discussion among scholars as to the basis on which the prophets indicted Israel. Much of this stemmed from the view that the covenant was a late development in Israel. In our view this is false, and the covenant is rightly traced back to Moses and the events at Mount Sinai (Ex 19–24), and it is striking in Hosea how clearly he refers to the covenant as the basis for the lawsuit he brings against Israel (and Judah—see Hos 12:2).[20] The word *covenant, bərît*, first occurs in Hosea 2:18 in the passage we will examine in the next chapter. However, it is in Hosea 6:7 and Hosea 8:1 that the charge against Israel is clearly articulated: they have broken the covenant and rebelled against Yahweh's law (*tôrâ*).

The covenant at Sinai bound the Israelites into a legal relationship with Yahweh whereby he committed himself to be their God and they agreed to be his people and to live in obedience to him. The pentateuchal laws that follow the covenant at Sinai give expression to how the Israelites are to live

---

[20]See Craig G. Bartholomew, *God Who Acts in History: The Significance of Sinai* (Grand Rapids, MI: Eerdmans, 2020). Note that in the Pentateuch the Israelites leave Sinai only in Num 10. There are several significant intertextual OT links in Hosea apart from the covenant: In Hos 12, he manifests awareness of the story of Jacob and Esau; he clearly knows of the exodus from Egypt (Hos 11:1; etc.); he knows of the gift of the land—note "Yahweh's land" in Hos 9:3; he is aware of the golden calf incident at Baal-Peor (Hos 9:10); he is aware of pentateuchal law (Hos 5:10); and he not only knows about the Sinai covenant but is fully aware of the creation-wide implications of the covenant (Hos 2:18), as we will see in the next chapter.

as his people. At the heart of these is the Decalogue. Hosea finds Israel guilty of breaking both the first and second tablets of the law. Central to his indictment is the breaking of the first commandment (Ex 20:3), as noted above. Having the living God in one's midst was a tricky business, and not surprisingly the first three commandments deal with how Israel is to relate to, or in Hosea's language, to "know" God (Hos 4:6; see also Hos 2:22 [2:20]). However, the second tablet, which deals with how we relate to our neighbors, is also clearly in view.

As with the Decalogue, so in Hosea abandonment of Yahweh has catastrophic consequences for interpersonal relationships. The breaking of the first tablet of the law inevitably leads to transgression of the second. Hosea 4:2 contains a list of five infinitive absolutes that refer to forbidden activities all relating to one's neighbor and akin to the second table of the law:

1. *'lh* (cursing) refers to the cursing of another person by the ceremonial invocation of Yahweh's name, specifically forbidden by the third commandment (Ex 20:7).

2. *kḥš* (lying) refers to deceiving and cheating a neighbor, especially in relation to the lawcourts and in business (see Ex 20:16, 17).

3. *rṣḥ* (murder) refers to premeditated murder (see Ex 20:13).

4. *gnb* (stealing) first of all signifies kidnapping in the Old Testament, a crime worthy of death (see Ex 20:15; 21:16).

5. *n'p* (adultery) denotes adultery, specifically forbidden in Exodus 20:14.

The five infinitive absolutes evoke in a graphic way the relational breakdown in Israel. This theme is found throughout the book. In Hosea 6:7-9 the reference to breaking the covenant is immediately followed by descriptions of bloodstained footprints, with even bands of priests engaging in murder.

Indeed in Hosea the leadership of Israel is singled out for accountability. In Hosea 4 the lack of knowledge among the Israelites is related to the failure of the priests who have exchanged the glory of God for something disgraceful and have turned their sacred duty into a business, feeding on the sins of the people. In Hosea 5:1 the Israelites are sandwiched between the priests and the royal house. Hosea 5:10 notes, "*Judah's* leaders are like those who move boundary stones," a crime condemned in the Torah. The result is that in Hosea 7 the people have become like the leaders, and they fire one another up to become depraved. After the death of Jeroboam II, the monarchy in the north was notoriously unstable, as noted above, and in

Hosea 7–8 Israel is castigated because they set up kings without God's approval (Hos 8:4); none of the rulers call on God (Hos 7:7), and ironically the people devour their self-appointed rulers (Hos 7:7).

The leaders would have played the key role in international relations, and Israel is found guilty not only of "religious" idolatry but also of political promiscuity. In the words of Hosea 12:2 [12:1], Ephraim "makes a treaty with Assyria and sends olive oil to Egypt" (NIV). In fact, religious idolatry could not be separated from political idolatry in Hosea's context, for an alliance with Assyria would mean allegiance to its gods. Abraham Heschel notes of Assyria, "Ashur was its god, plunder its morality, cruelty and terror its means."[21] In not relying on Yahweh and in colluding with foreign powers, Israel played a dangerous game. Hosea 7 uses the imagery of a bakery to evoke the state of Israel, and in Hosea 7:8 it is noted that she mixes with the nations and is like a flat loaf not turned over. In Hosea 7:11 she is like a senseless dove, now calling to Egypt, now to Assyria. Israel is increasingly feeling the pressure of Assyria, and it is Assyria that God will use to destroy the northern kingdom and take Israel's survivors off into exile (Hos 14:1 [13:16]).

JUDGMENT AND SALVATION: THE LOVER AND THE LION

Hosea depicts as do few other biblical books the passionate and agonized love of God for his people and creation. The agony of his love comes to the fore most clearly in Hosea 11:8-11. The four questions in Hosea 11:8 marked by a twofold "how" (*'ēk*) in the Hebrew evoke the agony within God. Wolff rightly notes that *ntn* ("give") and *mgn* ("hand over") here have the meaning "surrender completely."[22] God knows better than his wanton partner Israel just what the coming judgment will entail, and we have a picture here of him churned up inside at the prospect of handing them over to it.[23] Admah and Zeboyim allude to Deuteronomy 29:23, where with Sodom and Gomorrah they are mentioned as cities overthrown by Yahweh in his wrath. Romans 1:28 speaks of God "giving over" sinners to a depraved mind to do what ought not to be done. Hosea reminds us that such surrender—let alone when it comes to his people—is never easy for Yahweh. It is the agony of separation with all that follows.

---

[21] Abraham J. Heschel, *The Prophets: An Introduction* (New York: Harper & Row, 1962), 40.
[22] Wolff, *Hosea*, 201.
[23] Understandably, many react negatively to the final verses of Ps 137 and to its wish for the destruction of children. There is a parallel to this in Hos 13:16: the people of Samaria must bear their guilt, and this will have dire consequences for them and for their children.

Intriguingly, Yahweh's commitment to ultimate salvation is related in Hosea 11:9 to God's *holiness* and not, as we might suspect, to his love. His reason for not extinguishing Israel forever is, "For I am God, and not a human being—the Holy One among you." Holiness and love here embrace in surrendering Israel to Assyria—they have sown the wind and will reap the whirlwind (Hos 8:7)—while God remains committed to his promises to Abraham to bless all the nations through Israel.

A metaphor for God as holy judge in Hosea as in Amos is that of a roaring lion about to pounce on its unsuspecting prey (Hos 5:14-15; 13:7, 8). For a predominantly rural people, this would have been a terrifying image of imminent and brutal attack. Amazingly, in Hosea 11:10-11 the metaphor of God as a lion is again invoked, but this time in redemption. His holiness is unaltered; his children come *trembling*, but now not in order to be ripped apart but to be settled again in their homes.

Hosea holds before us, as he did to the rebellious Israelites of his day, Yahweh as the great Lover and as the Lion. If "lover" sounds demeaning to our view of God, it is because of our culture's demeaning of love. God seeks the well-being of his people and of his world relentlessly, and this is of course what love is really about. He longs for intimacy with those he created for this very purpose, but it is intimacy with the uncreated, holy God, who will not brook rivals to his affection.

It would be fascinating to know the reception history of Hosea's powerful sermons, but, as with Jonah, Hosea is more interested in knowing how we the readers respond to this God than to the immediate hearers'/readers' responses or what ultimately happened to Jonah.

The Theology of Hosea

Hosea in Old and New Testaments. Hosea yields a rich theology. Within the Old Testament Hosea has close connections with Genesis, Exodus, Deuteronomy, and 2 Kings, and with his contemporary prophets especially Isaiah, Jeremiah, Amos, and Micah. The wisdom element in Hosea should not go unnoticed: the book concludes in Hosea 14:9 with a poignant question, namely, "Who is wise?" and responds in the language of wisdom and the doctrine of the two ways. Hosea's distinctive development of the metaphor of marriage and adultery cannot be doubted, but even this is a development of the covenant theology of the Old Testament. Exodus 19:4, for example, speaks in eloquent terms of how Yahweh rescued Israel from

Egypt and brought her *to himself*. The novel in Hosea is a development of that which is implicit in the old. He returns to Israel's historical traditions in order to contextualize them for his day and to cast a searing light on the present, a light above all of judgment but also of hope in line with the promises to Abraham.

The Nestle-Aland edition of the Greek New Testament (NA[28]) lists approximately forty-three places in the New Testament where Hosea is referenced. Many of these are in Revelation, where Hosea's language of judgment would appear to be used to envision God's eschatological judgment. Perhaps the most well-known text from Hosea is Hosea 11:1—"Out of Egypt I have called my son"—quoted in Matthew 2:15 and seen as fulfilled in Joseph, Mary, and Jesus' escape from Egypt. As multiple scholars since the work of C. H. Dodd have noted, this is not fanciful exegesis but typological; Jesus is understood by Matthew as recapitulating in himself—fulfilling and taking forward—the vocation of Israel as the son of Yahweh.[24]

Remarkably, this Son takes on himself the judgment of God. As Wolff rightly says,

> It becomes clear that in the end Hosea's prophecy points in the direction of Pauline theology. God's struggle for his people and his suffering under their guilt is sealed by Jesus Christ (2 Cor 5:19-21), in whom this suffering bears fruit for all nations. In the light of this goal, the prophecy of Hosea in Israel becomes a model for the struggle carried on by Jesus' messengers on behalf of man in today's world.[25]

Nothing is lost in the New Testament of Hosea's image of God as Lover and Lion; the difference is that this image of God is enacted more fully and decisively in Jesus.

Not surprisingly, parts of the New Testament draw on Hosea in elaborating the fruits of Jesus' life and death for all nations. In Romans 9, in which Paul works through his own anguish over Israel, he draws inter alia on Hosea 1–2 to articulate the inclusion of the Gentiles into the people of God. One presumes that he identified deeply with Yahweh's anguish as depicted in Hosea. In a similar way, 1 Peter 2:10 uses Hosea 1:9 to articulate the

---

[24]See C. H. Dodd, *According to the Scripture: The Sub-structures of New Testament Theology* (London: Nisbet, 1952), 75-78, 102. On Hos 11 see Joy Philip Kakkanattu, *God's Enduring Love in the Book of Hosea: A Synchronic and Diachronic Analysis of Hosea 11, 1-11*, Forschungen zum Alten Testament 2/14 (Tübingen: Mohr Siebeck, 2006).

[25]Wolff, *Hosea*, xxix. Wolff finds evidence in Hosea that God turns his wrath in on himself.

marvelous news that those who were "not a people" are now the people of God; once they had not received mercy, but now they have. In this way the New Testament inhabits the narrative of the Old Testament, including Hosea, but restructures it around its fulfillment in Jesus.

God: Lover and Lion. It is not uncommon to find the Old Testament God of wrath contrasted with the New Testament God of love. Such a dichotomy is utterly false, and the New Testament is one with the Old in depicting God as both Lover and Lion. Jesus taught us to pray "Our Father who art in heaven"—the perfect balance between the intimacy of our relationship with God in Christ and a reminder that this Father is the transcendent God. Amid the Christianity lite of so much Western Christianity, few things would help us as much as a recovery of God as Lover *and* Lion.

Theologically, Hosea raises critical questions about the traditional view of God as impassible.[26] While we affirm unequivocally that in terms of his character and person God does not change, Hosea provides us with an insight into the rich inner life of God, and it *is* highly emotional. Heschel rightly notes that in Hosea, "God is conceived, not as the self-detached Ruler, but as the sensitive Consort to Whom deception comes and Who nevertheless goes on pleading for loyalty, uttering a longing for a reunion, a passionate desire for reconciliation. Of all the prophets, only Jeremiah has sensed a wider scale of personal relations, a more intense subjectivity."[27] In any development of a doctrine of God we need to beware of taking on Greek concepts of God as emotionless. C. S. Lewis rightly points out that God is at least personal; he may be more than personal, but he is not less.[28]

True religion: Inwardness. There is a false inwardness that is an expression of human autonomy and is reaping the whirlwind in Western culture today. It has been tracked in masterly fashion by Charles Taylor in his *Sources of the Self*, from Augustine through Descartes and on to the Romantics and into our present individualistic, hedonistic culture. However, there is also a true inwardness, a living *coram Deo* from the heart. Cultic ritual—for us, church and devotional practices—is of great importance, but, as Hosea reminds us, these things become vacuous and dangerous if the heart is not fully engaged. Hence Yahweh's radical statement in Hosea 6:6, "For I desire

---

[26]See Colin E. Gunton, *Act and Being: Towards a Theology of the Divine Attributes* (Grand Rapids, MI: Eerdmans, 2002), 22-23, 125-32. Gunton specifically refers to Hos 11:8 (*Act and Being*, 129).
[27]Heschel, *Prophets*, 48.
[28]C. S. Lewis, *Mere Christianity* (London: William Collins, 1952), 77.

mercy, not sacrifice, and acknowledgment of God rather than burnt offerings" (NIV). Jesus quotes this verse in response to the Pharisees' criticism of him (Mt 9:13; 12:7). The letter of the law is no good without its spirit.

Healthy inwardness is not easily attained. It involves (re)formation at the deepest levels of our being. Wolff perceptively states that Hosea may be a model for Jesus' followers today. Indeed so. Hosea is a model, like Jeremiah, of the sort of spiritual formation that may be necessary if we are to be bearers of the light in today's world. Jesus, like Yahweh in Hosea, wept over Jerusalem's failure to respond to him. Paul anguished over the Israelites' failure to respond to Jesus. Between the coming of the kingdom and its final consummation—the act of the drama of Scripture in which we live—there will be much to anguish amid a world so often bent on destruction. How will we find the resources to keep hoping, to keep loving? Only through deep spiritual formation of the sort that Hosea underwent until our hearts beat with God's heart in relation to his world.

Hosea ministered for some thirty-eight years without any success amid the deathworks (see below) of Israel while living the agony of his broken relationship with Gomer and with his children a constant reminder of Israel's adultery. Often, or so the great spiritual thinkers of the past tell us, God's service will involve, as with Hosea, intense suffering. Indeed, there is an analog between the agony of God in having to surrender Israel to her punishment and a central spiritual discipline, namely that of letting go, of surrendering.[29] The crucial difference, of course, is that we are *not* God, and as we surrender things out of our control to him, we are able to see beyond the immediate to his good and eternal purposes. Nevertheless, as many on the spiritual journey have discovered, letting go is far from passive. It has its own agonies as one surrenders again and again to God's mysterious purposes in life.

Only thus formed will we be in a position to compassionately engage the ideologies of our day, to engage in mission as part of the *missio Dei*. Wolff rightly notes, "This unfolding of Hosea's theology in polemical dialogue with the cultus and mythology of Canaan provides us with a fundamental example of faith's dialogue with contemporary ideology."[30] Like the culture

---

[29] Frederick Bauerschmidt notes the radicalness of detachment: "We do not detach ourselves from things because of the risk they pose for us by their impermanence; we detach ourselves from them as a way of recognizing that we are not their source and they are not our destiny. Part of the burden that the ego places upon itself is the role of being the source of things and circumstances." Bauerschmidt, *Why the Mystics Matter Now* (Notre Dame, IN: Sorin Books, n.d.), 68.
[30] Wolff, *Hosea*, xxvi.

of Hosea's day, ours abounds with idols both outside and inside the church. Deep formation will be required to resist these idols and to confront them without becoming pessimistic and discouraged.

Societal breakdown: Marriage and modernity. Hosea is an important source for a biblical understanding of marriage. In line with Genesis 1–2 and the Ten Commandments, the marriage relationship is clearly regarded as sacrosanct, and prostitution and adultery are regarded as violations of the marriage relationship and of God's law. Gordon Hugenberger draws substantially on Hosea in his work on marriage as a covenant.[31] The Old Testament data on marriage and sexuality is more complex and nuanced than that of the New Testament, and feminist interpreters have found Hosea to be a fertile source for patriarchy.[32] However, there is no suggestion that Hosea is free to engage in adultery and prostitution while Gomer is not. The entire book presupposes fidelity from both partners. Hosea 4:14 is notable in this respect; God says that he will not punish daughters when they turn to prostitution or daughters-in-law when they commit adultery because *the men* are the major part of the problem, consorting as they do with prostitutes.

As with the Israel of Hosea's day, we too live amid a culture in which marriage is breaking down and in which diverse sexual practices outside (and inside) marriage are welcomed and even celebrated. Hosea would, we think, remind us that this is to sow the wind and be in danger of reaping the whirlwind. God's law is not an alien addition to nature but mirrors the grain of creation. As we will see in the next chapter, Hosea is well aware that God's covenant is rooted in creation (Hos 2:20 [2:18]) so that the normativity of marriage applies to the non-Christian as much as the Christian. The family is the backbone to any society, and its fracture cannot but have negative consequences for a culture.

Hosea provides us with a window into a collapsing society, and his diagnosis is that its *social order* is collapsing because its *sacred order* is in disarray. Of course, once one concedes that the sort of God Hosea serves is the author of this world, then his logic is impeccable. Intriguingly, this is a theme that Jewish sociologist Philip Rieff deals with in his trilogy Sacred Order/Social

---

[31]Gordon P. Hugenberger, *Marriage as a Covenant: Biblical Law and Ethics as Developed from Malachi* (Eugene, OR: Wipf & Stock, 1994).

[32]For feminist and postmodern readings of Hosea, see Yvonne Sherwood, *The Prostitute and the Prophet: Reading Hosea in the Late Twentieth Century* (Sheffield: Sheffield Academic Press, 1996); Alice A. Keefe, *Woman's Body and the Social Body in Hosea* (London: Sheffield Academic Press, 2001).

Order.[33] Rieff notes that culture is always the translation of sacred order into social order and that the health of any culture depends on what he calls "v-i-a"—the vertical in authority. Our age, late modernity, which Rieff evocatively describes as one of "deathworks," is unique in its attempt to abolish the *via*. For Rieff such a culture is unsustainable.

We live in pluralistic cultures and are not a covenant theocracy like Israel, and this certainly complicates matters. However, Christians need to work with their cobelligerents in advancing a new commons in the West and elsewhere in which a life-giving and life-sustaining ethos is upheld, one informed by God's good order for his creation.

RECOMMENDED READING

Anderson, Francis I., and David N. Freedman. *Hosea*. AB 24. New York: Doubleday, 1980.
Dearman, J. Andrew. *The Book of Hosea*. NICOT. Grand Rapids, MI: Eerdmans, 2010.*
Evans, Mary J. "Hosea, Book of." In *Dictionary of Theological Interpretation of the Bible*, ed. Kevin J. Vanhoozer et al., 307-10. Grand Rapids, MI: Baker Academic, 2005.*
Heschel, Abraham J. *The Prophets: An Introduction*. New York: Harper & Row, 1962. Chapter 3.
Moon, Joshua. *Hosea*. AOTC. Downers Grove, IL: IVP Academic, 2018.
Strawn, Brent A. *What Is Stronger than a Lion? Leonine Image and Metaphor in the Hebrew Bible and the Ancient Near East*. OBO 212. Göttingen: Vandenhoeck & Ruprecht, 2005.

Recommended reading marked with a "*" indicates introductory works.

---

[33]Philip Rieff, *My Life Among the Deathworks: Illustrations of the Aesthetics of Authority*, ed. Kenneth S. Piver, Sacred Order/Social Order 1 (Charlottesville: University of Virginia Press, 2006).

4

A Tale of Two Futures

HOSEA 2:16-25 [2:14-23]

THE SECOND HALF OF HOSEA 2 envisages a radically different future from the judgment of Hosea 2:2-13. The particle translated "therefore" (Hos 2:16 [2:14]; *lākēn*) is often used in prophetic texts where it introduces a declaration by Yahweh after the statement of the grounds for it.[1] "Therefore" connects Hosea 2:16-25 [2:14-23] to the exposure of Israel's adultery in Hosea 2:4-15 [2:2-13], but it does so in a most unexpected way. The same word for "therefore" has already occurred twice in Hosea 2, in Hosea 2:8 [2:6] and in Hosea 2:11 [2:9]. In both these cases "therefore" introduces strong statements of God's judgment on the basis of Israel's adultery as expressed in Hosea 2:8-15 [2:6-13].[2]

The reader, therefore, rightly expects this third occurrence of "therefore" to introduce further judgment, and nothing quite prepares us for the surprise that follows. Instead of judgment, Yahweh promises to woo adulterous Israel once again, to bless her in every way, and to extend his blessing through Israel to the whole creation. What are we to make of these two radically different futures? We should remember that the Old Testament prophets primarily bring God's word to his people in their historical situations, although this often includes a predictive, future element as well. These two aspects are not antithetical, but it is vital to remember the primacy of the first, often referred to as *forth*telling as opposed to *fore*telling.

---

[1]BDB, 486. J. Andrew Dearman suggests "even so" as the translation, but, as we will argue, this flattens out the contradictory juxtaposition. Dearman, *The Book of Hosea*, NICOT (Grand Rapids, MI: Eerdmans, 2010), 120.

[2]James L. Mays reads Hos 2:4-17 [2:2-15] as a separate section, punctuated by the three "therefores." Mays, *Hosea*, OTL (Philadelphia: Westminster, 1969), 34-45. We follow most recent works on Hosea in seeing Hos 2:16-25 [2:14-23] as a separate section following on from the first part of Hos 2.

We need to ask, therefore, "What could these two very different approaches possibly have meant to the Israelites listening to Hosea or reading his book?" In our view this *juxtaposition of contrary futures* is quite deliberate. The reader is meant to be struck by the contrast and to try to negotiate it. Literary scholars would say that the juxtaposition opens up a gap in the reading that engages the reader, who is forced to try to negotiate the gap. In our view, the gap that opens up is directly related to the fact that Hosea tells a tale of two possible futures for his hearers. God's judgment is coming, but there is still time to repent and to align oneself *now* with the *hopeful* future that Yahweh will pursue with or without Hosea's audience. If God ordered history fatalistically, there would be no need for him to give his word to Hosea to proclaim to the Israelites. The very fact of Hosea's tough ministry implies that there is still time, there is still hope. The Israelites have come to a crossroads: either they can continue to indwell their tragic story of rebellion and adultery, which will lead to terrible judgment, to divorce from Yahweh (see Hos 1:8 [1:9]), or they can repent and become part of a very different story, one of hope for Israel and the world. There is clearly, as we will see below, a predictive element in Hosea 2:16-25 [2:14-23], but it is vital that we recognize what this prophecy would have meant for its earliest audience.

A danger with the Bible is that we become too familiar with it. This second part of Hosea 2 is an extraordinary, mind-blowing text. A helpful way to defamiliarize ourselves with it is to imagine ourselves as part of Hosea's audience: idolatrous Israelites who have betrayed Yahweh in myriad ways and who know in our hearts that we deserve the worst. We have already heard two searing statements of judgment following "therefore," and now here comes a third. But wait, this is different. Can it be true? Is this really possible?

Interpretation

> Therefore I am now going to allure her;
>> I will lead her into the wilderness
>> and speak tenderly to her.
> There I will give her back her vineyards,
>> and will make the Valley of Achor a door of hope.
> There she will respond as in the days of her youth,
>> as in the day she came up out of Egypt.

The first line of Hosea 2:16 has an unusual word order, which marks it as the opening statement of a new section.[3] The word order emphasizes that the initiative will be Yahweh's. Lines 2 and 3 of Hosea 2:16 are in parallel, as are lines 1 and 2 and lines 3 and 4 in Hosea 2:17. Such parallelism is typical of Hebrew poetry. Parallelism rarely just repeats the earlier idea; normally, there is an intensification of some sort, and we need to be sensitive to this as we read this section.

Allure can mean "seduce," "entice," or "court," but clearly the latter meaning is in view here. The Lord is going to woo his adulterous bride once again. The remainder of Hosea 2:16-17 indicates how he will do this.

He will lead her into the wilderness. The same word *wilderness* (NIV "desert") occurs in Hosea 2:5 [2:3], where it has a decidedly negative connotation. Here, however, it refers back to that period when God rescued the Israelites from Egypt and entered into a covenant with them in the wilderness at Mount Sinai (Ex 1–24). We should not think that Hosea was unaware of the difficulties in the wilderness period; Hosea 9:10 indicates an awareness of both the wonderful intimacy of Yahweh's early relationship with Israel as well as her tendency toward idolatry. Hosea refers in Hosea 9:10 to Israel's shameful behavior at Baal-Peor (Num 25:1-11; Deut 4:3-4).

Positively, Hosea 9:10 describes the wilderness period as like finding grapes in the wilderness (NIV "desert"), an unexpected and wonderfully refreshing surprise, a lot like Hosea 2:16-25 [2:14-23]. It is to this positive, exhilarating early experience of Israel in the wilderness with Yahweh that Hosea refers to when he says that God will "lead her into the wilderness" (see Jer 2:2-3). The Lord will lead Israel back into this experience. This is metaphorical language and does not mean that he will literally lead her back into the desert. Rather, he will court her again and recover the very best of those early times in his relationship with her.

He will court Israel again. Literally the Hebrew reads "I will speak to her heart," "her" being Israel. Ibn Ezra understands this as to persuade Israel with words, but there is more going on here than this.[4] This is the language

---

[3]In Hebrew the normal word order in a sentence is verb, subject, object. In the first line of Hos 2:16 [2:14], the order is particle (Therefore), particle of exclamation (*hinneh*), subject (I), verb (will allure), object (her). The pronoun *I* is often part of the verb in Hebrew, but here a separate word is used for *I*, stressing the subject of the action, namely, Yahweh.

[4]Ibn Ezra, *The Commentary of Rabbi Abraham Ibn Ezra on Hosea*, ed. Abe Lipshitz (New York: Sepher-Hermon, 1988), 30.

of courtship, as is evident from Genesis 34:3; Ruth 2:13; and Judges 19:3, in which the same idiom is used. James Mays rightly says, "Measured against Yahwism's studied aversion for speaking of God in any sexual terms, the picture is astonishing. Yet precisely at this point the allegory is not to be taken lightly. For it is in this daring kind of portrayal that the passion of God becomes visible—a passion that does not hesitate at any condescension or hold back from any act for the sake of the beloved elect."[5]

He will give back her vineyards and turn the Valley of Achor into a door of hope. In Hosea 2:10-11 [2:8-9] part of the punishment of Israel is the destruction of her agriculture (see Deut 28:30, 39). If she will not acknowledge that the fruits of nature (Hos 2:10 [2:8]) come from God, then he will remove them. But now he will return fertility to the land, the great symbol of which is the vineyards. Wine is a major symbol of blessing in the Old Testament and evokes feasting and celebration. Pinot gris and cabernet will once again be readily available in the land.

This hope of the renewal of Israel's life in the land with Yahweh is further evoked by a reference to Israel's history. The valley of Achor ($'\bar{a}k\hat{o}r$ = trouble) was the scene of Joshua's confrontation with Achan for his sin (Josh 7:24-26). But now "Trouble Valley" becomes "Hope Valley" as Yahweh opens a door of hope. As is typical of poetry, this is rich, allusive language. A closed door can symbolize an end, but an open door evokes a way forward, a fresh start.

It is possible that there is further allusion to Joshua in this verse.[6] "Hope" (*tiqwâ*) has a homonym meaning "thread" or "cord," found in Joshua 2:18, 21, where it refers to the scarlet cord that Rahab, the Canaanite prostitute, had to tie on her house to avoid being killed by the conquering Israelites. That cord symbolized her hope, and Yahweh is similarly offering Israel—another prostitute—a way to avoid his punishment.

"The days of her youth" refers to the time after the exodus from Egypt when God led Israel to Sinai and established her in a covenant relationship with himself (Ex 19–24). As Yahweh says in Exodus 19:4, "I carried you on eagle's wings and brought you to myself" (NIV).

The result: Israel will respond with delight. And Israel will respond to God's courtship as the Israelites did at Sinai (see Ex 24:3-8). The verb *respond*

---

[5]Mays, *Hosea*, 44-45.
[6]Dearman, *Book of Hosea*, 123.

(*'ānâ*) occurs five times in Hosea 2:23-25 [2:21-22]. It can mean to respond or to sing (see Ex 15:21, "And Miriam *sang*"). In our view celebration is evoked by all six uses of this world in our passage, but *'ānâ* is best translated "sing" in Hosea 2:17 [2:15].[7] Israel will respond to God's courtship with joy and delight, simply bursting with song at the wonder of it all.

The remainder of our passage divides into three sections, each introduced by "In that day." "In that day" is technical term for the time when Yahweh will act decisively in judgment or salvation. It is a synonym for "the day of Yahweh," a phrase we encounter repeatedly in the Minor Prophets (see chap. one). Clearly there is an *eschatological* dimension to Hosea 2:18-25 [2:16-23] that goes way beyond the immediate situation of Israel. We have here not just *forth*telling but *fore*telling.

A useful illustration of such eschatological Old Testament passages is that of a range of mountains in the distance. From afar they look two-dimensional, but once you get close you see that they also have depth and are at different points on the horizon. It is only as we look back at passages such as this from the point of view of the kingdom coming in Christ and to be consummated in the future that we can tease out the different threads of fulfillment.

The stress in Hosea 2:18-25 [2:16-23] is clearly that God will act in *salvation*. What a salvation it is. Hosea 2:18, 21-22 [2:16, 19-20] speaks of a new relationship with Yahweh. Hosea 2:20 [2:18] speaks of a new covenant, and Hosea 2:23-25 [2:21-23] speaks of a renewed land.

A new relationship. We have already seen in Hosea 2:16 [2:14] that Yahweh will court faithless Israel again and in Hosea 2:17 [2:15] that she will respond in delight. Hosea 2:18 [2:16] indicates the result; Israel's marriage to Yahweh will be restored. Once again she will call Yahweh "my husband," with all the intimacy that entails. In the parallel line we learn what Israel will *not* call Yahweh, namely, "my master." It is important to note that this is the Hebrew word *ba'al*, which can mean "master" but was also the special name of the god of the Canaanites. Israel was guilty of an unhealthy syncretism in her worship, and this will now cease, as Hosea 2:19 [2:17] makes crystal clear.

Hosea 2:21-22 [2:19-20] elaborates on Yahweh's bridal gifts, the characteristics of this new relationship that he will establish with Israel: it will be

---

[7]Ibn Ezra suggests "play and sing" (*Commentary of Rabbi Abraham Ibn Ezra*, 30).

characterized by righteousness (*ṣedeq*), justice (*mišpāṭ*), love (*ḥesed*), compassion (*raḥămîm*), and faithfulness (*ʾĕmûnâ*). All of these are major Old Testament words. Above all they characterize God, but in this relationship his people will genuinely become like him.

Righteousness and *justice* are often paired together; they evoke wholeness in relationships; they can—and often do—have a legal focus but extend beyond that as well. *Love* refers to devoted loyalty that goes beyond the requirement of the law. An example is the sort of commitment demonstrated by Ruth to Naomi (Ruth 1:8; 3:10). *Compassion* or *mercy* speaks of gentleness and a generous and tender commitment to the well-being of the other. The root of this word in Hebrew is that same as that used for the name of Hosea's daughter, namely, No-Mercy. But now all is changed, and God's relationship with Israel is full of mercy, and Israel herself is merciful. *Faithfulness* speaks of constancy and stability. Indeed, at the start of Hosea 2:21 [2:19] Yahweh says that this new relationship will be "forever."

The final line of Hosea 2:22 [2:20] sums up what the new marriage will entail: they will acknowledge Yahweh. "Know" is a better translation of the verb *yādaʿ*, which the NIV translates as "acknowledge," for this is no mere acknowledgment. The verb is used in the Old Testament for the intimate relationship of marriage as two become one flesh, and here it similarly invokes the deepest intimacy.

A new covenant. Hosea 2:20 [2:18] speaks of a new covenant. This is the first of five uses of *covenant* in Hosea. William Dumbrell notes, "Hosea is a book thoroughly covenant-based, ringing with appeals founded upon God's love for Israel and indicating the countless ways in which this love had been demonstrated, but pointing also to the corresponding lack of response from Israel."[8] Actually, Hosea 2:20 [2:18] does not use the word *new*, and indeed this is no new covenant but a renewal of a very old one. The allusion here is clearly to God's covenant with Noah. In Genesis 9:8-10 God establishes his covenant with the second Adam, namely, Noah, with his descendants and "with every living creature that was with you" (NIV). God's covenant with Noah concerns not only humans but the whole creation. Indeed, as Dumbrell convincingly demonstrates, *the* basic covenantal

---

[8]William J. Dumbrell, *Covenant and Creation: An Old Testament Covenant Theology* (Milton Keynes, UK: Paternoster, 2013), 249.

text in the Old Testament is Genesis 1.⁹ The word for "covenant" in the Old Testament, *bərît*, first occurs in Genesis 9:9 to refer to God's covenant with Noah, but in looking at the terms of the covenant, it is quite clear that Noah is a second Adam and that God is reestablishing with Noah his original creation covenant.

Abraham is not mentioned here, but in Genesis 12:1-3 it is equally clear that God's covenant with him will eventually involve restoring blessing to God's whole creation. It is that picture of *šalôm* ("peace") that is evoked here. Central to it is relationship with God (see the last part of Hos 2:25 [2:23], which evokes this in the traditional language of covenant), but it involves far more. The negative condition of such peace is that war must cease, as articulated in the last part of Hosea 2:20 [2:18].

God intends for his creation to be in harmony and at peace, and as we will see again and again in the Minor Prophets, his concern extends to all his creation. His desire is that "all may lie down in safety" (Hos 2:20 [2:18]), including the animals. Dumbrell says, "That Hosea should have thought so inclusively about the renewal should cause no surprise in view of his fondness for referring to Israel's (and Judah's) older traditions (cf. 2:3; 9:10; 11:8; 12:4)."¹⁰

Modern scholars have suggested that covenant is a late prophetic development in the history of Israel, but we reject that view. The major Old Testament covenant in the history of Israel was that at Mount Sinai facilitated by Moses. The prophets, like Hosea, look back to the Sinai covenant and hold Israel accountable on its terms. Hosea knows the story of Israel well, and he repeatedly refers to and alludes to its story.¹¹ But on the basis of looking back he looks forward to how the story will come to fulfillment, and what a glorious vision it is of creational wholeness.

A renewed land. The new covenant involves not only Israel in relationship to God but also the animals and the land. We must not make the mistake of spiritualizing this vision of the future. Israel was a real people placed in a real land. William Temple once commented that Christianity is the most materialistic of all religions,¹² and we see that right here in Hosea. The

---

⁹See Dumbrell, *Covenant and Creation*. Long before Dumbrell, Karl Barth argued similarly that covenant is the inner dimension of creation, and creation the external basis of covenant.
¹⁰Dumbrell, *Covenant and Creation*, 248.
¹¹See, e.g., Else Kragelund Holt, *Prophesying the Past: The Use of History in the Book of Hosea*, JSOTSup 194 (Sheffield: Sheffield Academic Press, 1994).
¹²William Temple, *Readings in St. John's Gospel* (London: MacMillan, 1947), xx.

relationship God will establish with his people, spoken of again in the second half of Hosea 2:25 [2:23], will literally involve rain and thus fertile soils, grain, new wine, and olive oil.

Israel's adultery had shattered the nexus of relationships in which she was situated, namely, God–Israel–land. Her sin had called forth God's anger with devastating consequences for the land and all of its inhabitants. But now God will take the initiative to restore the relational ecology. The verb *respond* (ʿānâ) occurs five times in Hosea 2:23-26 [2:21-24], indicating the links in this ecological relational chain. Not surprisingly, God sets it going by responding to the skies, and they respond to the earth by watering it, and so on.

It is not easy to work out precisely how to understand *respond* in these verses. However, as Ibn Ezra points out, a helpful parallel usage is found in Ecclesiastes 10:19, "and money is the answer for everything" (NIV).[13] The same verb is used in this verse, and as Ibn Ezra notes, it means "provides for" everything. A similar usage is present here in Hosea: God provides for the skies, they provide for the earth, which provides grain, wine, and oil for the Israelites. As Andrew Dearman writes, "The whole cosmos responds as if its constituent parts are YHWH's household at work."[14]

Message and Theology

We witness in this passage the power and pathos of prophecy. It is the word of God for the people of God in their particular situation. What a powerful word it is. Israel is in a terrible mess, but God invites her to repent and become part of his purposes for his world. This seems irresistible, but although the door of hope has been opened Hosea 2:17 [2:15], it still has to be entered in order for Israel to become part of this story of hope and a future. Tragically, the northern kingdom and then the southern kingdom chose not to enter this doorway, and punishment fell as they were dragged away into exile, first in 722 BC and then in 586/7 BC. Such is the mysterious irrationality of sin.

God's holy love. This irrationality of sin comes into clear focus and is set against the backdrop of an extraordinary portrayal of God's love. Karl Barth notes,

---

[13] Ibn Ezra, *Commentary of Rabbi Abraham Ibn Ezra*, 31.
[14] Dearman, *Book of Hosea*, 131.

> So far as the written records go, Hosea was the first to declare expressly that the action of Yahweh in His covenant with Israel is in every respect and from the action of His love. He did so very graphically by using the picture of a marriage between Yahweh and His people; and his presentation is all the more impressive because it is set in contrast and connexion with the severest proclamation of judgment.[15]

Barth rejects Walther Eichrodt's view that this is a fresh development of the older view of covenant, which sought at all costs to maintain the distance between God and humankind.[16] Grace and love were present in the Sinai covenant from the outset, and what Hosea does is make that love explicit in his circumstances, circumstances in which God's love could ironically no longer be assumed to be understood by his rebellious audience.

In John and in the Johannine Epistles we find the doctrine of God's love in full bloom. Colin Gunton writes, "John's theology of the *economy* of love—for it is that with which he is concerned—is grounded in a conception of God's *being* as love."[17] However, as Barth notes, we find an indication, a foretaste, if you like, of this doctrine in a passage such as Hosea 11:8. The Synoptics speak little of God's love, although it is everywhere presupposed. However, it is explicit in John, and in 1 John 4:8 we read, "Whoever does not love does not know God, because *God is love*" (NIV). God's love is the basis of our love. "The man who loves does so merely, but necessarily, because it comes to him 'of God' to do so. As he loves, he testifies that this is the case. . . . As against this, *he who does not love . . . bears witness to the terrible fact that he has not known God.*"[18]

At the outset of his doctrine of God, Barth speaks of "The Being of God as the One who Loves in Freedom."[19] Barth makes love central to the doctrine of God: "This unconstrained love for the unworthy other provides in turn the basis of a polarity or dialectic of love and freedom which forms a matrix within which the discussion of the [divine] attributes is formed."[20] For Barth, all God's perfections express simultaneously his love and freedom: "God is not first the One who loves, and then somewhere and somehow, in

---

[15]*CD* IV/2:761.
[16]*CD* IV/2:763.
[17]Colin E. Gunton, *Act and Being: Towards a Theology of the Divine Attributes* (Grand Rapids, MI: Eerdmans, 2002), 116.
[18]*CD* IV/2:754, emphasis added.
[19]*CD* II/1:257.
[20]Gunton, *Act and Being*, 98.

contradistinction to that, the One who is also free. And when He loves He does not surrender His freedom, but exercises it in a supreme degree."[21]

Gunton argues that when we reflect on God's love in sending his Son as a sacrifice, we do better to speak of the holiness of God's love: "God's love is indeed free, but its holiness encompasses far more adequately the shape of the love as involving the overcoming of the sin that brings men and women into enmity with God."[22] God's holiness and love, as we see so clearly in Hosea, are thus inextricably and gloriously interwoven, and we do well to resist the repeated attempts to separate them.[23] God's love is the basis for our love, first for him and second for our neighbors. Call always precedes our response.[24]

That day. Great twentieth-century missiologist Lesslie Newbigin says that the Bible does two things: it tells us the true story of the world, *and* it invites us to become part of it, to make it our story.[25] As we have seen, this is precisely what Hosea does in Hosea 2. We are further along in the development of the biblical story, in a different act in the great drama of Scripture, as it were. "That day" has dawned in Jesus, although now it has become clear to us that the mountain of his first coming is separated from the mountain of the final consummation of the kingdom. But his kingdom is the fulfillment of the vision Hosea articulates in this passage. The kingdom of God involves the recovery of God's original purposes for his entire creation, and we are invited now to be part of it. John's term for the kingdom of God is "eternal life," often misunderstood to mean life in heaven when we die. "Eternal life" actually means "the life of the age to come," the life of "that day," life as God intended it to be in all its rich materiality. The radicality of the New Testament is that it declares that in Jesus the new age has already dawned and now awaits its final fulfillment in a new heavens and new earth.

And what does eternal life involve? In words very similar to Hosea, John 17:3 tells us, "Now this is eternal life, that they know you the only true

---

[21] *CD* II/1:344-45.
[22] Gunton, *Act and Being*, 117.
[23] See the important older book by John W. Wenham, *The Goodness of God* (London: Inter-Varsity Press, 1974).
[24] See Jean-Louis Chrétien, *The Call and the Response*, trans. Anne A. Davenport (New York: Fordham University Press, 2004).
[25] See, e.g., J. E. Lesslie Newbigin, "The Bible: Good News for Secularised People." https://missionworldview.com/wp-content/uploads/2020/06/ea8a85_faf8a6551b14431db8fd326cdc197c6a.pdf.

God, and Jesus Christ, whom you have sent." Central to eternal life, to salvation, is *knowing* God. Such knowledge will certainly include knowing *about* God, but as Hosea reminds us, it involves the deepest level of intimacy.

To live is to love, and first we are called into an ever-deepening relationship with Jesus. Evangelicals speak a lot about knowing God, but what is often lacking is the deep existential dimension that knowing God involves. Too often we, like the Israelites, have lost our "first love" (Rev 2:4). Like Jesus, we need practices of prayer that will open us again and again to God and lead us ever deeper into his very life. A good marriage matures over time, and only as we practice the presence of God will we be formed to become like God (see Hos 2:21-22 [2:19-20]).

Deep spirituality is not easily attained, and it is intriguing that Yahweh leads Israel into the wilderness to woo her. This is what we might call desert spirituality, particularly associated with the desert fathers and mothers in the early church.[26] Thomas Merton points out that the desert fathers were not trying to escape the world. Their culture was becoming corrupt as the church became institutionalized under Constantine, and the only way for them to preserve their faith was to jump off the ship and swim for their lives. Once they found the firm ground in Christ, they could pull their whole culture with them. Deserts are dangerous and strip us of all our normal luxuries and crutches. The advantage is that they show us what really matters, namely, God. As we seek to be wooed again by God, we too will need our deserts into which we can withdraw from the hectic consumer culture in which we live and find the solitude and silence in which to be allured once again by God.

Like Hosea, what we will discover as we embrace the journey inward is that far from it taking us away from God's world, we will capture God's vision for the recovery of his purposes for his whole creation. Our journey inward will issue in a journey outward in his service in his creation. Salvation is not about an individualistic saving of our soul so it can go to heaven. Salvation is about "that day," about the renewal of the entire creation, the arrival forever of shalom. As believers, this is the story of which we are part, and we are called to live that story now. If Hosea is anything to go by, this will not be an easy journey, but it will be a journey of life and full of Jesus.

---

[26]See Douglas Burton-Christie, *The Word in the Desert: Scripture and the Quest for Holiness in Early Christian Monasticism* (New York: Oxford University Press, 1993).

RECOMMENDED READING

Anderson, Francis I., and David N. Freedman. *Hosea*. AB 24. New York: Doubleday, 1980.
Bartholomew, Craig G. *The Old Testament and God*. Old Testament Origins and the Question of God 1. Grand Rapids, MI: Baker Academic, 2022. Pages 438-43.*
Dearman, J. Andrew. *The Book of Hosea*. NICOT. Grand Rapids, MI: Eerdmans, 2010.*
Gunton, Colin G. *Act and Being: Towards a Theology of the Divine Attributes*. Grand Rapids, MI: Eerdmans, 2002. See the index for his discussions of God's love and holiness.
Moon, Joshua. *Hosea*. AOTC. Downers Grove, IL: IVP Academic, 2018.
Wenham, John W. *The Goodness of God*. London: Inter-Varsity Press, 1974.

Recommended reading marked with a "" indicates introductory works.*

5

Joel

THE VALLEY OF DECISION

THE PROPHETS ARE IN NO DOUBT that God intervenes in history and is altogether capable of what theologians call "special divine action." Among the Minor Prophets, it is the short book of Joel that perhaps holds pride of place in this respect, with its majestic theology of the day of Yahweh. Joel serves thus as a "hermeneutical key to the Twelve," disclosing the day of Yahweh, God's climactic intervention in history.[1]

THE CONTEXT OF JOEL

Joel sits rather loose to history when compared to other books in the Twelve. The precise dating of the book, its historical context, and immediate audience are all unsure. Joel the prophet is not named in the rest of the Old Testament, preventing us from finding a comparable timeframe within which to place him. Finally, the book lacks the fuller superscriptions we find in other books in the Twelve, preventing us from clearly identifying the original context or audience.[2] Because of this, the book is comprehensible against various historical backdrops. Indeed, the canvas of the Old Testament provides the frame in which to understand the book. Joel alludes to or quotes other prophetic texts in diverse ways (e.g., Joel 3:5 [2:32] and Obad 17; Joel 4:16 [3:16] and Amos 1:2; Joel 4:18 [3:18] and Amos 9:13; Joel 1:15

---

[1] Jörg Jeremias, "The Function of the Book of Joel for Reading the Twelve," in *Perspectives on the Formation of the Book of the Twelve: Methodological Foundations—Redactional Processes—Historical Insights*, ed. Ranier Albertz, James D. Nogalski, and Jakob Wöhrle, BZAW 433 (Berlin: de Gruyter, 2012), 77; see also Tchavdar S. Hadjiev, "Reading Joel Within and Without the Book of the Twelve," in *Reading the Book of the Twelve Minor Prophets*, ed. David G. Firth and Brittany N. Melton, SSBT (Bellingham, WA: Lexham Academic, 2022), 30-45.

[2] For various proposals, see: Miloš Bič, *Das Buch Joel* (Berlin: Evangelische Verlagsanstalt, 1960), 106-9; Ellie Assis, "The Date and Meaning of the Book of Joel," *VT* 61 (2011): 163-83, here 164.

and Is 13:6; Joel 2:13 and Jon 4:2; Joel 2:14 and Jon 3:9; Joel 4:10 [3:10] and Is 2:4 // Mic 4:3).[3] Other connections emerge as well, notably Exodus 10 and Exodus 34 (but see also Deut 28 and possibly 1 Kings 8).[4]

Structure

The book is a complex but unified composition, dividing roughly into two distinctive parts: the first half about judgment and the second half about salvation.[5]

Joel 1:1–2:17	The impending destruction coming in the day of the Lord and the call to repentance
Joel 1:1-7	Description of locust horde(s)
Joel 1:8	Call to lament
Joel 1:9-12	Description of ravaged land
Joel 1:13-14	Call to lament and consecrate a fast
Joel 1:15-18	Coming day of Yahweh
Joel 1:10-20	Appeals to Yahweh by humanity and beast
Joel 2:1-11	Day of the Lord has come!
Joel 2:13-14	Call to turn back to God
Joel 2:15-17	Call to consecrate a fast and pray in penitence
Joel 2:18–4:21 [2:18–3:21]	The promised future restoration of Zion and judgment against the nations in the day of the Lord
Joel 2:18-20	God's compassionate response
Joel 2:21-24	Land, beasts, and children of Zion restored
Joel 2:25-26	Restoration from locust horde and shame

---

[3] See Jeremias, "Function of the Book"; John Day, "Prophecy," in *It Is Written: Scripture Citing Scripture*, ed. D. A. Carson and H. G. M. Williamson (Cambridge: Cambridge University Press, 1988), 48-50; James L. Crenshaw, *Joel*, AB (New York: Doubleday, 1995), 27-28.

[4] John Strazicich, *Joel's Use of Scripture and the Scripture's Use of Joel: Appropriation and Resignification in Second Temple Judaism and Early Christianity*, BIS 82 (Leiden: Brill, 2007); Ruth Scoralick, *Gottes Güte und Gottes Zorn: Die Gottesprädikatationen in Exodus 34,6f. und Ihre Intertextuellen Beziehungen zum Zwolfprophetenbuch*, HBS 33 (Freiburg: Herder, 2001). See also the foundational work of Siegfried Bergler, *Joel as Scrhiftinterpret*, BEATAJ 16 (Frankfurt am Main: Peter Lang, 1998).

[5] See H. W. Wolff, *Joel and Amos*, Hermeneia (Philadelphia: Fortress, 1977), 7; J. D. Nogalski, *The Book of the Twelve: Hosea–Jonah*, SHBC (Macon, GA: Smyth & Helwys, 2011), 203. Interconnected elements integrate the structure of the book and help define the nature of Israel's God, revealed in Joel 1:1. See Willem S. Prinsloo, *The Theology of the Book of Joel*, BZAW 163 (Göttingen: de Gruyter, 1985), 122-26.

Joel 2:27	Self-disclosure of Yahweh: "You shall know..."
Joel 3:1-5 [2:28-32]	God's Spirit poured out
Joel 4:1-3 [3:1-3]	Valley of Jehoshaphat
Joel 4:4-8 [3:4-8]	Oracle against Nations (Tyre, Sidon, Philistia)
Joel 4:9-13 [3:9-13]	Battle and judgment in the valley of Jehoshaphat
Joel 4:14-16 [3:14-16]	Day of Yahweh in the valley of decision
Joel 4:17 [3:17]	Self-disclosure of Yahweh: "You shall know..."
Joel 4:18-21 [3:18-21]	Restoration of Zion (Jerusalem/Judah), judgment on Egypt and Edom

INTERPRETATION

Joel 1:1-7. Joel 1:1 is a typical introduction: "The word of the LORD came" to the prophet. Joel 1:2 commands hearers to listen to what is said in God's "word," complemented with a command "to recount/tell" (Joel 1:3) the message for days to come. The imperatives *listen* and *give ear* echo the invocation of Psalm 78, which recites God's wondrous deeds. The story needing a recounting is, however, one of *destruction*. A "locust plague" (Joel 1:4) has annihilated the agriculture of the land, creating trauma for God's people.[6]

The devastation clearly lies in the past, marked by the perfect verbs of Joel 1:6-20. But a break in the perfects appears in Joel 1:15, wherein the day of Yahweh "shall come" (imperfect of the root *bwʾ*) like havoc from Shaddai (the Almighty). Still, the imminence of that day of Yahweh is closely associated with the devastation of Joel 1:3-14. Indeed, the exclamatory particle *ʾăhâ*, "Alas!" (Joel 1:15), highlights that the day of Yahweh brings dread, terror. If the locust plague is bad, the day of Yahweh will be worse.

The meaning of "locust plague" is ambiguous, drawing together an image of environmental disaster and a metaphor for an invading and devastating army. First, these verses join the locust plague (Joel 1:4) with the "nation" that has gone up against God's land (Joel 1:6). The language of the enemy "going up" against God's people in Joel 1:6 at least echoes the language of God's locust plague that "goes up" against Egypt in Exodus 10:12. Second, metaphors surrounding Joel 1:6 offer complementary pictures of the invading army: the metaphor of a locust plague (Joel 1:4) and the simile of a predatory lion (Joel 1:6) surround "for a nation has invaded my

---

[6]Nogalski (*Book of the Twelve*, 218-19) thinks that the four locusts mentioned are a series of four locust plagues, corresponding to the four generations mentioned in Joel 1:3.

land" (Joel 1:6). The locust plague devours the agriculture of the land, and the lion devours the living animals of the land. Third, the poetic presentation of the enemy nation as a lion invites a nonliteral reading: both lion and locust are metaphors for devastating invasion. Fourth, the locusts in Joel 1 connect with the mention of the locust in Joel 2:25, so that the "northern" army in Joel 2:20 narrows down the semantics of locusts from Joel 1: the locust plague is a metaphor for an invading army rather than simply a natural disaster.[7] Whatever else may be said, the poetry correlates locusts and the army as indicators of the coming day of Yahweh, evoking comprehensive devastation.

Joel 1:8-19. "Human response" from God's people appears with the imperatives of Joel 1:2-3, 5, which continue in Joel 1:8, 13-14. God's people (here personified as Zion) should lament (Joel 1:8, 13) and mourn over the loss of Yahweh.[8] Joel 1:9, 13 carries the image of loss forward. The priests suffer from the loss of people bringing sacrificial meals and are called to repent and mourn (see Deut 18:1-8). The whole land is ravaged (Joel 1:12). God calls for a formal fast at the temple (Joel 1:14). The culminating imperative is "cry out" (*wəzaʿăqû*) to Yahweh in Joel 1:14, an appeal that appears in Exodus 2:23 (see also Ps 130:1). True worship and transformation for the people, then, will begin with a cry of help before their God where he may be found—the environs of the temple. If Joel 1:14 signals the need to cry out to Yahweh, Joel 1:15-16 defines the content of that plea (note the shift in pronouns from Joel 1:15 to Joel 1:16). The lament continues through the next two verses as well, as they remember the suffering of the land (Joel 1:17) and beasts (Joel 1:18). God's people, God's land, and God's creatures—everything—suffer in his judgment.

A dark picture of devastation coalesces in Joel 1:15-18, which sets the agenda for the day of Yahweh in the Twelve.[9] "Imminent" and coming quickly, the day "draws near."[10] Joel 1:15 echoes Isaiah 13:2; in both cases Israel's God is described with the title *Shaddai*, but in Joel it works in a wordplay with "desolation" (*šōd*): God (Shaddai) brings his "desolation" (*šōd*).

---

[7] So Pablo R. Andiñach, "The Locusts in the Message of Joel," *VT* 42, no. 4 (1992): 433-41.
[8] See Crenshaw, *Joel*, 97.
[9] See Rolf Rendtorff, "How to Read the Book of the Twelve as a Theological 'Unity,'" in *SBL Seminar Papers 1997* (Atlanta: Scholars Press, 1997), 423-25.
[10] The nearness of the day of Yahweh is found also in Obad 15 and Zeph 1:7, 14, focused on different groups. In Joel 1:15, the day of the Lord is imminent for God's people, as in Zeph 1:7. In Obad 15, the day of Yahweh's appearing is imminent for the nations (so too Joel 4:14 [3:14]).

Petitions shift from the third-person plural "we" (Joel 1:15-16) to the first person singular "I" (Joel 1:19), echoing individual appeals in the Psalter: "To you, O Yahweh, I call!" (see Ps 4:2-4; 17:6; 18:7 [18:6]; 28:1, etc.).[11] Joel 1:20 reveals that the beasts of the field *also* cry out to God, reminding us that Yahweh is responsive not just to humans but also to animals languishing in the fields (see Jon 4:11). God cares for the animals because he is the Creator and Lord who cares for everything he has made.

Joel 2:1-11. Joel 2:1 and Joel 2:11 frame the section describing Yahweh's day. It is imminent (Joel 2:1), "great," and "terrible" (Joel 2:11), adjectives repeated in the Minor Prophets (Joel 2:2; Zeph 1:15; Mal 3:23 [4:5]). Repeated commands to "blow a horn in Zion" (Joel 2:1, 15) accompany "day" language. The first sounding of the horn marks an alarm: the day of Yahweh draws near! The second sounding summons God's people to fast and pray. The repeated command to fast reveals a tension in the chapter. On the one hand, the day of Yahweh's destruction is certain. However, the question of who can endure the day is precisely answered by those who call out to Yahweh, particularly in the fast in Joel 2:15. Those who recognize Yahweh's *imminent* day of judgment make the people ready: they "sound an alarm" (Joel 2:1), and they call on the Lord with prayer and supplication at the fast (Joel 2:15). Those who will "endure" (Joel 2:11) in the coming day of the Lord, then, are expectant, penitent, and dependent on their God.

The historical invasion of the army (either the invading soldiers or the army of locusts, if one interprets the siege as a metaphor for natural disaster) becomes *cosmic in scope* by Joel 2:10.[12] Such apocalyptic language is also found in Isaiah 13:10-13 and Ezekiel 32:7-8. These texts, as here in Joel, show how an event can be impregnated with cosmic metaphors extrapolated to refer to *the* decisive time when God acts to vindicate his people and set all things right.

Joel 2:12-17. The call in Joel 1:19 is elaborated as a call for return in Joel 2:12. What does returning to Yahweh mean in Joel 2:12-14? Because there is no overt expression of rebuke or admission of sin, some think the call for

---

[11] The appellant ("I") may well be the prophet, who mediates between the people and their God even as he sits as one of the petitioners. If the prophet prays to God, he does so within the corporate plight of God's people.

[12] See Ronald L. Simkins, "God, History, and the Natural World in the Book of Joel," *CBQ* 55 (1993): 435-52.

returning does not mean repentance from sin.[13] Mark Boda demurs, arguing that penitence from sin is exactly what is in view in Joel 2:12-14.[14] We agree that the appeal is penitential.

Joel 2:13 emphasizes *inward* devotion and turning to God. Yahweh desires not only rending of garments but also rending of the heart. The covenantal language of Exodus 34:6-7 appears in Joel 2:13, affirming Yahweh's gracious character in responding to his people's repentance.

Table 5.1. Reception of Exodus 34:6-7 in Joel 2:13

JOEL 2:13	EXODUS 34:6-7
gracious	merciful
merciful	gracious
slow to anger	slow to anger
abounding in steadfast love	abounding in steadfast love and faithfulness
relenting over punishment	*keeping steadfast love for thousands*
	forgiving iniquity and transgression and sin

The italicized words in table 5.1 indicate what is not reiterated in Joel's reception of the Exodus passage. Further, this is the first time the Twelve uses Exodus 34:6-7. Elsewhere it appears in Joel 2:13; Jonah 3:10; Micah 7:18-20; Nahum 1:2-3; Malachi 1:9.[15] Jakob Wöhrle argues this "grace-corpus" of Exodus 34:6-7 funds as a larger redactional framework governing the Minor Prophets. Elements of Exodus 34:6-7 appear at the beginning, the middle, and ending of the Book of the Twelve.[16] Table 5.1 and table 5.2 are adapted from Wöhrle.[17]

In terms of *how* Exodus 34:6-7 appears and which elements emerge and where, Wöhrle sees a general pattern. The full set of divine characteristics emerges in Joel 2:13 and in Jonah 4:2, but the other books use only some elements. Nahum 1:3 emphasizes Yahweh as "slow to anger," the only other place where that language appears outside Joel 2:13 and Jonah 4:2.

---

[13]Crenshaw, *Joel*, 40-43.
[14]Mark J. Boda, "Penitential Innovations Within the Twelve," in *On Stone and Scroll: Essays in Honour of Graham Ivor Davies*, ed. James K. Aitken, Katherine J. Dell, and Brian A. Mastin, BZAW 420 (Berlin: de Gruyter, 2011), 391-408, esp. 401-2.
[15]See Jakob Wöhrle, "So Many Cross-References! Methodological Reflections on the Problem of Intertextual Relationships and Their Significance for Redaction Critical Analysis," in Albertz, Nogalski, and Wöhrle, *Perspectives on the Formation*, 14.
[16]Wöhrle ("So Many Cross-References," 14n38) omits Hosea from consideration.
[17]Wöhrle, "So Many Cross-References," 14.

Table 5.2. Wöhrle's distribution of grace-corpus elements in the Book of the Twelve

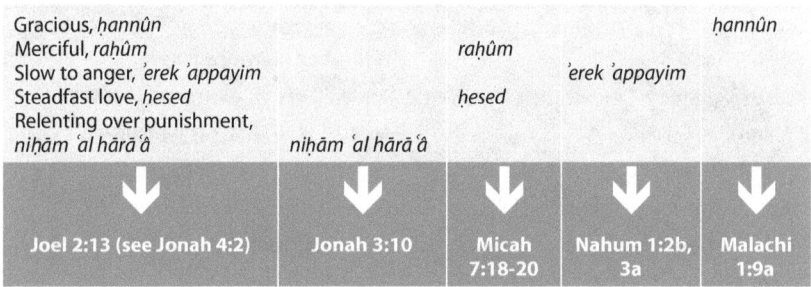

In this way, Exodus 34:6-7 is a "theological superstructure" for the Twelve. However, grace is matched by judgment: Yahweh is slow to anger, but he will not clear the guilty, whether those culpable are Israel or the nations (Joel 2:13; Nahum 1:3). The positive characteristics diminish across the Twelve.

Still, Yahweh's positive characteristics appear first in Joel's text. This fact reveals Yahweh's radical commitment to his people, if they turn to him. The phrase "relenting over punishment" stands out because of its close linkage to prayer. The work of (1) mourning and fasting, coupled with (2) the turn to God, is set within prayer; prayer becomes the means by which God becomes the source of hope for the people. God alone provides the possibility of transformation, for which they pray. The text offers no explicit sacrificial terminology of purification or atonement. Rather, God's people anticipate an outpouring of God *himself* as expressed in his covenantal character: his grace, his mercy, and his covenant love. Yahweh relents from punishment and responds to prayer.

Nevertheless, Joel 2:14 affirms the freedom of God, his sovereignty. Divine forgiveness is *expected* but not *guaranteed*. The phrase "Who knows?" (Joel 2:14) does not imply fatalistic resignation to one's fate. Rather, the question recognizes the radical freedom of Yahweh to act as he wishes in response to immediate appeals of his people. That Yahweh stands committed to his covenant, while at the same time free, strangely energizes God's people and their appeals for divine help.

Joel 2:18-27. This section marks a critical turn in the book, where the prayers mentioned in Joel 1:19-20 and Joel 2:12-17 receive their first divine response. The second response comes in Joel 3:1-5 [2:28-32]. True to his covenantal fidelity in Exodus 34 // Joel 2:13, the Lord is roused (Joel 2:18) and responds (Joel 2:19) with compassion. In this restoration oracle, Yahweh responds to the distresses mentioned in the first two chapters of the book.

Table 5.3. Recurrence of distress and divine response in Joel 1–2

DISTRESSES	DIVINE RESPONSE
locusts (Joel 1:4)	restoration from locust plague (Joel 2:25-26)
army (Joel 1:6)	driving the northerner away (Joel 2:20)
dearth of new wine/grain/oil (Joel 1:5, 10, 18)	restoration of new wine/grain/oil (Joel 2:19, 24)
lack of offering/libation (Joel 1:9, 13)	abundance of grain, wine, oil (Joel 2:24)
mourning land (Joel 1:10)	"Fear not, O soil!" (Joel 2:21)
groaning beasts (Joel 1:18)	"Fear not, O beasts of the field!" (Joel 2:22)
withered land and crops (Joel 1:11-12, 16-17)	fertile land (Joel 2:22)
drought (Joel 1:20)	early and latter rain (Joel 2:23)
mourning people; joy has dried up (Joel 1:12-14)	joy, no more shame (Joel 2:23, 26, 27)

The important theological recognition formula "you shall know" in Joel 2:27 (see Is 45:5-6) reveals that restoration in Joel 2:18-27 is the *second* of the two-step rhythm of God's judgment *and* restoration in Joel. God reveals himself, and God's people know him in and through this revelation. The repetition of the root *yd'* in Joel 2:14, 27 reveals that the question raised in Joel 2:14 finds its answer in Joel 2:27. The divine judgment described in Joel 1:3–2:17 is transformed, reversed, made new in the divine restoration of Joel 3–4.

Joel 3:1-5 [2:28-32]. The second promise of restoration after Joel 2:18-27, the promise of Joel 3:1-5 [2:28-32], carries the theme of restoration further. The opening phrase of Joel 3:1, "and it will be after that," connects the action depicted in what follows with the vision of Joel 2:18-27. In this future time after judgment, God's Spirit will accompany restoration. Spirit empowerment is for the future, as it does not occur in Joel 2 and is not anticipated in the book to this point.

The closest parallel to Joel's idea of the Spirit of God being poured out comes in Ezekiel 36:27: "I will put my spirit in your midst." Similar images of Spirit restoration appear in Ezekiel 37:14; 39:29. Isaiah, too, depicts a coming restoration where God will pour out his Spirit, though without using the verb *I will pour out* (*'ešpôk*) as in Joel 3:1-2 [2:28-29] (see Is 42:1; 44:3-4; 59:21). In Isaiah 59:21, for example, God sets his Spirit on the judged and restored remnant of Israel, in which God—through his Spirit—puts his own words in the mouths of God's people, their children, and their children's children, for all of time (*wəʿad ʿôlām*). This

Isaianic text, along with Ezekiel 36:27, connects with the substance of Joel 3:1-2 [2:28-29].[18]

The terminology "all flesh" (Joel 3:1 [2:28]) and "upon male and female slaves" (Joel 3:2 [2:29]) signal a universal restoration.[19] These may be either foreign slaves obtained from war conquest or Israelite slaves who find themselves financially indebted to an overlord and working to pay off their obligations.[20] Both are possible. If the former, then a universalistic emphasis accompanies the gift of prophecy. God pours out his Spirit on those of both high and low estate, male and female, Israelite and foreigner. A democratization of God's Spirit comes on *all peoples* who are brought together as God's people. All shall be prophets: Yahweh has judged and restored his people, placed his Spirit in them, and now they speak his words (see Is 59:3, 13).[21]

Joel 4:1-13 [3:1-13]. The final sections of Joel depict a time when Yahweh will restore Judah and Jerusalem, but he will judge the nations. Joel 4:2 [3:2] and Joel 4:12 [3:12] indicate the place that frames the section: "the valley of Jehoshaphat." Not a location identifiable on a map, this valley is a prophetic picture of divine judgment: *Jehoshaphat* in Hebrew means "Yahweh judges." Yahweh judges "all nations" (Joel 4:2 [3:2]), and he "will contend" with them.

Taken on its own, Joel 4 may give the impression that somehow Israel's God is xenophobic or racist. The book's canonical context, however, prevents us from such shortsightedness. First, Joel 1–2 reminds us that Yahweh judges sinful Israel just as he does sinful nations. Joel 3:1-5 [2:28-32] indicates a democratizing of the Spirit of Yahweh, as discussed above. Finally, Jonah's message in the Book of the Twelve reminds us that Yahweh is merciful to *all* nations that turn in repentance to him (see esp. Jon 4:2).[22] Xenophobia, then, on a canonical reading of the Twelve, is excluded.

---

[18]Wolff, *Joel and Amos*, 67.
[19]"All flesh" may not mean "all nations." "All flesh" may be a designation of all societal groups in the people of Israel, namely, sons, daughters, elders, and young men (Joel 3:1). Crenshaw, however, believes Joel's vision in this section is only for Judahites remaining in the former nation of Judah in the late postexilic period (*Joel*, 43).
[20]Victor H. Matthews and Don C. Benjamin, *Social World of Ancient Israel: 1250–587 BCE* (Grand Rapids, MI: Baker Academic, 1993), 199-205.
[21]See Rodrigo J. Morales, *The Spirit and the Restoration of Israel*, Wissenschaftliche Untersuchungen zum Neuen Testament 2/282 (Tübingen: Mohr Siebeck, 2010), 24-25.
[22]See Thomas B. Dozeman, "Inner-Biblical Interpretation of Yahweh's Gracious and Compassionate Character," *JBL* 108, no. 2 (1989): 207-23.

Yahweh's plan for the reconciliation of *all things* comes through the particular people of Israel.[23] Joel teaches that Yahweh's demands for justice and righteousness impinge on both Israel *and* the nations, but it is Israel that Yahweh has chosen (the particular) to be the instrument of salvation to the nations (the universal). Those nations that stand against Yahweh and the people he has chosen are bound for judgment.

In fact, Joel 4:4-8 [3:4-8] reminds us that the ways of those against Yahweh will rebound on their own heads. This is retribution, and the retribution principle in the prophets can be stated rather simply: as he is just, Yahweh rewards people justly according to their actions, whether good or bad, whether individually or communally.[24] Judgment comes against these enemy nations in the form of a divine army. Enemies come to the valley of Jehoshaphat to engage Yahweh and his warriors in battle (Joel 4:9-13 [3:9-13]). But such posturing by sinful nations remains vain. Yahweh does not fight but "sits" in judgment (Joel 4:12 [3:12]). The blending of warfare and viticultural imagery in Joel 4:13 [3:13] makes the point clear: the wine/blood that flows and overflows belongs to the enemy nations.[25]

Joel 4:14-21 [3:14-21]. This final section opens with a variation on terminology in Joel 4:14 [3:14]: the "valley of Jehoshaphat" becomes the "valley of decision." When the two terms are compared, the judgment that was *going* to take place in the valley of Jehoshaphat takes on a note of certainty, even *finality*, with the change into the moniker "valley of decision." It is twice used in Joel 4:14 [3:14], highlighting the certainty of Yahweh's action: nothing shall turn it back. His judgment against enemy nations is *done*. That the twofold valley of decision surrounds the day of Yahweh in Joel 4:14 [3:14] enables us to see a different facet to the day itself: it is a time of *Yahweh's final judgment* against his enemies. In the context of Joel, the valley of decision lies somewhere beyond Zion. Why? Because Zion is a place of perfect peace as Yahweh dwells there (Joel 4:17, 21 [3:17, 21]). But the valley is the location where Yahweh judges his enemies through warfare.

---

[23]Richard Bauckham, *The Bible and Mission* (Grand Rapids, MI: Eerdmans, 2003), 11.

[24]On the difficult text of Joel 4:4-8 (3:4-8), see Heath A. Thomas, "Hope Through Human Trafficking? Theodicy in Joel 4:4-8," in *Theodicy and Hope in the Book of the Twelve*, ed. Colin Toffelmire, Beth Stovell, George Athas, and Daniel Timmer, LHBOTS 705 (London: T&T Clark, 2021), 88-110.

[25]Note the viticultural tools that nations transform into instruments of warfare in Joel 4:10 [3:10]. Joel clearly uses the language of Mic 4:3 // Is 2:4, or at least a common source that informed all three texts, and inverts the language to depict the horrible fate of the enemy nations.

Two theological points emerge from Joel 4:15-17 [3:15-17]. First, *creation's tumult* reveals the Creator God. God's world is responsive in the judgment of the Lord. It is through his judgment that the world is prepared for renewal, centered in Zion (see Joel 4:16-21 [3:16-21]). Second, God's care for *his people* in Zion reveals the *covenantal God*. God does his work in and through his election of his people, Israel. In this way, creation and covenant, two threads that run through the Old Testament in general and the Minor Prophets, conjoin, albeit in a cosmic eschatological vision.

Joel 4:18-21 [3:18-21] provides an eschatological vision of restoration that moves beyond the localized portrait of restoration mentioned in Joel 2. The opening phrase "and it will be in that day" (Joel 4:18 [3:18]) is a typical transition that indicates an eschatological prophetic vision. The day of Yahweh has taken on cosmic significance: Israel's God has judged the nations, made his people and city pure and holy; he rightly reigns on the throne in Zion; and the world produces fertility and vitality from Yahweh's dwelling, with a life-giving river sprouting from it (see Ezek 47). In short, Zion becomes the source of life for the world because Yahweh dwells there with his purified people.

However, two historical archetypal enemies of Israel (Egypt and Edom) get their just deserts in the vision.[26] True, both Egypt and Edom figure in visions of restoration in other texts, but here the emphasis is on the judgment of these enemies and the restoration of God's people. These nations will become desolate wastes, but Judah and Jerusalem will be full of people forever, and there will be fecundity on an unprecedented scale: "Mountains shall drip with wine and the hills shall flow with milk; all the channels of Judah will be full of water" (Joel 4:18 [3:18]). After judgment, Yahweh will rule in Zion with his people forever.

JOEL IN THE NEW TESTAMENT

The vivid imagery of the day of Yahweh is central to Joel's reception in the New Testament. Paul draws on Joel to present the appropriate response to God in the face of the impending judgment. In 1 Corinthians 1:2, Paul greets the Corinthian church as those who "call upon the name of the Lord Jesus Christ." He invokes Joel 3:5 [2:32], but with a crucial difference. The name of the Lord, which for Joel is Yahweh, now becomes the name of the Lord

---

[26]See Bert Dicou, *Edom, Israel's Brother and Antagonist: The Role of Edom in Biblical Prophecy and Story*, JSOTSup 169 (Sheffield: Sheffield Academic Press, 1994).

Jesus the Messiah. In this way, Paul blends the understanding of repentance and faith with an acclamation that Jesus is God, Lord, and Messiah.

His statement is staggering for its theological depth. Paul sees in Jesus the fulfillment of the kingdom of God, in his life, death, burial, and resurrection. Those who have called on *his* name are saved. But this same Jesus is both Israel's God and Israel's Messiah. However, this acclamation is not simply a response to the call of God ("called to be saints") or a past affirmation (as in they previously *called* on the Lord). Rather, Paul calls the church at Corinth the church who are *calling* on the name of our Lord Jesus Christ. The participle indicates that a mark of the church is that they are ones who perpetually identify with Jesus and call on his name.

Pentecost inaugurates the age of the church, and Peter reaches for Joel to explain to his audience what they are witnessing. Peter uses Joel 3:1-5 [2:28-32] in Acts 2, identifying the activity of the Spirit of God at Pentecost as a fulfillment of prophecy and the eschatological inauguration of the day of Yahweh. Peter quotes closely LXX Joel 3:1-5 in Acts 2:17-21. For Peter and the believers at Pentecost, the day of salvation depicted in Joel comes in and through Jesus, who is in fact the Lord. Both judgment and salvation coalesce with the day of Yahweh in Joel; in Acts 2 the emphasis lies in God's salvation. Peter adapts LXX Joel 3:1 in Acts 2:17 by using the words "in the last days" instead of the Greek word for "afterward" from Joel. The last days, the eschaton, had broken into the present, and Peter proclaims this in his adaptation of Joel.[27]

Revelation engages Joel intertextually in at least three passages to depict the consummation of that kingdom in the day of the Lord as a day of wrath not against Israel but against the world in the final judgment: Revelation 6:12-17; 9:7-9; 14:14-20. Revelation 6:12-17 evokes Joel's depiction of the day of Yahweh in general (as "darkness"; Joel 2:2, 10), but Revelation 6:12 clearly employs the "moon turns to blood" in Joel 3:4 [2:31] to describe the "wrath of the Lamb" that comes on worldly powers on the day of the Lord. In this, John affirms that the day of the Lord is a day of judgment, but his vision affirms that this day is part of God's work in Christ Jesus, who is the "Lamb" (Rev 6:16). The question that those terror-ridden nonbelievers ask is quite simply, "Who can stand" on the day of wrath? Their question finds its antecedent in the description of Yahweh's day in Joel 2:11, "For great is the

---

[27]Huub van de Sandt, "The Minor Prophets in Luke–Acts," in *The Minor Prophets in the New Testament*, ed. Maarten J. J. Menken and Steve Moyise, LNTS 377 (London: T&T Clark, 2009), 63.

Day of the LORD, and exceedingly terrible: Who can endure it?" as well as Nahum 1:6, "Who can stand before his indignation? Who can endure the heat of his anger?"

The answer is, of course, no one. The only exception comes for those who repent and believe in the Lord. Those who have trusted in the Lord will find escape and be saved in Zion (LXX Joel 3:5). If this is not said explicitly in Revelation 6, the intertextuality between Revelation 6:17 and Joel 2:11 (and Nahum 1:6) "creates these expectations in the readers."[28] Whenever human beings accept God's dominion through the Lamb of God, "place is made for God's renewing lordship over his world."[29]

Revelation 9:7-9 uses Joel's depiction of the locust plague (Joel 1–2) to depict the coming day of the Lord. Marko Jauhiainen argues that Joel's locust plague causes the people of Israel to tremble, but in Revelation 9, the locust plague is universalized and the *whole world* trembles. In both texts nothing escapes the locusts on the day of the Lord, except those who have the seal of the living God; they escape divine judgment.

The terror of the locust imagery in Revelation 9:7-9 is matched by the harvest imagery in Revelation 14:14-20, which clearly draws on Joel 4:1-21 [3:1-21], especially Joel 4:13 [3:13]: "Swing the sickle, for the crop is ripe! Come and tread, for the winepress is full! The vats are overflowing for great is their punishment!" The harvest imagery certainly combines the punishment of wickedness with blood of grapes, signifying the punishment of sin. However, the harvest imagery may also imply, especially in its deployment in Revelation 14:14-20, a kind of gleaning of firstfruits of the harvest (Rev 14:4). That is to say, the harvest may separate the righteous in harvest and a treading of unrighteousness, combining the judgment and salvation that accompanies the day of the Lord both in Joel and in Revelation.[30]

THE THEOLOGY OF JOEL

Joel presents a deep and rich theology that resonates with other prophetic books. We will attend specifically to the day of Yahweh in the next chapter.

Divine justice. Divine justice in the book of Joel envisions Yahweh's activity with his people *and* the nations. God's covenant people are called to repent

---

[28]Marko Jauhiainen, "The Minor Prophets in Revelation," in Menken and Moyise, *Minor Prophets in the New Testament*, 163.
[29]Jürgen Roloff, *Revelation*, Continental Commentary (Minneapolis: Fortress, 1993), 93.
[30]See the discussion of Jauhiainen, "Minor Prophets in Revelation," 168.

and turn to God under the stipulations of the covenant. Yet, for Joel, Yahweh does not establish justice with *only* his covenant people. Yahweh's day dawns over the nations as well. The book of Joel exhibits Yahweh's imperial power: Yahweh dispenses judgment on Israel (Joel 1), the "northerner" (Joel 2:20), "all nations" (Joel 4:2 [3:2]), Tyre and Sidon (Joel 4:4 [3:4]), Philistia (Joel 4:4 [3:4]), and Egypt and Edom (Joel 4:19 [3:19]). He also uses foreign nations to do his bidding (Joel 2:11). "In sum, Israel's prophets serve as heralds for a cosmic God. As such, they offer an international perspective for what happens to Israel even as they affirm the importance of God's covenant with Israel."[31]

The Spirit of God. Joel's description of the Spirit of God in Joel 3:1-5 [2:28-32] displays certain affinities with Isaiah 59:21; Ezekiel 36:27; 37:27. The difference between these texts, however, is marked. God's provision of the Spirit in Isaiah 59:21 enables God's people to follow his words (divine instructions as in Josh 1:8-9). The Spirit in Ezekiel 36:27, too, enables God's people to follow God's judgments and statutes. The Spirit in Ezekiel 37:27 provides *life* for God's people. But the Spirit in Joel 3 enables God's people to do the work of prophecy: to hear from God and speak God's word.

One sees a progression of vision of the Spirit in Joel 1:1–3:5 [1:1–2:32]. In Joel 1–2, God's people worship at the temple with the priests at the lead; they repent at the temple with the priests at the head of the penitential liturgy. This liturgical worship, in its hierarchical and mediated form, contrasts starkly with the shift to God's Spirit coming on all peoples in Joel 3:1-5 [2:28-32]. There is *no* hierarchical mediation in this oracle: all people are imbued with the Spirit of God and the gift of prophecy and vision. This picture accords well with the New Testament image of God's people *becoming* the spiritual house of God and replacing the temple. Of course, in the New Testament, Jesus is the cornerstone and the head of the temple. The point, however, remains salient: Joel 3:1-5 [2:28-32] casts a vision of the presence of Yahweh being poured on his people without mediation, without prophets or priests to stand between God and the people. What God once bestowed on anointed leaders in Israel's past has now become the mark for *all peoples who call on the name of the Lord*. This marks Joel as a Spirit book and important for any theology of the Spirit of God.

The kingdom of God. Joel 4 [3] depicts Zion as the center of Yahweh's kingdom, where he reigns without opposition. In fact, Joel 4:18-21 [3:18-21]

---

[31]David L. Peterson, *The Prophetic Literature: An Introduction* (Louisville: WJK, 2002), 39.

connects with a number of elements of Zion theology that celebrate the reign of God in his cosmic mountain: the healing water that flows from Zion (Joel 4:18 [3:18]), divine triumph over enemies and salvation for Zion (Joel 4:19 [3:19]), and God's eternal reign in his eternal dwelling (see Joel 4:17 [3:17]).[32] The phrase "and Yahweh dwells in Zion" (Joel 4:21 [3:21]), which closes the book, discloses an eschatological vision of the kingdom of God: all of God's (restored) people, living in God's (restored) land, under God's (abiding) rule. The kingdom of God thematically links to the day of the Lord.

"And it will be in that day" (Joel 4:18 [3:18]) is a key phrase that marks eschatological renewal visions. Joel anticipates and envisions the kingdom of God without employing the terminology normally associated with it in Second Temple Judaism (*malkuth Adonai*) or the New Testament. In Joel 4 [3], the following themes coalesce with the coming of the kingdom of God:

- Yahweh's kingdom appears at the initiative of Yahweh on the day of the Lord (Joel 4:1, 14 [3:1, 14]).
- Yahweh's kingdom appears with cosmic manifestations (Joel 4:15-16 [3:15-16]).
- Yahweh's kingdom appears with Yahweh's judgment against those who oppose him (Joel 4:12 [3:12]).
- Yahweh's kingdom appears with the restoration of his people (Joel 4:16-18, 20 [3:16-18, 20]).
- Yahweh's kingdom appears by re-creating the broken world, so that there is no more threat (Joel 4:17-18 [3:17-18]).
- Yahweh's kingdom appears in Zion, which brings healing (waters) for the remainder of the world (Joel 4:18 [3:18]).
- Yahweh's kingdom is enjoyed by those who recognize his work and call on him (Joel 4:17 [3:17]; see Joel 3:5 [2:32]).

Recommended Reading

Assis, Ellie. "The Date and Meaning of the Book of Joel." *VT* 61 (2011): 163-83.
Bergler, Siegfried. *Joel as Scrhiftinterpret*. BEATAJ 16. Frankfurt am Main: Peter Lang, 1998.

---

[32]See Heath A. Thomas, "Zion," in *Dictionary of the Old Testament Prophets*, ed. Mark J. Boda and J. Gordon McConville (Downers Grove, IL: InterVarsity Press, 2012), 907. See also Jon Levenson, *Sinai and Zion: An Entry into the Jewish Bible* (New York: Harper & Row, 1985), 111-35.

Hadjiev, Tchavdar S. "Reading Joel Within and Without the Book of the Twelve." In *Reading the Book of the Twelve Minor Prophets*, ed. David G. Firth and Brittany N. Melton, 30-45. SSBT. Bellingham, WA: Lexham Academic, 2022.*

Jeremias, Jörg. "The Function of the Book of Joel for Reading the Twelve." In *Perspectives on the Formation of the Book of the Twelve: Methodological Foundations—Redactional Processes—Historical Insights*, ed. Ranier Albertz, James D. Nogalski, and Jakob Wöhrle, 77-87. BZAW 433. Berlin: de Gruyter, 2012.*

Nogalski, J. D. *The Book of the Twelve: Hosea–Jonah*. SHBC. Macon, GA: Smyth & Helwys, 2011.

Scoralick, Ruth. *Gottes Güte und Gottes Zorn: Die Gottesprädikatationen in Exodus 34,6f. und Ihre Intertextuellen Beziehungen zum Zwolfprophetenbuch*. HBS 33. Freiburg: Herder, 2001.

Strazicich, John. *Joel's Use of Scripture and the Scripture's Use of Joel: Appropriation and Resignification in Second Temple Judaism and Early Christianity*. BIS 82. Leiden: Brill, 2007.

Thomas, Heath A. "Hope Through Human Trafficking? Theodicy in Joel 4:4-8." In *Theodicy and Hope in the Book of the Twelve*, ed. Colin Toffelmire, Beth Stovell, George Athas, and Daniel Timmer, 88-110. LHBOTS 705. London: T&T Clark, 2021.

Wöhrle, Jakob. "So Many Cross-References! Methodological Reflections on the Problem of Intertextual Relationships and Their Significance for Redaction Critical Analysis." In *Perspectives on the Formation of the Book of the Twelve: Methodological Foundations—Redactional Processes—Historical Insights*, ed. Ranier Albertz, James Nogalski, and Jakob Wöhrle, 3-20. BZAW 433. Berlin: de Gruyter, 2012.

Recommended reading marked with a "*" indicates introductory works.

6

The Day of the Lord

THIS CHAPTER CONTINUES OUR DISCUSSION of Joel as we focus on the day of the Lord and its connection with the kingdom of God in the Minor Prophets. While tracing the phrase in the Old Testament is of value, the concept of the day of the Lord far exceeds the strictures of precise terminological data (*yôm* + deity), relating to a wider set of terms, concepts, and metaphors in the Minor Prophets. When read together, this terminology indicates that the day of the Lord comprises a patterned event of divine revelation wherein God acts in the world for salvation, which also implies judgment, to establish his reign.

THE OLD TESTAMENT CONCEPT OF THE DAY OF THE LORD

According to Moshe Weinfeld, the day of the Lord stems from a "belief in the advent of God to save Israel and mankind. This salvation involves both the eradication of evil through cosmic war and the establishment of cosmic redemption. It is only natural that the people see in this day of divine theophany the promise of national redemption through which, in their view, the God of Israel's kingship will be manifested."[1] The day of the Lord thus evokes God's reign, his kingdom, wherein Yahweh vanquishes evil and establishes justice, righteousness, and peace.

The origin of the concept remains debated.[2] Weinfeld thinks the concept of the day of the Lord did not originate within a certain institution or social

---

[1] Moshe Weinfeld, *Normative and Sectarian Judaism in the Second Temple Period*, LSTS 54 (London: T&T Clark, 2005), 79-80.
[2] Mowinckel's view is that the concept of the day of the Lord originated in the cult, particularly the New Year's festival in Israel. By contrast, von Rad suggests the concept originated in Israel's warfare traditions, in which Yahweh battles and defeats Israel's enemies. See Sigmund Mowinckel, *The Psalms in Israel's Worship* (Grand Rapids, MI: Eerdmans, 2004), 106-19; Gerhard von Rad, "The Origin of the Concept of the 'Day of Yahweh,'" *JSS* 4 (1959): 97-108.

context, whether cultic or military. However, the day of the Lord may have emerged in other quarters, such as the daily liturgy of Jewish prayer.[3] This resonates with Jesus' (Jewish) teaching on prayer, in which the concepts of the day of the Lord and the kingdom of God connect and grow thematically (Mt 6:10; see Mt 6:13).

Because the day of the Lord marks the epochal intervention of God in the world, individual events in the history of Israel can be identified with the day, but no singular event of the past exhausts its final, ultimate horizon in history. Each instance of the day of the Lord in the Minor Prophets is like a tile in an expansive mosaic that, when taken together, composes the full vision of the final, eschatological day of the Lord that is yet to come. But as the tiles in the mosaic, all are related, creating the whole image. The composite image affords a kind of divine economy of judgment and salvation in the intervention of God. Each text pushes toward the eschatological day; this advent of God into the world will bring God's *final* judgment of the wicked and *ultimate* vindication of the righteous. Further, after this day, God will bring his final and glorious kingdom on earth.

The Day of the Lord and the Kingdom of God

Working through Joel as a guide to the concept, it is apparent that the day of the Lord and the kingdom of God—the central theme of Jesus' teaching—correlate. Note the following:

- The day of the Lord is a *time* and *event*, not a singular day (Joel 4:1 [3:1]). This enables a flexibility as to its application in varied contexts.
- The day of the Lord therefore emerges in more than one historic moment in the history of God's people: past, present, or future (Joel 1:15; 2:2, 11; 3:1 [2:28], 3:4 [2:31]; 4:1 [3:1], 4:14 [3:14]).
- The day of the Lord emerges with/after momentous cosmological events (Joel 2:1-2, 10; 3:3-4 [2:30-31]; 4:15 [3:15]).
- The day of the Lord is a time of restoration and salvation (Joel 3:1-5 [2:28-32]; 4:1 [3:1], 4:18 [3:18]). It is followed by peace and harmony: Yahweh reigns (Joel 3:5 [2:32]; 4:17 [3:17], 4:20 [3:20]).
- The day of the Lord is a time of judgment and punishment (Joel 1:15; 2:1-2, 11; 4:1 [3:1], 4:14 [3:14], 4:19 [3:19]).

---

[3]Weinfeld, *Normative and Sectarian Judaism*, 77.

- The day of the Lord presses forward eschatologically. It anticipates a *coming* (sometimes conceived of as *final*) vindication of the righteous and punishment of the wicked (Joel 4:1-3 [3:1-3], 4:9-21 [3:9-21]).
- The day of the Lord correlates with the coming reign of God, which can also be identified as the coming kingdom of God (Joel 4:16-18 [3:16-18], 4:21 [3:21]).
- The day of the Lord is a day of refuge and restoration for those who, in humility and fidelity, call on the Lord and wait for him (Joel 3:5 [2:32]).
- The day of the Lord reveals the just and restorative character of Yahweh (Joel 2:27; 4:17 [3:17]).

These characteristics derive from a synthetic description of the day of the Lord in Joel and so intertwine concepts traditionally held apart by historians of biblical prophecy. Joel's presentation sets the stage for how the day of the Lord might be understood in the other Minor Prophets. It is a significant theme that ties the twelve prophetic books together, and each of the other prophets highlights this or that feature, but none draw together all of the elements identified above as Joel does.[4] In fact, we agree with Weinfeld's assessment, "No two prophets have quite the same conception of the Day of the Lord."[5] But even though the prophets differ in how they apply the concept to their historical contexts, nonetheless corporately they touch on the characteristics identified above. Correlated, the Twelve display a universal vision of the day of the Lord, and Joel synthesizes the day-of-the-Lord concept. Joel's conception of the day of the Lord is more holistic in part because his book takes up other texts on the day of the Lord from the other prophets.[6]

THE DAY OF THE LORD AND ANCIENT NEAR EASTERN CONTEXTS

No texts from the ancient world, so far as we are aware, use the language "*yôm* + deity" to communicate a day of either judgment or salvation.

---

[4]On the day of the Lord as a theme that ties the Twelve together, see Rolf Rendtorff, "Alas for the Day! The 'Day of the LORD' in the Book of the Twelve," in *God in the Fray: A Tribute to Walter Brueggemann*, ed. Tod Linafelt and Timothy K. Beal (Minneapolis: Fortress, 1998), 186-97; Rolf Rendtorff, "How to Read the Book of the Twelve as a Theological 'Unity,'" in *SBL Seminar Papers 1997* (Atlanta: Scholars Press, 1997), 423-25; James D. Nogalski, "The Day(s) of YHWH in the Book of the Twelve," in *Thematic Threads in the Book of the Twelve*, ed. Paul L. Redditt and Aaron Schart, BZAW 325 (Berlin: de Gruyter, 2003), 192-212; Paul R. House, "Endings as New Beginnings: Returning to the Lord, the Day of the Lord, and Renewal in the Book of the Twelve," in Redditt and Schart, *Thematic Threads*, 313-38.
[5]Weinfeld, *Normative and Sectarian Judaism*, 80.
[6]Thus we read Joel late, belonging to the Persian period (or later).

However, in some texts from the ancient world (particularly from ancient Akkad and Babylon), there *is* a concept of judgment, decreed by a deity, that is demarcated by the language "day of *X*." Usually, however, this is described as a "day of judgment" associated with a divinely ordained storm. In Lamentation over the Destruction of Sumer and Ur, the high gods Enlil and An decree destruction by way of a storm on a "day."[7] These texts are well known as city laments, though the term *lament* is a generic classification that may not exactly fit the material. In them there is an indication that the day of judgment is given by a deity (or a set of deities) and comes in the form of a storm, fire, pestilence, and an invading army. The day described in these texts, like the day of the Lord in the Old Testament, is not a *singular* twenty-four-hour day but a period of time, an event, in which destruction is ordained. Thus in both the Bible and the city laments a day of destruction or salvation cannot be confined to a twenty-four-hour period but should be understood as an event.

It is possible biblical material reflects city-lament tradition, especially in the book of Lamentations. One of the primary characteristics of the city lament in the Bible is the divine agent of destruction (Yahweh), who comes against his people and land in judgment on the day of the Lord.[8] Old Testament prophets modify the facets of the pagan city lament for their theological contexts, but nonetheless some characteristics of this genre appear in biblical contexts.

One other point of comparison needs to be recognized. In contrast to Israelite prophecy, when the day of judgment is employed in ancient Near Eastern city laments there is nowhere a reference to a glorious reversal of fortune that eventuates in an *Endzeit* where the deity reigns supreme and the people live in peace. By contrast, eschatological visions of Israelite prophecy associated with the day of the Lord hold *precisely* this in view. This coming of God presents "a culminating and ameliorative end to the historical process," as Bill Arnold writes, whereas Israel's neighbors do not share this universalistic vision.[9] The notion that the day of the Lord brings to culmination sin-bound history is certainly correct, but N. T. Wright rightly argues that the day does not come with an end to the historical

---

[7]Jacob Klein, "Lamentation over the Destruction of Sumer and Ur," *COS* 1:535-39.
[8]F. W. Dobbs-Allsopp, *Weep, O Daughter of Zion: A Study of the City-Lament Genre in the Hebrew Bible*, Biblica et Orientalia 44 (Rome: Pontifical Biblical Institute, 1993), 63.
[9]Bill T. Arnold, "Old Testament Eschatology and the Rise of Apocalypticism," in *The Oxford Handbook to Eschatology*, ed. Jerry T. Walls (Oxford: Oxford University Press, 2008), 31.

process, full stop, as Arnold's comments imply.[10] The day of the Lord does not transform the world into an otherworldly world of forms akin to Greek dualistic thought. Rather, the day of the Lord inaugurates the kingdom of God in history and in the creation.

THE DAY OF THE LORD IN SECOND TEMPLE LITERATURE

The concept was received in Second Temple Judaism (ca. 500 BC–AD 100) with some flexibility. Like Joel, Jews could find in the day of the Lord messages of both impending judgment against the wicked and salvation for God's people. Some representative texts that use and adapt the day of the Lord are, among others, 1 Enoch (concerned with day of judgment throughout, but see 1 Enoch 27.3-4; 108.1-3), 4 Ezra, Jubilees, Assumption of Moses 10.1-13, 2 Baruch 59.9, Testament of Judah 24.2-6, and Testament of Levi 3.9. These works indicate the tumult that accompanies the day of the Lord, identifying it in various ways.

Qumran material reflects the concept of the coming day of the Lord as a day of judgment. For example, the Qumran pesher of Habakkuk understands the vision in Habakkuk 2:2-4 as the coming day of the Lord, his end-time judgment, and the time in which God's righteous will be vindicated and the wicked will be judged. This first-century BC text identifies those being judged as wicked Jerusalemites (especially the high priest) who do not follow the strictures and viewpoints of the community that received the pesher. The Qumran community's Teacher of Righteousness will be vindicated in the day of judgment, but Jerusalem's high priest and his compatriots will be judged. In this way, the pesher links the day of the Lord with a final judgment that happens at the end.[11]

Other Jews living in the third through first century BC received the day of the Lord tradition(s) to emphasize the universal, final judgment, which finds resonance with Joel 4 [3]. Several factors help us understand the emphasis, not least being the social and historical circumstances of being governed and oppressed by and large by foreign rulers: Persian (539–331 BC), Greek (331–146 BC), and then Roman (146 BC–AD 395). Those under constant threat from occupiers longed for a word of comfort that would remind them of God's ultimate sovereignty over *all* nations, that Israel's God would provide the ultimate vindication and judgment, installing his reign with his

---

[10]N. T. Wright, *Paul and the Faithfulness of God*, Christian Origins and the Question of God 4 (Minneapolis: Fortress, 2013), 1047-61.

[11]For a critical edition of the pesher, see William H. Brownlee, *The Midrash Pesher of Habakkuk*, Society of Biblical Literature Monograph Series 24 (Missoula, MT: Scholars Press, 1979).

king forever. Second Temple literature, especially apocalypses, provided these Jews this hope. The final judgment on display, then, is similar to the final judgment on display in Joel.

Although Second Temple Jewish apocalypses use the day-of-the-Lord concept, it is too much to say that apocalyptic literary tradition derives genetically from the day-of-the-Lord concept. Jewish apocalyptic texts (such as 1 Enoch 1–36 [The Book of Watchers], 2 Jubilees, 2 Baruch, or the Testaments of Levi and Judah) do not simply expand the day-of-the-Lord teaching to create a new genre that scholars identify as "apocalypses." Rather, Jewish apocalypses go their own way; they tend to be revelatory in the sense that secrets of this world are revealed by God, filled with dreams and visions, replete with heavenly messengers, and often contain various kinds of polarities between the heavenly and earthly realms. Jewish apocalypses in the Second Temple period remain complex literary works. They integrate the day-of-the-Lord concept into their larger arguments in various ways.

THE DAY OF THE LORD IN THE NEW TESTAMENT

The New Testament takes up the concept of the day of the Lord variously but most often associates the day of the Lord with the coming and revelation of Jesus. The day of the Lord in the New Testament coincides with the pouring out of the Spirit, the coming of Christ (parousia), divine judgment, and the reign of God. The New Testament as a whole presents the day of the Lord as "the day when God will visit the world to bring this age to an end and to inaugurate the Age to Come. This term is not to be thought of as a single calendar day but as the entire period that will witness the final redemptive visitation of God in Christ."[12] Some themes emerge in New Testament usage of the day of the Lord:

The parousia. The first point that emerges is that the day of the Lord has to do with the coming of God into the world, often called the parousia in New Testament studies. All in all, the parousia depicts the coming of God into the world, and this usually means the coming of Christ into the world *after* his ascension (1 Thess 5:2; 2 Pet 3:10; Rev 3:3, 16:15).[13] So the day of the Lord is transformed into the Christian "day of Jesus Christ," or elsewhere "day of Christ" (Phil 1:10; 2:16) or "day of our Lord Jesus Christ" (1 Cor 1:8). The

---

[12] G. E. Ladd, *A Theology of the New Testament*, rev. ed. (Grand Rapids, MI: Eerdmans, 1993), 600.
[13] See Adela Yarbro Collins, *Cosmology and Eschatology in Jewish and Christian Apocalypticism*, JSJSup 50 (Leiden: Brill, 1996), 186.

thought of New Testament writers is that, when Jesus comes again, he will perform two functions. First, Jesus will pronounce judgment on human beings (Acts 17:31; 2 Tim 4:1; 2 Clement 1.1). Second, as Savior, Jesus will transform our bodies and bring freedom from death (Phil 3:20-21). On this second point, Jesus is the vindicator of the righteous who comes at the "end" (1 Thess 1:10).

Divine final judgment. God's judgment accompanies the parousia. We see this in Matthew's presentation of Jesus. Jesus affirms that there will be days of tribulation, and then there will be cosmic signs that mark the coming day of judgment (Mt 24:29-31). The wicked will be judged, but the righteous will be gathered to God. Something similar appears in Luke's presentation of Jesus' teaching about the day of the Son of Man. Here, the day-of-the-Lord imagery from the prophets blends with the image of "one like a Son of Man" in Daniel 7. The blend is unique but powerful. Daniel presents the Messiah as one who comes with the clouds of glory and receives dominion and power from the Ancient of Days. The Son of Man then defeats the enemies of God and ushers in an eternal kingdom. Jesus in Luke presents the coming of the Son of Man with cosmic upheaval in his day of judgment (Lk 17:22-26; see Mt 24:29-31). In Luke 17, then, the coming day of the Lord is transformed into the coming day of the Son of Man. Judgment comes at the hand of Jesus in the final day of the Lord.

What is the nature of God's judgment in Christ? Is Jesus' judgment a divine *no* to God's creation? Not at all. The New Testament depicts God as *affirming* his creation even as he comes in judgment. This becomes evident in, for instance, the teaching of 2 Peter 3, where the day of the Lord is one of judgment, to be sure, but not a denial of creation. Rather, 2 Peter 3 affirms that God's judgment on his day brings an end to the wicked age, but in that same day God purifies the created order with fire. What remains after judgment will be a renewed created order.

The pouring out of the Spirit. Connected to the day of the Lord is a time period known as the "last days" in the New Testament. For Luke, the last days have come with Jesus and the pouring out of his Spirit. Peter's sermon of Acts 2 crystallizes the relationship between the day of the Lord, Jesus, and salvation. As the Spirit of God pours out on those in Jerusalem at Pentecost, Peter identifies the activity as a fulfillment of prophecy from Joel. From Acts 2, the day of salvation depicted in Joel is met in the person and work of

Jesus, who is in fact the Lord. Salvation comes through him just as judgment comes for those who reject him.

How do the last days relate to the day of the Lord? For Acts, the last days have broken into the present in the work of Jesus. His life, death, burial, resurrection, and ascension mark the last days, in which the day of the Lord is present. Pentecost, then, marks the salvation on the day of the Lord that anticipates another coming of Jesus, namely, the parousia mentioned above. The last days are here, Peter argues, because the day of the Lord Jesus has come. But Jesus is coming again. G. E. Ladd reckons this strange intermixing of ideas to be the result of a particular way of thinking about the coming of the kingdom of God. The day of the Lord, like the kingdom of God, is present now because of Jesus' first coming, but it is not consummated yet because his second coming awaits. The church experiences the last days now because Jesus has already come and inaugurated a new age, but the final consummation of the new age will appear when Jesus comes on his last day and brings in his kingdom.[14]

Conclusion

> When we shall have come to that judgment, the date of which is called peculiarly the day of judgment, and sometimes the day of the Lord, we shall then recognize the justice of all God's judgments, not only of such as shall then be pronounced, but, of all which take effect from the beginning, or may take effect before that time. And in that day we shall also recognize with what justice so many, or almost all, the just judgments of God in the present life defy the scrutiny of human sense or insight, though in this matter it is not concealed from pious minds that what is concealed is just.[15]

Saint Augustine's blending of the universal and particular aspects of the day of the Lord is appropriate. The day of the Lord affirms the justice of God, whether in the particular days of prophets or in the universal day of judgment. God is just, and his ways are right. But Augustine's description could be taken further, connecting the day of the Lord and the kingdom of God. The two ideas go hand in hand in a fully orbed biblical theology. The

---

[14]See G. E. Ladd, *The Presence of the Future: The Eschatology of Biblical Realism* (Grand Rapids, MI: Eerdmans, 1974); Ladd, *The Gospel of the Kingdom: Scriptural Studies in the Kingdom of God* (Grand Rapids, MI: Eerdmans, 1959).

[15]Saint Augustine, *The City of God*, trans. Marcus Dods (Peabody, MA: Hendrickson, 2009), book 20, section 2, p. 643.

day of the Lord is the advent of God into the world in judgment and salvation to usher in his kingdom.

Recommended Reading

House, Paul R. "Endings as New Beginnings: Returning to the Lord, the Day of the Lord, and Renewal in the Book of the Twelve." In *Thematic Threads in the Book of the Twelve*, ed. Paul L. Redditt and Aaron Schart, 313-38. BZAW 325. Berlin: de Gruyter, 2003.*

Ladd, G. E. *The Presence of the Future: The Eschatology of Biblical Realism*. Grand Rapids, MI: Eerdmans, 1974.

Nogalski, James D. "The Day(s) of YHWH in the Book of the Twelve." In *Thematic Threads in the Book of the Twelve*, ed. Paul L. Redditt and Aaron Schart, 192-212. BZAW 325. Berlin: de Gruyter, 2003.

Rad, Gerhard von. "The Origin of the Concept of the 'Day of Yahweh.'" *JSS* 4 (1959): 97-108.

Rendtorff, Rolf. "Alas for the Day! The 'Day of the LORD' in the Book of the Twelve." In *God in the Fray: A Tribute to Walter Brueggemann*, ed. Tod Linafelt and Timothy K. Beal, 186-97. Minneapolis: Fortress, 1998.*

Weinfeld, Moshe. *Normative and Sectarian Judaism in the Second Temple Period*. LSTS 54. London: T&T Clark, 2005.

Yarbro Collins, Adela. *Cosmology and Eschatology in Jewish and Christian Apocalypticism*. JSJSup 50. Leiden: Brill, 1996.

Recommended reading marked with a "*" indicates introductory works.

7

Amos

YAHWEH, THE "MASTER OF GEOPOLITICS," AND THE AFFLICTION OF JOSEPH

Amos was the first of the so-called writing prophets in Israel, that is, prophets from whose ministries scrolls/books resulted.[1] A long history of prophecy preceded them. Moses is described as the prophet par excellence in Deuteronomy 18:15, and in the eleventh century BC, around the time of Samuel, groups of prophets appeared. Some two hundred years later, and one hundred years before Amos, the first major prophets distinct from Israel's kings and priests emerged on the scene in the northern kingdom, namely, Elijah and Elisha. There is significant continuity between their ministries and that of the writing prophets, but the written, edited residue of the latter's ministries marks a significant difference. As James Mays notes, Amos is "the point of departure for the study of the prophetic movement and its literature. His book is the testing ground for every thesis about the nature of prophecy and its developing history."[2]

The writing prophets emerged as first the northern kingdom and then the southern one headed down toward the horrific judgment of exile. The fixing of their ministries in books alerts us not only to Yahweh's repeated pleas to his rebellious people to repent but also to the role of these prophets in enabling Israel to understand his judgment and to see beyond it to a greater fulfillment of his purposes.[3] With the writing prophets, *eschatology* thus

---

[1] The literature on Amos is immense. A helpful resource is M. Daniel Carroll R., *Amos—The Prophet and His Oracles: Research on the Book of Amos* (Louisville, KY: Westminster John Knox, 2002).

[2] James L. Mays, "Words About the Words of Amos: Recent Study of the Book of Amos," *Interpretation* 13, no. 3 (1959): 259-72, here 259. See also Claus Westermann, *Elements of Old Testament Theology*, trans. Douglas W. Scott (Atlanta: John Knox, 1982), 127-29.

[3] Westermann (*Elements of Old Testament Theology*, 128) notes, "Only from Amos onward is the announcement of destruction directed to the whole people; previously this was not the case."

moves firmly into view. Amos was the first of the writing prophets and could have preceded Hosea by two decades.

Amos and His Context

Martin Buber notes, "Every prophet speaks in the actuality of a definite situation. The situation, however, serves the prophet not only as a starting point, but he throws the word of God into this actuality according to His injunctions, and only if we try ourselves to delve into this actuality, can we grasp the concrete reality of the word."[4] This is certainly true of Amos; it is only as we attend to the particular context of his ministry that we uncover the universality of his message. Amos is dynamite, and one can only imagine the power of his prophecies in their original context. Amos 1:1 tells us that Amos prophesied during the reigns of Uzziah king of Judah (790–740 BC) and Jeroboam II king of Israel (the northern kingdom; 786–746 BC).[5] Jeroboam II, "son of Jehu," was the last king in the dynasty of Jehu, established in 842.

Jeroboam II's reign was a time of peace and prosperity, but alas, also one of terrible social injustice. He succeeded in subduing the Aramaeans, Israel's dangerous proximate enemy (2 Kings 14:23-29). There was no war with Judah during his reign, and Israel reached its height of economic prosperity. Agriculture flourished, as did international trade, leading to large-scale urbanization and the creation of a wealthy upper class. As they moved to the cities, many Israelites were displaced from their land and became subject to exploitation by the upper class. Israel remained as religious as ever (Amos 4:4-5), but it was a perverse form of religion that enabled it to remain comfortable with the injustice practiced. It is even possible that oracles such as Amos 4:4-5 were preached at Bethel and/or Gilgal as the Israelites went about their religious devotions.

"Two years before the earthquake" (Amos 1:1) has evoked considerable discussion. For the recipients of the book, this was clearly a well-known historical marker; indeed, in Zechariah 14:5 it is simply "the earthquake in the days of Uzziah." Since earthquakes were not uncommon in Israel, "the earthquake" must refer to one of unparalleled severity, and this is confirmed by archaeology.[6] Some argue, on the basis of verses such as Amos 8:8 and

---

[4]Martin Buber, *The Prophetic Faith* (New York: Harper & Row, 1949), 96.
[5]Hosea is the only other prophetic book that includes the names of kings of both nations.
[6]See David N. Freedman and Andrew Welch, "Amos's Earthquake and Israelite Prophecy," in *Scripture and Other Artifacts: Essays on the Bible and Archeology in Honor of Philip J. King*, ed. Michael Coogan et al. (Louisville, KY: Westminster John Knox, 1994), 188-89.

Amos 9:1, 5, that Amos foresaw and predicted the earthquake and that its occurrence marked the termination and confirmation of his career as a prophet. It is also possible that it was at this time that Amos's oracles were gathered together by him or a follower, with the title attached or expanded after the earthquake "that was the occasion for the book's publication in substantially its present form."[7]

We cannot be sure of these details. What is clear is that "the earthquake" in the superscription has more than a literal reference; it symbolizes theophany and judgment (see Judg 5:4; 2 Sam 22:8; Ps 29; 46; 1 Kings 19:11-12) and thus the appropriate note of doom, right at the outset of Amos. Earthquake imagery is implicit in Amos 3:13-15; 4:11; 8:8 and explicit in Amos 9:1-5. Indeed, the verbal form of "earthquake" occurs in Amos 9:1. David Freedman and Andrew Welch note, "While Yahweh brings fire upon Israel and foreign nations alike, Yahweh reserves earthquake exclusively for Israel."[8] As in a dramatic film, even while the title is coming up the music alerts the viewer that conflict and trouble are brewing.

Nothing is known about Amos apart from what we find in this book. In Amos 1:1 we learn that Amos was from Tekoa, a town about six miles south of Jerusalem. Amos 1:1 describes him as a shepherd (*nqd*), a word used elsewhere in the Old Testament only to refer to the king of Moab (2 Kings 3:4).[9] In Amos 7:14, in which Amos explains his call to the priest of Bethel, Amaziah, he says that he was a shepherd (*bôqēr*) and a tender (*bōlēs*) of sycomore fig trees.[10] There has been much discussion about both words translated "shepherd," and they probably indicate that Amos was more than

---

[7]Francis I. Andersen and David N. Freedman, *Amos*, AB 24A (New York: Doubleday, 1989), 25.
[8]Freedman and Welch, "Amos's Earthquake and Israelite Prophecy," 190.
[9]Craigie, on the basis of Ugaritic evidence, notes, "Taken together, the evidence indicates that Amos was engaged extensively in agricultural business, being involved in cattle and fruit-farming, in addition to sheep. And it was from this large and responsible position that Amos was called to be a prophet, a vocation to which he responded willingly." P. C. Craigie, *Ugarit and the Old Testament* (Grand Rapids, MI: Eerdmans, 1982), 73-74. See also R. C. Steiner, *Stockmen from Tekoa, Sycomores from Sheba: A Study of Amos' Occupations*, Catholic Biblical Quarterly Monograph Series 36 (Washington, DC: Catholic Biblical Association of America Press, 2003).
[10]Concerning shepherds, Steiner (*Stockmen from Tekoa*) argues that *bôqēr* carries the same socioeconomic nuances as *nōqēd* but refers more specifically to the owner or manager of cattle. The term is used by Amos to claim financial self-sufficiency, since cattle were relatively expensive. Furthermore, concerning tenders and to ensure good fruit, the farmer had to slit the top of each tree, and the obscure Hebrew word *bōlēs* may refer to this practice. Steiner (*Stockmen from Tekoa*) argues that Hebrew *bls* came to refer to the unique process of harvesting sycomores. Also, Steiner adopts the spelling "sycomores" to distinguish the *sycomores* from unrelated *sycamores* of the US and Europe. Finally, Steiner's work is a thorough study of the words in Amos 1:1 and Amos 7:14-15 that describe Amos's occupation. Steiner argues that Amos worked with both livestock and

just a shepherd but rather a farmer of some wealth. M. Daniel Carroll R. concludes, "In sum, the evidence suggests that Amos was possibly an owner and manager of flocks and herds. He would have been a man of responsibility and influence, with the means to travel to Israel and market his stock in the North."[11] Prophets come in all shapes and sizes, and whereas it would have been hard to see Hosea without reflecting on his wayward wife and children with such strange names, as a distinguished, wealthy farmer and businessman used to trade and negotiations, Amos would have cut an altogether different figure.

In Amos 7:15 Amos tells how he was called by Yahweh to "Go, prophesy to my people Israel" (NIV). The close relationship between Yahweh and his prophets is evoked in Amos 3:7-8. The prophet has unique access to what God is up to, but he remains God's *servant* (Amos 3:7). In Amos 7:14 Amos denies being a prophet (*nābî*ʾ) or son of a prophet.[12] The passion driving his ministry is that *the sovereign Yahweh has spoken,* so "who can but prophesy?" (Amos 3:8).

The description of the book of Amos in Amos 1:1 as "The words of Amos" is unusual among the titles of prophetic books (see Jer 1:1). Francis Andersen and Freedman propose translating *dibrê ʿāmôs* as the story of Amos, Amos's record or Amos's report.[13] Either way, the unusual description does not detract from the authority of Amos in comparison with the sort of more common title we find in Hosea, "The word of Yahweh," as the repeated "This is what the LORD says" or its equivalents in Amos demonstrate.[14] *Dibrê* (words) refers to the totality of his ministry, as evidenced by the fact that Amos 1:1 literally reads, "The words . . . which he saw," alluding thereby to the visions in Amos 7:1–9:6 that are central to the book.

---

sycomores; he was a stockbreeder, a member of a sort of collective, and one who also harvested sycomore figs from trees that he did not own, in order both to sell and to provide fodder.

[11]M. Daniel Carroll R., *The Book of Amos*, NICOT (Grand Rapids, MI: Eerdmans, 2020), 206.

[12]In the Hebrew there is a nominal sentence construction without a verb. The tense is thus unclear, and the NIV is justified in translating "I was neither a prophet nor the son of a prophet."

[13]Andersen and Freedman, *Amos*, 185.

[14]Contra James R. Linville, who argues that "There is an implied tension between the prophet and God that will come to the surface later." Linville, *Amos and the Cosmic Imagination*, Society for Old Testament Study Monographs (Aldershot, UK: Ashgate, 2008), 6. See also Aaron Schart, "The First Section of the Book of the Twelve Prophets: Hosea-Joel-Amos," *Interpretation* 61, no. 2 (2007): 138-52, here 140. Schart similarly, but incorrectly in our view, argues, "However, it is noteworthy that only in Hos 1:1 and Joel 1:1 (not in Amos 1:1) does the phrase 'Word of YHWH' designate the *Gattung* of the corpus that follows. Although Amos' words are declared to have originated from a visionary experience, it is not stated as precisely that they are the pure word of YHWH. His writing may, therefore, have been seen as inferior in authority to those of Hosea and Joel."

In context Israel in Amos 7:14 clearly refers to the northern kingdom, and it does seem that Amos's ministry was primarily directed to the north. However, there are several references to Judah in the book, and we should not restrict his ministry in this respect. Especially as it became clear that Judah would not escape the judgment of the northern kingdom, and once Amos's book became available in writing, the relevance of Amos's message to the whole people of God would have become ever clearer.

That Uzziah is mentioned first in Amos 1:1 probably indicates that the book was edited into its final shape by a Judean. As with most Old Testament books, historical criticism has tended to identify numerous sources and layers in Amos, with a goal often being to identify original Amos material from the book.[15] Underlying such approaches is a radical reconstruction of the history of Israel and the view that Amos reached its final form over a long period of editing. A bewildering variety of conclusions has been reached, demonstrating the speculative nature of the source-, form-, and redaction-critical enterprise. Mercifully, as Andersen and Freedman note, "The enterprise seems to have exhausted itself in its conduct along the lines laid down in the nineteenth century."[16] They question the underlying presuppositions of the historical-critical approaches at four points essential to their viability: (1) the cosmic theology of the hymns in Amos is early and not late in the life of Israel, (2) the roots of eschatology are likewise ancient, (3) it is untrue that fulfilled prophecies could only have been written after the events in which we discern their fulfillment, and (4) Amos was a versatile literary craftsman quite capable of using cultic and wisdom motifs as well as prophetic oracles. Therefore, they rightly say,

> We have come to the conclusion, after working through the whole business many times and weighing all arguments, that there are no compelling reasons against accepting most if not all of the book as possibly, indeed

---

[15]See Gerhard F. Hasel, *Understanding the Book of Amos: Basic Issues in Current Interpretations* (Grand Rapids, MI: Baker, 1993) 17-27, 91-99, for a useful overview. More recently see Carroll R., *Book of Amos*, introduction. For a recent analysis of redactional layers see Tchavdar S. Hadjiev, *The Composition and Redaction of the Book of Amos*, BZAW 393 (Berlin: de Gruyter, 2009). On the modern history of interpretation of Amos see Carroll R., *Amos—The Prophet*, 3-72.

[16]Andersen and Freedman, *Amos*, 143. This has not stopped many scholars from continuing to work in terms of layers and multiple sources. Graham R. Hamborg, for example, discerns four redaction layers in Amos 2:6-16. Hamborg, *Still Selling the Righteous: A Redaction-Critical Investigation of Reasons for Judgment in Amos 2.6-16*, LHBOTS 555 (London: Continuum, 2012). Amid the pluralism of postmodernism, a variety of ideological readings have flourished. See, e.g., Linville, *Amos and the Cosmic Imagination*.

probably (we can never say "certainly") Amos. We have two main reasons for deviating from traditional criticism. . . . First is the cumulative demonstration of the *literary coherence* of all of the diverse ingredients in the whole assemblage. . . . It is a highly structured unity. Second is the diverse and divergent . . . points of view we account for as reflecting successive phases in the prophet's career.[17]

We follow Andersen and Freedman in reading Amos as a literary whole and as rooted in the historical ministry of Amos. However, Amos 1:1 and Amos 7:10-17 are written in the third person, indicating at least another hand in the composition of the book. It is also possible that the book was updated for Judah in its publication. As with all such prophetic books, we need to remember that the books were edited into shape because of the ongoing relevance of the prophet's ministry for later generations so that a book like Amos has more than one rhetorical trajectory.[18]

Outline

Amos contains a variety of types of literature and content: judgment oracles, exhortations, hymns, woes, oaths, visions, plagues, and eschatology. We follow Andersen and Freedman in dividing the book into four major sections plus the title in Amos 1:1 and the theme in Amos 1:2. Amos 1:3-16 is made up of oracles against nations unified by a repeated formula.[19] However, it is hard to know where the oracle against Israel starting in Amos 2:6 ends. It could go right through to Amos 4:12, with "Israel" in Amos 4:12 indicating an *inclusio* with Amos 2:6.[20] Woes dominate Amos 5–6, and Amos 7:1–9:6

---

[17]Andersen and Freedman, *Amos*, 143-44. See also S. Paul, *Amos: A Commentary*, Hermeneia (Minneapolis: Fortress, 1991).

[18]See, e.g., Jason Radine, *The Book of Amos in Emergent Judah*, FAT 2/45 (Tübingen: Mohr Siebeck, 2010).

[19]Kurt Koch's analysis of the structure of Amos has been very influential. See Kurt Koch und Mitarbeiter, *Amos. Untersucht mit den Methoden einer strukturalen Formgeschichte*, 3 vols. (Neukirchen-Vluyn: Kevelaer, 1976). For Koch the principal markers of division are the extensive $\check{s}m^{\,\prime}$ formulae and the long doxologies. The structure of the book is, in his view: Amos 1–2: speech to the nations; Amos 3–4: doom against his own people as (divine) admonition; Amos 5:1–9:6: doom against his own people as a prophetic funeral lament. Amos 9:7-15 is left over as a kind of appendix. More recently see Adri van der Wal, "The Structure of Amos," *JSOT* 26 (1983): 107-13, who seeks to resurrect the older view of the major break in Amos occurring between Amos 1–6 and Amos 7–9. Paul Noble discerns the following structure in Amos: superscription (Amos 1:1); part I: Yahweh's word to the nations (Amos 1:2–3:8); part II: a palistrophic judgment oracle (Amos 3:9–6:14); part III: the destruction and reconstitution of Israel (Amos 7:1–9:15). Noble, "The Literary Structure of Amos: A Thematic Analysis," *JBL* 114, no. 2 (1995): 209-26.

[20]Van der Wal ("Structure of Amos," 109) discerns an *inclusio* in Amos 1:2 and Amos 3:8.

is the most obviously unified section. Amos 9:7-15 is the eschatological conclusion. As with so many Old Testament books, Amos has more of an *organic* than a clear logical unity, and there are multiple interconnections in the book, such as echoes, inclusions, announcement of a theme that is only later developed, the placing of three hymn fragments (Amos 4:13; 5:8; 9:5-6) at strategic points, and so on. We divide up the book as follows:

Amos 1:1	Title and earthquake
Amos 1:2	Theme: The lion will roar
Amos 1:3-4:13	Doom!
Amos 5:1-6:14	Woes
Amos 7:1-9:6	Visions
Amos 9:7-15	The end and the beginning

INTERPRETATION

Amos 1:2-4:13. Amos's vocation was primarily to the north as a prophet of judgment, but he is clear that judgment comes from the temple, namely, Zion/Jerusalem (Amos 1:2), where Yahweh dwells among his people, a central theme in the Book of the Twelve. The northern kingdom had set up alternative centers of worship at Bethel and Gilgal, centers that will call down Amos's wrath (see Amos 4:4-5), but already this locating of Yahweh in Jerusalem would have alerted northerners to potential trouble. In the Hebrew word order the gathering momentum in Amos's opening salvo is clear: "Yahweh—*from Zion*—he roars." The typical Hebrew word order of verb, subject, object is subverted, with the verb coming last in the sequence. This delay creates tension—what will Yahweh do from Zion? The answer is unequivocal. Amos's imagery is evocative: Yahweh roars like a lion.[21] Lions stalking prey only roar, however, as they attack (see Amos 3:4), with the roar designed to paralyze the prey. The roar indicates that the lion is now leaping toward it prey, and in this way the imagery captures the utter *imminence* of judgment for the north.

This evocative imagery inclines us to translate the verbs in Amos 1:2 with their normal future tense: "The LORD will roar . . . the pastures will dry up."[22]

---

[21] See Karl Möller, *A Prophet in Debate: The Rhetoric of Persuasion in the Book of Amos*, JSOTSup 372 (Sheffield: Sheffield Academic Press, 2003), 160-64. The terrifying image of Yahweh as a lion is common in the Minor Prophets; see Hos 5:14; 11:10; 13:7; Joel 3:16.

[22] The tense of these verbs is debated. See Andersen and Freedman, *Amos*, 219-22, who argue for a perfect-tense translation. In our view there is thus a movement from Amos 1:2 (future) to Amos 3:8 (perfect = has roared). In this way the imminence of judgment is intensified.

Amid the affluence of the north, it must have seemed that all was well, but already Yahweh, the lion, was quietly and invisibly stalking his prey. When the roar comes, it will be too late. The effect will be devastating on the entire land; the pastures of the shepherds, the lowlands, will mourn, and the top of Mount Carmel, a lush mountainous area in the north, will dry up.[23] As with the earthquake, there is a literal and symbolic reference to these judgments. In Amos 9:3 the top of Carmel is contrasted with the bottom of the sea as places where the Israelites might try to hide from Yahweh's judgment. "Hence what is described in our verse [Amos 1:2] is a merism, meaning that every person and place is affected."[24]

Amos 1:3–2:16. Amos's rhetorical strategy in this masterly sermon is devastating; he declares Yahweh's judgment on the surrounding nations, then Judah, and then . . . the northern kingdom. The oracles proceed from foreign nations to blood relations and are also arranged geographically so that they slowly but steadily close in on the northern kingdom. "The geographical orientation thus moves from the northeast (Aram) to the southwest (Philistia), the northwest (Phoenicia), the southeast (Edom, Ammon, Moab) and finally to Judah and Israel."[25] As Christopher Wright notes, the effect is "to throw a kind of geographical noose around Israel and thus to make the climactic accusation against her even more devastatingly powerful."[26] With his numerical trope of escalating disobedience—"For three sins . . . even for four"—implying multiplicity and growing intensity, the word Amos uses for the repulsive sins of the nations is *peša'*, meaning "to rebel, to fall away."

1. Amos 1:3-5: Damascus (Amos 1:3) was the capital of Aram/Syria. The capital city stands for the nation—see "The people of Aram" in Amos 1:5—and is condemned because "she threshed Gilead, her southern neighbor, with sledges having iron teeth."[27] The sledge, or more precisely the threshing board (*ḥārûṣ*), was either a sledge dragged across grain or a wagon with the underbelly mounted with flint or iron teeth. This image could literally refer to a terrible form of torture in

---

[23]See Andersen and Freedman, *Amos*, 163-64.
[24]James C. Okoye, *Israel and the Nations: A Mission Theology of the Old Testament* (Maryknoll, NY: Orbis, 2006), 70.
[25]Okoye, *Israel and the Nations*, 195.
[26]Christopher J. H. Wright, *Living as the People of God: The Relevance of Old Testament Ethics* (Leicester, UK: Inter-Varsity Press, 1984), 123.
[27]With G, L, and 5QAm, Stuart translates, "Because they threshed the pregnant women of Gilead," which he reads as a metaphor for the gruesome treatment of the Gileadites by invading Aramaean soldiers. Douglas Stuart, *Hosea–Jonah*, WBC 31 (Nashville: Nelson, 1987), 304.

which a threshing sledge was dragged across people tied to the ground, but it may alternatively be an agricultural metaphor for savage and inhuman conquest of Gilead, what we would call war crimes.[28]

2. Amos 1:6-8: This second oracle deals with Philistia in the southwest; the major cities mentioned are Gaza, Ashdod, Ashkelon, and Ekron. She is condemned because she took captive whole communities—men, women, and children—and sold them to Edom, thus treating human beings as a mere consumer product with no concern for their welfare. Exodus 21:16 condemns this kind of kidnapping and assigns the death penalty to it.

3. Amos 1:9-10: Phoenicia is likewise condemned for selling whole communities of captives to Edom and disregarding a treaty (covenant) of brotherhood. Tyre was a slave-trading city, and this kind of sale of communities, again to Edom, is condemned. It is unclear who the treaty was with, but most probably Israel, which had a long relationship of cooperation with the Phoenicians.

4. Amos 1:11-12: Edom was a brother to Israel, according to the Pentateuch (Gen 25:24-26; Deut 2:4; 23:7). She opposed Israel en route to the land "with the sword" (Num 20:14-21), and there was a long history of enmity between her and Israel. She is condemned for this ongoing volatile enmity and indiscriminate slaughter of Israelite women.

5. Amos 1:13-15: The Ammonites are condemned for brutal warfare aimed at extending their borders. The description here of torture may well be literal.

6. Amos 2:1-3: Moab is condemned for burning to ashes the bones of the king of Edom, reminding us that not all the sins condemned were against Israel. It is unclear exactly what transgression is in view here; it could have been a violating of the sanctity of the tomb from which the body was taken and the bones burned, or it could be an attempt to ensure eternal death and prevent any possibility of resurrection.[29]

Carly Crouch asserts, "The most concentrated single source of information on ethics in the biblical prophetic literature, if not the entire Hebrew Bible,

---

[28]There is Assyrian evidence for the practice of torture in which a threshing sledge was dragged across people tied to the ground.

[29]Andersen and Freedman, *Amos*, 288; Stuart, *Hosea–Jonah*, 314-15.

is the first chapter of the book of *Amos*."[30] Amos 1:3–2:3 is indeed a rich and extraordinary passage in which the nations surrounding Israel are held to account for their treatment of other human beings. This is political theology, and this section embodies an ethic of international relations. Political leadership—see "the king" in Amos 1:5, 8, 15, and "her ruler" in Amos 2:3, as well as the parallel reference to "the one who holds the scepter" in Amos 1:5, 8 and "officials" in Amos 1:15; 2:3—is held accountable for human rights atrocities. It is no wonder that scholars debate from where Amos got this ethic, a topic we will return to under the theology of Amos below.

7. Amos 2:4-5: Judah. The noose tightens as the southern kingdom is now indicted. Judah is part of God's covenant people, and the terms of indictment thus differ: she has rejected the law (*tôrâ*) of Yahweh, as manifested in her violation of the first commandment.

8. Amos 2:6-16: Finally, Israel. She is condemned for multiple offenses: selling the innocent and needy into slavery for gain, however minimal; denying justice to the poor and the oppressed; sexual immorality; and perverse religious practices using the fruits of their injustice.

Amos is the great prophet of divine judgment, and in the oracles fire and destruction are the repeated elements that evoke the coming judgment of God (note how fire recurs in Amos 1:4, 7, 10, 12, 14; 2:2, 5). The imagery here is probably that of war resulting in cities being burned to the ground.

The oracle against Israel is much expanded, and it is hard to know where it ends; Amos has much to say to the northern kingdom. Amos 2:9-12 reminds the Israelites of all that God has done for them in the exodus from Egypt (Amos 2:10), the granting of the land (Amos 2:10), and the raising up of religious leaders such as Nazirites and prophets. Amos 2:11-12 provides a literal example of the attempt to prevent the prophets from prophesying (Amos 2:12). Despite God's grace, the Israelites continue to rebel, and thus in Amos 2:13-16 Amos pronounces God's coming judgment. He will crush Israel into the ground, and no form of human strength—neither the swift, nor the strong, nor the warrior, nor the archer, nor the soldier, nor the horseman—will avail against his judgment.

Amos 3:1–4:13. These two chapters continue Amos's pronouncement of guilt and judgment against Israel. There are three major sections, each

---

[30]Carly L. Crouch, *War and Ethics in the Ancient Near East: Military Violence in Light of Cosmology and History*, BZAW 407 (Berlin: de Gruyter, 2009), 97.

introduced by "Hear this word" (Amos 3:1, 13; 4:1). In Amos 3:13 this phrase is followed by "and *testify against* the descendants of Jacob," indicating that the imagery in Amos 3–4 is that of God's lawsuit (*rîb*) against Israel, a common motif in prophetic literature. The covenant, like marriage (see Hosea), is a *legally* binding relationship, and Israel is here, as it were, called to court to account for her behavior.

In Amos 3:1-2, God's election of his people and the exodus are the basis for the coming judgment. Amos 3:3 serves as a reminder that Israel had agreed to be God's covenant people (see Ex 19–24). Amos 3:4-6 contain six rhetorical questions, all relating to the connection between a scary noise or action and its associated disaster. The first question, for example, about whether a lion roars if it has no prey, harks back to Amos 1:2. Indeed, Amos 3:4 and Amos 3:8 function as an *inclusio*, with the repeated imagery of the lion roaring, and in the process echo Amos 1:2. Just as the roar of the lion signifies that it has prey, so Yahweh's roar means that judgment is inevitable.

In highly evocative legal imagery, the Philistines and the Egyptians, Israel's great enemies, are called to bear witness to the unrest and oppression in Israel (Amos 3:9). *Fortresses* occurs three times in Amos 3:9-10, and they are personified so that the foreign fortresses are called to bear witness to the unjust means by which Israel has filled her fortresses. Fortresses (*'armnôt*) were royal, multilevel buildings in which the upper class lived and worked. Even foreigners would have been shocked by the terror and oppression used to maintain this lifestyle in Israel. The Israelites no longer know how to do "right" (Amos 3:10; *nəkōḥâ*); the word means "what is decent, honest, and just." Thus judgment will come; an enemy will overrun Israel and in the process destroy the great symbols of injustice (Amos 3:11-14).

Amos 4:1-12 informs Israel that the crushing of Amos 2:13 will involve going into exile (Amos 4:2-3), which happened in 722 BC when the Assyrians conquered the northern kingdom. The inevitability of this is established by Yahweh swearing an oath (Amos 4:2). The precise imagery at work in Amos 4:2 is unclear. The Israelites could be compared to fish caught by hooks and carried away. Alternatively, *ṣinôt* (hooks) could mean "ropes," and we know from Assyrian images engraved on stone that prisoners were lead away by a rope fastened to a hook that pierced the nose or lower lip.

The perverse religiosity of the Israelites is depicted in Amos's ironic exhortations in Amos 4:4-5. Jeroboam I made Bethel a rival shrine to Jerusalem (1 Kings 12), and it appears that Gilgal had also become an alternative center for northern worship. As noted, the Israelites were deeply religious, but it was an empty form devoid of holiness.

Amos 4:6-11 reminds the Israelites of God's patient discipline in a variety of forms but is punctuated throughout with the phrase "yet you have not returned to me" (Amos 4:6, 8, 9, 10, 11). The climax is reached in the chilling exhortation of Amos 4:12, "Prepare to meet your God" (NIV). Doubtless the Israelites thought they encountered Yahweh regularly in their worship, but now they must prepare for a real encounter with Yahweh the judge.

Amos 4:13 contains the first of the three creation hymns in Amos. We will examine these in detail in the next chapter. Suffice it here to note that they could be excerpts from hymns used in the liturgy and thus serve as poignant reminders of who the God is whom they must prepare to meet. He is the majestic, transcendent Creator but also the immanent God who is closely involved in the creation. He exercises his lordship over the creation actively—he "treads on the heights of the earth"—and reveals his thoughts to humankind.[31] This God is well able and justified in exercising judgment.

Amos 5:1–6:14: Woes. The rhetoric of Amos is profoundly creative. In Amos 5:2 Amos pronounces or sings a lament over Israel as though she were already dead. However, as Amos 5:3-17 makes clear, the intention even at this late stage is to call forth repentance in Israel, as the urgent imperatives in Amos 5:4, 6, 14, 15 indicate. The first two of these imperatives relate to Israel's relationship to Yahweh: seek Yahweh and live! The second two imperatives, as does most of this section, relate to good and evil, to injustice and justice. As a manifestation of her false worship (Amos 5:5; see Amos 5:22-23, 25-26) Israel is condemned for hating legal justice and true testimony (Amos 5:10); preventing the poor from building homes—straw was an essential component in bricks—and using the money gained unjustly to build massive homes for themselves (Amos 5:11); and depriving the poor of justice in the courts (Amos 5:12).[32] As Amos 5:7 notes, "There are those who turn justice into bitterness and cast righteousness to the ground" (NIV). True religion, by comparison, involves maintaining justice in the courts (Amos 5:15; see also Amos 5:24; 6:12).

---

[31]That is, God's thoughts, not humankind's thoughts, as E. Hammershaimb argues in *The Book of Amos: A Commentary* (Oxford: Basil Blackwell, 1970), 75. See Amos 3:7.

[32]See the fascinating chapter by Edward F. Campbell, "Archaeological Reflections on Amos's Targets," in Coogan et al., *Scripture and Other Artifacts*, 32-52. See p. 48 for a line drawing of House 1727 in Shechem at this time. The drawing evokes the opulence and wealth Amos condemned.

Amos 5:18 and Amos 6:1 introduce two woe sections. The theme of Amos 5:18-27 is the day of the Lord. Amos 5:18 is one of the earliest—if not the first—occurrences of "the day of Yahweh," which "becomes a *Leitmotif* in prophetic discourse and is central to a theology of the Bible."[33] Presumably, it meant something important to Amos's audience, but exactly what we cannot be sure. It would appear that they looked to the day of Yahweh as a time when Yahweh would act to thwart all their enemies and establish them unequivocally as his people. Amos tells them this day is indeed coming, but for them it will be pitch darkness and not light (Amos 5:18, 20). Yahweh will send them into exile beyond Damascus (Amos 5:27).

The inclusion of Zion (Jerusalem) in Amos 6:1 reminds us that Amos's ministry is also directed at his own people in the south. Amos's central target is Samaria (the north), but Judah is not excluded. Andersen and Freedman discern a sevenfold woe in Amos 6:1-7. Amos 6:2 expands on the woe of Amos 6:1, and woe is implied in Amos 6:3, 4, 5, 6. Amos 6:7 concludes this symbolic totality of woe with another announcement of exile, with the wealthy and indulgent leading the way.

Part of our title for this chapter comes from Amos 6:6, "you do not grieve over the ruin/affliction of Joseph." In Amos, the house of Joseph is the northern kingdom, of which the Joseph tribes were the most important. "Master of geopolitics" is universal, whereas "ruin of Joseph" is particular and specific, as injustice always is.[34] The Israelites were immersed in injustice and false religion so that despite Israel's apparent prosperity, from God's point of view it was in ruins.

In Amos 6:8 we find the second of the three times that "Yahweh has sworn" occurs in Amos (see Amos 4:2; 8:7), a declaration of coming judgment involving total defeat (Amos 6:14). Lebo-Hamath was Israel's northernmost border and the Valley of the Arabah its southernmost. In the depiction of the siege of Israel in Amos 6:8-11, "city" in Amos 6:8 and "the great house" in Amos 6:11 are probably collectives referring to the totality of Israel. The terrible call for silence because "We must not mention the name of the LORD" in Amos 6:10 implies that "Yahweh will have become foe, not friend."[35]

---

[33] Andersen and Freedman, *Amos*, 521. See also chap. 6.
[34] "Master of geopolitics" in this chapter's subtitle is taken from Andersen and Freedman, *Amos*, 191.
[35] Stuart, *Hosea-Jonah*, 364. Silence is another motif found in the Book of the Twelve. See Hab 2:20.

Amos 7:1-9:6: Visions. This section contains a series of five visions, with two pairs of visions and one separate one:

Amos 7:1-3	Locusts
First Pair	
Amos 7:4-6	Fire
Amos 7:7-8	Plumb line
Second Pair	
Amos 8:1-2	Ripe fruit
Amos 8:3-14	*That* day
Amos 9:1-4	Destruction of altar and temple

The first two visions show God preparing types of judgment—a locust plague (see Joel 1:2-5) and divine fire—of which he relents on Amos's intercession. There is also dialogue in the second pair of visions, but now it is initiated by Yahweh, who asks Amos about familiar objects—a plumb line and a basket of ripe fruit—and thereby draws him into the coming judgment, with intercession no longer being possible. The meaning of *'ănāk* ("plumb line" in NIV), which occurs twice in Amos 7:7 and twice in Amos 7:8, is uncertain. In antiquity *'ănāk* was understood to refer to a metal. That Yahweh is about to put it "among [*bəqereb*] my people Israel" and not against (*'al*) them, as one would expect with a plumb line, suggests that it is some kind of metal object, perhaps a crowbar, a chisel, or even a battering ram.[36]

Between the third and fourth vision, we have a third-person narrative description of Amos's encounter with Amaziah the priest of Bethel, to which we referred above. In context it makes crystal clear that the coming judgment will be one of *exile*, a message clearly grasped by Amaziah (Amos 7:11) *and* articulated by Amos (Amos 7:17). Amos's denial of being a prophet or son of a prophet is a nominal sentence construction, and so the verb has to be supplied, and he could thus be saying "I was . . ." or "I am . . . ." The former is easily understood because his call to prophesy would have changed his status, whereas the latter would imply a radical alignment with the people and especially the poor by eschewing all hierarchy or office. Karl Barth reads the phrase in the latter way and notes that Amos "proclaims Yahweh as the God of the fellow-man who has been wronged and humiliated and

---

[36]See Andersen and Freedman, *Amos*, 758.

oppressed by man, and as the Avenger who has been challenged to direct and implacable action by what has been done to him."[37] Not surprisingly, there is good ancient Near Eastern evidence that kings took a close interest in what "their" prophets were prophesying.[38]

In the fourth vision (Amos 8:1-2), Yahweh shows Amos a basket of summer fruit; *qāyiṣ* means "summer fruit" and not necessarily "ripe fruit," as the NIV translates it. There is a play on *qāyiṣ* in Amos 8:2, which literally reads "The end [*haqqēṣ*] is coming for my people Israel." The vision is followed by a "that day" section in which the horror of the judgment and its causes are evoked. Social injustice is focused on as the major trigger of that day of judgment. This injustice is bound up with a distorted religiosity (Amos 8:5), and part of the judgment will be a famine of hearing the words of Yahweh (Amos 8:11-12). The heavens will be silent when Israel most needs to hear God's word.

Amos 9:1-4 is the final vision. "The altar" indicates that this is a sanctuary, possibly that at Bethel. In the Hebrew God is seen standing "on" (*ʿal*) the altar, a more evocative image than "by." Standing on the altar God (*ʾădōnay*) immediately pronounces judgment on the sanctuary and the people. "Pillars . . . thresholds" mark the extremities of the sanctuary, symbolizing its total destruction. Whereas in the Psalter God's all-seeing eye is a comfort, here his inescapability is a cause for terror (Amos 9:1-4). Amos 9:5-6 is the third and final hymn fragment in Amos, evoking God as Creator, who is immanently involved in his creation. Yahweh is the Creator, and the Creator is Yahweh: "Yahweh is his name" (Amos 9:6).

9:7-15: The end and the beginning. The material before and after the hymn fragment (Amos 9:5-6) pivots around it. God's judgment of Israel is the judgment not of the local or national deity but of the Creator, and creation also provides the basis for the further declaration of judgment in Amos 9:7-10. As the Creator, God is also the God of the Philistines and the Aramaeans, Israel's sworn enemies, and they too had their own exodus (Amos 9:7). Amos 9:8 pronounces the end of the northern kingdom, and yet even in Amos 9:8-10 there is some hope of a remnant, with "the sinners among my people" (Amos 9:10) being singled out for mention amid *my people*. Extraordinarily at this point of virtual extinction, Yahweh does not declare *lō-ʿammî*, as does Hosea, but "my people" (*ʿammî*). This hints at a future beyond exile and leads us to the

---

[37] *CD* IV/2:447.
[38] See J. Blake Couey, "Amos vii 10-17 and Royal Attitudes Toward Prophecy in the Ancient Near East," *VT* 58, no. 3 (2008): 300-314.

remarkable final section of Amos. Whereas "that day" has rung with overtones of judgment, here in Amos 9:11-15 it sounds forth restoration and renewal.

Amos 9:11 is framed by two temporal references: "In that day . . . as it used to be." The reference to David's booth or shelter (*sukkat*) has led many to argue that this is a much later addition, written after the exile of Judah in 587/6 BC. This is possible but not necessary. The destruction of the northern kingdom would be a major shattering of David's extensive kingdom, and the double reference to Israel in Amos 9:14-15—if taken as is mostly the case in Amos—to refer to the northern kingdom would confirm that this is authentic Amos material. The prophecy clearly refers to a restoration of Israel from exile, but the language used is highly metaphorical and evokes a far greater vision than restoration to the land.

Amos 9:12 moves quickly and in parallel from "the remnant of Edom"—those who survive God's judgment (see Amos 1:11-12)—to "all the nations that bear my name" (NIV).[39] In the Hebrew Amos 9:12 has its complexities, and it is probably best to understand the *wə* at the start of Amos 9:12b as epexegetic or emphatic, with "all the nations" being the subject of the verb *yîrəšû* ("they will possess") in Amos 9:12a.[40] This expression, "all the nations that bear my name," harks back to "all the nations" in Amos 9:9 and certainly includes Egypt, Philistia, and Aram (Amos 9:7). Indeed, universal redemption in the Abrahamic sense of "all nations will be blessed" (see Gen 12:1-3) is in view here. Wonderful agricultural imagery is used to evoke the shalom that will result (Amos 9:13-14). Exodus 15:17 speaks of Yahweh planting the Israelites on the mountain of "your inheritance"; in Amos 9:15 we have an intertextual allusion to this part of the Song of Moses so that Israel will once *again* be planted in the land, but now never again to be uprooted.

The Theology of Amos

The Lion. If Hosea portrays Yahweh as Lover and Lion, it is Yahweh *as Lion* that dominates in Amos. Especially in the hymn fragments, Yahweh is portrayed

---

[39]Amos 9:11-12 is quoted in Acts 15:16-18, but the quote largely follows the Old Greek text. The main and key difference is in Amos 9:12. The MT reads, "so that they may possess the remnant of Edom," whereas the Old Greek and Acts read, "that the rest of mankind may seek the Lord [NT] / me [Old Greek]." See R. Timothy McLay, *The Use of the Septuagint in New Testament Research* (Grand Rapids, MI: Eerdmans, 2003), chap. 1, for a detailed discussion; see also Craig G. Bartholomew, *Introducing Biblical Hermeneutics: A Comprehensive Framework for Hearing God in Scripture* (Grand Rapids, MI: Baker Academic, 2015), chap. 6.

[40]Andresen and Freedman, *Amos*, 918.

as the Creator, and evident throughout the book is his particular relationship with Israel as Redeemer and covenant God. In the theme of judgment, his roles as Creator and Redeemer come together. It is *from Zion* that the Lion roars. This evocative image of God speaks of imminent and real judgment for Israel as well as for the surrounding nations. Yahweh is not just the local deity but the Creator of heaven and earth and therefore rightly able to execute justice.

Theologically, Amos confronts us with the *holiness* and *wrath* of God, attributes that are neither popular nor politically correct today. Amos compels us to come to grips with the otherness of God, both ontologically—he is *God*—and morally—he is full of goodness and without sin. Amos is a theist; his God is transcendent, personal, and immanently concerned with his creation and its history. As Creator he is omnipotent, and though patient, he is not endlessly so. Amos's God is particular; he is Yahweh, the God of Israel, whom he declares "my people."

God, as portrayed in Amos, is dangerous, especially for sinners, for those who insist on doing things their way and refuse to submit to his way. Some version of *sin* and *sinner* occurs throughout Amos, helping us to rehabilitate further politically incorrect vocabulary, namely, *sin* and *sinner*. Before the Holy One sin calls forth judgment, and as we will see below, this is as true of the New Testament as the Old. But what does sin look like in actual practice? To that subject we now turn.

The "master of geopolitics": Religion, social justice, and sin. There are many popular misconceptions about sin. One is that sinners are people who are not religious and do not attend church. Of course, there is some truth in this; as the psalmist notes, "The fool says in his heart, 'There is no God'" (Ps 14:1 NIV). However, what is intriguing about Amos is that the sinners who are ripe for God's judgment are *highly religious* and somewhat orthodox in their belief. Religious practice, from this perspective, is not enough, and much turns on the sort of religious practice in view. In his *People of the Lie*, psychiatrist and author Scott Peck argues that counselors ought to be able to name evil. Amos would heartily agree. In the course of his book, Peck perceptively notes that evil is particularly attracted to religion because there it can most easily masquerade as the light. It is as though evil thinks that if it can just wrap itself in a cloak of religion, no one will ever notice its real character. Barth points out that Amaziah was a representative of the church of Yahweh; he falsely regarded the union of throne, altar, and mammon as self-evident. Amos proclaims the pitiless judgment he does *because* Israel was so religious a society.

A second common misconception about sin is that it is always personal and relates chiefly to issues such as not attending church, not reading one's Bible, not praying, not evangelizing, and so on. Once again, there is truth in this; true religion is highly personal, as we see, for example, in Amos's relationship with Yahweh, but it is far more than personal. James Muilenberg asks,

> What is it, then, that Israel ought to do? The prophets would answer that she *ought* to walk the good road that leads to Sinai; she *ought* to live out of gratitude for what is vouchsafed her; she *ought* to keep covenant and to obey the injunctions of the Teaching; she *ought* to live as God wills her to live, in conformity to his righteous purpose; she *ought* to continue to give allegiance to the One to whom she has committed her life and destiny.[41]

As we have seen with Amos, this is correct. However, it is still capable of being read in terms of a personal and individualistic ethic. Muilenberg adds, "What makes the message of the prophets so compelling is not only that they speak with passion and earnestness, but also that they direct their attention *to every facet of Israel's historical life*."[42] In this respect he identifies five areas they speak to: (1) the political order, (2) the economic order,[43] (3) the land, (4) the administration of justice, and (5) the world of nations. Amos focuses particularly on items 1, 2, 4, and 5. Sin manifests itself *as social injustice*, and the remarkable feature of Amos as the first to sound this prophetic note is that his message is virtually confined to it. "That is why we cannot fail to hear him. That is why his particular contribution to the biblical message is that *the affair of God is the affair of man*; the affair of the fellow-man who is so severely championed and defended by God."[44]

Barth notes how one-sidedly specific and concrete Amos is. Only a century has passed since Elijah and Elisha, and yet there is no focus in any detail on the Baal cult:

> His accusation . . . is simply and solely the inhumanity of the social relationships obtaining in this kingdom which so seriously and radically and blatantly challenges Amos—and in the first instance Yahweh himself—that there can be proclaimed to it only His wrath. . . . His accusation . . . is focused with

---

[41]James Muilenberg, *The Way of Israel: Biblical Faith and Ethics* (New York: Harper & Row, 1961), 77.
[42]Muilenberg, *Way of Israel*, 77, emphasis added.
[43]See Robert R. Ellis, "Amos Economics," *Review and Expositor* 107, no. 4 (2010): 463-79.
[44]Muilenberg, *Way of Israel*, 448, emphasis added.

astonishing exclusiveness upon the one point that in this state one man does not live and deal with others as he ought to according to the will of Yahweh; that wrong is done on the horizontal level of human relationship and therefore on the vertical level of the relationships of the people to Yahweh Himself as the Creator and Lord of its history.[45]

The gates were the lawcourts of the day, but even there the voice of righteousness was not heard. "Thus Yahweh alone was left as the friend and Champion and Helper and just Judge of the weak and poor who had suffered through this development—no, through the inhumanity of man to man."[46]

We noted above the rich ethic in Amos 1:3–2:3. We find in this passage an ethic of international relations. The definitive work on ancient Near Eastern international relations is Amnon Altman's rigorous *Tracing the Earliest Recorded Concepts of International Law: The Ancient Near East (2500–330 BCE)*.[47] He finds evidence for an ethic of international relations among some of the nations, but also an example with Assyria of the sheer celebration of the worst forms of brutality. In Amos 1:1–2:3 it is fascinating that God holds the nations surrounding Israel to account, *not for ignoring him*—that is reserved for Israel—but for their mistreatment of others. Sometimes one wonders how much has changed since Amos's day.[48]

This is why, in the history of interpretation, Amos has either been neglected or the source of movements that reawakened the conscience of the church to issues of social justice. In Amos's context, the oppressed neighbor was nearby; nowadays the oppressed neighbor may well be nearby but is likely to be a child laborer in a foreign country or a peasant who cannot sell their crops because of "free trade." Social and economic injustice is desperately real in the world in which we live, and Amos warns us that when we reach a situation in which there is only God left to champion the poor, then judgment lies just around the corner.[49]

It is not, however, just believers who need to take this message to heart. As we have seen, Amos also condemns the surrounding nations for their

---

[45] *CD* IV/2:447.
[46] *CD* IV/2:450.
[47] Amnon Altman, *Tracing the Earliest Recorded Concepts of International Law: The Ancient Near East (2500–330 BCE)* (Leiden: Brill, 2012).
[48] See M. Daniel Carroll R., "Imagining the Unthinkable: Exposing the Idolatry of National Security in Amos," *Ex Auditu* 24 (2008): 37-54.
[49] See Craig Bartholomew and Thorsten Moritz, eds., *Christ and Consumerism: A Critical Analysis of the Spirit of the Age* (Carlisle, UK: Paternoster, 2000).

unjust practices. There is a debate about whether they are guilty on the basis of natural law or covenantal law.[50] This, however, is a false dichotomy; the law of Israel *is* that of the Creator God, so the legal *principles* of the covenant are universally valid.[51] The oracles of judgment directed at nations other than Israel are a powerful reminder to the Israelites—for whose hearing the oracles are declared—that Yahweh, who dwells in Zion, is indeed the Lord of all nations, of the whole creation.

Amos in the New Testament

Novum Testamentum Graece lists some thirty-two references to Amos in the New Testament, almost all in the Synoptic Gospels, Acts, and Revelation. In terms of the relationship of Amos to the New Testament, some are more helpful than others.

In terms of biblical eschatology, Amos's theology of the day of Yahweh and his conclusion not surprisingly form part of the data with which the New Testament interprets the Christ event, as we saw in chapter six. In many ways Amos bears close comparison with John the Baptist, with his searing pronouncements of judgment. Both mention fire as part of divine judgment (Amos 7:4; Mt 3:11).[52] As prophets, both John and Jesus were rejected by many, as was Amos (see Amos 7:10-17; Acts 16:20; Amos 7:12; Lk 13:31, etc.). Amos 8:9 is directly referenced in the events surrounding Jesus' death in Luke 23:44 // Matthew 27:45 // Mark 15:33.

In Acts 15:16-17, Amos 9:11-12 is quoted by James to justify the inclusion of the Gentiles in the early church. The New Testament tends to use the LXX when it quotes the Old Testament, and James's quote of LXX Amos 9:11-12 is much discussed as a test case of the New Testament use of the Old Testament. James does indeed appear to be using the LXX, and there are some important differences between the LXX and the MT of Amos—see Acts 15:17-18 with Amos 9:12.[53] However, as Craig has argued elsewhere,

---

[50]John Barton, *Amos's Oracles Against the Nations* (Cambridge: Cambridge University Press, 1980), argues for a natural-law perspective.

[51]Möller, *Prophet in Debate*, 185-91. Stuart perceptively notes, "The 'crimes' . . . are violations of the implicit world-wide covenant, i.e. rebelliousness against Yahweh's sovereign law" (*Hosea-Jonah*, 310). In our view, Crouch is simply wrong when she writes, "There is a lack of cosmological language in *Amos*" (*War and Ethics*, 98).

[52]Fire is a common image in Amos.

[53]See Karen H. Jobes and Moisés Silva, *Invitation to the Septuagint* (Grand Rapids, MI: Baker Academic, 2000), 194-95; for a detailed discussion, see McLay, *Use of the Septuagint*, chap. 1. See also James A. Meek's useful chapter in his *The Gentile Mission in Old Testament Citations in Acts: Text,*

James's use of LXX Amos does not contradict the meaning of MT Amos but is in line with the eschatological vision of Amos 9:11-15.[54]

These textual links are helpful in alerting us to the role of Amos in biblical eschatology. However, *a broader concept of theological intertextuality* is required to open up the wider and richer connections between Amos, Jesus, and the New Testament.[55] There is, for example, far more about judgment in the Gospels than is often recognized, so that any false dichotomy between the God of the Old Testament and of the New needs to be rejected. Jesus, as many have noted, is above all else a prophet, and judgment forms a strong part of his ministry, as it does with Amos.[56] Of course, Jesus is in a different act of the drama of Scripture from Amos and is far more than a prophet. Nevertheless, his continuity with the prophetic tradition is real.

As does Amos, so Jesus takes social justice very seriously as a mark of discipleship. There are many examples of this; suffice it to take that of the Beatitudes, the characteristics of the citizens of the kingdom. "Blessed," says Jesus, "are those who hunger and thirst for righteousness, for they will be filled" (Mt 5:6 NIV). This beatitude cannot be limited to personal righteousness or justification, as important as those are. It surely includes a hungering for justice and righteousness in all areas of life, just as in the Lord's Prayer disciples are taught to pray, "Your kingdom come . . . on earth as it is in heaven" (Mt 6:10 NIV). Such a prayer commits the one praying or the community praying to the searing spirit of Amos in the quest for justice in all areas of human life—political, economic, social, and so on.

Amos resonates with recent work on Pauline theology as a critique of empire.[57] However, intriguingly, the New Testament books perhaps most

---

Hermeneutic, and Purpose (London: T&T Clark, 2008), 56-94; Sabine Nägele, *Laubhütte Davids und Wolkensohn: Eine auslegungsgeschichtliche Studie zu Amos 9,11 in der jüdischen und christlichen Exegese*, Arbeiten zur Geschichte des antiken Judentums und des Urchristentums 24 (Leiden: Brill, 1995).

[54]See Bartholomew, *Biblical Hermeneutics*, chap. 6. John A. Dunne argues that "David's tent" in Amos 9:11 refers to the temple, so Amos 9:11-12 refers to the rebuilding of the eschatological temple in the messianic era. Dunne, "David's Tent as Temple in Amos 9:11-15: Understanding the Epilogue of Amos and Considering Implications for the Unity of the Book," *Westminster Theological Journal* 73, no. 2 (2011): 363-74.

[55]See Mark Daniel Carroll R., *Contexts for Amos: Prophetic Poetics in Latin American Perspective*, JSOTSup 132 (Sheffield: Sheffield Academic Press, 1992).

[56]On Jesus as a prophet, see N. T. Wright, *Jesus and the Victory of God*, Christian Origins and the Question of God 2 (London: SPCK, 1996). On judgment in Jesus' ministry, see John W. Wenham, *The Goodness of God* (London: Inter-Varsity Press, 1974), an excellent work on this topic.

[57]See, e.g., Richard A. Horsley, *Paul and Empire: Religion and Power in Roman Imperial Society* (Harrisville, PA: Trinity Press International, 1997).

in tune with Amos's social critique are James and Revelation. Richard Bauckham shows that the commercial excesses of the Roman Empire are mercilessly critiqued in this closing salvo of the canon. If the James of Acts 15 is the same James who is the author of James, namely, the brother of Jesus, then although James never quotes Amos, he was clearly familiar with it, as he would have been with the teaching of his brother Jesus.[58] We will have more to say about comprehensive prophetic critique in our chapter on the theology of the Book of the Twelve.

Recommended Reading

Andersen, Francis I., and David N. Freedman, *Amos*. AB 24A. New York: Doubleday, 1989.
Carroll R., M. Daniel. *The Book of Amos*. NICOT. Grand Rapids, MI: Eerdmans, 2020.
Heschel, Abraham J. *The Prophets: An Introduction*. New York: Harper & Row, 1962. Chapter 2.*
Möller, Karl. "Amos, Book Of." In *Dictionary for Theological Interpretation of the Bible*, ed. Kevin J. Vanhoozer, et al., 36-38. Grand Rapids, MI: Baker Academic, 2005.*

Recommended reading marked with a "" indicates introductory works.*

---

[58]William M. Tillman Jr., "Social Justice in the Epistle of James: A New Testament Amos?," *Review and Expositor* 108, no. 3 (2011): 417-27. Tillman rightly concludes, "In summary, James brought to his constituency all the facets of justice that Amos articulated" (423).

8

Amos and Creation

THE HYMN FRAGMENTS

*The earth and all that is in it is important only because
in its totality it belongs to the Lord who comes from Zion.*

KARL BARTH, *CHURCH DOGMATICS* 3.3.

THERE ARE THREE HYMN FRAGMENTS, hymns, or verses of hymns in Amos, namely, Amos 4:13; 5:8; 9:5-6.[1] Scholars are generally agreed that these were not written by Amos and that they probably do not come from a single hymn.[2] They have in common an emphasis on Yahweh as the Creator and contain numerous participles from a stock of vocabulary familiar from other texts that deal with creation.

Historical critics generally see these as late additions, but such a view depends on a doctrine of creation being late in Israel, a view we reject.[3] Some view of creation was universal in the ancient Near East, and it is highly unlikely that Israel lacked a view of Yahweh as Creator from very early on. Bruce Waltke and Michael O'Connor furthermore note, "The use of participial titles for God is especially important in the old poetry of the Pentateuch (e.g., Deut 32:39) and former Prophets (e.g., 1 Sam 2:6-8)."[4] Most likely, these hymns were well known in the liturgies of Israel, and Amos or the editor of the book draws on them to remind the Israelites of the nature

---

[1]Shalom M. Paul refers to them as "doxologies." Paul, *Amos: A Commentary on the Book of Amos*, ed. Frank M. Cross, Hermeneia (Minneapolis: Fortress, 1991), 152.
[2]But see James Luther Mays, *Amos*, OTL (Philadelphia: Westminster, 1969), 83.
[3]See Paul (*Amos*, 152-53) for a useful overview of critical scholarship.
[4]Bruce K. Waltke and M. O'Connor, *An Introduction to Biblical Hebrew Syntax* (Winona Lake, IN: Eisenbrauns, 1990), 618n28.

of the God who is going to judge them. One can well imagine the use of a poignant verse from a hymn in the context of prophecy.[5] Perhaps these hymns were still sung at Bethel and Gilgal, and the Israelites had become anesthetized to their powerful content. Through his use of these familiar verses, Amos seeks to rouse the Israelites from their slumber.

Amos 4:13

> He who forms the mountains,
>   who creates the wind,
>   and who reveals his thoughts to [humankind],
> who turns dawn to darkness,
>   and treads on the heights of the earth—
>   the Lord God Almighty is his name. (NIV)

In the Hebrew Amos 4:13 begins *kî hinneh*, an expression that draws attention to what follows and should be translated "Behold" or "See." This expression (*kî*) also links the hymn fragment to what precedes it, namely, "prepare to meet your God [Elohim]." A major problem with the Israelites was their view of God, and this extract from their liturgy serves to jolt them into reality as to the nature of the God they must now prepare to encounter.

Amos 4:13 contains five participles, all denoting the great acts of God:[6]

1. He forms (*yôṣēr*) the mountains (A)
2. He creates (*bōrē'*) the wind (B)
3. He reveals (*maggîd*) his thoughts to humankind (C)
4. He turns (*'ōśēh*) dawn to darkness (B')
5. He treads (*dōrēk*) on the heights of the earth (A')

As Francis Andersen and David Freedman point out, this verse is a recitation of the great deeds of Yahweh rather than a poem characterized by parallelism. However, it does appear to have a chiastic structure of ABCB'A', as

---

[5]K. Cramer argues that the hymns are genuine Amos material. Cramer, *Amos: Versuch einer theologischen Interpretation*, Beiträge zur Wissenschaft vom Alten und Neuen Testaments 51 (Stuttgart, 1951), 92. He thinks they are among the most important parts of the prophet's message and were sung by him (93).

[6]Francis I. Andersen and David N. Freedman suggest that the five participles may intentionally match the five plagues in Amos 4:6-11. Andersen and Freedman, *Amos*, AB 24A (New York: Doubleday, 1989), 455. So also M. Daniel Carroll R., *The Book of Amos*, NICOT (Grand Rapids, MI: Eerdmans, 2020), 432.

indicated above. The mountains (A) are those heights of the earth on which Yahweh treads (A'). B and B' refer to the rhythms of nature. C refers to God's engagement with humankind.[7] Furthermore, the first and last pairs of participles are in the *qal* stem, while C is in the *hiphil*.

"To humankind" (*lə 'ādām*) could also be translated "to Adam."[8] Such a translation would fit with the reference to creation, and Adam is not only a historical figure but also a paradigmatic one, the representative of humankind. Either way, this phrase clearly portrays Yahweh as a God who is deeply involved in and with his creation. However, there is considerable debate about the meaning of *śēḥô*, "his thoughts," which occurs only here in the Hebrew Bible. Most exegetes treat it as a by-form of *śîaḥ* meaning his wishes/thoughts/plans.[9] Duane Garrett argues that it normally means "complaint."[10] If this is correct, then the hymn fragment has strong overtones of judgment. M. Daniel Carroll R. points out, "In 3:7–8, the prophet is said to be the channel of revelation, and the speech formulas throughout the book reinforce this idea of divine disclosure of the basis and consequences of his displeasure."[11] Similarly, B' could refer to an apocalyptic type of darkening (but see below) and A' to God's crushing judgment. Garrett notes of A', "Amos probably implies a combination of ideas, that YHWH is vigorous, that he is a cosmic figure stepping across the earth, and that he is a warrior before whom nothing can stand (the parallel to Mic 1:3 is especially telling)."[12]

Although a different word is used for "plan" in Amos 3:7, C echoes that verse, depicting Yahweh as not just transcendent but also immanent. As the center of the chiasm, C summarizes the heart of Amos's message—it is particularly to his people that God has revealed his thoughts.[13] The apostle Paul notes of the people of Israel in Romans 9:4, "Theirs is the adoption to sonship; theirs is the divine glory, the covenants, the receiving of the law, the temple worship and the promises" (NIV). As we saw in the previous chapter,

---

[7] The opening participle (*yōṣēr*) and the final word before the climactic declaration of God's name ("earth," *'āreṣ*) have the final two consonants in common but in reverse order.

[8] Andersen and Freedman, *Amos*, 453.

[9] Paul, *Amos*, 154.

[10] Duane A. Garrett, *Amos: A Handbook on the Hebrew Text* (Waco, TX: Baylor University Press, 2008), 128.

[11] Carroll, *Book of Amos*, 434.

[12] Garrett, *Amos*, 129.

[13] As with Amos 3:7, we do not think the reference is to God's revealing humankind's thoughts to humankind; this would make no sense.

Amos has been at pains to stress God's grace toward Israel and not least his revealing his thoughts via his prophets to them.

What AB and B'A' do is affirm in the strongest possible fashion that this revealer God who has been so deeply involved with Israel is none other than the Creator. The verbs *form*, *create*, and *make* ("turn") are found in Genesis 1–3 and in Isaiah 43:7; 45:7, 18 in relation to creation, as here. In Isaiah 40:12; Psalm 65:6; Proverbs 8:25, mountains are mentioned as part of God's creative activity.[14] Wilhelm Rudolph makes an evocative suggestion as to why mountains and wind are mentioned together: "If Yahweh is the creator of the mountains and of the wind, then thereby the most stable and the most moveable are juxtaposed, that which cannot be overlooked and the invisible. The combination of opposites always expresses the totality. . . . The first two participial phrases indicate Yahweh as creator of everything."[15]

"Wind" (*rûaḥ*) can also mean "spirit," and of course in Genesis 1–2 we find the *rûaḥ ĕlōhîm* brooding over the waters of creation, and Yahweh Elohim also breathes his *rûaḥ* into humankind. However, the context of cosmic creation makes "wind" more likely, as does the use of the verb *bārā*ʾ, normally used of God's creative activity.

There is some disagreement as to whether "darkness" comes from the root ʾ*yp* (= be dark) or from the root *yp*ʿ (shine out or forth), with ʾ*yp* being a metathesized form of *yp*ʿ.[16] If one follows Paul's latter understanding, then this phrase refers to Yahweh as turning darkness into dawn, that is, it is a further articulation of his control over creation and its rhythms. As Carroll notes, "the terrible power of the Creator is emphasized by the assertion that Yahweh is able to reverse the fundamental processes of nature."[17] If, with most commentators, one reads it as Yahweh turning dawn into darkness, it still emphasizes his control over nature but has a more threatening dimension and anticipates Amos 8:9 in this respect. Such a reading fits well with the final verse, with its evocative imagery of Yahweh treading on the high places (see Deut 32:13; Is 58:14; Mic 1:3), an image of victory *and* judgment. Douglas Stuart rightly notes

---

[14] Note that Gen 1–2 does not deal with the creation of mountains.
[15] Wilhelm Rudolph, *Joel, Amos, Obadja, Jona*, Kommentar zum Alten Testament 13.2 (Gütersloh: Gütersloher Verlaugshaus Gerd Mohn, 1971), 182 (our translation).
[16] For the latter view see Paul (*Amos*, 155), who translates this phrase, "Who turns blackness into glimmering dawn" (137).
[17] Carroll, *Book of Amos*, 434.

that Yahweh "is 'shaper'... creator... revealer... maker... and walker / treader... i.e., in control of everything and everyone. The created order answers to him."[18]

As with each of the three hymn fragments, Amos 4:13 climaxes in its concluding phrase: "the LORD God Almighty is his name."[19] "Almighty" is *ṣəbā 'ôt*, which can refer to the starry hosts of heaven or to the heavenly army. The latter is most likely in view here and emphasizes the power of God and thus the terror of having him come against one. In this way the hymn connects back to Amos 4:12, with its concluding imperative "prepare to meet your God." Yahweh is the all-powerful Creator who is immanently involved with his creation, and Israel stands no chance against him when he comes in judgment. Amos 4:13 also flows naturally into the lament of Amos 5:2. If this God is against her, then judgment is unavoidable and there will be no one to help her when he strikes. "The LORD God Almighty" also occurs in Amos 5:16, and his passing through Israel's midst (Amos 5:17) will result in wailing and cries of anguish.

Amos 5:8

He who made [*'ōśēh*] the Pleiades and Orion,
    who turns [*hōpēk*] midnight into dawn
    and darkens day into night,
who calls [*qōrē'*] for the waters of the sea
    and pours them out over the face of the land—
    the LORD is his name. (NIV)

Amos 5:8 occurs in the midst of Amos 5:4-15, and many commentators regard it as a late addition because it appears to interrupt Yahweh's arraignment of Israel.[20] However, this is speculative, and as we will show, Amos 5:8 fits in its context and functions powerfully as part of God's case against Israel. There is, furthermore, a catchphrase linking Amos 5:7 with Amos 5:8, namely, the verb *hpk* (turn). There are those in Israel who *turn* justice into bitterness, but Yahweh *turns* midnight into dawn. In Amos 5:7 the Israelites "turn" and "cast," but their actions pale into insignificance against Yahweh, who "made," "turns," "darkens," "calls," and "pours." Amos 5:8 is a celebration of Yahweh's creative power, with overtones of this

---

[18]Douglas Stuart, *Hosea–Jonah*, WBC 31 (Nashville: Nelson, 1987), 340.
[19]Paul (*Amos*, 155-56) sees this final phrase as an addition to the hymn.
[20]Paul, *Amos*, 167.

power used in judgment.²¹ As with Amos 4:13, participles dominate in this hymn, occurring three times, as indicated above.

As in Genesis 1, the stars are demythologized; they are not deities but God's creation. He made the Pleiades and Orion.²² The Pleiades (*kîmâ*) is a group of seven stars forming part of the Taurus constellation. Orion (*kəsîl*) is a further constellation. Pleiades and Orion are mentioned together in Job 9:10; 38:31, where Yahweh's creative power is similarly evoked. These constellations were associated with the New Year and the change of season so that Yahweh is here also praised as the one who regulates the seasons.

The next two phrases are arranged chiastically in an ABB'A' structure, as illustrated below:

who turns **midnight** into *dawn*
and darkens *day* into **night**

Yahweh controls not only the seasons but also the rhythm of day and night, an emphasis also found in Amos 4:13. The latter phrase, with its use of "day" (*yôm*), foreshadows the day of Yahweh in Amos 5:18. That Yahweh turns "day into night" also hints at judgment, a possibility strengthened in the following phrase: "who calls for the waters of the sea and pours them out over the face of the land," an allusion to the judgment of the flood in Genesis 6–9 (Amos 9:6 NIV).²³ "A whole ocean is tipped over the entire world."²⁴

As with Amos 4:13, the hymn ends with the name of God: "Yahweh is his name." The theology of Yahweh is articulated in particular in Exodus 3; 6. It is preeminently the name of the covenant God, the God who rescues his people from slavery in Egypt and brings them to himself. But the Sinai covenant is a legally binding relationship that commits Israel to obey him and live as his people. There are consequences for disobedience, and they are serious and will be perpetrated by this God, who is not just the local or national deity but the Creator God.

Readers should note that there is some debate as to whether the hymn ends at this point. Andersen and Freedman, for example, treat Amos 5:8-9

---

[21]For Amos 5:8 as part of a chiasm in Amos 5:1-17, see Carroll, *Book of Amos*, 437-38. Carroll argues that "Yahweh is his name" stands at the center of the chiasm (460).

[22]See S. Mowinckel, "Die Sternnamen im Alten Testament," *Nederlands theologisch Tijdschrift* 29 (1928): 5-75.

[23]The verb *he makes it dark* is unequivocal. See Andersen and Freedman, *Amos*, 488. Compare Amos 8:9.

[24]Andersen and Freedman, *Amos*, 491. They argue that the reference could either be to the undoing of the action of the third day of creation in Gen 1 or to the flood.

as the second hymn.[25] Since Amos 4:13 and Amos 9:5-6 *end* with God's name, we are inclined to see just Amos 4:13 as the hymn. However, Amos 5:9 does extend the thought of Amos 5:8 in terms of God's judgment in history: "The Lord controls not only the laws of nature (v 8) but also determines the destiny of nations."[26] A similar note is struck repeatedly in the Old Testament; suffice it to mention two examples: First, Psalm 1 and Psalm 2, the introduction to the Psalter. In Psalm 1 the individual is in view, but in Psalm 2 we hear the noise of the nations, the point being that the law of Yahweh relates to both individual and nation. Psalm 19, our second example, moves from creation in Psalm 19:1-6 to the wonderful relevance of the law of Yahweh for the believer in Psalm 19:7-14. As throughout the Bible, and here in Amos, redemption/judgment and creation are held inseparably together.

Amos 9:5-6

The Lord, *the* Lord *Almighty—*	A
he touches *the earth* and it melts,	B
and all who live in it mourn;	
the whole land rises like the Nile,	
then sinks like the river of Egypt;	
he builds his lofty palace in the heavens	C
and sets its foundation on the earth;	
he calls for the waters of the sea	B′
and pours them out over the face of *the land—*	
the Lord *is his name.* (NIV)	A′

This hymn concludes the fourth part of Amos, namely, Amos 7:1–9:6, the section dealing with Amos's visions. As we noted in the previous chapter, the visions have to do with the coming judgment, and this hymn rounds them off like a crescendo. Unlike the two previous hymns, Amos 9:5-6 begins and ends with the name of God, which functions as an *inclusio*.

The first name, literally ʾ*adōnāy YHWH ṣǝbāʾôt*, is similar to that in Amos 4:13; "Almighty" is *ṣǎbāʾôt* and refers to the God who commands the armies of heaven. The final name is the same as Amos 5:8, the name of Israel's covenant God, Yahweh. This envelope structure alerts us to the fact that Yahweh is going to encounter Israel in his power as judge.

---

[25] Andersen and Freedman, *Amos*, 486-94.
[26] Paul, *Amos*, 169.

The hymn has a chiastic structure, as set out above. This is indicated by the recurrence of the name of God at the beginning and end, the repetition of 'ereṣ in B and B', and the parallel in content between B and B'. The NIV translates 'ereṣ as "land" in B'. There are three participles—indicated in bold above—that speak of the activity of God: he touches, he builds, he calls. His touching and his calling relate to his activity of judgment, whereas his building is about his activity of creation. Whereas in Amos 4:13 God's revelation was central to the hymn, here it is his creation.

The Lord Almighty touches the earth and it melts. Although different verbs are used, one is reminded of Uzzah reaching out to take hold of the ark when David was bringing it into Jerusalem (2 Sam 6:6) and was struck dead. Humans need to be careful around the holy, and even more so when the Holy One reaches out merely to touch the earth. As Shalom Paul notes of the verb *melt* (*mwg*), "It describes the reeling and undulating motion of the earth also in Ps 46:7; 75:4."[27] It also occurs in Nahum 1:5, and the root reappears in Amos 9:13 ("flow").

The comparison of the land to the Nile repeats the image already found in Amos 8:8: "the whole land rises like the Nile, then sinks like the river of Egypt." "The cosmic upheaval of both land and sea are by-products of the theophany of the Deity who appears in order to execute judgment."[28] Similarly, Andersen and Freedman note that Amos 9:5 "is positively eschatological. It describes the dissolution of the earth at the touch of God, the opposite of its solidification out of the primal water, as in various creation stories. The reference to the waters of the sea, which is used twice (Amos 5:8b; 9:6b), achieves the same effect."[29] This is correct, but one must be careful in interpreting the imagery here. The New Testament draws on this type of prophetic imagery for the final judgment, and the sort of language Amos uses is sometimes taken to refer to the complete dissolution of the earth. However, this is metaphorical language of coming judgment and must be read as such. If, for example, the earth literally dissolves in response to God's touch, then there would be no one left in the land to mourn. Cosmic as the language is, the focus is on coming judgment on the northern kingdom. Thus the NIV is probably right in translating 'ereṣ as "land" in B'. It could be "the earth" and refer to eschatological judgment on the whole creation,

---

[27] Paul, *Amos*, 280n70.
[28] Paul, *Amos*, 280.
[29] Paul, *Amos*, 489.

but in context it is more likely a reference to the northern kingdom, hence "the land." As with Amos 5:8, the judgment of the flood is evoked: "**he calls** for the waters of the sea and pours them out over the face of *the land*," as a reminder to Israel of whom they are dealing with. At the center of the hymn stands "**he builds** his lofty palace in the heavens and sets its foundation on the earth."

It is not entirely clear how to translate "lofty palace" (*m'lwtw* [*ketiv*]) or "foundation" (*'ăguddâ*). The latter word means something like "cluster," something that is firmly held together, and so probably "storeroom" here.[30] The word *mă'ălôt* usually refers to "steps" so that some read this as a reference to steps in a multistoried heaven.[31] We follow many commentators in deleting the first *m* as a case of dittography and read *'ăliyātō*, "his chamber." As Stuart notes, "The particular metaphors for heaven and earth . . . (probably 'upper room' and 'storeroom'), seem to liken creation to a house or palace. The point is clear enough: Heaven and earth are Yahweh's handiwork and domain in which all elements are subject to him. What he made he controls."[32] This imagery is similar to what we find elsewhere in the Old Testament of heaven as God's throne and earth as his footstool. As his particular domain, heaven is superior to earth, but earth is his creation, and he remains deeply involved with and in it. He is Lord of heaven and earth, and his purposes with the earth will prevail, regardless of Israel's disobedience.

God's judgment as expressed in B and B' is an extension of his being Creator (C). The hymn ends with "Yahweh is his name," and the audience can be in no doubt that Yahweh is, as Genesis 2:4-5 puts it, "Yahweh Elohim." The covenant God of Israel—Yahweh—is the Creator God—Elohim—and this is bad news for rebellious Israel.[33] This vision of God's cosmic power and immanence concludes the section of the book containing Amos's vision and looks forward to the conclusion. The universality in Amos 9:7 and in Amos 9:12's "all the nations" is an extension of Yahweh's being the Creator.

Theology

Creation and revelation. It seems obvious from Amos and the other Minor Prophets that Yahweh speaks, but nowadays a theology of God speaking is

---

[30]Paul, *Amos*, 280n77 (see Ex 12:22; 2 Sam 2:25; Is 58:6; Stuart, *Hosea–Jonah*, 389n6b.
[31]Paul, *Amos*, 280n75. See Ex 20:26; 1 Kings 10:19-20; 2 Kings 9:13; Neh 3:15.
[32]Stuart, *Hosea–Jonah*, 393.
[33]Elohim is the name used for God in Gen 1.

often contested. In his award-winning *Revelation and Authority: Sinai in Jewish Scripture and Tradition*, Benjamin Sommer leans on Maimonides for a radically minimalist view of what happened at Sinai:

> When the Torah describes God as talking, it does not mean that God communicated using a voice and words. Indeed, for Maimonides, it cannot and must not mean that. It refers only to volition or thought. Further, it cannot refer to an act of volition or thought that Moses could receive through some sort of extrasensory perception. For if God acted at a given moment to think a specific thought or to express a particular wish . . . *then God is not eternal and unchanging*. Whatever happened to Moses at Mount Sinai, it did not involve his ears hearing God speaking any words to him, or even his mind "hearing" God silently expressing specific volitions. Both Moses and Israel had some intellectual experience of God at Sinai; but in light of Maimonides's statement in I:65, even Moses's deeper perception there did not involve the medium of language, even silently.[34]

How does a believing Jew such as Sommer reach such a view? The answer is his doctrine of God, as the italicized sentence above indicates. Maimonides drew deeply on Greek philosophy, which results in a view of God as being unable to speak or convey a thought. Fortunately, there is absolutely no reason for us to follow him on this, and the Minor Prophets—indeed, both Old Testament and New Testament—provide us with a very different view of God. When it comes to revelation, one's doctrine of God and of creation are crucial.

Indeed, the doctrine of creation backs into the doctrine of God. This is clear from the creation hymns in Amos, which could just as easily be called Yahweh hymns. Amos prophesies because *God* has spoken (Amos 3:8), and in his prophecies he calls Israel back to a true view of God. In these hymns he uses their liturgy to confront them with the true view of God as he has revealed himself. In the process Amos shows himself to be a theist. Yahweh is utterly transcendent; he is the Creator God and ontologically of an entirely different order from that of creation. He is the uncreated God who is the source of the creation. Yet he is not a God far off, as the deists would have it; Yahweh is deeply involved in history, and not only in Israel's history but that of all the nations (see Amos 9:7).

---

[34]Benjamin D. Sommer, *Revelation and Authority: Sinai in Jewish Scripture and Tradition* (New Haven, CT: Yale University Press, 2015), 83, emphasis added. See Craig G. Bartholomew, *God Who Acts in History: The Significance of Sinai* (Grand Rapids, MI: Eerdmans, 2020) for a detailed engagement with Sommer's view.

We are able to know this God truly because "he reveals his thoughts to humankind" (Amos 4:13). God is at least personal if not more than personal. This is demonstrably the case in Amos. God involves himself in the life of an ancient Near Eastern nation, Israel, which he takes as his people. He reveals himself *to them* and accompanies them in their journey. When they go off the rails, he raises up prophets to bring his word to them, in this case a word of judgment. Yahweh is thus personal and particular. He is not god in general or a pantheistic force in the universe but Yahweh, the God of creation and covenant and of history and eschatology. We could not know God apart from him showing himself to us, and he has done this particularly and definitively in the Old and New Testament, in the life of Israel and in the Christ event. His involvement with Israel and his presence in the church is inseparably connected with his purposes for the whole creation, for that day when all the nations will bear his name (Amos 9:12).

Colin Gunton points out that the fundamental philosophical distinction is not that between spirit and matter, between the creation and that which negates it, between immanence and transcendence, but that between *the uncreated God and his creation.* As he observes, "An adequate doctrine of creation will affirm that the creator makes a world that is other than he, but not opposed to him—apart from sin, that is."[35] Words and language are a good gift of God, and from this perspective there is nothing surprising about the Creator God empowering certain humans to use language to speak truthfully about him. Amos 4:13 is poignant in this respect, with God's revealing his thoughts to humankind nested amid strong statements about creation.

We should not underestimate what is at stake here: it is the chasm between the impersonal God of Greek philosophy, who neither speaks nor reveals himself, and the living God of the Minor Prophets, who thinks, speaks, and acts.

Creation and life. There are few doctrines which are paid as much lip service while being ignored as the doctrine of creation.[36] There is a good reason why the opening act of the drama of Scripture is creation, and if one diminishes this act, then every other act is diminished accordingly, and one easily

---

[35]Colin E. Gunton, *Act and Being: Towards a Theology of the Divine Attributes* (Grand Rapids, MI: Eerdmans, 2002), 47.
[36]See Bruce R. Ashford and Craig G. Bartholomew, *The Doctrine of Creation: A Constructive Kuyperian Approach* (Downers Grove, IL: IVP Academic, 2020).

ends up with a reductionist view of salvation as only personal and with a God who has no interest in social justice or politics.

How was Amos able to keep the focus on God and yet prophesy in relation to all dimensions of the life of Israel? From where did Amos get this wide-ranging vision that works the religion-society trajectory so relentlessly? From more than one source, but, as the hymns demonstrate, above all from his view of Yahweh as the Creator. If God is the Creator, then all of life belongs to him, and his people are required to live *coram Deo*, before the very face of God, in all dimensions of life as he has made it. This doctrine funds Amos's focus on politics, international relations, *and* religion.

Creative preaching. The worldview of Amos, rooted in Yahweh, opening out onto all dimensions of the life of God's covenant people and the whole of God's creation, funds his explosive message. How might we similarly land the message from God right in the midst of our twenty-first-century congregations?[37] Karl Möller proposes that Amos in his book conducts an extended debate with Israel.[38] William Doan and Terry Giles pick up on this in relation to the hymns in Amos as *performative* prophecy.[39] One can only imagine Amos pausing while prophesying to sing a verse from a hymn in Israel's liturgy. Amos reaches for a whole variety of genres and strategies to drive his message home, and we can learn from his creativity.

Bearing in mind the discontinuity and continuity between prophecy and preaching, there is surely much we can learn from Amos about preaching. Like Amos, we face major obstacles in our hearers that need to be subverted. In the West, Christianity is increasingly dominated by two forms of Christianity: first, that of the mainstream, which has little time for the transcendent, holy God Amos confronts us with, the God with nonnegotiable standards and a God not just of love but also of terrible judgment. Second, that of the evangelical churches, which embody a strong sense of the supernatural but tend to restrict God to church life and have little interest in or

---

[37]See Craig G. Bartholomew, *Excellent Preaching: Proclaiming the Gospel in Its Context and Ours* (Bellingham, WA: Lexham, 2015), on this issue. See also the important work by M. Daniel Carroll R., *Contexts for Amos: Prophetic Poetics in Latin American Perspective*, JSOTSup 132 (Sheffield: Sheffield Academic Press, 1992).

[38]Karl Möller, *A Prophet in Debate: The Rhetoric of Persuasion in the Book of Amos*, JSOTSup 372 (Sheffield: Sheffield Academic Press, 2003).

[39]William Doan and Terry Giles, *Performance and Power: Performance Criticism of the Hebrew Bible* (Edinburgh: T&T Clark, 2005). See also Joyce Rilett Wood, *Amos in Song and Book Culture*, JSOTSup 337 (Sheffield: Sheffield Academic Press, 2002).

time for the sociopolitical world, and thus often end up by default on the side of the political right.

Such generalizations need far more nuance, but they are helpful in beginning to alert us to the challenging context in which we preach today. As Martin Buber reminded us in the previous chapter, prophetic preaching is *always contextual*. It is no use calling the poorest of the poor to repent of the sins of Western corporations, and it is no use calling corporate North Americans to repent of the temptation to violence experienced on a daily basis by the oppressed. Amos reminds us that preaching requires an acute sense of the context and of the lives of those to whom we are preaching. Only thus will we be able to bring God's word to *these* people in *this* situation.

Anyone who has served in mainstream Western churches will be familiar with what we call "heritage Christianity": the assumption that just because one is part of a church, all is well, and we just need to limp along in fundraising to maintain the building and activities. Northern Israel shared this spirit of Christendom, and Amos worked tirelessly to disabuse the Israelites of it. So too will we need to find multiple strategies to disabuse pew sitters that all is well just because they are there. Like Amos, we will need to find creative ways to disrupt this unhealthy comfort and sense of ease.

Liberal Christianity has much to say about *love* and will rightly resonate with Amos's and Yahweh's concern for the oppressed and poor. However, as Jean Mouroux perceptively notes, "But if love is generally recognized as the supreme value, the idea of love has been so distorted and falsified that we shall need a very special effort to recover it in all its purity."[40] Mouroux notes that love is written into the fiber of the universe: "It is borne along on the wave of a measureless desire, written in the secret depths of every being, and drawing all towards God." However, as he points out, it is in the love of God that all other loves are rooted. Love is profoundly wounded by sin, and it is *only* through conversion to God via repentance and faith—love and obedience are inseparable—that "then begins the drama of the slow, difficult and magnificent growth of the children of God. The 'miracle of miracles' is thus the visible apparition of the eternal Love among men."[41]

Even as some evangelical preachers work to open up all of life as the terrain of God's kingdom for their congregations, so other preachers in

---

[40] Jean Mouroux, *The Meaning of Man*, trans. A. H. G. Downes (New York: Image, 1961), 182. See 182-241 for a very useful treatment of this topic.
[41] Mouroux, *Meaning of Man*, 182, 221, 193.

mainline congregations that are smug about their progressive views will need to find myriad ways in which to preach so as to enable their congregations to prepare to meet their Maker again and again. The sheer dynamism of Amos exalts the office of preaching. In this way Amos helps us to see the importance and weight of preaching, and few things would strengthen the church as much today as a retrieval of such preaching.

RECOMMENDED READING

Ashford, Bruce R., and Craig G. Bartholomew. *The Doctrine of Creation: A Constructive Kuyperian Approach*. Downers Grove, IL: IVP Academic, 2020.

Carroll R., M. Daniel. *Contexts for Amos: Prophetic Poetics in Latin American Perspective*. JSOTSup 132. Sheffield: Sheffield Academic Press, 1992.

Hasel, Gerhard F. *Understanding the Book of Amos: Basic Issues in Current Interpretations*. Eugene, OR: Wipf & Stock, 1991. Chapter 8.*

Recommended reading marked with a "" indicates introductory works.*

9

Obadiah

EDOM'S FALL AND YAHWEH'S KINGDOM

OBADIAH REMAINS UNDEREXPLORED but is a theological powerhouse. On the face of it, it seems to be a bleak book spelling doom for the Edomites. However, it also proclaims Judah's restoration as the inverse to Edom's devastation. The primary audience for Obadiah is suffering Judahites rather than the people of Edom.[1] God's word against Edom is matched by God's word against Assyria in Nahum, Babylon in Habakkuk, all nations in Micah 4:1-2; Haggai 2:21-22; and Malachi 1:11. If its audience is specific, its message ranges across all nations (Obad 15).

THE CONTEXT OF OBADIAH

How Obadiah fits in Israel's story remains unclear. Many scholars associate the book with (or after) the exile of Judah in 587 BC because of the animosity toward Edom reflected in exilic texts.[2] Edom either rejoiced at Judah's demise at the hands of the Neo-Babylonian Empire or profited from it afterward (see Lam 4:21-22; Ps 137:7-8; Jer 49:7-22).[3]

However, Obadiah may depict a general animosity toward the traditional rival of Israel/Jacob, the brother-nation of Edom/Esau rather than a specific historic moment (Gen 25–26; 2 Sam 8:12-14; 1 Kings 11:14-22; 2 Kings 8:20-22;

---

[1]Terence E. Fretheim, *Reading Hosea–Micah: A Literary and Theological Commentary* (Macon: Smyth & Helwys, 2013), 160.
[2]Paul R. Raabe, *Obadiah*, AB (New York: Doubleday, 1996), 47-56; John Barton, *Joel and Obadiah*, Interpretation (Louisville, KY: Westminster John Knox, 2001), 120-23.
[3]Bruce C. Cresson, "The Condemnation of Edom in Postexilic Judaism," in *The Use of the Old Testament in the New and Other Essays: Studies in Honor of William Franklin Stinespring*, ed. J. M. Bird (Durham, NC: Duke University Press, 1972), 125-48; Bert Dicou, *Edom, Israel's Brother and Antagonist: The Role of Edom in Biblical Prophecy and Story*, JSOTSup 169 (Sheffield: Sheffield Academic Press, 1994); J. Lindsay, "Edomite Westward Expansion: The Biblical Evidence," *Ancient Near Eastern Studies* 36 (1999): 48-89.

2 Chron 28:16-19; Is 63:1-6). If so, then the patriarchal animosity is universalized so that Edom becomes the paradigm of the enemy nation that has set itself up against God and his people.[4] The story of Edom becomes a cipher for all Israel's enemies (and what will come of them).[5] It is difficult to choose between these options.

We should also mention Obadiah's position between Amos and Jonah. Obadiah offers a comprehensive vision of *divine judgment* against Edom—a message of divine judgment that becomes effective for all nations as well. Amos, too, teaches God's wrath in judgment over all nations (but *especially* Israel). Yet this teaching on divine wrath against nations is nuanced by the theology of the nations in Jonah.

Outline

Based on its content, the book divides into two sections: Obadiah 1-15, 16-21.[6]

Obad 1-15	Prophecy against Edom
Obad 1	Superscription
Obad 1	Call for battle against Edom
Obad 2-4	Judgment oracle 1
Obad 5-14	Judgment oracle 2
Obad 15	Summative judgment statement and the day of the Lord
Obad 16-21	Prophecy of restoration for God's people
Obad 16	Cup of God's wrath against Edom
Obad 17-18	Ascension of God's remnant
Obad 19-21	Restoration of God's remnant

Interpretation

The book opens with a sparse introductory formula: "The vision of Obadiah" (Obad 1a). None of the introductory formulae in the Twelve contain as little detail as Obadiah. Obadiah is the "envoy" (*ṣîr*) sent by Yahweh to proclaim a word against Edom (Obad 1). The message? "Arise and let us go up against

---

[4] Fretheim, *Reading Hosea–Micah*, 161.
[5] See Barton, *Joel and Obadiah*, 121; Ehud Ben Zvi, *A Historical-Critical Study of the Book of Obadiah*, BZAW 242 (Berlin: de Gruyter, 1996).
[6] Two helpful summations are Raabe, *Obadiah*, 18-22; Barton, *Joel and Obadiah*, 118-19.

her for battle!" It is curious that Obadiah 1b reads, "We have heard a report from Yahweh." Yahweh has issued a "report" that his envoy shall declare among the nations. Who is the "we" speaking? It could be the divine council or the nations. In either case, Yahweh's message is not a local prophecy restricted *just* to Edom. The envoy is sent among the nations to proclaim a message about Edom. Although a message for Edom, the nations (and perhaps the heavenly council) are called to attend to Yahweh's report. The message has to do with Edom (Obad 1-15) *and* the day of the Lord, Israel's restoration (Obad 16-20), and ultimately the kingdom of God (Obad 21).

Edom's great reversal occurs in Obadiah 2-15. It is not uncommon for the Bible to contrast two opposing states: the proud and the humble, the rich and poor, the old and the young, the righteous and the wicked.[7] But this device is taken further when biblical literature differentiates former versus present reality, which might be identified as the motif of catastrophe, the fall from high estate to a low estate due to a tragic flaw. In the case of Edom, the flaw is nothing less than sin, Edom's "arrogant heart" (Obad 3; see also Obad 10-14 below).

Obadiah 2-4 denounces Edom's pride and (false) sense of security. The spatial metaphor of "height" or "high place" enables the reader to visualize Edom's stability and presumed security: from the heights Edom looked down arrogantly on other nations, enjoying military advantage and security from invasion (e.g., the "clefts of the rock, in your lofty abode," Obad 3). This spatial metaphor extends to hyperbole when the poetry places Edom's "nest" among the "stars" (Obad 4). Who can approach the stars? Edom seems inaccessible and impervious to harm, untouchable as the heavens.

Yet Yahweh will "pull you down from there" (Obad 4b). This final line is accompanied by the oracular formula "utterance of Yahweh." At Yahweh's word, Edom will be torn from their high place and brought to the depths of ruin. The spatial metaphor of high to low works effectively to present a reversal motif.

Obadiah 5-7 takes the reversal further, using examples of harvest and burglary as a comparison of Edom's downfall. Thieves and harvesters only take what is needed and leave a portion behind (Obad 5-6). However, those who have harvested Edom leave absolutely *nothing*; the nation is left completely bereft. Finally, the reversal is completed with betrayal.

---

[7]Luis Alonso-Schöckel, *A Manual of Hebrew Poetics,* SubBib 11 (Rome: Pontifical Biblical Institute, 2000), 85-94.

Former allies have now become foes (Obad 7). The transitional phrase of Obadiah 7b reveals that Edom's wisdom is nothing but a lack of discernment.[8] Those they believed were allies (and ate bread with them, likely indicating a formal covenantal partnership) placed snares under Edom's steps. Without these capacities, no one will survive the "battle" reported in Obadiah 2: "everyone will be cut off from Mount Esau by slaughter" (Obad 9).[9]

Obadiah 10-14 provides the rationale for the downfall: Edom is guilty of fraternal sins, as each of the things mentioned in these verses implies some sort of breach with "Jacob." Obadiah 10 opens with Esau's "violence" (*ḥāmās*) against Jacob. Terence Fretheim notes that the fraternal language in these verses evokes the Jacob narrative (Gen 25–36). "Esau" appears in Obadiah 6, 8, 9, 18, 19, 21. The patriarchal name for Israel, "Jacob," appears in Obadiah 10, 17, 18. The term "your brother Jacob" appears in Obadiah 10, confirming the patriarchal connection between Esau/Edom and Jacob/Israel in the verses. Esau has betrayed Jacob and sinned against him. For this, Esau will undergo a reversal of fortunes.

What are Esau's sins against his brother besides the "violence" listed?

- betraying Israel, who was being invaded in war (Obad 11)
- delighting in Israel's downfall in war (Obad 12)
- exploiting Israel's downfall in war by laying hold of their seized goods (Obad 13)
- assisting in Israel's invasion (Obad 14)

Obadiah 15 summarizes Edom's fate:

> For the day of the LORD is near
>   [it is] against all nations;
> Just as you have done, it shall be done to you
>   Your recompense shall return on your head.

We have seen this concept already in Joel 4:4, 7 [3:4, 7], and most scholars believe that Joel draws it from Obadiah 15. Does the statement concern Yahweh *punishing* Edom for their fraternal sins, or does the statement concern a kind of mechanical retribution that suggests what goes around

---

[8]Edom's connection with wisdom appears in Obad 7-8; Jer 49:7. Note the connection between Edom and the figure of Job. Job is clearly an Edomite, from the land of Uz (Job 1:1-5).
[9]Translation ours, following the exegesis of Barton, *Joel and Obadiah*, 143.

comes around? At this point, it is enough to note that Edom's reversal links with the coming of the day of the Lord.[10]

The turn to Israel's reversal appears in Obadiah 16-21. Obadiah 16 employs the metaphor of a cup of wrath to describe Edom's ultimate demise.[11] The cup metaphor appears in various Old Testament texts, often as an image of divine judgment. Wine and the cup of wrath sometimes correlate in biblical texts, as in Psalm 75:9 [75:8]. Yet, the metaphor remains somewhat enigmatic in one major respect. Normally, when the metaphor appears in biblical texts, it appears as a cup of wrath *in Yahweh's hand*, as in Psalm 75:9 [75:8]. That is to say, Yahweh pours out the cup of wrath on those experiencing divine punishment. This is not strictly the way the metaphor works in Obadiah 16. The hand of Yahweh is not present. One may assume that it lies in the background, but metaphors function on what is said as well as what is not said. What is not stated clearly is direct divine involvement with Edom's demise. Yahweh's hand does not hold the cup of wrath. Rather, Edom drinks the cup of wrath, as it were, holding it with her own hand. The nations, too, drink continually by their own hand.

In contrast to the fate of Edom and the nations, Obadiah 17 declares that there will be a "remnant" in Zion, which will be "holy." The effect of Obadiah 17, then, is to project a time in the future when nations that are set against Yahweh and Yahweh's people (like Edom) will experience a great reversal; God's dejected and abused people will experience a turnabout in which they will survive and be sanctified through their suffering ("they will be holy"), and the house of Jacob/Israel will regain its strength, its capital city Jerusalem, and its land, dispossessing the occupying forces. This is a future time closely associated with the day of the Lord, which is near (Obad 15).

The contrast between God's people and enemy nations, particularly Edom, appears in Obadiah 18: no "survivor" remains for Edom, but Yahweh's people shall remain. It is interesting that the same term for "survivor" (*śārîd*) in Obadiah 18 describes those who find shelter and rescue on the day of the Lord in Joel 3:5 [2:32]: "Anyone who calls upon the name of the LORD will be . . . among the survivors [*śərîdîm*]." The contrast becomes

---

[10]We follow the MT here. Some scholars prefer to emend the MT. See Barton, *Joel and Obadiah*, 149-50. Raabe (*Obadiah*, 188-90) prefers the MT reading. Either reading is sensible.

[11]It is entirely possible that the plural "you" of Obad 16 intends the people of Israel, who have drunk the cup of God's wrath (e.g., via Babylonian invasion), but now all nations will undergo their reversal and Israel will be restored. Still, we prefer to follow Raabe (*Obadiah*, 202-6) and read the plural "you" as referring to Edom.

clear: Edom will have no survivor, but when read with the co-text of Joel, there *will be survivors* among God's people—namely, those who call on the name of the Lord. Unlike Joel, there is no call for repentance, no fast. The world works in such a way that those who oppress will have their oppression turn back on them.

The last phrase of Obadiah 18, "for Yahweh has spoken," reminds us that Yahweh is present in some way with the reversal of Edom and the restoration of Israel. Yahweh's involvement, however, remains oblique when compared with his direct action in, for instance, the restoration of God's people in Joel. The house of Jacob and the house of Joseph will resettle southern and northern Palestine, up to Phoenicia in the north and down to the wilderness in the south. The resettlement, then, is a kind of repossession of the land given to God's people by Yahweh, so that by Obadiah 21, the resettlement is summarized with the statement: "and the dominion shall belong to the LORD."

The Theology of Obadiah

Obadiah touches on many of the great prophetic themes in the Old Testament, including: divine judgment, the day of Yahweh, talionic punishment, the cup of wrath, Zion theology, the land, and the kingship of Yahweh.[12]

Divine judgment. Is it true that Obadiah clearly presents a theology of divine punishment against wayward nations by Yahweh? Fretheim thinks not. His argument is that Obadiah presents a theology of creation that avoids a retribution theology. Fretheim states:

> A key theological issue for Obadiah is God's created moral order. "As you have done, it shall be done to you; your deeds shall return on your own head" (v. 15). This order of creation should *not* be understood in judicatory terms, as "punishment." Rather, this *creational reality* has to do with the workings of an order—a moral order—that is "built into" creation and that God the Creator continues to oversee, though not with precision. To use an image of cloth, the created moral order is more like burlap than silk.[13]

If Fretheim is correct, then the theology of Obadiah cannot be abbreviated as "an eye for an eye," but it could be summarized as "what goes around comes around." That is to say, under the moral world that God has created,

---

[12]Raabe, *Obadiah*, 3.
[13]Fretheim, *Reading Hosea–Micah*, 161-62.

if you sow the wind, you will reap the whirlwind. Sinners receive the natural outcome of their sin: it comes back on their own heads.

This idea has some truth to it. Wisdom material indicates a character-consequence relationship, where a life of wickedness turns back on the wicked, and the life of fidelity to God turns for good on the faithful. It is certainly true that Edom drinks the cup of God's wrath rather than God forcing it down its gullet (Obad 16). For the nations, likewise, their recompense comes back on their own heads: they are responsible for their own sin.

However, we can also affirm that Obadiah envisions divine justice administered on the day of the Lord. *God* as an agent administers judgment and punishment. Note, for instance, the way God is the active agent of judgment in Obadiah 2-4, 8. That judgment comes back on the head of Edom in Obadiah 15 exposes (1) the folly of Edom's sinful actions and (2) the justice of God in administering justice on his day. Divine and human responsibility remain thus intertwined: Edom is fully responsible for her demise, but God is fully responsible for meting out justice in his day. In our estimation, Fretheim fails to note adequately that the order built into the creation is actively sustained by Yahweh so that Yahweh's interventions and his sustaining of the creation work together.

Sin and rebellion. By railing against common breaches of God's order, Obadiah presents for *all peoples* the folly and horrific outcome of sin and rebellion against God and neighbor. In light of the sins listed in Obadiah 10-14, we see that Edom/Esau is held to account for her betrayal of her fraternal twin, Israel/Jacob. As it has come to Edom, so it shall come to all nations (Obad 15-16). The list of sin and rebellion listed above should (at the *very least*) give modern peoples pause. The twentieth century has been described as the most brutal in history.[14] Despite advances in medicine, science, and technology, the modern world is too often a bloody war machine.

The day of the Lord and the kingdom of God. As in Joel, the day of the Lord is a day of judgment and salvation. Obadiah 15-16 blends the judgment against Edom and the universal judgment against all nations. God will judge them on his holy mountain. Yet, the day *also* proves a day of salvation for God's people, Israel. As the wicked find judgment, the righteous find salvation.

---

[14]George Steiner, *Grammars of Creation: Originating in the Gifford Lectures of 1990* (London: Faber & Faber, 2001), 2-4.

In this way, the concept of the remnant stands out. Obadiah's vision of the remnant is somewhat different from, say, the remnant concept in Joel (Joel 3:5 [2:32]), Isaiah (Is 10:19-22; 11:11-16; 46:3), Amos (Amos 5:15), or Zechariah (Zech 8:11-12). In these texts, the remnant represents God's people who have been judged by God yet remain *after* judgment. In Obadiah, this remnant that was abused and betrayed by Edom now experiences a reversal at the hand of God. In the reversal, the land they lost they now regain—with extended borders. The reversal enables the remnant to regain Jerusalem (its loss described in Obad 12-14) *as well as* expanded borders beyond Jerusalem. Land, then, stands out in the configuration of the kingdom of God mentioned in Obadiah 21.

Obadiah's ending is poignant: "And the dominion shall belong to the LORD" (Obad 21). Dominion, or reign, belongs to the Lord after the great reversal that comes on his day (Obad 15). The day of the Lord brings the kingdom of God. *God's ultimate aim is not just a reversal of his people's fortunes but his reign over his good world.*

The similarity between Obadiah 21 and Psalm 22:29 [22:28] is striking, particularly in the phrase, "For to the LORD belongs the dominion [*kî ləYHWH hamməlûkâ*], and he rules over the nations" (Ps 22:29). "For Obadiah, YHWH's ultimate objective is not simply the defeat of enemies or the restoration of Israel but his kingship over the whole world."[15] It is, to be sure, an eschatological hope raised in Obadiah through the downfall of Edom. But that particular downfall in history served as a sign of the coming universal reign of God.

OBADIAH AND THE OLD TESTAMENT

As bad as was the Jacob-Esau relationship in Genesis, Obadiah tells another chapter in the "story of this dysfunctional family."[16] Fraternal strife sets the background for this new and momentous betrayal. Jeremiah 49; Ezekiel 35; Psalm 137; and Obadiah reflect on this betrayal each in its own way.

The close lexical and thematic connections between Jeremiah 49:7-22 and Obadiah lead to all sorts of questions concerning their relationship. We present here the connections, using Obadiah as the base text for comparison (see table 9.1).

---

[15] Raabe, *Obadiah*, 271.
[16] J. D. Nogalski, *The Book of the Twelve: Hosea-Jonah*, SHBC (Macon, GA: Smyth & Helwys, 2011), 393.

Table 9.1. Parallels between Obadiah and Jeremiah 49

JEREMIAH 49:7-22 (NRSV)	OBADIAH 1-16 (NRSV)
⁷ᵃ Concerning Edom. Thus says the Lord of hosts:	¹ The vision of Obadiah. Thus says the Lord God concerning Edom:
¹⁴ I have heard tidings from the Lord, and a messenger has been sent among the nations: "Gather yourselves together and come against her, and rise up for battle!"	We have heard a report from the Lord, and a messenger has been sent among the nations: "Rise up! Let us rise against it for battle!"
¹⁵ For I will make you least among the nations, despised by humankind.	² I will surely make you least among the nations; you shall be utterly despised.
¹⁶ The terror you inspire and the pride of your heart have deceived you, you who live in the clefts of the rock, who hold the height of the hill. Although you make your nest as high as the eagle's, from there I will bring you down, says the Lord.	³ Your proud heart has deceived you, you that live in the clefts of the rock, whose dwelling is in the heights. You say in your heart, "Who will bring me down to the ground?" ⁴ Though you soar aloft like the eagle, though your nest is set among the stars, from there I will bring you down, says the Lord.
⁹ If grape-gatherers came to you, would they not leave gleanings? If thieves came by night, even they would pillage only what they wanted.	⁵ If thieves came to you, if plunderers by night —how you have been destroyed!— would they not steal only what they wanted? If grape-gatherers came to you, would they not leave gleanings? ⁶ How Esau has been pillaged, his treasures searched out!
¹⁰ But as for me, I have stripped Esau bare, I have uncovered his hiding-places, and he is not able to conceal himself. His offspring are destroyed, his kinsfolk and his neighbors; and he is no more.	⁷ All your allies have deceived you, they have driven you to the border; your confederates have prevailed against you; those who ate your bread have set a trap for you— there is no understanding of it.
⁷ᵇ Is there no longer wisdom in Teman? Has counsel perished from the prudent? Has their wisdom vanished?	⁸ On that day, says the Lord, I will destroy the wise out of Edom, and understanding out of Mount Esau. ⁹ Your warriors shall be shattered, O Teman, so that everyone from Mount Esau will be cut off.
¹² For thus says the Lord: If those who do not deserve to drink the cup still have to drink it, shall you be the one to go unpunished? You shall not go unpunished; you must drink it.	¹⁶ For as you have drunk on my holy mountain, all the nations around you shall drink; they shall drink and gulp down, and shall be as though they had never been.

Did Obadiah draw from Jeremiah's prophecy or vice versa? After all, they both address Edom explicitly. Alternatively, was there a common source from which both Jeremiah and Obadiah drew, or is there no dependence whatever?[17] It is not our purpose to solve those questions here. It is enough to recognize that Jeremiah 49:7-22 and Obadiah both reflect the prophetic way of speaking against Edom.

Psalm 137:7-8 and Ezekiel 35 also denounce Edom. Ezekiel 35, like Obadiah, denounces Edom's treatment of God's people at the hands of the Babylonians. This fraternal betrayal equates to a betrayal of God (Ezek 35:10-14). Jeremiah 49; Ezekiel 35; and Obadiah each fit a type of prophetic speech that scholars have designated as Oracles Against Nations (OAN).[18] These oracles pronounce destruction of an enemy nation and the salvation of God's people. Psalm 137 remembers Edom's betrayal in its liturgical testimony, a point that leads to a terrifying blessing for vengeance against Edom's babies. The turn toward the kingdom of God is nowhere mentioned in the psalm, but the following psalm presents the majesty of God among the nations as he delivers his afflicted people. Indeed, Psalm 138:4-5 declares that all the kings of the earth will praise the majesty of Israel's God because he has rescued them.

In the Minor Prophets, Obadiah connects closely with the end of Amos. James Nogalski notes several similarities between the texts (see table 9.2). The connections indicate that Obadiah may borrow from Amos. Theologically, however, another significant point emerges.

Amos's vision in Amos 9 indicates a restoration of Judah, Jerusalem, and the Davidic line, all of which are bound for judgment in the earlier portions of Amos. Obadiah, however, expands the vision of restoration and depicts the repossession of lands that surround Jerusalem and Judah. In short, Obadiah's vision expands the picture of restoration in Amos 9. The way the restoration of Israel is achieved, however, is through the downfall of Edom.

It must be noted that Obadiah's portrayal of God's work with Edom is very negative. God's kingship comes through the demise of "Mount Esau." Yet it is important to recognize Obadiah's placement in the Minor Prophets. It precedes Jonah. As discussed in this volume, Jonah evokes the possibility

---

[17]See Leslie C. Allen, *The Books of Joel, Obadiah, Jonah, and Micah*, NICOT (Grand Rapids, MI: Eerdmans 1976), 131-33; Ben Zvi, *Historical-Critical Study*, 99-109; J. D. Nogalski, *Redactional Processes in the Book of the Twelve*, BZAW 218 (Berlin: de Gruyter, 1993), 61-74.

[18]J. H. Hayes, "The Usage of Oracles Against Foreign Nations in Ancient Israel," *JBL* 87 (1968): 81-92; Hayes, "Amos's Oracles Against the Nations (1:2-2:16)," *Review and Expositor* 92 (1995): 153-67; Graham S. Ogden, "Prophetic Oracles Against Foreign Nations and Psalms of Communal Lament: The Relationship of Psalm 137 to Jeremiah 49:7-22 and Obadiah," *JSOT* 24 (1982): 89-97.

of the nations' repentance. Jonah's hope for the nations balances Obadiah's dark vision for Edom.

Table 9.2. Parallels Between Obadiah and Amos 9

STRUCTURAL/THEMATIC PARALLELS	AMOS 9	OBADIAH
vision	9:1	1
five "if/though" clauses	9:2-4	4-5
"from there I will bring them/you down"	9:2	4
destruction/remnant motifs (agrarian image)	9:7-10	5
is it not (*halo*)	9:7	8
thematic shifts / "on that day"	9:11	8
"utterance of YHWH"	9:7,8,13	8
Eschatological "day"	9:11	15
allusion to destruction of Jerusalem	9:11	16
restoration of Davidic kingdom	9:11	19ff.
"possession of Edom and other nations"	9:12	17, 19
agricultural abundance	9:14	missing
restoration of exiles/captivity	9:14	19ff.
restoration/reclamation of cities	9:14	20
concluding promise for restoration of land	9:15	21

Source: J. D. Nogalski, *The Book of the Twelve: Hosea–Jonah*, SHBC (Macon, GA: Smyth & Helwys, 2011), 372-73, table on 372.

Obadiah and the New Testament

The New Testament never directly quotes Obadiah. However, some themes do emerge. As Obadiah draws attention to God's judgment against all nations that rebel against him (Obad 15-16), John draws attention to the same theme, though without directly attributing it to Obadiah. Obadiah is written to remind God's people that his reign is coming, and the pain of injustice will be set to rights. John reminds the church in his day that God's reign is coming, and the pain of injustice in their day is not the last word. Christ will come and judge ultimately, finally (see Rev 11:15). Obadiah envisions a day when the reversal will be complete: when Edom—and all nations that betray and rebel against God and his plan—will be judged, and the suffering righteous exonerated. So too the suffering saints of John's Revelation. The hope on display in both texts lies in the coming kingdom of God: "And the kingship will belong to the Lord" (Obad 21).

Obadiah's vision of renewal and reign after judgment arrives in the kingdom of Christ.

Obadiah for Today

In light of the New Testament mandate to love one's enemies and live peaceably with all people as best one can, how do we receive a text that celebrates a nation's downfall? We need to remember that it is not wrong to long for God to set wrongs right. That God is just and will judge is good news. As Paul says to the Christians in Rome, "Beloved, never avenge yourselves, but leave it to the wrath of God, for it is written, 'Vengeance is mine, I will repay, says the Lord'" (Rom 12:19 ESV). The point is clear. God *will* set the wrongs of the world to rights, and it is acceptable for Christians to long for that day. And it will be *God*, rather than us, who has the final word of judgment. Thus we can trust divine justice rather than taking justice into our own hands. In this way, Obadiah provides a voice for the suffering church today as we long for the coming kingdom of God. We can trust the long arm of divine justice against oppression and sin.

The answer for our world's ills is the gospel of the kingdom, not brute politics on the right or left. Still, it remains naive and evasive for the church to avoid politics. Although the kingdom is coming, the church is called to be salt and light *today* in whatever sphere of life that God has placed it. In this way, Obadiah does not demand a retreat from the world in light of the coming kingdom but rather a firm *reengagement* of the world in light of the coming kingdom. In the meantime, the church is called to witness to the coming kingdom and remind a broken world of his reign: "And the kingship will belong to the Lord" (Obad 21).

Recommended Reading

Barton, John. *Joel and Obadiah*. Interpretation. Louisville, KY: Westminster John Knox, 2001.

Nogalski, James D. *The Book of the Twelve: Hosea–Jonah*. SHBC. Macon, GA: Smyth & Helwys, 2011.*

Ogden, Graham S. "Prophetic Oracles Against Foreign Nations and Psalms of Communal Lament: The Relationship of Psalm 137 to Jeremiah 49:7-22 and Obadiah." *JSOT* 24 (1982): 89-97.

Raabe, Paul R. *Obadiah*. AB. New York: Doubleday, 1996.

Recommended reading marked with a "" indicates introductory works.*

10

Jonah

THE PATIENT GOD

Introduction

Amid the Minor Prophets, Jonah is an exceptional book.[1] Rather than containing the oracles of the prophet, it is a third-person narrative about a prophet, namely, Jonah.[2] What a story it is. Apart from this book, Jonah is only mentioned once in the Old Testament, in 2 Kings 14:25. Speaking of king Jeroboam II, 2 Kings notes, "He was the one who restored the boundaries of Israel . . . in accordance with the word of the Lord, the God of Israel, spoken through his servant Jonah son of Amittai, the prophet from Gath Hepher."

Jonah 1:1, with its designation of Jonah as "son of Amittai," clearly intends us to identify Jonah with the prophet who prophesied about the recovery of territory by the northern kingdom.[3] This tells us three important things: *first*, Jonah was a northern prophet; *second*, unlike Amos (see Amos 7:10-17), Jonah's ministry was—as far as we know—well received in the northern kingdom. Prophesying successfully about a recovery of territory would have been most welcome by Jeroboam and priests such as Amaziah. We can

---

[1]On the history of the interpretation of Jonah see Yves-Marie, *Le Livre de Jonas dans la Littérature Chrétienne grecque et latine: Sources et influence du Commentarie sur Jonas de saint Jérôme* (Paris: Études Augustiniennes, 1973); Barbara Green, *Jonah's Journeys*, Interfaces (Collegeville, MN: Liturgical Press, 2005).

[2]Jonah contains only one prophetic oracle, in Jon 3:4, consisting of five words in the Hebrew. The name "Jonah" (*yônâ*) means "dove." André Lacocque and Pierre-Emmanuel Lacocque suggest that there may be an intertextual connection with Is 60, in which the nations come to Jerusalem like "doves" (*yônîm*, Is 60:8), and at their head are ships of Tarshish (Is 60:9). Lacocque and Lacocque, *The Jonah Complex* (Atlanta: John Knox, 1981), 11-13.

[3]On the intertextuality of Jonah and 2 Kings 14 see Catherine L. Muldoon, *In Defense of Divine Justice: An Intertextual Approach to the Book of Jonah*, Catholic Biblical Quarterly Monograph Series 47 (Washington, DC: Catholic Biblical Association of America Press, 2010), 102-21.

perhaps imagine Jonah being feted in royal circles and a regular guest at elite dinner parties. From the little that we know about him, we can guess that nothing would have prepared him for the mission he was now called to.

Third, even if Jonah is historical—see below—the story of his mission to Nineveh is told for a later generation(s). It is always important to remember when dealing with biblical narrative that it is not generally written for the people involved in the action but for later generations to learn from what happened. Such awareness is fundamentally important if we are after the message of a book rather than the events behind the text. Hermeneutically, this is vital because we need to read this story in the light of Assyria's rise to superpower status and as *the* enemy who would take the northern kingdom into exile.

We simply cannot be sure of the date of composition of Jonah, but it is an Old Testament book and written first for God's Old Testament people.[4] As we will see below, in the Gospels Jonah is a type of Jesus, and this has led some authors, such as E. J. Young, to argue that the message of Jonah is Jesus.[5] In our view, this is a manifestation of a distorted Christocentric rather than a trinitarian hermeneutic that obscures the message of Jonah as much as it does the way in which Jonah informs the Gospels.[6] As part of Scripture, Jonah is written for all God's people, but it is through close attention to what Brevard Childs calls the discrete witness of the Old Testament that we will find our way to Jonah's use in the New Testament and its message for today.

Jonah as Narrative

From 2 Kings it is clear that there was indeed a historical prophet called Jonah son of Amittai. However, the *historicity of the book* Jonah has been much debated in recent centuries. There is no doubt that Jonah is carefully

---

[4]Douglas Stuart notes that Jonah is not datable except within the wide range of 750–250 BC. Stuart, *Hosea-Jonah*, WBC 31 (Nashville: Nelson, 1987), 432-33. The majority of scholars date Jonah to the postmonarchic period. See Ehud Ben Zvi, *Signs of Jonah: Reading and Rereading in Ancient Yehud*, JSOTSup 367 (Sheffield: Sheffield Academic Press, 2003), 7-8n19.

[5]Edward J. Young asserts, "The fundamental purpose of Jonah is not found in its missionary or universalistic teaching. It is rather to show that Jonah being cast into the depths of Sheol and yet brought up alive is an illustration of the death of the Messiah for sins not His own and of the Messiah's resurrection." Young, *An Introduction to the Old Testament* (Grand Rapids, MI: Eerdmans, 1984), 263.

[6]See Craig G. Bartholomew, "Listening for God's Address: A *Mere* Trinitarian Hermeneutic for the Old Testament," in *Hearing the Old Testament: Listening for God's Address*, ed. Craig G. Bartholomew and David J. H. Beldman (Grand Rapids, MI: Eerdmans, 2012), 3-19.

crafted literature in the best tradition of Hebrew storytelling. The question, however, is whether it is *historical* narrative, the validity of whose message depends on the events narrated having happened.

Douglas Stuart argues that there is a great deal at stake in its historicity: "If it really happened, it is really serious."[7] He rightly notes that we should not reject the historicity of the book because of the presence of the miraculous. He suggests that a general repentance in Nineveh is not unlikely, bearing in mind that during the first half of the eighth century BC things were not going well for the Ninevites. It is in his view possible that Nineveh had a king (Jon 3:6-7), and it is possible that at this time Nineveh functioned as a royal residence if not the capital of Assyria. Stuart notes, with many others, the similarities between Jonah and the Elijah-Elisha narratives and argues that there are parallels between Jonah's mission to Nineveh and Elijah's to Sidon and Elisha's to Syria, as well as the clustering of miracles around these figures.[8]

In our view, it is unlikely that this issue can be resolved with the present state of our knowledge. What does, however, need to be challenged is Stuart's assertion, "If it really happened, it is really serious." This is to make truth overly dependent on historicity. It is more accurate to say, "If it is really *true*, it is really serious." Literature can be true without being historical, and this could be the case with Jonah. Neither the genre, nor the poetics, nor the debate about the ancient Near Eastern historical evidence can finally decide the historical question, and in our view Jonah's message is not diminished if one takes it as carefully crafted literature *and* fiction. God is as able to speak his truth to us through fictional story as through historical narrative.

Indeed, whichever view one takes on historicity, to hear Jonah in all its power, one *must* imagine oneself among a group of Israelites listening to this story being told.[9] It is superb storytelling, and only through attending to its poetics in this way do we begin to see just how powerful it must have been in its original context and how powerfully it continues to speak to us today.[10]

---

[7]Stuart, *Hosea–Jonah*, 440.
[8]John H. Stek similarly defends its historicity. Stek, "The Message of the Book of Jonah," *Calvin Theological Journal* 4 (1969): 23-50.
[9]See Raymond F. Person, *In Conversation with Jonah: Conversation Analysis, Literary Criticism, and the Book of Jonah* (Sheffield: Sheffield Academic Press, 1996); Shimon Levy, "Jonah: A Quest Play," in Levy, *The Bible as Theatre* (Brighton: Sussex Academic, 2002), 161-72.
[10]See Kenneth M. Craig, *A Poetics of Jonah: Art in the Service of Ideology* (Macon, GA: Mercer University Press, 1999).

The shape of the narrative. Jonah begins, "And it was that the word of Yahweh [came] to Jonah son of Amittai, saying."[11] Listeners would immediately recognize this as a *prophetic* narrative, with the characteristic feature of prophetic revelation "the word of Yahweh came to . . . ." There follows in Jonah 1–2 the well-known story of Jonah's rebellion and attempted flight to Tarshish. Yahweh providentially redirects Jonah, and in Jonah 2 we have the psalm he prayed from inside the great fish. Jonah 2 ends with Jonah vomited up onto dry land.

The first four words of Jonah 3:1 are exactly the same as in Jonah 1:1, signaling part two of the book. Jonah is recommissioned and fulfills his mission in Nineveh, albeit reluctantly. In one sense, therefore, the narrative divides into two halves:

Jonah 1–2   Act 1: Rebellion
Jonah 3–4   Act 2: Obedience

Of course, the actual story has far more twists and turns than this basic division. Jonah has been subject to detailed literary, discourse, and rhetorical analysis, and in our discussion of the book below we will draw, where appropriate, on the insights of such work. A temptation of scholars is to try to find the objective structure of a biblical book apart from its content. In this respect Phyllis Trible's comment is a healthy corrective: "Form and content are inseparable. Hence proper articulation of form-content yields proper articulation of meaning."[12] An example of this issue is found in Jonah 4. In Jonah 4:4 and Jonah 4:9 Yahweh's question is repeated almost verbatim. This repetition appears to function as an *inclusio* holding Jonah 4:1-11 together as a single scene in act 2. Alternatively, we could take Jonah 4:1-4 as a scene and Jonah 4:5-11 as a—closely connected—following scene. The point to note is that *discourse analysis* yields a different breakdown of the chapter, namely:[13]

Jonah 4:1-4   Jonah prays and Yahweh responds
Jonah 4:5-7   Jonah and the leafy plant
Jonah 4:8-11   Yahweh's concern

---

[11] Our translation. The sentence is a nominal one, and the verb has to be supplied.
[12] Phyllis Trible, *Rhetorical Criticism: Context, Method, and the Book of Jonah*, Old Testament Series (Minneapolis: Fortress, 1994), 91.
[13] See W. Dennis Tucker, *Jonah: A Handbook on the Hebrew Text* (Waco, TX: Baylor University Press, 2006). The headings are ours, but the division of the text is Tucker's, decided according to discourse analysis, which focuses on syntax at the expense of content.

It is, of course, difficult to be certain about the literary structure of an ancient Near Eastern text, but we favor Trible's rhetorical-type approach while drawing on the insights of others but insisting that form and content have to be attended to *together*. It is through reading the book as attentively as possible that we are most likely to become aware of its implicit structure.

There is considerable symmetry between acts 1 and 2. Trible discerns the symmetry in table 10.1.[14] In terms of the literary structure of the book, the debate about the psalm in Jonah 2 requires comment. Most critical scholars argue that Jonah 2:2-11 is a later addition to the book. They argue that the psalm may be excised without loss of continuity to the narrative; indeed, the psalm disturbs the structure of Jonah; the psalm conflicts with Jonah's opposition to his mission to Nineveh throughout the narrative; and a thanksgiving psalm is inappropriate in a context of misery.

Table 10.1. Symmetry between acts 1 and 2 of Jonah

ACT 1	ACT 2
word of Yahweh to Jonah (Jon 1:1)	word of Yahweh to Jonah (Jon 3:1)
content of the word (Jon 1:2)	content of the word (Jon 3:2)
response of Jonah (Jon 1:3)	response of Jonah (Jon 3:3-4a)
impending disaster (Jon 1:4)	impending disaster (Jon 3:4b)
response (Jon 1:5)	response (Jon 3:5)
avoiding disaster (Jon 1:6)	avoiding disaster (Jon 3:6-9)
sailors and Jonah (Jon 1:7-15)	Ninevites and God (Jon 3:10)
response of the sailors (Jon 1:16)	response of Jonah (Jon 4:1)
Yahweh and Jonah (Jon 2:1-11 [1:17–2:10])	Yahweh and Jonah (Jon 4:2-11)

None of these arguments is decisive, and it is speculative to reconstruct an original Jonah when we have no textual evidence for such an alternative text. However, the most helpful response is to focus on the contribution the psalm makes to the book as a whole, a matter to which Childs made a major contribution.[15] Childs notes that the introduction of the psalm means that Jonah 4 is strongly influenced by Jonah 2. In Jonah 2, Jonah

---

[14]Trible, *Rhetorical Criticism*, 107-22.
[15]Brevard S. Childs, *Introduction to the Old Testament as Scripture* (London: SCM Press, 1979), 422-26. See also G. M. Landes, "The Kerygma of the Book of Jonah," *Interpretation* 21 (1967): 3-31; Jonathan Magonet, *Form and Meaning: Studies in Literary Techniques in the Book of Jonah*, BET 2 (Frankfurt: Peter Lang, 1976), 39-54; André Lacocque and Pierre-Emmanuel Lacocque, *Jonah: A Psycho-Religious Approach to the Prophet* (Columbia: University of South Carolina Press, 1990), 94-113.

prays to God *from* the belly of the great fish. It is a prayer of thanksgiving for deliverance *already* granted because the fish was God's means of deliverance from drowning in the sea. The psalm is a "veritable catena of traditional phrases from the Psalter. Jonah prays in the stereotypical language of the psalms which every faithful Jew had always used."[16] Jonah is grateful for his deliverance and praises God for it: "Salvation comes from the LORD" (Jon 2:8 [2:9]).

In Jonah 4, Jonah again prays to Yahweh (Jon 4:2), and again he uses traditional language. However, this time Jonah's appeal to the same attributes of God involves a negative, angry response from Jonah. "Jonah is thankful for his own deliverance, but resentful of Nineveh's inclusion within the mercy which had always been restricted to Israel."[17] The prayers in Jonah 2 and Jonah 4 provide an insight into the persona of Jonah. He is portrayed as a typical Jew who shares Israel's faith; in trouble he calls to God and gives thanks for his deliverance. In this way, as Childs perceptively notes,

> The effect of the prayer from a canonical perspective is to typify Jonah! The lesson which was directed to Jonah now also serves a larger audience. The book addresses those other faithful Jews who have been set apart from the nations by the Mosaic covenant, and who were sustained by the sacred traditions of their Psalter. . . . His role has been expanded by fashioning him into a representative figure and thus establishing a link between Israel and the heathen.[18]

OUTLINE

Our outline of Jonah is as follows:

Jonah 1–2	Act 1: Rebellion
Jonah 1:1-3	Jonah's call and his response
Jonah 1:4-6	Yahweh's response to Jonah's response
Jonah 1:7–2:1 [1:7-17]	The sailors' response and Jonah's confession—Jonah overboard
Jonah 2:2-11 [2:1-10]	Jonah's psalm of thanksgiving—Jonah back on dry land

---

[16]Childs, *Introduction to the Old Testament*, 423.
[17]Childs, *Introduction to the Old Testament*, 424.
[18]Childs, *Introduction to the Old Testament*, 424-25. Note that Childs accepts that the psalm is an addition but relates this to the "canonical process" and argues that the reshaping of the original story merely extended its original point. The original story—without the psalm—stressed God's right to override his prophetic word for the sake of the whole creation.

Jonah 3–4	Act 2: Obedience
Jonah 3:1-4	Jonah recommissioned
Jonah 3:5-10	The Ninevites repent and God repents
Jonah 4:1-4	Jonah prays and Yahweh responds
Jonah 4:5-7	Jonah and the leafy plant
Jonah 4:8-11	Yahweh's concern

INTERPRETATION

And so to the narrative itself.

Jonah 1-2: Act 1—Rebellion. *Jonah 1:1-3: Jonah's call and his response.* Jonah begins with the Hebrew verb *wayhî*, which Dennis Tucker notes is a discourse marker generally indicating something following a preceding event. The verb signals "it is therefore part of the mainstream of a greater narration."[19] This is a strange way to start a book, but as the following words make clear, Jonah and his mission are indeed part of God's larger story, part of his work with Israel and his world. "The word of Yahweh came to" is typical language for God's revelation to his prophet, and a Hebrew audience would have immediately recognized that this is a story about a prophet.

Jonah 1:1 introduces us to the two main characters of Jonah: Yahweh and the prophet Jonah. We do not know how well known Jonah son of Amittai was, and the audience may have scratched their heads and consulted with the more informed listeners before they remembered that Jonah was the one who prophesied the expansion of the northern kingdom under Jeroboam II. We have no knowledge of what Jonah thought about prophesying about the extension of Israel under Jeroboam II, the same king whom Amos and Hosea castigate. Jeroboam II's reign was a time of stability, affluence, and terrible injustice.

If Jonah was aware of the prophesying of Amos and Hosea, then his role in pronouncing the extension of Israel's boundaries should have caused him to reflect on Yahweh's purposes closely. Above we suggested that Jonah may have enjoyed the fruits of his "positive" prophecy; an alternative is that his response was to doubt Yahweh's reliability in bringing about his

---

[19]Christo J. H. van der Merwe, Jackie A. Naudé, and Jan H. Kroeze, *A Biblical Hebrew Reference Grammar*, Biblical Hebrew 3 (Sheffield: Sheffield Academic Press, 1999), 331-32. Albert H. Kamp suggests that this verbal form divides Jonah up into five sections: Jonah 1:1-4a; Jonah 1:4b–2:1a; Jonah 2:1b-11b; Jonah 3:1a–4:7c; Jonah 4:8-11c. Kamp, *Inner-Worlds: A Cognitive Linguistic Approach to the Book of Jonah* (Leiden: Brill, 2004), 89-91.

promised judgment, a doubt that would be magnified and confirmed in his new mission.[20]

A Hebrew audience would be familiar with the word of Yahweh commissioning a prophet, and his command to Jonah to "Arise, Go!" would not have surprised them. Nothing, however, would have prepared them—or Jonah—for what followed: "to the great city of Nineveh and preach against it, because its wickedness has come up before me." Nahum's entire prophecy, as we will see in chapter fourteen, is directed against Nineveh, which he describes as "the city of blood, full of lies, full of plunder, never without victims" (Nah 3:1 NIV). "Nineveh's reputation as a center of savage power is reason enough for Jonah to have made out of it a paradigm for utter wickedness reprieved by utter mercy."[21] Nineveh became the capital of Assyria around 700 BC, and it was Assyria who was God's instrument to conquer the northern kingdom and to take Israel into exile in 722 BC. How, a Hebrew audience would wonder, is the prophet going to respond to this mission? Yes, Assyria was evil, but . . . to go *there* and proclaim God's judgment *there*?

Using the same verb from Jonah 1:2, "arise," Jonah 1:3 begins "and Jonah arose." Is he going to rise to this extraordinary challenge? "To flee to Tarshish away from the presence of Yahweh!" Jonah's response to the word of Yahweh is immediate, but it is immediate *rebellion*. His descent from Yahweh is marked by the repetition of the verb *to go down* (*yārad*) in Jonah 1:3 ("went down" and "went aboard"), in Jonah 1:5 ("had gone below"), and in Jonah 2:7 [2:6] ("I sank down"). Tarshish is in the diametrically opposite direction from Nineveh and a long way from Israel. "From the presence of Yahweh" occurs twice in Jonah 1:3. Some suggest that this indicates a view of Yahweh as confined geographically to Israel, but Jonah 1:9 contradicts this view. Geographically, Jonah perhaps hopes to get as far away as possible from the locale of God's presence on earth, namely, the temple (see Jon 2:4), but he may also aim at severing his part in God's covenant people.

Jonah 1:4-6: Yahweh's response to Jonah's response. Jonah is sorely mistaken if he thinks he can escape Yahweh, but he tries his hardest. Israel was not a seafaring nation, but this does not prevent Jonah from buying a ticket for the earliest departure to Tarshish. Jacques Ellul notes, "To achieve damnation he pays his passage. The story of Jonah is indeed the story of all of us. What sacrifices are we not ready to make to be far from the face of God, unable as we

---

[20]See Muldoon, *In Defense of Divine Justice*, for this view.
[21]Jack M. Sasson, *Jonah*, ABC (New Haven, CT: Yale University Press, 2007), 70.

are to accept that it is God himself who fulfills his impossible will!"[22] Humans have an appropriate creaturely degree of freedom, and Yahweh allows Jonah to flee and to find passage on the boat to Tarshish, thereby entangling his life with pagan sailors, not unlike those to whom he was sent in Nineveh.

As Jonah confesses in Jonah 1:9, Yahweh is master of sea and land, and his hurling of a great wind into the sea demonstrates his omnipotence. Jonah 1:5 introduces Jonah's unknowing companions, the sailors. Remarkably, while the sailors are desperate to come to grips with the threat to their lives, Jonah is asleep below deck. Intertextually, one is reminded of Jesus being asleep amid a comparable storm while his disciples panic. Jonah's sleep is of a different order, perhaps an exhausted collapse in the hope that he is at last on the way as far from Yahweh as he can get.[23] The sailors are not part of the covenant people, but they know that prayer, a major theme in the book, is required and call Jonah to prayer. Ellul provocatively notes of non-Christians,

> They rouse them [Christians], i.e., they make Christians see what is really going on. A remarkable thing about even the active Christian is that he never really has much more than a vague idea about reality. He is lost in the slumber of his activities, his good works, his chorales, his theology, his evangelising, his communities. He always skirts reality. He views the storm from outside. . . . The world puts God and the Christian to the test when it needs to, and this test knots the drama around Christians.[24]

Jonah 1:7–2:1 [1:7-17]: The sailors' response and Jonah's confession—Jonah overboard. The sailors assume a logic of responsibility/causality for the storm and cast lots to see who is responsible. The lot falls on Jonah, and the sailors interrogate him with five searching questions as they probe his identity. Ironically, these questions from the heathen call Jonah back to his true identity, and in his response he gets to the heart of it: "I am a Hebrew and I worship the Lord, the God of heaven, who made the sea and the dry land" (Jon 1:9 NIV).[25] The Hebrew for "worship" is *yārē'* ("fear, reverence"), and the unusual word order of object, subject, verb places the emphasis on Yahweh, literally reading, "Yahweh, the God of heaven, I fear, who made the sea and

---

[22]Jacques Ellul, *The Judgment of Jonah*, trans. Geoffrey W. Bromiley (Grand Rapids, MI: Eerdmans, 1971), 28.
[23]In Hebrew the word for "to sleep" is very similar for "to go down."
[24]Ellul, *Judgment of Jonah*, 31.
[25]The coupling of Yahweh and Elohim occurs on the model of Gen 2–3 in Jon 1:9; 2:2 [2:1]; 4:6. See J. L'Hour, "Yahweh Elohim," *Revue Biblique* 81 (1974): 524-56, on the significance of the coupling in Genesis.

the dry land." That "the sea" is mentioned first also alerts us to the fact that Jonah knows exactly what is happening, as he acknowledges in Jonah 1:12.

Jonah says he "fears" Yahweh, but the word *fear* occurs repeatedly in this section, and it is mainly a characteristic of the sailors, *not* Jonah. Fear can mean "reverential worship," but it can also mean "dread." The same expression that uses the verb *fear* twice occurs in Jonah 1:10 and in Jonah 1:16, functioning as an *inclusio*. The sailors move from fear of the sea to fear and worship of Yahweh, and they make this journey via compassion (Jon 1:13) and prayer (Jon 1:15).[26]

As Ellul notes, "The word enlists man in an adventure into which he carries all those around him."[27] "Thus the elements and many men, especially the sailors, are engaged in the adventure of Jonah and with him and because of him. One sees here the weight and seriousness of vocation."[28] Ironically, the pagan sailors, unlike Jonah, act like true Israelites, casting lots, praying, and worshiping Yahweh.

Jonah is thrown overboard, presumably to certain death (Jon 1:15). But Yahweh provides a huge fish—no mention of a whale—and he is held in this state for three days and three nights.[29] In the Old Testament the number three is significant, used slightly less only than the number seven. "An act is repeated three times to bring it to full effect" (see 1 Kings 17:21; Dan 6:10; Gen 42:17; 2 Kings 20:8).[30]

Jonah 2:2-11 [2:1-10]: Jonah's psalm of thanksgiving.[31] As he is trapped in the dark of the belly of the big fish, the three days does its work, and Jonah prays (Jon 2:2 [2:1]). Prayer and worship are a major theme in Jonah; prayer is mentioned multiple times (Jon 1:5, 6; 2:2-3 [2:1-2], 2:8 [2:7]; 3:8; 4:2). Some see this prayer of thanksgiving as misplaced in its context since Jonah is still in the belly of the fish. However, it is the fish that has been the means of salvation, and for this he gives thanks.

The prayer shifts the language of the book from prose to poetry, and it is full of typical language from the Psalter, as any study Bible will reveal.[32]

---

[26]See Jon 1:5, 10, 16. The escalating language is an example of what Magonet (*Form and Meaning*, 31-33) calls "the growing phrase."
[27]Ellul, *Judgment of Jonah*, 22.
[28]Ellul, *Judgment of Jonah*, 25.
[29]See Sasson's sane comments on historicity in this respect (*Jonah*, 150-51).
[30]Sasson, *Jonah*, 153. See also G. M. Landes, "The 'Three Days and Three Nights' Motif in Jonah 2:1," *JBL* 86 (1967): 446-50.
[31]H. Gunkel classifies it as a "Dankpsalm." Gunkel, *Ausgewählte Psalmen*, 3rd ed. (Göttingen, 1911), 289. On the structure of the prayer as one of thanksgiving see Stuart, *Hosea–Jonah*, 472-73.
[32]See Magonet, *Form and Meaning*, 44-49. Various analyses of the structure of the poem have been proposed. See, e.g., Sasson, *Jonah*, 165-67; Trible, *Rhetorical Criticism*, 157-73; Thomas M. Bolin,

However, as Jonathan Magonet says, "A close reading of the text reveals certain stylistic features which it has in common with the narrative parts of the book, and which distinguish it in significant ways from other thanksgiving psalms."[33] Magonet notes of Jonah 2:6-7 [2:5-6],

> Now the language becomes totally unfamiliar, and as it progresses an oppressive feeling of claustrophobia, of utter helplessness, grows and closes in upon the speaker: the reeds wrap about his head, he sinks down and down to the bottom of the mountains, the earth, like bars, closes over him. And at the moment of greatest darkness and despair, when no human action can release him, God breaks through all these suffocating layers, and draws his life out to safety. And then only does he respond, almost as a disembodied soul, without his human arrogance, utterly dependent upon, and secondary to, God.[34]

Intriguingly, Jonah's *descent* marks his spiritual *ascent* as he moves from hoping to look again toward the temple (Jon 2:5 [2:4]) to remembering Yahweh and having his prayer rise to the temple (Jon 2:8 [2:7]).[35] Jonah 2:7 [2:6] is the center around which the psalm turns. The two verbs, *yāradtî* ("I went down"; NIV, "sank down") and *watta ʿal* ("you brought up"), capture Jonah's movement of descent and ascent, both literal and spiritual. The cause of this redemption is entirely the act of Yahweh, as we see in Jonah 2:7c [2:6c]: "But you, LORD [Yahweh] *my* God, brought my life up from the pit." The mention of sacrifice and vows (Jon 2:10 [2:9]) parallels the sailors' action in Jonah 1:16.

Finally, in Jonah 2:11 [2:10] Jonah is returned to dry land. He has literally and metaphorically been taken through a dark night of the soul, and his prayer indicates a reawakening to Yahweh, but intriguingly there is no mention of his willingness to carry out his mission or repentance of his rebellion. It remains to be seen how deep the work in his life has been.

Jonah 3–4: Act 2—Obedience. *Jonah 3:1-4: Jonah recommissioned.* Jonah 3:1-2 repeats Jonah's commission with the intensification of "a second time." One can imagine the audience listening with bated breath to see what Jonah's response will be *this* time. Jonah 3:3 begins in the Hebrew "And he arose"

Freedom Beyond Forgiveness: The Book of Jonah Re-examined, JSOTSup 236 (Sheffield: Sheffield Academic Press, 1997), 97-120; etc.
[33]Magonet, *Form and Meaning*, 40.
[34]Magonet, *Form and Meaning*, 51.
[35]See Magonet, *Form and Meaning*, 40.

(Jon 3:3a; see Jon 1:3) "and he went to Nineveh."³⁶ Jonah 3:3 stresses the size of Nineveh, a motif that will recur in Jonah 4:11. Intriguingly, in the Hebrew it says, "Nineveh was a large city *lē ʾlōhîm*." Literally, *lē ʾlōhîm* means "to the gods" or "to God." Several interpretive possibilities present themselves: *lē ʾlōhîm* could turn the phrase into a superlative meaning "an exceedingly great city"; mean "to the gods," speaking of the religious nature of Nineveh; or mean "to God," stressing that Nineveh belongs to God and is important to him.

Perhaps the narrator intends there to be some ambiguity in this expression, with elements of all three meanings in play. By Jonah 4:11 it will become clear that Nineveh matters to God and why. That Nineveh "took three days to go through it" (Jon 3:3) has generated much discussion, with some suggesting it is an anachronistic description or betrays lack of knowledge of the smaller size of Nineveh. At its height Nineveh was three miles on its widest axis, about eight miles in circumference, and occupied approximately 1,850 acres. Jack Sasson rightly remarks, "'Three-days' merely establishes that a large space separates two positions."³⁷ It also sets up a contrast with the "one day" of Jonah 3:4: "The contrast in number means to sharpen our perception of a prophet who is very much in a hurry to do what God asks of him, whether earnestly or enthusiastically or just to get it over with."³⁸ Early in his ministry he "cries out" (see Jon 1:2; 3:2) to the Ninevites the bad news: "Forty more days and Nineveh will be overthrown" (Jon 3:4 NIV). Jonah clearly understands *nehpāket* as "turned" in the sense of "overthrown." It is possible, however, that the meaning is deliberately ambiguous, with "turned" in the sense of repenting also a possibility.³⁹

Jonah 3:5-10: The Ninevites repent, and God repents. For listeners to the story, this is a poignant moment. How will the Ninevites respond? Will Jonah survive? The response is a model of submission and obedience, unlike that of Jeroboam II and of Jonah but akin to the sailors. The king leads as he should; he repents and decrees that the whole of Nineveh should do the same. People *and animals* are called to a fast, and all are covered in sackcloth. The motif of animals being covered in sackcloth is evidence for some that this is a legendary tale; Sasson, however, comments, "That animals should

---

³⁶Jonah 1:3 includes an infinitive, "to flee." Here consecutive imperfects are strung together to emphasize his obedience. See Sasson, *Jonah*, 227.
³⁷Sasson, *Jonah*, 230-31.
³⁸Sasson (*Jonah*, 224) translates, "Hardly had Jonah gone into town a day's journey when he called out . . ."
³⁹Sasson, *Jonah*, 236, 233-34.

be clothed in sackcloth is itself not an absurdist touch."⁴⁰ Even today it is not uncommon for animals to be dressed up for important ceremonies. God's (Elohim's) *call* has been heard through Jonah, and now the people are to *call*—the same verb—urgently on God (Elohim) and to repent. Certainly the king has also understood *nehpāket* as "overthrown."

The king raises the possibility of God repenting (*nāḥam*), and this is indeed what he does in Jonah 3:10.⁴¹

Jonah 4:1-4: Jonah prays, and Yahweh responds. If the Ninevites are thankful Jonah is not! "Seemed very wrong" (Jon 4:1) is *wayēraʿ*, meaning "it was evil," and in Hebrew the sentence literally reads "And it was evil to Jonah, a great evil." The narrative thus "continues to feature *rāʿâ*, which, once removed from Nineveh, comes to lodge in Jonah himself."⁴² Jonah prays "to Yahweh," not "Yahweh, my God," as in Jonah 2:6, and he explains that he fled to Tarshish from being "at home" because he knew this is what God would do and his flight was an attempt to compel God to execute judgment. "Isn't this what I said LORD when I was at home" is intertextually related to Exodus 14:12, "Didn't we say to you in Egypt . . ." "Take away my life" (see Jon 4:8, 9) and evokes 1 Kings 19:4, where Elijah, having fled from Jezebel, despairs. "The effect is to set up a series of very powerful 'echoes' in which each text interacts with the other, and both react within the 'Jonah' context itself. . . . However, it is difficult to see how far the author of 'Jonah' intended the ripple of his associations to spread."⁴³

The dark night in the belly of the big fish has not done its work deeply enough, and Jonah verges on blasphemy here, calling God's compassion evil. "At home" is *ʾadmātî*, whereas in Jonah 1:8 the word for "country" is *ʾereṣ*. This creates a link with "people" (*ʾādām*) in Jonah 4:11. Ironically, Jonah quotes from Exodus 34:6-7, where Yahweh reveals himself to Moses after graciously restoring Israel after the golden calf incident.⁴⁴ Significantly, Jonah does not refer to Exodus 34:7, which stresses that Yahweh's patience is not endless. Thus Jonah cites an ancient and well-known creed listing Yahweh's attributes, first found in Exodus 34:6 and also in Numbers 14:18;

---

⁴⁰Sasson, *Jonah*, 257.
⁴¹See Joel 2:14 and see our comments in chapter 3.
⁴²Sasson, *Jonah*, 272.
⁴³Magonet, *Form and Meaning*, 75-76.
⁴⁴See Joel 2:13. On Joel and Jonah see Magonet, *Form and Meaning*, 77-79. On Ex 34:6-7, see Muldoon, *In Defense of Divine Justice*, 103-12. Muldoon refers to Ex 34:6-7 as the DAF, the Divine Attribute Formula.

Psalm 86:15; 103:8; 145:8; Nahum 1:3; Nehemiah 9:17; and, of course, Joel 2:13, but uses it to indict Yahweh. His retrospective justification of his rebellion also casts him in the best possible light, albeit perversely. In Jonah 4:2 the Hebrew reads literally, "Was this not *my word*" (*dəbārî*), whereas it was the word (*dābār*) of Yahweh that commissioned him.

Yahweh's response to Job is framed with two questions (Jon 4:4, 9). There is no answer recorded to Yahweh's first question.

Jonah 4:5-7: Jonah and the leafy plant. Instead, Jonah goes outside the city, finds some shade, and waits to see what will happen to the city. NIV translates "had gone out," which is possible but not necessary. The verb can also be translated simply as "went." His action is better seen as following the first question; presumably he is waiting to see whether God will come around to *his* way of seeing things.

Jonah 4:8-11: Yahweh's concern. Through Jonah's experience of and care for the leafy plant, Yahweh repeats the question to Jonah with the addition of "the plant" (Jon 4:9). Jonah's response is the same as in Jonah 1:3.

Jonah concludes with a lesson from the plant and a question. Jonah 4:11 is an extraordinary evocation of Yahweh's compassion. There is much discussion about the meaning of "cannot tell their right hand from their left." Sasson suggests that it means that Nineveh is so full of life that the Ninevites cannot tell who their neighbors are.[45] We suggest that it is a metaphor that evokes the darkness in which they live without the light of Yahweh and his *tôrâ*, such a deep darkness that they are disoriented to the extent that they cannot even discern which is which hand, as it were.

Most intriguing are the final two words of the book, which Sasson translates "and animals galore."[46] In the history of interpretation, many proposals have been made in relation to what this means. However, in our view it means what it says; God is profoundly concerned about the whole of life in Nineveh, since it is all his creation. Jonah was depressed about the death of his shade-giving plant. God's concern extends to the whole of his creation.

As a novel or film script, Jonah would never do, for we never hear how he responds to Yahweh's searching question. What must our audience have thought? By now they would surely have realized that Jonah is . . . themselves, namely, Israel. As becomes apparent especially in Jonah 4, they are the ones who have benefited again and again from Yahweh's compassion.

---

[45]Sasson, *Jonah*, 315.
[46]Sasson, *Jonah*, 300.

When early Israel committed idolatry with the golden calf, God forgave them and restored the covenant despite it literally having been shattered. In so many ways they have acted as God's enemy, and yet he has been endlessly gracious; how then could they not be gracious to their own enemies?

The Theology of Jonah

It will be apparent from our journey through Jonah that the book is a veritable mine of theology. There is so much to learn from the book, and we confine ourselves here to some of the major themes.

God. The central character in Jonah is Yahweh. He has the first word and the last. The first is a commission, the last a question. This is no deist view of God but one of a sovereign, transcendent God—he commands the sea and its creatures—but not a God far off. He is intimately involved with his creation and his people, highly personal, and as capable of posing questions as giving commands.

As we will note below, Jonah above all evokes the patience of God but never at the expense of his justice. Karl Barth rightly says, "God does not renounce His government when He exercises patience."[47] An important insight into their mutuality is that God's love and patience are *not* unconditional, contrary to much of what Western Christianity tells us today. He is just and holy and cannot tolerate sin, and his love and patience *create the space for repentance*, not for endless, sustained rebellion. As noted earlier, in this respect Jonah is an important complement to Amos, Joel, and Obadiah. As we will see with Nahum, Nineveh *was* eventually destroyed. God's sending Jonah to Nineveh is not a sign that he has abdicated his holiness and justice; rather, the very sending of a prophet implies the possibility of repentance.

Barth says of God's patience,

> We define God's patience as His will, deep-rooted in His essence and constituting His divine being and action, to allow to another—for the sake of His own grace and mercy and in the affirmation of His holiness and justice—space and time for the development of its own existence, thus conceding to this existence a reality side by side with His own, and fulfilling His will towards this other in such a way that He does not suspend and destroy it as this other but accompanies and sustains it and allows it to develop in freedom.[48]

---

[47] *CD* II/1:414.
[48] *CD* II/1:409-10.

Barth rightly notes that God's patience is central to the message of Jonah. Intriguingly, Barth finds the "decisive moment of the biblical testimony to God's patience" in Hebrews 1:3, according to which God sustains all things by his powerful word. This holding of creation in existence against the background of human rebellion and repentance cannot depend ultimately on our action but on God's patience. "The abyss in the heart of God is so deep that in it the other, the reality distinct from God, can be contained in all its wretchedness."[49]

Barth is perceptive and right in connecting God's patience to the doctrine of creation. This connection is affirmed in Jonah, with the king of Nineveh calling all of Nineveh, including the animals, to fast and repent and in God's final question, in which he articulates his concern for humans and animals.

Needless to say, Jonah is a powerful call for God's people to be like God, holy *and* compassionate. As we know in practice, these characteristics are not antithetical, although they are too often wrenched apart in contemporary culture. Compassion is often so prized today that is gets elevated above God's order for his creation and thereby denatured. And in some church circles a brand of orthodoxy is upheld that affirms the doctrine of grace but manifests no grace interpersonally. God's patience creates the space for the other, and so should ours (see 1 Pet 3:15, "with gentleness and respect"). This, indeed, is at the heart of a healthy societal pluralism, working to create the space for difference without affirming the direction much difference takes. Thus, in our view, for example, Christians should be deeply concerned for the rights of Muslims in Western culture—and for the rights of Christians and others in Muslim societies—without this meaning that we affirm Islam as on a par with Christianity, which we do not. God's patience is the context within which the space was created for us to find our way home to God, and we ought similarly to protect and create such space for others. God's patience is the space for and of mission. Part of the message of Jonah is that pagans sometimes manifest Christian virtues where Christians do not.[50] Jonah calls us to display integrity—wholeness—in our beliefs and praxis.

Spirituality. In the following chapter we will focus on the psalm in Jonah 2 and on the spiritual theology of Jonah. Suffice it here to note that, like Job

---

[49]*CD* II/1:413-14, 416, 411.
[50]Jonah certainly bears on the relationship between Christianity and other religions, as does Amos 9:7.

and so much of the Old Testament, this is a book about transformation at the deepest level so that we become like God. Ellul perceptively notes of Jonah, "Throughout his adventure he is alone."[51] Yet his aloneness has implications for so many. As with the patriarchs in Genesis 12–50, if Jonah is to bear God's promise and his word, then he must become like that promise and word. He must undergo transformation; he must enter the dark night of the soul, where his deepest issues are dealt with. The mission entrusted to Jonah was his worst nightmare come true precisely because it touched those parts of his life that most needed transformation. So it often is with the dark night. If Jonah was "published" during the exile, one can only imagine what it felt like to listen to this story. The exile was for the Israelites the equivalent of Jonah's descent, in which it must have seemed as though God had completely abandoned them.

Saint John of the Cross argues that in the dark night God's light is so present that it seems to us like utter darkness, just how it would have seemed to Jonah in the dark belly of the fish. We do not know how Jonah eventually responded to God's penetrating question in Jonah 4:11. It does not matter. What is crucial is that the dark night invites *us* into a deeper, transforming experience of God. We can respond to suffering and the radically unexpected like Jonah, or we can listen for God's question in our struggle and seek the grace to embrace what comes our way and so to become more like God and the message we carry.

Mission. Jonah *is* an extraordinary Old Testament anticipation of New Testament mission.[52] It ties in closely with Israel's vocation to be a royal priesthood, a sign to the nations of what life under God's reign should look like (see Gen 12:1-3; Ex 19:4-6). In his *Transforming Mission*, great missiologist David Bosch has, alas, little to say about the Old Testament and mission and dismisses Jonah in this respect: "Even the book Jonah has nothing to do with mission in the normal sense of the word. The prophet is sent to Nineveh not to proclaim salvation to non-believers but to announce doom. Neither is he himself interested in mission; he is only interested in destruction."[53]

---

[51]Ellul, *Judgment of Jonah*, 22.
[52]See Stephen B. Chapman and Laceye C. Warner, "Jonah and the Imitation of God: Rethinking Evangelism in the Old Testament," *JTI* 2, no. 1 (2008): 43-69.
[53]David Bosch, *Transforming Mission: Paradigm Shifts in Theology of Mission* (New York: Orbis, 1991), 17.

Proclamation of judgment is, however, part of mission, and while Jonah may only be interested in destruction, Yahweh is not. Indeed, far more helpful are Bosch's earlier comments on Jonah in his *Witness to the World*.[54] Bosch's comments come in chapter six, where he deals with the first element of a biblical foundation for mission, namely, *God's compassion*. Bosch notes that Jonah is "a matchless object lesson of Yahweh's compassion." He rightly asserts, "The concern of the book is rather with Jonah himself—a 'missionary' without a missionary's heart—and through Jonah with Israel." Jonah is "a call to Israel to allow themselves to be converted to a compassion comparable to that of Yahweh. . . . a compassion that knows no boundaries." Jonah becomes so angry "for no other reason than that God is treating those outside his covenant the same as he is those within."[55]

JONAH AND THE NEW TESTAMENT

Jonah is most clearly connected to the New Testament through Jesus' comments in Matthew 12:38-42; 16:4; and Luke 11:29-32, that no other sign will be given to "this generation" than that of Jonah. As Jonah was in the belly of the big fish three days and three nights, so the Son of Man will be three days and three nights in the heart of the earth. The Ninevites and the Queen of the South will arise and condemn "this generation" because something greater than Jonah and Solomon is present. Jesus' use of Jonah clearly connects with the theme of judgment. The Pharisees ask for a sign (Mt 12:38), but as with the Ninevites, no other sign will be given than the life, death, and preaching of Jesus.

However, contained within Jesus' teaching are major clues as to what his life is all about. The "Son of Man" title evokes the Son of Man in Daniel 7, who is given sovereignty over all the nations. But this Son of Man will descend into the belly of the earth. As the Apostles' Creed puts it: he "descended into hell." There has been much theological ink spilled over this phrase in the creed, and perhaps Jonah can help us to understand it. Jonah's descent, as we have seen, is to a point of complete and utter abandonment and separation from God. It is such agony that Jesus will take on himself in his death. But he is "something more than Jonah," and through his resurrection he will break the hold of death and usher in the new creation. Even

---

[54]David Bosch, *Witness to the World: The Christian Mission in Theological Perspective* (Louisville, KY: Westminster John Knox, 1980).
[55]Bosch, *Witness to the World*, 53.

in his anger with the Pharisees, he evokes the sign that is available to them also for redemption.

As we note at several other places in this book, the Old Testament–New Testament relationship should not be confined to quotations. A broader view of intertextuality is required. If in the direct references to Jonah Jesus evokes the theme of judgment, then it is in his weeping over Jerusalem that we witness his compassion. Especially in the Johannine version of the Great Commission, "As the father has sent me, so I send you," we hear the strong echoes of Jonah 4:11.

Recommended Reading

Allen, Leslie C. *The Books of Joel, Obadiah, Jonah and Micah*. NICOT. Grand Rapids, MI: Eerdmans, 1976.

Barth, Karl. *Church Dogmatics*. Edited and translated by Thomas S. Torrance and Geoffrey Bromiley. Edinburgh: T&T Clark, 1936–1969. II/1:406-39.

Chapman, Stephen B., and Laceye C. Warner. "Jonah and the Imitation of God: Rethinking Evangelism in the Old Testament." *JTI* 2, no. 1 (2008): 43-69.*

Craig, Kenneth M. *A Poetics of Jonah: Art in the Service of Ideology*. Macon, GA: Mercer University Press, 1999.

Walton, John H. "Jonah, Book of." In *Dictionary for Theological Interpretation of the Bible*, ed. Kevin J. Vanhoozer et al., 401-4. Grand Rapids, MI: Eerdmans, 2005.*

Recommended reading marked with a "" indicates introductory works.*

11

Spiritual Formation

JONAH AND HIS CANTICLE: JONAH 2:3-10 [2:2-9]

The story of Jonah is not only a religious manifesto; it is also a psychological tableau of the human condition. Jonah . . . is human, he is everyone. . . . Jonah qua *human, exemplifies our call to task. He is also a paradigm of our resistance.*

ANDRÉ LACOCQUE AND PIERRE-EMMANUEL LACOCQUE, *JONAH: A PSYCHO-RELIGIOUS APPROACH TO THE PROPHET*

IN HIS BOOK OF POEMS ON JONAH, Thomas Carlisle makes the point that one can be so obsessed with what is going on inside the "whale" that one can miss the drama taking place inside Jonah.[1] By slowing the narrative down and through the shift from prose to poetry, to say nothing of the content, Jonah 2 prevents us from doing this. Jonah is confined to the belly of the fish, and our attention is confined to Jonah. Jonah is compelled to face up to his situation, and we are granted a glimpse into his inner life. Poetry is peculiarly suited to evoking the richness of experience, and it does that here. Jonah 2 "allows us to follow Jonah's movement from numbness to meaningfulness. Integral to this movement, paradoxically, is the deliberate suspension of the plot. At last Jonah takes time to reflect upon his existence."[2] And so must we. Jonah is about many things, as befits its genre, but it is certainly about spiritual formation, as we will see.

---

[1] Thomas Carlisle, *You! Jonah!* (Grand Rapids, MI: Eerdmans, 1968).
[2] André Lacocque and Pierre-Emmanuel Lacocque, *Jonah: A Psycho-religious Approach to the Prophet* (Columbia: University of South Carolina Press, 1990), 96.

Jonah 1

The formation of Jonah begins in Jonah 1:1, when the word of Yahweh comes to him. "Particular in its recipient, the vocation is universal in its structure and implications."[3] In order to see this connection between God's call to Jonah and its universal implications, one needs to note the theological connection between the particularity of the word of Yahweh coming to Jonah—or to any prophet—and the word of God in creation. It is *through* his word that creation is called into existence (Gen 1:1–2:3), and it is *by* his word that Adam and Eve are addressed. André Lacocque and Pierre-Emmanuel Lacocque perceptively note that the command of Genesis 1:28 is properly an *order-benediction*.[4] Because the order of creation is God's good handiwork, commandment is not alien to being human but its very possibility. Thus God's command to Jonah—for that is what it is—is simultaneously *an invitation* to go beyond, to escape the crowd and to become more fully himself; ultimately it is a call not for a divorce from society but to deep formation so that one can make a true contribution to society, as we will see.[5]

Such a call means that whatever happens, life will never be the same again. We see this in Jonah making no attempt simply to remain in Israel; something must now give, and he resists the formation to which he is invited by fleeing to anonymity in Tarshish. Ironically, his fleeing demonstrates just how relevant is *this* call to his formation; it touches something very deep within him. Carl Jung writes, "We are susceptible only to those suggestions with which we are secretly in accord."[6] This secret is, however, buried deep within Jonah, and it is time for it to surface and find expression. But that will be no easy task.

Such resistance to deep change has been noted by many psychologists. Frank Manual was the first to label this resistance the "Jonah syndrome," although we owe its development to Abraham Maslow.[7] Jung similarly refers to it as the "Jonah-and-the-Whale" complex.[8] The Jonah complex is the attempt to run away from social responsibilities and growth. It involves

---

[3] Lacocque and Lacocque, *Jonah: A Psycho-religious Approach*, 173.
[4] Lacocque and Lacocque, *Jonah: A Psycho-religious Approach*, 190.
[5] Lacocque and Lacocque, *Jonah: A Psycho-religious Approach*, 69.
[6] Carl G. Jung, *Modern Man in Search of a Soul* (New York: Harcourt, Brace & World, 1933), 65.
[7] Abraham H. Maslow, "Neurosis as a Failure of Personal Growth," *Humanitas* 3 (1967): 153-6.9
[8] Carl G. Jung, *Symbols of Transformation* (New York: Pantheon, 1967), 419. See also Robert Assagioli, *The Act of Will* (Baltimore: Penguin, 1973), 112-13.

the fear of being different, alone, and of losing control.[9] Ironically, it is pervasive in Western "individualism," as many psychologists have noted.[10]

Jonah understandably "feels threatened by an appeal that singles him out so completely that it makes him a being of exception in the world."[11] Lacocque and Lacocque relate this to the human vocation: "*The Hebrew Scripture posits that human vocation involves a certain quality of life, a becoming that brings humans to be themselves by means of an ongoing dialogue with the source of life, namely, God.*"[12] This is a profound insight, entirely in tune with Hans Rookmaaker's question, "Why does God save us?" and his penetrating answer, "To make us fully human!" Or as Irenaeus poignantly puts it, "The glory of God is the human person fully alive." Creation is the very stuff of redemption, and thus salvation or becoming part of God's covenant people is not about religious practices unrelated to creation but about the recovery of God's purposes for his creation and for us as his creatures in the *imago Dei*.

Being a prophet or a minister or a Christian *does not* exempt one from this vocation; on the contrary, it places us before the face of God, which is precisely where such work begins. Theologically our word for this is *sanctification*, "becoming holy," which rightly understood involves becoming whole. This needs to be said because there is a widespread tendency nowadays to see and embrace religion as a means of avoiding such formation. As we see with Jonah, when God gets to work things become messy, and such mess is the last thing many churches or Christian institutions want nowadays. Jonah, at least, sees the need to escape from the cultus as quickly as possible if he is to avoid God's "madness." We, however, have a tendency to wrap ourselves in the cultus of ritual and religious practice lest God should actually get to work. Externally and internally the pressure is on clergy and Christians to have it all together, as though conversion delivered the whole person in one fell swoop. Tragically, we would easily see someone like Jonah as burned out and certainly unemployable. Fortunately Yahweh sees him very differently.[13] Jerome rightly speaks in Yahweh's voice when he notes,

---

[9]See André Lacocque and Pierre-Emmanuel Lacocque, *The Jonah Complex* (Atlanta: John Knox, 1981).
[10]Lacocque and Lacocque, *Jonah: A Psycho-religious Approach*, 197.
[11]Lacocque and Lacocque, *Jonah: A Psycho-religious Approach*, 73.
[12]Lacocque and Lacocque, *Jonah: A Psycho-religious Approach*, 74, emphasis original.
[13]Eugene Peterson has written some of the best material on spirituality today, certainly within the Reformed tradition. In his *Under the Unpredictable Plant: An Exploration in Vocational Holiness* (Grand Rapids, MI: Eerdmans, 1992), he tells of a crisis in his life as a pastor and how he found Jonah a major resource for his journey.

"Jonah, that headstrong prophet, once fled from me, but in the depths of the sea he was still mine."[14]

The reader may rightly wonder how widely one can legitimately extrapolate from Jonah's experience. It is, after all, unique in so many ways. However, what is intensely personal is often most universal. In the history of Christian spirituality, to say nothing of the Scriptures, it is commonly recognized that deep formation involves a crisis of some sort or another. We see this, for example, with Abraham (Gen 22) and the patriarchs, including Joseph, with Job and Qohelet, as Craig Bartholomew has noted elsewhere, with Elijah, with Jeremiah and Hosea, with Jesus in the wilderness being tempted, with Paul, and with the saints down through the centuries.[15] Saint John of the Cross coined the expression "the dark night of the soul" for such deeply transformative experiences and refers to Jonah as an example. He, too, notes how strong the temptation is to avoid them. As we stated in the previous chapter, Saint John of the Cross perceptively notes that amid the dark night God's light is so intense that it appears to the person undergoing the experience as though all is utter darkness. Certainly this was the case with Jonah.

There is a storm brewing within Jonah, and events progress to mirror that internal storm. Jonah desperately seeks to get away from God's cultic presence, but God pursues him like the hound of heaven. Jonah descends *and* descends until he is asleep amid the bottom of the boat amid the storm; this is not a sleep of peace but of depression and despair. He has turned against himself and into himself, as we tend to do when things get really out of control.

Psychologists tend to read Jonah symbolically and see the waters, the great fish, and its belly as symbols of disintegration and inner transformation. The belly of the fish is seen as a uterus, which will enable rebirth. Thus Lacocque and Lacocque note that whereas "fish" in Hebrew is normally

---

[14]Jerome, *Letter* 29.3, in *The Principal Works of St. Jerome*, trans. W. H. Fremantle, G. Lewis, and W. G. Martley, Nicene and Post-Nicene Fathers, Series 2 (Grand Rapids, MI: Eerdmans, n.d.), 51.

[15]Craig G. Bartholomew, *Ecclesiastes*, BCOTWP (Grand Rapids, MI: Baker Academic, 2009); Bartholomew, "Hearing the Old Testament Wisdom Literature: The Wit of Many and the Wisdom of One," in *Hearing the Old Testament: Listening for God's Address*, ed. Craig Bartholomew and David J. H. Beldman (Grand Rapids, MI: Eerdmans, 2012), 302-31. For example, there are some remarkable parallels between Jeremiah and Jonah. See, e.g., Jer 51:34, 44. Also, central to the temptations of Jesus is the possibility of avoiding the cross. Thereby Jesus' vocation is strongly focused. Furthermore, Peterson (*Under the Unpredictable Plant*) draws a parallel between the shipwreck Paul experienced and Jonah. Finally, for more recent examples, see, e.g., Mother Teresa's diaries, published after her death.

masculine, in Jonah 2:2 [2:1] it is feminine. However we interpret these elements of the story, we must note just how bad things get before the process of change begins. God will take Jonah to hell, and there precisely is God waiting for him.[16]

Lacocque and Lacocque rightly say that the real issue is Jonah's unwillingness to perform his priestly role in the world. As we see with the storm and the sailors, his failure in this respect endangers the whole world, as it does with us. Fyodor Dostoevsky perceptively notes, "We are all responsible for all."[17] Ironically, Yahweh uses his disobedient prophet to bring the pagan sailors to worship him, a foretaste perhaps of what awaits in Nineveh.

Things go from bad to worse for Jonah, and he is tossed into the sea, where all control is surrendered. It is at this moment that the stage is set for his "conversion." Without Jonah 2, the story would be entirely different, and it is this chapter that provides profound insight into his—and our—spiritual formation.[18]

Jonah 2: A Canticle of Thanksgiving

In Jonah 2:3 [2:2] there is a shift from prose to poetry. Recent decades have witnessed extensive work on the nature of Hebrew poetry, and there is considerable disagreement, not least in relation to how Jonah 2 functions as poetry.[19] The best recent work on Hebrew poetry is that by Benjamin Hrushovski.[20] Hrushovski affirms the centrality of parallelism to Hebrew poetry but argues rightly that parallelism is more than semantic; it is also grammatical and phonological, and these different forms of parallelism overlap and interact. Poetry cannot be determined by exact rules since it is common throughout diverse cultures for poets to bend the rules.

Kenneth Craig subjects Jonah 2 to this sort of analysis and concludes that it is indeed poetry and contains all three types of parallelism. Craig

---

[16]Lacocque and Lacocque, *Jonah: A Psycho-religious Approach*, 76-80.
[17]Quoted in *Jonah: A Psycho-religious Approach*, 86.
[18]See Lacocque and Lacocque, *Jonah: A Psycho-religious Approach*, 96-97.
[19]As Kenneth Craig demonstrates through an examination of the views of Jerome T. Walsh, Duane L. Christensen, and Frank M. Cross. See Kenneth M. Craig, *A Poetics of Jonah: Art in the Service of Ideology* (Macon, GA: Mercer University Press, 1999), 113-16. Thomas M. Bolin argues, "What is patently evident among the many attempts to delineate a structure to Jonah's psalm is that no two offering are alike, which justifies the suspicion that there is no recoverable structure to be found." Bolin, *Freedom Beyond Forgiveness: The Book of Jonah Re-Examined*, JSOTSup 236 (Sheffield: Sheffield Academic Press, 1997), 105. *Justifies* is a strong word but not logical. A variety of approaches may just mean that some or one is right and others are not.
[20]"Prosody, Hebrew," in *Encyclopedia Judaica*, ed. Cecil Roth (Jerusalem: Keter, 1971), 13:1195-1203.

concludes his foray into the parallelism of Jonah 2 by writing, "The weight of these isolated examples of parallelisms indicates that the poet uses grammar as a whole, morphology and syntax, to convey meaning and images which are particularly relevant to the action which is narrated in chapter 1."[21] Poetry and narrative are not by any means antithetical, and there is a strong narrative dimension to Jonah's canticle, including an important role played by dialogue. We translate Jonah 2 as follows:

And he [Jonah] said:	
In my trouble I called to Yahweh,	A
and he answered me.	
From the belly of Sheol I called for help;	B
you heard my voice.	
You cast me into the depths,	C
into the heart of the waters,	
and a current *enveloped* me	
and your waves and billows swept over me.	
And I said, "I have been banished from before your eyes.[22]	D
Surely,[23] I will again look to your *holy temple.*"	
Water surrounded me up to my neck,	E
the deep *enveloped* me,	
seaweed was wrapped around my head.	
To the base of the mountains I went down,	
The bars of the netherworld shut behind me forever.	
But you brought me up from the grave alive,	F
Yahweh my God.	
As I was losing consciousness I remembered Yahweh.	E'
And my prayer reached you at your *holy temple*.	D'
Those who hold to vain emptiness abandon their loyalty.	C'
But I with a voice of thanksgiving will sacrifice to you	B'
That which I have vowed I will carry out.	
Salvation belongs to Yahweh.	A'

---

[21]Craig, *Poetics of Jonah*, 123.

[22]This idiom is common in the OT, referring either to God's vigilance with respect to humankind or to being good or bad in the sight of God (Jack M. Sasson, *Jonah*, ABC [New Haven, CT: Yale University Press, 2007], 178). The latter meaning is in operation here; see Ps 34:16-17.

[23]The demonstrative *'ak* is capable of three meanings: a temporal one ("just as"), an emphatic one ("surely"), and an adversative one ("nevertheless"). See BDB, 36. One's grasp of the context will determine the meaning assigned.

Jonah's canticle is a prayer of thanksgiving.[24] As he is trapped in the dark of the belly of the big fish, the three days does its work, and Jonah prays (Jon 2:2 [2:1]). The fish has been the means of salvation, and for this he gives thanks, hence the use of the past tense. Various literary analyses have been made of the canticle; our approach will be to follow it through and then to reflect on the literary structure, bearing in mind Phyllis Trible's perceptive comment about form and content being inseparable.[25]

In terms of narrative, the canticle starts in Jonah 2:3 with a summary of Jonah's experience. He was "in trouble" and descended to the "belly of Sheol," the place of the dead and departed, when he called to Yahweh and was answered. The final cry in Jonah 2:10 [2:9] summarizes this summary: "Salvation belongs to Yahweh," and thus the two function as an *inclusio*. The canticle is about Yahweh's saving of Jonah. It is not uncommon in Hebrew oral/literary narrative for the plot to be declared early on and then unpacked, as here.[26]

Jonah 2:4 looks back to when Jonah was thrown overboard and enveloped by the waves. The sailors threw him overboard, but now he declares to Yahweh, "*You* cast me into the depths." The reflective space created by his confinement enables Jonah to reinterpret what has happened to him and to find the meaning in it. The experience offers him a transfigured existence; as with the transfiguration, it is the same existence, but now endowed with meaning. Whereas Jonah slept in the boat, now he is conscious and attentive in the darkness. Jonah 2:4-5 [2:3-4], ironically, marks the start of Jonah's spiritual ascent. He addresses Yahweh directly for the first time, thereby evoking the I-Thou relationship that is at the heart of being human. He acknowledges that Yahweh is in control and that rather than it simply being his choice to flee, it is Yahweh who has banished him from his presence.

Jonah 2:5b [2:4b] is notoriously difficult to translate. We translate *'ak* as "Surely" in order to evoke the turmoil of his experience. Jonah's experience at this point is one of disintegration before there can be

---

[24]See Jon 2:10 [2:9], "I with a voice of *thanksgiving*. . . ." H. Gunkel classifies the prayer as a *Dankpsalm*. Gunkel, *Ausgewählte Psalmen*, 3rd ed. (Göttingen, 1911), 289. On its structure as one of thanksgiving see Douglas Stuart, *Hosea–Jonah*, WBC 31 (Nashville: Nelson, 1987), 472-73.

[25]Various analyses of the structure of the poem have been proposed. See, e.g., Sasson, *Jonah*, 165-67; Phyllis Trible, *Rhetorical Criticism: Context, Method, and the Book of Jonah*, Old Testament Series (Minneapolis: Fortress, 1994), 157-73; Bolin, *Freedom Beyond Forgiveness*, 97-120; etc.

[26]See Craig G. Bartholomew, *Introducing Biblical Hermeneutics: A Comprehensive Framework for Hearing God in Scripture* (Grand Rapids, MI: Baker Academic, 2015), 487-88.

reintegration, and despair—"I have been banished"—and hope are juxtaposed in high tension. At this stage, it would appear that the very best he can hope for is that he will one day somehow look on the temple in Jerusalem once again. Jonah 2:6-7a [2:5-6a] describes his further descent. Various metaphors evoke his drowning and certain, imminent death. As is evident from our translation, the parallelism evokes the terrifying and intensifying descent of Jonah.

Jonah 2:7c [2:6c] marks the turning point of the canticle. His ascent, both literal and spiritual, is the result of Yahweh's gracious intervention and is likened to resurrection. Its correlate inside Jonah is found in Jonah 2:8 [2:7]: he remembered Yahweh and the prayer *contained in* such remembrance reached Yahweh at his holy temple.[27]

Jonah 2:9 [2:8] is intriguing. Jonah compares himself with those who abandon loyalty. Has he not done precisely this? There can be no doubt that Jonah has indeed undergone a profound transformation, but Jonah 2:9 [2:8] raises the question of just how profound the transformation actually is. Jonah 4 will accentuate this doubt.

The prayer is full of typical language from the Psalter, but this language is contextualized in terms of Jonah's experience.[28] For example, the stages of descent in his experience are "described with almost 'geographical' exactitude: at first the 'flood,' the breakers and waves pass over him; he descends further to the base of the mountains till the very earth closes over him. Every other such description in the Psalter consists only of a series of synonymous phrases, any of which are interchangeable, but no other consecutive descent is described."[29]

The repetition of *sābab*, translated as "enveloped" in Jonah 2:4 [2:3], 2:6 [2:5], and of "the temple" in Jonah 2:5 [2:4], 2:8 [2:7] mark this descent. He moves downward from being surrounded by the seas (Jon 2:4 [2:3]) to being surrounded by the deep (Jon 2:6 [2:5]; *təhôm*), to the roots of the mountains.

Finally, in Jonah 2:11 [2:10] Jonah is returned to dry land. He has literally and metaphorically been taken through a dark night of the soul, and his

---

[27] Remembrance is a rich OT theme. See Eccles 12:1 and see the comments in Bartholomew, *Ecclesiastes*. Remembrance here is about far more than a mental reminder; it is rather a jolt of recognition of who Yahweh really is.

[28] See Jonathan Magonet, *Form and Meaning: Studies in Literary Techniques in the Book of Jonah*, BET 2 (Frankfurt: Peter Lang, 1976), 44-49.

[29] Magonet, *Form and Meaning*, 40.

prayer indicates a reawakening to Yahweh. It remains to be seen how deep the work in his life has been.

The structure of the canticle. As we noted, there is wide disagreement about the structure of the canticle. Above we attended to its narrative development, beginning as it does with a summary. In our view, a chiastic structure to the canticle can be discerned, which we indicate above.

It is difficult to be conclusive when it comes to chiasm. Our evidence for the above is as follows. We have already noted the *inclusio* in Jonah 2:3 [2:2] and Jonah 2:10c [2:9c]. Jonah 2:3b [2:2b] repeats Jonah 2:3a [2:2a] and thus is part of this summary, but the repetition of "voice" (*qôl*) in Jonah 2:3b [2:2b] and Jonah 2:10ab [2:9ab] inclines us toward seeing Jonah 2:3b [2:2b] and Jonah 2:10ab [2:9ab] as related chiastically. Jonah 2:4 [2:3] and Jonah 2:9 [2:8] are ironically related, since it is Jonah's lack of loyalty (*ḥesed*) that underlies his being cast into the depths, but there are also notable similarities between the consonants of the verbs in Jonah 2:4c [2:3c] and Jonah 2:9 [2:8]. Jonah 2:5 [2:4] and Jonah 2:8 [2:7] both contain the reference to "your holy temple," negatively in the former and positively in the latter. Jonah 2:6 [2:5] and Jonah 2:7ab [2:6ab] both speak of Jonah's final descent. F stands at the center, telling us what the psalm is about, namely, Jonah's deliverance, and connects in this way with the summaries in A and A'.

JONAH 3–4

Lacocque and Lacocque rightly note that Jonah emerges from the belly of the fish transformed. He passes from what they call prior self to authentic self, from narcissism to self-oblation.[30] Biblically speaking he *repents*, a major theme in Jonah. Paul Tillich defines repentance as "the act of the whole person in which he separates himself from elements of his being, discarding them into the past as something that no longer has any power over the present."[31] Repentance is never final this side of eternity, nor is formation through the dark night. The dark night is followed by rebirth, and as we see with Jonah, this can be challenging.

Jonah is now ready to obey Yahweh and does so, but clearly elements from his past continue to dog his ministry. If he has moved from terror at the call, to depression in the boat, to fear in the waters, he now manifests

---

[30] Magonet, *Form and Meaning*, 94-113.
[31] Paul Tillich, *The Eternal Now* (New York: Scribner's Sons, 1963), 128.

anger. This time, however, he does not flee but prays and expresses his anger to Yahweh in no uncertain terms. Leslie Allen says that Jonah "considers it intolerable that Israel's experience of Ex. 32 should be mirrored in Nineveh; he cannot stomach Yahweh's cheapening his mercy by offering it to all and sundry."[32] Gabriel Cohn perceptively notes, "It is his very zeal *for* God that turns Jonah against God."[33]

Jonah has come a long way since his attempted flight, but there is more work to be done. He does not flee, but he still resists. Issues central to his becoming fully human and exercising his priestly role in the creation still need to be dealt with. In his anger and response to God's mercy, "two different conceptions of justice and grace confront one another."[34] One is struck by Yahweh's patience in dealing with Jonah at this point. He creates the space for Jonah to shift his perspective and provokes this growth by asking questions.

Intriguingly, a friend of mine who has practiced as a psychologist for many years says that she has noticed in her practice that when people start to get better, or turn the corner from illness back to health, they usually start by getting angry first. It seems to be the first sign of real, authentic life. Thus perhaps we, like Yahweh, must be more patient with Jonah and more optimistic about his development beyond the book.

At stake is nothing less than Jonah becoming like Yahweh, holy, patient, just, and merciful. For Jonah to exercise his priestly role in the world, he needs more than his desire for justice; he also needs longsuffering, compassion, and patience. Albert Schweitzer searched for an answer to the question of how life can be judged as successful and meaningful. On the third day of a boat trip wresting with this issue, the phrase "reverence for life" entered his mind. He describes it thus:

> The great fault of all ethics hitherto has been that they believed themselves to have to deal with the relations of man to man. In reality, however, the question is what his attitude to the world and all life that comes within his reach. A man is ethical only when life as such, is sacred to him, that of plants and animals as that of his fellow men, and when he devotes himself helpfully to all life that

---

[32] Leslie Allen, *The Books of Joel, Obadiah, Jonah, and Micah*, NICOT (Grand Rapids, MI: Eerdmans, 1976), 227.

[33] Gabriel Cohn, *Das Buch Jona* (Assen: Van Gorcum, 1969), 100. Translation is that of Lacocque and Lacocque, *Jonah: A Psycho-religious Approach*, 138.

[34] Lacocque and Lacocque, *Jonah: A Psycho-religious Approach*, 144. Lacocque and Lacocque note that this exemplifies the debate between Jerome and Origen (145).

is in need of help. . . . Only by means of reverence for life can we establish a spiritual and human relationship with both people and living creatures within our reach. . . . Through reverence for life we become, in effect, different persons [i.e., beings-for-the-world].[35]

As Creator, God appropriately respects and loves his creation and if we are to do the same then we must become like God. This is precisely what spiritual formation is all about; we are made in the *imago Dei*, and we need to become the *imago Dei*. Indeed, this is what makes the book of Jonah so universal, for "apart from the vocation to become fully human, nothing else equalizes us that would not be accidental." "The problem therefore is not whether some have a vocation like Jonah, while some do not; the problem is for all men and women to fulfill their humanness."[36]

We are left at the end of Jonah with no idea what happened to him. Did he come around to God's way of thinking? We simply do not know. This is intentional, for the important question is *what is happening with us*. Are we like God or like Jonah? From Jonah we can learn many things, but one thing stands out; it is primarily through the practice of prayer that we open ourselves to this formative work of the Spirit. Within the catholic church there is a great tradition and great resources in this respect, but they need to be excavated and reintroduced in our day. Only thus will the church produce not just prophets but saints.

Recommended Reading

Lacocque, André, and Pierre-Emmanuel Lacocque. *Jonah: A Psycho-religious Approach to the Prophet*. Columbia: University of South Carolina Press, 1990.

———. *The Jonah Complex*. Atlanta: John Knox, 1981.

---

[35]Albert Schweitzer, *Albert Schweitzer: An Anthology*, ed. C. R. Joy (New York: Harper & Row, 1947), 271-72, Quoted in Lacocque and Lacocque, *Jonah: A Psycho-religious Approach*, 204.
[36]Lacocque and Lacocque, *Jonah: A Psycho-religious Approach*, 175, 205.

12

Micah

DIVINE FORGIVENESS AND THE REMNANT

PROPHETS HAVE AN UNCANNY habit of cutting to the core of issues, and Micah embodies this ability. If we want to know what true religion is really about, then Micah is our book. Micah presents Yahweh as the one who forgives sin and preserves a remnant through judgment. It balances divine forgiveness and judgment for Israel and the nations. Burkard Zapff sees Micah as a kind of "core" to the Twelve, providing theological ballast for the negative portrayal of the destiny of the nations that one finds, for instance, in Nahum-Habakkuk-Zephaniah.[1]

THE CONTEXT OF MICAH

From Micah 1:1 we learn that the prophet belongs in the southern kingdom, as Micah comes from Moresheth, ministering during the reigns of Jotham (758–743), Ahaz (743–714), and Hezekiah (727–698). Moresheth is southwest of Jerusalem, near Judah's border with Philistia. The regnal formulae in Micah 1:1 indicate that the prophet is a rough contemporary of the prophet Isaiah, and indeed Micah echoes the language of Isaiah of Jerusalem (Mic 4:1-3 // Is 2:2-4; Mic 4:11-13 // Is 17:12-14; Mic 5:9-13 // Is 2:6-21; Mic 2:2 // Is 5:8-10). The Assyrian threat lay on the horizon, particularly during the reigns of Tiglath-pileser III (744–727), Shalmaneser V (726–722), Sargon II (721–705), and Sennacherib (704–681). The fall of Samaria in Micah 1 testifies to the imminent downfall of the northern kingdom in 722 BC at the hands of Assyria. However, the impending destruction of Judah/Jerusalem

---

[1]Burkard M. Zapff, "The Book of Micah—the Theological Center of the Book of the Twelve?," in *Perspectives on the Formation of the Book of the Twelve: Methodological Foundations—Redactional Processes—Historical Insights*, ed. Ranier Albertz, James D. Nogalski, and Jakob Wöhrle, BZAW 433 (Berlin: de Gruyter, 2012), 129-46.

depicted in Micah 1:5, 13; 3:9-12; 6:9-16 connects with 701 BC, when the Assyrian king Sennacherib successfully campaigned in the Levant, destroyed many cities in Judah, and laid siege to Jerusalem without capturing it.[2]

Broadly speaking, redaction critics view Micah 1–3 as belonging (partially) to the eighth century BC (even if edited finally in the exilic period), while other texts are exilic (Mic 6:1–7:7) or postexilic (Mic 4–5).[3] Our study does not discount redaction criticism but focuses on the final form of Micah.

Outline

One can divide the book into three major units: (1) a book of doom (Mic 1:2–3:12), (2) a book of visions (Mic 4:1–5:14 [4:1–5:15]), and (3) a book of contention and conciliation (Mic 6:1–7:20).[4] However, Kenneth Cuffey offers a compelling proposal that the restoration visions of Micah 2:12-13; 4:1-8; 5:1-14 [5:2-15]; 7:7-20 offer structural markers. The term "remnant" (šəʾērît) appears in the restoration visions, marking a vital concept emerging in both Micah and the Twelve (see table 12.1).[5]

Table 12.1. Structure of Micah

MICAH 1–2	MICAH 3:1–4:8	MICAH 4:9–5:14 [4:9–5:15]	MICAH 6–7
Theme: The God Who Regathers	Theme: The God Who Rules His Own	Theme: The God Who Leads to Victory	Theme: The God Who Forgives His People
Subunit 1: Micah 1:2–2:11 the problem: sin with the land; lose land	Subunit 1: Micah 3:1-12 the problem: inadequate human leadership	Subunit 1: Micah 4:9-14 [4:9–5:1] the problem: defeat and inability	Subunit 1: Micah 6:1–7:6 the problem: sin and depravity

---

[2] Kyle H. Keimer, "Sennacherib's Invasion of Judah and Neo-Assyrian Expansion," in *Behind the Scenes of the Old Testament: Cultural, Social, and Historical Contexts*, ed. Jonathan S. Greer, John W. Hilber, and John H. Walton (Grand Rapids, MI: Baker Academic, 2018), 299-305.

[3] For discussion, see James D. Nogalski, *The Book of the Twelve: Micah—Malachi*, SHBC (Macon, GA: Smyth & Helwys, 2011), 511-16; Burkard M. Zapff, *Redaktionsgeschichtliche Studien zum Michabuch im Kontext des Dodekapropheton*, BZAW 256 (Berlin: de Gruyter, 1997); Simon J. De Vries, "Futurism in the Preexilic Minor Prophets Compared with That of the Postexilic Minor Prophets," in *Thematic Threads in the Book of the Twelve*, ed. Paul L. Redditt and Aaron Schart, BZAW 325 (Berlin: de Gruyter, 2003), 252-72, here 256.

[4] Francis I. Anderson and David Noel Freedman, *Micah*, AB 24E (New York: Doubleday, 2000), 7.

[5] Kenneth H. Cuffey, *The Literary Coherence of the Book of Micah: Remnant, Restoration, and Promise*, LHBOTS 611 (New York: Bloomsbury T&T Clark, 2015), 258. For šəʾērît in the Twelve, see Amos 9:12; Mic 2:12; 4:7; 5:7-8; 7:18; Zeph 2:7-9; Hag 1:12-14; 2:2; Zech 8:6-12.

MICAH 1-2	MICAH 3:1-4:8	MICAH 4:9-5:14 [4:9-5:15]	MICAH 6-7
Subunit 2: Micah 2:12-13 God regathers	Subunit 2: Micah 4:1-8 God rules	Subunit 2: Micah 5:1-14 [5:2-15] God leads to victory	Subunit 2: Micah 7:7-20 God forgives
Key indicator: šə 'ērît in Micah 2:12	Key indicator: šə 'ērît in Micah 4:7	Key indicator: šə 'ērît in Micah 5:6-7 [5:7-8]	Key indicator: šə 'ērît in Micah 7:18

Adapted from Kenneth H. Cuffey, *The Literary Coherence of the Book of Micah: Remnant, Restoration, and Promise*, LHBOTS 611 (New York: Bloomsbury T&T Clark, 2015), 258; his original is fig. 6.2.

Interpretation

Micah 1-2. Micah 1:1 echoes the superscriptions of Hosea 1:1 and Amos 1:1. In this way, Micah is a co-text to these other books, giving the impression that the ministry of these prophets was roughly contemporaneous.[6]

Table 12.2. Ministries of Hosea, Amos, and Micah

HOSEA 1:1	AMOS 1:1	MICAH 1:1
Jeroboam II (789-748)	Jeroboam II (789-748)	
Uzziah (758-743)	Uzziah (758-743)	
Jotham (758-743)		Jotham (758-743)
Ahaz (743-714)		Ahaz (743-714)
Hezekiah (727-698)		Hezekiah (727-698)

Micah 1:2-7 depicts Yahweh's judgment. He comes from the heavens to the earth to tread on the high places of the earth (Mic 1:3). Beneath his feet, the mountains melt and run down into the valleys, like wax flows when melting from fire (Mic 1:4). Note the juridical imagery in Micah 1:2: the nations and the earth are witnesses, as the word of the Lord is a "witness" against the peoples (Mic 1:2).

Micah 1:5 offers the reason for the judgment: "all this" (*kol-z 'ōt*), Yahweh says, is because of "rebellion" and "sins" of Israel/Jacob. More specifically, these sins are further clarified as "Samaria" for Israel and the "high place" in Jerusalem (Mic 1:5). Some form of illicit worship is in view, as the "high place" (*bāmôt*) of Jerusalem indicates a shrine for worship (the temple?). The northern kingdom of Israel (Jacob) has committed a "crime" (*pešaʿ*), defined

---

[6]See also Aaron Schart, *Die Entstehung des Zwölfprophetenbuchs: Neuarbeitungen von Amos im Rahmen schriftenübergriefender Redaktionsprozesse*, BZAW 260 (Berlin: de Gruyter, 1998), 39.

as "Samaria."[7] Since the days of king Jeroboam II (789–748 BC), shrines devoted to deities other than Yahweh emerged in Samaria. This makes sense of the mention of idolatry in Micah 1:7: "All her images shall be beaten to pieces, all her wages shall be burned with fire, and all her idols I will lay waste; for as the wages of a prostitute she gathered them, and as the wages of a prostitute they shall again be used" (NRSV).[8]

Alternatively, the Jerusalem/Samaria connection in Micah 1:5 may connote the royal palaces that were built in these locations. If so, then the crime and sin of Samaria and Jerusalem, respectively, is directed to the royal administration of Israel and Judah. This reading anticipates Yahweh's castigation of the leaders in other texts (see Mic 3:1-3, 9-12; 6:9-16). It makes good sense of the emphasis on social justice in Micah, especially in Micah 6, as we will see in the next chapter.

Whichever is in view, Micah 1:5 indicates the failure of the people in their covenantal relationship with Yahweh. Idolatry and social injustice remain outside the parameters of how his people are to live in the land. Yahweh will discipline them, purifying his people in judgment, calling them back to their purpose in his world. Their failure demands divine discipline. Following the divine verdict of Micah 1:7, we see mourning and wailing in Micah 1:8. Jeremiah's image of the "incurable wound" (Jer 15:18; 30:12) emerges first in Micah 1:9.

Micah 1:10-15 mourns the destruction of Judah—the cities mentioned in Micah 1:10-15 are located there. Moreover, the geographic locations are part of a wordplay in the Hebrew that crystallizes the fate of the city.[9]

Micah 2 develops the message of judgment through a change in forms: a woe oracle (Mic 2:1-5), a prophetic disputation (Mic 2:6-11), a salvation oracle (Mic 2:12-13). The woe oracle, identifiable by the generic "Alas" or "Woe!" (*hôy*) in Micah 2:1, preserves an accusation with a judgment decree. Those who devise "evil" in their beds (Mic 2:1) break the tenth commandment in Micah 2:2, as they "covet" (*wəḥāmədû*) fields and seize them (see Ex 20:17). In an agrarian society, the act of seizing fields leaves the victim destitute, without home or food. Instead of allowing this injustice to persist, a great reversal will take place, delineated in Micah 2:3-4. Those who have

---

[7] For the linkage of Jacob with the northern kingdom, see Andersen and Freedman, *Micah*, 171.
[8] See discussion of Bruce K. Waltke, *A Commentary on Micah* (Grand Rapids, MI: Eerdmans, 2007), 59.
[9] See the "topography of terror" from Stephen G. Dempster, *Micah*, THOTC (Grand Rapids, MI: Eerdmans, 2017), 66.

performed evil against their countrymen in Judah will have their own unjustly gained fields parceled out to their captors (Mic 2:4).

Micah 2:6 opens the disputation, in which the prophet and the evildoers described in Micah 2:1-5 engage one another. The evildoers do not want Micah to preach, but the prophet responds in Micah 2:7 that his words *must* be said. Their evil leaves those exploited like vulnerable travelers (Mic 2:8), like homeless mothers (Mic 2:9), like deprived children (Mic 2:9), and the land itself becomes unclean (Mic 2:10).

The utter failure of the leadership calls for judgment, and Micah 2:12-13 reveals that Yahweh will do it. God will lead refugees, his people, if the current rulers refuse to lead. Introduced by an intensive construction (infinitive absolute + *yiqtol* verb), Micah 2:12 provides the surety of the divine act: "I will certainly gather, O Jacob, all of you. I will surely collect the remnant of Israel." Yahweh as the shepherd leads the refugees back home; the king closely follows Yahweh in this redemptive act (Mic 2:13).

Micah 3:1-4:8. Yahweh castigates Israel's leaders (Mic 3:1-4), prophets (Mic 3:5-8), and rulers (Mic 3:9-12) for their inability to enact justice. Repetition of the verb *šimʿû-nāʾ* ("Listen") in Micah 3:1, 9, coupled with the new audience in Micah 3:5 ("Thus says Yahweh regarding the prophets"), demarcates the accusations. Instead of loving the good, these evildoers fill Zion with inequity (Mic 3:9), wrongdoing (Mic 3:10), and bribery (Mic 3:11). They exploit the vulnerable (Mic 3:2-3) and cause starvation (Mic 3:5). These leaders should know justice but exhibit perversity in relation to their fellow humans.

Micah 3:1-3 addresses the "heads of Jacob" (*roʾšē yaʿăkōb*) and the "rulers of the house of Israel" (*ûqəṣînē bêt yiśrāʾēl*). These refer to the king and the aristocracy. Kings especially should pursue justice above all else, as justice and fairness mark the good king (e.g., Is 32:1; see also 2 Sam 8:15; 1 Kings 10:9; Jer 22:15; Ps 72). Micah interrogates and thereby accuses the leadership: "[But] you hate good and love evil" (Mic 3:1-2a).

Horrific imagery accompanies Micah's accusation. Food is a gift that should be celebrated, but Micah 3:2-3 presents the vulnerable of the land as meat for a celebratory meal (see Ezek 24:1-14). The injustice present among the people leads to destruction. Cannibalistic imagery in the Old Testament is reserved for the most dreadful moments (see Lam 2:20; 4:10; Ezek 11:3, 7, 11; 24:1-14; Jer 19:9). The sins of leaders will not be absolved, as Micah 3:4 reveals: "When they cry out for help to Yahweh, he will not answer them. He will hide his face from them in that time because their deeds were so evil."

Micah 3:5-8 rails against false prophecy. "Prophets who lead my people astray" (*hannəbî'îm hammat'îm*, Mic 3:5) is vivid and portrays false leaders. The hiphil participle *hammat'îm* speaks of those who cause the people to believe or act in a way that diverges from those of Yahweh. Their sin is their greed, enacting violence if they do not get their way (Mic 3:5b). Divine judgment follows the accusation in Micah 3:6, governed by the imagery of darkness and night as opposed to vision and visibility. Instead of honor, these prophets will not speak and will experience shame (Mic 3:7).

Contrasted with these false prophets is the *true* prophet, who speaks the word of judgment. The true prophet is overwhelmed with power (*kōaḥ*), judgment (*mišpāṭ*), might (*gəbûrâ*), and the spirit of Yahweh (*rûaḥ YHWH*; see Is 11:2). The point is clear: Micah is anointed with the spirit of Yahweh and filled "to declare to Jacob his crime and to Israel his sin" (Mic 3:8b). Opposing false prophets, Micah declares the truth of the leaders' sin.

We turn again in Micah 3:9 to the imperative *šim'û-nā'* ("Listen"), opening the third portion of this section. It comprises an accusation of sin against the leaders (see Mic 3:1). Their crimes vary: leaders abhor justice (Mic 3:9); leaders pervert what is right (Mic 3:9); leaders build Zion with bloodshed and wickedness (Mic 3:10); leaders, priests, and prophets take bribes (Mic 3:11); leaders assume Yahweh's presence despite their sin (Mic 3:11). Leaders remain depraved, disconnected from Yahweh, and lead Zion astray; as a result, Zion will be "ploughed like a field" (Mic 3:12).

Micah 4:1-8 shifts away from the desolation of Zion to focus on her restoration in "the last days" (*bə'aḥărît hayyāmîm*). This strange phrase appears in Hosea 3:5 and Micah 4:1 in the Minor Prophets. These "last days" are described sometimes as an "end of history," "the last days," or sometimes translated "the latter days."[10] The concept connotes not an end of history, *full stop*; rather, it is a radical end to the kind of history we find in Micah 3—a history wrecked with sin, injustice, and horrors.

Hope breaks forth in Micah 4:1-4 (which is virtually identical to Is 2:1-4). In the future order of things, all nations will make pilgrimage to the house of Yahweh and be taught in the ways of Yahweh (Mic 4:1-2). Zion will be a place of perfect peace: there will be no more fighting and war. Each person will experience safety and security, as swords will be

---

[10]See Stephen Dempster, "At the End of the Days" (בְּאַחֲרִית הַיָּמִים) An Eschatological Technical Term? The Intersection of Context, Linguistics and Theology," in *The Unfolding of Your Words Gives Light: Studies on Biblical Hebrew in Honor of George L. Klein*, ed. Ethan C. Jones (University Park, PA: Eisenbrauns, 2018), 118-41, esp. 119-20.

fashioned into plowshares and spears into pruning hooks (Mic 4:3). Everyone will have a place to live and eat, "each person will sit under his own vine and fig tree, and there will be no one to disturb" (Mic 4:4). This radical upending of the sinful order of things described in Micah 4:2-3 is only possible because "The mouth of Yahweh of Armies has spoken" (Mic 4:4b). Human initiative cannot re-create Zion. Only Yahweh's word effects a new world.

Micah 4:5 shifts to a first-person plural "we," signifying the commitment of restored Zion (Israel and the nations) to their God. The nations will "walk" in the name of their deities, but the inhabitants of Zion will "walk" in the name of Yahweh ("our God") forever. To be associated with the name of a deity implies both relation and belonging. Yahweh's name becomes the banner under which restored Zion lives.

"In that day" (*bayyôm hahû'*) in Micah 4:6 correlates to the same time frame as "the last days" (*bə'aḥărît hayyāmîm*). Micah 4:7-8 discloses Yahweh's reign in the future (*mālak YHWH*), and his rule will extend "from now until forever." When Yahweh reigns, the "sovereignty" of Zion and Jerusalem will return, presumably forever.

Zion's inhabitants are described as the "remnant" (*šə'ērît*) in Micah 4:7, while Micah 4:6-7 lists the inhabitants: the lame, dispersed, formerly afflicted, those driven off. The remnant who are drawn back into Zion are those who have experienced the judgment of Yahweh and survive. This "remnant" is no longer weak or debilitated, but Yahweh makes them into a "strong nation" (*gôy 'āṣûm*). This community of restored exiles has been made whole and powerful under the aegis of Yahweh.

The Davidic house emerges in Micah 4:8 and anticipates Micah 5:2, as the restoration oracle testifies that the former sovereignty will return to the "hill of the daughter of Zion" (*'ōpel bat-ṣiyyôn*), likely referring to a portion of the eastern hill of Jerusalem that David captured (see 2 Sam 5:7). With this allusion, the salvation oracle correlates the future reign of Yahweh *and* the restoration of the Davidic dynasty. Yahweh will rule, once again and forevermore, through the Davidic king.

Micah 4:9–5:14 [4:9–5:15]. Micah 4:9 reverts from the glorious future back to the present, asking the people why they cry out for help. A king in this verse reminds the people that the *current* king is unable to provide and protect the people in the face of international threat. This king will be unable to prevent exile, as the following verses reveal.

The poetry shifts, focusing on Zion among the nations in Micah 4:10–5:14 [4:10–5:15]. Zion *must* go into exile even to Babylon (Mic 4:10). Once there, Yahweh will redeem his people and rescue them. Micah trades on the imagery of labor pains to illustrate the anguish and deferred salvation. Nations believe Zion is vulnerable (Mic 4:11), but Micah reminds Zion, "But they do not know the thoughts of Yahweh" (Mic 4:12a). Although it looks as though Zion will be defeated in exile and oppression, appearances are deceiving. In fact, Yahweh prepares his people for future strength (Mic 4:13). Salvation through judgment and pain is the plan of Yahweh for Zion; Zion's present pangs will give birth to a new age.[11]

This new age is depicted with a royal figure in Micah 4:14–5:5 [5:1-6], and the oracle presents Bethlehem Efrat as the location from which the ruler will emerge. This "ruler" (*môšēl*) belongs to Yahweh, as Micah 5:1 [5:2] indicates; God raises him up "for me" (*lî*). Yahweh's ruler in the new age will be devoted completely to him. Bethlehem Efrat echoes the birthplace of David, the king of Israel (see 1 Sam 17:12). Yahweh's king will see the reunification of Israel and Judah (Mic 5:3 [5:4]).

The future king's rule will extend throughout the world as he provides for the nations "in the majesty of the name of Yahweh, his God" (Mic 5:3 [5:4]). This verse also reveals that the future king will "tend his flock." Technically, our translation includes "the flock," which is not present in Hebrew. However, the term *wərā'â*, "he will tend," is a shepherding metaphor for the future king. This term is used to describe God's shepherding his people (Hos 4:16; Is 40:11), but also the king shepherding the people (2 Sam 5:2; Jer 3:15; 23:2). In our text, the picture is one of the future king pasturing his flock in the strength and name of Yahweh.

Micah 5:6-7 [5:7-8] depicts the "remnant of Jacob" (*šə'ērît ya'ăkōb*) with ambiguous metaphors: dew, rainfall, and predatory lions. We have witnessed "remnant" language in Micah 2:12 and Micah 4:7, drawing together the complex theme of the remnant in the book. That Yahweh will preserve a remnant testifies to Yahweh's judgment, for how will a remnant remain unless the majority have been removed, now dwelling among "many peoples" (*'ammîm rabbîm*)? Despite this external threat, the remnant will be like dew, showers, and predatory lions.

On the face of it, these metaphors confuse. How can natural phenomena of dew and rainfall somehow relate to predation? The images are not

---

[11] Waltke, *Commentary on Micah*, 249.

equivalent but rather increasingly present the powerlessness of humanity to prevent these phenomena. Jacob will be like "dew" and "showers" in Micah 5:6 [5:7], natural phenomena that humans cannot—and thereby (on the analogy) the nations cannot—prevent.

Yahweh's miraculous act of preserving the remnant will not be stopped. The positivity with the image of dew and showers on the ground speaks to the blessing that the people will be among the nations. Water and dew refresh the parched earth, and thereby Yahweh's preservation of the people in the midst of the nations will somehow be a blessing to the nations (see Gen 12:1-3). This positive image in Micah 5:6 [5:7] jars against the negative image in Micah 5:7 [5:8]. Strikingly, the nations represent the sheep:

Remnant of Jacob // lions
Nations & many nations // flocks of sheep

The sheep will be powerless to prevent the predation just as the nations will be unable to prevent Israel's presence among them. Yahweh's unrivaled power, depicted through analogy in Micah 5:6-7 [5:7-8], guarantees the bold declaration of Micah 5:8 [5:9]: "Your hand will be exalted over your enemies, and all your foes will be cut off." Because Yahweh guarantees the certainty of Jacob's ascendancy, the nations will be powerless to prevent it, just as people are impotent to prevent natural phenomena.

Micah 5:9-14 [5:10-15] matches Micah 4:1-6 in its eschatological emphasis. "In that day" (*bayyôm hahû'*) in Micah 4:6 correlates with "in that day" (*bayyôm hahû'*) in Micah 5:9 [5:10]. Interestingly, the fate of the nations in Micah 4 is largely positive, as joint participants in renewed Zion. In Micah 5, however, the nations emerge as objects of Yahweh's wrath: "I will enact vengeance in anger and rage against the nations who do not obey me" (Mic 5:14 [5:15]). The distinguishing characteristic between nations that inhabit Zion and those that are judged largely depends on their devotion to Yahweh. Those nations characterized by participation in renewed Zion self-identify as those who want to go up to the mountain of Yahweh to be instructed in his ways and to walk in his paths (Mic 4:2). By contrast, those nations who stand under divine judgment trust in their own sources of security: horses and chariots (Mic 5:9 [5:10]), cities and strongholds (Mic 5:10 [5:11]), sorcery and soothsayers (Mic 5:11 [5:12]), and carved idols and standing stones (Mic 5:12 [5:13]), as well as sacred poles (Mic 5:13 [5:14]). Yahweh will "cut off" these from the nations; the hiphil verb from the root *krt* (repeated 3× in Mic 5:9-11 [5:10-12]) indicates divine action against these sources of security: military, fortified strongholds, and religious practices that do not accord with Yahweh devotion. In this eschatological vision, all opposition and false securities will be removed so that Yahweh worship and devotion to his supremacy will remain.

Micah 6-7. These chapters focus back on the present and away from the eschatological future. In fact, they parallel the accusation against Yahweh's people in Micah 2-3.[12] We will explore Micah 6:1-8 in the next chapter in our discussion of Micah's vision for justice. However, for now it is enough to note that through the lawsuit metaphor, Yahweh highlights the people's lack of understanding of what is required of them. Rather than extravagant sacrifices, Yahweh simply requires justice between fellow human beings, kindness toward fellow human beings, and humility before Yahweh.

Micah 6:1 and Micah 6:9 serve as bookends to what comes between them with the repetition of the imperative "Listen!" (*šimʿû*). However, the use of the imperative in Micah 6:9 comes after an appeal to listen to the voice of Yahweh, who speaks to the city and declares the wisdom of "fearing" Yahweh's name. Yahweh calls these people to listen to the "rod" and the one who appoints it. The rod image indicates divine discipline for the people (Is 30:31; Lam 3:1). The reasons for divine discipline emerge in Micah 6:10-16, all predicated on Yahweh's speech in Micah 6:9 to the inhabitants of the city. Yahweh decries ill-gotten gains (short *ephah* measures; Mic 6:10); wicked scales and fraudulent weights, which give rise to unjust gains (Mic 6:11); rich, violent men, with the general term *violence* employed (Mic 6:12); and liars and deceivers, which, by all counts, is sin (Mic 6:12; see Ps 34:13; 41:6; 109:2; 120:2-3; Prov 14:25; 19:1; 30:8).

The divine response: "Therefore I will make you ill, striking you down, desolating you because of your sins" (Mic 6:13). The outcome of divine action is elucidated in Micah 6:14-15:

- The people will not be satisfied with food but continue to hunger (Mic 6:14).
- The people will conceive without giving birth (Mic 6:14).

---

[12]Gunnar Begerau, "Micah, Prophet of Hope Through Judgment," in *The Lion Has Roared: Theological Themes in the Prophetic Literature of the Old Testament*, ed. H. G. L. Peels and S. D. Snyman (Eugene, OR: Wipf & Stock, 2012), 65-75, here 69.

- If birth is granted, then the child will be killed (Mic 6:14).
- The people will sow but not reap (Mic 6:15).
- The people will make oil but not be able to use it (Mic 6:15).
- The people will make wine but not be able to drink it (Mic 6:15).

Interestingly, divine action nullifies enjoyment of foodstuffs and cash crops (olive oil and wine) when false measuring devices and fraudulent weights are used to gain them, as depicted in Micah 6:10-12. Instead of enjoying the fruit of injustice, ironically, those who practice these actions will *not* enjoy their labor.

The meaning of the practices of Omri and the house of Ahab in Micah 6:16 is unclear, but it may refer to 1 Kings 21 and the unjust seizure of Naboth's vineyard. At the very least, it evokes the sin of the northern kingdom, which was judged, and reminds the inhabitants of Jerusalem (in the south) that Yahweh will judge the south for injustice just as he has the northern kingdom.

Micah 7 presents the city as one who is forlorn over the sad state of the people.[13] In Micah 7:1-6, Zion witnesses the absence of faithful and upright people. Instead, predatory inhabitants lie in wait to shed innocent blood. Leaders among God's people (officials and judges) take bribes, and the leaders plot wicked schemes. The faithful are completely alone, with friends and companions unable to help those who are exposed. Social order gives way to chaos as children revolt against parents, and the household is a place of enemies instead of a haven for help and support.

In the face of this chaos, Zion stands up and looks to Yahweh for help. "But I shall wait expectantly with Yahweh; I shall wait for the God of my salvation. My God will hear me!" (Mic 7:7). This language depicts a prayer for deliverance, funded by the hope that God will see and hear the prayer based on his divine goodness and power. Micah 7:7 is a prophetic mode of prayer in which the petitioner prays that God's justice and salvation would be activated in a dire social context.[14]

Because of faith in Yahweh, Zion can respond to the pain of Micah 7:1-6 with a new confidence. She speaks directly, indicated by the first-person "my" and "I" in Micah 7:8-10. Zion affirms she will experience God's

---

[13]This is the personification of the city of Jerusalem as a female mother, "Lady Zion." See the discussion of Mark S. Gignilliat, *Micah*, ITC (London: T&T Clark, 2019), 260.

[14]James Leo Garrett Jr., *Systematic Theology: Biblical, Historical, and Evangelical* (Grand Rapids, MI: Eerdmans, 1995), 2:401-5.

salvation, but only through judgment. Shame (Mic 7:8, 10), sin (Mic 7:9), and current devastation give way to restoration, forgiveness, and rebuilding in Micah 7:11-13.

In Micah 7:14, Zion calls for the shepherd-king who will rule the restored people of God. Some ambiguity emerges in terms of the identity of the shepherd-king. Is the prayer calling for *Yahweh* to care for the flock as the good shepherd (see Mic 2:12), or is it calling for the eschatological, *Davidic* shepherd-king to rule (see Mic 5:1-5 [5:2-6])? Likely, the divine-shepherd king takes priority, for Zion uses the language "your inheritance" (*naḥălātekā*) to describe the people (as we find in covenantal contexts: Deut 4:20; 9:26, 29). "The logic of election is at work in the prayer of Zion. Zion's only status and leverage for intercession is their identity as Yhwh's very own, his inheritance."[15]

Yahweh responds to Zion's prayer in Micah 7:15-17, indicated by the hiphil imperfect first-person singular verb *I shall demonstrate miracles* (Mic 7:15). These miracles echo Yahweh's miracles "in the days of your exodus from the land of Egypt." Yahweh, who delivered God's people through judgment in the past and brought them to the Promised Land, will again restore his people miraculously, vindicating them. Unevenly presented to this point in the book, the nations emerge as those who stand in awe of God's work with his restored people. Instead of mocking Zion's downfall (as in Mic 7:8-10), the nations "will come in dread to Yahweh our God, and they will be afraid before you" (Mic 7:17). It is unlikely the nations are incorporated into Zion as we saw in Micah 4:1-6, because the sense of Micah 7:16-17 is only a reversal: from mocking Zion to revering and fearing God's restoration of Zion.

The chapter concludes with a hymn that exults in the covenant characteristics of Yahweh, evocative of Exodus 34:6-7. Micah's emphasis on the forgiveness of Yahweh (Mic 7:18-19) and divine commitment to his people through election (Mic 7:20) makes this hymn a climactic affirmation of Yahweh's unfailing fulfillment of the promise of Abraham. Despite the perennial problem of sin among Yahweh's people, God will fulfill his purposes through them: he will bless them to be a blessing, and all the nations of the earth will be blessed through them (see Gen 12:1-3). This shall be accomplished by Yahweh preserving a "remnant of his inheritance" (*lišē'rît naḥălātô*). Again, the "remnant" language unites the four major sections of the book, highlighting Yahweh's commitment to mercy and forgiveness even while judging sin.

---

[15]Gignilliat, *Micah*, 271.

The Theology of Micah

Micah 7:18—"Who is a God like you?"—is a call to "reflective discernment" wherein the reader must assess the question in the light of the entirety of the canonical book but also in the light of the disclosure of the divine name and divine character presented in Exodus 34:6-7.[16] The theological themes explored here draw the reader to reflect on Yahweh and his ways with Israel.

The God who preserves a remnant. Micah depicts Yahweh's commitment to his people so that they are preserved beyond judgment. The covenant is the theological substructure for Yahweh's fidelity to Israel. If remnant stands out as a theological emphasis, then a theology of divine election emerges as well. Divine election recognizes that Yahweh has chosen his covenant people, Israel, and it will be this people through whom divine blessing proceeds. Through judgment, Yahweh preserves a remnant so that Yahweh's purposes to bless all of creation will follow through them, so that human sin never speaks the last word in this covenantal context.

The God who forgives. Yahweh's people do sin in Micah. Yahweh judges sin, portrayed with unblinking certainty. Jacob's "crimes" and "sins" lead to "disaster" at the hand of Yahweh (Mic 1:12). Based on divine holiness and justice, Yahweh exerts judgment against any form of wickedness, either among his people or other nations.

However, Micah concludes the book with a focus on overwhelming divine *forgiveness.* "Who is a God like you?" (Mic 7:18) finds an answer in the very next line in the same verse: Yahweh pardons the sin and passes over the crimes of the remnant of his heritage. We have seen how Micah draws on Exodus 34:6-7, emphasizing divine forgiveness in affirming the covenant characteristics of Yahweh. Divine forgiveness is not a theological reality that one takes for granted, but it is a truth about God in which Micah exults. That God preserves a remnant speaks to the overwhelming grace present with divine forgiveness.

The beautiful final lines of the book deserve mention, as here one discovers the evocative image of Yahweh casting sins into the depths of the sea (Mic 7:19). In previous days, Yahweh hurled the horse and rider of the Egyptian army into the sea, as Exodus 15:1-11 rehearses. Now Yahweh casts sin into the depth of the sea, concluding the book while emphasizing divine forgiveness.

---

[16] We agree with Gignilliat's assessment (*Micah*, 81).

The future age and messianic king. Micah exposes a tension between present sin and future hope, particularly in Micah 4–5. As is well known, Micah differentiates between eschatological future and present reality through distinctive terminology:

Present: "now" (*'attâ*), Micah 4:9, 14
"but now" (*we'attâ*), Micah 4:11

Future: "in the last days" (*bə'aḥărît hayyāmîm*), Micah 4:1
"in that day" (*bayyôm hahû'*), Micah 4:6; 5:9 [5:10]

The phrases *bə'aḥărît hayyāmîm* and *bayyôm hahû'* signal the future hope. The messianic king will be Davidic, and the restoration of Zion will incorporate both Israel redeemed and the nations called to follow Yahweh's ways. In this way, the messianic hope of Micah 5 is correlated with the hope of Zion restored. Although the future messianic king will emerge under the work of Yahweh (Mic 5:1-4 [5:2-5]), the prayer still is that Yahweh (the divine-shepherd king) will shepherd his people (Mic 7:14). The canonical text enfolds historical moments within God's economy with Israel: present distress where Israel faces enemy threat, and a future period that includes "pilgrimage of the nations, alongside a restitution of Israel that includes both the simultaneous return of the Diaspora under Yahweh's kingship and a final purification of Israel combined with a final judgment against those nations which are disobedient."[17] The future king will lead God's people under the power of the divine king, or as Micah 5:3 [5:4] affirms, "He [the future Davidic king] will stand and shepherd in the strength of Yahweh, in the majestic name of Yahweh, his God."[18]

God and the nations. Micah proclaims Yahweh as sovereign over Israel and all nations. The nations' judgment and future salvation leads to some confusion. For instance, Micah 7 depicts the future judgment of the nations. But Micah 4:1-5 depicts a restoration for Israel *and* the nations. Yahweh's future restoration of Israel *and* the nations in the last days reminds readers of his divine care for the entirety of creation. But when does judgment and salvation occur for the nations? In Micah, the timing is somewhat unclear. Stephen Dempster observes:

---

[17]Zapff, "Book of Micah," 134-35.
[18]For discussion, see Gregory Goswell, "Davidic Rule in the Prophecy of Micah," *JSOT* 44, no. 1 (2019): 153-65.

God uses the nations to refine his people and to judge them, but their attempt to destroy the people will meet with final defeat. Then when God reforms his people, this will become the nations' opportunity for salvation. They will see their plight and hear the word of the Lord go out from Zion, and this will result in their pilgrimage to Zion and repentance in which they give up their ways of war.[19]

Thus the nations are caught up in the grand movement of judgment and salvation that reveals the work of Yahweh. Micah presents the way to a future hope: through repentance, attending to the word of Yahweh and hoping in him rather than any other source of trust. "The nations who set themselves over against Yhwh both now and in the future will know Yhwh as a roaring lion. While those who take refuge in him will find an extended hand of mercy from a relenting God whose mercy can cede his severity."[20]

Living in the light of God's requirement. What does God require of his people? The next chapter explores this more fully in relation to the famous requirement of Micah 6:8. However, in a whole-book perspective, Micah clearly calls those who are known by Yahweh to live with a particular shape, or way, to life:

- a way of life that embraces Yahweh, rejects idolatry, and recognizes sin (Mic 1:5-7; 3:8)
- a way of life that cares for the vulnerable rather than grasping at power (Mic 2:1-2, 8-9; 3:1-3, 9-12)
- a way of life that is honest and fair rather than exploitative (Mic 6:9-16; 7:2-3)
- a way of life that trusts in Yahweh more than any other source of hope, "fearing" Yahweh and his name (Mic 6:9; 7:7)
- a way of life that does justice, loves kindness, and walks in humility before Yahweh rather than offering something Yahweh does not require (Mic 6:8)
- a way of life that embraces divine forgiveness, even in the face of judgment (Mic 7:18-20)

---

[19]Dempster, *Micah*, 206.
[20]Gignilliat, *Micah*, 77.

Micah and the New Testament

There are two explicit citations of Micah in the New Testament: Micah 5:1 [5:2] in Matthew 2:6; Micah 7:6 in Matthew 10:35-36 and Luke 12:53.[21] We discussed Micah 5:1 [5:2] in chapter one. The second appears in Jesus' teaching found in Matthew 10:35-36. In these verses, Jesus teaches that his message and work will bring division rather than consensus. Micah 7:6 speaks about the sinful community at odds with the faithful speaker of Micah 7. They are faithless, but the sufferer at odds with the community waits for Yahweh's salvation. Micah 7:6 appears in Jewish messianic texts that speak of the division that comes in communities and families when the Messiah appears in the last days.[22] Interestingly, this text also appears in Luke as well (Lk 12:53), and both emphasize the hostility and division that comes when Messiah (Jesus) appears.[23] In Matthew's vision, division emerges as a result of Jesus' claim to messiahship and the consequent rejection of his claim by some Jewish leaders.

Micah for Today

Micah sets future hope in dialogue with this present darkness. Micah weighs, with unflinching honesty, human oppression, resultant pain, and grief born from human sin. Micah's vision especially flags (un)just leadership. The critique of leadership in Micah 1-3, as well as the concomitant call for faithful leadership, reminds readers today that God desires leaders who will pursue justice, mercy, and humility, not as a tactic but as an ethos. Micah's persistent vision of leaders who refuse the good but instead oppress, exploit, subvert, and chop up people like meat for the cooking pot (Mic 3:3) vividly exposes the leadership vacuum that is present in the ancient and modern worlds.

On the one hand, such a leadership vacuum invites better leaders to the table. That is certainly the case, as we find Yahweh's requirement in Micah 6:8. Better leaders will be humble, dependent on the Lord, and will look to the benefit and good of all rather than just the benefits of the elite or

---

[21] Zapff, "Book of Micah," 129-46.
[22] See Clay Alan Ham, "The Minor Prophets in Matthew's Gospel," in *The Minor Prophets in the New Testament*, ed. Maarten J. J. Menken and Steve Moyise, LNTS 377 (London: T&T Clark, 2009), 48-49. See also S. T. Lachs, *A Rabbinic Commentary on the New Testament: The Gospels of Matthew, Mark, and Luke* (Hoboken, NJ: Ktav, 1987), 186.
[23] See Huub van de Sandt, "The Minor Prophets in Luke-Acts," in Menken and Moyise, *Minor Prophets in the New Testament*, 59-60.

privileged. Their eyes will be those of Jesus, who looks to care for the least of these in the community.

Micah's vision of *future* leadership in the inbreaking of the kingdom of God in Micah 4–5 expresses the radicality and utter necessity of God's intervention and healing of the brokenness of the world. The coming king of Micah 5:3 [5:4], for instance, will shepherd the flock in the strength and name of Yahweh, revealing that this future leader's prestige, power, and efficacy will be measured in strength that belongs properly to Yahweh rather than the king; the greatness of the king will be in how the leader leads under the aegis of Yahweh rather than establishing one's own name or prestige. Only when the leader properly gives power and glory to God will the people experience peace (Mic 5:4 [5:5]).

When Jesus entered into the world as *this future king*, those captured by his claims experienced the peace Micah 5:4 [5:5] envisions. Those who long for such peace in our present world look to our leaders but recognize that, even at their best, today's leaders anticipate God's future king, who will make all things new and provide perfect peace. This focus on the *future hope* enables people of faith to see present leaders—for all their brokenness and blessing—in the light of the return of Christ and his future kingdom. We will be unable to valorize or idolize today's leaders even while holding them to high standards because we are a people radically committed to the future hope.

Recommended Reading

Begerau, Gunnar. "Micah, Prophet of Hope Through Judgment." In *The Lion Has Roared: Theological Themes in the Prophetic Literature of the Old Testament*, ed. H. G. L. Peels and S. D. Snyman, 65-75. Eugene, OR: Wipf & Stock, 2012.

Cuffey, Kenneth H. *The Literary Coherence of the Book of Micah: Remnant, Restoration, and Promise*. LHBOTS 611. New York: Bloomsbury T&T Clark, 2015.

Dempster, Stephen G. "At the End of the Days" (בְּאַחֲרִית הַיָּמִים) An Eschatological Technical Term? The Intersection of Context, Linguistics and Theology." In *The Unfolding of Your Words Give Light: Studies on Biblical Hebrew in Honor of George L. Klein*, ed. Ethan C. Jones, 118-41. University Park, PA: Eisenbrauns, 2018.

———. *Micah*. THOTC. Grand Rapids, MI: Eerdmans, 2017.

Gignilliat, Mark S. *Micah*. ITC. London: T&T Clark, 2019.*

Goswell, Gregory. "Davidic Rule in the Prophecy of Micah." *JSOT* 44, no. 1 (2019): 153-65.

Recommended reading marked with a "*" indicates introductory works.

13

He Has Told You What Is Good

MICAH 6:6-8

Introduction

The Old Testament reveals that justice (*mišpāṭ*) was intended to penetrate every sphere of Israel's life—legal, familial, social, religious, political, and so on—yet its precise denotation remains elusive.[1] Like wisdom, justice is a *totality concept*, driving one to speak about everything.[2] Justice relates to the totality of the created order and can and should be instantiated in a multitude of ways in multiple spheres of culture.[3] Micah 6:6-8 serves (with Amos 5:24) as a touchstone for appropriate, just social action in the world.[4]

Interpretation

Micah 6 functions within a larger structural unit of Yahweh's accusation against his people. Micah 6:1-8 exposes the people's sin and depravity and parallels the disputation of Micah 2–3: Yahweh's accusation against the leaders of God's people (Mic 2–3) // Accusation against the people of God (Mic 6:1–7:7).[5] God's people are perplexed about two issues: they assume Yahweh's presence among them exempts them from any kind of suffering or

---

[1] Rolf Knierim, *The Task of Old Testament Theology: Methods and Cases* (Grand Rapids, MI: Eerdmans, 1995), 88.
[2] Raymond van Leeuwen, "Wisdom Literature," in *Dictionary for Theological Interpretation of the Bible*, ed. Kevin Vanhoozer et al. (Grand Rapids, MI: Baker Academic, 2005), 848.
[3] Knierim (*Task of Old Testament Theology*, 89-114) outlines various conceptualizations of justice (sixteen of them!) in the OT.
[4] H. G. M. Williamson, *He Has Shown You What Is Good: Old Testament Justice Then and Now* (Cambridge: Lutterworth, 2012).
[5] See Gunnar Begerau, "Micah, Prophet of Hope Through Judgment," in *The Lion Has Roared: Theological Themes in the Prophetic Literature of the Old Testament*, ed. H. G. L. Peels and S. D. Snyman (Eugene, OR: Wipf & Stock, 2012), 65-75, here 69. See also Leslie C. Allen, *The Books of Joel, Obadiah, Jonah and Micah*, NICOT (Grand Rapids, MI: Eerdmans, 1974), 260.

adversity (Mic 3:10-11), and they believe what Yahweh requires is regular, burdensome sacrifice. If they offer sacrifice, then they have fulfilled the letter of the law, so to speak (Mic 6:6-7).[6]

On both counts, Yahweh counters their misunderstanding with a dose of reality.

Micah 6:1-5. This section presents a court scene in which Yahweh stands to present the *rîb YHWH*, "the dispute of Yahweh" (Mic 6:2). The *rîb* is a technical form of legal disputation in the prophetic texts, in which Yahweh is prosecutor and judge.[7] This dispute arises in a covenantal context. Micah flags covenant breach and announces Yahweh's accusation. In Micah 6:3, Yahweh asks his people how he has "wearied" them.

Yahweh contrasts the people's false perception of him (Mic 6:3) with reality (Mic 6:4-5). Yahweh delivers, saves, and provides rather than placing exhausting burdens on them. Micah 6:4-5 rehearses, in abbreviated form, the exodus from Egypt. Micah 6:5 recalls the events of Numbers 23–24, with the threat of Balak and Balaam. Instead of cursing, Yahweh drew Balaam to bless God's people, thwarting the Moabite threat. In this short sweep of salvation history, Yahweh defends his activity for Israel: rather than being exhausting or a burden, Yahweh delivers, protects, and provides. Micah 6:5 closes by describing these events as the *ṣidqôt YHWH*, "the righteous acts of Yahweh."

Micah 6:6-7. Micah 6:6-7 opens a new section. The first-person verbs belong to a worshiper (perhaps going to the temple to petition Yahweh), whose questions ascend climatically from the ordinary to ridiculous.[8]

> With what should I [the worshiper] come before Yahweh?
>   Should I bow before Yahweh, most high?
> Should I come before him with whole burnt offerings,
>   With year-old calves?
> Would Yahweh be pleased with thousands of rams,
>   With multitudes of rivers of oil?
> Should I offer my firstborn [son for] my transgression,
>   The fruit of my womb [for] the sin of my life?

---

[6]Mignon R. Jacobs, "Micah, Book of," in Vanhoozer, *Dictionary for Theological Interpretation*, 514; Jacobs, *Conceptual Coherence of the Book of Micah*, JSOTSup 322 (Sheffield: Sheffield Academic Press, 2001), 157-95.

[7]See chap. 1; Kirsten Nielsen, *Yahweh as Prosecutor and Judge: An Investigation of the Prophetic Lawsuit (rib-Pattern)*, JSOTSup 9 (Sheffield: JSOT Press, 1978).

[8]Bruce K. Waltke, *A Commentary on Micah* (Grand Rapids, MI: Eerdmans, 2007), 358.

The first and third verbs, *should I come/should I come before him*, derive from the Hebrew root *qdm*, which in the stem (piel in both verbs) denotes an encounter between friends or relations. Only in Micah 6:6 does the root depict an encounter between Yahweh and the worshiper in a cultic setting (but see Ps 95:2). The second verb, *should I bow before (Yahweh)*, derives from the root *kpp*, which in Isaiah 58:5 suggests a pious person who bows his head and fasts (but compare with Ps 145:14; 146:8). Wolff says, "With the word [*kpp*] *niphal* he describes a person in an attitude of deep humility who, self-abased at prayer, *bows down* his whole body before" Yahweh most high.[9]

The piety of the language mirrors the purpose of the offering. The worshiper brings the offerings to atone for unspecified sins in Micah 6:6. "Whole burnt offerings" (*ʿōlôt*) signify the basic offering that atones for human sinfulness (the year-old calf is specified for the "whole burnt offering" in Lev 9:3).

"Thousands of rams" and "multitudes of rivers of oil" are an exaggeration of normal sacrificial practice. In the Torah, a ram is offered up as "a whole burnt offering" (Lev 8:21; 9:2), or "a guilt offering" (Lev 5:15, 18; 6:6) and "well-being offerings" (*šəlāmîm*; Lev 9:4; Num 6:14, 17). The "rivers of oil" may refer to anointing oil of the well-being offering, but this is a bit unclear. Still, if the oil is for well-being offering, then the worshiper speaks about bringing offerings to manage covenant breach (*ʿōlâ* and *ʾāšām* offerings) and (possibly) to celebrate the relationship between the worshiper and Yahweh (*šəlāmîm*?). However, the question is *how many of these offerings* would "please" (*rṣh*) Yahweh.

"Pleasing" Yahweh through sacrifice is technical language of the Israelite cult (Lev 1:4; 7:18; 19:7; 22:23, 25, 27). The only other instance where "thousands" of rams are offered appears in 1 Kings 3:4; 1 Chronicles 29:21; 2 Chronicles 29:33 (all describing the same kind of incident). Accompanying this possibly royal sacrifice are "multitudes of streams of oil," a sacrificial unit only here. The oddity of the absurd amount of oil draws one to question the authenticity of the question. Does the worshiper revere or ridicule Yahweh with the question? Apparently, the worshiper is *desperate* for Yahweh to accept the sacrifice to ameliorate the breach in relationship and deliver from whatever distress the worshiper encounters.

The climactic question, "Should I offer my firstborn [son for] my transgression, the fruit of my womb [for] the sin of my life?" is horrific, even "the pinnacle of human delusion."[10] This query reveals one of two things: either

---

[9]Hans Walter Wolff, *Micah: A Commentary*, trans. Gary Stansell (Minneapolis: Augsburg, 1990), 177.
[10]Delbert R. Hillers, *Micah*, Hermeneia (Philadelphia: Fortress Press, 1984), 78.

it exposes the *lack* of piety present in the worshiper's questions because of the perceived failure of Yahweh with the worshiper, or it reveals the worshiper has confused what Yahweh fundamentally desires in vital relationship, despite sincere piety.[11]

The final query raises the possibility of child sacrifice. Should the worshiper *follow through* with the sacrifice? Would that please Yahweh? Some think of an Abrahamic intertext here, but Isaac was not the "firstborn" (bəkôr). Closer to the notion of the "first-born" (bəkôr) of Micah 6:7 is the language of Exodus 22:29: "You shall give me the firstborn among your sons." Such human sacrifices "were more than mere possibilities, both in other nations of the time and in Israel, at least in certain periods."[12] Jon Levenson supposes the authenticity of this dark piety in Micah, believing that offering the firstborn mentioned in Micah 6:7, as in Exodus 22:29, reflects ancient devotion to Yahweh. The speaker of Micah 6:7 asks Yahweh whether it is right to follow through giving the firstborn child to Yahweh as a sacrifice, following this early practice.[13] If the worshiper did *that*, would it meet Yahweh's requirement?

But the major concern of Micah 6:7 is not an abstract notion of devotion, as Levenson supposes. Micah 6:7 is concerned with divine *forgiveness* for "my transgression" and "the sin of my life." The repeated first-person singular suffixed pronoun *my* indicates the motivation for the sacrifice: to restore the sinner's broken relationship with Yahweh because of individual sin. The request does not come from a position of thanksgiving (like a well-being offering) but of a position of need.

To gain atonement, the worshiper wonders whether Yahweh desires the firstborn as a substitute for the parent. If this is devotion, it represents a dark devotion indeed. What parent would reasonably give up the life of one's firstborn child to save one's own skin? This is not a reasonable, pious, or legitimate request, as we will see.

Micah 6:8. Yahweh's response "ignores both the substance and desperation of the questions with what seems a studied disdain. The proposals and the

---

[11]Wolff (*Micah*, 178-79) argues that the speaker "exaggerates in the extreme by pushing his examples of boundless sacrifices toward what is plainly frivolous." Mays and Hillers argue the worshiper's questions expose a sense of desperation or anxious uncertainty. James Luther Mays, *Micah*, OTL (Philadelphia: Westminster, 1976), 141; Hillers, *Micah*, 78-79.

[12]Hillers, *Micah*, 78.

[13]Jon D. Levenson, *The Death and Resurrection of the Beloved Son: The Transformation of Child Sacrifice in Judaism and Christianity* (New Haven, CT: Yale University Press, 1993), 10-12.

assumption on which they are based are simply disregarded."[14] The instruction to "do justice, love mercy, and walk humbly with your God" (Mic 6:8) negates engaging in behavior (regardless of the devotion) that would threaten the life of another human being, not least one's firstborn child. It is difficult to "do justice" for the child if the parent is busy immolating the child to atone for the parent's own "transgression" (Mic 6:7). It would seem a profound absence of mercy to sacrifice one's own child to deal with personal "sin." It would seem a disastrous display of pride to view a parent's own forgiveness more valuable than the very breath of one's child. Cruel violence and justice cannot belong together.

The appeals of Micah 6:6-7 reveal a deep and abiding failure among the people to discern the shape of true faithfulness. Thus, Micah 6:8 completely disregards the queries raised by the worshiper, and the divine response redirects the worshiper who misses the point.

The Hebrew root *ngd* ("He has told you," *higgîd ləkā*, Mic 6:8) appears in Micah 1:10; 3:8, and in the latter text, the proclamation testifies to the crimes of Judah. Micah 1:10 instructs the prophet *not* to proclaim (*ngd*) a word of judgment in Philistia (Gath) because judgment is coming on Judah. In these prior texts the content of the "telling" (*ngd*) is judgment against Judah. In Micah 6:8, however, God (through the prophet) declares (*ngd*) what is "good," thus not a word of judgment but of virtue. The term "good" (*ṭôb*) is semantically flexible. Prophets often describe the requirements of Yahweh by using the term *ṭôb*: Isaiah 1:17; 5:20; Amos 5:14-15; Micah 3:2. In these texts, *ṭôb* is diametrically opposed to evil.

In Isaiah 1:17, the notion of the good refers to social engagement, provision, and care for those who are vulnerable (oppressed, fatherless, and widow) after a litany of injustice and sin. Thus the "good" (*ṭôb*) teaching Yahweh has given extends to the social spheres of life, establishing justice for the vulnerable (which the people are not doing). Amos, too, frames the good (*ṭôb*) after describing a litany of covenant violation. In this broad context, Yahweh calls his people to seek *ṭôb*, "good" (Amos 5:14), and "hate evil" (Amos 5:15), which is immediately followed with maintaining justice in the court (Amos 5:15).

To narrow the semantic range, "what is good" (*ṭôb*) couples with "and what Yahweh is seeking from you" in Micah 6:8. When read in the broader context, Micah 6:8 contrasts with Micah 6:6. See the repetition of language in table 13.1, noting the interchange between the worshiper and Yahweh.

---

[14]Mays, *Micah*, 141.

Table 13.1. Interchange between worshiper and Yahweh in Micah 6

MICAH 6:6	MICAH 6:8
With what (bammâ)	What is good and what (mâ-ṭôb ûmâ)
shall I bring Yahweh (ʾăqaddēm YHWH)	Yahweh requires from you (YHWH dôrēš mimməkâ)

Repeated language in Micah 6:6 and Micah 6:8 (mâ + YHWH + interchange between "I"/"you") flags how God redirects the worshiper's misdirected expectations of what is required to please Yahweh. Yahweh does not require an extravagant sacrifice, whether thousands of animals or one's own child. Rather, Yahweh requires the very life of the worshiper ("what Yahweh requires of you"). "The concentration on the thing offered [in Mic 6:6-7] is shifted to a focus on the quality of life that is lived. Good is what Yahweh requires and what is good is the one thing needful to know."[15]

Micah 6:8 is the only instance in the Old Testament in which the combination of justice, mercy, and humility ever appears with the verbs *to do, to love,* and *to walk*. However, the combined verbal concepts of loving and walking and Yahweh's requirement resonate with Deuteronomy. The combination of the verbs *to love* and *to walk* as paradigmatic of the faithful life is broadly Deuteronomic and emerges elsewhere (Deut 10:12; 11:22; 19:9; 30:16: Josh 22:5; 1 Kings 3:3, 6; 8:3). However, the combination in Micah 6:8 is unusual.

Table 13.2. Parallels between Deuteronomy 10:12-13 and Micah 6:8

DEUTERONOMY 10:12-13	MICAH 6:8
What Yahweh your God requires (mâ + šōʾēl)	What Yahweh requires (mâ + dôrēš)
Love Yahweh (ûləʾahăbâ ʾōtô)	Love kindness (wəʾahăbat ḥesed)
Walk in all his ways (lāleket bəkol dərākāyw)	Walk humbly with your God (wəhaṣnēʿa leket ʿim-ʾĕlōhêkā)

When read together, Deuteronomy 10:12-13 and Micah 6:8 depict the vertical and horizontal relationships in Yahweh's "requirement." What God requires (šōʾēl) in Deuteronomy 10:12-13 is a vertical commitment to Yahweh in devotion/love to him (ûləʾahăbâ ʾōtô) and walking in his ways (lāleket bəkol dərākāyw). What Yahweh requires (dôrēš) in Micah 6:8 is a horizontal devotion to one's fellow humans, to love kindness (wəʾahăbat ḥesed) *as well*

---

[15] Mays, *Micah*, 141.

as walking humbly before Yahweh (*wəhaṣnēʿa leket ʿim-ʾĕlōhêkā*).[16] In the light of the linguistic resonance between texts, walking and loving in Deuteronomy 10:12-13 and Micah 6:8 depict a love for Yahweh and a love for humanity. These verses set in broad canvas the requirements of the faithful life, echoed in Jesus' teaching, "You shall love the Lord your God with all your heart, and with all your soul, and with all your strength, and with all your mind; and your neighbor as yourself" (Lk 10:27 NRSV).

Yahweh requires Israel to "do justice." This notion does not appear in Deuteronomy 10:12-13, but it does appear, for instance, in Proverbs 21:3, "To do [*ʿăśōh*] righteousness and justice [*mišpāṭ*] is more acceptable to Yahweh than sacrifice." The infinitive *ʿăśōh* of Proverbs 21:3, like the infinitive of Micah 6:8 (*ʿăśōt*), intends embodied enactment of something; it could be translated "to enact justice" or even "to act justly." In this sense, "justice" (*mišpāṭ*) intends a way of living one's life to be fair and right in one's dealings with others. This way of living accords with the God of justice, who deals fairly and rightly with Israel and the nations: "For Yahweh is a God of justice [*mišpāṭ*]; blessed are those who wait for him" (Is 30:18). For Israel, the "whole idea of justice was wrapped up with the qualities and characteristics of the Lord, their God, and especially connected to the covenant relationship between Israel and the Lord. Justice is essentially relational and covenantal."[17]

Yahweh requires those who follow him to embody that same fairness and right-dealing with others, especially those who are vulnerable in society. God's people need "spiritual rehabilitation that makes them people who can accurately reflect God's character to the world."[18] The notion of justice reflected in Micah 6:8 is wide ranging and "means that the orders of justice that are maintained and reinstituted by peaceful actions, by just court decisions and by conciliation within the community."[19] Justice is embodied and enacted by everyone in the society. Justice in Micah equates to fair dealing with fellow human beings.

The phrase "to love kindness" is akin to doing justice, and the emphasis does not fall on emotion but rather on one's covenantal obligation to fellow

---

[16]So Daniel L. Smith-Christopher states, "Here the notion is not that justice is performed toward God; instead it is how people behave toward one another." Smith-Christopher, *Micah: A Commentary*, OTL (Louisville, KY: Westminster John Knox, 2015), 196.
[17]Christopher J. H. Wright, *Old Testament Ethics for the People of God* (Downers Grove, IL: IVP Academic, 2004), 258-59.
[18]B. P. Irwin, "Social Justice," in *Dictionary of the Old Testament Prophets*, ed. Mark J. Boda and J. Gordon McConville (Downers Grove, IL: IVP Academic, 2012), 727.
[19]Wolff, *Micah*, 180.

human beings. Emotion may lie in the background of wə ʾahăbat ḥesed, "to love kindness," but ḥesed, "kindness," is inherently covenantal and often appears in the Old Testament in contexts of one person delivering another out of dire straits, even when it was not necessary to take that action.[20] So Robin Routledge states, "At the heart of ḥesed is loving commitment within the context of a relationship. It represents both the attitude of loyalty and faithfulness to the relationship and to the related parties, and the corresponding kind and dutiful action, often expressed as help or deliverance, that arises from it."[21] Bruce Waltke draws the notions of justice and kindness together: "It is now apparent that the practice of ḥesed is closely related to mišpāṭ: both pertain to the deliverance of an oppressed, weaker party by the stronger party, but whereas mišpāṭ puts the emphasis on the action, ḥesed puts it on the attitude of the action."[22]

"Loving" ḥesed intends a fully orbed embrace of fellow human beings, helping those in dire straits and less fortunate. Help can be accomplished with a negative attitude, driven purely by cold obligation. But loving kindness requires one to serve with joy, exuberant in the act of service itself. Obligation in that sense is not cold but comprises a mutuality one feels toward another in the community. As God's people "love kindness," they embody love for the powerless and vulnerable, imitative of Yahweh's actions for his people (Mic 6:3-5).

The hiphil infinitive absolute wəhaṣnēʿa, "to be humble," is a hapax legomenon. The widespread divine desire for humility emerges with the term ʿānāw in various texts (Ps 25:9; 34:2; 149:4; Prov 3:34; 11:2; Zeph 2:3). Yahweh requires a life journey marked by humility before him. Humility in this sense is not equated with *humiliation* or shame. Rather, the humble disposition depicted here is a life lived in utter dependence on Yahweh, who is revered as the God, king, protector, and provider described in Micah 6:4-5. If one lives in dependence on Yahweh, one will be far less likely to exploit one's neighbor.

The final question emerging from this discussion is the meaning of ʾādām, which we have translated as "O human." Grammatically, this is a vocative ("O human") rather than a proper noun ("Adam"). If the verses are set within the context of a covenant lawsuit, then does Yahweh's address to ʾādām

---

[20]Katherine Doob Sakenfeld, *The Meaning of Hesed in the Hebrew Bible*, HSM 17 (Missoula, MT: Scholars Press, 1978), 233.
[21]Robin Routledge, "Hesed as Obligation: A Re-Examination," *Tyndale Bulletin* 46, no. 1 (1995): 195.
[22]Waltke, *Commentary on Micah*, 394.

intend an Israelite in covenant relationship with Yahweh and one another *only*? If so, then why include the term at all? It is possible to omit the word for clarity, with the context of the individual worshiper in place. If this is the case, it is possible that the worshiper from Micah 6:6-7 serves the referent of the second-person singular "you" of Micah 6:8a: "He has told you." Otherwise, it may include the broad sweep of humanity, including all human beings as a group into Yahweh's address. The most sensible explanation comes in the context. As the covenant lawsuit is intoned from Micah 6:1-8, usage of *'ādām* reminds the Israelite of their creaturely relationship with the Creator. Yahweh has reminded human beings what is good and what Yahweh seeks from them.

JUSTICE IN MICAH AND TODAY

Micah and our concern for justice flows from God being just. As God has liberated, protected, and provided for his people (Mic 6:4-5), his people are to "do justice" and "love kindness" in a way analogous to what God has done for his people. Justice is something that must be done and is thus always historical and particular. To do justice we have to become aware of injustice in our time and place(s). Oliver O'Donovan argues that attentiveness to the time in which one lives is necessary for appropriate action in the world: "World and self are co-present only in the moment of time which is open to us for action."[23]

What kind of justice does Micah 6:6-8 evoke, attending to the world, time, and agency represented in the text? We see justice as liberation of Israel's poor from oppression as the conception at work. Rolf Knierim rightly draws attention to the fact that the prophets often promote liberation for Israel's underprivileged or poor as an act of justice, and it appears that this is the case here (e.g., Is 1:17; Jer 9:24; 21:12; Amos 5:15; Ps 140:12; 146:7).[24] Micah 6:8 typifies a notion of justice that is liberative in scope and broad in its application, rather than narrow and only juridical.

Still, it is possible to narrow the scope further, historically. Because of Micah's concern for the land (along with Isaiah of Jerusalem), some view the issue of justice central to Micah in unjust land seizure: the wealthy of Jerusalem appropriate the land of the poor rural folk. This would explain, for

---

[23]Oliver O'Donovan, *Self, World, and Time*, Ethics as Theology 1 (Grand Rapids, MI: Eerdmans, 2013), 15.
[24]Knierim, *Task of Old Testament Theology*, 94-96.

instance, the critique of Micah 2:1-5 ("they covet fields and seize them"), but more significantly the critique of the rich in Micah 6:9-16 immediately following our text. Micah 6:9-16 derides the rich and wealthy, whose storehouses of grain are somehow evil. If the storehouses were filled with produce unjustly seized from the poor of the land, then it would give a social backdrop for determining why these storehouses are described so negatively.[25] Such activity in ancient Israel may be socially advantageous, economically viable, and (possibly) authorized by the crown, but Yahweh reveals it to be profoundly unjust. While the social profile outlined above remains evocative, justice evokes a way of life in which followers of God deal fairly with their neighbors, especially those who are most vulnerable in society.

What does the moral vision expressed in Micah 6:8 look like today? Broadly speaking, to do justice for the vulnerable and powerless inevitably, for the modern West, means that the church must attend to the land and work in solidarity with the poor while rejecting the consumerist materialism that distinguishes itself as an idol of our age. One begins where one lives, in the community in which God has placed one.

Attending to the land in one's place is especially pertinent here. The eighth-century prophets like Micah were keen to appropriate positive and fair use of land as opposed to the exploitative and lavish use of the land for only a few in the region around Jerusalem and Judah.[26] Land use, then, properly engaged means that everyone should have a place to call home. Land must be understood as a divine gift for the good of all, not just a few. Reception of the land as gift must be done at a local level. To do justice in Micah's language means the church ought to treat the land in which they live with care as a steward rather than an owner, as the world belongs to God. To love God well, one must love one's neighbor and ensure place for all in the land. The church has the opportunity to live on the land in such a way that love of God and neighbor is exemplified. Of course, this call for appropriate land usage will take different accents as the needs of local place are variable.

---

[25]See David N. Premnath, *Eighth Century Prophets: A Social Analysis* (St. Louis: Chalice, 2003), 104-7, 117-20. Blessing Onoriode Boloje argues along similar lines in "Economic Piracy and Land Confiscation (Micah 2:1-5): Micah's Portrayal of Evil-Doers, Evil-Doing, and Yahweh's Action," *Journal for Semitics* 28, no. 1 (2019): 1-15.

[26]Heath A. Thomas, "Building House to House (Isa. 5:8): Theological Reflection on Land Development and Creation Care," *BBR* 21, no. 2 (2011): 189-212. The discussion that proceeds here is drawn from the insights of this essay. For other discussion, see Ellen F. Davis, *Scripture, Culture, and Agriculture: An Agrarian Reading of the Bible* (Cambridge: Cambridge University Press, 2009).

For instance, I (Heath) live in Oklahoma, where land and land use remains a complex challenge. This is not simply because of problems of poverty and homelessness in my community or other cities in the state. It is not only because rental markets in cities, concentrated and proliferated among wealthy few, prevent homeownership among lower income families. It is also because of the complexity of land ownership between the state and First Nations peoples and tribes (Native Americans). Christians in this space must navigate these complexities as we strive to uphold the land as a gift and the land as a place for all, not just for a few. To do justice with one's neighbor in Oklahoma, the church must take account of these complexities with seriousness and creativity even while upholding Micah's call for proper and fair dealing one with the other.

With this example in view, we can see that expectations for proper habitation in God's land are no longer confined, as it were, to the borders of Canaan in light of God's kingdom inaugurated in Jesus. Israel's use (and misuse) of land becomes paradigmatic for proper use of land in the church. Responsibilities that belonged to Israel to care for the land in Micah now belong paradigmatically to those who have faith in Christ, who are now "fellow citizens with the saints and members of the household of God" (Eph 2:19). As such, just land use in the church serves as a sign of the reign of God and God's love for humanity. The various ways in which Christians live on this land—now—may be understood in the light of kingdom land ethics, which are designed to produce "fruits of the kingdom" (Mt 21:43)—signs that God reigns in Christ and that he is reconciling the world to himself. If the church *fails* to live justly on the land, then no doubt they do *not* do justice, love mercy, or walk appropriately with their God. The church must learn receive the earth as a gift from God, being reconciled to God through Christ (Col 1:15-20), and being responsible for just action on the earth, caring for neighbors in the community in which God places them. The entirety of the world is the theater for God's justice and righteousness to be performed.

The example in Oklahoma reminds us that the church must live out just land practices concretely, and somewhere; the best place to start is where God has placed one. Understanding what actions regarding the land are in fact beneficial for all is impossible if the church remains ignorant of local place. The church, then, will develop God's land in ways that accord with the rhythms of whatever particular place—whether coastal, mountain, plain, swamp, or the like, with the particular communal and political realities that impinge on land use. The church must be aware of and live into the environment where it finds itself proclaiming Christ and his kingdom.

Micah also invites us to attend to the poor and vulnerable, in our local places. Bob Goudzwaard and Craig Bartholomew speak to both a preferential option for the poor (or developing an economy of care) and a rejection of consumerism, most recently in their analysis of the modern world.[27] For the church to bear witness to the justice of God in Christ, we must recognize the most vulnerable in our world is the Majority World in the Global South, who suffer in poverty while the modern West, including the church, is captivated by an unwritten edict, "I shop, therefore I am." The purchase of cheap material goods promulgates inequality among the nations and reinforces material prosperity as the ultimate good in the western world.

And just like Sheol, the gaping maw of the consumerist, materialistic world never says "Enough!" The rich increase their wealth, while the poor and vulnerable—children, Majority World countries, those without health care or help—bear the brunt of the burden. The words of Micah become more vibrant with this injustice in view: "Alas for those who devise wickedness and evil deeds on their beds! When the morning dawns, they perform it, because it is in their power. They covet fields, and seize them; houses, and take them away; they oppress householder and house, people and their inheritance" (Mic 2:1-2 NRSV). The powerful exploit the weak and vulnerable, *because it is in their power*.

The church of Jesus Christ must speak and embody a different word to the idols of our time and the injustices of our day. Because of the complexity of the globalized economy and the interconnectedness of the Global North and Global South economically, to give due to our neighbors means to attend to the ways in which the Majority World lags behind the modern West. The church must attend to the inequity and live a different way as we attend to the poor.

The gospel of Jesus Christ must be borne in word *and* deed. Jesus' forgiveness of sin and liberating power through his death and resurrection must be proclaimed with our lips and promoted with our lives. Those who

---

[27]Bob Goudzwaard and Craig G. Bartholomew, *Beyond the Modern Age: An Archaeology of Contemporary Culture* (Downers Grove, IL: IVP Academic, 2017). See also Bob Goudzwaard and Harry de Lange, *Beyond Poverty and Affluence: Toward an Economy of Care* (Grand Rapids, MI: Eerdmans, 1995); Craig G. Bartholomew and Thorsten Moritz, eds., *Christ and Consumerism: A Critical Analysis of the Spirit of the Age* (Carlisle, UK: Paternoster, 2000).

have tasted the justice of God displayed in Jesus will enact justice in their world. We will do justice and love kindness as we walk humbly with our God. As one Baptist theologian says:

> The Christian mission is to do all the good he can in every realm of life, in every possible way. He is to make regnant the will of God in the whole extent of human life and society. There is no conflict between serving God and helping men. Surely the Christ who healed the bodies of men and performed a miracle to feed the hungry multitude does not represent a God who is displeased with anything that makes this world a better place in which to live. . . . The only way to regenerate society is through the regeneration of the individual units of society. And the only power that can regenerate the individual is the gospel of Jesus Christ. Nor has the gospel done its full work in the life of the individual unless he is made right in every relation to life. The gospel makes a man live right in the world, not withdraw from the world.[28]

Recommended Reading

Boloje, Blessing Onoriode. "Economic Piracy and Land Confiscation (Micah 2:1-5): Micah's Portrayal of Evil-Doers, Evil-Doing, and Yahweh's Action." *Journal for Semitics* 28, no. 1 (2019): 1-15.

Goudzwaard, Bob, and Craig G. Bartholomew. *Beyond the Modern Age: An Archaeology of Contemporary Culture*. Downers Grove, IL: IVP Academic, 2017.

Jacobs, Mignon R. *Conceptual Coherence of the Book of Micah*. JSOTSup 322. Sheffield: Sheffield Academic Press, 2001.

———. "Micah, Book of." In *Dictionary for Theological Interpretation of the Bible*, ed. Kevin J. Vanhoozer et al., 512-15. Grand Rapids, MI: Baker Academic, 2005.*

Knierim, Rolf. *The Task of Old Testament Theology: Methods and Cases*. Grand Rapids, MI: Eerdmans, 1995.

Premnath, David N. *Eighth Century Prophets: A Social Analysis*. St. Louis: Chalice, 2003.

Smith-Christopher, Daniel L. *Micah: A Commentary*. OTL. Louisville, KY: Westminster John Knox, 2015.*

Wolff, Hans Walter. *Micah: A Commentary*. Translated by Gary Stansell. Minneapolis: Augsburg, 1990.

Recommended reading marked with a "" indicates introductory works.*

---

[28] W. T. Conner, *The Gospel of Redemption* (Nashville: Broadman, 1945), 221-22.

14

Nahum and Zephaniah

GOD, THE NATIONS, AND ISRAEL

WE ADDRESS THESE TWO SHORT BOOKS together because of their common focus on Yahweh's engagement with Israel and the nations. Each addresses Assyria and its capital Nineveh (Nahum 1:1; 3:18; Zeph 2:13), with Babylon the focus in Habakkuk, the book between them (Hab 1:5-11). Together the three books reveal how Yahweh allows imperial might to hold sway, even for a time, within the scope of his sovereignty.

Context

Nahum anticipates the destruction of Nineveh, which places it firmly in the latter third of the seventh century BC. Amos, Hosea, Micah, Nahum, and Zephaniah all emerge from this context. Nahum 3:8-10 mentions the fall of Thebes to the Neo-Assyrians in 663 BC. Thus, Nahum must come after that event. Klaas Spronk thinks the book emerged in Jerusalem around 660 BC, while Marvin Sweeney thinks the book likely emerged after the fall of the Neo-Assyrian Empire, with the sacking of Nineveh in 612 BC.[1] The content and tone of Nahum 3:1-7, 18-19 support Sweeney's view.

Connections between Nahum 1 and Habakkuk 3 encapsulate the books.[2] These hymns correlate the fall of Nineveh (Nahum) and the march of Yahweh to deliver Judah from Babylonian power (Habakkuk) through shared imagery and language. Yahweh is on the move, and he will judge the wicked

---

[1]Klaas Spronk, *Nahum*, HCOT (Kampen: Kok Pharos, 1997), 1, 12-13.
[2]Ranier Kessler, "Nahum-Habakuk als Zweiprophetenschrift: Ein Skizze," in *Gotteserdung: Beitrage zur Hermeneutik und Exegese der Hebraischen Bibel*, ed. R. Kessler, Beiträge zur Wissenschaft vom Alten und Neuen Testament 170 (Stuttgart: Kohlhammer, 2006), 137-45; Walter Dietrich, "Three Minor Prophets and the Major Empires," in *Perspectives on the Formation of the Book of the Twelve: Methodological Foundations—Redactional Processes—Historical Insights*, ed. Ranier Albertz, James D. Nogalski, and Jakob Wöhrle, BZAW 433 (Berlin: de Gruyter, 2012), 147-56.

and deliver his people. In this way, one can understand why some interpret portions of Nahum as a late monarchic to exilic text. However, Assyria becomes, with Egypt, a paradigmatic enemy for Israel, conjoined as it is with Egypt in some texts mentioning their doom (Hos 7:11; 11:5, 11; 12:1; Zech 10:11; see also Jer 2:18, 36; Lam 5:6). In this way, Assyria and Egypt (and indeed Babylon) become paradigmatic enemies. When a reader of the Twelve perceives any of them, one may hear echoes of empire and envision structures of oppressive and violent power. As such, Assyria becomes a metaphor of imperial violence that Yahweh will thwart by his just rule.

Outline

We follow Walter Dietrich's bipartite structure for the prophecies:[3]

Nahum 1:1	Superscription
Nahum 1:2–2:1 [1:2–1:15]	Yahweh's vengeance and power
Nahum 2:2–3:19 [2:1–3:19]	Poems of Nineveh's demise

Interpretation

Nahum 1:1. Nahum 1:1 states that what follows is a *maśśā'* oracle concerning Nineveh, "a writing of the vision of Nahum" (*sēper ḥăzôn naḥûm*). This latter phrase is unusual but finds a parallel in Deir 'Alla: "A warning from the writing [*spr*] of Balaam, son of Beor, a man of vision [*ḥzh*] of the gods."[4]

Nahum 1:2-10.[5] Nahum 1:2 opens the book with a chiasm:[6]

A   A jealous God
B   Yahweh is an avenger
B' Yahweh is an avenger
A' And a master of wrath

Nahum 1:2 sets the stage for the theme of the book: Yahweh judges in his wrath and avenges his honor. God's vengeance is an expression of his justice: the verbal form *nqm* is used in the Old Testament to describe Yahweh's vengeance against sinful Israel, who is oppressing the poor, needy, underprivileged, and exposed (Lev 26:25; Is 1:24; Jer 5:9; Ezek 24:8). In this sense,

---

[3]Walter Dietrich, *Nahum, Habakkuk, Zephaniah*, IECOT (Stuttgart: Kohlhammer, 2016), 21.
[4]Spronk, *Nahum*, 30.
[5]The broken acrostic of Nahum 1:2-8 is much discussed. See Thomas Renz, "A Perfectly Broken Acrostic in Nahum 1?," *JHS* 9, no. 23 (2009): doi:10.5508/jhs.2009.v9.a23.
[6]Spronk, *Nahum*, 33.

Yahweh is a "jealous" God (see Josh 24:19; Ex 20:5-6; Deut 5:9-10); the language indicates divine passion for sole worship and how worship then fuels proper action in the world.[7] A subtle play on words may emerge between *nōqēm*, "avenger," repeated in B and B' of the chiasm, and the prophet's name, *naḥûm*. God's vengeance against the oppressor and comfort for the oppressed emerge in the wordplay.

Nahum 1:3 draws on the self-disclosure formula in Exodus 34:6-7, witnessed elsewhere in the Minor Prophets. Nahum draws the characteristics of Yahweh into his broader argument of divine activity against the foe. Nahum 1:3a draws on these verses to argue that Yahweh is slow to anger but by no means clears the guilty. Nahum's placement in the Book of the Twelve, as well as its overarching message of judgment, affirms that Yahweh is a God who is slow to anger, but his divine patience has limits: at a certain point Yahweh's anger breaks forth to deliver the oppressed from the oppressor. However, we should remember that human sin has cost Yahweh as well, as "God has chosen to bear the people's sins rather than deal with them on strictly legal grounds."[8]

Nineveh is called the "city of bloodshed" (*'îr dāmîm*) in Nahum 3:1; Habakkuk 2:12 describes Babylon with similar language (*hôy bōneh 'îr bədāmîm*). However, in the Book of the Twelve Jerusalem can be designated with similar language to these bloody cities. Micah 3:10 describes Jerusalem's leaders as building "Zion with bloodshed and Jerusalem with injustice [*bōneh ṣiyyôn bədāmîm wîrûšālaim bə'awlâ*]." Yahweh judges *all* cities guilty of bloodshed; in Nahum 1:2-8, Yahweh traverses the south to the northeast, the normal route ancient travelers would take on their way to Nineveh. Judgment is sure, as Nahum 1:6 confirms: "Before his indignation who shall stand, and who will rise in the heat of his anger?"

Nahum 1:7, 12-15 shifts to present a word of hope for the Judahites. Nahum 2:1 [1:15] exhorts the audience:

> Look! Upon the mountains
>   the feet of one bringing news of victory,
>   One proclaiming peace
> Make pilgrimage, O Judah, [to] your feasts!
> Complete your vows!

---

[7] Against Steven Tuell, who argues that a "note of ambiguity" persists about Yahweh's rationale for action. Tuell, *Reading Nahum–Malachi*, ROT (Macon, GA: Smyth & Helwys, 2016), 22-23.

[8] Terence E. Fretheim, *The Suffering of God: An Old Testament Perspective*, Overtures to Biblical Theology (Philadelphia: Fortress, 1984), 148; see 138-48.

For a scoundrel will never again cross through you.
He has been completely cut off.

Nahum 2:1 [1:15] resonates with Isaiah 52:7: "How beautiful upon the mountains are the feet of the messenger who announces peace, who brings good news, who announces salvation, who says to Zion, 'Your God reigns'" (NRSV). Both texts depict an oracle in which the messenger (the prophet?) proclaims peace, the absence of war or oppression. In both texts, Yahweh's people find comfort in the divine action against Babylon (Isaiah) and Nineveh (Nahum). Yahweh defeats the Assyrian threat ("He has been completely cut off"), enabling Judah to make pilgrimage to Jerusalem and worship Yahweh. The "scoundrel," presumably Assyria, will never enter the territories of Judah again.

Nahum 2:1-13. In Nahum 2:2 [2:1], the "scatterer" (NRSV translates "shatterer") against Nineveh may be (1) Yahweh or (2) the instrument of divine judgment (Babylon, which sacked Nineveh in 612 BC). Nahum 2:3 [2:2] addresses God's people, reminding them that Yahweh "is restoring the majesty of Jacob as well as the majesty of Israel." This strange insertion combines Jacob *and* Israel in the vision of restoration, perhaps indicating royal dynasty and nation.[9]

Nahum 2:4-14 [2:3-14] portrays the attack on Nineveh. A third-person speaker observes the army charge (Nahum 2:4-7 [2:3-6]) and overwhelm the city. The attack is a flood: "gates of the rivers are opened, and the palace is dissolved" (Nahum 2:7 [2:6]). After invasion, prestige is gone (Nahum 2:8-14 [2:7-13]): the city is stripped of beauty (Nahum 2:9-11 [2:8-10]), wealth (Nahum 2:10 [2:9]), and people. Devastation is captured through consonance and assonance, *bûqâ ûməbûqâ ûməbūllāqâ* ("emptiness, and void, and waste!"; Nahum 2:11 [2:10]), and the shift to a metaphor of predation, with lions and their cubs on the hunt. Predation imagery, particularly of lions, is familiar in the Minor Prophets (Joel 1:6; Amos 3:4; Mic 5:7 [5:8]; Zeph 3:3; Zech 11:3), appearing now with the most evocative presentation in the Book of the Twelve (Nahum 2:12-13 [2:11-12]).[10] The lion and the cubs attack and maul Nineveh and fill their den with the kill.

Nahum 2:14 [2:13] shifts from third person description to first-person speech. Yahweh speaks against Nineveh:

---

[9]See J. J. M. Roberts, *Nahum, Habakkuk, and Zephaniah*, OTL (Louisville, KY: Westminster John Knox, 1990), 64-65.

[10]For discussion of the lion metaphors, see Thomas Renz, *The Books of Nahum, Habakkuk, and Zephaniah*, NICOT (Grand Rapids, MI: Eerdmans, 2021), 141-47; Brent A. Strawn, *What Is Stronger than a Lion? Leonine Image and Metaphor in the Hebrew Bible and the Ancient Near East*, OBO 212 (Göttingen: Vandenhoeck & Ruprecht, 2005).

> Behold! I am against you,
>> Utterance of Yahweh of Armies.
> And I will burn up her chariot in smoke;
>> And a sword will consume your young lions.
> And I will cut off your prey from the land;
>> And the voice of her messengers will never again be heard.

Nahum 2:14 [2:13] shifts to the "young lions" (young leaders) of Nineveh consumed by the sword of the enemy. The royal house ceases to exist (no royalty means neither royal messages nor royal messengers). Nahum 2:14 [2:13] also reverts to a gendered presentation of Nineveh as female. We retain the third-person feminine singular pronouns found in the Hebrew text ("her chariot"; "her messengers"). Nineveh and Jerusalem are depicted as females, as befits ancient Near Eastern convention.[11]

Nahum 3:1-19. Yahweh once again speaks (Nahum 3:5-6) against Nineveh: "I am against you" (Nahum 3:5 // Nahum 2:14 [2:13]). Utilizing the horrific imagery of a raped woman, Yahweh will "lift up" Nineveh's skirts over Nineveh's face "and display your nakedness to the nations" (Nahum 3:5). This spectacle reverses the former honor of the city, and now the enemies look on Nineveh's shame (Nahum 3:5b). Moreover, Yahweh will "throw filth" on the city, her degradation complete.

Nahum 3:8-9 remembers Assyria's conquered nations and cities of ages past: No-Amon (Thebes), Cush, Egypt, Put, and Libya. However, these fallen kingdoms now call out against their oppressor, Assyria. Nineveh experiences the desolation formerly meted out against others by herself. Nahum 3:15-17 portrays the invading armies as a swarm of locusts (see Joel 1:4) that devour everything. In the face of the impending destruction, the king of Nineveh offers no defense or help (Nahum 3:18). The demonstrated cruelty of Assyria will come back on its head, and nothing remedies its fate: "Your wound is severe" (Nahum 3:19).

THE CONTEXT OF ZEPHANIAH

From Nahum we turn to Zephaniah, who is "a relentless critic of his age."[12] The prophet's unyielding critique of his people stems from their pervasive

---

[11]Cynthia R. Chapman, *The Gendered Language of Warfare in the Israelite-Assyrian Encounter*, HSM 62 (Winona Lake, IN: Eisenbrauns, 2004), 104-5.
[12]Maria Eszenyei Szeles, *Habakkuk and Zephaniah: Wrath and Mercy*, ITC (Edinburgh: Handsel, 1987), 63.

rebellion against Yahweh. Judah's leaders had effectively turned their backs on their covenant God to worship pagan deities such as Baal, a Canaanite storm deity (Zeph 1:4), and possibly to astral worship (Zeph 1:5).[13] God's people are idolatrous to their core.

The book is familiar with the topography, streets and gates, and social structures of Jerusalem, so Zephaniah may have emerged from the royal court of Judah around 630 BC or from the leadership of Jerusalem.[14] Based on the superscription, Zephaniah ministered in the first half of Josiah's reign (639–609 BC), just prior to the royal reform movement around 622 BC (see 2 Kings 22:3–23:23).[15] Zephaniah's preaching warns God's people of their infidelity to him and their need to "seek the LORD" (Zeph 2:3).

Outline

Zephaniah 1:1	Superscription
Zephaniah 1:2-18	Divine judgment on the day of the Lord
Zephaniah 1:2-3	Creation
Zephaniah 1:4-13	Judah and Jerusalem
Zephaniah 1:14-18	The day of the Lord
Zephaniah 2:1-3[16]	Call for repentance
Zephaniah 2:4-15	Oracles against the nations
Zephaniah 2:4-7	Philistia
Zephaniah 2:8-11	Moab and Ammon
Zephaniah 2:12	Cush
Zephaniah 2:13-15	Assyria
Zephaniah 3:1-20	Zion judged and restored

---

[13]See Adele Berlin, *Zephaniah*, AB (New Haven, CT: Yale University Press, 2008), 75-77.

[14]The prophet readily denounces the palace its practices (Zeph 1:8). He knows international and royal practices of other major kingdoms (Zeph 2). Zephaniah also is familiar with Jerusalem's leaders (Zeph 3:3), the religion and cult (Zeph 3:4), and the city's tradesmen and their practices (Zeph 1:11).

[15]It is possible that Zephaniah's preaching occurred just after the reforms as well, when they did not take hold as Josiah had hoped. We prefer to see Zephaniah's preaching as early in Josiah's reign.

[16]Perlitt takes this section to be distinct from Zeph 1:2-18 on a formal level. Lothar Perlitt, *Die Propheten Nahum, Habakkuk, Zephanja*, Das Alte Testament Deutsch 25/1 (Göttingen: Vandenhoeck & Ruprecht, 2004), 118. We have included it with the day of the Lord judgment because of the call to repentance in Zeph 2:1-3 is *still* set in the context of the "day of the LORD's wrath" (Zeph 2:2-3).

| Zephaniah 3:1-8 | Judged Zion |
| Zephaniah 3:9-20 | Restored Zion |

Nowadays it is common to think that the book of Zephaniah did not reach its final form until the postexilic (Persian) period.[17] Some believe portions of the book belong with the earliest grouping of texts in the Minor Prophets, called the "Book of the Four," which includes (portions of) Hosea, Amos, Micah, and Zephaniah.[18] However, Zephaniah "now presents itself rhetorically and structurally as a unified work."[19]

INTERPRETATION

Zephaniah 1:1. Read alongside the co-text of 2 Kings 22–23, it is clear that the prophet preaches in a time of upheaval and transition. Josiah begins in earnest to bring God's people back to Yahweh. Zephaniah is largely sympathetic to this reform, warning of impending doom and calling God's people in Judah to seek Yahweh once again.

Zephaniah 1:2–2:3. The introductory oracle of Zephaniah 1:2-3 draws on creation language (Gen 1:20-28) only to invert it: God will no longer create—he will *de*-create. "I will utterly sweep away everything." Those living things populating God's world (humans, animals, birds, fish) will be "wiped off" its face. Although the next verses focus on Judah and Jerusalem, the universal vision of destruction is unmistakable in Zephaniah 1:2-3. God, as the creator of the world, exerts his authority to be its *destroyer*.

Zephaniah 1:4-6 unpacks the rationale for the decree. God will stretch out his hand in judgment against Judah and "all the residents of Jerusalem" (Zeph 1:4). The universal frame by which God's judgment is understood in Zephaniah 1:2-3 narrows to God's chosen land and city: Judah, the southern kingdom, which remained after the destruction of the northern kingdom in 722 BC, and "all the residents of Jerusalem," those who live in the capital city of Judah and worship at Yahweh's temple. Zephaniah 1:4 indicates that this central place of devotion had become corrupted by Baal worship. Either Baal was worshiped exclusively in Jerusalem, according to the prophet's critique, or more likely Baal was worshiped alongside Yahweh in Jerusalem. Hence the phrase "I will cut off from this place the remnant of Baal" in Zephaniah 1:4.

---

[17] James D. Nogalski, *The Book of the Twelve: Micah–Malachi*, SHBC (Macon, GA: Smyth & Helwys, 2011), 698-706.
[18] Nogalski, *Book of the Twelve*, 492-93, 700-701.
[19] Berlin, *Zephaniah*, 20.

Zephaniah 1:4 makes clear that the inhabitants of Jerusalem venerate a pagan deity in the heart of Yahweh's own temple. The term "this place" in Zephaniah 1:4 also indicates where Yahweh reigns and judges: the temple. Yahweh, the great lover of his people (see the chapter on Hosea), announces his bride's infidelity in their bridal chamber, the temple itself.

Zephaniah 1:4b-6 narrows Yahweh's judgment. The priesthood has forfeited their duties, and the priests are the subject of Zephaniah 1:4b-6. The judgment oracle presupposes that the pagan priestly practices are in full swing at the temple. Yahweh will no longer endure it; he will "cut off" the very name of those pagan priests from his house.

Zephaniah 1:5-6 escalates the intensity of apostasy. Not only are there pagan Baal priests serving in the temple of Yahweh, but they worship the stars or astral deities *and* swear by Yahweh *as well as* the pagan deity Molek (or Milcom). Zephaniah 1:6 summarizes: these priests no longer *seek* (*lō ʾ- biqšû*) Yahweh, nor do they inquire of (*lō ʾ dərāšūhû*) Yahweh. The true priest should guard knowledge and "seek" (*bqš*) Yahweh's instruction (Mal 2:7). A priest "inquires" (*drš*) of the Lord for direction and discernment, likely at the request of others (2 Kings 22:13). Although not exclusively a priestly duty, that "seeking" and "inquiring of" Yahweh appear in Zephaniah 1:6 with cultic activity immediately preceding them (Zeph 1:5) draws the focus of the rebuke in Zephaniah 1:4-6 to the idolatrous priests, who have led God's people astray.[20]

Zephaniah 1:7 flags Yahweh's judgment against God's people, especially the wayward priests. "Be silent from before the Lord Yahweh, for the day of the LORD is near." It is likely the temple constitutes the spatial location of Yahweh's decree of judgment (see Hab 2:20).

Feasting is a wonderful time in the liturgical calendar of God's people. But Zephaniah's prophecy strikes a discordant note regarding feasts. Yahweh calls a feast and consecrates his guests, but it is a festival of *divine wrath* rather than celebration and joy (Zeph 1:7b-8). As strange as it may be in the modern West, pilgrimage, homecoming, and sacred meals fueled Israel's social and cultic experience and way of knowing God.[21] Worship, feasting, and pilgrimage marked Israel's identity so that Israel was herself as she worshiped. Moreover, Israel knew God precisely through ritually shaped

---

[20]The motif of "seeking" (*bqš*) Yahweh recurs in Zephaniah.
[21]Dru Johnson, *Knowledge by Ritual: A Biblical Prolegomenon to Sacramental Theology*, Journal of Theological Studies Supplement Series 13 (Winona Lake, IN: Eisenbrauns, 2016).

disclosures of divine identity. Often these rituals required sacrifices. The term *sacrifice* in Zephaniah 1:7 is *zebaḥ*, an offering in which a portion is immolated at the altar and certain portions are reserved as food for the priests and the one who brings the sacrifice.

Zephaniah 1:7-8 introduce a metaphor that inverts the normal order of liturgical sacrifices. Instead of worshipers bringing and offering to Yahweh and worshiping before the Lord, in these verses Yahweh prepares the sacrifice and offers it. Instead of an animal for sacrifice, Yahweh brings the royal and cultic leaders as the offering. Indeed, the entirety of Judah is the target of the sacrifice, if one takes Zephaniah 1:2-17 in view. This inversion is unexpected and shocking, designed to evoke the horror of Yahweh sacrificing humans for their sin as a form of punishment. This new ritual way of knowing Yahweh exposes a new view of consecration as well: "consecrated" guests of Yahweh for his sacrifice (Zeph 1:7). Are these consecrated to celebrate the meal with Yahweh? Or are they consecrated as the sacrificial animal?

Early Christian opinion diverged. Jerome, Cyril of Alexandria, and Theodore of Mopsuestia identify those consecrated as those whom God appointed for executing his divine judgment against Judah. As such, the guests are the Babylonians. But Theodoret of Cyrus (ca. AD 431–440) is the earliest commentator to identify the guests as those consecrated for punishment, namely, the people of Judah: "You see, since what is really holy is set aside and marked off from the profane, he calls *sanctified* those set aside for punishment, in being set aside by the God of all himself."[22] Although ambiguous in terms of who/what is consecrated, the larger point of the metaphor is to evoke terror. Yahweh ritually offers his own people, enabling a fearsome new way of understanding God.

Thus, those who would blithely say to themselves, "The LORD will not do good, nor will he do harm" (Zeph 1:12 NRSV), are proven to be horrifically naive, blinded by their own apathy toward Yahweh. Apparently, apathy was common from those in Jerusalem with wealth, as Zephaniah 1:10-13 indicates. Wealth perhaps enabled these Judahites to be indifferent, thinking Yahweh would do nothing to dislodge them from their prestige. Yahweh's response to such indifference and apathy toward his rule is terrifying: the day of Yahweh (Zeph 1:14-18).

---

[22]Theodoret of Cyrus, *Commentaries on the Prophets*, vol. 3, *Commentary on the Twelve Prophets*, trans. Robert Charles Hill (Brookline, MA: Holy Cross Orthodox Press, 2006), 209.

Echoes of Joel 1:15 appear in Zephaniah 1:14: "for the day of Yahweh is near" (Joel 1:15) // "the great day of Yahweh is near" (Zeph 1:14). Both texts highlight the imminence of Yahweh's judgment. Like Amos 5:18, 20 and Joel 2:2, for Zephaniah 1:15 the day of Yahweh is "darkness," but Zephaniah takes the gloomy picture further in Zephaniah 1:15-16: a day of fury, distress and melting, devastation and desolation, gloom and darkness, cloud and heavy clouds, a day of horn and war cry against the fortified cities and against high corners. Piling up ominous images of devastation and warfare (especially against the walls and fortifications of the city, Zeph 1:16) allows the reader to taste the horrors of divine judgment.

Finally, Zephaniah 1:18 subtly exposes the pride of the inhabitants, the object of Yahweh's wrath. The inhabitants of Jerusalem have trusted in their "silver and gold" for security and salvation. In this way, Zephaniah 1:18 gives some clarity to the meaning of Zephaniah 1:17: "because they sinned against Yahweh." God's people commit the sin of misplaced trust: they trusted in wealth to save when Yahweh is their only salvation.

Yahweh's day of darkness is graphic: an enemy army spreads through the business district and wealthy areas from the northwest (Fish Gate, Zeph 1:10) to the southwest (Second Quarter, Zeph 1:10) and then to the south and southeast. The sound of warfare, clanging, battle, and wailing is matched with the overriding darkness and gloom accompanying the invasion. In short, Yahweh's day is dreadful and distressing.

The cosmic significance of the event comes with the last line of Zephaniah 1:18: "And in the fire of his zeal, the whole earth shall be consumed. For a full, indeed a terrible end he will make to all the inhabitants of the earth." With this concluding statement, the reader is drawn back to the cosmic imagery of Zephaniah 1:3, where Yahweh has decreed that he will wipe humanity off the face of the earth. The poetry reinforces the inescapability of divine judgment. There is truly nowhere to hide or escape the divine verdict. How should the people respond?

Zephaniah 2:1-3 calls for *repentance*, a response that restores the broken covenant relationship with Yahweh. The call begins with difficult verses that are on all counts obscure. Zephaniah 2:1-2 is unclear, leading the Latin Vulgate, the Old Greek (LXX), and modern translations to render the verses variously. However, Zephaniah 2:1 indicates the necessity of gathering together, most likely the nation of Judah (the referent to the Hebrew *haggôy*, "the nation"), and Zephaniah 2:2 indicates the timeframe of the gathering:

"before the burning anger of Yahweh comes upon you" (*bəterem lō'-yābô' ălêkem yôm 'ap-YHWH*). The construction of this Hebrew phrase is difficult, as is its syntactical relation to the beginning of the verse. The construction remains difficult because *lō'-yābô'*, "it will not come upon you," combined with the adverb *bəterem*, "before," presents a double negative. It is impossible for something to occur before it happens! Adele Berlin suggests the construction marks emphasis: repent before Yahweh's day comes.[23]

The other option is a purpose clause: "In order that the burning anger of Yahweh not come upon you." This option is possible if the phrase is syntactically dependent on Zephaniah 2:1. Thus, the meaning of the verses would be a call to gather together and repent (Zeph 2:1) so that "the burning anger of Yahweh will not come upon you."

Whereas Zephaniah 2:1-2 remain difficult, the sense of Zephaniah 2:3 is clear. The text reads, "Seek Yahweh, all humble ones of the land, those who do his judgment; seek righteousness, seek humility, [and] perhaps they may be hidden on the day of the anger of Yahweh." The notion of being hidden from Yahweh's wrath is a way of saying that one will be preserved from the judgment of God. Opposed to those experiencing wrath on the day of Yahweh, those who are hidden on judgment day display a radically different disposition, distinguished by a quest: a search for Yahweh, for righteousness, and for humility. Those who are marked by this quest are defined as "all the poor/humble of the land who do his [Yahweh's] command" (Zeph 2:3).

Zephaniah 2:3 presents the command "seek!" three times in the plural imperative *baqqəšû*, followed by the objects of the commands: seek Yahweh (*baqqəšû YHWH*), seek righteousness (*baqqəšû ṣedeq*), and seek humility (*baqqəšû 'ănāwâ*). The commands mark a quest for the things of God in the face of loss or lack of direction (see Deut 4:29; Is 51:1; Jer 29:13; Hos 3:5). This quest provides a pathway of survival in the day of divine anger. A word should be said about the pursuit of righteousness (*ṣedeq*). Hemchand Gossai avers:

> In essence then צדק [righteousness] is not simply an objective norm which is present within society, and which must be kept, but rather it is a concept which derives its meaning from the relationship in which it finds itself. So we are able to say that right judging, right governing, right worshipping and gracious activity are all covenantal and righteous, despite their diversity.[24]

---

[23]Berlin, *Zephaniah*, 97.
[24]Hemchand Gossai, *Justice, Righteousness and the Social Critique by Israel's Eighth-Century Prophets*, American University Studies 141 (New York: Peter Lang, 1993), 55-56.

By seeking righteousness (*ṣedeq*), the faithful seek Yahweh, who is "upright" (*ṣaddîq*). The status of harmony in the covenant is threatened by sin. Yahweh enjoins his people to seek the harmonious relationship ("righteousness") and to do so by being humble and doing Yahweh's decrees.

Zephaniah 2:4-15. This section presents oracles against Philistia (Zeph 2:4-7), Moab and Ammon (Zeph 2:8-11), Cush (Zeph 2:12), and Assyria (Zeph 2:13-15). These nations exerted power, according to Berlin, sometime between 633 and 618 BC. Moab, Ammon, and Philistia were vassals of the Assyrian Empire during that era (though Cush, it must be admitted, seems a bit of an outlier). In Zephaniah 2:4-15, divine judgment goes from the east (Philistia) to the west (Moab and Ammon) and the south (Cush) to the north (Assyria; see Amos 1–2). The four major cities of Philistia parallel one another in Zephaniah 2:4: Gaza // Ashkelon, Ashdod // Ekron. These are complemented by correspondence between Moab and Ammon (Zeph 2:8-9), whose destruction echoes Sodom and Gomorrah, respectively (Zeph 2:9).

The Moabites/Ammonites display "pride" (*gā'ôn*, Zeph 2:10), a negative characteristic often appearing in judgment texts against the nations (Ex 15:7; Ezek 16:56; 32:12; Zech 9:6; 10:11; Amos 6:8) and against Israel and Judah (Amos 6:8; Hos 5:5; 7:10; Jer 13:9). Pride demarcates its owner as fundamentally opposed to Yahweh and his purposes with humanity. By contrast, Yahweh seeks those who are humble (*'ănāwâ*, Zeph 2:3).

Oracles against Cush (Ethiopia) and Assyria follow in Zephaniah 2:12-15. The prophecy against Cush is short and abrupt, giving the impression its presence (Zeph 2:12) balances the geographical array between north/south and east/west. No sin is mentioned by Cush in Zephaniah 2:12, only judgment. Expansive judgment against Assyria appears in Zephaniah 2:13-15. Self-adulation is the target: Yahweh castigates Nineveh (the capital of Assyria) as the "exultant city" who believed "I am, and there is no other!" (Zeph 2:15). Nineveh's self-declaration of independence jars against Yahweh's virtually identical revelation in Isaiah 45:5:

> Zephaniah 2:15: "I am, and there is no other!" (speech of Nineveh)
> Isaiah 45:5: "I am Yahweh, and there is no other!" (speech of God)

Zephaniah 3:1-20. Zephaniah 3 is of a piece, devoted to the judgment (Zeph 3:1-8) and restoration (Zeph 3:9-20) of Zion. Zephaniah 3:1-5 speaks in the voice of an external observer viewing the immorality of

Jerusalem. A general sense of depravity, predation, and faithlessness emerges among the leaders of the people (judges, Zeph 3:3; prophets, Zeph 3:4; priests, Zeph 3:4). Zephaniah 3:2 presents the general malaise: "She does not obey; she takes no instruction; in Yahweh she does not trust; to God she does not draw near." The city and people rebel against Yahweh, the covenant Lord of Israel.[25] In response, Yahweh judges his own people due to covenant failure, exemplified in social breakdown and oppression (Zeph 3:3-5).[26]

Apart from their covenantal rebellion, Zephaniah 3:5 declares, "Yahweh is righteous [*ṣaddîq*] in her midst; he does no wrong. Morning by morning he renders his judgment in the light." Yahweh is the righteous covenant partner. Noted above in Zephaniah 2:3, Yahweh remains upright (*ṣaddîq*) in the way he relates to his people, but they know no "shame" (Zeph 3:5).

His enacted judgment against nations (Zeph 2:4-15) would surely draw the city of Zion to "fear" Yahweh, but Zephaniah 3:7 exposes that it did not: "they were eager to corrupt all their deeds." As a result, Yahweh judges the sins of Judah (and the nations). Those who eschew humility and instead embody pride and haughtiness will be put to shame. The phrase in Zephaniah 3:11, "For then I will remove from your midst *your proudly exultant ones*" (NRSV), draws on language already witnessed in Zephaniah: the "exultant" city of Nineveh (Zeph 2:15) // the "exultant ones" of Jerusalem (Zeph 3:11).[27] Both Nineveh *and* Jerusalem fall under the weight of their pride and the overwhelming judgment of God against them.

However, those who exhibit humility and lowliness (Zeph 3:12) and those who take shelter in "the name of Yahweh" will be preserved in judgment, also called "the remnant of Israel" (Zeph 3:13). The remnant reminds God's people of hope beyond judgment, and so this people exhibit humility, faithfulness, and seeking him in the present day (see Zeph 2:3). This remnant will be composed of peoples, presumably both Israel *and* the nations, with "pure speech" who will call "upon the name of Yahweh" (Zeph 3:9). Whereas, prior to divine intervention, their speech may have been defiled, it is purged now of sin (hence the Hebrew adjective *bərûrâ*, "pure"). A final image of peace

---

[25] Dietrich (*Nahum, Habakkuk, Zephaniah*, 231) views the language as late.
[26] Against Dietrich (*Nahum, Habakkuk, Zephaniah*, 231), who views the covenantal overtones of Zeph 3:2 separate from the theme of social failure and oppression in Zeph 3:3-5. In our view, covenantal failure on the part of the people (Zeph 3:1-2) is exemplified in the oppression of the leadership (Zeph 3:3-5).
[27] ʿālîz ("exultuant") is used in both.

and security in Zion concludes this section: "They will pasture and lie down, and no one will make them afraid" (Zeph 3:13 NRSV).

Zephaniah 3:14-20 invokes redeemed and restored Zion to celebrate Yahweh's vindication in song. The city is personified as female, as is often the case in prophetic texts, calling the city of Jerusalem the "daughter of Zion" (Zeph 3:14). The title "daughter of Zion" becomes a polyvalent metaphor, used here to emphasize the place of renewal and security under the reign of God. Zion is a judged but renewed city whose king (Yahweh) is in her midst (Zeph 3:15).[28] Yahweh celebrates Zion's redemption with singing "as on a festival day" (Zeph 3:18), contrasting with the dark feast of Zephaniah 1:7. Yahweh enables the traverse from shame to honor, from judgment to restoration. He restores Zion's fortunes, a phrase that connotes future life before God in the land.

THE THEOLOGY OF NAHUM AND ZEPHANIAH

God, Israel, and the nations. These books present Yahweh's justice displayed among Israel and the nations, or Yahweh's imperial power.[29] That so small a nation as Judah would assert the cosmic power of Yahweh over Assyria is no small feat. God enfolds the fate of the nations into his larger purposes of creation renewal, here in Nahum and Zephaniah as (primarily) object lessons of divine judgment against sin. Divine punishment of nations reveals Yahweh's fundamental commitment to justice instead of a raw exercise of imperial power. "There are limits to brute power, and the curb on such brutalizing, arrogant power is the indefatigable resolve of Yahweh, which regularly defeats the greatest powers, who thought they were situated for success to perpetuity."[30]

Nahum castigates Assyria for serial crime, which Yahweh judges: plotting evil against Yahweh (Nahum 1:11), enslavement (Nahum 1:12-13), idolatry (Nahum 1:14), injustice/bloodshed (Nahum 3:1), and prostitution/sorcery and selling/exploiting nations (Nahum 3:4). These crimes, and Yahweh's response, lead Walter Brueggemann to rightly argue that the "emotive aversion

---

[28] For full discussion of Zion and the Daughter of Zion, see Heath A. Thomas, "Zion," in *Dictionary of the Old Testament Prophets*, ed. Mark J. Boda and J. Gordon McConville (Downers Grove, IL: IVP Academic, 2012), 907-14.

[29] David L. Petersen, *The Prophetic Literature: An Introduction* (Louisville, KY: Westminster John Knox, 2002), 38-39.

[30] Walter Brueggemann, *Theology of the Old Testament: Testimony, Dispute, Advocacy* (Minneapolis: Fortress, 1997), 504.

to brutality is located in the heart of Yahweh, so that political abuse becomes, in the end, theological reality.... Assyrian imperialism is contained Yahwistically in the categories of mandate-violation of mandate-sanctions. The empire cannot outflank Yahweh, who wills compassion in the political process."[31] Yahweh's repugnance for injustice among the nations matches divine revulsion of injustice among his people.

What is only hinted at in Nahum (Nahum 1:15; 2:2) takes its full form in Zephaniah (Zeph 3:9-13). The nations will be judged (Zeph 2:4-15), but Yahweh will restore the peoples so that "all of them may call on the name of Yahweh and serve him with a single purpose" (Zeph 3:9). These restored peoples will be present in Zion: "The king of Israel, Yahweh, is among you; you shall no longer fear" (Zeph 3:15). In this way, Yahweh's purpose with Israel and the nations becomes clearer: both may be judged, but Yahweh's ultimate vision of the future is one of restoration, with his reign assured in Zion. What will *not* be allowed in this restoration vision, however, is a lack of devotion to Yahweh. Rather, Yahweh draws into Zion those who are "meek" and "humble," who take refuge in Yahweh's name (Zeph 3:12). This remnant of those preserved after divine judgment will have nothing to make them afraid (Zeph 3:13).

God and violence. God's relationship with violence has been a perennial problem in the Christian church since the days of Marcion in the second century AD, whose perception of divine violence in the Old Testament led him to divest the God of the Old Testament from association with Jesus and the New Testament. Clearly Nahum and Zephaniah present the violent God, a divine warrior attacking Nineveh/Assyria (Nahum 1:2-8) and Jerusalem/Judah (Zeph 1:2-18). Regina Schwartz argues that violence, inherent in the Bible, establishes a violent legacy for the church. Biblical violence begets communal violence.[32]

In light of Schwartz's proposal, we must clearly unpack what one means by *violence*, divine or otherwise, and what it might mean for community.[33] Violence is "an act or deportment that causes pain (physical, social, emotional, psychological, or even spiritual) to an Other."[34] If this definition holds,

---

[31] Brueggemann, *Theology of the Old Testament*, 509.
[32] Regina Schwartz, *The Curse of Cain: The Violent Legacy of Monotheism* (Chicago: University of Chicago Press, 1998).
[33] Jerome F. D. Creach, *Violence in Scripture*, IBC (Louisville, KY: Westminster John Knox, 2013).
[34] Heath A. Thomas, "Suffering Has Its Voice: Divine Violence, Pain and Prayer in Lamentations," in *Wrestling with the Violence of God: Soundings in the Old Testament*, ed. M. Daniel Carroll R.

then Nahum and Zephaniah present Yahweh as violent, causing Judah and Assyria pain.

Still, violence may be associated with pain but not necessarily correlated with additional experiences of evil. An experience can be painful (and thereby violent) but beneficial. Parental discipline and physical exercise underscore the difference between experiences of pain and harm/evil. Discipline and exercise may be violent, but it does not follow that these actions or actors should be further defined as harmful or evil.[35] Rather, they may be violent *and* good, or at the very least beneficial (Prov 13:24; 22:15; 23:13; 29:15).

Nahum and Zephaniah reveal Yahweh to be violent but also to be profoundly good, as he acts in the interests of the oppressed and against the oppressor, whether the oppressor is Nineveh/Assyria (Nahum) or Jerusalem/Judah (Zephaniah). Rescue and salvation of the oppressed means violence against the tormentor. Yahweh's violence is real, but divine violence works in service of divine justice, as Abraham Heschel notes: "Since justice is His nature, love, which would disregard the evil deeds of man, would contradict His nature. Because of his concern for man, His justice is tempered with mercy. Divine anger is not the antithesis of love, but its counterpart, a help to justice as demanded by true love."[36] Yahweh's patience is extensive, as we have seen in Jonah, but his nature as just drives God to enact justice for the oppressed and for his name. In this light, the covenant characteristics of Yahweh's jealousy and vengeance tempered with divine patience in Nahum 1:2-3 make sense. Nevertheless, some critics remain unconvinced.

Julia O'Brien states, "In Nahum, Nineveh's cruelty provokes Yahweh's anger; that anger leads Yahweh to take vengeance on enemies; and the destruction of those enemies is described as the sexual assault of a woman."[37] One cannot justify divine violence if that means the violation of a female body. Judith Sanderson extends O'Brien's point: "No aspect of God's relationship with humankind can be represented in the modern world by an image that depends on a destructive view of women's bodied selves." Because Nahum's divine warrior against the (female) city of Nineveh "is dangerous to women's health, lives, and well-being," she says, it "must be recognized as

---

and J. Blair Wilgus, Bulletin for Biblical Research Supplement Series 10 (Winona Lake, IN: Eisenbrauns, 2015), 94.

[35]Thomas, "Suffering Has Its Voice," 94-95.

[36]Abraham J. Heschel, *The Prophets*, Perennial Classics ed. (New York: HarperCollins, 2001), 380-81.

[37]Julia M. O'Brien, *Challenging Prophetic Metaphor* (Louisville, KY: Westminster John Knox, 2008), 112.

such. In a society where violence against women is epidemic, it is extremely dangerous to image God as involved in it in any way."[38]

Leonard Maré and Johan Serfontein similarly argue that the book depicts human values rather than divine ones:

> The violent YHWH in Nahum should perhaps not be associated with the God humankind is struggling to know and comprehend. . . . Humankind creates a god that serves its needs and ideologies. Thus, the god of Nahum becomes a rhetorical-ideological construct of the expectations of the society and ideologies of the world in which Nahum's author and audience once lived.[39]

They regard the god of Nahum as a human construct they can reject, enabling a constructive counterreading. Because Maré and Serfontein resist Nahum's ideological presentation, they create space to construct "a God who is compassionate and loving to those in need."[40]

But on what basis is their construction of God better than the god of Nahum depicted in the text? To have a God "compassionate and loving to those in need" may mean the deity enacts or allows violence to preserve justice. In the Minor Prophets, again and again God allows—without endorsing their methods—nations to conquer others, with all the associated brutality, as part of his purposes of justice. In the world presented by Nahum and Zephaniah—much less the modern world—it is difficult to conceive of protective or compassionate action toward the oppressed that may not simultaneously be violent toward the oppressor.

To O'Brien and Sanderson's objections, one could resist and excise the text altogether from theological ethics to avert the theological problem.[41] This move, however, could prevent engagement with a text to shock the reader in potential complicity in shame, degradation, or violence.[42] Alternatively, this move may prevent the strange pathway Nahum provides for

---

[38] Judith E. Sanderson, "Nahum," in *Women's Bible Commentary*, expanded ed., ed. Carol A. Newsom and Sharon H. Ringe (Louisville, KY: Westminster John Knox, 1998), 235-36.

[39] Leonard Maré and Johan Serfontein, "The Violent, Rhetorical-Ideological God of Nahum," *Old Testament Essays* 22, no. 1 (2009): 175-85.

[40] Maré and Serfontein, "Violent, Rhetorical-Ideological God," 184.

[41] Joseph Jensen omits Nahum and Zephaniah from consideration in *Ethical Dimensions of the Prophets* (Collegeville, MN: Liturgical Press, 2006).

[42] As does Hugh Pyper when reading monstrous violence against the female in Lamentations. See Pyper, "Reading Lamentations," *JSOT* 95 (2001): 55-69. He argues the shaming character of the text should not be expunged but read and, as such, presents a potentially salutary shock in exposing *readers* to potential complicity in such shameful activity.

healing when facing extraordinary violence in a modern context, as Jacob Onyumbe Wenyi demonstrates in a reading of Nahum from an African context (Congo).[43] Removing bits of the Bible readers find distasteful may limit the transformative or shocking potential of Scripture.

Hans Boersma's work provides a different valence on the question of God and violence, offering divine hospitality to comprehend divine violence. Boersma argues:

> God's hospitality requires violence, just as his love necessitates wrath. This is not to say, of course, that God's violence and wrath are his essential attributes. God *is* love, not wrath; he *is* a God of hospitality, not a God of violence. There is an absolute primacy, therefore, of hospitality over violence. Hospitality bespeaks of the very essence of God, while violence is merely one of the ways to safeguard or ensure the future of his hospitality when dealing with the humps and bumps of our lives. Divine violence, in other words, is a way in which God strives toward an eschatological situation of pure hospitality.[44]

The Christian God, in his essence, is love and pure hospitality. Boersma posits pure divine love and hospitality compose the destination of all creation. God provides, through creation and (especially) new creation, the perfect love for God, self, one another, and the world lived out and borne before the presence of God.

However, in a broken world, violence—even divine violence—is necessary for the revelation of God's love to take hold in the real world. "Love, it seems, requires passionate anger toward anything that would endanger the relationship of love."[45] Divine violence ensures the possibility of the pure hospitality and love.

Divine violence in Nahum and Zephaniah is act of compassion toward and salvation for the oppressed, and divine vengeance emerges from Yahweh's desire for justice and love. In the Book of the Twelve, "Nahum focusses on what some might call the 'dark side' of God, while Jonah portrays God's mercy and compassion toward the same wicked city. Both aspects are essential for an understanding of divine nature."[46]

---

[43]Jacob Onyumbe Wenyi, *Piles of Slain, Heaps of Corpses: Reading Prophetic Poetry and Violence in African Context* (Eugene, OR: Cascade, 2021).
[44]Hans Boersma, *Violence, Hospitality, and the Cross: Reappropriating the Atonement Tradition* (Grand Rapids, MI: Baker Academic, 2004), 49.
[45]Boersma, *Violence*, 49.
[46]Duane L. Christensen, *Nahum: A New Translation with Introduction and Commentary*, AB (New Haven, CT: Yale University Press, 2009), 3.

God and restoration. Divine restoration towers in Zephaniah. Zephaniah 3:9 depicts a future restoration where the nations are purged of their wickedness so that their very speech is transformed that they all "call on the name Yahweh." Judah, too, is caught up in this restoration; the final destiny of Zion culminates as the nations and Israel unite in Zion. "The LORD has taken away the judgments against you, he has turned away your enemies. The king of Israel, the LORD, is in your midst; you shall fear disaster no more" (Zeph 3:15 NRSV).

Restoration of fortunes in Zephaniah 3:14-20 exposes the past sins of God's people only to traverse former sin by the redemptive power of Yahweh. In this renewed relationship, Yahweh reestablishes his people into their land, where they will be productive and remain in their place, under the reign of Yahweh, their God. Note that the phrase that Yahweh is "in your midst" recurs in Zephaniah 3:15, 17, highlighting Yahweh's presence and rule in this restoration. Yahweh will reign perfectly, Israel will be completely devoted to their God, and they will be renowned among the nations.

NAHUM AND ZEPHANIAH IN THE NEW TESTAMENT

Zephaniah is virtually absent from the New Testament in terms of explicit quotation. Revelation may obliquely allude to Zephaniah in Revelation 14:5, "no lie was found in their mouth; they are blameless" (*kai en tō stomati autōn ouk eurethē pseudos: amōmoi eisin*), which echoes LXX Zephaniah 3:13: "the remnant of Israel will do no wrong, and they will speak no empty thing, and there will be no deceitful tongue found in their mouth" (*kai ou lalēsousi mataia, kai ou mē eurethē en tō stomati autōn glōssa dolia: dioti autoi nemēsontai*). This connection, however, is dubious.

Romans 10:15 alludes to Nahum 2:1 [1:15], which speaks to the need for a messenger to proclaim the good news of Jesus Christ.[47] "And how are they to proclaim him unless they are sent? As it is written, 'How beautiful are the feet of those who bring good news!'" (Rom 10:15 NRSV). The logion "as it is written" indicates that what follows is a quotation of Hebrew Scripture. This citation, however, is not direct and shares language with Isaiah 52:7.

There may be an echo of Nahum 3:4 in Revelation 17:2, with the apocalypse's description of Babylon fitting Nahum's depiction of Assyria: "Because of the countless debaucheries of the prostitute, gracefully alluring, mistress of sorcery, who enslaves nations through her debaucheries, and peoples

---

[47] Christensen, *Nahum*, 18.

through her sorcery" (Nahum 3:4 NRSV). Beyond these, little of Nahum emerges in the New Testament except for thematic correspondence between divine judgment against the nations, particularly Babylon in Revelation.

Nahum and Zephaniah Today

Nahum and Zephaniah portray God's work in the world, accenting divine judgment against exploitation and oppression. Yahweh will not abide oppression, and Yahweh will act—even in violence—against such injustice. Yahweh has made humanity to cultivate, rather than domineer, the created order. With each act of imperial oppression and exploitation, both Israel and the nations reveal themselves as threats to the good created order and worthy of divine judgment so as to liberate the rest of creation from oppressive rule.

For Christian faith, the judgment and salvation of God, so clearly on display in Nahum and Zephaniah, is preeminently answered in the cross of Jesus Christ. God has spoken against the world powers and their perceived permanence in the paradoxical humiliation and glory of the cross. In the suffering, shame, death, and resurrection of Jesus, God has won eternal victory. Jesus bears the sin and shame of humanity, defeating the powers through his resurrection. Now Jesus victoriously reigns as King of kings and Lord of lords.

This fact of divine judgment against exploitation reminds the church of God's *continued* opposition to national oppression and exploitation in our day. It would not be too far a stretch to note the significant ways in which the Two-Thirds World suffers at the hands of the One-Third World. Does this exploitation of the most vulnerable not offend God? The church of Christ must be the agents for positive change and reform.

Craig Bartholomew and Bob Goudzwaard offer a way forward even while delineating the challenges of our modern world—including poverty, global economic exploitation, and greed.[48] Central in their proposal is the church of Christ as responding to the demands of the gospel—to live as Christ has lived and lean on Christ for ultimate security, strength, and power. As we center ourselves in Christ, we will begin to embrace a preferential option for the poor, confess our complicity in world powers (especially in global consumerism), and then work toward positive change. The journey into Christ will drive the church to serve the world; instead of living complicit with the

---

[48]Bob Goudzwaard and Craig G. Bartholomew, *Beyond the Modern Age: An Archaeology of Contemporary Culture* (Downers Grove, IL: IVP Academic, 2017), 189-273.

world powers (whether Assyria, Babylon, or the modern Western world), the church will live as those who are "a people humble and lowly, they shall seek refuge in the name of the Lord" (Zeph 3:12 NRSV).

Recommended Reading

Christensen, Duane L. *Nahum: A New Translation with Introduction and Commentary.* AB. New Haven, CT: Yale University Press, 2009.

Dietrich, Walter. *Nahum, Habakkuk, Zephaniah.* IECOT. Stuttgart: Kohlhammer, 2016.

———. "Three Minor Prophets and the Major Empires." In *Perspectives on the Formation of the Book of the Twelve*, ed. Ranier Albertz, James D. Nogalski, and Jakob Wöhrle, 147-56. BZAW 433. Berlin: de Gruyter, 2012.*

Kessler, Ranier. "Nahum-Habakuk als Zweiprophetenschrift: Ein Skizze." In *Gotteserdung: Beitrage zur Hermeneutik und Exegese der Hebraischen Bibel*, ed. R. Kessler, 137-45. Beiträge zur Wissenschaft vom Alten und Neuen Testament 170. Stuttgart: Kohlhammer, 2006.

Renz, Thomas. *The Books of Nahum, Habakkuk, and Zephaniah.* NICOT. Grand Rapids, MI: Eerdmans, 2021.

Wenyi, Jacob Onyumbe. *Piles of Slain, Heaps of Corpses: Reading Prophetic Poetry and Violence in African Context.* Eugene, OR: Cascade, 2021.*

Recommended reading marked with a "*" indicates introductory works.

15

Habakkuk

A PROTESTING AND PATIENT FAITH

How shall we live when life turns completely upside down? Habakkuk speaks to this question, and its message stands at the intersection of interrelated challenges of life: evil and divine justice, the essence of faith, meaning in suffering, and the power of prayer. As one processes these complicated relationships, Habakkuk becomes a feast, albeit a challenging one, for those who will take the time to dine at the table.[1]

Context

If Habakkuk the prophet emerged from the cult in Jerusalem, then the book is in some way part of cultic liturgy for God's people there.[2] Still, Habakkuk's originating cultic associations, whatever they may have been, remain obscure in the final form of the book.[3] The book does not convey a biography of the prophet as much as it proclaims the messages of Yahweh *through* the book. Habakkuk serves as a distinctive character in each of the three poems and as such plays a role in its theological message.[4]

---

[1]This chapter draws on Heath A. Thomas, *Habakkuk*, THOTC (Grand Rapids, MI: Eerdmans, 2018). For a different perspective using discourse analysis, see David J. Fuller, *A Discourse Analysis of Habakkuk*, Studia Semitica Neerlandica 72 (Leiden: Brill, 2020).

[2]Psalmic language in Hab 3:1 (e.g., *prayer* and *shigionoth*; see Ps 7:1); *watchtower* and *watchpost* of Hab 2:1 may be language indicating oracular prophecy at the temple (as in Neh 13:30; 2 Chron 7:6; 8:14; 35:2); For the role of the cultic prophet, see Aubrey R. Johnson, *The Cultic Prophet in Ancient Israel* (Cardiff, UK: University of Wales Press, 1962).

[3]Heath A. Thomas, "Hearing the Minor Prophets: The Book of the Twelve and God's Address," in *Hearing the Old Testament: Listening for God's Address*, ed. Craig G. Bartholomew and David J. H. Beldman (Grand Rapids, MI: Eerdmans, 2012), 356-79; Francis Watson, *Paul and the Hermeneutics of Faith* (London: T. & T. Clark, 2004), 78-163.

[4]Marvin Sweeney rightly notes his importance as the major character identified in Hab 1:1; 3:1. Sweeney, "Structure, Genre, and Intent in the Book of Habakkuk," *VT* 41, no. 1 (1991): 63-83.

Still, it is possible to read the book broadly within the waxing of the Neo-Babylonian Empire and the waning of the Judahite state. This sets the stage for Habakkuk roughly between 620 and 587 BC. Habakkuk reads best against the context of the reign of Jehoiakim prior to the fall of Jerusalem in 587 BC.[5] Through Habakkuk's eyes, we see the sin of Judah matched by the greed of the Neo-Babylon Empire. Judah is internally corrupt, while the Neo-Babylonians gobble up people and resources. Judah lies directly in their path of destruction. From this base, it is possible to read the book of Habakkuk more broadly within the Minor Prophets, with each of the books a fertile co-text.[6]

Outline

Habakkuk is a unity composed of two major parts.[7] The first is the oracle introduced in Habakkuk 1:1, and the second is the prayer of Habakkuk in Habakkuk 3:1. These two components are identifiable by the superscriptions.

Habakkuk 1:1	Oracle
Habakkuk 1:2-4	First complaint
Habakkuk 1:5-11	First divine response
Habakkuk 1:12-17; 2:1	Second complaint
Habakkuk 2:2-20	Second divine response
Habakkuk 3:1	Prayer
Habakkuk 3:2	Programmatic introduction
Habakkuk 3:3-15	The divine march to the south
Habakkuk 3:16-19	Human response
Habakkuk 3:19	Liturgical note

Habakkuk 1:1 refers to the "oracle" (*maśśā'*) Habakkuk saw. *Oracle* is a generic term indicating divine revelation given to a prophet that explains

---

[5] Sweeney, "Structure, Genre, and Intent"; Sweeney, *The Twelve Prophets*, Berit Olam (Collegeville, MN: Liturgical Press, 2000), 2:455-56. But see a different understanding of Habakkuk within Jehoiakim's reign: Robert D. Haak, *Habakkuk*, VTSup 44 (Leiden: Brill, 1992), 107-49. See also Thomas, *Habakkuk*, 28-29.

[6] Thomas Renz, "Habakkuk and Its Co-Texts," in *The Book of the Twelve: An Anthology of Prophetic Books or the Result of Complex Redactional Processes?*, ed. Heiko Wenzel, Onasbrücker Studien zur Jüdischen und Christlichen Bibel 4 (Göttingen: Vandenhoeck & Ruprecht, 2018), 13-36.

[7] Thomas Renz, *The Books of Nahum, Habakkuk, and Zephaniah*, NICOT (Grand Rapids, MI: Eerdmans, 2021), 199; Thomas, *Habakkuk*, 9-30; see also J. J. M. Roberts, *Nahum, Habakkuk, and Zephaniah*, OTL (Louisville, KY: Westminster John Knox, 1990), 82-85. For an alternative view, see Michael H. Floyd, *Minor Prophets: Part 2*, Forms of the Old Testament Literature (Grand Rapids, MI: Eerdmans, 2000), 81-86.

God's intentions in human affairs. The *maśśā'* also provides direction for human response in light of God's revelation.[8] God reveals his activity after the complaints of Habakkuk 1:2-4 and Habakkuk 1:12-2:1. God's activity revealed in Habakkuk 1:5-11 and Habakkuk 2:2-20 responds to Habakkuk's questions and gives him deeper knowledge and understanding of God's ways in his context. Finally, the prayer of Habakkuk 3 complements the oracle as a skillful addition to the book, reinforcing its overall emphasis.

INTERPRETATION

Habakkuk 1:1-2:1. In Habakkuk 1:2-4, our prophet calls out to God regarding "violence" that is being perpetrated by the "wicked" (Hab 1:4), who surround the "righteous" (Hab 1:4). Traditional lament language dominates in Habakkuk's speech: "how long" (Hab 1:2) and "why" (Hab 1:3) typify complaints to God about situations of distress. Habakkuk highlights two forms of injustice: (1) cries of "violence" (Hab 1:2) God neither hears, nor from which he delivers; and (2) God makes the prophet "look upon" iniquity, trouble, destruction, and violence (Hab 1:3). The first form of injustice is one perpetrated against the righteous, and Yahweh remains passive (Hab 1:2). The second complaint, however, does not object to Yahweh's passivity but to his *active* role in making Habakkuk look on injustice in his day.[9]

Habakkuk offers, then, a twofold complaint. Real, valid complaining in the Bible is not petulant or petty. The Old Testament reinforces complaint speech over and again. The New Testament follows this impulse as well (see Lk 18:1-8). The prophet sees that violence, destruction, contention, and dispute remain the basic order of the day. God, as he sees it, has either passively watched this situation arise or (worse) *caused* the prophet to witness this reality.

The general and negative term "violence," *ḥāmās*, appears in Habakkuk 1:2, which indicates manifestations of unjust action against God or other people. It describes creation-denying actions God detests (see Gen 6:11, 13). Yahweh usually counteracts such violence in his world, as in the purifying flood of Genesis 6-9. In the face of violence, Habakkuk addresses Yahweh in prayer because of Yahweh's commitment to justice.

---

[8] Richard D. Weis, "A Definition of the Genre *Massa'* in the Hebrew Bible" (PhD diss., Claremont Graduate School, Emory University, 1986). For an alternative proposal envisioning the *maśśā'* as an editorial marker, see Mark J. Boda, "Freeing the Burden of Prophecy: Maśśā' and the Legitimacy of Prophecy in Zech 9-14," *Biblica* 87, no. 3 (2006): 338-57.

[9] Note the hiphil stems in Hab 1:3: "Why do you make me look upon [*tar'ēnî*] iniquity?" and "[Why] do you cause me to visage [*tabbîṭ*] trouble?"

The text reminds us that *faithlessness* does not mark Habakkuk's cry to God but rather a deep and abiding faithfulness *to* Yahweh and a deep allegiance to the faithfulness *of* Yahweh, whom he knows as the great one who sets wrongs right. Habakkuk appeals to God because Yahweh is committed to his creation and to his covenant people. Habakkuk's cries expose the brokenness and violence in the world; his cries confirm the need of divine deliverance.

Yahweh responds in Habakkuk 1:5-11. The Lord proclaims that he is going to do a "wonder" (Hab 1:5), namely, by raising up "the Chaldeans [Neo-Babylonians], that bitter and hasty nation" (Hab 1:6). God routinely uses foreign nations to discipline his people for sin. The prophetic books testify to this fact repeatedly (e.g., Is 10; Jer 5:14-17). But that God would raise up this nation remains a challenge. God himself describes their "justice" as proceeding from themselves in Habakkuk 1:7. Further, they swallow up the world in "violence," *ḥāmās* (Hab 1:9). The repetition of this same word in Habakkuk 1:2, 9 shows that God clearly responds to his people's violence by raising up a violent nation whose justice proceeds from themselves. This is, to be sure, a wonder, but not a particularly transparent disclosure of God's will and God's justice. When God's justice seems like *in*justice, then what should the prophet say?

When faced with this quandary, Habakkuk responds with Habakkuk 1:12-17, by all counts another complaint to God. This time, however, his voice is not raised about his own people's wickedness and violence. He questions God about the Chaldeans and the justice of raising them up for punishment. How could God use *this* people? How can God respond to violence with violence? Habakkuk 1:12-14 is most likely questions to God, with the exception of Habakkuk 1:13a, "You are too pure of eyes to look upon evil, and you are not able to gaze upon trouble." The prophet questions God's actions, and he *affirms* God's character. In fact, the character of Yahweh enables the prophet to wonder about divine actions: If God is good and pure, how can he use a vile and violent nation to achieve his purposes in the world? Habakkuk 1:15-17 also reveals why Habakkuk cannot understand God's pronouncement concerning the Neo-Babylonian juggernaut: they are idolaters. After they do God's work in punishing and reproving God's people (Hab 1:12), they will not give the Lord the glory. Rather, they will make sacrifices to their gods, typified by the terms *dragnets* or *fishnets* in Habakkuk 1:17. Habakkuk knows the sin of idolatry because he knows the instruction of the Lord (Hab 1:4).

Habakkuk 2:2-20. The prophet concludes his second line of questioning in Habakkuk 1:12-17 with what appears to be an interior monologue or soliloquy in Habakkuk 2:1. The prophet takes his stand on the watchpost to "see" what God will say to him. He has uttered his complaint. Now the prophet waits to hear the verdict of the divine judge.

Habakkuk 2:2-20 constitutes the divine response. Specifically, Habakkuk 2:2-5 highlights God's judgment *against* idolatrous Babylon and emphasizes the vitality of faith in God. Habakkuk 2:6-20 presents woe oracles against the nation (Babylon) that operate out of violence and oppression rather than the manifest will of God. It is appropriate to focus in on two primary texts in Habakkuk 2 that are vital to understanding the chapter. The first is Habakkuk 2:2-5, and the second is Habakkuk 2:20. We shall take each in turn.

Habakkuk 2:2-5 reveals God's initial response to the prophet, clearly demarcated by the phrase "The LORD answered me." The divine response is a command to the prophet that he would "write down" the "vision" on tablets so the "one who reads it may run."[10] The vision here is a word given by the Lord, particularly a word of judgment that is close to being fulfilled. The great challenge of the command, of course, is that it *confirms* God's message to the prophet in Habakkuk 1:5-11: judgment is coming, and Habakkuk is to write it down for all to see. The prophet's complaints here have not moved Yahweh to answer the prophet directly. God *addresses* the prophet's questions without *answering* them as the prophet has asked them. Habakkuk 2:3 seemingly offers a contradictory word, as Donald Gowan rightly notes. God's word is coming, and it will not delay; still, it awaits its own time in coming to fruition. "At this point we are frankly left with a mystery, because we cannot calculate the time, we do not understand why the time is not Now. Only God knows that. And that is where faith comes in."[11]

More will be said in the next chapter about the famous and stimulating affirmation that the "righteous one will live by its faithfulness" (Hab 2:4b). However, suffice it to note here that this point is central to the book and that God's encouragement to the prophet is a call to faith and faithfulness. God calls the prophet to believe and trust in God's word, his vision of discipline through the Neo-Babylonian threat. The vision is indeed coming. When it will be fulfilled will be clear in its own time. In the meantime, however, God

---

[10]For discussion of Hab 2:2, see Thomas Renz, "Reading and Running: Notes on the History of Translating the Final Clause of Hab 2:2," *VT* 69 (2019): 435-46.
[11]Donald E. Gowan, *The Triumph of Faith in Habakkuk* (Atlanta: John Knox, 1976), 41.

calls his righteous to faithfulness. It is the slow and steady obedience before God in the face of impending death.

By embracing pain, the righteous ones remain faithful to their Lord: they "will live" (Hab 2:4). It is unclear whether this life means survival, resurrection, or eternal life. Likely, in its immediate context, it means a vision of survival for God's people beyond the Neo-Babylonian threat. However, it may intend a kind of death and resurrection of God's people: they will be judged, but they will not be eradicated completely. Rather, a remnant will rise from the death of their judgment (see Hos 6:1-2).

Further, Yahweh discloses that he will deal with Babylonian pride. Habakkuk 2:5-20 shows that Yahweh simply will not allow the violence of Babylon to persist through five woe oracles (see table 15.1). The woe oracles in Habakkuk 2:6-17 reinforce Babylon's great reversal.[12] The very ones the Babylonians oppressed will render parables and mocking songs taunting their destruction. Habakkuk 2:18-19 exposes the futility of Babylon's idolatry and provides a response to Habakkuk's complaint in Habakkuk 1:16-17.

Table 15.1. Five woe oracles of Habakkuk 2

WOE	HÔY	INTERROGATIVE	SIN	THREAT	REPETITION/ INTERTEXT
Habakkuk 2:6-8	Habakkuk 2:6b; 8b	How long? Will not?	unjust pledges	proverb and ridicule	Habakkuk 2:8 // Habakkuk 2:17
Habakkuk 2:9-11	Habakkuk 2:9; 10b	Is not?	evil profits	shame for the house; debtors arise suddenly	
Habakkuk 2:12-14	Habakkuk 2:12	Is it not?	city of murder	???	Micah 3:10 // Habakkuk 2:12 Proverbs 24:3 // Habakkuk 2:12 Habakkuk 2:13 // Jeremiah 51:58 Numbers 14:21 // Habakkuk 2:14 Isaiah 11:9 // Habakkuk 2:14

---

[12] Walter Dietrich argues for six rather than five oracles of woe in a three-step redactional process in *Nahum, Habakkuk, Zephaniah*, IECOT (Stuttgart: Kohlhammer, 2016), 156. Heath A. Thomas argues the woes present a logic of hope in the book in "Hope Through Woes in Habakkuk," in *Hope in the Old Testament: Gordon McConville Festschrift*, ed. Alison Lo and Jamie Grant (forthcoming). Hope in Habakkuk is explored more broadly in George Athas, Beth M. Stovell, Daniel C. Timmer, and Colin M. Toffelmire, eds., *Theodicy and Hope in the Book of the Twelve*, LHBOTS 705 (London: T&T Clark, 2021), esp. 22-39, 173-93, 194-213.

WOE	HÔY	INTERROGATIVE	SIN	THREAT	REPETITION/ INTERTEXT
Habakkuk 2:15-17	Habakkuk 2:15		causing friend to drink; gazing on nakedness	shame; cup of wrath	Habakkuk 2:17 // Habakkuk 2:8
Habakkuk 2:18-20	Habakkuk 2:19a	What?	folly of idolatry	???	Habakkuk 2:20 // Psalm 11:4

In light of God's call for faithfulness and his own divine faithfulness to his people and world, revealed in Habakkuk 2:2-19, it is fitting that Habakkuk 2:20 highlights the cosmic rule of the Lord in the temple. "The LORD is in his holy temple. Be silent before him, all the earth!" Even though Zion will be judged in sin and punished for it, God's reign is undiminished. His disclosure of justice and his ways with creation draw the faithful to silence before his majesty. Indeed, all the earth is called to wonder at the mystery and majesty of God.

Habakkuk 3:1-19. As God's will has been disclosed, the prophet utters a "prayer." The terminology in Habakkuk 3:1 and Habakkuk 3:19 is evocative of the psalmic superscriptions. This powerful and difficult poem presents the prophet's praise to the God of life. The prophet "heard" Yahweh's word and "saw" Yahweh's "wondrous deed" (Hab 3:2; see Hab 1:5). This recognition drives him to embrace the judgment that is coming. In Habakkuk 3:3-15, Yahweh is the divine warrior, with spear and bow in hand. Heavens and earth shudder before him, and he goes to war. Typically, this language is used in contexts that remember Yahweh fighting *for* his people, as Exodus 15 reminds us: "Yahweh is a warrior! Yah is his name" (Ex 15:3). He is pictured in a similar manner in Habakkuk 3:3-15.

Habakkuk reflects on the historical memory of Yahweh in the exodus and reads it through God's cosmic rule and defeat of wickedness and death. He proclaims, "You have gone out to save your people, to save your anointed. You have smashed the head of the house of the wicked; you have uncovered it from foundation to the top" (Hab 3:13). God *will* save, but it will be through judgment. In this, Habakkuk horrifyingly embraces pain. If the world turns upside down, even so Habakkuk affirms that he will "rejoice in the God of my salvation" (Hab 3:18). The stunning imagery of agrarian life is revealed in Habakkuk 3:18, replete with cattle, grain, figs, olives, sheep, and grapes. But Habakkuk affirms that even if God were to remove such life-giving sustenance, and God's good world would be turned into the wasteland, *even so*, he will "rejoice in the God of my salvation."

Rejoicing in God no matter the cost haunts Gowan: "Faithfulness means to go on doing the right thing, no matter what happens, Whether anybody ever rewards you or not—do the right thing, because that is what God wants.... Faith means that you *know* the God who puts these demands upon you, and to know God makes you rejoice, no matter what."[13] Habakkuk's vow to rejoice is a commitment to a pilgrimage with God through the wasteland. Again, in his embrace of death the prophet ironically finds the life that was immediately under threat in Habakkuk 1:2-4. His steps, however, are not heavy and cold on the hard earth. Rather, with Yahweh, he walks like the deer, and the Lord makes him tread the heights (Hab 3:19).

Habakkuk in the New Testament

Thematically, Habakkuk stands as a crucial bridge to the nature of faith and faithfulness in the Bible.[14] Paul's citation of Habakkuk 2:4 diverges from the MT and LXX in both Romans 1:17 and Galatians 2:20 (his citation exhibits neither the third-person pronoun "his/its" from the Hebrew nor the first-person pronoun "my" from the Greek). According to Peter Stuhlmacher, Romans 1:17 is essential in Paul's larger argument to demonstrate God's righteousness (or faithful activity of God), which believers (i.e., the righteous) embrace by faith in Jesus. By placing their faith in Christ, these faithful become part of the righteousness of God: living testimonies of God's faithfulness and righteousness.[15] Jesus epitomizes that faithfulness to the Lord by following God, even to the point of his death. But his death means life for those who believe in him, as well as the re-creation of all things.

In Galatians 3, Paul depicts the type of person who embraces God's faithfulness, whom Paul distinguishes from the kind of person who is essentially self-reliant, trusting in one's adherence to works of law. By contrast, Paul argues, the faithful trusts and believes in God's faithfulness, which is manifest in the gospel of Jesus Christ. Bae Gil Lee says of Galatians 3:11, "Paul emphasizes that both Jews and Gentiles must respond to God's eschatological provision for their deliverance from the curse, by having faith in

---

[13]Gowan, *Triumph of Faith*, 84.
[14]Heath A. Thomas, *Faith amid the Ruins: The Book of Habakkuk*, Transformative Word Series (Bellingham, WA: Lexham, 2016), 79-89.
[15]Peter Stuhlmacher, *Paul's Letter to the Romans: A Commentary* (Louisville, KY: Westminster John Knox, 1994), 25-32.

Christ crucified."¹⁶ In other words, the text is not using Habakkuk 2:4 to predict the coming Messiah but rather to refer to the one to whom we should look in faith to see the incarnation of God's faithfulness in this present age.

Hebrews 10:38 uses Habakkuk 2:4b to encourage faithfulness and perseverance in the face of suffering. Hebrews 10:37 employs the Greek rendering of Habakkuk 2:2-4a to depict the coming Messiah (particularly the second coming of Jesus), but it does so to encourage the saints to persevere in their faith. Jesus is coming, so do not shrink back from following the Lord. "God is worthy of faith precisely because of his extraordinary divine faithfulness, both in guaranteeing the vision (vv. 2-3) and in guaranteeing Christ the Lord (per the New Testament evidence). Placing faith in God's faithfulness exhibits the fitting behavior of the follower of God."¹⁷

In Habakkuk, the notion of faith is not opposed to works-based righteousness. Rather, faith and faithfulness are crystallized as fidelity to God by believing God's testimony, his promise, of divine salvation through judgment. Habakkuk 2:2 reminds the prophet and the faithful that God's vision of judgment *will* come, but through this judgment, salvation springs forth as well. As the prophet and the righteous people of God place their trust in the God who brings salvation through judgment, as he says he will do, then God will ensure that they will "live." Habakkuk 2:4b, "The righteous in his faithfulness will live," becomes a foundation for what it means to live and live well before God, even in the face of seeming disaster.

In this way, there is a dual focus to faith in the book of Habakkuk, and indeed a dual focus in the reception of Habakkuk in the New Testament. On the one hand, Habakkuk teaches the faithfulness of God to do what he promises to do: to bring salvation, even through judgment. In this way, the faithfulness envisioned in Habakkuk 2:4b clearly envisions *God's* faithfulness in his redemptive purposes. Faith is not trusting in what *humans* do but what *God* does in and through his victorious acts. The emphasis on God's actions seems to be in play in Paul's usage of Habakkuk 2:4b in Romans 1:16-17, where God's righteousness is revealed from "faith to faith" (Rom 1:16). God's people, then, are called to place their faith in *this* God, who is faithful to them (Rom 1:17). This second aspect of faith—namely, what believers do when they get a glimpse of the faithful God—is clearly taught in the book of

---

¹⁶Bae Gil Lee, "A Developing Messianic Understanding of Habakkuk 2:3-5 in the New Testament in the Context of Early Jewish Writings" (PhD diss., Southwestern Baptist Theological Seminary, 1997), 141.
¹⁷Thomas, *Habakkuk*, 163.

Habakkuk. Habakkuk teaches the believer to trust in the God of salvation. Faith in the God who saves, not in works, is salvific. This point is drawn on in Galatians 3:11 particularly in the New Testament.

Theology

The mystery of faith. Habakkuk teaches the mystery of faith. Sometimes Christian understanding of faith can be tamed into mere mental assent to God's characteristics and definitions of his ways: omnipotence, omniscience, and the like. Yet the doctrines are there to draw us into the dance of faith—faith in the living God. Such an encounter with the living God is not safe, but it is good. Habakkuk presents the "wild, untameable God," who, as in Isaiah, reveals himself to be "the creator, the Lord of the ends of the earth."[18] He is the God who can speak a new and wondrous yet confusing word.

Habakkuk's experience with God leads him to an intellectual and existential crisis of faith. The God he knows has created the world (see Hab 1:14 and the echoes of Gen 1:28) and founded the world in justice. Habakkuk recognizes the eternality of the Lord and the place of Israel in God's redemptive plan. He is the King who is "in his holy temple," with "all the earth silent" before him. The facts Habakkuk knew about God were good and right. Yet it is this very knowledge of God in Scripture that leads him to question the ways and designs of the divine.

From this quandary, Habakkuk teaches the mystery of deep spiritual formation as believers rest in the confusing designs of God (confusing, at least from the perspective of mere mortals). The church often finds itself in the place of Habakkuk, challenged and unsure. God's wondrous ways leave us asking, "How?" and "How long?" and "Why?" The church, like the prophet, discovers there is a mystery of faith that transcends arid formulation of doctrines divorced from the manifest presence of the living God. Still, Habakkuk teaches the church to embrace God's clear word even if he (or we) cannot understand God's precise designs. This is a deep and abiding trust in God despite clear perception of the will of God.

The extraordinary affirmation of Habakkuk 3:16, that the prophet will "rest" in "the day of distress," exposes a spirituality of a faith developed in and through his abandonment to the mystery of God. Habakkuk does not know *why* God is doing what he is doing with the Babylonians. He only knows *that* God is doing it, and the Babylonians will be judged by a just God for their

---

[18] N. T. Wright, *For All God's Worth* (Grand Rapids, MI: Eerdmans, 1997), 37.

pride. God's revealed message is understandable, even if not fully comprehensible. Once understood, Habakkuk embraces the mystery of God and abandons himself to the providence of the Lord. He can even face the potential infertility of God's creation (Hab 3:17) because Yahweh has spoken, and Yahweh will act. In turn, Habakkuk will "rejoice in the LORD," who is the "God of my salvation" (Hab 3:18).

The mystery of faith is borne in prayer and suffering. It is embraced in both, because God may take his follower to extraordinary depths of pain and confusion. The whys and hows of human experience in God's world are often never answered. And sometimes, Habakkuk teaches, when God *does* answer, it raises even more questions. But this little poem teaches how humans are deeply formed, from the inside out, in the mystery of faith. Our questions call out for response. But finally, the word that God offers is extraordinarily a word of rest and peace, even if it means our suffering and a "day of distress." Habakkuk calls its readers to abandon themselves to divine providence. God is not safe, but he is good. He is the King.

Faith and prayer. Habakkuk teaches prayer.[19] Some understand the structure of the book of Habakkuk as a transition from doubt to faith. Habakkuk traverses from doubt (Hab 1:2–2:3) to faith (Hab 2:4–3:19). Habakkuk 3 reveals the appropriate response to the mystery of God: believe God in faith and patiently wait on him. The book teaches that *faith* overcomes *fear*. True spirituality learns that doubt/complaint will be overcome by faith/praise.

Various biblical and theological sources may reinforce this thinking. A variety of texts in the New Testament indicate that suffering should be borne with rejoicing or that suffering is a soul-building exercise (Rom 5:2-4; Phil 3:10; Col 1:24; 2 Tim 1:12; 1 Pet 1:6-9; 3:8-22; 4:1-19).[20] Why, then, would we, like Habakkuk, want to lament in the face of "light and momentary afflictions," especially when the "weight of glory" awaits us (2 Cor 4:17)? Paul's admonition in the book of Romans becomes instructive toward rebuffing lament in the face of suffering: "Be joyful in hope, patient in affliction" (Rom 12:12). Paul has said enough, then, to rebuff lament. It represents doubt-filled speech when God expects hope and patience in suffering.

However, the careful interpreter will note that Paul concludes the verse by stating: "Be joyful in hope, patient in affliction, faithful in prayer" (Rom 12:12). *Prayer*—what of this action, of prayer? How does this last

---

[19]Thomas, *Faith amid the Ruins*, 57-71.
[20]Note too Jas 1:2; 5:7-10.

phrase by the apostle press toward faithful lament prayer? Karl Barth rightly instructs that prayer is "a quite precise action. Placed as we are and grievously oppressed, how can we avoid calling upon God? How can we avoid being of the company of those who, like the Psalmists, saw things as they really are, and in their misery cried out unto God? . . . Uncomfortably this energy of prayer presses into the world of men."[21]

We may avoid lament prayer because it is not happy enough for modern Western Christians. Still, it is right to consider whether the rush to praise in the modern church, although filled with the right intentions, might gloss over the way things really are: a broken world and awaiting its redemption day. Paul encourages joy, to be sure. He admonishes patience, yes. But these virtues are borne in faithful prayer—lament prayer included. Lament prayer cries out to God about the discordance between what is hoped for in the age to come and what is experienced in the world today.

Habakkuk's prayers reveal such radical faith. His complaints are not faithless, as they *lean forward* toward the God he knows in the face of hardship and an unknown future. His complaints *anticipate* that God's divine care and justice (which has shown itself to be sure in the past) will be made *real* in the real world. Habakkuk's praise in Habakkuk 3 *looks back* at what God has said and done in response his questions. The important thing to note in this book, however, is that the prophet does not come to praise without his persistent lament. The praise evinced in the third chapter is not so much faith *overcoming* doubt but rather faith *recognizing* the power and work of God and rejoicing in him for it.

Similarly Christ guides us in our weariness, pain, and questions toward the new world that he has established: the no-tears and no-pain world of the new heavens and earth. In the meantime, we cry out with Jesus, "Your kingdom come and your will be done on earth as it is in heaven" (Mt 6:10). The church, with Habakkuk, cries "How long?" With Saint John we cry, "Even so, come quickly, Lord Jesus" (Rev 22:20).

Treasure in broken jars. Paul reminds the church we have treasures in jars of clay, which display God's glory (2 Cor 4:7). These jars are broken and shattered but not destroyed. Habakkuk's experience of brokenness is one such picture of the broken vessel. He is shattered in confusion, broken because of his people's sin, confused because of God's word of judgment. Of course, God's message

---

[21]Karl Barth, *The Epistle to the Romans*, trans. E. C. Hoskyns (Oxford: Oxford University Press, 1975), 458.

of salvation is sure, but it is the prophet's brokenness that stands out *first*. Yet his wounds made visible in his book help to heal the church and world.

This is so because Habakkuk reveals affliction as part and parcel of the faithful life before God. Suffering is horrific and debilitating. It is shameful in some cultures. Suffering, at least for Job, brought the stigma that there was something wrong or *sinful* about him, and such perceptions may continue in the modern church. Nevertheless, the Scriptures reveal suffering to be at the heart of the earliest Christian message. Jesus commanded his followers to take up their cross in following their master (Lk 9:23). A cross meant death and pain. For the church, suffering is a battle in spiritual growth, it is a marker of a broken world, and it is part what it means to be "in Christ." Yet Ann Jervis is right to say that by "virtue of our being caught between the time of Christ's resurrection and the time of our own, we recognize that we will suffer as we hope for glory."[22]

Our wounds will become a source of healing for others. Paul reminds the Corinthian church that it is God "who comforts us in our afflictions so that we in turn may be able to comfort others in any of their afflictions and to share with them the comfort that we ourselves receive from God. For as the sufferings of Christ overflow to us, so our comfort overflows to Christ" (2 Cor 1:4-5). Henri Nouwen remarkably says that the Christian is called in this world "to be the wounded healer, the one who must look after his own wounds but at the same time be prepared to heal the wounds of others."[23] Habakkuk's experience reminds the church of the treasure that hides among the shards. He calls the church to persevere, take up our cross, and embrace the pain when it (inevitably) comes.

Recommended Reading

Athas, George, Beth M. Stovell, Daniel C. Timmer, and Colin M. Toffelmire, eds. *Theodicy and Hope in the Book of the Twelve*. LHBOTS 705. London: T&T Clark, 2021.

Dietrich, Walter. *Nahum, Habakkuk, Zephaniah*. IECOT. Stuttgart: Kohlhammer, 2016.

Fuller, David J. *A Discourse Analysis of Habakkuk*. Studia Semitica Neerlandica 72. Leiden: Brill, 2020.

Renz, Thomas. *The Books of Nahum, Habakkuk, and Zephaniah*. NICOT. Grand Rapids, MI: Eerdmans, 2021.

———. "Habakkuk and Its Co-Texts." In *The Book of the Twelve: An Anthology of Prophetic Books or the Result of Complex Redactional Processes?*, ed. Heiko Wenzel, 13-36.

---

[22]L. Ann Jervis, *At the Heart of the Gospel: Suffering in the Earliest Christian Message* (Grand Rapids, MI: Eerdmans, 2007), 109.

[23]Henri J. M. Nouwen, *The Wounded Healer* (London: DLT, 1994), 83.

Onasbrücker Studien zur Jüdischen und Christlichen Bibel 4. Göttingen: Vandenhoeck & Ruprecht, 2018.

———. "Reading and Running: Notes on the History of Translating the Final Clause of Hab 2:2." *VT* 69 (2019): 435-46.

Thomas, Heath A. *Faith amid the Ruins: The Book of Habakkuk*. Transformative Word Series. Bellingham, WA: Lexham Press, 2016.*

———. *Habakkuk*. THOTC. Grand Rapids, MI: Eerdmans, 2018.*

———. "Hope Through Woes in Habakkuk." In *Hope in the Old Testament: Gordon McConville Festschrift*, ed. Alison Lo and Jamie Grant. Forthcoming.

Recommended reading marked with a "" indicates introductory works.*

16

Faith in the Faithful God

HABAKKUK 2:2-4

HABAKKUK 2:2-4 COMPOSES some of the most difficult and most profound verses in the book. Here we find God's response to Habakkuk's second complaint. Yahweh draws Habakkuk's gaze to a "vision" (Hab 2:2) that will engender appropriate response to Yahweh during distress. That appropriate response is faithfulness to the faithful God. A close exegetical examination of these verses is warranted so we might gain a greater perspective on Habakkuk's vision of faith and the Christian faith.

YAHWEH'S VISION

In Habakkuk 2:2 Yahweh "answers" Habakkuk's questions in Habakkuk 1:12-17, where the prophet complained about Yahweh using the Babylonians for his purposes of judgment. Habakkuk believes Yahweh is subverting the very moral order of God's creation in doing so. He draws in creation imagery from Genesis 1:26-27 in Habakkuk 1:14, asking whether Yahweh presides over a topsy-turvy world.

God's response is found in Habakkuk 2:2-5, and then it is elaborated further in Habakkuk 2:6-20. For our purposes, we focus on the former verses. Yahweh says to the prophet, "Write a vision, and make it plain upon tablets, so that the one who reads it may run into it" (Hab 2:2). Writing prophecy or visions down has some analog in the prophets (Is 30:8). Writing down the vision likely serves as a witness and confirmation of the validity of God's message as well as a source of hope when it is read by the faithful.

Heath Thomas argues that the image of "running into" (*yārûṣ qôrē᾽ bô*) the vision, although unusual, is a metaphor for seeking security and help in the vision. The closest parallel to the Hebrew construction in Habakkuk 2:2 appears in Proverbs 18:10: "The name of Yahweh is a strong tower; the righteous *run into it* [*bô-yārûṣ*] and find security."[1] Yahweh provides a vision that will engender hope and security when the faithful will pursue it with all they have: they *run into* the content of the vision.

Habakkuk 2:3 delineates the imminence of the vision identified in Habakkuk 2:2. Yahweh instructs that the vision is for an "appointed time," and it is for "the end." The collocation "end" (*qēṣ*) and "appointed time" (*mô 'ēd*) occurs in Daniel 8:19. It speaks of the time in which eschatological events unfold in Daniel's vision (see similar constructions in Dan 11:27, 29, 35). In the book of Daniel, this vision includes both cosmic and local judgment. If this meaning of the collocation holds for Habakkuk 2:3, then Yahweh draws attention to a vision that concerns itself with cosmic judgment that will engender hope for God's people as they read the vision and "run into it." Likely, this vision addresses the complaint of Habakkuk in Habakkuk 1:12-17, that Yahweh governs a topsy-turvy world that operates outside the moral order. This is especially true, Habakkuk complains, if Yahweh uses the Babylonians for divine judgment of the Judean nation.

Habakkuk 2:3 is strange. The vision encourages, but it seems to delay, and the faithful need reassurance that the vision hastens to the appointed time. Yahweh reassures Habakkuk that the vision "will not lie," and if it seems to tarry, the faithful are to "wait for it" because "it will surely come and it will not delay" (Hab 2:3). "Although there may be a long wait for the vision to be realised, there can be no question of its ultimate failure. It is therefore a word of reassurance which takes into account a general feeling about the question of delay but denies the ultimacy of such pessimism."[2]

Still, the exact timeline is unspecified, affirming the radical freedom of God to enact the vision. Recognition of divine freedom opens the possibility of faith in God: "Faith means being faithful to God rather than relying upon a specific timeline. Temptation seduces believers when they begin to rely on God's *schedule* for security and hope rather than on God *himself*. This is a kind of disordered love, which will lead to disordered lives. A timeline may take our eyes away from the One who gave it."[3] These verses instruct simultaneously in divine freedom and faithfulness as a doorway to faith in God. God hears the cries and complaints of the people of God, and if it seems odd that he does not answer or respond in the ways or times we might wish, we

---

[1] Heath A. Thomas, *Habakkuk*, THOTC (Grand Rapids, MI: Eerdmans, 2018), 108-9.
[2] Robert P. Carroll, "Eschatological Delay in the Prophetic Tradition?," *ZAW* 94, no. 1 (1982): 52-53.
[3] Thomas, *Habakkuk*, 111.

can take hope that God's salvation *will come* because God is both free and faithful. But in the meantime, we are called to live in faithfulness before the Lord of time. Waiting in faith leaves us open to see God break open future salvation into the present moments of life.

The meaning of the verity of Habakkuk 2:2-3, then, emerges: God's vision is faithful and true testimony that does not lie or deceive. Because the vision is written down, it serves as inscribed testimony. It memorializes and consecrates the verity of God's vision.[4] In contrast to Habakkuk's complaint in Habakkuk 1:12-17, God's world *is* ordered and *is* comprehensible, not because everything is sensible to human perception but because God is free and faithful to his word. The faithful who hear or read the vision can trust God, his word, and his world. They can trust in God's salvation.

In regard to the tablets mentioned, several options emerge in regard to their content. It may be the message of Habakkuk 2:4, "Behold! It is inflated— his soul is not upright in him. But the righteous one shall live in his/its faithfulness." This message is the core teaching of Habakkuk. But given the size of the stone or wood tablets being used, would more than one tablet be necessary? After all, the "tablets" of Habakkuk 2:2 indicates more than one plaque. Unless Habakkuk writes poorly or with very large characters, one finds little reason to use more than one tablet to write such a message. So, the tablets likely held more material than Habakkuk 2:2. Some think some portion (or all) of Habakkuk 3 encompasses the message on the tablets.[5] However, this is not definitive. We believe the best option for the content of the vision written on the tablets is Habakkuk 2:4-20.[6]

Habakkuk 2:4-20 reveals Yahweh's commitment to vindicate his faithful and judge the wicked. Habakkuk 2:4-5 demonstrates a contrast between the righteous and the wicked, and Habakkuk 2:6-20 exposes the great reversal and fate that will befall the wicked. They will fall before the authority and justice of Yahweh. This message enables a robust theodicy, so that God's

---

[4]We agree that Hab 2:2b has the connotation of writing and "confirming" the vision on tablets, following David Toshio Tsumura, "Hab 2:2 in Light of Akkadian Legal Practice," ZAW 94, no. 2 (1982): 294-95. However, we do not fully follow Tsumura's recent argument on Hab 2:2c, as the better co-text with which to read Hab 2:2c is Prov 18:10.

[5]See J. J. M. Roberts, *Nahum, Habakkuk, and Zephaniah*, OTL (Louisville, KY: Westminster John Knox, 1990), 81; see the discussion of M. H. Floyd, "Prophecy and Writing in Habakkuk 2,1-5," ZAW 105 (1993): 462-81, esp. 472.

[6]See Floyd, "Prophecy and Writing," 472-73, who also suggests that at minimum Hab 2:4 is the content of the vision mentioned in Hab 2:2-3, but then in a footnote offers his view that Hab 2:4-20 is the whole of it.

people come to understand that God's actions fit within his moral order. God's people *can* live before him in absolute faith and trust in God's faithfulness (Hab 2:4) precisely because chaos will not persist indefinitely. At an appointed time, God will set all things right (Hab 2:5-19). His reign is sure, and the world is rightly established in Zion (or in the temple, in Hab 2:20). This message written on the tablets was available to those who would read them, encouraging them in faith despite the coming judgment at the hand of the Babylonians.

THE FAITHFUL'S RESPONSE

Habakkuk 2:2 invokes the faithful to "run into" the vision. Habakkuk 2:3 calls the faithful to wait for the vision. Although the Babylonian threat lies ahead, God's people can trust Yahweh because God will enact justice. This comprises a rich and complex vision of divine justice. By proclaiming the sure punishment of Babylon's pride (esp. in Hab 2:5-20), God demonstrates to his own faithful people that they will be vindicated and not put to shame. The faithful, then, should read, run into, and wait for the vision's fulfillment.[7]

With the backdrop of Habakkuk 2:2-3 established, we turn to Habakkuk 2:4. Jewish and Christian traditions recognize this verse as clarifying faithful life before God. For Jews, this text distills the entirety of the law. Rabbi Simlai in the third or fourth century AD suggested that all 613 precepts in the Torah were reduced to eleven by King David (e.g., Ps 15), to six by Isaiah (Is 33:15-16), to three by Micah (Mic 6:8), to two by Isaiah (Is 56:1), then to one by Amos (Amos 5:4). However, it is Habakkuk who bases all the teaching of the Torah into one principle: "The righteous shall live by his faith" (Hab 2:4; Babylonian Talmud Makkot 23b-24a).

For the apostle Paul, this verse clarifies the essence of the gospel for Christians. "Hab 2:4 is *the* crucial Old Testament text for Paul," as evidenced in Romans 1:17 and Galatians 3:11.[8] Martin Luther says of Habakkuk 2:4:

> The godly people are waiting for Yahweh; therefore, they live, therefore they are saved, therefore they receive what has been promised [namely, life through

---

[7]Heath A. Thomas, *Faith amid the Ruins: The Book of Habakkuk*, Transformative Word Series (Bellingham, WA: Lexham, 2016), 73-89.

[8]J. Christiaan Beker, "Echoes and Intertextuality," in *Paul and the Scriptures of Israel*, ed. Craig A. Evans and James A. Sanders, Journal for the Study of New Testament Supplement Series 83 (Sheffield: JSOT Press, 1993), 64-69, here 68.

the good news of Jesus Christ]. They receive it by faith, because they give glory to the God of truth, because they hold the hand of Yahweh. And so the prophet is looking not only to this promise but to all the other promises about preaching the Gospel or revealing grace.[9]

Luther believes the vision God gives is "a prophecy about the Christ and the kingdom of the Christ, which had been prophesied earlier in all the prophets."[10] Further, Christian interpreters through the ages have leaned on Habakkuk 2:4 for inspiration, guidance, and encouragement. Irenaeus uses this verse as a key text to identify the kind of faith Abraham displayed and the kind of faith that justifies believers in Christ, apart from obedience to the law.[11] In his defense against Marcionism, Irenaeus argues for the impossibility of the New Testament testifying of a different deity from the Old Testament. His proof is the prophetic witness of Jesus Christ, who foretold all of Christ's works and even pronounced the end of the law. Irenaeus draws on Habakkuk 2:4 and says, "But this point, that the Just shall live by faith had been foretold by the prophets."[12] Habakkuk 2:4 is central for the Christian life.

But Habakkuk 2:4a remains hermeneutically difficult. First, the verb translated "it is puffed up" or "it is inflated" (*'uppəlâ*) is underdetermined. The root occurs only in Numbers 14:44, where the meaning of the verb is contested, and in Habakkuk 2:4. The verb could mean "to be presumptuous" or "impudent": the Israelites "were impudent to ascend the hill" (Num 14:44). When used as a substantive, the root may mean something that is raised up or puffed up, either a raised hill (Is 32:14; Neh 3:26) or a boil (see 1 Sam 5:6). The ESV translates *'uppəla*, "Behold, his soul is puffed up."

We believe the two strongest possibilities are (1) J. J. M. Roberts's emendation, dividing *'uppəla* into *'āp lōh* ("the one who faints before it"), and (2) the traditional reading maintained by the ESV ("Behold, his soul is puffed up; it is not upright within him"). Whatever reading one follows, Habakkuk 2:4a presents contrast, as Thomas argues:

---

[9]Martin Luther, *Luther's Works*, vol. 19, *Lectures on the Minor Prophets II*, ed. Hilton C. Oswald (St. Louis: Concordia, 1974), 123.
[10]Luther, *Lectures on the Minor Prophets II*, 121.
[11]Saint Irenaeus, *The Demonstration of the Apostolic Preaching*, trans. J. Armitage Robinson (London: SPCK, 1920), §§35, 102.
[12]Saint Irenaeus, *Five Books of Saint Irenaeus Against Heresies*, trans. John Keble (Oxford: James Parker, 1872), §4.34.2-3, 414-15.

1. *Babylonian King vs. Faithful Israelite*: If we follow the ESV, the "inflated" soul is the Babylonian king (and that soul is not upright). That prideful king is contrasted with the righteous follower of YHWH, who relies on the surety of God's vision and trusts in his faithfulness. This follower of YHWH responds in faith to God's faithful vision. Or . . .

2. *Faithful vs. Faithless Israelite*: If we follow Roberts's emendation of 2:4a, the one whose soul "faints" within him after hearing the vision (of vv. 2-3) reveals that his soul is not established. This faltering follower of God, revealed as faithless, contrasts with the righteous one who hears the vision (from vv. 2-3) and embraces God's vision in faith.[13]

In either case, God calls the righteous to live faithfully before him, trusting God's vision as reliable. The verse calls for a deep faith in the faithfulness of God, and it encourages God's faithful to live their lives on the basis of that faith.

If the soul of the Babylonian king is the subject of the verbs (option 1 above), then Habakkuk 2:4a is resonant with, for instance, Isaiah 10. Isaiah 10:5-15 reveals the king of Assyria is the instrument of God's judgment: the "rod" of God's anger and the "instrument" of his wrath. But, as he is guilty of pride, Yahweh will punish the king's pride and arrogance (Is 10:12-15). Habakkuk 2:4 serves as the prelude of divine judgment on the Babylonians, fully described in Habakkuk 2:5-20. Habakkuk 2:4 *confirms* the great reversal described in Habakkuk 2:2-3, where the righteous are vindicated and the wicked judged. This reinforces the theology of divine justice depicted there.

But if we follow the second option above, then the verse calls the faithful to perseverance. Yahweh calls the faithful to wait expectantly for Yahweh to fulfill his salvific vision and judge the wicked. The faithful should remain true to God against all odds. We should note that invocations for perseverance and patience are common in the Minor Prophets: Habakkuk 2:2-3; 3:16; Hosea 12:6; Micah 7:7; Zephaniah 3:8.

With the options of Habakkuk 2:4a in view, it is time to turn to the latter half of the line. The Old Greek (LXX) translates Habakkuk 2:4b differently from what one finds in the Hebrew reflected in the Masoretic Text. See in table 16.1 the translation of the Greek and Hebrew of the whole text of Habakkuk 2:4, taking account of options described in Habakkuk 2:4a above.

---

[13]Thomas, *Habakkuk*, 114.

Faith in the Faithful God

Table 16.1. LXX and MT of Habakkuk 2:4

HABAKKUK 2:4 (LXX AND ENGLISH TRANSLATION)	HABAKKUK 2:4 (MT AND ENGLISH TRANSLATION)
ean hyposteilētai, ouk eudokei hē psychē mou en autō: ho de dikaios ek pisteōs mou zēsetai.	hinnēh ʿuppəlā lōʾ-yāšərâ napšô bô wəṣadîq be ʾĕmûnātô yiḥyeh
If he shrinks back, my soul is not pleased in him; but the just one will live by my faithfulness (or "will live by faith in me")[a]	Behold! The one who faints before it [or, "Behold! It is inflated"], His soul is not upright within him; But the righteous one shall live in its faithfulness.

[a] If one reads the genitive construction *ek pisteōs mou* as a subjective genitive, God's faithfulness is in view: "God's faithfulness" rather than "faith in God." If one reads the genitive construction *ek pisteōs mou* as an objective genitive, human faithfulness is in view: "faith in God" rather than "God's faithfulness." For discussion see Francis I. Andersen, *Habakkuk: A New Translation with Introduction and Commentary*, ABC 25 (New York: Doubleday, 2001), 209-16.

A significant difference between the Greek and Hebrew traditions emerges in the pronouns in Habakkuk 2:4b: "my (God's) faithfulness" (LXX) or "his/its faithfulness" (MT). Whose faithfulness is in view in these words?[14]

- The MT may emphasize the faith *of the righteous follower of Yahweh*, if we take the third-person masculine singular pronoun affixed to the noun *faithfulness* to mean the faithful person who anticipates the vision to be fulfilled.

- Alternatively, the MT may emphasize the faithfulness of *Yahweh's vision*, if we take *vision* to be the antecedent of the third-person masculine singular pronoun affixed to the noun *faithfulness*.

- The LXX lays emphasis on "God's faithfulness," because of the first-person singular pronoun given, "*my* faithfulness" (and Yahweh clearly distinguishes himself as the speaker).

The LXX version of Habakkuk 2:4 ties closely with Habakkuk 2:3. Rendered with explanatory glosses, the text translates, following Wolfgang Kraus, roughly, "If (he) shrinks back [or rebuffs God's statements in Hab 2:2-3], my soul [God himself] is not pleased in him. But the righteous will live by my faithfulness [i.e., the righteous will trust in God's faithfulness to fulfill God's statements in Hab 2:2-3]."[15] The LXX highlights "God's faithfulness," because

---

[14] This section leans heavily on Thomas, *Habakkuk*, 117-19.
[15] Thomas, *Habakkuk*, 117. See Wolfgang Kraus, "Hab 2:3-4 in the Hebrew Tradition and in the Septuagint, with Its Reception in the New Testament," in *Septuagint and Reception: Essays Prepared for the Association for the Study of the Septuagint in South Africa*, ed. Johann Cook, VTSup 127 (Leiden: Brill, 2009), 101-17, here 111-13. Kraus views the contrast in Hab 2:4 (in the LXX) between

of the first-person singular pronoun given, "*my* faithfulness," and the speech is in the mouth of God.

However, the MT deserves greater attention. Does the verse speak to God's faithfulness, the faithfulness of the just one, the faithfulness of the people, or something else? It is often thought that the Hebrew MT emphasizes the faithfulness of the righteous follower of Yahweh. However, the faithfulness in view may refer neither to God nor to faithful people, at least in the Hebrew text. What is "trustworthy" and "faithful" is the *vision* that God gives in Habakkuk 2:2-3. The grammar allows this view, and the third-person masculine singular suffix on "faithfulness" (*be'ĕmûnātô*) could refer to "the vision" as much as it could refer to Yahweh, "since it is the reliability of the vision that is in question (c.f. Hab 2:3a)." So Robert Haak translates Habakkuk 2:4b: "but the righteous because of its fidelity [God's vision in Hab 2:2-3] will live."[16]

We take Haak's point, but we note the difficulty of distinguishing the vision's faithfulness from Yahweh's fidelity. Even Haak admits, "It is difficult, and probably not desirable, however, to draw too sharp a distinction between the vision, the content of the vision . . . , and the author of the vision (Yahweh). Their reliability is interdependent."[17] For this reason, we believe the faithfulness of Habakkuk 2:4b refers to God and the vision of vindication of Habakkuk 2:2-3.[18]

The Righteous One

If this is so, can we identify the righteous/just one? The just one or righteous one of the "righteous one will live" may be a messianic prophecy: "The righteous one [i.e., the Messiah] will live by faith." Richard Hays thinks both intertestamental literature and in the New Testament interpretation of Habakkuk 2:4 reinforce this reading. "The Righteous One" is a messianic title for Jesus. Paul declares the Righteous One (who is Jesus) will live by the faithfulness of God in Romans 1:17. Paul's reuse of Habakkuk 2:4 in Romans 1:17 testifies that the faithful and righteous sufferer is Jesus, who dies but experiences resurrection by God's faithfulness.[19] This could be, but we

---

the faithful who hear God's vision and trust in God's faithfulness (Hab 2:4b) and the faithless one who hears the vision and "shrinks back" away from both its content and from God himself.

[16] Robert D. Haak, *Habakkuk*, VTSup 44 (Leiden: Brill, 1992), 59, 25.

[17] Haak, *Habakkuk*, 59.

[18] So too Thomas Renz, *The Books of Nahum, Habakkuk, and Zephaniah*, NICOT (Grand Rapids, MI: Eerdmans, 2021), 290.

[19] Richard B. Hays, *The Conversion of the Imagination: Paul as Interpreter of Israel's Scripture* (Grand Rapids, MI: Eerdmans, 2005), 119-42.

believe Habakkuk 2:4 is not first an eschatological prediction about the Messiah, even if it could be applied that way.

The righteous likely refers to the faithful people who persevere even through Yahweh's judgment. Second century AD Judaism understood Habakkuk 2:4 in this way. A Jewish targum on Habakkuk reads the "righteous" with a nonmessianic understanding: "The wicked think that all these things are not so, but the righteous live by the truth of them."[20] This represents a different reading from the messianic one, highlighting the faithfulness of followers of Yahweh deemed as righteous precisely because they live in accordance with the ways of Yahweh. Similarly, the Qumran Habakkuk pesher envisions that the faithful ones are "righteous" because they live in accordance with Yahweh's *tôrâ* and the instruction of the Teacher of Righteousness.[21] The reception of Habakkuk 2:4b in 2 Baruch indicates a nonmessianic understanding of the righteous, emphasizing a contrast between those who are wicked and those who are righteous in their faith in God (2 Baruch 54.16–18). Still, these indicators are not unanimous. Another Qumran text, 8Ḥev1 (Naḥal Ḥever Twelve Prophets in Greek), does read *dikaios* as a messianic title, "Righteous One."

We believe the identity of the righteous one in Habakkuk is one(s) who trusts in God and lives faithfully before him.[22] James Mulroney demonstrates, through extensive and close analysis of the Old Greek of Habakkuk 2:4, that although the verse *could be applied* to a messianic figure, in the original Greek text it is not necessary that one reads the text in that way. Nor is it essential in the Hebrew text. It is possible but not essential. The "righteous one" was *applied* to Jesus as the fulfillment of the one who embraced God's plan, even to the point of his death, and who brought life. His life, death, and resurrection constitute the fulfillment of the eschatological vision of the "appointed time" and the "end," and thereby those who trust in Jesus are caught up in that movement as well.[23]

One discovers an inbuilt human response to the vision of God's faithfulness, namely, *faith* in God's fidelity to enact justice. This is true whether

---

[20]Kevin J. Cathcart and Robert P. Gordon, *The Targum of the Minor Prophets*, AB 14 (Wilmington, DE: Glazier, 1989), 150-51.

[21]For a fresh reading of the Qumran pesher on Habakkuk, see Timothy H. Lim, *The Earliest Commentary on the Prophecy of Habakkuk*, Oxford Commentary on the Dead Sea Scrolls (Oxford: Oxford University Press, 2020).

[22]See the discussion in Renz, *Books of Nahum, Habakkuk, and Zephaniah*, 288-89.

[23]James A. E. Mulroney, "Revisiting Hab 2:4 and Its Place in the New Testament Eschatological Vision," *STR* 6 (2015): 3-28.

one reads the righteous as the faithful followers of Yahweh or a messianic identity. The Messiah *and* the faithful demonstrate their allegiance to Yahweh precisely because they trust Yahweh to the end, both in judgment and salvation. The Greek and Hebrew versions closely relate God's response to the prophet in Habakkuk 2:2-4. Both versions present God's response to the prophet in Habakkuk 2:2-3 as the *divine answer* to the prophet's questions concerning the enemy nation. The righteous will trust Yahweh and his vision because he is faithful, as is Yahweh's vision. "The revelation promises that the innocent victims of aggression who remain loyal to God will live, while the swollen appetite of the oppressors will be their downfall. The promise does not so much call the arrogant to repent and adopt faith in God as urge those who put their trust in God to continue to do so."[24] God will vindicate the righteous and in so doing will prove the veracity of the vision.

This vindication of God (where the righteous will be delivered and the enemy will be defeated) is for the appointed time, *the end*. God's people should persevere in patience and faith, waiting for this time to come. Habakkuk 2:4, then, in both the Greek and Hebrew versions, reiterates that God is faithful and those who are righteous will then respond in faith to God's faithfulness.

Life

Another significant question that emerges from this verse is the meaning of the statement "the righteous will live" in Habakkuk 2:4b. In Habakkuk 1:12, the prophet asks God, "O Lord, will we not die?" when confronted with the Babylonian threat. Habakkuk 2:4b responds to this question. Yahweh affirms the faithful will *not* die but in fact will *live*. For those who pledge their allegiance to Yahweh and live faithfully before him, life is guaranteed: "the righteous one, by its faithfulness, will *live*."

But what life lies in view? Luther interprets life with the coming of Christ's kingdom: "If you wish to abide and be preserved, you must believe this inscription on the tablet [from Hab 2:2-3], which says that the Christ will come with His kingdom."[25] Life in Christ's kingdom comes by "belief" or faith in God's promise. We like Luther's reading, but the precise nature of life envisioned in Habakkuk 2:4b remains ambiguous, firing our imaginations to fill the content with contextual evidence.

---

[24]Renz, *Books of Nahum, Habakkuk, and Zephaniah*, 290.
[25]Luther, *Lectures on the Minor Prophets II*, 197.

Faith in the Faithful God

The text may indicate that the righteous will not be swept away in the Babylonian onslaught but rather will be exiled and live in a foreign land. This makes sense of the immediate context of Habakkuk 2:1-2. Life understood in this context affirms that Yahweh will judge his people by the hand of Babylon, but Yahweh will enable them to survive and restore them to Zion. Habakkuk 2:4b, then, reveals that God will not destroy his people due to their sin, but he will preserve a remnant that is made pure through the fires of judgment. Life, then, is a grace of God as he preserves Israel in salvation *through* judgment.

The meaning of *life* in Habakkuk 2:4b may be understood a bit more broadly. Because the vision in Habakkuk 2:2-3 is about the end, life in Habakkuk 2:4b may connote a kind of resurrection. As Thomas notes, Habakkuk 6:1-2 instructs that judgment against God's people will not be final. They will die in exile, but they will be revived: "In two days he will make us whole again, on the third day he will raise us and we shall *live* before him" (Hos 6:2). Death in this text is real: Israel dies in the wilderness of exile, but God raises them back to vitality and returns them to the land. For our purposes with the connection to Habakkuk, in this verse the root *hyh* is the same as one finds in "the righteous will *live* [*hyh*] in his faithfulness" in Habakkuk 2:4b. A similar thought appears in Zechariah 10:9: "Though I sowed them among the nations, yet in far countries they shall remember me, and with their children they shall *live* [*hyh*] and return." The metaphor of God sowing his seed among the nations indicates that God's people have been scattered, have been broken open on the ground of the nations in death, and yet through their death they spring forth into new life. God revives them, and they will live. The concept of God drawing life out of death for Israel stands in Hosea and Zechariah and may emerge for Habakkuk 2:4 as well.[26]

However construed, Habakkuk 2:4b is a word of encouragement for those who believe God will do what he says he will do: Yahweh will give life beyond death! His grace is his divine prerogative, and so it is not in some way earned. Nonetheless, Yahweh provides life to those who would believe in him by faith. The vision reminds the faithful that whenever Yahweh's vindication takes hold, the faithful can trust in Yahweh's faithfulness: all will be set to rights and God's people will live, not die. Even if they experience the reality of judgment, Yahweh pronounces life over them still.

---

[26]Thomas, *Habakkuk*, 120-21.

Conclusion

In the Christian faith, dying to self and rising to new life is indicative of the cruciform life. Such a commitment to the way of Christ is the essence of expressing allegiance to Christ. Jesus instructs: "If any want to become my followers, let them deny themselves and take up their cross and follow me. For those who want to save their life will lose it, and those who lose their life for my sake will find it" (Mt 16:24-25 NRSV). Yet ironically in our death we do not die but are raised to new life in our Savior. We can say with Saint Paul: "I have been crucified with Christ; and it is no longer I who live, but it is Christ who lives in me. And the life I now live in the flesh I live by faith in the Son of God, who loved me and gave himself for me" (Gal 2:19-20 NRSV). Habakkuk testifies to a cruciform life in the vision and instruction of Habakkuk 2:2-4: the faithful will trust Yahweh to the point of death, living in allegiance to him alone, believing that his grace and faithfulness will bring them life. This is true of Jesus; it will be true of those who follow Jesus as well.

Recommended Reading

Carroll, Robert P. "Eschatological Delay in the Prophetic Tradition?" *ZAW* 94, no. 1 (1982): 47-58.

Kraus, Wolfgang. "Hab 2:3-4 in the Hebrew Tradition and in the Septuagint, with Its Reception in the New Testament." In *Septuagint and Reception: Essays Prepared for the Association for the Study of the Septuagint in South Africa*, ed. Johann Cook, 101-17. VTSup 127. Leiden: Brill, 2009.

Lim, Timothy H. *The Earliest Commentary on the Prophecy of Habakkuk*. Oxford Commentary on the Dead Sea Scrolls. Oxford: Oxford University Press, 2020.

Mulroney, James A. E. "Revisiting Hab 2:4 and Its Place in the New Testament Eschatological Vision." *STR* 6 (2015): 3-28.*

Renz, Thomas. *The Books of Nahum, Habakkuk, and Zephaniah*. NICOT. Grand Rapids, MI: Eerdmans, 2021.

Thomas, Heath A. *Faith amid the Ruins: The Book of Habakkuk*. Transformative Word Series. Bellingham, WA: Lexham Press, 2016.*

———. *Habakkuk: A Commentary*. THOTC. Grand Rapids, MI: Eerdmans, 2018.

Recommended reading marked with a "" indicates introductory works.*

17

Zechariah

PRISONERS OF HOPE

Haggai and Zechariah began their prophetic ministries in the same year, namely, 520 BC.[1] Zechariah's ministry began two months after Haggai's, and his visions began two months after Haggai's last oracles.[2] This moves us firmly into the postexilic Persian period, and in our chapter on Haggai, we discuss the indispensable historical context for understanding these books. Prophecy—and preaching—is always contextually specific, and as we listen to the Minor Prophets it is vital to be aware that Haggai, Zechariah, and Malachi are rooted in the postexilic period and differ in this way from the rest of the Twelve, with the possible exception of Jonah, which is notoriously difficult to date.

Zechariah, Prophet and Priest

In Zechariah 1:1 (see also Zech 1:7) we are introduced by an editor to "Zechariah son of Berekiah, the son of Iddo." The standard formula for prophetic revelation "the word of Yahweh came to" clearly identifies Zechariah as a prophet. "Son of Berekiah, the son of Iddo," however, indicates he was also a priest. Ezra 5:1; 6:14 also identifies Zechariah as a descendant of Iddo. In Nehemiah 12:4 Iddo is identified as one of the priests and Levites who returned to Jerusalem from exile in Babylon with Zerubbabel and Joshua. In Nehemiah 12:16 Zechariah is referred to as the head of the priestly family of

---

[1] The date headings for both Haggai and Zechariah are reckoned in relation to Darius I, who became king around October 5, 522 BC, and ruled until his death in November 486 BC. See the chart in Carol L. Meyers and Eric M. Meyers, *Haggai, Zechariah 1–8*, AB (New York: Doubleday, 1987), xlvi, for the chronological data. The eighth month in Zech 1:1 could be November or December.
Our subtitle for this chapter comes from this evocative expression in Zech 9:12. See Al Wolters, *Zechariah*, HCOT 19 (Leuven: Peeters, 2014), 287.

[2] Meyers and Meyers, *Haggai, Zechariah 1–8*, 89–90.

Iddo. "*Son of Berekiah*, the son of Iddo" identifies Zechariah more closely as the grandson of Iddo rather than his son. In Ezra 5:1; 6:14 the expression in Hebrew is *bar-ʾiddô*. *Bar* normally means "son" in later Hebrew, but "son" can mean actual son or descendant.

Marvin Sweeney suggests that the designation of Berekiah is meant to associate Zechariah with Jeberekiah in Isaiah 8:1-4, one of two named as witnesses of the birth of Isaiah's son, so that Zechariah's book is to be seen as a witness to the fulfillment of Isaiah's prophecies.[3] There are undoubtedly, as we will see, strong connections between Isaiah and Zechariah, but it seems to us unlikely that such a designation would be invented for this purpose. Zechariah 1:1 is concerned to locate the ministry of Zechariah precisely, and the introduction of a fictitious genealogy would subvert this. What the editor is concerned to do is to alert us that Zechariah is both a prophet and a priest, as the repetition of his dual pedigree in Zechariah 1:7 makes clear. Indeed, there is much priestly imagery and cultic focus in Zechariah.

Zechariah's genealogy alerts us to exile in Babylon as a formative influence on the book and on Zechariah. We do not know whether he himself was in exile and returned from it, but that scenario is highly likely. If so, he would have known in his bones the reality of exile from the land and the struggle of the Israelites to adjust to exile, as well as the jubilation *and* struggle of returning. As a priest, he would have been well equipped to prophesy about the reconstruction of the temple and the cultus in Jerusalem. He would also have known Israel's tradition and Scriptures well, and not surprisingly, Zechariah is chock-full of intertextual resonances to earlier parts of the Old Testament.

Outline

As we will explain below when we work through Zechariah, the chronological headings in Zechariah 1:1; 1:7; 7:1 indicate the overarching shape of the book.

Part I:	Zechariah 1–6	An invitation and eight visions
	Zechariah 1:1-6	Introduction: An invitation to return
	Zechariah 1:7–6:15	Eight visions
	Zechariah 1:7-17	Vision 1: A problematic peace and a God of compassion

---

[3] Marvin A. Sweeney, *The Twelve Prophets*, Berit Olam (Collegeville, MN: Liturgical Press, 2000), 2:563; see Meyers and Meyers, *Haggai, Zechariah 1–8*, 91-92, who suggest four possibilities.

	Zechariah 2:1-4 [1:18-21]	Vision 2: Powerful nations and Yahweh ṣəbā'ôt
	Zechariah 2:5-17 [2:1-13]	Vision 3: An international city
	Zechariah 3:1-10	Vision 4: The high priest
	Zechariah 4:1-14	Vision 5: Lampstand
	Zechariah 5:1-4	Vision 6: The flying scroll
	Zechariah 5:5-11	Vision 7: A basket and three women
	Zechariah 6:1-15	Vision 8: Four chariots and two crowns
Part II: Zechariah 7–14		
	Zechariah 7:1–8:23	A question and a long answer
	Zechariah 9–14	Two pronouncements
Zechariah 9–11		A prophecy
	Zechariah 9:1-8	Judgment against the nations and redemption
	Zechariah 9:9-17	Prisoners of hope
	Zechariah 10:1-12	The restoration of Judah
	Zechariah 11:1-17	Revoking the covenant
Zechariah 12–14		A prophecy
	Zechariah 12:1-14	Judgment on the nations and mourning in Israel
	Zechariah 13:1-6	Cleansing from sin and the cessation of prophecy
	Zechariah 13:7-9	Strike the shepherd, refine the sheep
	Zechariah 14:1-21	The day of Yahweh: A new exodus and a new creation

INTERPRETATION

Zechariah 1:1-6: Introduction—An invitation to return. The opening six verses introduce the book of Zechariah and record his first sermon as well as summarize his ministry. We have already noted the importance of the postexilic context as the time when Zechariah was prophesying (Zech 1:1). Zechariah 1:1 dates this opening address within a few weeks of the start of the rebuilding of the temple. Zechariah 1:2 is in the third person, and this shifts to Yahweh speaking in the first person in Zechariah 1:3b-6a. Zechariah 1:2 introduces a theme that is central to this opening salvo, namely, "your ancestors," which occurs four times in Zechariah 1:2-6. A version of the root for "anger" in Hebrew (*qṣp*) opens and closes Zechariah 1:2; hence the NIV translation "very angry." The combination of the verb and noun expresses the "very angry," but it is unusual to have the noun placed at the end of the sentence. In this way however, anger functions as an *inclusio* for the opening words of Zechariah. "Your ancestors" refers to the Israelites who went into exile as part of God's judgment on them, enclosed in his wrath. As we have seen in Amos and elsewhere in the Minor Prophets, a common name for God that expresses his character as holy, omnipotent judge is Yahweh *ṣəbā'ôt* ("the LORD Almighty"). "Almighty," or "of Hosts," as it is often translated, evokes here Yahweh as the commander in chief of the armies of heaven—his hosts—coming against *his people* in judgment, as he did in the exile. This language thus recalls the judgment of exile and with "your ancestors" asks Zechariah's audience to look back and learn.

In Zechariah 1:4 Zechariah summarizes the message of the "earlier prophets" as "Turn" (*šûbû*). However, as Zechariah 1:4-5 notes, they did not turn, and they were overtaken by Yahweh's words and decrees. In Zechariah 1:3, in which the postexilic community is invited to return to Yahweh, the word for "return" is also *šûbû*. Yahweh has not changed, and neither has his requirement for his people, but in his patience he again makes the offer of reconciliation: "The prophet repeats the old, old story, claiming no originality for his central message."[4] If they will turn to him, then he will turn to them. Physically they have returned, but they need to return in their hearts and lives. Peter Craigie notes, "The work on the temple would become a monument to folly, unless it was accompanied by spiritual reconstruction."[5] As we see in the latter part of Zechariah 1:6, the people do turn—the word for repent is the same verb, *šûb*—and acknowledge the justice of God's judgment in the exile.

The reference to the earlier or Former Prophets is significant in more ways than one. Zechariah is familiar with the work of the prophets who preceded him and the overarching tradition of the Old Testament, and although he never *cites* Isaiah, Jeremiah, and Ezekiel, he *alludes* to them repeatedly as well as to other Old Testament books, such as Genesis, Leviticus,

---

[4]Peter C. Craigie, *Twelve Prophets*, The Daily Study Bible OT (Philadelphia: Westminster, 1985), 2:160.
[5]Craigie, *Twelve Prophets*, 2:162.

Deuteronomy, and Lamentations. We therefore need to be alert to echoes of these earlier books in our reading of Zechariah.[6]

Zechariah 1:7–6:15—A call to imagine. This section consists of eight visions introduced by a single date in Zechariah 1:7, approximately February 15, 519 BC.[7] All of them appear to have occurred "in the night" (Zech 1:8; see also Zech 4:1), but the use of the verb *to see* (*r'h*; NIV "I had a vision") "points to a wakeful prophetic experience rather than to any somnambulistic or dreamlike state on the part of the prophet."[8] In a very different context Wendell Berry notes, "Devotion to any particular place now carries always the implication of heartbreak."[9] For those who had returned from exile, this was certainly the case. They had suffered immensely and now lived amid the ruins of the old Jerusalem. Where were they to find the hope and faith required for a new start?

Berry appropriately defines faith as "difficult belief—of waiting, of patience, of endurance, of hanging on and holding together." They were to find the strength to wait, to endure, to hang on, from God, certainly, but it is fascinating to note the extent to which Zechariah 1–6 requires *an engaged imagination*. As Berry notes, imagination "is the power to make us *see*, and to see, moreover, things that without it would be unseeable."[10] This is certainly the case with the visions of Zechariah 1–8, which are remarkable in their metaphorical and imaginative intensity. The reader is further drawn in to exploring the visions by the presence of the angel and the dialogue between the angel and Zechariah. Zechariah himself does not generally know what the visions stand for and has to ask the angel or messenger.

Vision 1: Zechariah 1:7-17—A problematic peace and a God of compassion. In Zechariah 1:6 we read that the Israelites responded to God's invitation in Zechariah 1:3 and turned to Yahweh. The first vision culminates in Zechariah 1:16 with the declaration by Yahweh, "*I have turned* [*šabtî*] *to Jerusalem with mercy*." The verb is in the perfect tense and, unlike the NIV, should be

---

[6]On the intertextuality of Zech 1:1-6 see Michael R. Stead, *The Intertextuality of Zechariah 1–8* (London: T&T Clark, 2009), 75-86. Stead discerns echoes of Jeremiah, Ezekiel, Lamentations, Is 52; 54, and Deuteronomy.

[7]For a very useful reflection on hermeneutics and these visions, see Al Wolters, "Confessional Criticism and the Night Visions of Zechariah," in *Renewing Biblical Interpretation*, ed. Craig Bartholomew, Colin Greene, and Karl Möller, Scripture and Hermeneutics Series 1 (Grand Rapids, MI: Zondervan, 2000), 90-117.

[8]Meyers and Meyers, *Haggai, Zechariah 1–8*, 109. But see Sweeney, *Twelve Prophets*, 2:576.

[9]Wendell Berry, *Imagination in Place* (Berkeley: Counterpoint, 2010), 21.

[10]Berry, *Imagination in Place*, 183, 186-87.

translated as "have turned." In this way Zechariah 1:16 links the visions with the opening section and alerts us to Yahweh's fulfillment of his promise that if they return to him, he will return to them.

In accord with the name of God Yahweh ṣabāʾôt ("the LORD Almighty"), the first vision is a military one. Horses were almost exclusively used for military purposes in the ancient Near East, and that is the case here. Zechariah sees a man mounted on a red horse standing in a ravine amid myrtle tress, with horses behind him, red, brown, and white ones.[11] The myrtle is an evergreen shrub, which grows to a height of about two meters and is found in low-lying places and on hillsides. Here it adds to the sense of concealment.[12]

It is uncertain whether the mention of the myrtle trees and the colors of the horses are significant. Sweeney suggests they are. Following K. Seybold, he notes that myrtles played a role in ancient mythologies because their evergreen leaves and long roots suggested they reached down to the subterranean waters. *Məṣulâ* (ravine) may, he suggests, be related to *ṣulâ* ("ocean deep"; see Is 44:27) and *məṣôlâ* ("depth/deep"; see Ex 15:5; Mic 7:19; Jon 2:4 [2:3]; Zech 10:11). The mention of myrtle trees is vital because the colors of their flowers—white and sometimes rose—correspond to the colors of the horses. In the Old Testament the myrtle is one of four types of plants waved at the Festival of Sukkoth (Lev 23:40; Neh 8:15) "to symbolize the rebirth of creation in the fall at the time when the rainy season of Israel begins."[13] Sukkoth was when Solomon dedicated the first temple (1 Kings 8:65-66), when Jeroboam dedicated the temple at Beth El (1 Kings 12:32), and when Zerubbabel and Joshua dedicated the altar of the Second Temple (Ezra 3:1-7). Sweeney suggests that the vision is of a site near the site of the temple so that the myrtle at Sukkoth, symbolizing rebirth and new creation, would fit with the view of the temple as the center of the creation.[14]

---

[11] The primary meaning of *rkb* is "to be mounted," although it can also mean "to ride." See Meyers and Meyers, *Haggai, Zechariah 1-8*, 110. The Hebrew for "horses" and the adjectives signifying color are in the plural and do not specify the number of horses. On horse colors in general see "Equine Coat Color Genetics," UC Davis Veterinary Genetics Laboratory (accessed December 9, 2022), http://www.vgl.ucdavis.edu/services/coatcolorhorse.php. We are unaware of any work done on how Israelites classified horse colors, but red and sorrel should probably be thought of as variants of what we call *chestnuts* in the equine world. White is what is commonly called "gray."

[12] The word the NIV translates "ravine" is *məṣulâ*, a hapax legomenon probably derived from *ṣl* or *ṣll*, "to be or grow dark" (Zech 1:8). Thus Meyers and Meyers, *Haggai, Zechariah 1-8*, 110, translate it "in the shadows."

[13] Sweeney, *Twelve Prophets*, 2:577; see Is 41:19; 55:13.

[14] But see Meyers and Meyers, *Haggai, Zechariah 1-8*, 113.

We find this an attractive hypothesis but not certain. There does not seem to be as close a correspondence between the colors of the myrtle flowers and the horses as Sweeney suggests. In our view the horses were probably a ruddy brown, brown, and gray. The cultic and historical links with Sukkoth are more convincing, but there is no evidence that the vision is at a site close to the temple, and it is unclear to us that Sukkoth represents the rebirth of creation. Zechariah does have close links with Isaiah, and the mention of myrtles here *may* resonate with Isaiah 55:13.

Sukkoth is about exodus into a new land, and it is likely that myrtle trees in flower at this time and as the season of fertility beckons combine to create an expectation of a new act of God, the dawning of a new day, and real return from exile. Thus there may well be a new-creation motif at work here, but if so, it is subtle and less pronounced than Sweeney suggests.

The horses represent God's military forces, and whereas in the final vision they are drawing chariots, here they lack chariots in order to stress swiftness. Such swiftness is required for their role of surveillance throughout the earth (Zech 1:10). They return and report that the world is at peace, a report that is less an empirical geopolitical analysis than an underlining of Yahweh's immanence and sovereignty over the earth and a description of stark contrast with the broken state of Jerusalem. The contrast is glaringly obvious, and the angel of Yahweh intercedes on behalf of Jerusalem and Judah in the form of a lament. "How long?" he asks.[15] The verb for "withhold mercy" (*lōʾ-təraḥēm*) is from the same root as the name of one of Hosea's children, namely, "No-Mercy" (*lō-ruḥāmâ*). Yahweh has withheld mercy for the seventy years of exile (see Jer 25:11; 29:10), but now he speaks comforting words—literally "good words, comforting words"—to the angel (see Is 40:1), who then gives Zechariah an oracle to proclaim to the Israelites.

The proclamation reiterates Yahweh's covenant commitment to Israel. Various forms of the root for "jealous" (*qnʾ*, Zech 1:14) are commonly used in the Old Testament for Yahweh's special relationship with his people. Here his jealousy for his people and anger with the nations indicate that his anger with Israel has ceased. Zechariah 1:16 picks up on the angel's lament and on the repeated "turn" in Zechariah 1:1-6 with its statement that Yahweh has *turned* to Jerusalem with mercy (*bəraḥămîm*). The sign of this is that his house, the temple, will be rebuilt, and Jerusalem and Judah will prosper. In the Hebrew, "again" occurs twice in Zechariah 1:17b. Yahweh will again

---

[15]A characteristic element in laments, but see also Is 6:11.

comfort Zion and again choose Jerusalem. All of this evokes the full restoration of Yahweh's relationship with his people. Even as the oracle is proclaimed, Yahweh speaks of "my house" and "my towns." Yahweh will take up habitation again among his people in his land.

How, one wonders, would the inhabitants of Jerusalem have received this vision and oracle from Zechariah? Doubtless the military presence of the Lord Almighty's troops in close proximity would raise fears and doubt about what would follow. They had tasted what this could mean in exile. This casts a different light on Zechariah's question in Zechariah 1:9. The question is a nominal sentence without a verb, which has to be supplied. Literally it reads, "What these, my Lord?" Thus it could be translated, with the NIV, as "What are these, my lord?" but if we are right in thinking that Zechariah and his hearers would immediately recognize them as a (divine) military presence, then the force of the question is rather "What is the meaning of these (soldiers), my Lord?" From their experience of exile Israel knew only too well what they could mean, and we can imagine a certain anxiety in Zechariah's question and in his audience.

This is confirmed by the angel's answer, which explains their mission rather than who they are. It is really only with the angel's lament and Yahweh's response that it becomes clear that the soldiers are not a threat to Jerusalem. Yahweh has not changed; he remains commander in chief of his hosts, but now that his people have turned, he has turned in mercy to them. To hear this God speak of "my house" and "my towns" would have been an extraordinary comfort and motivation to Zechariah's congregation as well as a reminder that Yahweh's mercy is never cheap grace.[16]

Vision 2: Zechariah 2:1-4 [1:18-21]—Powerful nations and YHWH ṣəbā 'ôt. In vision 1 Yahweh asserts his anger with the nations, and this theme is picked up in the short second vision. The horn is a symbol of strength, and that there are four probably implies a more general reference to all nations of the earth from the four points of the compass, especially to those nations hostile to Israel and that scattered not only Judah but Israel also.[17] The number four may also allude to the four horns of the typical Israelite altar (see Ex 27:2), especially if, as Sweeney suggests, these horns symbolize Yahweh's power throughout the world.[18] A notable feature in this vision is

---

[16]See Dietrich Bonhoeffer, *The Cost of Discipleship* (London: SCM Press, 1959), for the distinction between cheap and costly grace.

[17]Four is a significant number in Zechariah. There are four horns, four winds in Zech 2:10 [2:6], four winds and four chariots in the sixth vision, Zech 6:1, 5.

[18]Sweeney, *Twelve Prophets*, 2:582.

that in Zechariah 2:3 [1:20] *Yahweh himself* shows Zechariah the four smiths and explains their role to defeat the nations who so terrorized Israel.[19]

Like the first vision, the second indicates that Yahweh has not changed. He remains sovereign over the nations. But now this sovereignty is exercised on Israel's behalf and for the protection of his people so that they need not fear. It is also a reminder that God has not abandoned justice.

Vision 3: Zechariah 2:5-17 [2:1-13]—An international city. The surveyor portrayed in Zechariah 2:5-6 [2:1-2] echoes the theme of the measuring line in Zechariah 1:16, although a different word is used in Zechariah 2:5 [2:1] for "measuring line." The image of being scattered to the "four winds" likewise echoes the four horns of the previous vision. In Zechariah 1:16 the measuring line is a symbol of restoration (see Jer 31:38-39), but here the prevention of the young man from carrying out his survey of Jerusalem—as if by a startling incoming message from heaven/the temple (Zech 2:7 [2:3])—opens up an eschatological vision of the future of Jerusalem and indeed of the world.[20] Haggai and Zechariah were deeply involved in the rebuilding of the temple, and that eventually involved the walls of Jerusalem as well in circa 445 BC (Neh 2–6). But now a vision is presented of a city so great that walls cannot contain it except that Yahweh himself will be a wall of fire around it.[21]

Yahweh has already declared that he has returned to his people and to Jerusalem (Zech 1:16), but now another return is envisaged, not only of exiles but also of Yahweh himself (Zech 2:14 [2:10]). The language of "that day," that is, the day of Yahweh, resurfaces, and now it is a day of salvation—albeit following judgment (Zech 2:15 [2:11])—when many nations will be joined with Yahweh as part of his people.[22] Yahweh will again inherit Judah as his portion in the holy land and will again choose Jerusalem.

---

[19] The word (*ḥārāšîm*) refers to "craftsmen," but if the horns are made of metal, then the craftsmen would be smiths or metalworkers. Sweeney (*Twelve Prophets*, 2:583) notes, "The identification of YHWH as the one who shows the prophet this vision is important because it points to YHWH as the source of the visions shown to the prophet by the angel."

[20] Perhaps the prevention of the young man from carrying out his survey of Jerusalem is an early indication that Yahweh is rousing himself in the temple (Zech 2:17 [2:13]). In Amos 7:7-9 the measuring line is a symbol of coming judgment.

[21] David L. Petersen (*Haggai and Zechariah 1–8: A Commentary*, OTL [Philadelphia: Westminster, 1984], 171) suggests a parallel with the Persian royal city of Pasargadae, which was constructed without walls and contained many fire altars to represent the Persian god Ahura Mazda. Sweeney (*Twelve Prophets*, 2:586) notes, "The restoration of YHWH's presence or 'glory' to Jerusalem is thus presented as an analogy to Ahura Mazda's presence in Pasargadae and thus to Persian imperial power."

[22] There are some difficulties in determining who the speaker is in Zech 2:12-13 [2:8-9] and Zech 2:15 [2:11]. In our view, in Zech 2:12-13 the saying, although introduced as the word of

Zechariah 2:17 [2:13] sets out the only adequate response, namely, for all flesh (*bāśār*) to be still before the presence of Yahweh because he has roused himself for action in his holy dwelling, the temple. In Habakkuk 2:20 and Zephaniah 1:7 there is a similar exhortation to silence *by all the earth*, but there it is in the context of his judgment. Here the silence prefaces his acting for international salvation so that Jerusalem will truly become an international city, including *many animals* (Zech 2:8 [2:4]), a theme found repeatedly in the Minor Prophets.

Doubtless this vision had immediate messages for its hearers. Zechariah 2:8-9 [2:4-5] announces the restoration of Jerusalem. Conventional thinking would have been that Jerusalem must have walls if it was to be restored, whereas this vision serves as a reminder that the future may be different from the past. The assumption of Yahweh's active presence as a protecting wall of fire around Jerusalem and in the temple would also have been a great encouragement. The call for exiles to return would encourage those who had returned to dig in and participate in Yahweh's restoration of Jerusalem.[23] Likewise, the description of Jerusalem and its inhabitants as "the apple of his eye" would have provided reassurance that Yahweh was indeed again jealous for his people (see Zech 1:14).

The language of "inheritance" and "choosing," drawn from the traditions of Israel and the unique description of Israel as the holy land, would have indicated unequivocally that Israel had a future with Yahweh. Nevertheless, an eschatological dimension dominates the vision and looks way beyond the present context into a glorious future. Indeed, as Sweeney notes, even the image of the "four winds" in Zechariah 2:10 [2:6] "recalls the role of the Temple as cosmic center, i.e., YHWH as sovereign of the cosmos."[24]

Vision 4: Zechariah 3:1-10—The high priest and the branch.[25] Restoration of Jerusalem as Zion requires an altar, a temple, and a high priest. In this fourth vision Zechariah is shown—presumably by the angel of the other

---

Yahweh, oscillates between an angel—note the reference to the angel of Yahweh in Zech 3:1—speaking and Yahweh speaking. Meyers and Meyers (*Haggai, Zechariah 1-8*, 162) thus rightly place "for whoever . . . plunder them" and "They will be a people to me, and I will dwell in your midst" (Meyers and Meyers's translation) in quotation marks as the speech of Yahweh.

[23]The reference to Babylon as "the land of the north" (Zech 2:10 [2:6]) recalls Jeremiah's reference to the judgment from the north (Jer 1:14; 4:6; 10:22). Babylon lay east of Judah, but one would reach it via a northern route.

[24]Sweeney, *Twelve Prophets*, 2:587.

[25]There is considerable discussion about the integrity of this section as well as the vision being an addition to an original set of seven visions. See Sweeney, *Twelve Prophets*, 2:592-93.

visions—the ordination of the high priest Joshua in the courts of heaven.[26] The ordination of the high priest is set out in Exodus 29 and Leviticus 8–9. Here that ritual is followed only in a generalized fashion, but the symbolic element is crystal clear. The vision follows a three-part narrative sequence:

Zechariah 3:1-2: Joshua accused by Satan and defended by Yahweh

Zechariah 3:3-5: Joshua purified

Zechariah 3:6-10: Joshua commissioned and an announcement

The "angel of Yahweh" plays a central role in the proceedings in the heavenly courts, functioning as a kind of majordomo. Joshua is described by Yahweh as a burning stick snatched from the fire (see Amos 4:11; Is 7:4). The fire would be that of exile, during which he suffered but survived and returned to Jerusalem. That he went into exile connects him with the guilt of the people and makes him vulnerable to the Satan's accusations.[27] In the background lingers the question, Is tainted Israel really able to recover? The answer is found in the description of Yahweh as the one "who has chosen Jerusalem" (Zech 3:2; see also Zech 2:16 [2:12]).

The extent of Israel's taint is clear from the word *filthy* (*ṣôʾîm*), which is derived from the word meaning "vomit" or "excrement." Israel's sin has contaminated her to the very core of her existence, but now Joshua's filthy clothes are removed and replaced with "fine garments," a word used elsewhere only in Isaiah 3:22 and here referring to a tunic or the high priestly robe of the ephod. The ritual change of clothes is *prefaced* by an internal cleansing: "See, I have taken away your sin." In Zechariah 3:5 Zechariah interjects, calling for him to receive also a turban, which he does, with his festal garments. Zechariah's interjection may seem unusual, but it paves the way in the narrative for the reference to the stone in Zechariah 3:9, which was a rosette on the high priest's turban (see Ex 28:36-38; Zech 4:2, 10).

In Zechariah 3:6-7 the angel of Yahweh commissions Joshua on behalf of Yahweh. The shift in name to Yahweh *ṣəbāʾôt* fits with the seriousness of the commission. Like all leaders and Israelites, Joshua is to "walk in obedience to me," and in relation to his office as high priest he is to keep

---

[26]The motif of the heavenly court is also found in Gen 1:24-26; 1 Kings 22; Is 6; Job 1. Joshua is also identified as high priest in Hag 1:1, 12, 14; 2: 2, 4; Zech 3:8; 6:11.

[27]The Satan is found elsewhere in the OT, including in Job 1. There is much discussion as to whether or not this figure should be identified with Satan/the devil in the NT. See Victor Hamilton, "Satan," in *Anchor Bible Dictionary*, ed. David Noel Freedman (New York: Doubleday, 1992), 5:985-89.

his requirements for the cultus as set out in Leviticus. "My house" and "my courts" in Zechariah 3:7 refer to the temple. As high priest, Joshua would have access to the holy of holies, that is, to the very presence of Yahweh, thus sharing "a place among these standing here" (Zech 3:7 NIV) in the heavenly court.

Zechariah 3:8-9 is an announcement of the significance of the ordination of Joshua. It is not precisely clear who Joshua's "associates, seated before you" are. Most probably it refers to his priestly associates, including Zechariah. "Symbolic of" is a translation of the Hebrew *môpēt*, used in the Old Testament for God's miraculous acts as *signs* leading up to the Israelites' liberation from Egypt as well as of humans' and especially prophets' symbolic actions.[28] Joshua's ordination is thus a sign of more than the restoration of the temple.

Yahweh is going to bring his servant, "the Branch," a royal Davidic figure (Zech 3:8; see Is 11; Jer 23:5-6; 33:14-26), who, in a vision drawn from Micah 4:4 and Isaiah 2:2-4, will usher in shalom (Zech 3:10). The coming of the Branch is announced in Zechariah 3:8, but sandwiched in between this announcement and the declaration of what he will do in Zechariah 3:10 is a further reference to the priesthood in Zechariah 3:9. The seven eyes or facets on the stone on the front of Joshua's turban relate to the seven lamps, seven channels, and seven eyes of the next vision (Zech 4:2, 10). In line with the cosmic imagery of the temple, they evoke Yahweh's omniscience and immanent involvement in the world from Zion. The temple is about cleansing from sin, and the coming of shalom (Zech 3:10) will be preceded by the removal of the sin of "this land in a single day."

Zechariah 4:10 provides an evocative description of Jerusalem's condition at this time; it was a day of small things. It would have been very easy to become discouraged and to look around and compare the present unfavorably with past glory. In this context the vision of Joshua's ordination in the heavenly court would have spoken with tremendous power. Yes, the temple had to be rebuilt, but would Yahweh really indwell it again? This was a crucial question because the cultus functioned as the diplomatic corps mediating between the Israelites and Yahweh. Without Yahweh's presence and without a functioning temple, there was no future for Jerusalem. Yahweh's defense of Joshua and his ordination and purification provided assurance that Yahweh truly was back with his people. Not only had he truly

---

[28]See Meyers and Meyers, *Haggai, Zechariah 1-8*, 199.

turned to his people, but the ordination of Joshua was a sign of greater things to come.

Vision 5: Zechariah 4:1-14—A golden lampstand and two olive trees. The move from the coronation of the high priest Joshua to the golden lampstand is a natural one, since the lampstand was part of the furniture of the temple. As with the clothing of Joshua, the relationship with the cultic apparatus in the sanctuary and first temple is not exact, perhaps indicating continuity and discontinuity.[29] Zechariah is woken up to see this vision, an unusual note but one that fits with the rhetoric in this section (see the repetition in Zech 4:11-12), which draws attention to the significance of the vision. The reader too is to remain wide awake at this point.

The golden lampstand or menorah has its bowl on it, the bowl being the main basin in which olive oil was collected to feed the seven lamps. Each lamp has seven lips.[30] On either side of the lampstand are two olive trees. The first of Zechariah's three questions occurs in Zechariah 4:4. The reference to Zerubbabel laying the foundation of the temple in the power of the Spirit may seem a strange answer to Zechariah's question, but once we see in Zechariah 4:7 that the lampstand symbolizes God's presence in the temple as the center of the world, the logic becomes clear. Just as the Spirit of Yahweh hovered over the creation in Genesis 1:2, so here it is the Spirit who will usher in the new Jerusalem. The "mighty mountain" of Zechariah 4:7 is a metaphor for all the obstacles in the way of Zerubbabel generating the project of building the temple, and he will do it only with God's help. Yahweh is ready to help, as the cry "Favor, Favor" at the end of Zechariah 4:7 indicates.

On either side of the lampstand is an olive tree, and from Zechariah 4:11-12 it appears that it was these in particular that Zechariah did not understand. Olive trees, of course, produce oil for lamp fuel, but the fertility of the trees is also dependent on the lampstand, symbolizing Yahweh's presence. From Zechariah 4:14 we learn that the olive trees represent the two who are anointed, namely, the priest, Joshua, and the prince, Zerubbabel. "Just as the olive oil represents the fertility, light, and stability of creation, so the king and priest represent the stability of the people of Israel."[31] Craigie notes how this stresses the importance of human leadership and involvement in the

---

[29]The relationship to Ex 25:31-40; 37:17-24 is not clear.
[30]For the view that they are "lips" rather than channels, see Sweeney, *Twelve Prophets*, 2:605-6.
[31]Sweeney, *Twelve Prophets*, 2:607.

fulfillment of God's purposes: "The temple was the home of the lampstand, symbolizing both God's window on the world and God as light of the world. But it was the two olive trees, representing Joshua and Zerubbabel, which provided the fuel so that the lamp could burn brightly."[32]

For many in Jerusalem, it must have seemed as though this was indeed "the day of small things." This vision serves to jolt Zechariah's audience awake out of their nostalgia for the past and to focus them on the task at hand—the temple will be rebuilt—as well as the significance of being the people of Yahweh even at this time. Yahweh is no local deity confined by the vicissitudes of his people; from Zion he surveys the whole earth, and his anointed "serve the LORD of all the earth" (Zech 4:14).

Vision 6: Zechariah 5:1-4—The flying scroll. The high priest has been ordained and purified. But so too must the people be cleansed, and the next two visions deal with the eradication of evil among God's people. Jerusalem has another opportunity to be Zion, but Yahweh has not changed; he remains the holy, dangerous but gracious God. In this sixth vision Zechariah sees a remarkable thing: a large, unrolled flying scroll. The scroll is thirty by fifteen feet; normal scrolls were much narrower. Today's equivalent would be like seeing a drone from *YHWH ṣəbā'ôt* flying overhead. Sweeney notes, "The measurements of the flying scroll and their correspondence to the measurements of both the Temple vestibule, where the Torah was read to the people every seventh Sukkoth, and the cherubim which guarded the ark of the covenant where the tablets of the covenant were kept, suggest that the scroll is somehow to be identified with YHWH's Torah."[33] This is confirmed by what we are told about the writing on the scroll in Zechariah 5:3.

The scroll deals with covenant curse and has writing on both sides, the one side declaring that every thief will be banished and the other that everyone who swears falsely will be banished. There is some debate about the meaning of the verb *banished* (*niqqâ*). It means either "to be purged out" in the niphal, hence "banished," or "to be acquitted" in the piel stem. The pointing in the MT allows it to be either, but both Sweeney and Carol Meyers and Eric Meyers argue for the meaning "to be acquitted."[34] If this is the case, then the point is that there is lawlessness in Jerusalem, and neither the thief nor the one swearing falsely is being punished. In the end, the

---

[32]Craigie, *Twelve Prophets*, 2:179.
[33]Sweeney, *Twelve Prophets*, 2:616.
[34]Meyers and Meyers, *Haggai, Zechariah 1-8*, 286; Sweeney, *Twelve Prophets*, 2:617.

meaning is not altered by the translation one chooses, but in our view "purged" or "banished" fits better in the context, since the scroll is envisioned as having the power to purge and destroy (Zech 5:4). YHWH ṣəbāʾôt declares that he will send out this curse, and like a virus it will enter the house of every thief and everyone who swears falsely and remain in those houses until the entire building is destroyed.

One may wonder why these two social sins are the focus of the scroll. The word for thief is from the same root as "You shall not steal" in the Decalogue, and swearing falsely connects with the ninth commandment but is referred to specifically in several other contexts, such as Leviticus 6:3; 19:12; Jeremiah 5:2, as well as in Zechariah 8:17. In Zechariah 8:17 the context is clearly legal and thus closely connected with bearing false witness, which also has a legal referent. Stealing and corrupting the legal system are sure ways to destroy a society, and thus these utterly destructive actions are foregrounded as requiring eradication.

Vision 7: Zechariah 5:5-11—A basket and three women. The repetition of the verb *yṣʾ* ("go out") three times in Zechariah 5:5-6 ("came forward"; "appearing") conveys a sense of movement.[35] The angel draws Zechariah's attention to what is going out, perhaps from the temple, and it is an *ʾêpâ* ("basket"). Everywhere else in the Old Testament this word is used for a measure, but clearly here it refers to the container for such a measure rather than the measure itself. One should therefore translate it as "basket," "container," or "jar."[36]

In Zechariah 5:6 the angel explains the meaning of the basket. Literally the MT reads, "This is their eye [*ʿênām*] in all the land." *ʿÊnām* is commonly emended to *ʿăwōnām*, meaning "their iniquity."[37] The emended reading fits with the declaration in Zechariah 5:8 that the woman is "wickedness," but "their eye" also fits in the context. In Zechariah 4:10 the eyes of Yahweh range throughout the earth, whereas here "their eye" is removed. The referent for "their" is not indicated, but it probably refers to the Persian authorities who ruled over Judah from Babylon, to whom the woman in the basket is to be sent.[38] Additionally, it could refer to Persian and Israelite ways of seeing that

---

[35]NIV does not translate the third occurrence in Zech 5:6. Literally the angel answers, "This is the basket going forth."

[36]The word may also have a background in Mesopotamian for a cult room. If so, it would contain here a double entendre. See Meyers and Meyers, *Haggai, Zechariah 1-8*, 295-97.

[37]Following the LXX reading.

[38]See Sweeney, *Twelve Prophets*, 2:619-20.

subvert Yahweh's vision. External and internal contamination—"wickedness"—must be removed from Jerusalem, and Lady Wickedness is pushed back into the basket and carried off to Babylon by two female angels.[39] The use of *kikkar* ("the cover of lead") to refer to the lid appears to be deliberately ironic in this respect, as it literally means "a rounded cake," and the term is used for cultic ritual (Ex 29:23; see also Jer 7:18; 44:19).

As noted above, this vision relates closely to the previous one. If the returned exiles are truly to be God's people, they must be purified. Evil must be banished from Jerusalem. If we are right in seeing this basket as moving from the temple outward, then whereas the sixth vision dealt with the second table of the law, this one deals with the first table and the cleansing of Israel's worship from any idolatry.

Vision 8: Zechariah 6:1-15—Four chariots and two crowns. The final vision clearly connects back to the first with the horses, albeit now with chariots added, each with a set of different-colored horses and emerging from between two mountains of bronze rather than a shadowy ravine. Sweeney notes, "Whereas Zech 1:7-17 portrays the different colors of horses hidden in the myrtles awaiting the time when the Temple would be built, Zech 6:1-8 portrays the different colors of horses, now attached to chariots, emerging from the heavenly Temple to range through the earth as the process of Temple reconstruction commences."[40]

The chariots are interpreted by the angel as the four winds/spirits (see Zech 2:10 [2:6]) going out from the presence of the Lord of the whole world. The imagery reflects the Achaemenid Persian practice of using riders to maintain communications and keep the king apprised of any problems in his empire. Zechariah 6:8 must be understood in relation to the many prophetic warnings about trouble coming from the north. As noted previously, Persia was in the east but reached via a northern route. The giving of rest to the Spirit (Zech 6:8) signifies that the building of the temple can proceed, since no attack will be coming from the north.

In Zechariah 6:9-15 we read of a coronation, which flows from the start of temple construction and the establishment of peace in the north. Zechariah is instructed to acquire the requisite materials from three visitors from Babylon (Zech 6:10) and to have crowns made.[41] There is some disagreement

---

[39]For a good critique of misogynist readings of this section, see Sweeney, *Twelve Prophets*, 2:620.
[40]Sweeney, *Twelve Prophets*, 2:625.
[41]The MT is plural.

as to whether one or two coronations are in view in this passage. In Zechariah 3:8 the Branch is distinct from Joshua, but Sweeney thinks that there is one coronation in view and that Joshua is here identified as the Branch (Zech 6:12) who will build the temple. In our view, it is better to see two potential coronations as in view. Joshua is actually crowned, but Zechariah 6:12 is not a reference to Joshua but to a Davidic ruler, the Branch, presumably Zerubbabel. The high priest and the Davidic ruler are both viewed as ruling from their respective thrones and in harmony with each other.

Zechariah 7–14. In the following chapter we will focus on the eschatology of Zechariah 9–14 and on Zechariah 9:9-13 and Zechariah 14 in particular. Thus we will not deal with Zechariah 7–14 here in as much detail as we have done with Zechariah 1–6. This is definitely not because it is less important. Major messianic themes occur in Zechariah 9–14, such as the king coming riding on a donkey (Zech 9:9), the good shepherd (Zech 9:16), the cornerstone (Zech 10:4), the one they have pierced (Zech 12:10), living waters flowing from Jerusalem (Zech 14:8), and so on, themes that are taken up in the New Testament and seen as fulfilled in Jesus.

What must be noted here is that a legacy of historical criticism is the view that Zechariah 9–14 is from a different time and prophet(s).[42] This view continues to dominate Zechariah scholarship. Meyer and Meyers, for example, argue that Haggai and Zechariah 1–8 were edited into a single work in time for the dedication of the Second Temple.[43] Zechariah 9–14 is, however, from a different hand(s):

> Chapters 9–14 probably do not represent the sayings of a single prophet in response to a specific event or series of historical events. Rather, they represent the collected sayings of one or more individuals, who spoke within the framework of earlier prophecy as it had been transmitted at that time. . . . More specifically, the author or authors of Second Zechariah were undoubtedly individuals who emerged in the shadow of Zechariah, the prophet of the restoration, inasmuch as the language and themes of first Zechariah played a definitive role in shaping chapters 9–14. Some might characterize the author(s) of these chapters as belonging to a circle of prophets among whom

---

[42]See R. J. Coggins, *Haggai, Zechariah, Malachi*, Old Testament Guides (Sheffield: Sheffield Academic Press, 1987), 40-51; Childs, *Introduction to the Old Testament as Scripture*, 472-87. On the composition of Zechariah, see Mark J. Boda, *The Book of Zechariah*, NICOT (Grand Rapids, MI: Eerdmans, 2016), 16-37.

[43]Carol L. Meyers and Eric M. Meyers, *Zechariah 9–14*, AB (New York: Doubleday, 1993), 26.

the words of the earlier prophets were preserved and expanded upon, but among whom the words of Zechariah . . . were especially revered.[44]

Meyers and Meyers is some of the best work on Zechariah, but it is obvious from the above quote that the evidence for multiple Zechariahs is *underdetermined*.[45] It should be noted that first, as we will see below, Zechariah 9–14 is presented as part of the overarching structure of Zechariah from a literary point of view. Second, as Meyers and Meyers recognize, there are close connections between Zechariah 9–14 and the rest of the book. Third, while it is helpful to look for an appropriate social setting for Zechariah 9–14, we should not let the argument that "the nature of the responses contained in Zechariah 9–14 is comprehensible in light of the situation in the first half of the fifth century" be determinative. Zechariah 9–14 does seem to address a different context from that of Zechariah 1–8, but it is hard to be sure which context. These chapters are strongly eschatological, and one can imagine a variety of contexts in which they would have been meaningful.

For us the literary structure of the book is definitive, while we hold open the possibility that additional sources have been included in the final form of the book by the editor(s). The overall structure is closely related to the chronological data in Zechariah 1:1, 7 and Zechariah 7:1. As we have seen, Zechariah 1:1-6 is the introduction to the book, in which the narrator/editor presents what follows as the word of Yahweh to Zechariah. Zechariah 1:7–6:15 presents the visions of Zechariah, and Zechariah 7:1–14:21 his oracles and pronouncements, with each major section introduced by the dates when the word of Yahweh came to the prophet.

In Zechariah 7:1 and Zechariah 7:8 the narrator tells us, "The word of Yahweh came to Zechariah." The abbreviated form of the name compared with Zechariah 1:1, 7 and the introductory *waw*-consecutive indicate that Zechariah 7:1 is "structurally dependent upon 1:7 so that 1:7–6:15 and 7:1–14:21 form the two basic components of the larger block in 1:7–14:21."[46] The Yahweh word transmission formula also appears in Zechariah 7:4; 8:1, 18, but these are subordinate to Zechariah 7:1, 8. Zechariah 7:4 is in the first person: "Then the word of the LORD Almighty came *to me*." Zechariah 8:18 is the

---

[44]Meyers and Meyers, *Zechariah 9-14*, 27.
[45]See the discussion of Wolters on the A, B, and C corpora in Zechariah. He views the historical theories of Zech 9–14 as underdetermined (Wolters, *Zechariah*, 1-27, 253-473).
[46]Sweeney, *Twelve Prophets*, 2:635.

speech of the prophet, and contra the NIV and the NRSV, the Hebrew in Zechariah 8:1 does not identify the recipient but simply states, "And the word of the LORD of hosts came. . . ." Sweeney thus rightly notes,

> Although Zechariah 9–11 and 12–14 are generally considered to be independent compositions from a later time than that of the prophet Zechariah, they, too, must be considered components within the basic structure defined by the narrator's introductions in Zech 7:1 and 7:8. . . . The generic identification of the following material [Zech 9–14] that is inherent in each provides no indication of the setting or the addressee of the pronouncement that would establish them as structurally independent blocks in relation to Zech 1:1; 1:7; or 7:1. In the absence of such independent information, Zechariah 9–11 and 12–14 must be considered as structurally subordinate in the first instance to Zech 7:1, which provides the necessary information concerning the setting of the following oracular material, and in the second instance to Zech 7:8, which provides the introduction to a major thematic block concerned with the restoration of Jerusalem and Judah within Zech 7:1–14:21.[47]

Zechariah 7:1–14:21 is introduced by a question posed to Zechariah about mourning and fasting. Zechariah replies that the time for mourning should be seen as time for rejoicing because the nations will recognize Yahweh in Jerusalem as the temple is rebuilt. Zechariah 9–11 and Zechariah 12–14 articulate the process by which this will take place.

Zechariah 7–8: A question and a long answer. It is hard not to be gripped by the evocative metaphors of the visions. But how did the inhabitants of Jerusalem respond? Zechariah 7–8 is dated, according to Zechariah 7:1, to December 7, 518 BC, less than two years after Zechariah received the visions in Zechariah 1–6. These chapters give us some idea of the reception of the visions by the populace. Good preaching always calls forth questions, which in turn reveal a lot about those who ask them. So it is here. The people of Bethel send delegates to inquire of the priests of the temple whether they should mourn and fast in the fifth month as they have done for so many years.[48]

---

[47]Sweeney, *Twelve Prophets*, 2:635-36.
[48]There are three difficult issues in Zech 7:2. Can the town Bethel be the subject of "sent"? Second, the Hebrew reads "his men" rather than "their men," as in the NIV, but there are two antecedents to "his." Third, the men function as Israelites, but they have Babylonian names. Readers should see the commentaries for discussion of these issues. In our view the town Bethel can and does function as the subject of "sent." "His" probably refers to Regem-Melek's men. Finally it would not have been surprising for exiles to take Babylonian names while in captivity. The use of the

The mourning and fasting would have been for the destruction of the temple, and the query is about whether this should continue now that the temple is being rebuilt. The "fifth month" was Av, and Jewish tradition indicates that both the First and the Second Temple were destroyed on the ninth of Av.

Like a good therapist, Yahweh replies through Zechariah by *not* answering but asking a string of questions (Zech 7:4-7) designed to get the delegation and the broader population (note "all the people of the land" in Zech 7:4) thinking about their motivation and the appropriate response to the loss they experienced. Zechariah 7:7 is the climax of the series of questions and refers the hearers to the prophetic tradition (see Is 1:10-17; Hos 4; Mic 6:6-8; Amos 5; Jer 7).[49]

Sweeney sees Zechariah 7:8–14:21 in its entirety as Zechariah's response to Sharezer's question. In the immediate context Zechariah 7:8-14 highlights, as do so many of the prophets, the need for fasting to be accompanied by the *practice of justice*. Zechariah 7:9 (see also Zech 8:16) is one of those great Old Testament verses akin to Micah 6:8. A notable point in Zechariah 7:12 is the mention of "his Spirit," one of those places in the Old Testament in which we find an incipient theology of the Spirit.

Zechariah 8:1-23: The restoration of Jerusalem. In Zechariah 8:19 we see that Zechariah is still answering the question about fasting and mourning. The tenor of this entire chapter is that it is time now for mourning to become dancing and celebration, a time to love truth and peace (Zech 8:19c) because Yahweh is restoring Jerusalem, although there is a continued emphasis on justice (Zech 8:16) and a strong expression of Yahweh's distaste for injustice: "I hate all this"! Rhetorically, the chapter is also designed to encourage God's people to build the temple (Zech 8:9, 13). Much of what we find here is a repetition and development of emphases in Zechariah 1–6. For example, God's jealousy for Zion (see Zech 1:14) is strongly affirmed in Zechariah 8:2. Yahweh will return to and dwell in Jerusalem (see Zech 1:16). His anger has passed, and he will now do good to Jerusalem (Zech 8:14-15).

God's blessing on Jerusalem is elaborated in typical but evocative expressions. The elderly must have been decimated through the exile, but now once again men and women will live to a ripe old age (Zech 8:4). Children will play

---

first person in the question of Zech 7:3 may indicate that Sharezer is the leading figure of the delegation. See Sweeney, *Twelve Prophets*, 2:639.

[49]Sweeney, *Twelve Prophets*, 2:641.

in the streets (Zech 8:5). Agriculture will flourish (Zech 8:12). God's people will start to fulfill their vocation to be a blessing to the nations (Zech 8:13; see Gen 12:1-4). This is wonderfully represented in Zechariah 8:20-23.

Zechariah 9–14: Two pronouncements. The chapters move between judgment and salvation, reaching a crescendo in Zechariah 14.

Zechariah 9–11: A prophecy. Both Zechariah 9 and Zechariah 12 have the heading "A prophecy" or "burden" (*maśśāʾ*). In prophetic speech this usually means "that which is lifted up," "oracle," or "pronouncement." In Jeremiah 23:33-40 the word is used ironically to evoke the burden of his ministry amid false prophecy. Especially in Zechariah 11:4-17 and Zechariah 13:2-9, Zechariah makes extensive use of Jeremiah, and so some suspect a similarly ironic use of "burden" in Zechariah 9:1; 12:1. However, in Zechariah 9–14 the context is one of great hope and not that of false prophecy, as in Jeremiah 23, and so the word *maśśāʾ* should be understood as "prophecy" (NIV) or "pronouncement."

Zechariah 9:1-8: Judgment Against the Nations and Redemption. This pronouncement is reminiscent of Amos's opening sermon, but it does not end with an indictment of Jerusalem but the reverse: Yahweh will himself encamp at "my temple" to protect it and keep watch over it.[50] A further intriguing note is that his judgment of the Philistines by removing their forbidden drinking of blood from sacrifices will leave a remnant who will become a clan in Judah (Zech 9:7). Here again we see the recurring motif of God's judgment and *salvation* being extended to the nations through Israel.

Zechariah 9:9-17: Prisoners of hope. Our heading for this section, and this chapter of our book, comes from Zechariah 9:12: "You prisoners of hope."[51] Certainly this pronouncement as a whole would have had meaning for postexilic Israelites (see Zech 9:11, 12b; 13) but the eschatological dimension stretching into the future and the use of metaphors and imagery in this respect are strong, indeed overwhelming.[52] It is as though the connection

---

[50]Of the places mentioned in Zech 9:1-6, the move is from Hadrak in Syria in the north to the Philistine cities in the southwest. The sins calling forth this judgment are only elaborated on for Tyre—economic injustice—and the Philistines—eating the blood of sacrificial animals, a practice forbidden in Israel. "Take" (hiphil of *swr*) in Zech 9:7a is the same verb used for removing the filthy garments from Joshua in his heavenly ordination (Zech 3:4). Just as this enabled Joshua to become high priest so the Philistines will be able to "belong to God" (Zech 9:7).

[51]Prisons were not part of Israelite culture, nor probably of that of the ancient Near East. The reference is to confinement and especially that of exile.

[52]Zechariah 9:11 is noteworthy for its reference to the blood of the covenant (Sinai) as the basis for Yahweh releasing his people from the waterless pit, an image for exile.

with the immediate historical context lessens and the vision extends into the future.

Zion is called to rejoice greatly (Zech 9:9) because her king comes to her righteous and victorious but humbly, riding on a donkey and not on a warhorse (see visions 1 and 8). This king will proclaim and establish peace (*šālôm*) among the nations throughout the world (Zech 9:10). In the process the instruments of war will be removed from both Ephraim and Jerusalem.

Paradoxically, Zechariah 9:14-17 returns to the theme of judgment of the nations and salvation of God's people. We say paradoxically because, just having declared that instruments of war will be destroyed in Israel, these verses speak of Yahweh leading his people in conquering the nations: "They will destroy and overcome with slingstones" (Zech 9:15 NIV). Of course, this paradox is already present in Zechariah 9:13, and presumably the paradox is resolved by the fact that peace will emerge from judgment.

Zechariah 10:1-12: The restoration of Judah. A pernicious division between Yahweh as the God of history versus God as God of "nature" has bedeviled too much Old Testament scholarship. Clearly Zechariah envisions Yahweh as the God of history, but here in Zechariah 10:1 we see that there is no contradiction between history and nature. As Creator, Yahweh is as much the source of springtime and rain for agriculture for all people as he is the sovereign God ruling over history. Zechariah 10:1 is echoed in Matthew 5:45, where God is portrayed as the one who makes rain and sunshine for all. Undoubtedly, there is also an implicit critique here of idolaters who seek Baal to ensure fertility of the land.

Yahweh's goodness contrasts with the false leaders of his people: prophets (Zech 10:2), and the shepherds or leaders (Zech 10:3). Here Yahweh, by contrast, is portrayed as the good shepherd who will care for his flock. The result is that from Judah will come the cornerstone—an architectural image probably for a king—the tent peg, the battle bow, and every ruler. The precise reference of these items is unclear, but it is clear that strong leadership and military might will emerge from Judah so that her enemies will be destroyed (Zech 10:5). A recurring motif in Zechariah 9–14 is the vision of a reunited Israel including both north and south. So, for example, we find in Zechariah 9:1 a reference to "all the tribes of Israel." Zechariah 10:3-6 focuses on Judah, but in Zechariah 10:7-12 this vision is extended to Ephraim (the northern kingdom). Exiles from Assyria and Egypt will be brought back to live securely in Israel (Zech 10:10, 12) as by a new exodus (Zech 10:11).

Zechariah 11:1-17: Revoking the covenant. This oracle of judgment, by far the strongest in Zechariah, expands on Zechariah 10:3, where Yahweh declares, "My anger burns against the shepherds, and I will punish the leaders" (NIV). In Zechariah 10:10 Lebanon is a place of rest for returned exiles, whereas in Zechariah 11:1-3 it is to prepare for judgment. The picture in this oracle is one in which the worst practices of social injustice and false religion—"Praise Yahweh, I am rich!"—have reappeared among God's people so that the people are like "the flock marked for slaughter" (Zech 11:4-5 NIV). Zechariah is called to shepherd this flock marked for slaughter, which he does, but the flock detests him, and he grows wary of them (Zech 11:4, 7-8).

Judgment is depicted in four striking symbolic actions. Zechariah breaks his first staff called Favor, symbolizing God breaking the covenant he made with all the nations, namely, the covenant of creation.[53] Second, the flock he leads pays him thirty pieces of silver, and he throws them to the potter at the temple. Third, he breaks his second staff called Union, symbolizing a shattering of the bond between southern and northern kingdoms. Finally, he takes once again the attire of a "foolish shepherd" because God will raise up a worthless shepherd who will harass and destroy his people.

This is strong stuff, and one can only imagine what it felt like to hear such a declaration of final judgment. Zechariah 11:17 is crucial for the interpretation of the chapter as a whole since it indicates the illocutionary force of the oracle. God is incensed at the "worthless shepherd," at leaders who instead of facilitating his rule and care over his people lead them astray and thus call forth his judgment.

Zechariah 12: Judgment on the nations and mourning in Israel. Like Zechariah 9, Zechariah 12 contains the heading "A prophecy" or "burden" (*maśśā'*). As in Zechariah 10:1 and so often throughout the Minor Prophets, we find in Zechariah 12:1 another creation motif evoking Yahweh's transcendence and immanence—"who forms the human spirit within a person" (NIV)—as Creator.[54] The pronouncement conceives of "that day" when all the nations of the earth gather against Jerusalem. Yahweh will set out to destroy all the nations that attack Jerusalem (Zech 12:9) and will do so through Jerusalem. The three images of Jerusalem as a cup (Zech 12:2), an immovable rock (Zech 12:3), and a fire pot in a woodpile (Zech 12:6) are

---

[53]See William J. Dumbrell, *Covenant and Creation: An Old Testament Covenant Theology* (Milton Keynes, UK: Paternoster, 2013), for the exegetical base for this view.
[54]An allusion to Gen 2.

used to convey Jerusalem's role in the judgment envisaged. By comparison, Yahweh will "shield" Judah "so that the feeblest among them will be like David, and the house of David will be like God [Elohim], like the angel of the LORD [Yahweh] going before them" (Zech 12:8 NIV).

Rather than victory being accompanied by hubris, God's people are depicted in Zechariah 12:10-14 as pervasively mourning the ways in which their behavior has pierced Yahweh. This is a result of Yahweh pouring out a spirit of grace and supplication on his people. Here again in Zechariah we have a reference to the Spirit of Yahweh.

Zechariah 13:1-6: Cleansing from sin and the cessation of prophecy. Zechariah 13:1 speaks of a fountain being opened for the house of David and the inhabitants of Jerusalem to cleanse them from sin and impurity or corruption. With the meaning "fountain," *māqôr* is often paired with "waters of life" (Jer 2:13; 17:13) or elliptically with "life" (Prov 10:11; 13:14, etc.). "As such, it is part of the cosmic language associating Yahweh with the source of life and creativity. The waters of life are associated with Zion as the center of the universe and thus the focus of the Temple and the divine presence."[55]

In Zechariah 13:2-6 the effect of such cleansing is that the very names of the idols are banished from the land, and without idolatry there is no longer a need for prophets, so they too will be eradicated from the land. Zechariah 13:5 appears to allude to Amos 7:14. The root '*dm* occurs twice in Zechariah 13:5 and evokes a return to God's purposes for his creation, with his people working the land/ground (*'ădāmāh*) as they were created to do.

Zechariah 13:7-9: Strike the shepherd, refine the sheep. This oracle returns to the problem of bad leadership among God's people (see Zech 10:3; 11). The shepherd and many of the sheep are struck down, but a remnant is refined in the process, and they become God's people.

Zechariah 14: The day of Yahweh—A new exodus and a new creation. As we have seen, the theme of the day of Yahweh is a central one in the Minor Prophets, and it dominates this final chapter of Zechariah (Zech 14:1, 4, 6, 7, 8, 9, 13, 20, 21). Once again judgment and salvation are interspersed. Jerusalem itself will be judged (Zech 14:2), as will all the nations that fought against Jerusalem (Zech 14:12-15) *and their animals* (Zech 14:15). The language of "the plague" and the motif of the gathering of the wealth of the surrounding nations evoke the first exodus of Israel from Egypt.

---

[55]Meyers and Meyers, *Zechariah 9–14*, 362. See Zech 14:8.

The vision of salvation is climactic. Yahweh himself will fight against the nations attacking Jerusalem, and he is pictured as standing astride the Mount of Olives, which is split in two (Zech 14:3-4). The Jerusalemites will flee and then, says Zechariah, "The LORD [Yahweh] *my* God will come, and all the holy ones with him" (Zech 14:5c NIV). The holy ones are the heavenly court (see Zech 3) so that heaven, as it were, has now come down to earth, a vision that is taken up in Revelation of the heavenly city, the new Jerusalem, coming down to earth from heaven.

The eschatological dimensions of this final chapter in terms of a renewed creation are crystal clear in Zechariah 14:6-11. With distinct echoes of Eden, living water will flow out from Jerusalem, and once again Yahweh will be king over the whole earth. Zechariah 14:9b is a clear allusion to the Shema in Deuteronomy 6; here it is actualized in the whole world so that the mission of Israel is achieved. The survivors from all the nations are envisioned as making a pilgrimage to Jerusalem every year (see Ps 120–134, the Psalms of Ascent; Is 2:3; Mic 4:2) to worship "the King, Yahweh ṣəbā ʾôt," and to celebrate the Festival of Tabernacles, the festival associated with the Israelites living in temporary dwellings during the wilderness period (Lev 23:42).[56] It is hard to be sure why this festival is highlighted. Meyers and Meyers note that "it is clear that by some time in the fifth century, if not earlier, Booths was a festival of special significance—associated with the ark of the covenant and the Torah of Moses."[57]

Zechariah 14:20-21 brings the whole of Zechariah to a majestic conclusion, not surprisingly beginning *and ending* "on that day." As Meyers and Meyers rightly note, "If much of this prophet's message has been future directed, the ending of his oracle is emphatically so."[58] The images of bells and pots relate to warfare and subsistence. The horse was the military animal par excellence in the ancient Near East and "is thus an apt symbol of all that is antithetical to the conditions of the eschatological age of peace and universal divine sovereignty. As a beast of war and of human political aggression, it represents the antithesis of God's harmonious rule at the end of days."[59] It is, however, important to note that horses are not eradicated in this vision but now have the cultic vocabulary of "Holy to Yahweh" (see Lev 23:20; 27:30, 32; Josh 6:19; Ex 28:36) inscribed on their bells. This implies the end of

---

[56]The combination "the King, Yahweh ṣəbā ʾôt" is unique in the OT.
[57]Meyers and Meyers, *Zechariah 9–14*, 470.
[58]Meyers and Meyers, *Zechariah 9–14*, 478-479.
[59]Meyers and Meyers, *Zechariah 9–14*, 480.

warfare and the reign of peace. Pots were used in Israel in the cultus and for cooking. In the temple the pot was the lowliest item, whereas now it will be like the sacred bowls in front of the altar. *On that day* even lowly temple pots will "have their sanctity vastly intensified."[60]

Zechariah 14:21 is even more remarkable. The distinction between holy and unholy, between sacred and profane, was utterly central to the Levitical cultus. Here such distinctions are abolished. Every pot will be designated holy, and the foreigners who visit will borrow from these pots and cook in them. "All food will have the status of sacrifice, and all consumption of food will have a sacral quality. . . . The idea of everyday cooking pots becoming holy means that all food, and thus sustenance and life itself, will have the status of a sacrificial meal that people share with their deity. . . . The expression of holiness here is the culminating idea of this eschatological statement."[61]

ZECHARIAH AND THE OLD TESTAMENT

Especially since Rex Mason's influential doctoral dissertation, studies of intertextuality within Zechariah and between Zechariah and the Old Testament have mushroomed.[62] Mason examined the relationship between Zechariah 9–14 and Zechariah 1–8 and concluded that there is a continuing line of tradition between the two especially in the Zion tradition (Zech 9:9; 2:14 [2:10]), the purification of the community (Zech 3:5; 13:1), universal salvation (Zech 9:6-7; 14:16-21), the appeal to the Former Prophets, and provision of leadership as a sign of the new age. For Mason the same essential spirit of Zechariah 1–8 is found in Zechariah 9–14, but in Zechariah 9–14 there is a disillusionment with human leadership and a hope for direct intervention from God himself.

In a fine work both methodologically and exegetically, Michael Stead examines the intertextuality and intratextuality of Zechariah 1–8.[63] Intertextuality is a slippery concept, and Stead defines it carefully. He rightly notes that Zechariah 1–8 hardly ever uses citations or direct quotations but

---

[60]Meyers and Meyers, *Zechariah 9–14*, 486.
[61]Meyers and Meyers, *Zechariah 9–14*, 486-87.
[62]Mason's dissertation was completed in 1973 and published as Rex Mason, "The Use of Earlier Biblical Material in Zechariah 9–14: A Study in Inner Biblical Exegesis," in *Bringing Out the Treasure: Inner Biblical Allusion in Zechariah 9–14*, ed. Mark J. Boda and Michael H. Floyd, JSOTSup 370 (Sheffield: Sheffield Academic Press, 2003), 1-208. See also Boda, *Book of Zechariah*, 39-41.
[63]Michael R. Stead, *The Intertextuality of Zechariah 1–8*, LHBOTS 506 (London: T&T Clark, 2009).

prefers *oblique reference* to or echoes of other Old Testament texts.[64] This makes it harder to pin down intertextuality, but Stead's study reveals a number of interesting conclusions.

First, sustained allusion is a characteristic of Zechariah 1-8. In relation to Zechariah 2, he finds sustained allusions to Lamentations 2; Joel 2; Jeremiah 48-51; Ezekiel 38-39; and Isaiah 12-14; 40-55. In relation to Zechariah 1-8 he discerns repeated allusions also to Exodus 25-27; Deuteronomy 28-30; 2 Samuel 7; Isaiah 54, Jeremiah 30-33; and Ezekiel 40-48. As Stead notes, this means that "In order to understand Zech 1-8, one must read the various background passages and absorb their worldview and, only then, seek to read Zech 1-8 with this background in mind. The sustained allusions demonstrate that Zech 1-8 is a text 'written with other texts-in-mind,' and so we need to read it with the same texts in mind."[65]

Second, it is important to note that the intertextuality of Zechariah 1-8 is constituted in part by the development of composite metaphors constructed from multiple elements from different sources. In this way Zechariah 1-8 understands only some elements of the Former Prophets to apply to its historical context. Thus, third, Stead concludes that Zechariah 1-8 is historically conditioned. The most appropriate historical context is that of the dating formulae in Zechariah 1-8, confirmed by the strong restoration focus of the intertexts in Zechariah 4-5. Fourth, he finds that the thought world of Zechariah 1-8 is dominated intertextually by the Former Prophets and Deuteronomy. Zechariah 1-8 is aware of other traditions, such as the exodus, the Decalogue, and the priestly material in Exodus and Leviticus about the tabernacle, but Isaiah, Jeremiah, Ezekiel, and Deuteronomy are the dominant influences. Zechariah 1-8 assumes familiarity with these texts to the extent that the readers can recognize echoes apart from specific citations. As a literary text, Zechariah 1-8 contains many gaps, gaps that the intertextuality helps to fill. Stead argues that far from making Zechariah 1-8 a wax nose, the intertexts create a framework that limits the number of possible meanings. He concludes that study of the intertextuality in Zechariah 1-8 shows that Zechariah 1-8 applies the material of the Former Prophets in an imminent eschatology rather than a future one.

A fascinating question is that of the extent to which the prophecies of Zechariah 1-8 were in fact fulfilled. Some were clearly not, and Zechariah 1-8

---

[64]Stead, *Intertextuality of Zechariah 1-8*, 253.
[65]Stead, *Intertextuality of Zechariah 1-8*, 254.

leaves this question hanging. Stead suggests that it is precisely here that Zechariah 9–14 enters the picture. It is addressed to a later time and

> Whereas Zech 1–8 stresses the imminent (if partial) fulfillment of the classical prophets, Zech 9–14 stresses that the ultimate fulfillment of these prophets lies still yet in the future. Zech 9–14 does not contradict what has been said before in Zech 1–8, but goes on to affirm that what has been said before is not the end of the story, and that there are important things which need to be heard by a subsequent generation.[66]

Katrina Larkin has undertaken a detailed study of intertextuality and Zechariah 9–14, using the categories of mantology and innerbiblical exegesis from Michael Fishbane, and of typology.[67] Mantological exegesis is intended to solve cognitive problems and to foreground what is hidden. The Old Testament books that she finds Zechariah 9–14 engaged with are virtually the same as in Zechariah 1–8, with the addition of Amos and a stronger wisdom influence.

ZECHARIAH AND THE NEW TESTAMENT

Zechariah is the most influential of the twelve Minor Prophets in the New Testament. It is referred to in passages such as James 4:8 (Zech 1:3), but the majority of references are found in the Gospels and in Revelation.[68] The citations of passages such as Zechariah 9:9, about the king coming to Jerusalem on a donkey, and of the thirty pieces of silver (Zech 11:12-13; Mt 26:15; 27:9-10) and Judas are well known, but Zechariah's influence extends far beyond such citations.[69] Intertextuality has created awareness of the allusions and echoes of the Old Testament in the New, and although this makes it far harder to be certain of references in many cases, the result is a much richer, theological reading.

A strength of N. T. Wright's approach to the New Testament is his taking of the category of story seriously and in the process opening up the wide-ranging intertextuality between the New Testament and the Old. A result is that in his work on Jesus, Wright correctly identifies Zechariah as a major

---

[66] Stead, *Intertextuality of Zechariah 1–8*, 262.
[67] Katrina J. A. Larkin, *The Eschatology of Second Zechariah: A Study of the Formation of a Mantological Wisdom Anthology*, Contributions to Biblical Exegesis and Theology 6 (Kampen: Kok Pharos, 1994).
[68] See NA[28], 868-69.
[69] There are a number of tricky elements in the Gospels' use of Zech 11:4-17 in relation to Judas's betrayal of Jesus. Inter alia, see *CD* II/2:463-71.

influence. Wright shows that Zechariah lies behind much of Jesus' theology of the kingdom of God. Wright describes Zechariah 14:9 as one of the most explicit statements of the coming of the kingdom and notes,

> A book which, as we have already seen, was arguably of great influence on Jesus, and which contained dark hints about the necessary suffering of the people of YHWH, is of course Zechariah, particularly its second part (chapters 9–14). The writer promises the long-awaited arrival of the true king (9.9-10), the renewed covenant and the real return from exile (9.11-12), the violent defeat of Israel's enemies and the rescue of the true people of YHWH (9.13-17).[70]

Matthew, for example, contains many allusions to and quotations from Zechariah, but let us take Matthew 21:1-22 (// Mk 11:1-25; Lk 19: 28-48; Jn 12:12-19; 2:13-17) as an example of what a thicker, intertextual reading yields. This is the story of Jesus' entry into Jerusalem on a donkey and the cleansing of the temple. Wright argues that the whole incident "cries out to be seen, as various writers have recently argued, within the context of a deliberate reapplication of Zechariah."[71] Jesus' quasi-royal entry into Jerusalem and his authority over the temple evoke Zechariah 9:9; 6:12.[72] Matthew 21:5 quotes Zechariah 9:9, and clearly Jesus is seen as enacting this prophecy from Zechariah. Jeffrey Trumpbower notes that it is not unusual for first-century figures to deliberately act out scriptural prophecies, and this is what Jesus does here.[73] Wright sees Jesus' cleansing of the temple as a symbolic and prophetic enactment of judgment on it. Mark 11:16 adds a perplexing detail about Jesus' cleansing of the temple: he would not allow anyone to carry "a vessel" through the temple courts. Wright suggest this is a veiled allusion to the pots in Zechariah 14:20-21, thereby indicating that "the day" has come at last.

Clearly Jesus' crucifixion is constitutive of his vocation and of his ushering in the kingdom. Here too Zechariah plays an important part in helping us to understand the reasons for his death in conjunction with other major passages such as Daniel 7, certain psalms, and Isaiah 40–55. Matthew 26:31

---

[70]N. T. Wright, *Jesus and the Victory of God* (London: SPCK, 1996), 308, 586.
[71]Wright, *Jesus and the Victory of God*, 422. Wright also identifies other major OT backgrounds to this incident.
[72]Zechariah 6:12 refers to the Branch who will build the temple of Yahweh.
[73]Jeffrey A. Trumpbower, "The Historical Jesus and the Speech of Gamaliel (Acts 5:35-9)," *New Testament Studies* 39 (1993): 500-517, esp. 513.

has Jesus quote Zechariah 13:7 to explain his coming passion. Jesus uses shepherd imagery of himself on a number of occasions, and when

> we find Jesus quoting explicitly from Zechariah 13.7 . . . we should not expect a cunning insertion by a later exegetically minded Christian theologian, but should see this as an indication of Jesus' own mindset. This is, of course, strikingly confirmed not only by isolated sayings but by symbolic actions: Zechariah 9 focuses on the king riding into Jerusalem on a donkey, as the agent of the return from exile and the renewal of the covenant; Zechariah 14, which celebrates the coming of YHWH and his kingdom, ends with the Temple being cleansed of traders. There should be no doubt that Jesus knew this whole passage, and that he saw it as centrally constitutive of his own vocation, at the level not just of ideas but of agendas.[74]

The New Testament is eschatological through and through, and thus it is not surprising that Zechariah is drawn on so extensively to articulate Jesus' theology of the kingdom and the meaning of his death. Nor is it surprising that Revelation should draw on Zechariah at many points for its wealth of imagery and metaphors to evoke the meaning of the present and the future. Examples of these are the lampstands in Revelation 1:12 and the seven lamps of Revelation 4:5 (see Zech 4:2); the question "How long" in Revelation 6:10 (Zech 1:12); the motif of the measuring rod in Revelation 11:1; 21:15 (Zech 2:5 [2:1]); Satan as the accuser in Revelation 12:10 (Zech 3:1); the two olive trees and the two lampstands in Revelation 11:4 (Zech 4:11-12); the seven spirits of God in Revelation 5:6 (Zech 4:10); the four winds in Revelation 7:1 (Zech 6:5); and there being no night in the city in Revelation 21:25 (Zech 14:7). Zechariah is one of the wells from which Revelation draws its extensive source of images. This is not surprising given the metaphorical and eschatological nature of Zechariah. Perhaps more importantly, Zechariah shares with Revelation the vision of the kingdom coming, as articulated in Revelation 11:15: "The kingdom of the world has become the kingdom of our Lord and of his Messiah, and he will reign for ever and ever" (NIV; see Zech 14:9).

Matthew 23:35 refers to Zechariah the son of Berekiah as the final prophet murdered. Most scholars, however, take this to refer to Zechariah son of Jehoida in 2 Chronicles 24:20-22, which appears to be confirmed by Matthew's statement that he was murdered between the temple and the altar.

---

[74]Wright, *Jesus and the Victory of God*, 599-600. The word for "Canaanite" in Zech 14:21 could mean "merchant."

THEOLOGY

There are a myriad theological issues waiting to be explored in Zechariah. Clearly, we cannot pursue them all here. As is so typical with the prophets, we find a view of God as transcendent and holy and yet immanently involved with his people and his creation. The vision genre in Zechariah 1–6 facilitates eloquent testimony of a God who is not far off but active in history. We have noted in the other Minor Prophets a strong doctrine of creation, and Zechariah is no exception. Zechariah 10:1 and Zechariah 12:1 stand out in this respect, but the book as a whole evokes Yahweh's sovereignty over his whole creation, not least with the visions of the horses, and Zechariah 9–14 climaxes with a vision of a renewed creation, holy and resplendent. Zechariah was a priest, and the use of imagery from and of the temple, with its nature as the microcosm of the macrocosm of the world, repeatedly opens up a creation-wide vista.

The name *Zechariah* means "Yahweh has remembered," and this encapsulates the theology of the book. Produced in and for the postexilic context, Zechariah is above all else about calling forth hope in the future and thus also for the present. This is never at the expense of Yahweh's holiness and justice, but it is a great affirmation of his faithfulness to his people and his purposes for his creation. Starting in Zechariah 1:1-6, Zechariah also contains a rich doctrine of repentance, which is spelled out as the book develops. Philip Rieff alerts us to the indispensability of a "v-i-a," a vertical in authority, for the health of a society, and this is addressed directly in the visions of the flying scroll and of the woman in the basket. There are certain sins that destroy the very fabric of any culture.

Eschatology is central to Zechariah and especially to Zechariah 9–14, as we have seen. We will return to this issue in the following chapter. Here we want to focus on two related issues, imagination and a theology of hope. Zechariah exemplifies the title of Walter Brueggemann's deservedly well-known *Prophetic Imagination*. Again and again in the postexilic period, believers must have been tempted to despair, as are so many in our world today. How, in such contexts, does one sustain and spark hope? An answer from Zechariah is that one engages the imagination and provides images that will do this work. Zechariah ransacks the "earlier prophets," as it were, to create highly evocative images for the returned exiles, images that do create hope as they are allowed to refurbish tired minds and energize weary bodies. Karl Barth is well known for his caution about the use of imagination, but here in Zechariah we have ample theological support for it. What we have at work is not the free play of imagination in which we create our own worldviews but a use of the tradition to fire believers up anew with the traditional worldview of Israel for their time and place.

Christians have much to learn from this. Let us provide one example. When the great Christian philosopher Johann Hamann was writing in the eighteenth century, he drew on all his resources to confront the burgeoning Enlightenment spirit at its humanistic roots. He drew deeply and creatively on Scripture in his work and at several places on Zechariah. Indeed, one of his works is titled "Disrobing and Transfiguration: A Flying Letter to Nobody, the Well Known."[75] "Flying Letter" is an allusion to Zechariah 5:1-3. This text is a critique of Moses Mendelssohn's natural philosophy, and Hamann draws on a myriad of sources, not unlike Zechariah and including Zechariah, in order to make his point.[76] This is all in the service of the view that "These are sheer proofs of the indissoluble bond between the spirit of observation and the spirit of prophecy. Our knowledge is indeed in part, and our prophesying in part, united, however, it is a triple cord that is not quickly broken. If one falls, the other will lift up his fellow; if the two lie together, then they have heat."[77] In this creative, imaginative and humorous way—and Zechariah too does not lack the comic—Hamann welds together reason and faith in opposition to the Enlightenment tradition. That tradition remains dominant today, albeit in naturalist, postmodern, and historicist guise, and we need authors like Zechariah and Hamann who can imagine a different approach and enable us to see what might be.

We subtitled this chapter "Prisoners of Hope," and we have seen how this embodies the message and theology of Zechariah. In the sixties and seventies Jürgen Moltmann addressed this issue creatively in his *Theology of Hope* (1964).[78] Moltmann "learned to think of the Church as constituted by its mission to the world in the service of the coming universal Kingdom of God."[79] Moltmann was also one of the first to attend closely to Dietrich Bonhoeffer's theology, and drawing on the resources of Marxist philosopher

---

[75]Johann Georg Hamann, *Writings on Philosophy and Language*, Cambridge Texts in the History of Philosophy (Cambridge: Cambridge University Press, 2007), 219-39.
[76]See Hamann, *Writings on Philosophy and Language*, 232n62, for Hamann's use of Zech 12:2.
[77]Hamann, *Writings on Philosophy and Language*, 233.
[78]See Richard Bauckham, *Moltmann: Messianic Theology in the Making* (Basingstoke, UK: Marshall Pickering, 1987).
[79]Bauckham, *Moltmann*, 5.

Ernst Bloch, he developed his eschatological theology of hope. In the process Moltmann rightly saw that truly biblical eschatology illumines the present, provides a searching critique of the status quo, and leads to movements for change. Thus, as Richard Bauckham notes,

> If hope thrusts the Christian into the painful contradiction between the promise and present reality, it simultaneously thrusts him into the world. The contradiction arises from a hope for the world, for the whole of this worldly reality, which it exposes in all its god-forsakenness. The Christian's suffering is thus a loving solidarity with the whole of the suffering creation ... and a hopeful solidarity in expectation of the transformation of all creation.... Love and hope for this world involve the Christian in a movement towards world-transformation which has two movements: critical opposition and creative expectation.[80]

Zechariah is *a* major resource for this biblical vision of hope.

Recommended Reading

Boda, Mark J. *The Book of Zechariah*. NICOT. Grand Rapids, MI: Eerdmans, 2016.

——. *Haggai, Zechariah*. New International Version Application Commentary. Grand Rapids, MI: Zondervan, 2004.*

Wolters, Albert. *Zechariah*. HCOT. Leuven: Peeters, 2014.

——. "Zechariah, Book Of." In *Dictionary for Theological Interpretation of the Bible*, ed. Kevin J. Vanhoozer et al., 862-64. Grand Rapids, MI: Baker Academic, 2005.*

Recommended reading marked with a "" indicates introductory works.*

---

[80]Bauckham, *Moltmann*, 40.

18

The King Receives His Kingdom

ZECHARIAH 9:9-10

There is a strong eschatological dimension to Zechariah, and in this chapter we will focus on one of the central passages in Zechariah 9–14, namely, the Davidic king's entry into Jerusalem in Zechariah 9:9-10. Our aim in this chapter is to see how a theological reading that respects the discrete witness of Zechariah relates to the New Testament interpretation of this text.

Zechariah 9:9-10: The Davidic King's Entry into Jerusalem

Zechariah 9:9-10 in context. As noted in the previous chapter, Zechariah 9:1 is the start of a new section in Zechariah, with its heading of *maśśā'* (burden), and most agree that Zechariah 10:1 is the start of a new unit within Zechariah 9–11, beginning with the imperative "Ask."[1] There are clear thematic links between Zechariah 10:1 and Zechariah 9:17 and between the shepherds of Zechariah 10:3 and Yahweh as shepherd in Zechariah 9:16, but such links are common in Zechariah, and Zechariah 10 focuses on the issue of leadership among God's people and return from exile.[2] It would appear to be a distinct but related section.

Zechariah 9:1-8 is identifiable as a subunit within Zechariah 9 by its content, dealing as it does with Yahweh defeating Israel's enemies. The cities are listed because they were traditional enemies of Israel.[3] Their geography circumscribes the ideal land of Israel, and Zechariah 9:1-8 moves from north

---

[1]On Zech 9 as poetry, see Al Wolters, *Zechariah*, HCOT 19 (Leuven: Peeters, 2014), 257.
[2]See Mike Butterworth, *Structure and the Book of Zechariah*, JSOTSup 130 (Sheffield: Sheffield Academic Press, 1992); Katrina J. A. Larkin, *The Eschatology of Second Zechariah: A Study of the Formation of a Mantological Wisdom Anthology*, Contributions to Biblical Exegesis and Theology 6 (Kampen: Kok Pharos, 1994).
[3]But see Wolters, *Zechariah*, 257-60.

to south, starting with Syria and moving to Phoenicia, Philistia, and finally Judah. Paul Hanson notes, "The borders of that area are not arbitrarily set, but outline what ancient Israelite tradition held to be the ideal kingdom of the Jews."[4] The oracle thus envisions a restoration of the boundaries of the land as it was under David.

There is also an *inclusio* that further identifies Zechariah 9:1-8 as a subunit. In the Hebrew the word *eye/eyes* occurs in Zechariah 9:1 and Zechariah 9:8. *Eye* in Zechariah 9:1 is so unusual that it appears to be intentionally selected as an *inclusio*.[5] The *eye* repetition also links back into the motif of eyes in Zechariah 1–6. This subunit concludes in Zechariah 9:8 with Yahweh on guard at his temple in Jerusalem, the geographical center from which he will recover for Israel its heritage.

If Zechariah 9:1-8 thus deals with the restored land, then Zechariah 9:9-10 deals with the restored Davidic king receiving his kingdom.

> The two verses are at the center of the chapter and constitute the centerpiece of the entire poem from a theological, as well as a literary, point of view. The placement of these verses after the opening unit, which depicts the restored land of Israel, and before the final verses, which concern the restored people of Israel, suggests that the entire piece is carefully crafted: the restored royal figure is the lynchpin of the restored land and people.[6]

Zechariah 9:11-17 deals with the benefits of the restored king's rule. On the basis of the "blood of my covenant"—an expression found elsewhere only in Exodus 24:8—Yahweh will release his people from the waterless pit, a metaphor for exile, and through a new exodus (Zech 9:14-16) he will establish his people again in the land.[7] Anthony Petterson notes that if there is anything new in this section, it is the use of exodus imagery to describe the true end of Israel's exile.

INTERPRETATION

With Yahweh encamping at his house and guarding against oppressors (Zech 9:8), the prophecy envisages the coming of the king to Jerusalem.[8]

---

[4] Paul D. Hanson, *The Dawn of Apocalyptic: The Historical and Sociological Roots of Jewish Apocalyptic Eschatology*, 2nd ed. (Philadelphia: Fortress, 1979), 317.
[5] Carol L. Meyers and Eric M. Meyers, *Zechariah 9–14*, AB (New York: Doubleday, 1993), 163.
[6] Meyers and Meyers, *Zechariah 9–14*, 169.
[7] "Storms of the south" in Zech 9:14 is exodus imagery.
[8] "Encamping" may allude to the tabernacle.

Yahweh speaks in the first person in Zechariah 9:7-8, but in Zechariah 9:9-10 he uses the imperative. "Rejoice greatly" and "Shout" evoke a major cause for celebration and festivity. To rejoice greatly and shout echoes Zechariah 2:14 [2:10] (see also Zeph 3:14). "Daughter Zion," and its repetition in "Daughter Jerusalem," is a term of affection evoking a restored relationship with Yahweh. The reason for celebration: "Your king comes to you, righteous and victorious."

There is much debate about the identity of this king. He has been identified as

1. Yahweh,[9] but his riding on a donkey and being "saved" argue against this view.

2. Representing God's faithful people who will embody God's gracious rule to the nations through their covenant life.[10] This view rests largely on the parallels with Isaiah 55:1-5. However, in Zechariah 9:9-10, it is clearly an individual who is in view.[11]

3. The messianic Davidic king. This remains the majority view and in our view is the right one.[12] Zechariah 1–8 contains many references to a coming Davidic king, to the coming Shoot who will remove the iniquity of the land in one day, who will build the eschatological temple, who will usher in the day of peace. In Zechariah 9 this hope continues to be held out *after* the temple has been built, and it is this hope for a Davidic king that we find here in Zechariah 9:9-10. The description of the king as "*your* king," that is, Jerusalem's, and the allusion to Psalm 72:8, which we will discuss below, confirm that the Davidic king is in view.

The imagery here is highly evocative. In Zechariah 9:1-7 the land in its Davidic contours has been secured through the acts of Yahweh, and now the

---

[9]Hanson, *Dawn of Apocalyptic*, 292-324.
[10]So A. Leske, "Context and Meaning of Zechariah 9:9," *CBQ* 62 (2000): 663-78; Rex Mason, "The Use of Earlier Biblical Material in Zechariah 9–14: A Study in Inner Biblical Exegesis," in *Bringing Out the Treasure: Inner Biblical Allusion in Zechariah 9–14*, ed. Mark J. Boda and Michael H. Floyd, JSOTSup 370 (Sheffield: Sheffield Academic Press, 2003), 1-208.
[11]There are cases in the OT where an individual symbolizes Israel. The suffering servant in Isaiah and Jonah are examples. However in Zech 9:9 Israel is clearly distinguished from the coming king.
[12]See Wolters, *Zechariah*, 277-78; Mark J. Boda, *The Book of Zechariah*, NICOT (Grand Rapids, MI: Eerdmans, 2016), 563-70. Boda notes, "It is thus likely that 9:9-10 joins Hag. 2:20-23 in creating high expectations for Zerubbabel's rule. As will be seen in 11:4-16, these high expectations will soon be dashed, due to the fragility of human participants" (565).

king comes to receive his kingdom. The king is righteous (*ṣaddîq*) and "saved" (Zech 9:9, *nôšāʿ*, NIV "victorious"). Righteousness is an appropriate characteristic of the king, as we see, for example, in the last words of David (2 Sam 23:3-4).

"In the fear of God" is parallel to "righteousness" and alerts us that the good king is not only personally righteous but facilitates the rule of God over his people. Thus F. Laubscher is right when he speaks of *ṣaddîq* as the characteristic of the one who upholds *ṣedeq*, that is, "the ideal order," just as we find articulated in the law of the king in Deuteronomy 17:18-20.[13] Similarly, Jeremiah 23:5 looks forward to the day when a Davidic king will be raised up "who will reign wisely and do what is just and right in the land" (NIV). This is a clear case of *lex rex* rather than *rex lex* and was revolutionary in the ancient Near East but also *entirely* appropriate. The king enters the land as gift and is there to serve Yahweh and his people and creation.

The description of the king as "saved" requires exploration. With Yahweh's victory he has been saved, is a sign of salvation, and brings salvation. "Victorious" is an adequate translation, but it obscures the fact that "Thus, rather than a figure who enacts his own salvation, this king is one who has relied on the Lord for salvation."[14] This is confirmed by the description of the king as *ʿānî* (lowly) and riding on a donkey. As we have seen in Zechariah 1–8, the horse was the supreme animal of war; here, however, the king rides on a donkey, the humble domestic beast.[15] The contrast between the donkey and the horse is confirmed in Zechariah 9:10, in which the horse-drawn chariots and warhorses will be taken away from Jerusalem. As befits the Davidic king, his confidence is in Yahweh and not in military might. It is likely that Zechariah 9:9 alludes to Genesis 49:11, Jacob's blessing on Judah. As Rusty Reno notes, "The messianic potential of Jacob's blessing of Judah becomes explicit in the prophecies of Zechariah."[16]

---

[13] F. Laubscher, "The King's Humbleness in Zechariah 9:9. A Paradox?," *Journal of Northwest Semitic Languages* 18 (1992): 131-32.

[14] Mark J. Boda, *Haggai, Zechariah*, NIVAC (Grand Rapids, MI: Zondervan, 2004), 416. Twelfth-century Hebraist David Kimhi proposed "having salvation" as the meaning. Meyers and Meyers (*Zechariah 9–14*, 88) translate "saved is he" and compare the use of this verb with Deut 33:29 and Ps 33:16. They stress that the king is restored only as a result of Yahweh's intervention.

[15] This view has been contested. See Boda (*Haggai, Zechariah*, 417n30), for bibliographical details, as well as Antti Laato, *A Star Is Rising: The Historical Development of the Old Testament Royal Ideology and the Rise of the Jewish Messianic Expectations* (Atlanta: Scholars Press, 1987).

[16] Rusty R. Reno, *Genesis*, Baker Theological Commentary on the Bible (Grand Rapids, MI: Brazos, 2010), 288; see also Boda, *Haggai, Zechariah*, 417, for the contrasts between Zech 9:9 and Gen 49:11.

The relationship between Yahweh and this king is extremely close.[17] In Zechariah 9:10a Yahweh speaks in the first person; negatively, he will eradicate war and its instruments from Israel (Ephraim and Jerusalem).[18] Positively, *the king* will speak shalom (peace) *to the nations*. Zechariah regularly echoes Isaiah, and it is hard not to recall Isaiah 52:7-10 at this point. As in Zechariah 9:9-10, the atmosphere is one of jubilation. In Isaiah 52:7 we read of those who "proclaim peace," the peace of Yahweh's kingdom being reestablished as he returns to Zion. As in Zechariah 9:10b, salvation is extended to the ends of the earth.

The means of the king's proclaiming and establishing peace is his rule from sea to sea and from the river to the ends of the earth. This exact phrase is found in Psalm 72:8 (see also Ps 89:26 [89:25]). It speaks of his reign over all the earth: "In sum, the 'sea to sea' combination, intensified by the imagery of the next line ('river to the ends of the earth'), constitutes language that conveys the universality of the king's domain. The directional imagery functions as a kind of merism; all points and thus everything in between."[19] Mark Boda notes that Zechariah appears to generalize the boundaries of Exodus 23:31.[20]

The description of the extent of his reign also evokes the divergent descriptions of the extent of the land of Israel. In Genesis 15:18-21, "this land" is followed by a spatial merism: from the river of Egypt to the river Euphrates. As scholars note, this depiction is different from the precise delineation of the land in Numbers 34. Nili Wazana rightly says, "The difference in form and context reveal that these are two separate genres that convey two different *conceptions* of the Promised Land, but not two different *territorial units*." The concept and literary form of these spatial merisms has a compelling background in Neo-Assyrian imperial claims, in which they evoke world rule. Thus, in the Old Testament "the spatial merisms in promise terminology reflect a land that has no borders at all, only ever-expanding frontiers; they are referring to universal rule, using stock terminology typical of Neo-Assyrian royal inscriptions."[21] In Zechariah 9:10 the king fulfills the vocation of Israel to extend Yahweh's reign to the ends of the earth.

---

[17]See Anthony Petterson, *Haggai, Zechariah and Malachi*, AOTC (Nottingham, UK: Apollos, 2015), 138.
[18]Israel is reunited as under David.
[19]Meyers and Meyers, *Zechariah 9–14*, 137.
[20]Boda, *Haggai, Zechariah*, 418.
[21]Nili Wazana, "From Dan to Beer-sheba and from the Wilderness to the Sea: Literal and Literary Images of the Promised Land in the Bible," in Mary N. MacDonald, ed., *Experiences of Place* (Cambridge, MA: Center for the Study of World Religions, 2003), 63-64, 67-71; see Deut 11:25.

Zechariah 9:9-10 and the Gospels

The Gospels contain many allusions to and quotations from Zechariah, but in Matthew 21:1-22 (// Mk 11:1-25; Lk 19:28-48; Jn 12:12-19) we find the well-known application of Zechariah 9:9-10 to Jesus as he enters Jerusalem and then cleanses the temple.[22] According to Matthew 21:1, it was as Jesus and his disciples approached Jerusalem and came to Bethphage—probably Bethany—on the Mount of Olives overlooking Jerusalem that he sent two disciples to find a donkey and her colt. As we saw in the previous chapter, Zechariah 14:4 speaks of Yahweh standing on the Mount of Olives "on that day," and the Mount of Olives is the site from which Jesus ascends to heaven and to which he will return to consummate his kingdom (Lk 24:50-51; Acts 1:11-12). It is thus from a site pregnant with symbolism that Jesus initiates his entry into Jerusalem *to receive his kingdom*, for that is what the enactment of Zechariah 9:9 indicates.

Matthew stresses the divine ordering of the events that unfold with his "at once" in Matthew 21:2, Jesus' instruction that any query should be met with "the Lord needs them," and his citation of Zechariah 9:9 as fulfilled by Jesus in his entry into Jerusalem on a colt. Matthew's citation is closer in form to the Hebrew than our LXX versions, and he alone among the Gospel writers reads Zechariah 9:9 as referring to two animals. Donald Hagner notes that not only is it possible to read the Hebrew this way, but an unbroken colt would be accompanied by its parent when introduced into service so that "there is thus an *ipso facto* probability that historically two animals were involved in the entry of Jesus into Jerusalem."[23]

The first line of the quote from Zechariah 9:9 in Matthew 21:5 ("Say to Daughter Zion") differs from Zechariah 9:9 ("Rejoice greatly, Daughter Zion"). Hagner suggests the influence of Isaiah 62:11 on the form of this line, through conflation of memory or perhaps through liturgical use.[24] The effect is to omit the "Rejoice" and "Shout greatly" of Zechariah 9:9, but of course in practice in Matthew 21 and the parallel passages this is precisely what happens. A large crowd gathers and precedes and follows him in to Jerusalem, identifying him as the Davidic king with their shout, "Hosanna to *the Son of David*!"

Wright argues that the whole incident "cries out to be seen, as various writers have recently argued, within the context of a deliberate reapplication

---

[22]Only Matthew and John quote Zech 9:9.
[23]Donald A. Hagner, *Matthew 14–28*, WBC 33B (Nashville: Thomas Nelson, 1995), 594.
[24]Hagner, *Matthew 14–28*, 593.

of Zechariah."²⁵ Jesus' quasi-royal entry into Jerusalem and his authority over the temple evoke Zechariah 9:9 and the prophecy about the Branch building his temple in Zechariah 6:12.²⁶ Matthew 21:5 quotes Zechariah 9:9, and clearly Jesus is seen as enacting this prophecy from Zechariah.

THE THEOLOGY OF ZECHARIAH 9:9 AND MATTHEW 21

Zechariah 9:9 and its context is *kingdom theology*. The Davidic king enters Jerusalem to receive his kingdom; he proclaims peace to the nations, and his reign will extend over the entire world. We know from the Synoptic Gospels that the main theme of Jesus' teaching was the kingdom of God/heaven, and John has his equivalent vocabulary, at the heart of which is eternal life, a thoroughly Jewish concept of the life of the age to come, which has already broken in with the coming of the king.²⁷

How then does the fulfillment of Zechariah 9:9 in Jesus' entry into Jerusalem help us to understand the kingdom theology of the Gospels? It is illuminating in many ways.

First, it alerts us unequivocally that the hope of the kingdom is no otherworldly, spiritualized kingdom but the recovery of God's purposes for his creation, that is, *within* history. The Davidic king of Zechariah 9:9, clearly identified as Jesus in the Gospels, proclaims peace to the nations and extends his reign or kingdom to the entire world.

A tragic development in the history of the theology of the kingdom of God was the view that the kingdom evokes God's reign but not that over which he reigns.²⁸ This played into the hands of those who saw the kingdom as a spiritual phenomenon unconnected to the material, earthly, historical realm. *Kingdom* does indeed evoke the reign of God, but it is a multivocal symbol and certainly includes within its scope the creation as the focus of God's kingly rule. Dale Bruner rightly says,

> The word "kingdom" denotes both a place ... and a power.... The idea of space is by no means secondary. The kingdom is a *place* entered, where people sit and eat and drink at table; it is also a place from which people are rejected

---

[25]N. T. Wright, *Jesus and the Victory of God*, Christian Origins and the Question of God 2 (London: SPCK, 1996), 422. Wright also identifies other major OT backgrounds to this incident.

[26]Zechariah 6:12 refers to the Branch who will build the temple of Yahweh.

[27]Note that while the primary background to Matthew's use of Zech 9:9-10 is Zechariah, it would also speak eloquently to NT readers' experience of empire.

[28]See Craig G. Bartholomew, *Where Mortals Dwell: A Christian View of Place for Today* (Grand Rapids, MI: Baker Academic, 2011), for a detailed discussion of this issue.

or not allowed to enter; it is, in short, a house, a state, a realm—a king*dom*. At the same time the kingdom is also an activity in time—God's sovereignty, reign, rule, and indeed, even God's person—*king*dom.[29]

There is no hint in Zechariah of some kind of spiritualized kingdom disconnected with the creation. There is eschatology, yes, but it is an eschatology of the recovery of God's purposes for his creation, a vision of that day, as Psalm 85:10-11 so eloquently states it, when

> Love and faithfulness meet together;
> > righteousness and peace kiss each other.
> Faithfulness springs forth from the earth,
> > and righteousness looks down from heaven. (NIV)

C. H. Dodd taught us rightly that New Testament quotations from the Old Testament are not just prooftexts but generally cited with their broader context in view. With this in mind, it is simply impossible to read Matthew 21 and imagine that Jesus thought he would fulfill Zechariah 9:9 by ushering in a spiritual kingdom that had nothing to do with God's purposes for his creation. The point of Zechariah 9, as of the kingdom, is the eradication of that which distorts and misdirects the creation, namely, war and rebellion against Yahweh, *not* the eradication of the creation.

Second, it causes us to reflect on the identity of Jesus. In Matthew 21:10 we are told that Jesus' entry into Jerusalem stirs up the entire city and people ask, "Who is this?" In Matthew 21:11 the crowds answer, "*The prophet* from Nazareth in Galilee." Certainly Jesus was a prophet, as N. T. Wright and many others argue.[30] He is also a wise man, a priest, *and* the Davidic king. Jesus' enactment of Zechariah 9:9, however, draws attention not to his being a prophet but to his being the Davidic *king*, the Messiah, who is entering Jerusalem *to receive his kingdom*.

Third, that the crowds still did not see this alerts us to the humility, what Søren Kierkegaard calls the *abasement*, of Jesus. Jesus' humility is, of course, indicated in the king/his riding into Jerusalem on a donkey, but he embodies this humility and enacts it in ways we could never have expected from Zechariah. As Frederick Buechner evocatively notes, "*He set his face to go to Jerusalem*, the Gospels say, sets it like a table or a clock for a time

---

[29]Dale Bruner, *Matthew: A Commentary*, vol. 1, *The Christbook* (Grand Rapids, MI: Eerdmans, 2004), 140.
[30]See chap. 21.

which he does not have to be a God to know is coming as he latches his feet under the soft belly of the ass he rides."[31]

His triumphal entry into Jerusalem and his cleansing of the temple trigger the events that lead to his crucifixion. Amid messianic expectations of the time there was diversity, but no one was anticipating a crucified Messiah, let alone one who would receive his kingdom through crucifixion. In retrospect one cannot but relate "the one they have pierced" in Zechariah 12:10 to Jesus' crucifixion, but this is only in retrospect. Jesus fills out his Zechariah 9:9 kingship in a radically unexpected way. As he says in John 12:32, "And I, when I am lifted up from the earth, will draw all people to myself" (NIV). Kierkegaard has a meditation of more than one hundred pages on this verse in his *Practice in Christianity*.[32] He notes of Jesus, "Here on earth he walked around in lowliness, in the lowly form of a servant, in poverty and misery, a suffering one. This, indeed, was Christianity, not that a rich man makes the poor rich but that the poorest of all makes all rich, both the rich and the poor."[33] Karl Barth evocatively says of Jesus that he went into the far country in order that we might come home, and similarly Kierkegaard writes, "Indeed, he walked the infinitely long way from being God to becoming man; he walked that way in order to seek sinners."[34]

Both Barth and Kierkegaard rightly evoke the humility of Jesus, but they relate his death rightly but reductionistically to us as sinners. Jesus' entry in Jerusalem is followed by his cleaning of the temple, the microcosm of the macrocosm of creation, and when he dies the curtain in the temple is torn from top to bottom (Mt 27:51). Jesus will build the new temple of his people in a new creation, and Matthew concludes with Jesus asserting, "All authority in heaven and on earth has been given to me." The king has received his kingdom, but it is received through his abasement on the cross and his subsequent resurrection, ascension, and return.

Jesus' claim to be king is universal and exclusive. His story is the true metanarrative of the world, but what makes it so distinctive, as Lesslie Newbigin points out, is that at its heart is the cross, a humility evoked in his riding on a donkey into Jerusalem, his Father's home in the creation. As Kierkegaard rightly states, "Thus, Christianly understood, in this world

---

[31]Frederick Buechner, *The Faces of Jesus: A Life Story* (Brewster, MA: Paraclete, 2005), ix.
[32]Søren Kierkegaard, *Practice in Christianity*, ed. and trans. Howard V. Hong and Edna H. Hong (Princeton, NJ: Princeton University Press, 1991), 149-262.
[33]Kierkegaard, *Practice in Christianity*, 153.
[34]Kierkegaard, *Practice in Christianity*, 20.

loftiness is abasement. So Christ entered on high, but his life and work on earth are what he left for imitation: that true loftiness is abasement or that abasement is true loftiness."[35] This leads us to take history with the utmost seriousness but in a radically Christian perspective. As Karl Popper says,

> The life of the forgotten, of the unknown individual man; his sorrows and his joys, his suffering and death, this is the real content of human experience down the ages. If that could be told by history, then I should certainly not say that it is blasphemy to see the finger of God in it.[36]

Recommended Reading

Boda, Mark J. *The Book of Zechariah*. NICOT. Grand Rapids, MI: Eerdmans. Pages 560-74.
Duguid, Iain. "Messianic Themes in Zechariah 9-14." In *The Lord's Anointed: Interpretation of Old Testament Messianic Texts*, ed. Philip E. Satterthwaite, Richard S. Hess, and Gordon J. Wenham, 265-80. Carlisle, UK: Paternoster, 1995.*
France, R. T. *Jesus and the Old Testament: His Application of Old Testament Passages to Himself and to His Mission*. Vancouver, BC: Regent College Publishing, 1988.*
Treier, Daniel J. "Typology." In *Dictionary for Theological Interpretation of the Bible*, ed. Kevin J. Vanhoozer et al., 823-27. Grand Rapids, MI: Baker Academic, 2005.*

Recommended reading marked with a "" indicates introductory works.*

---

[35] Kierkegaard, *Practice in Christianity*, 259.
[36] Karl R. Popper, *The Open Society and Its Enemies*, vol. 2, *Hegel, Marx* (New York: Routledge, 1962, 1966), 364.

19

Haggai and Malachi

RESTORATION AND REMEMBRANCE

Haggai focuses on the restoration of the temple and the shape of life lived before the Lord in Persian Yehud. Questions abound in the book, centering on the validity and significance of the new temple built in Jerusalem. The people perceived the new temple as inferior to the glory of the temple destroyed by the Neo-Babylonian king in 586 BC. But God affirms: "The glory of this latter house will be greater than the former one" (Hag 2:9).

Malachi, too, explores the shape of life before Yahweh under Persian rule. With a (perceived) diminished temple and a diminished sense of authority, Israel questioned the validity of following Yahweh. As the messenger of the Great King, Malachi calls God's people back to faithfulness, contextualizing God's instruction for the people. Together they testify to the faithful life in and beyond the Persian era.[1]

THE CONTEXT OF HAGGAI

Although it is brief, we can place Haggai's work in the second year of the Persian king Darius I (521–486), even within *fifteen weeks* of 520 BC, according to date markers in the book (see table 19.1).[2]

Little is sure of the prophet's life, but we know he was "the messenger of Yahweh" (Hag 1:13), an honorific title applied to a prophet only in Isaiah 44:26 and 2 Chronicles 36:15-16.[3] He embodies the messenger role, employing

---

[1] See the excellent analysis of Mignon R. Jacobs, *The Books of Haggai and Malachi*, NICOT (Grand Rapids, MI: Eerdmans, 2017).
[2] For further discussion, see Jacobs, *Books of Haggai and Malachi*, 8-11.
[3] Haggai may have been a Judean survivor after the fall of Jerusalem who remained in the land, but this is inconclusive. See Pieter Verhoef, *Haggai and Malachi*, NICOT (Grand Rapids, MI:

Table 19.1. Dates in Haggai

DATE MENTIONED IN HAGGAI	MODERN EQUIVALENT
The twenty-first day of the month (Hag 1:1)	August 29, 520
The twenty-fourth day of the same month (Hag 1:15)	September 21, 520
The twenty-first day of the seventh month (Hag 2:1)	October 17, 520
The twenty-fourth day of the ninth month (Hag 2:10, 18, 20)	December 18, 520

messenger speech ("thus says the LORD") and prophetic utterances ("utterance of Yahweh").

Alongside Haggai, leadership of the process to restore the temple fell to Zerubbabel and Joshua (Hag 1:1, 12-15). When the movement to restore Jerusalem's temple occurred, it affected the very heart of the Persian Empire, according to Ezra 5:11–6:13. Within fifteen weeks of work, Haggai introduced a new period of Jewish history: the five hundred years that scholars now describe as the Second Temple period, from 515 BC to the first century AD. "The brief era of prophetic efficacy brought about the turn of an age."[4]

OUTLINE

Marvin Sweeney organizes Haggai into three major units displaying three major themes: temple building, future glory, and future restoration.[5] However, we prefer John Kessler's structure and recognize patterning of reproach and encouragement:[6]

A. Haggai 1:1-11	Reproaches against the people with a vison of hope
(Haggai 1:12-15)	(Brief narrative of the results of the prophetic word)
B. Haggai 2:1-9	Encouragement and promise
B'. Haggai 2:10-19	Reproaches against the people with a vision of hope
A'. Haggai 2:20-23	Encouragement and promise

Eerdmans, 1987), 6-7. He possibly was an exile who returned under Zerubbabel and Joshua, but he is not listed as a returnee (Ezra 2 or Neh 7).
[4]Hans Walter Wolff, *Haggai: A Commentary* (Minneapolis: Augsburg, 1988), 16.
[5]Marvin A. Sweeney, *The Twelve Prophets*, Berit Olam (Collegeville, MN: Liturgical Press, 2000), 2:532-33.
[6]John Kessler, *The Book of Haggai: Prophecy and Society in Early Persian Yehud*, VTSup 91 (Leiden: Brill, 2002), 247-51.

Interpretation

Haggai 1:1-11 (A). The word of Yahweh comes through Haggai to Zerubbabel (the governor of the Persian province of Yehud) and Joshua (the high priest in the temple-less age), leaders tasked to rebuild Jerusalem's temple (Hag 1:1). Much of what we find regarding these two leaders derives from Zechariah 3-4; 6:9-15 (see also 1 Chron 3:19; Ezra 2:2; 3:2, 8; 4:2-3; 5:2; 10:18; Neh 7:7; 12:1, 26, 47).

Haggai 1:2 surfaces the problem of the book (Yahweh's house lay in ruins) as well as the *cause* of the dereliction ("This people says, 'The time has not yet come to build the house of Yahweh'"). The people were disinclined to rebuild the temple while living in luxury. "Paneled houses" implies (cedar?) wood paneling on the inside of the house, presumably an expensive feature for the home. Rich Yehudites used paneling before the exile (Jer 22:14). Using language from Haggai 1:2, Haggai 1:4 raises a question. It is as if Haggai asks, "So is the time right for you to live in luxury in your house while Yahweh's house lies desolate?" The answer is obviously no.

Haggai 1:5, 7 calls the people to consider their ways in the light of the coming word of judgment (Hag 1:6). The idiomatic expression *śîmû ləbabkem 'al-darkêkem*, "set your heart on your ways," compels introspection in the life of faith. Personal gain, without attending to proper devotion to Yahweh, remains vacuous and will leave the people dissatisfied. Haggai 1:8 shifts and encourages change: "Go up on the hills, get wood, and rebuild the house. Then I will be pleased in it and I will be glorified." "Therefore" (*'al-kēn*) links the neglect of the people in Haggai 1:9 to divine judgment in Haggai 1:10: refusal to rebuild the temple results in God's absence, infertility, drought.[7]

The underlying logic is as follows:

fecundity of temple = fecundity of land
but
desolation of temple = desolation of the land

Echoes of covenant curse emerge in this logic (Lev 26:19-20; Deut 28:23-24, 30, 38-40, 48). God blesses the land when the people are faithful, but God curses the land when the people are faithless.[8] Even under Persian rule,

---

[7] Steven Tuell, *Reading Nahum-Malachi*, ROT (Macon, GA: Smyth & Helwys, 2016), 150.
[8] Anthony Petterson, *Haggai, Zechariah and Malachi*, AOTC (Nottingham, UK: Apollos, 2015), 61; Elie Assis, "Composition, Rhetoric and Theology in Haggai 1:1-11," *JHS* 7 (2007): 1-14, esp. 12-13.

Israel's covenantal calling as God's missional people in the world has not subsided (Ex 19:4-6). In the covenant, God expects the people to live faithfully, experiencing divine blessing.

(Haggai 1:12-15). Zerubbabel, Joshua, and "all the remnant of the people" (*wəkōl šəʾērît hāʿām*) heard the voice (*šmʿ* + *qôl*) of Yahweh and his prophet, and they "feared" (*wayyîrəʾû*) the presence of Yahweh (Hag 1:12). "Hearing the voice" evokes covenantal obedience to God's word; the same language emerges in Exodus 19:5. "Fearing" depicts awe and reverence for Yahweh, complementing "hearing" language. This verbiage exposes heart change: formerly ambivalent on hearing God's word, they now hear and fear Yahweh.

God responds to the people through Haggai, "I am with you" (Hag 1:13), a phrase indicating the promise of divine presence when fulfilling a divinely mandated task (Ex 3:12; Josh 1:5, 9).[9] "Their God" in Haggai 1:14 typifies the inner transformation of the people described in Haggai 1:12-13: Yahweh of Armies becomes *their God*. The genitive of relationship here indicates their allegiance to Yahweh. These no longer oppose the things of God: Yahweh's priorities are now theirs as well.

Haggai 2:1-9 (B). Between Haggai 1:15b and Haggai 2:1 is about a month of time, following the dated episodes (September 21, 520, Hag 1:15; October 17, 520, Hag 2:1). Apparently the "rousing" work of God (Hag 1:14) waned in only a few short weeks! Thus, the word of the Lord once again comes through Haggai to encourage Zerubbabel, Joshua, and the remnant of the people.

God interrogates the people:

Haggai 2:3: Who has seen the former temple that was destroyed? How does it look now? Is it not like it is nothing to you now?

Haggai 2:12: First question on priestly ruling

Haggai 2:13: Second question on priestly ruling

Haggai 2:19: Question about present supplies in the temple

Haggai 2:3 flags the overall lack of vision to see God's new work through the new temple.[10] Yahweh draws their attention from the past to the present: the former temple is gone. Then the prophet stresses the point: anyone who focuses on the former glory of the former temple is living in the past, but God has stirred up the work to do a new thing, a fresh work, among this people.

---

[9] *ʾănî ʾittəkem*, "I am with you" (masculine plural suffixed pronoun, intending the people).
[10] Elie Assis, "A Disputed Temple (Haggai 2,1-9)," *ZAW* 120 (2008): 582-96.

Haggai 2:4 encourages the people to "be strong" (*ḥăzaq*). The imperative echoes Yahweh's command to Joshua, son of Nun, in Joshua 1:6, 9, and the people's reiteration of the charge in Joshua 1:18: "be strong" (*ḥăzaq*). The imperative of Haggai 2:4, however, is coupled with another: "and get to work [*wa 'ăśû*]!" Haggai encourages with a word from Israel's past contextualized for the present: as God strengthened Joshua for his task, so too will Yahweh strengthen the people for this task. However, they must get on with it and get to work.

Haggai 2:5 continues the theme of divine presence by reminding the people of the covenant Yahweh "cut" with Israel when he delivered them from Egypt (Ex 19:4-6; 20-24). The closing words of Haggai 2:5 remain somewhat elusive: "And my Spirit was standing/is standing [*'ōmedet*] in your midst. Do not fear!" The participle *'ōmedet* may intend the memory of the exodus Yahweh rehearses for the people. However, the Spirit of God enables the craftsmen to do their work in the construction of the tabernacle (Ex 31:2-3; 35:30-31), so the image of Haggai 2:5 is likely that the Spirit encourages the people: they are divinely empowered to construct the temple. Finally, Haggai 2:5 concludes with *'al-tîrā'û*, "Do not fear!" This phrase is used often in the prophets to encourage those who face daunting tasks by reminding them of God's help and presence (Is 7:4; 35:4; 40:9; 41:10, 13; Joel 2:21-22; Zeph 3:16). Divine support for the building project would encourage their work.

Haggai remembers God's work in the past in Haggai 2:4-5 and shifts in Haggai 2:6-9 to an eschatological future where the nations' wealth will be brought to the new temple to adorn it. Although some were skeptical of the temple's restoration, these verses reveal that the new temple will exceed the glory of the former. The restoration of the temple will affect all of creation (Hag 2:6-7). Nations bringing their goods to Yahweh's temple is a theme that one finds in other prophetic texts, especially Isaiah 60. Yahweh glorifies his temple by the nations of the world bringing their wealth to his house (Is 60:7).

Reading Haggai 2:8 in the light of the Twelve, the gold and silver belonging to Yahweh, which was stolen by the nations (Joel 4:5 [3:5]), now come back to the temple from the nations. Haggai 2:8 shows divine retribution at work: Yahweh takes his silver and gold back to restore his house.[11]

---

[11] Assis briefly mentions this ("Disputed Temple," 585). For full discussion, see Heath A. Thomas, "Hope Through Human Trafficking? Theodicy in Joel 4:4-8," in *Theodicy and Hope in the Book of the Twelve*, ed. Colin Toffelmire, Beth Stovell, George Athas, and Daniel Timmer, LHBOTS 705 (London: T&T Clark, 2021), 88-110.

In this act of restoration, Yahweh constructs peace (Hag 2:9) in a currently disputed place. The glorious, restored temple will be far greater than anything that preceded it.

Haggai 2:10-19 (A'). These verses draw attention to the people's lack of obedience to God's law. Haggai 2:10 presents the date of the next prophetic word: December 18, 520, about three months after the prophecy given in Haggai 2:1. The date is significant, as it represents three months after the work begins (Hag 1:15) and two months after Haggai's word of encouragement to Zerubbabel, Joshua, and the remnant of the people (Hag 2:1). When contextualized with Zechariah 1–8, the date stands at the exact center of the narratives, with three dates preceding it and three dates following it (into Zech 1–8).[12] This date likely marks the refounding ceremony of the temple: the temple is rededicated in 515 BC (Ezra 6:14), but the temple is refounded in a ceremony to inaugurate its continuing role in the Jewish community.[13] On this day, Haggai brings a question to the priests about proper distinctions between holy, unclean, and the effective work of God.

Priests give rulings about holy and profane, clean and unclean.

holy	=	fit for ritual service
profane	=	unfit for ritual use, and it must be sanctified
clean	=	fit for regular use, but for ritual use must be sanctified
unclean	=	unfit for either regular or ritual use

When something holy or clean becomes defiled/unclean/profane, the person (or thing) must endure cleansing so that they/it might be useful again. In the case of holy service, sacrifice sanctifies, or makes something holy again. Leviticus prescribe the guidelines for priests to distinguish clean from unclean, holy from profane, as well as the processes of sanctification and ritual cleansing.

Holiness reflects the character of God, as Leviticus maintains: "Be holy, for I am holy" (Lev 11:44-45; 19:2; 20:7, 26; 21:8). But more to the point, holiness made the people fit for service. The motivation for Israel's holiness was nothing short of love and devotion to Yahweh, the God of holiness and the Lord of Israel's salvation: "I am the Lord your God" (Lev 18:2, 4).

---

[12]See the discussion of Tuell, *Reading Nahum–Malachi*, 154-55.
[13]Carol L. Meyers and Eric M. Meyers, *Haggai, Zechariah 1–8*, AB (New York: Doubleday, 1987), 59-64.

The two rulings presented to the priests in Haggai 2:11-12 and Haggai 2:13-14 reflect on holiness and the purpose of God's people. Haggai 2:11-12 queries whether holy food in someone's cloak, whose cloak then touches nonholy food (whether bread, stew, wine, olive oil, or anything else), sanctifies the nonholy food. The priest rules—no, the holy meat in the cloak does not consecrate or sanctify other objects. Haggai 2:13-14 then shifts to consider a person defiled by a corpse, whether their defilement makes other people and objects impure if they encounter them (see Num 19). As death represents the *ultimate* defilement, the priestly answer is in the affirmative. Haggai then gives the interpretation of the ruling, as corpse contamination defiles everything, "Thus is this people, and thus is this nation before me, and thus is all the work of their hands, so that which they bring there is unclean" (Hag 2:14).

The reasons for Haggai's questions to the priests remains a point of discussion.[14] Sweeney reasonably argues that Haggai's request for a ruling represents an argument *for* building the temple: because returning to the land does not sanctify, and because unclean people make the land unclean in the return, then it is necessary to build the temple so that God's people will have a means for sanctification through sacrifice.[15]

Haggai 2:15 and Haggai 2:18 bracket the verses in between with *śîmû-nā' ləbabkem min-hayyôm hazzeh*, "Please consider, from this day forward." This utterance draws God's people to reflect on what happened to them prior to their present state. The prophet reminds God's people that the exile is connected to covenant curse. Haggai returns to the phrase *śîmû-nā' ləbabkem min-hayyôm hazzeh*, "Please consider, from this day forward" (Hag 2:18). The call for God's people to reflect on their past is designed to draw God's people to renew their commitment to him in the present and future. As they commit to God, Yahweh says, "from this day I will bless you" (*min-hayyôm hazzeh 'ăbārēk*). With the restoration of the temple, Yahweh will bless the people and the land.

Haggai 2:20-23 (B'). For Haggai, Zerubbabel represents Yahweh's "signet ring" (*ḥôtām*), a rare term in the Hebrew Bible. The imagery is that of

---

[14]Tuell plausibly argues that Haggai represents a stream of Levitical tradition (non-Zadokite) that survived in the land during the temple-less age. In this restoration, Zadokites cannot suppose that their return simply means a return to the way things were prior to the exile. Returning to the place of their former authority does not "sanctify" their work (hence Hag 2:11-12), and instead they are still "unclean" (hence Hag 2:13-14). See Tuell, *Reading Nahum–Malachi*, 155-57.

[15]Sweeney, *Twelve Prophets*, 2:551-52.

Yahweh as king, and Zerubbabel is God's royal seal. Ancient Near Eastern kings used signet rings to seal various objects to indicate the object belonged to the king. Thus, Zerubbabel serves as the seal of Yahweh, whose leadership indicates his belonging to Yahweh. Three terms describe Zerubbabel's divine favor in these verses: "my servant," "my signet ring," and "chosen" one. Each term signifies the honor due to Zerubbabel as Yahweh's divine choice for leadership. Zerubbabel, however, is more than a random choice; he is a descendant of David, as Chronicles's genealogy depicts (1 Chron 3:17-19). In this way, the book concludes with an emphasis on temple restoration as well as Davidic restoration, without explicitly labeling Zerubbabel as king. These twin themes of temple and Davidic dynasty reconnect Haggai to the divine promises in the Davidic covenant (2 Sam 7:12-14).

However, the lack of explicit kingly language leaves the restoration of the Davidic house only suggestive rather than definitive. After all, Zerubbabel remains only a governor of Judah. At the close of the book, then, the promises of kingship, temple, and restoration appear only in a muted fashion. God's future blessing will exceed his present blessing. Yahweh once again "shakes" the heavens and the earth (Hag 2:6-8), this time as he appoints Zerubbabel (Hag 2:21).

Theology

Divine covenant and presence. Yahweh and his covenants (Sinai, Davidic) are central in Haggai. As Haggai asserts the importance of covenant, Yahweh's "house" (Hag 1:2-4, 8, 14) and presence (and the threats against divine presence) move to the fore. Haggai 1–2 depicts two sins that threaten divine presence: ambivalence about the temple's desolation (Hag 1:9) and the defilement of the people (Hag 2:14). But the temple mediates divine presence for Israel. Haggai 2:10-19 depicts the need for the temple to facilitate Israel's service once again. Sin and defilement must be addressed, so God's people are to take courage and get to work building the temple. Yahweh's blessing (Hag 2:19) will come with temple construction, as will his forgiveness. It is no wonder that the temple emerges as vital to the Persian Yehudi community.

Divine mediation. In addition to the word of the prophet and the temple, Yahweh mediates his presence through the Davidic king in the Davidic covenant. Zerubbabel is Yahweh's signet ring and the servant of Yahweh, whom

Yahweh has chosen (Hag 2:20-23). The latter language echoes the words of Psalm 89:3, where Yahweh says: "I made a covenant with my chosen one; I have sworn an oath with David, my servant." In this light, Yahweh's election of Zerubbabel is a direct evocation of the Davidic covenant, further elaborated in this distinct moment as Yahweh's signet ring.

Haggai and the New Testament

The New Testament alludes to Haggai only once, in Hebrews 12:25-29. Although this is not a direct citation of LXX Haggai 2:6 or Haggai 2:21, Hebrews 12:26 uses similar language:

"Yet once more I will shake not only earth but also heaven."
Eti hapax egō seisō ou monon tēn gēn alla kai ton ouranon. (Heb 12:26)

"Yet once more I will shake heaven and earth, and the sea and the dry land."
eti hapax egō seisō ton ouranon kai tēn gēn, kai tēn thalassan kai tēn xēran. (LXX Hag 2:6)

"I will shake heaven and earth, and the sea and the dry land."
Egō seiō ton ouranon kai tēn gēn, kai tēn thalassan kai tēn xēran. (LXX Hag 2:21)

Eti hapax, "yet once more," appears in both LXX Haggai 2:6 and Hebrews 12:26. The verb *seiō*, "I shake," as well as the terms *ton ouranon kai tēn gēn*, "heaven and earth," appear in these texts. In this way, Hebrews's writer looks to be splicing or combining both texts. But the author of Hebrews combines these Haggai verses in a way that also diverges from the previous text. Hebrews 12:26 inverts "heaven and earth" in Haggai to read, "I will shake not only earth but also heaven." The variation appears to be intended to inform his argument, as the writer augments the intertext with *ou monon . . . alla*, "not only . . . but also." Additionally, the writer inserts *Eti hapax*, "yet once more," to introduce the allusion, which does not appear in Haggai. Why is this the case?

Hebrews 12 distinguishes between the former reality (Sinai, Heb 12:18-21) from the present reality of Christ and the new Jerusalem (Zion, Heb 12:22-25). This new age/old age contrast is paralleled in the distinction between heaven and earth. The earth represents the people of God/Moses/Sinai in the past (Heb 12:25), but heaven represents the people of Christ/Zion/Jesus (Heb 12:25). A temporal and spatial contrastive logic emerges from the argument (see table 19.2).

Table 19.2. Contrasts in the logic of Hebrews 12:18-25

rejecting the one Speaking	contrasts	call to hear the one speaking
Sinai	contrasts	Zion
previous age (old covenant)	contrasts	present age (new covenant)
Moses	contrasts	Jesus
Earth	contrasts	heaven
Israel	contrasts	church
fear	contrasts	fidelity

The contrastive logic does not relegate the era of Sinai to irrelevance but sets the former age in relationship with the glory of God in Christ. Once the contrast is made between the people of God now and then, the writer inserts the allusion to Haggai in Hebrews 12:26. The shaking of the earth corresponds to the former age of Sinai. But now that Jesus has come and is speaking, he "shakes" the "heavens" (Heb 12:26). As a result, the writer of Hebrews draws the readers back to a central theme of the book: warning against falling away into apostasy. Instead of the sin that marked the people of God from the previous age of Sinai, considering the climactic work of Jesus and his shed blood (Heb 12:24), the church should ensure that they attend to the teaching and example of Christ and not fall away from it (Heb 12:25).[16]

THE CONTEXT OF MALACHI

Malachi concludes (1) the postexilic prophets (Haggai, Zechariah, Malachi), (2) the Minor Prophets (Hosea–Malachi), and (3) the Prophets (former and latter) in the tripartite Hebrew canon.

Malachi's dating is uncertain, though likely from the Persian era, and Malachi is an anonymous prophet. Unlike others in the Twelve, Malachi may be a literary construct rather than a historical person. The name *Malachi* (*malʾākî*) means "my messenger." Malachi 3:1, for example, uses the same term (*malʾākî*), meaning "my messenger" rather than a proper name.

Whether we understand Malachi as a historical prophet or a literary figure, if one cuts the book of Malachi, it bleeds Scripture.[17] Malachi engages

---

[16]P. Ellingworth, *The Epistle to the Hebrews: A Commentary on the Greek Text*, New International Greek Testament Commentary (Grand Rapids, MI: Eerdmans, 1993), 687.

[17]Karl William Weyde, *Prophecy and Teaching: Prophetic Authority, Form Problems, and the Use of Traditions in Malachi*, BZAW 288 (Berlin: de Gruyter, 2000).

the story of Jacob and Esau (Gen 25–36), the prophetic announcement of Edom's destruction (Num 20:14-21), and various prophetic texts that resemble Malachi's prophecies (Amos 1:11; Obad 7, 10, 12; Ezek 25:13; 32:29; 35:3-4, 7, 9, 14-15; 36:33-36; Is 34:14; Jer 49:12-13, 17).[18] Moreover, it evinces echoes of covenantal fidelity, especially with the language of Deuteronomy (Yahweh's love for Israel: Deut 5:10; 6:5; 7:13; etc., but see also Ex 20:1-2). In this way, Malachi closes the Minor Prophets with a concept begun in Hosea, the covenant love of Yahweh for Israel and the expected reciprocal love of Israel for their God. Michael Fox rightly argues that the book distinctly portrays both the royal messenger (Malachi, who delivers messages of the king) and the royal lord (Yahweh, the Great King).[19]

Fox reads Malachi as a counternarrative to kingship and authority in a Persian context. Yahweh is the Great King, but the king of Persia is not. Xerxes took the throne of the Persia after the death of Darius I (486 BC). Darius I was defeated by Greece in the Battle of Marathon (490 BC), which could have provided a sense of hope that Yahweh really was shaking the nations (Hag 2:7, 22) and the glory of Yahweh would be made evident in the Persian province of Yehud. However, by 486 BC, upon Darius's death, Xerxes took the throne and reasserted the dominance of Persia. Malachi's message is not tied necessarily to one historic moment.

Outline

Six prophetic discussions govern the structure of Malachi, offering a corporate dialogue with God unmatched in so small a book.[20] But more to the point, we find several messages from the messenger of the Great King, Yahweh.[21]

---

[18]Ranier Kessler, "The Unity of Malachi," in *Perspectives on the Formation of the Book of the Twelve: Methodological Foundation—Redactional Processes—Historical Insights*, ed. R. Albertz, J. D. Nogalski, and J. Wöhrle, BZAW 433 (Berlin: de Gruyter, 2012), 223-36.

[19]R. Michael Fox, *A Message from the Great King: Reading Malachi in Light of Ancient Persian Royal Messenger Texts from the Time of Xerxes*, Siphrut 17 (Winona Lake, IN: Eisenbrauns, 2015).

[20]Egon Pfeiffer, "Die Disputationsworte im Buche Maleachi: Ein Beitrag zur form-geschichtlichen Struktur," *Evangelische Theologie* 19 (1959): 546-68; Hans-Jochen Boecker, "Bemerken zur formeschichtlichen Terminologie des Buch Maleachi," *ZAW* 78 (1966): 194-212; Ranier Kessler, *Maleachi*, HThKAT (Freiburg: Herder, 2011), 41-51.

[21]Fox, *Message from the Great King*, 120-28. We diverge from Fox on the descriptions of Mal 3:1-7 and Mal 3:8-12. In our view, Mal 3:8-12 does not present a "divine gardener" image but rather resumes the vision of Yahweh's displeasure in his people's actions. Further, Fox names Mal 3:1-7 rather indelicately as a "reboot," where Yahweh informs his people what he will do to announce his action of judgment. We prefer to see this section as rehearsing the language of "messenger."

Malachi 1:1	A message from Yahweh, the Great King
Malachi 1:2-5	A report of the King's victory
Malachi 1:6–2:9	The King's displeasure
Malachi 2:10-17	Judah's unfaithfulness to the King
Malachi 3:1-7	The King brings a royal messenger
Malachi 3:8-12	The King's displeasure
Malachi 3:13-21 [3:13–4:3]	The return of the King
Malachi 3:22-24 [4:4-6]	The return of the messenger

INTERPRETATION

Malachi 1:1. The "oracle" (*maśśā'*, 18x in the OT) in the superscription depicts prophetic activity of some kind. Canonically, *maśśā'* connects Malachi to Nahum 1:1 and Habakkuk 1:1, effectively linking the final book in the Twelve with Nahum, the seventh book in the corpus, creating a subcorpus from Nahum to Malachi.[22] But the superscription also combines *maśśā'* with *dəbar-YHWH*. This latter prophetic terminology occurs in Zechariah 1:1; 9:1; 12:1, as well as the entirety of the Haggai-Zechariah-Malachi unit. By our count, in the Minor Prophets, the "word of Yahweh" (*dəbar-YHWH*) occurs thirty-four times. It is a technical term for divine revelation, and thus here it signifies the message comes from Yahweh himself.[23] Finally, the superscription indicates the *maśśā'* and *dəbar-YHWH* comes to Israel "by the hand of Malachi" (*bəyad mal'ākî*). This language resonates with prophetic action under the direction of Yahweh (Moses, Ex 6:1; Elijah, 2 Kings 9:36; prophets, 2 Kings 17:13; Isaiah, Is 20:2). The combination of the three terms (*maśśā'*, *dəbar-YHWH*, *bəyad mal'ākî*) reveals that this book carries the authority of Yahweh's royal messenger, the one who gives the divine king's message to the people.

Malachi 1:2-5. Hosea opens the Minor Prophets with the love of Yahweh (see chap. 3), and Malachi concludes the corpus by reasserting the truth: "I have loved you," Yahweh says to Israel in Malachi 1:2.[24]

---

[22] Giving credence to the view of Boda, who views *maśśā'* to be an editorial marker that bolsters prophecy in the Persian period: Mark J. Boda, "Freeing the Burden of Prophecy: Maśśā' and the Legitimacy of Prophecy in Zech 9–14," *Biblica* 87, no. 3 (2006): 338-57.
[23] See the discussions of Andrew E. Hill, *Malachi*, AB (New York: Doubleday, 1998), 40-41; Meyers and Carol L. Meyers, *Haggai, Zechariah 1–8*, 7.
[24] S. D. Snyman, *Malachi*, HCOT (Leuven: Peeters, 2015), 14; see also Kessler, *Maleachi*, 120.

Divine love is proved by Yahweh's exclusion of Esau and embrace of Israel. "Jacob I have loved but Esau I have hated" (Mal 1:2-3 NKJV) presents a confusing depiction of Yahweh's relationship. This language depicts fidelity in covenant relationship rather than pure emotion or xenophobia. This is precisely the usage of love in Deuteronomy (Deut 4:32-34, 37; 7:8-9; 13; 10:12, 14-15, 18-19; 11:1, 12, 22; 13:3; 19:9; 23:5; 21:15; 30:16) and in our more immediate context in the Twelve (Hos 11:1, 4; 14:5 [14:4]). "The declaration of Yahweh's love for his people may be an expression of emotion, but it is also, and perhaps foremost, an expression of covenantal relationship."[25] *Hate* signifies not loathing but Yahweh's noncovenantal relationship with Esau. Esau is decidedly *not* the line through whom the blessing of Yahweh will ensue. The downfall of Esau/Edom (echoing Deut 2:4-5) should be a sign of hope for Jacob, that Yahweh is true to his commitment to Israel.

Malachi 1:6–2:9. Yahweh's people (esp. priests) disregard Yahweh and divine love, evidenced by problems in the cult:

- Priests dishonor Yahweh by offering improper sacrifices (Mal 1:6-9).
- Priests and people present inadequate offerings to Yahweh (Mal 1:10-14).
- Priests do not follow Yahweh's covenant relationship with Levi (Mal 2:1-9).

Children honoring parents is well-established in Israel (Ex 20:12; Deut 5:16), but priests dishonor their "father" (Mal 1:6). Yahweh is the father and Israel the child (see Ex 4:22; Hos 11:1). Honor is due the father in both social and theological relationships, which means affording the honoree the appropriate consideration, regard, and deference in the relationship. The priests present defiled food on the altar (Mal 1:7), treat Yahweh's table with contempt (Mal 1:7), and offer blind animals for sacrifice (Mal 1:8). Each action violates the requirements for sacrifice prescribed in Leviticus 22:17-33 and thereby dishonors God as father. Yahweh's response is clear: he is displeased and will not accept offering from the priests' hands (Mal 1:10).

Haggai and Malachi both draw attention to failures of the priesthood, a reality borne throughout the Minor Prophets, as Mark Boda maintains.[26]

---

[25]Snyman, *Malachi*, 34.
[26]Mark J. Boda, "Penitential Innovations in the Book of the Twelve," in *On Stone and Scroll: A Festschrift for Graham Davies*, ed. Brian A. Mastin, Katharine J. Dell, and James K. Aitken, BZAW 420 (Berlin: de Gruyter, 2011), 291-308; Boda, "Penitential Priests in the Twelve," in *Priests and Cults in the Book of the Twelve*, ed. Lena-Sofia Tiemeyer, Ancient Near East Monographs 14 (Atlanta: SBL Press, 2016), 51-64; Boda, "Perspectives on Priests in Haggai-Malachi," in *Prayer and Poetry in the Dead Sea Scrolls and Related Literature: Essays in Honor of Eileen*

Joel 1–2 presents priests appropriately leading the people to penitence. Zechariah 7–8 depicts a failure of priestly leadership, and Malachi 1–2 reiterates this point. Their failure in Malachi 2:1-9 reveals priestly disregard for the covenantal obligations from their early commitments.

Malachi 1:14 shifts the metaphor from father to king.[27] Malachi 1:14 emphasizes Yahweh's authority as divine King whose honor/name will be *feared* among the nations. The connection to fearing Yahweh in Malachi 1:14 links back to the question of Malachi 1:6: "If I am a master, where is your *fear* of me?" Yahweh's authority, power, and prestige as the divine King over *all* nations should lead to honoring the Lord with appropriate sacrifices. However, the priests despise Yahweh's name (Mal 1:6, 14). Malachi 2:1-9 curses the priests for their lack of honor. Yahweh rebukes priestly descendants and dishonors *them* (e.g., spreading feces over the priests' faces using the animal waste of their defiled sacrifices, etc., in Mal 2:3). As unfaithful priests despise Yahweh (note the use of the root *bzh* in Mal 1:6), Yahweh will despise them (note the use of the root *bzh* in Mal 2:9).

Malachi 2:10-17. Malachi 2:11-17 exposes covenantal failure with Yahweh:

- profaning Yahweh's sanctuary and remarrying the daughter of a foreign god (Mal 2:11)
- lamenting and weeping over unaccepted offerings (Mal 2:13)
- unfaithfulness in marriage and divorce (Mal 2:14-16)
- questioning Yahweh's justice (Mal 2:17)

Such violation leads Yahweh to reject their offerings. This rejection leads the people to lament (unjustly) with weeping (Mal 2:13). Yahweh then explains why he rejects their offerings in Malachi 2:14-16, where he calls the people to remember the "wife of your youth" (Mal 2:14, 15), a phrase that indicates the first love in a relationship, which should satisfy the spouse forever (Prov 5:18). Husbands should embrace their wives as Yahweh has embraced (even wayward) Israel.

The people make Yahweh weary with their words (Mal 2:17), apparently twisting the clear teaching of Deuteronomy 18:12; 25:16. They finally ask,

---

Schuller on the Ocassion of Her 65th Birthday, ed. Jeremy Penner, Ken Penner, and Cecilia Wassen, Studies on the Texts of the Desert of Judah 98 (Leiden: Brill, 2012), 13-33.

[27] Divine kingship in the OT: Ps 10:16; 24:8, 10; 29:10; 47:2; 84:3; 93:1; 95:3; 96:10; 97:1; 98:6; 99:1; 103:19; Is 6:5; 33:22; 43:15; 44:6. See Shawn W. Flynn, *Yahweh Is King: The Development of Divine Kingship in Ancient Israel*, VTSup 159 (Leiden: Brill, 2014).

"Where is the God of justice?" Yahweh responds to their final question, but not as they might anticipate.

Malachi 3:1-7. These verses compose a salvation oracle that depicts the day of Yahweh (Mal 3:2), which is both a day of judgment and salvation. Yahweh declares he will send "my messenger" (*mal'ākî*), who will clear the way before Yahweh. The remainder of Malachi 3:1 relates the messenger with two other figures: "the lord" (*hā'ādôn*) and "the messenger of the covenant" (*mal'āk habbərît*). These two figures represent Yahweh, depicted through angelic personae.[28]

The message is a word of salvation and judgment. For the Levites and for those who seek Yahweh, who delight in his covenant, and who fear Yahweh (Mal 3:2-4), the day announced by the messenger comprises a day of salvation, purging sin and providing undefiled sacrifices. Divine pleasure in the sacrifices (Mal 3:4) indicates restored covenantal relationship with Israel. But divine judgment accompanies salvation. Yahweh judges "sorcerers and adulterers," "those who swear falsely," "those who oppress the wages of a hired laborer, the widow and the fatherless," and "those who thrust aside the resident alien" (Mal 3:5). The list of evildoers resonates with the Decalogue (adultery: Ex 20:14; Deut 5:18; swearing falsely: Ex 20:16; Deut 5:20), but the remainder of the list addresses social sin elaborated in the Torah (defrauding wages of laborers, Deut 15:18; not caring for the widow or fatherless or resident alien, Deut 24:17-22; 26:12-13). Even in judgment, Yahweh's covenant remains in place (Mal 3:6-7). God implores his people's return; he would, in turn, return to them (e.g., Joel 2:12-13; Zech 1:3).

Malachi 3:8-12. God's people retort, "How do we rob you?" when God inquires of the propriety of robbing him. Yahweh reminds the people of the tithe (Deut 14:22-29; 26:12-15; Lev 27:30), which apparently the people neglected. Yahweh offers a test: bring the tithe and see what happens: "See if I do not open the floodgates of heaven and pour out a blessing for you without end" (Mal 3:10). Devotion to God, no matter the hardship, yields blessings.

Malachi 3:13-21 [3:13–4:3]. Yahweh imitates the harsh words of the people: "It is vain serving Yahweh. What do we gain by walking mournfully and keeping his requirements, or when we walk as mourners before the presence of Yahweh of Armies?" (Mal 3:14). Their words invert the call of Yahweh in

---

[28]Snyman, *Malachi*, 130-35.

Deuteronomy 10:12-13, which reminds God's people that obedience is for their well-being. Instead of embracing this truth, they characterize obedience to Yahweh as "vanity."[29] God does not even respond to their speech. Stylistically, the absence of a divine response signals the conclusion of the discussions in the book.

A "book of remembrance" (*sēper zikkārôn*) is written before Yahweh memorializing those who feared Yahweh and esteemed his name (Mal 3:16; see Mal 1:6, 11, 14; 2:5). They will be remembered by Yahweh and preserved on the day, Malachi 3:17 proclaims: "'They will belong to me,' says Yahweh of Armies, 'my own treasured possession on the day which I am preparing. I will have compassion on them just as a father has compassion on his son, the one serving him.'" This covenantal language connotes mutuality: Yahweh will preserve those who fear Yahweh and revere his name (Mal 3:20 [4:2]) when he judges the wicked. But the wicked will experience "burning like a furnace" (Mal 3:19 [4:1]) and "will be ashes" (Mal 3:21 [4:3]).

Malachi 3:22-24 [4:4-6]. Malachi ends with two conclusions. The first appears in Malachi 3:22 [4:4]: "Remember the instruction of Moses my servant, the statutes and the ordinances I commanded him at Horeb for all Israel" (see Eccles 12:13). The mention of Horeb recalls the second giving of the law in Deuteronomy. Malachi rhetorically places the reader at Sinai once again, responsible for the "statutes" and "ordinances" that first generation failed to keep (see Deut 5:1-4). Over and again, Israel's faithlessness in Malachi has been met with Yahweh's action to preserve Israel in the future. Although both Malachi 3:22 [4:4] and Deuteronomy require following the letter of God's law, these texts show that this is not enough because Israel will fail in that obedience. As such, Malachi 3:22 [4:4] (no less Deuteronomy; see Deut 30:1-10) requires God's people ultimately to depend on Yahweh's saving work with their whole being in faith *despite* their waywardness.

Malachi 3:23-24 [4:5-6] frames future hope: "See! I am sending to you Elijah the prophet before the great and terrible day of Yahweh comes. And he will turn the heart of fathers to their sons, and the heart of sons to their fathers, lest I come and I strike the land with a curse." This second conclusion draws attention to the "second Moses," Elijah the prophet. On a narrative reckoning of the story of Israel, Moses and Elijah represent the great prophets of the periods of the exodus (Moses) and the early monarchy

---

[29]This is a different Hebrew word from the *hebel* (vanity) of Ecclesiastes, but the parallel is notable.

(Elijah), respectively; canonically, Moses and Elijah are shorthand for the Torah and Prophets, the two subsections of the tripartite Hebrew canon: the Torah (Moses) and the Prophets (Elijah).

The first and second conclusions of Malachi, then, subtly nod in the canonical direction by attributing remembrance to the "Torah of Moses" and "Elijah, the prophet." As the book concludes with an emphasis on the coming of the prophet before the coming day of Yahweh, an eschatological thrust is given to the end of the book and to the end of the Prophets. It opens the reader's horizon for the coming event of Yahweh's revelation of judgment and salvation, heralded by the coming of the prophet Elijah. When he comes, the day of Yahweh is not far behind.

Theology

Covenant. *Judgment and discernment.* While Malachi confirms divine judgment against sin, the book further argues that iniquity distorts human discernment to the degree that what is objectively evil is considered good (Mal 2:17). This perversion of human discernment "wearies" Yahweh and necessitates judgment. Judgment, on this account, purifies so that proper relationship with God ensues. Judgment also resets proper discernment so that humans now see reality properly: evil is evil and good is good.

Love. Although the book of Malachi reinforces over and again the notion of covenant breach, it accents human-divine relationship in terms of intimacy, self-giving, and communion and presents these relational connections as being absent (Mal 1:2-5). Covenantal love is neither cold nor contractual but a relationship of self-giving and trust.

Honor. The covenant relationship requires honor (Mal 1:6-14). Honor, once again, is not cold or calculating: "In all dealings with parents, respect, esteem, having regard and concern for, and showing affection, considerateness, and appreciation are all the order of the day."[30] The fatherhood of Yahweh coincides with the kingship of Yahweh. As the Great King (Mal 1:14), Yahweh exerts his rule over all creation. Now, one may consider divine kingship language as reinforcing a transcendent, far-removed image of Yahweh jarring against the familial imagery that has gone before. After all, Yahweh's kingship is immediately defined in terms of its greatness and reverence among the nations (Mal 1:14). There can be no doubt that the kingship of Yahweh reinforces his prominence and preeminence over all rival powers:

---

[30] Terence Fretheim, *Exodus*, Interpretation (Louisville: John Knox, 1991), 231.

Persia, Babylon, or whomever. However, if we understand the imagery of Yahweh's kingship to be connected to the immediate problem of cultic sacrifice and blemished animals for offering, then another way to envision Yahweh's kingship emerges.

The King's table. The discussion leading to the declaration of Yahweh's kingship (Mal 1:6-13) centers on polluted sacrifices brought to Yahweh's "table" (*šulḥan YHWH*, Mal 1:7), and speaks of the offerings in terms of "bread," "food," and "fruit" (Mal 1:7, 12). The altar and temple indicate the King's table and the King's house, with the sacrifices as the food for Yahweh. Thus, the kingship of Yahweh has been framed by the notion of the people and priests dining at the table of God. Yahweh's relationship with humanity, even in the light of his divine kingship, implies the intimacy and communion of a shared food. The relational capacity for friendship and fidelity in the shared table emerges only to be quashed by the relational breach and betrayal of blemished sacrifices. Yahweh is *not* honored or befriended at the table. He is neglected and spurned due to the indifference of his people.

God and the future. Malachi presents God as pressing forward to future renewal in the face of present rebellion and the break in communion. Yahweh's fifty-five or so direct addresses to the people in the book reveal a God who speaks to his people so they might "return" (Mal 3:7). Malachi presents Yahweh's future commitment to Israel as well. Because of Israel's intractability, Yahweh will enact a time when sacrifices will be pleasing to him (Mal 3:2-4) and relationship will be restored. Those relying on Yahweh with humility, honor, and fear will be those vindicated by Yahweh (Mal 3:14-16). Although family relationships are strained and broken (both in terms of divorce and remarriage in Mal 2:10-17 and in terms of the divine father's relationship with his son in Mal 1:6-8), Yahweh provides future reconciliation (Mal 3:17-18). Central to this future work of Yahweh is the messenger of Yahweh, who reveals the divine word "to prepare the way before" the work of God.

MALACHI IN THE NEW TESTAMENT

Malachi is especially prominent in the discussion of John the Baptist in the Gospels (Mt 11:10; Mk 1:2; Lk 7:27). These texts, with very little variation, cite Malachi 3:1 from the Greek translation of the Old Testament (LXX): "See, I am sending my messenger, and he will clear a way before me." The differences between the Gospels' citation and the original is the second-person "you" (*sou*) instead of the first-person "me." Thus the Gospels read: "See! I am sending my messenger ahead of you, who will prepare your way before you."[31] John the Baptist is the messenger of these Gospel texts, and the day being announced is the coming of Jesus in judgment and salvation. The second-person pronoun "you" refers to Jesus.

John the Baptist is Malachi's "Elijah" (Mal 3:23 [4:5]) who comes before the day of the Lord (Mt 11:14; 17:10-12; Mk 9:11-13; Lk 1:16-17). Jesus' arrival in judgment and redemption inaugurates the future hope. Luke presents John the Baptist as the fulfillment of Malachi's vision of the coming Elijah. Luke, however, takes the vision further by saying, "to make ready a people prepared for the Lord" (Lk 1:17), most likely meaning preparing the people for the coming of Jesus, the Messiah.

Paul's instruction in 1 Corinthians 10:21 may refer to Malachi 1:7, 12 in the use of the phrase "the table of the Lord." As indicated above, Malachi presents the altar as Yahweh's table and the sacrifice as the food. It uses an unusual phrase, "table of Yahweh," to refer to communion between Yahweh and his people, which has been sullied by sin. If Paul uses this same language, and indeed it is identical to Malachi 1:7, 12 in Greek ("table of the Lord," *trapeza kyriou*), then the apostle carries forward the theme of covenant loyalty through the shared communion in the Lord's Supper. As the people of God share in Communion at the Lord's table, then there should be no division within them, nor should there be division or breach in their relationship to Jesus. If this is accurate, then Paul has applied Malachi's intertext to reinforce a theme of enacted Communion and participation in the Lord's Supper as a means of covenant loyalty.

Finally, the apostle Paul uses Malachi 1:2-3 in his discussion of God's election of Israel in Romans 9:13: "Jacob I have loved, but Esau I have hated." Few texts generate as much discussion on theological topics such as election and/or predestination as this Pauline text does. Malachi's usage of Jacob/Esau is an affirmation of Jacob/Israel as the way God would bless the world through election and covenant. God's choice of Jacob is an affirmation of divine freedom, regardless of Israel's fidelity. In using this language from Malachi, Paul affirms the divine freedom God displays in his election of Israel in the covenant. It has nothing to do with works, fidelity, or what the covenant partner brings to the table.

---

[31] Mark 1:2 diverges from this by omitting "before you" at the end of the verse.

Paul reinforces the notion of divine freedom in election by revealing the originating moments of Israel's election: the birth of Jacob and Esau. "Israel is constituted by God only through his free elective grace," says Peter Stuhlmacher, and because of this, Paul argues that Jacob and Esau, though brothers born of the same mother, remain distinct in terms of divine election through the covenant.[32] Thus the older son (Esau) would serve the younger (Jacob), and the "God who elects and the God who justifies in and through Christ are one and the same; ever since Abraham, Israel stands and falls based on his [God's] action!"[33] God has freely chosen to work through Jesus to create a new Israel composed of Jews and Gentiles.

RECOMMENDED READING

Flynn, Shawn W. *Yahweh Is King: The Development of Divine Kingship in Ancient Israel.* VTSup 159. Leiden: Brill, 2014.

Fox, R. Michael. *A Message from the Great King: Reading Malachi in Light of Ancient Persian Royal Messenger Texts from the Time of Xerxes.* Siphrut 17. Winona Lake, IN: Eisenbrauns, 2015.

Jacobs, Mignon R. *The Books of Haggai and Malachi.* NICOT. Grand Rapids, MI: Eerdmans, 2017.*

Kessler, Ranier. *Maleachi.* HThKAT. Freiburg: Herder, 2011.

———. "The Unity of Malachi." In *Perspectives on the Formation of the Book of the Twelve: Methodological Foundation—Redactional Processes—Historical Insights,* ed. R. Albertz, J. D. Nogalski, and J. Wöhrle, 223-36. BZAW 433. Berlin: de Gruyter, 2012.

Snyman, S. D. *Malachi.* HCOT. Leuven: Peeters, 2015.

Tuell, Steven. *Reading Nahum–Malachi.* ROT. Macon, GA: Smyth & Helwys, 2016.*

Recommended reading marked with a "" indicates introductory works.*

---

[32] Peter Stuhlmacher, *Paul's Letter to the Romans: A Commentary* (Louisville, KY: Westminster John Knox, 1994), 147.

[33] Stuhlmacher, *Paul's Letter to the Romans,* 148.

20

The Theology of the Minor Prophets

ONE OF THE GLORIES OF THE BIBLE is that God has not revealed himself in a systematic, theological textbook—as much as we love these!—but in and through his immersion in the life of a nation. God created the world with a history, and he reveals himself in *a particular history*, namely that of Israel and climactically in Jesus of Nazareth. Particularly in the prophets, the result is that God's word is concrete, occasional, directed toward particular circumstances and situations. Henri Nouwen comments that the most personal is often the most universal,[1] and that is certainly true of the Minor Prophets. The books of the Minor Prophets as a whole came into existence over a long period of time, and they bear the marks of the individual personalities of the prophets or authors. Thus, even as we explore their common theology we need to be alert to the differences between them.[2]

There can be no question that the overwhelmingly central character in the Minor Prophets is Yahweh, the living God who has established Israel as his covenant people. *Everything* turns around him, and it is from him that the theology of these books flows. We do well to defamiliarize ourselves with the Minor Prophets so that we can catch a glimpse of the extraordinary God who stands in *their* midst and has come to us in Christ.

THE GOD WHO SPEAKS

C. S. Lewis notes that the God of the Bible is at least personal, if not more than personal.[3] This is certainly true of the God revealed to us in the Minor

---

[1] Henri J. M. Nouwen, *Bread for the Journey: A Daybook of Wisdom and Faith* (Toronto: HarperCollins, 1997), 77.
[2] See John Goldingay, "Twelve Books, One Theology?," in *Reading the Book of the Twelve Minor Prophets*, ed. David G. Firth and Brittany N. Melton, SSBT (Bellingham, WA: Lexham Academic, 2022), 171-92.
[3] C. S. Lewis, *Mere Christianity* (London: William Collins, 1952), 77.

Prophets. It is far too easy to take this for granted (see chap. 8). For example, in nine of the Minor Prophets the fact of God speaking is referred to in the opening verse; in Amos (see Amos 1:3), Nahum (see Nahum 1:14; 3:5), and Habakkuk (see Hab 2:2) the language of God speaking comes later, but throughout the Minor Prophets God is portrayed as a God who speaks—and acts—and this is what makes the books so powerful and dynamic. In all of the Minor Prophets the people of God are at a crossroads.[4] It is a time of empires, of threats at home and abroad, and in such contexts Yahweh speaks.

Hence we refer to the Minor *Prophets*. The prophets are the vehicles by which and through which Yahweh addresses his people (see Hos 12:11 [12:10]), as Amos 3:3-8 makes crystal clear. As Andersen and Freedman point out, *dābār* (nothing) cannot in Amos 3:7 mean "anything" or "nothing," since clearly God does most things without consulting a prophet first. "In the context the *dābār* is a specific course of action in response to an unusual situation . . . a departure from the norm that needs to be identified and explained as an act of God."[5] What Amos 3:7 does highlight is the *intimate relationship* between Yahweh and his prophets. At critical times in the life of his people, Yahweh entrusts his plans and his words to his prophets. This evokes the enormous privilege of being a prophet, of being one of "his servants" (Amos 3:7). Amos 3:8 speaks of the compulsion under which the servant prophet worked; when God has spoken, who can but prophesy?

Of course, God's speech is not always welcome. Francis Andersen and David Freedman suggest that Amos 3:3-8 is designed to solve the strangeness of Amos 3:2.[6] We might expect the fact that God has "known" only Israel among all the nations to be followed by a declaration of blessing, but instead it leads to punishment.[7] This is not a message that many of God's people wanted to hear, so *a* theme in the Minor Prophets is *the relationship between true and false prophecy*. The genuine prophet told the truth, whereas the false prophet told his hearers what they wanted to hear.

Amos's confrontation with Amaziah in Amos 7:10-17 is a great example of this. Amaziah was a priest at the sanctuary at Bethel and, having been exposed to Amos's searing preaching, reported him to king Jeroboam. Amaziah rightly understood that Amos's preaching was politically

---

[4]Jonah might appear an exception, but we take Jonah to be representative of the people of God.
[5]Francis I. Andersen and David N. Freedman, *Amos*, AB 24A (New York: Doubleday, 1989), 399; see 1 Sam 20:2.
[6]Andersen and Freedman, *Amos*, 384.
[7]NIV translates "chosen," but the verb is normally translated "known."

subversive and threatened the very existence of the northern kingdom. Amos's response is an oracle of terrible judgment.

Amos 7:16 has a close parallel in Micah 2:6. Micah 3:5 reveals to us clearly the strategy of the false prophets. The phrase "bite their teeth" is a synecdoche for "to eat." The root of the verb *nšk* (bite) has to do with snakes in ten of its other eleven uses and may thus metaphorically evoke the deadly effect of such prophets on their audience.[8] Their venom is found in prophesying *šālôm* (peace) when judgment is coming (see Jer 6:14; Zeph 3:4). As Micah notes in Micah 2:11, a prophet predicting plenty of wine and beer is just the sort of prophet for this people. The potential opposition to the true prophet is also referred to in Hosea 9:7-8.[9]

There is a note of tragic humor in Micah's statement, and this alerts us to the rich diversity of ways in which Yahweh addresses his people: prophecy full of arresting images, surprising metaphors, poetry, language from law courts, imaginative visions, the language of wisdom, and so on. Yahweh employs a full range of speech acts as he turns to his people at critical stages in their life.

THE COVENANT GOD

"I have been the LORD your God ever since you came out of Egypt" (Hos 12:10 [12:9]). God's address to his people through his prophets alerts us to his particular relationship with them. In recent decades historical criticism has tended to date the emergence of covenant as late in Israel, even as a prophetic invention. However, as we have seen in our examination of the Minor Prophets, Yahweh's covenantal relationship with his people is built into the DNA of these books. We will not repeat that level of detail here other than to note that the Minor Prophets show awareness of the covenant with Noah (see Hos 2:18), the Sinai covenant, the Davidic covenant, and especially the concomitant establishment of Jerusalem as Zion, a major motif found in every one of the Minor Prophets. If Hosea 6:7 refers to the covenant "with" Adam, then there is also an understanding of Genesis 1–3 as the basic covenantal text.

Yahweh's relationship with his people is based on his deliverance of them from Egypt (Amos 3:1; Mic 6:4; Hag 2:5), his establishment of them at Sinai

---

[8] Bruce K. Waltke, *A Commentary on Micah* (Grand Rapids, MI: Eerdmans, 2007), 159; see also D. K. Innes, "Some Notes on Micah," *Evangelical Quarterly* 41 (1969): 109.
[9] Intriguingly, Zech 13 refers to a time when prophets will be removed from the land.

as his covenant people, and his gift to them of the land. The repeated emphasis on Zion evokes Yahweh's covenant with David (2 Sam 7) and the building of the temple as the place where Yahweh dwells amid his people.

The primary background for the multivocal symbol of covenant for Yahweh's relationship with his people is that of a treaty between a Great King and a vassal. Perhaps the clearest expression of this is found in Zephaniah 3:15 in a wonderful sentence, literally, "The king of Israel, Yahweh is in your midst!" (see Ex 15:18). Yahweh is *the Great King*, and his people are bound to him legally by a covenant, on the basis of which they have sworn to obey him and to keep his commandments. It is on this basis that he calls them to account, as we will see below.

The portrayal of Yahweh as the God of the covenant, however, exceeds the treaty analogy and bespeaks intimacy of a far greater order than is evoked by a treaty. Hosea in particular is extraordinary in this respect, in which Yahweh is portrayed as *the husband* of his bride Israel. In Zechariah 1:14 Yahweh declares himself to be "jealous for Jerusalem and Zion." Within the intimacy of the covenant of marriage and of Yahweh's relationship with Israel, such jealousy is an appropriate emotion.

In Hosea 11:1 Israel is referred to as a "child" much loved by Yahweh in her youth, and in parallel with this we find the sentence, "And out of Egypt I called *my son*." This is *familial* language and evokes a deep intimacy between Yahweh and his people. In Hosea 11:8 God's internal agony over Israel, appropriate to familial breakdown, is set before us: "My heart is changed within me; all my compassion is aroused."

ZION, CITY OF THE GREAT KING

The Davidic covenant (2 Sam 6–7) is central to the Minor Prophets, with its theology of Zion. Zion is first referred to in 2 Samuel 5:7: "Nevertheless, David captured the fortress of Zion—which is the City of David." Zion thus became the name of the capital city of Jerusalem during the united and divided monarchies. We cannot be sure of the details of the origin of the rich Zion theology in the Old Testament other than that it must be connected with the establishment of Jerusalem as the capital of Israel under David, and in particular with the building of the temple there under Solomon.[10]

The term "Zion" (*ṣiyyôn*) is used throughout the prophets (48× in Isaiah, 17× in Jeremiah, 7× in Lamentations, 7× in Joel, 2× in Amos, 2× in Obadiah,

---

[10]Some historical critics distinguish between the David tradition and the Zion tradition.

7× in Micah, 1× in Zephaniah, 7× in Zechariah). Zion is referred to—albeit not by name—in Jonah 2:4, 7 and clearly presupposed in Haggai. Hosea speaks twice of the house of God (Hos 8:1; 9:15), a synonym for Zion. Indeed, the terminology of Zion and related language is far more prevalent in the Prophets than in the Pentateuch, Historical Books, or even the Writings (with the exception of the Psalter).

In Old Testament studies there has been much discussion about the tradition history of Zion theology.[11] The Zion tradition is extensive, and we cannot here examine the complex of texts that extend way outside the Minor Prophets, not least in the Psalms.[12] Even more so than covenant, Zion is a *multivocal* symbol that "has among its denotations the kingship of Yahweh and among its connotations Yahweh's exclusive prerogative to be the defender of and provide security for his people."[13] Zion is a multivocal symbol that functions amid a network of relationships, a network that in our view results from the transfer of the traditions of the older Israelite theology to the new geographical, political, and above all religious context once Jerusalem was established as "Zion."[14] Ben Ollenburger argues rightly that the Zion tradition is "an exegesis of the Ark and its tradition," with components added from Canaanite motifs such as the cosmic mountain.[15] Take covenant, for example. Central to covenant is Yahweh as king, and Ollenburger rightly notes that Yahweh's presence in Zion is most prominently referred to as "king" (see Ps 24:8-10; 68; 132). No Davidic king is ever referred to as "king

---

[11] See Heath A. Thomas, "Zion," in *Dictionary of the Old Testament Prophets*, ed. Mark J. Boda and J. Gordon McConville (Downers Grove, IL: IVP Academic, 2012), 907-14, for a comprehensive bibliography and for the history of research.

[12] See Ben C. Ollenburger, *Zion, the City of the Great King: A Theological Symbol of the Jerusalem Cult*; Richard J. Clifford, *The Cosmic Mountain in Canaan and the Old Testament*, Harvard Semitic Monographs 4 (Eugene, OR: Wipf & Stock, 1972); Richard Hess and Gordon Wenham, eds., *Zion, City of Our God* (Grand Rapids, MI: Eerdmans, 1999); Bernard F. Batto and Kathryn L. Roberts, eds., *David and Zion: Biblical Studies in Honor of J. J. M Roberts* (Winona Lake, IN: Eisenbrauns, 2004). Gunkel identifies Ps 46; 48; 76 as the major Zion Psalms. Ollenburger (*Zion, the City of the Great King*) rightly notes that there is probably not a group of Zion psalms; instead, the Zion psalms are individual expressions of a coherent theology of Zion that underlies most of the psalms. This is articulated most clearly in the songs of Zion and in the creation psalms. On Zion and the Psalms see Othmar Keel, *The Symbolism of the Biblical World: Ancient Near Eastern Iconography and the Book of the Psalms* (Winona Lake, IN: Eisenbrauns, 1997), 111-76.

[13] Ollenburger, *Zion, the City of the Great King*, 19.

[14] Ollenburger (*Zion, the City of the Great King*) refers to three theories of the origins of the Zion tradition. We agree with this third one.

[15] Ollenburger, *Zion, the City of the Great King*, 43. There is much discussion about the influence of pagan motifs on the theology of Zion. There is no reason why such motifs should not have been embraced by Israel and made subservient to its Yahwism, but such theories are inherently speculative.

of Zion," since this is reserved for Yahweh alone. This view of God as king agrees entirely with the treaty background to covenant, but now Yahweh has a residence in Jerusalem, namely, Zion. Yahweh's presence in the temple is real and not just symbolic. "Yahweh's heavenly rule is reflected in his earthly sovereignty, centered in the temple which unites heaven and earth."[16]

A central aspect of Zion theology is thus the *real presence* of Yahweh in the temple. In a delightful chapter titled "The Psalmody of Presence," Samuel Terrien rightly states, "It can hardly be doubted that the psalmists obtained their spiritual acuity from their Zion-centered theology."[17] It is this real presence, as we will explore below, that makes Zion both a refuge and a danger, because Yahweh really dwells there.

According to Zion theology, Yahweh exercises his kingship through his power as *Creator and defender*. Ollenburger notes that Zion symbolism is "fundamentally a theology of creation"; "it is preeminently through creation, rather than nature or history, that God is related to the world."[18] As scholars of the priestly literature of the Old Testament have rightly noted, the temple is a microcosm of the creation so that Zion inevitably evokes Yahweh as Creator and makes his abode the center of the creation. Ollenburger notes that scholars such as Rolf Rendtorff and Gerhard von Rad argued that the motifs of creation and redemption were first brought together by Second Isaiah. However, as he rightly points out, already in Exodus 15 they are woven together in a text that is acknowledged to be early.[19] Zion theology includes the notion of a universal world order.

The temple is central in Zion, reminding us that although the Davidic king is important, the divine King is ultimate. God rules his kingdom from Zion's temple, and as God's people worshiped at the temple, they found the deep meaning of their world. Jon Levenson captures the thought:

> The Temple is the epitome of the world, a concentrated form of its essence, a miniature of the cosmos.... The Temple is not a place in the world, but the world in essence. It is the theology of creation rendered in architecture and glyptic craftsmanship. In the Temple, God relates simultaneously to the entire cosmos, for the Temple (or mountain or city) is a microcosm of which the

---

[16]Ollenbuger, *Zion, the City of the Great King*, 34.
[17]Samuel Terrien, *The Elusive Presence: Toward a New Biblical Theology* (San Francisco: Harper & Row, 1978), 312.
[18]Ollenbuger, *Zion, the City of the Great King*, 161.
[19]Ollenbuger, *Zion, the City of the Great King*, 58.

world itself is the macrocosm. Or, to put it differently, the center (or navel or axis or fulcrum) is not a point in space at all, but the point in relation to which all space attains individualization and meaning.[20]

So Zion's temple does not just give a picture of the order of creation; in actuality, the temple orders the world as it relates to it. As spokes connect the outer rim to its central hub to form a functional wheel, Zion's temple serves as the center of God's world, by which the rest of the world is connected and from which it gains sensibility and stability. Without Zion, the meaning of the world is left undisclosed. But in Zion, the world is disclosed as God's kingdom, with God on his throne in the most holy place, where God calls worshipers to celebrate before him in unbridled worship. In this way Zion and the temple disclose the universal world order mentioned above.

We find the emphasis on Zion and creation helpful and correct. Inter alia it makes the creation hymns in Amos, for example, what we would expect rather than an addition. Where we would disagree is in claiming that Zion theology is a theology of creation and *not* one of history. This in our view perpetuates a false dualism between creation and history. And the *historical* dimension of Zion is important. Psalm 132 connects Zion with David and celebrates that "the LORD has *chosen* Zion, he has desired it for his dwelling" (Ps 132:13 NIV). The connection between Yahweh and Zion is a historical one and not a natural or eternal one, as with ancient Near Eastern temples. Othmar Keel writes,

> Yahweh's dwelling in Zion is thus a free act of grace. In it the exodus from Egypt and the settlement of the land find their full completion. The object of the exodus is the sovereignty of Yahweh, which produces life and salvation. That lordship will extend from Zion to include all nations (Ps 87; Mic 4:1-3). In the free election of Zion as an act of divine condescension lie the essence and the specifics of all Zion-theology, all Davidic theology, and finally, of the whole biblical theology of incarnation.[21]

Yahweh's choice of Zion means that he can also un-choose it. It is this that makes him dangerous for a sinful people. Keel notes in this regard that it is the nations and not the floods of chaos that rage against Yahweh (see Ps 46; 65; 76).[22]

---

[20]Jon D. Levenson, *Sinai and Zion: An Entry into the Jewish Bible* (New York: Harper & Row, 1985), 138-39.
[21]Keel, *Symbolism of the Biblical World*, 120.
[22]Keel, *Symbolism of the Biblical World*, 175.

The connection of Zion with creation is confirmed by the function of temples in the ancient Near East. Keel says of holy places in the ancient Near East, "The creator-god made his appearance on the primeval hill; the ordered world had its origin from it." Temples were built on mountains and symbolized the cosmic mountain. Keel notes, "Zion possesses all the prerogatives of the cosmic mountain."[23] Zion was in fact a modest hill made exceptional by the one who dwelt there. As with the tabernacle, it has close connections with Eden. The creation dimension alerts us that Yahweh's kingship extends over all nations. Nineveh is thus not only the object of his compassion (Jonah) but also rightly of his wrath (Nahum). In the visions that open Zechariah, Yahweh's worldwide reign is clearly set forth.

The effect of Yahweh's being King in Zion means that Zion symbolizes *presence* and thus security, refuge, and life. Joel ends on the climactic note: "Yahweh *dwells* in Zion!" The presence, the *dwelling*, of Yahweh in the temple must not be spiritualized; he really lives there, even while the whole creation cannot contain him. This brought tremendous comfort: "In Zion, the psalmists were at home as the guests of Yahweh. It is therefore to be expected that an overwhelming sense of divine nearness permeated their personal prayers."[24] Terrien describes the psalmists evocatively as "Poets of the interior quest," a reminder of the effect of Yahweh's proximity in Zion on spirituality.[25] The shaping of human interiority by Yahweh's proximity in Zion is powerfully represented by Hosea and Jonah. Hosea is called to enact Yahweh's agony in his own marriage and family, and Jonah discovers through a deeply formative journey that one can flee Jerusalem but not Yahweh. As the Creator-Redeemer, Yahweh's presence literally means life and blessing. In Haggai, Zion's sacramental power is evoked in the effects on the land of not having rebuilt the temple (Hag 1:5-11).

Ollenburger notes that a surprising conclusion of his research is the pervasive concern for *justice* in the Zion traditions. All this and more we find in the Minor Prophets. Certainly the Zion motif in the Minor Prophets alerts us to the danger of having *the* King in Zion in the face of persistent disobedience. A major feature in the Minor Prophets is their exploration of the implicit threat in having Yahweh as one's refuge and defender. If Yahweh *of Hosts* is particularly associated with Zion theology, as some scholars

---

[23]Keel, *Symbolism of the Biblical World*, 113, 116.
[24]Terrien, *Elusive Presence*, 307.
[25]Terrien, *Elusive Presence*, 279.

argue, then the danger is that the armies of Yahweh get turned against his own people.

Creator

In Amos's hymns the doctrine of creation comes most clearly to the fore in the Minor Prophets (Amos 4:13; 5:8; 9:5-6). However, a theology of creation pervades the Minor Prophets, as we have seen, for example, in its Zion theology. Joel 2:3 refers to the Garden of Eden. Jonah confesses in Jonah 1:9, "I am a Hebrew and I worship the Lord, the God of heaven, who made the sea and the dry land" (NIV), a succinct confession of the doctrine of creation.

In poetic language similar to that in Isaiah, Zechariah begins Zechariah 12, "The Lord, who stretches out the heavens, who lays the foundation of the earth, and who forms the human spirit within a person." In these few words Zechariah summarizes the message of Genesis 1-2. In their judgment and salvation oracles the Minor Prophets repeatedly extend Yahweh's judgment and salvation to all nations (Joel 3:2, for example), indeed, to the whole cosmos. Such a comprehensive vision reflects their foundation in a doctrine of creation, as does the concern with international relations (Amos 1:3-2:16) and with the capital of Assyria—Nineveh—in Jonah and Nahum. Obadiah is extraordinary for its vision of the kingdom of God, concluding with a statement reminiscent of Revelation 11:15: "And the kingdom will be the Lord's" (Obad 21 NIV).

The theology of Old Testament wisdom is one of creation, and we find wisdom motifs in the Minor Prophets, notably the ending of Hosea in Hosea 14:9. In Micah 6:9 is a virtual paraphrase of Proverbs 1:7, "and to fear your name is wisdom." A noteworthy element of creation theology in the Minor Prophets is the concern with the land and with animals. We have noted how Haggai connects the flourishing of the land with the rebuilding of the temple. In Jonah a huge fish is the vehicle of Jonah's redemption; the animals are included in the fast and repentance in Nineveh (Jon 3:7-9); and most remarkably the final words of Jonah are *ûbəhēmâ rabbâ* ("and many animals"), as Yahweh seeks to rouse Jonah to compassion (see also Joel 1:18, 20).

Yahweh—and Israel—amid the Empires

The Minor Prophets exercised their ministries amid the emergence of the superpowers of Assyria, Babylon, and Persia. It was a new period in the ancient Near East, and the small countries that Israel had struggled with in the past were now replaced by superpowers. The smaller countries, such as Israel, were being swallowed up by the empires. The first major superpower on the scene was Assyria, and by far the largest number of references to Assyria in the Minor Prophets is found in Hosea (Hos 7:11; 8:9; 9:3; 10:6; 11:5, 11; 12:2 [12:1]; 14:4 [14:3]). Assyria conquered the northern kingdom of Israel and took them into exile in 722 BC. The empire of Babylon succeeded Assyria and conquered the southern kingdom of Israel in 587 BC and took them into exile.[26] Not surprisingly, Minor Prophets from this time, such as Micah and especially Habakkuk, refer to the looming threat of Babylon. Micah says directly to Judah, "You will go to Babylon" (Mic 4:10). Habakkuk wrestles with the alarming notion that *Yahweh* is raising up the Babylonians, and not least to punish Judah.

We need to defamiliarize ourselves with texts such as Hosea in order to begin to grasp the geopolitical realities with which they deal. Marc Van de Mieroop writes, "The history of the New East in the first millennium until the late seventh century was dominated by one power: Assyria. Through its military might, this state gradually expanded its control over a vast area from western Iran to the Mediterranean and from Anatolia to Egypt, dominating political and economic life."[27]

There were two major phases in Assyria's imperial expansion, the first in the ninth century and the second, more expansive phase beginning in the mid-eighth century, right around the time Hosea was prophesying. Religion drove the imperialism of Assyria. As the representative of the god Aššur, the king represented order, and his duty was to bring order to the whole world through military expansion. "All that was foreign was hostile, and all foreigners were like non-human creatures. Images of swamp-rats or bats, lonely, confused, and cowardly, were commonly applied to those outside the king's control."[28] The style of warfare was brutal, generally involving terrorizing the enemy into submission through means such as torture, rape, pillaging, and razing houses and fields.

At the time of Hosea, Israel was feeling the long shadow of Assyria pressing down on it. It was in the context of such realpolitik amid overwhelming power and with terrifying consequences that Hosea prophesied. J. H. Bavinck notes, "For anyone who thought deeply on these things two

---

[26]On the Babylonian and Persian Empires see Marc Van De Mieroop, *A History of the Ancient Near East ca. 3000–323 BC*, 3rd ed. (Oxford: Wiley-Blackwell, 2016), 270-301.
[27]Quoted in Van De Mieroop, *History of the Ancient Near East*, 229.
[28]Van De Mieroop, *History of the Ancient Near East*, 260.

possibilities existed: Israel would either be spiritually and politically absorbed into the contemporary world, or Israel must itself become a living power by means of which the nations would be drawn into the light of the salvations of Israel's God."[29]

Facing down an empire is a real test of faith, and the northern kingdom failed dismally. Hosea castigates Israel for turning to Assyria for help and forging foreign alliances (Hos 5:13; 7:11; 8:9; 10:6; 11:5). Realistically, we might wonder, What was the alternative? For Hosea the answer was clear: to trust Yahweh and to obey his leadership. Lest we write this off as pie in the sky, it is worth listening to Van De Mieroop's comment: "The resilience of the states surrounding Assyria shows that the empire was not always fully dominant and could be successfully opposed."[30] Hosea (Hos 5:13) is clear that the great king of Assyria "is not able to cure you, not able to heal your sores" (NIV). The obvious implication is that Yahweh *can* do these things. As the Creator, he is also *the* great physician and able to heal in all dimensions of life.

Astonishingly, in terms of the relative insignificance of Israel in the ancient Near East of its day, Hosea makes quite clear that Assyria's conquest of the northern kingdom will be *Yahweh's* doing, *his* punishment of Israel. Similarly, Habakkuk speaks of Yahweh raising up the Babylonians. As throughout the Minor Prophets, Yahweh is viewed as both transcendent and *immanently involved* in his world. He not only speaks but acts, and his acting is evoked in a myriad ways in the Minor Prophets, one of which is through the acts of the superpowers. What must not be missed is the colossal vision of Yahweh, who handles the great empires of the day as merely his instruments.

In the eighth century it must have seemed as though Assyria would rule forever, but Hosea already looks beyond Assyria's reign to a time when Israelites will return from Assyria (Hos 11:11). By their very nature and ideology empires appear indestructible, but their collapse can come quickly, as it did with Assyria in the sixth century. It takes the eye of faith, the agonized eye of Hosea, to look beyond the realities staring one in the face and to see beyond and above . . . to see Yahweh. It takes prophetic vision to speak of the realities to which Joel refers and end his book, "The LORD dwells in Zion!"

Oliver O'Donovan titled his political theology *The Desire of the Nations*, a title that comes from Haggai 2:7. In the postexilic period it must have been

---

[29]J. H. Bavinck, *An Introduction to the Science of Missions*, trans. David H. Freeman (Phillipsburg, NJ: Presbyterian & Reformed, 1960), 19.

[30]Van De Mieroop, *History of the Ancient Near East*, 256.

near impossible to see how Israel would recover and be anything like it was in the past centuries. But even in this context the prophets never lose their geopolitical antennae, and Haggai prophesies of a time when Yahweh "will shake all nations, and what is desired by all nations will come." From Hosea to Malachi, the Minor Prophets present us with a vision of the world, including government and politics, as rightly finding its place in submission to Yahweh. O'Donovan is perceptive in titling his book as he does; it is only as the nations bow before Yahweh and submit to his instruction that they will flourish and be fulfilled *as nations*. In this sense the Minor Prophets are like a midrash on Psalm 2. Patrick Miller notes that Psalms 1–2, the introduction to the Psalter, move from the individual believer in Psalm 1 to the tumult of the nations in Psalm 2.[31] "Blessed" (Ps 1:1; 2:12) functions as an *inclusio* for the introduction to the Psalter and alerts us that the way of *blessing* for individual *and* nation is found by following Yahweh's *tôrâ*. The Minor Prophets would shout a hearty "Amen."

GOD THE JUDGE, THE LORD OF HOSTS

A theme that runs through the Minor Prophets like a lightning bolt in the sky is that of judgment. This is never an easy message, and Habakkuk, perhaps above all the Minor Prophets, wrestles existentially with the problem of *his* God raising up the Babylonians to punish Judah. However, Hosea is right there next to him, encountering on a daily basis his wayward wife and his children, with their names evoking coming judgment. Jonah might be thought not to deal with judgment, but as we listen to the story of the prophet Jonah, we gradually become attuned to the sting in its tail; Jonah *represents Israel*, and its journey to redemption, like that of Jonah, will be through the death of drowning, doubtless a powerful image of exile.

Yahweh is the "Holy One" (Hab 1:12) in covenant relationship with his people.[32] As he is the Holy One in Zion, his presence becomes dangerous to those who rebel against him, worshiping other gods and practicing injustice. The Minor Prophets remind us again and again of Yahweh's patience and his endless attempts to call his people back to faithfulness, but to no avail. The danger of Yahweh in one's midst is evoked by a favorite name for God in the Minor Prophets, namely, the Lord of Hosts. Taken together as

---

[31]Patrick Miller, *Interpreting the Psalms* (Philadelphia: Fortress, 1986), 87-93.
[32]The epithet "Holy One" is particularly common in Isaiah. In the Minor Prophets it occurs only in Hos 11:9, 12; Hab 1:2; 3:3; Zech 14:5.

the Book of the Twelve, the Minor Prophets contain a higher occurrence (98x) of this name than anywhere else in the Old Testament.

As we have seen, *Hosts* most likely refers to the armies of heaven so that this title evokes Yahweh as a royal warrior with immense forces at his disposal. Amos 4:13 uses this title in one of the creation hymns, alerting us that the Creator God, while transcendent, is immanent too, and dangerously so for those who persistently rebel against him. One is blessed indeed to have the Lord of Hosts on one's side, but it is utterly catastrophic to have him turn against one, far more serious than Assyria or Babylon.

The remarkable number of occurrences of "Yahweh of Hosts" in the postexilic Haggai, Zechariah, and Malachi requires some comment. In most of its usages in these books, it is used to comfort and reassure postexilic Israel, and there are good reasons for this. The Israelites had returned from the harrowing experience of exile to what must have appeared like a failed state. It appeared even more vulnerable than before to foreign powers. In this context it needed to know that the Lord of the armies of heaven was with it for blessing, so that it could build and move forward. Hence the recurrence of this name of Yahweh.

In terms of God's judgment *the* major theme in the Minor Prophets is undoubtedly the day of Yahweh. It ties the twelve prophetic books together, and each of the other prophets, apart from Jonah, highlights this or that feature, but none draw together all of the elements identified above as clearly as does Joel, as we have seen.[33] It functions, like Zion, as a multivocal symbol amid a network of references and is thus flexible in terms of its application. The Minor Prophets exploit this flexibility to maximum benefit, and not least in terms of judgment. It was too easy for recalcitrant Israelites to focus on the day of the Lord as a time of blessing, when Israel's enemies would be vanquished. The Minor Prophets turn this around and confront Israel with the day of the Lord as one of judgment *for them.*

The Minor Prophets are nothing if not rich in evocative metaphor and poetry as they warn God's people of coming judgment. In Hosea Yahweh is

---

[33]Rolf Rendtorff, "Alas for the Day! The 'Day of the LORD' in the Book of the Twelve," in *God in the Fray: A Tribute to Walter Brueggemann*, ed. Tod Linafelt and Timothy K. Beal (Minneapolis: Fortress, 1998), 186-97; Rendtorff, "How to Read the Book of the Twelve as a Theological 'Unity,'" in *SBL Seminar Papers 1997* (Atlanta: Scholars Press, 1997), 423-25; James D. Nogalski, "The Day(s) of YHWH in the Book of the Twelve," in *Thematic Threads in the Book of the Twelve*, ed. Paul L. Redditt and Aaron Schart, BZAW 325 (Berlin: de Gruyter, 2003), 192-212; Paul R. House, "Endings as New Beginnings: Returning to the Lord, the Day of the Lord, and Renewal in the Book of the Twelve," in Redditt and Schart, *Thematic Threads*, 313-38.

portrayed above all as the aggrieved husband. In Hosea, Amos, and Joel we find the recurring motif of Yahweh as a lion about to pounce on his prey (Hos 5:14; Amos 1:2; 3:4; Joel 4:16 [3:16]). In Hosea 13:7-9 Yahweh is depicted as a lion, then as a leopard, and then as a bear, all poised to destroy Israel. In Hosea 5:14 we also find the image of Yahweh as a lion, and in Hosea 5:15 Zion has become his lair from which he emerges to hunt Ephraim down. Like the day of the Lord, the concept of Yahweh as a lion can also be used positively as in Hosea 11:10: "They will follow the Lord; he will roar like a lion. When he roars, his children will come trembling from the west." In Micah 5:8 the remnant of Jacob is itself depicted as a devouring lion.

Gracious and Compassionate

Judgment is *never* easy for God in the Minor Prophets. If we encounter his terrifying wrath in these books—as indeed we do—so too we encounter him as endlessly gracious and compassionate. The very existence of the Minor Prophets testifies to this since their ministries are designed to alert Israel to the danger it is in and thereby to keep open the possibility of repentance and grace. Yahweh's internal agony as he moves to judge his people is powerfully embodied in the person of Hosea. Jonah's journey is designed to form him into a prophet *like Yahweh*, and the characteristic of Yahweh that emerges in Jonah is not just Yahweh's wrath but his *compassion*, and remarkably his compassion for Nineveh.

Jonah 4:2 and Joel 2:13 intentionally recall the great depiction of God in Exodus 34:6-7. This depiction of Yahweh occurs *after* Israel's heinous sin in building a golden calf even while Moses was up on Mount Sinai with God. It would thus have spoken with exceptional power to those who heard the Minor Prophets, reminding them of Yahweh's holiness and his grace.

Within the Minor Prophets are many images of God as gracious and compassionate. In Hosea, despite Israel's waywardness he is the forgiving husband and lover who pledges to woo Israel again and to "speak tenderly to her" (Hos 2:14) so that Israel will again call Yahweh "my husband" (Hos 2:16). He is the God who "answers" (NIV translates "respond to") the skies and to the earth so that the earth in turn answers with great fertility (Hos 2:23-24 [2:21-22]). Yahweh is the great physician who heals (Hos 5:13–6:3; 7:1; 11:3). He comes like the winter rains (Hos 6:3). He is like a loving father with a little child (Hos 11:4). Again and again he is the one to whom Israel can turn (Hos 14:2; Joel 2:12-14; Mic 7:18). He loves Israel deeply

(Hos 9:10; 11:1). He is appalled by the oppression of the innocent and poor (Amos 5:12; 8:4-6). As the wise God, he provides ways of righteousness for his people (Hos 14:9). And so we could continue.

Sin and Repentance

A major task of the Minor Prophets is to persuade God's people of the need to repent. As we have seen, like good preachers, they employ multiple strategies in order to rouse Israel from its slumber amid the terrible storm that is on the horizon. Think of Amos's masterful sermon as he pronounces judgment on the surrounding countries . . . then on Judah . . . and then on the northern kingdom. Or of Zechariah's drone-like scroll that flies from the temple over the people of God (Zech 5:1-4), the curse that will enter the house of the thief and of anyone who swears falsely by the name of Yahweh, and those houses will be utterly destroyed. No one could accuse the Minor Prophets of a lack of imagination when it comes to sin.

Fundamentally, the Minor Prophets relate sin to Israel's breaking of her covenant with Yahweh. They call Israel to account on the basis of *her history with God*. As Claus Westermann rightly notes, there is one word that makes this connection clear, the word *forget*.[34] *Forgotten* is not a common word in the Minor Prophets, but in Hosea 8:14 we find the devastating statement, "Israel has *forgotten* their Maker and built palaces; Judah has fortified many towns. But I will send fire on their cities that will consume their fortresses" (NIV). In the case of the Minor Prophets, the more common word is *remember*, the correlate of *forget*. Malachi 4:4 could be a heading for the Minor Prophets as a whole: "*Remember* the law of my servant Moses, the decrees and laws I gave him at Horeb for all Israel" (NIV).

The imagery of the lawcourt we find in the Minor Prophets flows from Israel forgetting the covenant. Her covenant with Yahweh is a *legally* constituted and binding relationship, and blessings and curses follow obedience and disobedience, respectively. The classic passage in this regard is Micah 6. Micah 6 describes a courtroom scene in which Yahweh is lodging a charge against Israel (Mic 6:2). As Israel's covenant God, Yahweh claims her obedience in *all areas* of her life. The result is that "the various spheres of life of the people are all mentioned in the accusations of the prophets."[35] The religious sphere, the

---

[34]Claus Westermann, *Elements of Old Testament Theology*, trans. Douglas W. Scott (Atlanta: John Knox, 1982), 121.
[35]Westermann, *Elements of Old Testament Theology*, 129; see also 130-34.

political sphere, and the social sphere are all scrutinized. There is never any suggestion that Israel is not religious, but her form of religion is denounced.

Religion and its practices are never condemned as such (see Joel 2:15-17), but what is condemned is their corruption and radical misdirection. "The prophets considered the worship service to be just as necessary as the rest of the people thought. Their accusation served a cleansing, reflecting, and reawakening of worship."[36] Her defection to other gods is prominent in Hosea, but in the other Minor Prophets it is mainly the corruption of her worship that is in view. Amos 5:21-26 shows this clearly. In Haggai, Zechariah, and Malachi it is, of course, the restoration of Israel's worship that is focused on.

Westermann perceptively notes that prior to Amos's preaching, prophetic judgment was announced to individuals. "Now the prophets attributed responsibility to the people, something which was also highly significant politically."[37] In Westermann's view, a major break with Amos onward was a release from the conception of "sacral kingship," which saw the king as representing the people, so that now judgment is directed at the people as a whole. While it is true that apart from figures such as Amaziah (Amos 7:10-17) the Minor Prophets direct their attention to the people as a whole, the leaders do come in for particularly scathing attacks. We see this, for example, very clearly in Micah 3.

The consequence of persistent sin for Israel is *judgment*, and the Minor Prophets make this excruciatingly clear. Prophecy was not unique to Israel, but Westermann observes,

> Only in Israel has there been this succession of prophets from Amos to Jeremiah and Ezekiel, who through this long period of time have steadfastly announced the intervention of a god against his own people. The prophecy of judgment is the most noticeable religious phenomenon in a particular stage of Israel's history, the stage from the beginning to the end of the monarchy. . . . In a history of Israel's religion as well as in a history of the people and a history of Israel's literature, the prophecy of judgment occupies the most important position in this stage next to kingship.[38]

The primary judgment announced is that of exile, first of the northern kingdom by Assyria and then of the southern kingdom by Babylon. An

---

[36] Westermann, *Elements of Old Testament Theology*, 133-34.
[37] Westermann, *Elements of Old Testament Theology*, 128.
[38] Westermann, *Elements of Old Testament Theology*, 125-26.

intriguing phenomenon that Westermann indicates as accompanying this judgment prophecy is that now the prophet's life cannot be separated from his message. "The history of the prophets themselves as a story of suffering becomes an integral part of the history of prophecy."[39] The prophets share in the collateral damage brought on by Israel's disobedience.

In terms of judgment, an important motif is that of God's patience, which is longsuffering until eventually judgment falls. In the Book of the Twelve an intriguing way in which this is depicted is through a comparison of Jonah and Nahum. Jonah reveals God's patience with Nineveh; Nahum the judgment that finally falls.

Ethics

Growing up as Craig did in apartheid South Africa, he is still amazed how most white South African evangelicals and Reformed Christians managed to acquiesce—even support—racist apartheid with the Minor Prophets in their Bibles. Heath grew up in the American South and Midwest and remembers the tragic reality that various states worked through toward racial integration in schools and public life, while churches by and large remained some of the most segregated places in the country. Surely this is a reality that God's prophets would denounce. Ethically, the Minor Prophets are sheer dynamite. It is hard to imagine what courage it must have taken to preach as they did, and it is hard to imagine what would happen in our churches if we really recovered these books for today.

As we retrieve the Minor Prophets, we will need to take note of the following characteristics of their ethics. First, we must note that the ethic of the Minor Prophets is utterly *comprehensive*. There is no area of Israel's life to which Yahweh does not lay claim. Second, we must note therefore that the ethic embodied in the Minor Prophets *resists any kind of dualism*. In contemporary language, it is never a question of worship and evangelism *or* social justice. Worship and life—cultus and covenant—are held integrally together. Yahweh, of course, is to be their first priority, as is his worship, but from this fundamental allegiance flows a lifestyle in which the people are called to embody his character in every area of their national life.

Third, we must embrace the concern for societal and international justice as a major theme of the Minor Prophets. We find in the Minor Prophets an incipient ethic for international relations. The great empires overshadow the

---

[39]Westermann, *Elements of Old Testament Theology*, 129; see also Hos 6:5.

Minor Prophets, but in places such as Amos 1–2 we also find a consideration of relations between Israel and its neighbors. This is an area that is starting to receive attention in ancient Near Eastern studies, and the contribution of the Minor Prophets should be noted.[40] The Minor Prophets simply will not let us explore such relationships apart from Yahweh, making the religious dimension central. As noted in our chapter on Amos, although the nations are not condemned for abandoning Yahweh, as is Israel, Israel's covenantal ethic mirrors Yahweh's order for his creation so that all nations are accountable to his order for human life.

Spirituality

As will be clear from our discussion thus far, the Minor Prophets have much to teach us about true worship. In the process they also give us important insights into a deep spirituality. Habakkuk is a major resource for living faithfully amid judgment. Jonah is about spiritual formation to become worthy of one's calling as a prophet. Hosea's suffering alerts us to what may be involved in becoming like Yahweh and in sharing in the *missio Dei*. It is not by chance that Jonah sits in the middle of the Minor Prophets as a narrative of formation. If we ask how these prophets were able to exercise such extraordinary ministries, the answer is Jonah: formation. Comparably, in the Sermon on the Mount (Mt 5–7), the Lord's Prayer sits right in the center of Jesus' ethical teaching.

Spirituality has much to say about *silence*, and this is a motif that recurs in the Minor Prophets. Habakkuk 2:20 calls the whole earth to be still before Yahweh. Similarly, Zephaniah 1:7 exhorts its hearers to "Be silent before the Sovereign Lord." Zechariah 2:17 [2:13] says, "Be still before Yahweh, all humankind, because he has roused himself from his dwelling." Admittedly, all these verses relate to coming judgment, but their illocutionary effect on the hearers and readers is to stop, come to stillness, and attend contemplatively to Yahweh. This move is utterly central to spirituality.

Eschatology

> For the earth will be filled with the knowledge of the
> glory of the Lord as the waters cover the sea.
> Habakkuk 2:14

---

[40]See, e.g., Raymond Cohen and Raymond Westbrook, eds., *Amarna Diplomacy: The Beginnings of International Relations* (Baltimore: Johns Hopkins University Press, 2000).

Jonah ends, as it were, with a question mark. Will Jonah, after all that he has gone through, come around to God's way of thinking, or will he persist in his anger and stubbornness? Jonah represents Israel, and if his descent to death in the big fish represents the death of exile, then Jonah raises in the most poignant fashion the question of Israel's future. The Minor Prophets have much to say about Israel and the future.

It will be obvious from our discussion above that the Minor Prophets brought the word of the living God to a particular people in a particular context; that is, *forthtelling* was the major part of their ministries. "The prophets appeared because Israel had threatened its own existence by turning away from its God."[41] However, God's very concern with Israel's death-wish alerts us to his refusal to allow his purposes to run into the sand. As Westermann notes, the prophets can only be understood between *a before* and *an after*, and they are the crucial hinge between the two. Amid the chaos and desolation of exile, they bring Yahweh into the picture in no uncertain terms and thereby open up a future beyond exile and judgment. As Westermann writes,

> Just as *the prophets were the messengers of God's judgment*, so also they are the messengers of the saving, healing, forgiving God who brings about a turn of events. God's judgment and God's compassion are in the Old Testament the elements of a history; one cannot bring them together into a static relationship. That is why we encounter God's judgment and his compassion in the words of the prophets in an active, changing relationship which never comes to rest.[42]

It is no easy task to tease apart the different strands in the salvation elements in the Minor Prophets. Westermann rightly says, "*The history of salvation prophecy* encompasses an extremely varied and diverse complex which until now has not been adequately disclosed."[43] Multiple elements blend into one another as the Minor Prophets assure their hearers of a future to come.

One strand is an assurance that exile will not be the end of Israel and that a remnant at least will return from exile. Indeed, the salvation prophecies in the Minor Prophets are all what J. H. Bavinck calls "Israel-centric," focused on the restoration of Israel and of Zion in particular.[44] A second strand is

---

[41] Westermann, *Elements of Old Testament Theology*, 126.
[42] Westermann, *Elements of Old Testament Theology*, 141.
[43] Westermann, *Elements of Old Testament Theology*, 143.
[44] J. H. Bavinck, *Introduction to the Science*, 24.

that of the emergence of a purified Israel who will truly be the people of God. This one reason why the theme of judgment never entirely disappears even amid the salvation oracles. A third strand is the judgment of the nations, which crops up repeatedly in the salvation prophecies. A fourth strand is that "it is particularly characteristic of the salvation portrayals that the transformed future reality transcends the present reality in various ways."[45] Bavinck rightly notes in this respect,

> One can therefore hardly speak of the promise of missions within the framework of the Old Testament. It is more glorious than that. The nations shall of themselves journey to Israel's God, as though drawn by a magnet.... That which shall make the missionary calling powerful and effective is not so much the force of the call itself, but the fact that God shall have glorified Israel.[46]

This is Israel-centric, but far more than that, it is extraordinarily comprehensive and thoroughly theocentric. As Bavinck observes, "The event of salvation shall thus indeed be fulfilled in an *Israel-centric* fashion, but in its depths, it is *theocentric*, it concerns God and his name and his glory."[47]

What needs to be noted is how the immediate future and the eschatological future are blended together so that it is nigh impossible to sort out the different strands. This is why such prophecy is often compared to a range of mountains that, when viewed from afar, look as though they are all together, and only as one approaches them do the different ranges and the space between them come into view.

A fifth strand is the emergent messianic predictions. We have attended to these in the chapters on individual books. Suffice it here to note how the Davidic kingship imagery is regularly taken up and depicted in terms of a future ruler who is intimately related to the triumph of the kingdom of God. In the following chapter we will examine the relationship between the Minor Prophets and Jesus, and the so-called messianic prophecies will be the focus of our attention. Here it should be noted that in the Minor Prophets we also find an astonishing Spirit theology, which is closely connected with the last days. This is a particular feature of Joel but also present in Haggai 2:5; Zechariah 4:6; 6; 12:10.

---

[45]Westermann, *Elements of Old Testament Theology*, 144.
[46]Bavinck, *Introduction to the Science*, 22. The centripetal or what we call the "plausibility" motif of OT mission remains alive in the NT and needs to be recovered.
[47]Bavinck, *Introduction to the Science*, 24.

A sixth strand is that of the end of history and the ushering in of a new creation under God's reign. Westermann refers to this as the apocalyptic element and notes that it is this element that makes a conception of world history possible.[48] We see this, for example, in Zechariah 14:5-11.

It is typical of such apocalyptic vision that catastrophic imagery is used, hence our description of such visions as new-creation ones. However, there is no indication that the creation will be destroyed. Rather, all evil and opposition to Yahweh will be eradicated. The result will be the arrival of the kingdom of God: "The LORD will be king over the whole earth. On that day there will be one LORD, and his name the only name."

Recommended Reading

Bartholomew, Craig G. *The Old Testament and God*. Old Testament Origins and the Question of God 1. Grand Rapids, MI: Baker Academic, 2022. Pages 443-51.

Bavinck, J. H. *An Introduction to the Science of Missions*. Translated by David H. Freeman. Phillipsburg, NJ: Presbyterian and Reformed, 1960.

Dumbrell, William J. *Covenant and Creation: An Old Testament Covenantal Theology*. 2nd ed. Milton Keynes, UK: Paternoster, 2013.

Hess, Richard S., and Gordon J. Wenham, eds. *Zion: City of Our God*. Grand Rapids, MI: Eerdmans, 1999.

Thomas, Heath A. "Zion." In *Dictionary of the Old Testament Prophets*, ed. Mark J. Boda and J. Gordon McConville, 907-14. Downers Grove, IL: IVP Academic, 2012.*

Recommended reading marked with a "" indicates introductory works.*

---

[48] Westermann, *Elements of Old Testament Theology*, 151.

21

The Minor Prophets and Jesus

> *Jesus was seen as, and saw himself as, a prophet; . . .*
> *a prophet like the prophets of old, coming to Israel with*
> *a word from her covenant god, warning her of the imminent*
> *and fearful consequences of the direction she was travelling,*
> *urging and summoning her to a new and different way.*
>
> N. T. WRIGHT, *JESUS AND THE VICTORY OF GOD*

IF WE THINK OF THE OLD TESTAMENT as a series of streams emerging out of Eden, then it is important to realize that they *all* converge in Jesus of Nazareth. Matthew, who refers to the Minor Prophets more than the other Gospels, rightly makes much of Jesus as the *fulfillment* of the Old Testament. Closely related to the motif of fulfillment is that of eschatology. Jesus not only fulfills the Old Testament but is the climax of history, the pivot around which the whole of creation revolves. One cannot understand Jesus without the Old Testament, but the Christ event is also an explosion of good news, new and unexpected. Ben Witherington perceptively notes,

> Jesus lived at a time when the rivers of the prophetic, apocalyptic, and sapiential traditions had already flowed together; indeed, apocalyptic was itself a hybrid of wisdom and prophetic materials. It is not surprising that Jesus himself reflected this situation in his words and deeds and in his self-understanding as a messianic prophet, a northern prophet, an apocalyptic eschatological sage, a Son of Man.[1]

---

[1] Ben Witherington III, *Jesus the Seer: The Progress of Prophecy* (Minneapolis: Fortress, 2014), 191.

Thus, it is inadequate to attend only to those places where the Minor Prophets are explicitly quoted or alluded to in the Gospels as we attend to the Minor Prophets and Jesus. Such quotes provide important nodal points, as we will see below. However, especially since the work of C. H. Dodd, we are aware that quotations and citations in the New Testament generally take the context from which they were quoted seriously. Thus, the quotes, the citations, the allusions, and intertextuality push us back into the Minor Prophets as a whole, then forward again to Jesus, then back again into the Minor Prophets, and so on and so forth. In the process we need to have the whole of the Minor Prophets before us lest we miss many of the multifaceted ways in which Jesus fulfills them. An example of this is the use of Amos in the Gospels. Amos is quoted in Acts but not in the Gospels, and yet, as the quote from N. T. Wright in the epigraph indicates, Amos may have had a formative influence on how Jesus perceived his ministry.

Indeed, we could take the previous chapter and explore how every theme we discussed is developed in the Gospels in relationship to Jesus. The motif of the *God who speaks* is intensified beyond our imagination in the Gospels. As John in particular alerts us, Jesus is the Word of God incarnate. Jesus is the Word in a way that we could never have imagined from the Minor Prophets alone. Jesus is portrayed as prophet, priest, king, and wise man in the Gospels, but many argue that preeminently he is portrayed as *prophet*, the one who in word and life brings the climactic message of God to us. Covenant is a major New Testament theme, and not least in the Gospels. Matthew presents Jesus in his genealogy as son of Abraham and son of David, alerting us to Jesus as the fulfillment of the Abrahamic and Davidic covenants. A significant motif in the Gospels is that of Jesus as a second Moses, evoking Jesus as the fulfillment of the Sinai covenant. Jerusalem, and thus Zion, is central to all the Gospels. Covenant also features, of course, in the Last Supper. The Gospels are awash with new-creation motifs and are also full of teaching about judgment, and, of course, grace upon grace. Ethical teaching abounds, as does Jesus' practice of spirituality, the suffering prophet par excellence.[2]

Perhaps most significantly is the centrality of eschatology in the Gospels. If in the Minor Prophets the distant mountains appear together,

---

[2]See Heath A. Thomas, "Hearing the Minor Prophets: The Book of the Twelve and God's Address," In *Hearing the Old Testament: Listening for God's Address*, ed. Craig G. Bartholomew and David J. H. Beldman (Grand Rapids, MI: Eerdmans, 2012), 378-79.

in the Gospels they are prised apart into the coming of the kingdom in Jesus and its final consummation when he returns. We need to be conscious of this shift as we explore the relationship between the Minor Prophets and Jesus.

Now, of course, all of these themes are also found in the other parts of the Old Testament, so that often we cannot pinpoint the Minor Prophets as *the* source for fulfillment in the Gospels. This makes the identification of precise relationships far harder, but it simultaneously opens up a richer stream of theology finding its fulfillment in Jesus. With intertextuality one sometimes has to sacrifice certainty for overarching lines of fulfillment, a price that is not only worth paying but needs to be paid.

Our approach in this chapter will be as follows. We will begin, as is traditional, with quotes and allusions to the Minor Prophets in the Gospels and then back in from there to the broader theology of the Minor Prophets and how they are fulfilled in Jesus. The Minor Prophets, and Zechariah in particular, play an important part in all the Gospels, but especially so in Matthew.[3] We will therefore use Matthew as our framework and draw in passages from the other Gospels as appropriate.

Matthew and the Minor Prophets

Matthew cites the Minor Prophets ten times, far more than any of the other Gospels.[4] Three of these are among Matthew's formula quotations, in which he specifically introduces them (Mt 2:15; 21:5; 27:9-10); seven are spoken by characters in the Gospel, six by Jesus (Mt 9:13; 10:35-36; 11:10; 12:7, 40; 26:31) and one by the chief priests and scribes (Mt 2:6). Two occur within the birth narrative (Mt 2:6, 15), two within the passion narrative (Mt 26:31; 27:9-10); five occur in the middle of the Gospel, mainly in the context of controversy and resistance (Mt 9:13; 10:35-36; 11:10; 12:7, 40); one appears in the lead-up to the passion (Mt 21:5).

Of these citations, half are found in other Gospels (Mt 10:35-36; 11:10; 12:40; 21:5; 26:3) and half only in Matthew. Matthew's ten citations are drawn from Hosea, Jonah, Micah, Zechariah, and Malachi. These ten account for

---

[3]See, e.g., Charlene McAfee Moss, *The Zechariah Tradition and the Gospel of Matthew* (Berlin: de Gruyter, 2008); Christopher Tuckett, ed., *The Book of Zechariah and Its Influence* (New York: Routledge, 2003).

[4]For the data that follows see Clay Alan Ham, "The Minor Prophets in Matthew's Gospel," in *The Minor Prophets in the New Testament*, ed. Maarten J. J. Menken and Steve Moyise, LNTS 377 (London: T&T Clark, 2009), 56.

one-fifth of Matthew's citations from the Old Testament, indicating the Minor Prophets' importance for him in telling the story of Jesus.

On Jesus' lips. To any disciple the question "What did Jesus say?" is of fundamental importance. We will begin our examination of the references to the Minor Prophets in the Gospels by examining those sayings that occur on the lips of Jesus.

Hosea 6:6 in Matthew 9:13; 12:7: Diagnosing the problem. It is fascinating to note that six of Matthew's ten citations of the Minor Prophets are found on the lips of Jesus. Also intriguing is that the first one occurs immediately after Jesus' call to Matthew, the tax collector, to follow him, that is, to become his disciple. Jesus has dinner with many tax collectors and sinners at Matthew's house, causing the Pharisees to ask his disciples, "Why does your teacher eat with tax collectors and sinners?" In his reply Jesus makes the ironic point that it is not the healthy but the sick who need a doctor, and then he says, quoting Hosea 6:6, "But go and learn what this means; 'I desire mercy, not sacrifice.' For I have not come to call the righteous but sinners" (NIV).

Jesus also quotes Hosea 6:6 in Matthew 12:7 in relation to controversy about his disciples eating heads of grain in the grain fields on the Sabbath. In reply Jesus refers to what David and his companions did (1 Sam 21:2-7 [21:1-6]) and to what the priests do in the temple (Num 28:9-10) and then says: "I tell you that something greater than the temple is here. If you had known what these words mean, 'I desire mercy, not sacrifice,' you would not have condemned the innocent. For the Son of Man is Lord of the Sabbath."

Both passages are triple-tradition texts, but neither Mark nor Luke includes Hosea 6:6. In Matthew 9:13 Jesus introduces the quote from Hosea 6:6 with, "But go and learn what this means," and in Matthew 12:7 with, "If you had known what these words mean." Hosea 6:6 is the only Old Testament quotation repeated in Matthew.

If Matthew the tax collector and disciple of Jesus is the author of Matthew's Gospel, and if we take the historicity of the Jesus sayings seriously, then Matthew 9 gives us an important insight into the origin of drawing on the Minor Prophets in order to understand Jesus. This tradition stems directly from Jesus, and one can well understand how Matthew *and* the Pharisees would be driven back to Hosea and to the Minor Prophets in order to understand what Jesus was getting at in his quote from Hosea 6:6. In fact, with the way he introduces the quote in Matthew 9:13 and Matthew 12:7, Jesus literally pushes his hearers to go and reflect on Hosea and what is going on in Hosea 6. For any of his hearers, and especially the Pharisees, going back to Hosea 6 would generate a real shock.

Hosea 6:6 occurs in the section Hosea 6:4-10. In this section Israel and Judah are indicted because their love for Yahweh is so transient (Hos 6:4). The covenant is being broken; priests plan and execute murder; and Israel is given to prostitution. The situation could hardly be worse. In Hosea 6:6 *ḥesed* ("mercy") and "knowledge of God" are in parallel, indicating what God desires above sacrifice.[5] As noted above, Yahweh is not against sacrifice but desires [*ḥāpaṣtî*] cultic service to be a ritual expression of lives characterized by *ḥesed* and knowledge of him. Jesus' point, as with Hosea, is that ritual practices without a lived faith are empty and vacuous.

Jesus' quotation of Hosea 6:6 and his statement that he has come for the sick and not the healthy are doubly ironic. Hosea 6:6 raises the question of the spiritual health of Israel and thus of the Pharisees themselves. Hosea 6:6 also alerts us to the sickness of Israel that brought about God's judgment, and so the question is raised of whether the Pharisees are indeed healthy while the sinners and tax collectors are sick. As Michael Shepherd comments, "The point of course is not that the Pharisees are righteous but that they are righteous in their own eyes. They too are sinners, but they have not recognized this fact in the way that some of the tax collectors and 'sinners' have about themselves."[6]

Yahweh as the one who heals is a central motif in the Minor Prophets, and it could well inform Jesus' rhetoric in Matthew 9. What the Pharisees need to grasp is that Jesus is not fraternizing with sinners in order to confirm them in their sinfulness but in order to bring them to repentance so that their lives might manifest *ḥesed*.

Jesus' use of Hosea 6:6 thus illumines his ministry on a number of levels:

- Judgment and the people of Israel: the resistance of the Pharisees is implicitly related to Israel's resistance to Yahweh's words through Hosea.
- His ministry is in continuity with the prophetic tradition.
- His view of healthy religion: he attends to those who acknowledge their sickness and calls them to be his disciples. Indeed, at the end of Matthew 9:9-13 Jesus provides his hearers with a summary statement

---

[5] "Knowledge of God" is a better translation of the Hebrew than NIV's "acknowledgment of God."
[6] Michael B. Shepherd, *The Twelve Prophets in the New Testament*, Studies in Biblical Literature 140 (New York: Peter Lang, 2011), 14.

of his mission: "For I have not come to call the righteous, but sinners." His quote from Hosea 6:6 provides an important and ironic clue as to what the righteous and sinners look like.

- What is implicit in Matthew 9 is made explicit in Matthew 12, namely, *the identity of Jesus*. In Matthew 9 Jesus touches the underlying unease of the Pharisees; namely, they did not know what to make of Jesus and would have found his statement "I have not come to call the righteous, but sinners" disturbing, to say the least, because of the implicit authority involved. In Matthew 12 the question of Jesus' identity is heightened by Jesus' statement, "I tell you that something greater than the temple is here" (Mt 12:6 NIV). Sacrifice is relativized since one greater than the temple is present. Who could be greater than the temple, other than Yahweh? Implicitly Jesus associates himself with Yahweh, as he does more explicitly in Matthew 12:8, "For the Son of Man is Lord of the Sabbath" (NIV).

- In terms of his identity, Jesus feels free to critique the Jewish oral tradition. Plucking grain on the Sabbath was forbidden, not in the Old Testament but in the oral law (Mishnah Shabbat 7:2).

Jesus thus uses Hosea 6:6 twice to diagnose the problem with the Israel of his day.[7] In this we see him as firmly and consciously in line with the Minor Prophets and especially Hosea, Joel, Amos, Jonah, and Micah. As Wright notes,

> That which was wrong with the rest of the world was wrong with Israel, too. "Evil" could not be located conveniently beyond Israel's borders, in the pagan hordes. It has taken up residence within the chosen people. The battle against evil—the correct analysis of the problem, and the correct answer to it—was therefore of a different order from that imagined by his contemporaries.[8]

Jesus uses Hosea 6:6 to push his hearers toward an accurate diagnosis of the current situation, and in the process he invites them to wrestle with the nature of his identity. The diagnosis is much the same as that of Hosea in his day, but the day is different; indeed, it is *the* day of which the prophets spoke.

Micah 7:6 in Matthew 10:35-36: Mission, division, and a new family. Matthew 10 is the second of the five discourses of Jesus in Matthew's Gospel. The chapter deals with Jesus' instruction to the Twelve as he sends them out

---

[7]See Wright, *Jesus and the Victory of God*, 446-63, a section titled "What's Wrong?"
[8]Wright, *Jesus and the Victory of God*, 446-47.

on a mission to the "lost sheep of Israel" and to proclaim the coming near of the kingdom in word and deed (Mt 10:7). His teaching makes it clear that they will meet with resistance and polarized responses. Toward the end of the discourse Jesus quotes Micah 7:6:

> For a son dishonors his father,
> > a daughter rises up against her mother,
> > a daughter-in-law against her mother-in-law—
> > > a man's enemies are the members of his own household.

Micah 7 laments the deterioration of the land and social disintegration. An example of the latter is the familial breakdown of Micah 7:6. On Jesus' lips the quote is used to indicate the *effect* his ministry and life will have on those who hear his message. Part of a disciple's taking up of one's cross will be living with the familial and social divisions that following Jesus causes. In Micah 6 the familial breakdown is a symptom of Israel's disease; in Matthew 10 such divisions will be *caused* by differing responses to the message of the kingdom. The condition of Israel remains in the picture, but in the new situation of Jesus' coming the discord is aggravated by those who receive the message and those who reject it.

As Wright notes, such sayings by Jesus would have been shocking in first-century Palestine, in which the family was a major symbol of Jewish identity. In relation to Jesus' related command to "leave the dead to bury their dead" Wright says, "The only explanation for Jesus' astonishing command is that he envisaged loyalty to himself and his kingdom-movement as creating an alternative family. The same impression is given very strongly by Jesus' quotation of Micah 7.5-6, and the comment which follows."[9] Although the illocutionary force of Jesus' use of Micah 7:6 is different from that in its original context, the context in Micah 6 alerts us to the judgment overtones in Jesus' teaching, overtones that are intensified amid the eschatological urgency of the times.

Malachi 3:1 in Matthew 11:10:[10] *Jesus is the Messiah.* The quote in Matthew 11:10 is a conflation of Malachi 3:1 and Exodus 23:20. In context, John the Baptist, who is in prison, sends his disciples to ask Jesus whether he is truly the one who is to come. Because of the very real opposition to him, Jesus cannot come out

---

[9]Wright, *Jesus and the Victory of God*, 401.
[10]See Mal 3:1 and Ex 23:20 in Mk 1:2b; Mal 3:22-23 LXX in Mk 9:11-13; Mal 3:1 and Ex 23:20 in Lk 7:24-30.

and simply say, "Yes, I am the Messiah." Instead he cryptically refers to Isaiah's prophecies about the Messiah as being fulfilled and then speaks to the crowd about *the identity of John*. He asks them what they went out into the wilderness to see—a reed swayed by the wind? As his chosen symbol, Herod had an image of a Galilean reed embossed on his coins. Thus, Jesus is asking the crowd, as it were, Were you looking for another Herod-like king?[11] Surely not, and Jesus suggests they went out to see *a prophet* and *more than a prophet*. They went out to see the one about whom it is written, "I will send my messenger ahead of you, who will prepare your way before you."

Malachi 3:1 is closely related to Malachi 3:23 [4:5], which identifies the messenger as Elijah. Jesus makes the same connection in Matthew 11:14. Jesus' discussion of John the Baptist is an indirect way of discussing his own identity. As Wright says, "Well then: if John was the last of the preparatory prophets, where are we now? . . . If John is Elijah, this means, without question, that Jesus is the Messiah. The whole discussion of John turns out to be a veiled discussion of Jesus himself."[12]

This is confirmed by the changes Jesus makes in his quotation of Malachi. Jesus changes "me" in the Hebrew to "your" and "you" in the second line, thus adding a third person—himself—into the picture and making himself the object of this preparation, so that the coming of Jesus is nothing less than the coming of Yahweh.[13]

Jonah 2:1 [1:17] in Matthew 12:40: Judgment on the wrong sort of kingdom. Jesus' reference to Jonah as a sign for this "wicked and adulterous generation" follows on from his healing a demon-possessed man (Mt 12:22-23). This raises the question of the satanic, and the Pharisees suggest that it is only by Beelzebul that Jesus drives out demons. Jesus responds (Mt 12:25-37), and then, remarkably, some of the Pharisees request a sign, presumably in order to substantiate Jesus' power. Jesus replies with his reference to Jonah as the only sign they will be given.

There is more than one dimension to the analogy between Jonah and Jesus.[14] In Matthew 12:40 the analogy is between Jonah's three days in the belly of the big fish and the Son of Man's three days in the heart of the earth.[15]

---

[11]Wright, *Jesus and the Victory of God*, 496.
[12]Wright, *Jesus and the Victory of God*, 496.
[13]In the Hebrew of Mal 3:1 there is no pronominal adjective before "way."
[14]The parallel pericope in Lk 11:29-32 speaks of the sign of Jonah but makes no reference to the three days and nights in the fish.
[15]This analogy is not mentioned in the parallel passages in Mark and Luke.

In Matthew 12:41 the analogy is between Jonah's preaching of imminent judgment and Jesus' predicting imminent judgment on Israel. The Ninevites repented; Jesus' opponents do not, and "now something greater than Jonah is here" (Mt 12:41).

As Wright notes, Jesus' opponents opt for precisely the wrong sort of kingdom, which, by implication, is that of Satan. The reference to Jonah associates Jesus' opponents with the Ninevites, in danger of imminent judgment because of their godlessness.[16] "What then must Jesus have thought was going on? . . . The battle he himself had to fight was with the satan; the satan had made its home in Israel, and in her cherished national institutions and aspirations."[17] Shepherd comments, "The sign of Jonah is thus identical to the message of the text of Jonah, an indictment against Israelite (and later Jewish) rejection of God's plan in the midst of Gentile faith and inclusion."[18] Jesus embodies the true kingdom, casting out evil and bringing healing. The entire episode and teaching depends, of course, on the identity of Jesus and the nature of the true kingdom of God.

Zechariah 13:7 in Matthew 26:31:[19] *The true shepherd.* Zechariah 13:7 is quoted on Jesus' lips in Matthew 26:31 and Mark 14:27. In Zechariah 13, the section from which Jesus quotes is preceded by a section in which Yahweh says he will cut off the names of the idols, the false prophets, and the spirit of impurity from the land "in that day" (Zech 13:2-6). Then Yahweh commands the sword, "Awake, sword, against my shepherd, against the man who is close to me! . . . Strike the shepherd, and the sheep will be scattered, and I will turn my hand against the little ones" (Zech 13:7 NIV). The text indicates that two-thirds will perish (Zech 13:8), but the remaining third will be refined in the fire to be the true covenant people of God (Zech 13:9).

Zechariah 13:2-9 thus deals with the purification of religion and the purification of leadership. The "shepherd" would be a false leader: "False leaders must be dealt with if the people are to be restored to a full relationship with God."[20] Jesus regularly uses the imagery of shepherds and sheep for his ministry, but what is striking here is how Jesus uses this quote

---

[16]Wright (*Jesus and the Victory of God*, 166) suggests that a similar sign will validate Jesus' message too; after forty years (see forty days in Jonah), Jerusalem will be destroyed.
[17]Wright, *Jesus and the Victory of God*, 461; see 459-61.
[18]Shepherd, *Twelve Prophets*, 13.
[19]See Mk 14:27. On the historicity of this statement by Jesus see Wright, *Jesus and the Victory of God*, 533-34.
[20]Peter C. Craigie, *Twelve Prophets*, The Daily Study Bible OT (Philadelphia: Westminster, 1985), 2:217.

from Zechariah *to predict his passion*. He alters the quoted text to "I will strike . . ." In Zechariah 13 the false shepherd is removed, but here *Jesus, the true shepherd*, will be dealt a deadly blow and the disciples scattered. This is a powerful image of Jesus taking on himself the punishment Zechariah indicated would be leveled against Israel (see Mk 10:45). After he is risen, he will shepherd his sheep and go ahead of them to Galilee (Mt 26:31).

Hosea 10:8 and Luke 23:30. Hosea 10 is a declaration of coming judgment against Israel. The effect of this judgment will be so traumatic that the people "will say to the mountains, 'Cover us!' and to the hills, 'Fall on us!'" (Hosea 10:8 NIV). In Luke's account of Jesus' crucifixion, as Jesus is led away to be crucified many women mourn and wail for him. Jesus turns to them and warns the "Daughters of Jerusalem" not to weep for him but for themselves and their children, for terrible times are coming in which the barren woman will count herself *blessed*, and then Jesus quotes Hosea 10:8.

Wright asks what caused Jesus to express such a terrible beatitude as this at such a time of his imminent crucifixion. It is one final warning of the cost to Israel of rejecting "the things that make for peace" (Lk 19:42). Wright notes that the context of Hosea 10 is important for understanding Jesus' saying:

> It is all there: the vine that has become proud and gone to ruin, the judgment on the sanctuary, the rejection of YHWH and of the king, the terrible judgment which will result from trusting in military power, the dire warning to the mothers and the children—and, finally, the death of the king. The application to Jesus' contemporaries fits at every point with the picture we have drawn overall. The judgment of which Jesus was warning the women of Jerusalem was the devastation which would result from the city's rejection of him as the true king, and his message as the true way of peace. His own death at the hands of the Romans was the clearest sign of the fate in store for the nation that had rejected him.[21]

As Wright says, this also enables us to make sense of Jesus' final cryptic saying: "For if people do these things when the tree is green, what will happen when it is dry?" (Lk 23:31). "He was the green tree, they the dry."[22]

It is helpful to pause and reflect on what insights we gain from the use of the Minor Prophets on Jesus' lips alone:

---

[21]Wright, *Jesus and the Victory of God*, 569.
[22]Wright, *Jesus and the Victory of God*, 569.

- With his emphasis on *ḥesed*, Jesus positions himself as the true prophet pronouncing judgment on Israel. His way is that of the true Israel, of true *covenant loyalty*, and implicitly he positions himself as Yahweh.
- With his emphasis on the message of the kingdom causing family divisions, he alerts us to the emergence of a new family that the kingdom message will create.
- Through his discussion of John the Baptist, he reveals himself as the Messiah; with John as Elijah, the day of Yahweh has come, and Jesus is that Lord.
- Through his use of Jonah 2 and Hosea 10, Jesus pronounces judgment on the Israel of his day and points toward the nature of the true kingdom of God, one in which the real problem of evil is being dealt with.
- Through his adaptation of the shepherd text from Zechariah, Jesus presents himself as the true shepherd (king) who takes on himself the punishment pronounced on Israel.

Just by focusing on these texts we get a rich insight into how Jesus is retelling the story of Israel with himself as its fulfillment. What is striking is how strong the theme of judgment is and the remarkable turning of that judgment against Jesus himself. Assuming, as we do, that this material comes from Jesus himself, it is not hard to see how the writers of the Gospels, and Matthew in particular, would search the Minor Prophets for further clues to the Christ event.

Fulfillment of the Minor Prophets in Matthew. Matthew's fulfillment formula—"all this took place to fulfill"—occurs ten or eleven times (Mt 1:22; 2:15, 17, 23; 4:14; 8:17; 12:17; 13:35; 21:4; 27:9, and probably 2:5). R. T. France writes that these fulfillment quotations (apart from Mt 2:5-6) "are editorial comments on the events being narrated. Some of them draw on well-known prophetic texts, whose fulfillment in the coming of Jesus is widely recognized among Christians (Mic 5:1[2]; Isa 9:1-2; 42:1-4; 53:4; Zech 9:9), but others would not have been on a list of 'obvious' messianic prooftexts."[23] Of these two are from the Minor Prophets: Hosea 11:1 and Zechariah 11:13.

"Fulfillment" for Matthew operates at multiple levels, and not least the level of the overarching story of Israel rather than simply prophetic

---

[23]R. T. France, *The Gospel of Matthew*, New International Commentary on the New Testament (Grand Rapids, MI: Eerdmans, 2007), 12.

predictions. Matthew, we might say, engages in a typological understanding of the Old Testament in relationship to Jesus, an approach informed by what he had learned *from Jesus himself.* A feature of Matthew's use of the Old Testament that has attracted attention is the Old Testament text he used. His quotes often do not "correspond to the LXX text, which is the basis of most of his (and the other NT writers') quotations."[24] On occasion he appears to provide an independent translation of the Hebrew, but his translation does not always fit with Hebrew texts we are familiar with. His textual freedom "suggests that Matthew was sometimes willing to modify the wording of the text" to make clear how it was fulfilled in Jesus.[25] Sometimes two or more Old Testament texts are conflated into one quote, as in Matthew 2:6; 21:5 and most elaborately in Matthew 27:9-10 in the Zechariah/Jeremiah quote.

Five of Matthew's fulfillment quotations occur in Matthew 1:18–2:23. Of these five, two are from the Minor Prophets, namely, Micah 5:1 [5:2] in Matthew 2:6, and Hosea 11:1 in Matthew 2:15. As we come to this section in Matthew, it is important to remember that it is preceded by the genealogy of Matthew 1:1-17, which clearly portrays Jesus as the son of Abraham, the son of David. The messianic manifesto of Matthew 1:18–2:23 is designed to show from the start that Jesus truly is the Messiah.

Micah 5:1 [5:2] in Matthew 2:6: The Messiah of lowly origins. Matthew flags his concerns clearly in the birth narratives of Jesus in Matthew 1:18: "This is how the birth of *Jesus the Messiah* came about" (NIV). In Matthew 1:18–2:23 the first fulfillment citation is in Matthew 1:22. The quote of Micah 5:1 [5:2] in Matthew 2:6 is the first of four citations in Matthew 2. The wording of Matthew's quote differs from the LXX and MT.

Micah 5:1 [5:2] occurs in the section Micah 4:14–5:5 [5:1-6]. In this section there is a move from present distress to future salvation. Judah is called on to form a troop to defend herself, most probably during Sennacherib's siege of Jerusalem.[26] *Troop* rather than *army* indicates her smallness. The salvation oracle contrasts Bethlehem's role with the present distress. Bethlehem is small and insignificant in terms of leadership and military might, but from her will emerge a ruler over Israel who will unite Israel (Mic 5:1 [5:2]), shepherd his flock in the strength of Yahweh (Mic 5:3 [5:4]), become great to the ends of the earth (Mic 5:3 [5:4]), and be the one of peace

---

[24]France, *Gospel of Matthew*, 13.
[25]France, *Gospel of Matthew*, 13.
[26]Bruce K. Waltke, *A Commentary on Micah* (Grand Rapids, MI: Eerdmans, 2007), 296.

(Mic 5:4 [5:5]). It is likely that Micah has in mind David at this point, a king whose father was Jesse *of Bethlehem* (1 Sam 16:1).

Micah 5:1 [5:2] is a well-recognized messianic prophecy. However, the last eight words of Matthew's quotation—"for out of you will come a ruler who will shepherd my people Israel"—more directly "echo . . . 2 Samuel 5:2: 'a leader' (*hēgoumenon*) is the term in 2 Samuel 5:2 [in the LXX] for David's role, as against 'ruler' in Mic 5:1[2], and 'who will be the shepherd of my people Israel' echoes God's call to David in 2 Sam 5:2," as France writes.[27] The latter phrase also reflects the language of Micah 5:3 [5:4], "He will stand and shepherd his flock in the strength of the Lord."

We have already noted that Micah had David in view in his oracle, and the links between Micah 5:1 [5:2] and 2 Samuel 5:2 in Matthew 2:6 confirm this connection. 2 Samuel 5:2 speaks of God's original call of David, and Micah 5:1 [5:2] describes the role of the coming Davidic king. France rightly notes, "Matthew's combined quotation of these two passages draws out the integral connection between them more effectively than a more pedantic exegetical commentary."[28]

Matthew makes further alterations to Micah 5:1 [5:2]. He changes the name "Bethlehem Ephrathah" to the more geographically specific "Bethlehem, in the land of Judah." The change is not needed to distinguish this Bethlehem from the other in Galilee; instead, it is to emphasize Jesus' origins in Judah (see Mt 2:1, 5). "Judah" now appears twice in Matthew's quotation, and it invites the reader to recall that his genealogy in Matthew 1 traces the dynastic line through Judah. This is vital for Matthew's presentation of Jesus the Messiah because only a member of the tribe of Judah could occupy the throne of David.

Micah describes Bethlehem as "small among the clans of Judah," and the LXX makes it "smallest"; Matthew alters it to "by no means least." Matthew's negative is "emphatic," and it "derives not from the text of Micah but from Matthew's reading of the text in the light of its fulfillment" in the birth of Jesus in Bethlehem.[29] Now that the Messiah has been born in small, insignificant Bethlehem, Bethlehem's status has been transformed. It should be noted that Matthew by no means misinterprets Micah but interprets it in the light of the new situation even as he quotes it.

---

[27]France, *Gospel of Matthew*, 71-72.
[28]France, *Gospel of Matthew*, 72.
[29]France, *Gospel of Matthew*, 72-73.

Matthew's use of Micah 5:1 [5:2] is thus pregnant with meaning. Jesus is the promised Messiah. He fulfills the Davidic covenant, and like the origins of David, he too is lowly and despised. As in Micah, Yahweh remarkably bypasses Jerusalem and raises up his Messiah from insignificant Bethlehem. As with David, Jesus is the true ruler over Israel. As commentators note, there is in this passage an implicit contrast between the violent rule of Herod and that of Jesus.[30] Herod cannot tolerate any challenge to his rule, but Jesus is the humble ruler, the good shepherd, from Bethlehem. The context of Micah 5:1 [5:2] in Micah alerts us to other dimensions of Jesus' rule as Messiah. His rule will extend to the ends of the earth (see Mt 28:18), and his rule will be one of peace, of shalom.

Hosea 11:1 in Matthew 2:15: Jesus the true Israel and initiator of the new exodus. Matthew 2:13-23 contains three episodes: first, the Lord directs Joseph to take Jesus and his mother to Egypt; second, Herod orders the murder of the children in Bethlehem; and third, an angel of the Lord instructs Joseph to return to Nazareth. Each episode concludes with a fulfillment quotation. The quotation from Hosea 11:1 occurs at the end of the first scene but anticipates the second and especially the third.

In Hosea 11 the verse quoted refers to the exodus and Yahweh's grace toward his people, grace that failed to receive the appropriate response of love and obedience. Initially this verse strikes one as quite different from Micah 5:1 [5:2], which is clearly a prophecy. However, it is an important verse since it alerts the reader that Jesus the Messiah redoes the history of Israel; he recapitulates it, as it were, signaling that he is *the true Israel* and will inaugurate the *new exodus*, not just an exodus from Egypt but ultimately the liberation of the creation from sin and evil. Dale Bruner perceptively comments, "As Matt 1 taught the *New Genesis* by the birth of the promised Son of David, so Matt 2 teaches the *New Exodus* in the migration in and out of Egypt by Jesus the new Moses."[31]

Zechariah 9:9 in Matthew 21:5: Zion's King. We have already examined Zechariah 9:9 and its use in the New Testament in chapters 1 and 18.[32] By the

---

[30]See D. R. Bauer, "The Kingship of Jesus in the Matthean Infancy Narrative: A Literary Analysis," *CBQ* 57 (1995): 306-23, who notes the contrast between Herod's and Jesus' kingship and the radically different responses to Jesus represented by the magi and Herod.

[31]Dale Bruner, *Matthew: A Commentary*, vol. 1, *The Christbook* (Grand Rapids, MI: Eerdmans, 2004), 75-76.

[32]See Zech 9:9 in Jn 12:15. Maarten J. J. Menken notes, "The peculiar form which Zech 9.9 has taken in Jn 12.15 is largely due to the fourth evangelist, that he probably worked with a LXX text, and that he uses it to emphasize that Jesus comes as a peaceful king for the benefit of the world."

time Jesus enters Jerusalem with his passion ahead of him, he no longer needs to guard his identity as he had done. Jesus deliberately enacts Zechariah 9:9 to draw attention to his being the Davidic *king*, the Messiah, who is entering Jerusalem *to receive his kingdom*. He does this humbly on a donkey, well aware of what lies ahead of him and that his journey to kingship will involve terrible suffering.

Zechariah 11:12-13 in Matthew 27:9-10. Zechariah 11:12-13 occurs in a judgment section in Zechariah (Zech 11:4-17) dealing with the two shepherds. Yahweh instructs a shepherd to shepherd the "flock marked for slaughter." He does so and cares in particular for the oppressed, but he meets great resistance, revokes his calling, and requests that the flock give him his pay. They pay him thirty pieces of silver, the price of a slave (Ex 21:32).

Fulfillment, as we have noted, operates on different levels in Matthew, and that is certainly the case here. First, we should note that Matthew attributes this quote to Jeremiah, and it is likely that the quote is a conflation of Zechariah 11:12-13 and Jeremiah 19:1-13. France notes, "This is, however, not a simple quotation of a single text, but a mosaic of scriptural motifs, some of which do in fact come from Jeremiah."[33] France rightly says,

> Echoes of all these Jeremiah passages, especially Jer 19:1-13, would no doubt be heard by readers well versed in the OT, so that they would recognize Matthew's adapted version of Zech 11:13 not as a quotation of that text alone but as a mosaic of familiar and related prophetic motifs. This is not simple prooftexting, but the product of long and creative engagement with Scripture which delights to draw connections between passages and to trace in the details as well as in the basic meaning of the text the pattern of God's fulfillment of his prophetically declared agenda.[34]

Of particular import is Matthew's threefold use of the Greek root for "price" in comparison to Zechariah's twofold use. This emphasizes the low view of Jesus held by Judas and the Jewish leaders.

In Zechariah and in Jeremiah the context is one of betrayal and judgment. Paying the shepherd of Zechariah the money for a slave is an indication that his service is regarded as of no worth. The association of Judas and the

---

Menken, "The Minor Prophets in John's Gospel," in Menken and Steve Moyise, eds., *The Minor Prophets in the New Testament*, Library of New Testament Studies 377 (London: T&T Clark, 2009), 79-96, 85.

[33]France, *Gospel of Matthew*, 1042.
[34]France, *Gospel of Matthew*, 1043-44.

Jewish leaders with this text is a terrible indictment. They are the leaders of God's people but, as in the days of Jeremiah and Zechariah, unable to see the good shepherd when he stands in front of them. Indirectly, this quote reaffirms Jesus' identity as the good shepherd, the true king.

The fulfillment of Zechariah 12:10 in John 19:37. Of the Minor Prophets, John manifests a clear preference for Zechariah and especially Zechariah 9–14. We include John 19:37 in this section because it is clearly referred to as a Scripture fulfilled in the crucifixion of Jesus. John refers to Jesus' legs not being broken as part of this fulfillment (Ex 12:46; Ps 34:21) and then quotes Zechariah 12:10. B. F. Westcott sees here the dual attestation of the Law and the Prophets.[35]

Zechariah 12 deals with judgment on the nations and mourning in Israel. Zechariah 12:10 comes in the context of that mourning: "They will look on me, the one they have pierced, and they will mourn for him as one mourns for an only child, and grieve bitterly for him as one grieves for a firstborn son" (NIV). This is Yahweh speaking, and as such it is an astonishing statement. Also intriguing is the shift from "on me" to "for him." Andreas Köstenberger notes that this is significant since, although John and Revelation 1:7 read only "on him," John presupposes that Yahweh is represented by the Messiah and that to pierce him is to pierce Yahweh himself.[36] Remarkably, in Zechariah it is not the nations but "the house of David and the inhabitants of Jerusalem" (Zech 12:10) who have pierced Yahweh. In Zechariah 12:10-14 the pouring out of the Spirit leads to terrible grief over what they have done.

John clearly understands Jesus' crucifixion as a fulfillment of that piercing of Yahweh referred to in Zechariah. Jesus is the crucified Messiah. "Significantly, the fulfillment entails a reversal; it is as the one pierced that Jesus becomes the source of salvation for those who look on him in faith."[37] John earlier speaks of Jesus as the living water, and it is noteworthy that Zechariah 12:10-14 is followed by a section dealing with a fountain being opened and providing cleansing from sin.[38] Thus, the broader context in Zechariah alerts us to the effects of Jesus being pierced.

---

[35] Frederick Dale Bruner, *The Gospel of John: A Commentary* (Grand Rapids, MI: Eerdmans, 2011), 1131-32.
[36] Andreas J. Köstenberger, "John," in *Commentary on the New Testament Use of the Old Testament*, ed. G. K. Beale and D. A. Carson (Grand Rapids, MI: Baker Academic, 2007), 415-512, here 505. Köstenberger's discussion as a whole is useful (504-6).
[37] Köstenberger, "John," 505.
[38] See Jn 7:38, which may well allude to Zech 14:8.

Allusions. Apart from the clear quotes and citations of the Minor Prophets, there are myriad (possible) allusions. In John, for example, some of the possible allusions are as follows:

- John 7:38: "living waters" may allude to Zechariah 14:8.
- John 1:21 "I am not" may allude to Malachi 3:23 [4:5].
- John 3:28 may allude to Malachi 3:1.
- John 1:47, with its "in whom there is no deceit," may allude to Zephaniah 3:13.
- John 2:16 may allude to Zechariah 14:21; by declaring temple and trade incompatible, Jesus fulfills Zechariah's prophecy.
- John 7:42 alludes to Micah 5:1 [5:2].
- John 8:41, with its "only father," may allude to Malachi 2:10. The expression "one father" is unique in the Old Testament, and in John "it creates a subtle irony: the Johannine Jews take pride in a statement about their relation with God that in Malachi functions as the beginning of a passage in which the prophet indicts the faithlessness of God's people (Mal 2.10-16)."[39]

So we could continue. In Mark 4:35-41, to provide a final example, it is highly likely that a deliberate parallel is being drawn between Jonah (Jon 1:4, 10) and Jesus, thereby focusing powerfully on Jesus' power as the Son of God. The comparison equates Jesus with Yahweh.

Conclusion

As we noted at the outset, all the streams of the Old Testament converge in Jesus. The Minor Prophets are only one of those streams, but, as we have seen, it *is* a significant one. Matthew quotes more from the Book of the Twelve than from any other Old Testament source, and the Old Testament is utterly foundational to his Gospel. Of Mark, Cilliers Breytenbach concludes,

> Finally, quotations from and allusions to Zechariah play an important role in portraying the Messianic expectations that the crowd were associating with Jesus (11.1-11), the prediction of the dispersion and gathering of the Twelve (14.27), the ransoming effect of the Son of Man's death (10.45; 14.24), and the announcement of his eschatological advent (13.27). Thus, although Mark's use

---

[39]Menken, "Minor Prophets in John's Gospel," 94.

of the Minor Prophets is not as extensive as the Book of Isaiah, it nevertheless plays an important role in the narrative.[40]

The Minor Prophets play less of a role in Luke's Gospel but are significant in Acts. And we have seen above the importance of the Minor Prophets for John.

If we reflect on how significant a stream the prophets are for understanding the Christ event, it needs to be said that *without the prophets the story of Jesus could not be told*, at least not in the form we have it. The prophets are grounded in the law and covenant, but we would have no sense of the climactic, *eschatological* nature of Jesus' arrival apart from the prophets. In this respect the Minor Prophets box way above their size. Isaiah and Daniel in particular but also Jeremiah and Ezekiel are indispensable for understanding Jesus. However, so too are the Minor Prophets.

One way to see this is to take N. T. Wright's five worldview questions and to see how substantial the contribution of the Minor Prophets is to answering them. The five are:

Who are we?

Where are we?

What's wrong?

What's the solution?

What time is it?[41]

Who are we? Wright's answer is that we are Israel, the chosen people of God, in the process of being redeemed at last and for the sake of the world. Jesus wrestles with Israel and its identity throughout his ministry, and particularly in his controversies, and so do the Minor Prophets. The Minor Prophets direct their ministries to Israel, and so, on the whole, does Jesus. This is especially clear in Matthew 10, where Jesus sends the Twelve on a mission with the firm instruction, "Do not go among the Gentiles. . . . Go rather to the lost sheep of Israel" (Mt 10:5-6). This instruction is revealing; Israel is God's people, but they are "lost sheep." Matthew 10 is, of course, one of the passages in which Micah 7:6 is quoted, in Matthew 10:35-36, indicating that Jesus will cause terrible division among the people of God and of families in

---

[40]Cilliers Breytenbach, "The Minor Prophets in Mark's Gospel," in Maarten J. J. Menken and Steve Moyise, eds., *The Minor Prophets in the New Testament*, Library of New Testament Studies 377 (London: T&T Clark, 2009), 27-38, 37.

[41]See Wright, *Jesus and the Victory of God*, 443-47.

particular. We are Israel, but a new Israel is being formed, and it will divide the old Israel. A new family and a different kind of kingdom are emerging.

This is what makes the fulfillment motif so important, and we have seen how the Gospels draw on the Minor Prophets to show that Jesus is indeed the promised Messiah of the Old Testament. We are the people of God, and in Jesus Yahweh is bringing his work set out in the Old Testament to fulfillment. As Heath Thomas rightly notes, the New Testament use of the Twelve affirms the inherent continuity of the narrative arc of Scripture:

> The expectation built into the Twelve, anticipating God's work of salvation in which all creation is renewed, is carried further in the New Testament. There, this expectation is met in the person and work of Jesus Christ, who makes all things new. God's Christ-work enables the outpouring of the Spirit of God on those who believe (Joel 2; Acts 2). The reader is called to be liberated by this Jesus and the world of faith he opens up.[42]

Where are we? Wright's answer is that we are still in exile, needing to be brought home in a final and true way. Wright notes that Jesus says little about the land; indeed, he undermines adherence to the land as a major Jewish symbol. A different kingdom was coming into existence that would embrace the whole creation. As we have noted in our chapter on Zechariah, we do find the motif of returning from exile even in the postexilic books. However, it is not as central as in Wright's work. What is clear in the Gospels is that Israel is at *a crossroads*. She was also at a crossroads, albeit in different ways, when the Minor Prophets prophesied. This is particularly true of the preexilic and exilic Minor Prophets. Jesus draws from their explosive ministries to alert Israel to the greater crossroads at which she finds herself now, and exile is an appropriate motif for that situation. Jesus' use of "ḥesed and not sacrifice" and his pronouncement of Jonah as the only sign that will be given an unbelieving generation evoke the perilous situation in which Israel finds itself.

What's wrong? According to Wright, Israel had failed to live up to its calling. It had been duped by the accuser. The struggle coming to a head was not with Rome but cosmic. The real enemy was the Satan: "The battle he himself has to fight was with the satan; the satan had made its home in Israel, and in her cherished national institutions and aspirations."[43]

---

[42]Thomas, "Hearing the Minor Prophets," 378-79.
[43]Wright, *Jesus and the Victory of God*, 461.

This is strong language but an analysis that finds its parallel in the Minor Prophets. Gustavo Gutiérrez speaks of "religion as a tranquilizer," and both the Minor Prophets and Jesus attack such religion head-on.[44] Thomas notes, "New Testament citation of the Twelve reinforces the concept of judgment and salvation that comes in the Day of the Lord. The use of this concept from the Twelve is perhaps the most extensive theological theme explored."[45] In Luke's Gospel, even as he is led to be crucified, Jesus is still warning the "Daughters of Jerusalem" about the danger they are in. In the process he quotes Hosea 10:8.

In the Minor Prophets, and in Jesus' ministry, the theme of judgment is terribly strong, and Jesus draws on the analysis of the Minor Prophets in this respect. Israel is the people of God, but a people under threat of judgment.

What's the solution? In brief, as Wright notes, the solution is the kingdom of God. Israel needed to return from exile; evil needed to be defeated, and Yahweh needed to return to Zion. Jesus saw himself as a prophet like his predecessors, and his fate would be the same as theirs. He retold the story of Israel as his story.

A *new exodus* is required, and Matthew, with his quote from Hosea 11:1, alerts us that Jesus is the true Israel and that in and through him the new exodus is taking place. Clay Ham concludes, "The evangelist makes a striking portrayal of Jesus as the true Israel, whose sojourn in and departure from Egypt intimates a 'new exodus,' during which Jesus proves faithful where Israel has not been."[46] This is an exodus that will, however, lead the whole creation out of bondage to sin and evil.

The Minor Prophets play an important role in the Gospels in confirming that Jesus really is the Messiah. Matthew's quotation of Zechariah 9:9 (Mt 21:1-11), for example, affirms that Jesus is not just the anticipated Davidic king of Israel but king over the kingdom of God. His reign extends over the whole of creation (see Mk 11:1-11; 12:35-37; 13:27; see also Rev 21:5).[47] This vision of the reign of the messianic king comports with the creation-restorative vision of the Twelve on the same (see Amos 9:12; Mic 4:2-3; Zech 2:11; 8:22-23; 9:9-13). That the ruler comes from Bethlehem is important in helping to explain his

---

[44]Gustavo Gutiérrez, *The Power of the Poor in History*, trans. Robert R. Barr (Maryknoll, NY: Orbis, 1983), 123-24.
[45]Thomas, "Hearing the Minor Prophets," 374.
[46]Ham, "Minor Prophets in Matthew's Gospel," 45.
[47]L. Schenke, *Das Markusevangelium* (Stuttgart: Kohlhammer, 2005), 264; Breytenbach, "Minor Prophets in Mark's Gospel," 33-34.

The Minor Prophets and Jesus

identity. Jesus is lowly and apparently insignificant but is indeed the ruler, the great shepherd. The Gospels' unusual use of the "striking of the shepherd" metaphor from Zechariah points toward the fact that Jesus will himself be struck dead, but then he will go on to shepherd his sheep. John's use of Zechariah 12:10 alerts us that in the crucifixion Yahweh himself was being pierced.

The Minor Prophets' answer to this question is *Yahweh and his Messiah*. The Gospels' answer is *Jesus and his kingdom*. The latter is explicated with vocabulary and theology from the Minor Prophets. The solution is also, of course, for Israel to repent and embrace Jesus.

What time is it? It is the time of the inauguration of the kingdom. As Wright says, "By labelling John as 'Elijah,' and by linking his own movement in direct sequence to John's, Jesus leaves his hearers no choice. Either he is an imposter, or he is indeed inaugurating the kingdom."[48] As we have seen, Malachi is crucial in setting out the link between the return of Elijah and the arrival of Yahweh in his temple (Mal 3:1). Jesus' delineation of John the Baptist as Elijah clearly turns the spotlight on himself as the Messiah, *as Yahweh* coming to his temple.

The Minor Prophets play a vital role in helping us to see the eschatology at work in Jesus' life and ministry. In Jesus the day of Yahweh has arrived; the kingdom of God is present because the King is here. In the Minor Prophets there is never any indication that the day of the Lord will usher in a spiritual kingdom with no connection to the creation. Rather, the evil from the creation will be eradicated, and a purified people of God will emerge with consequences for all creation, for all nations. In this way the Minor Prophets are an indispensable help in enlarging our understanding of Jesus and his kingdom.

The hermeneutic of this chapter, indeed of this book, is important, however inadequately we have executed it. We take the discrete witness of the Minor Prophets seriously and move from them to Jesus. The Gospels push us back into the Minor Prophets to explore New Testament references in their contexts, and this in turn pushes us back to Jesus. It is a *dialectical hermeneutic*, with the Minor Prophets illumining Jesus, Jesus casting his light back on the Minor Prophets, and so on.

The end result is *a colossal view of Jesus*. He is the Messiah, Yahweh himself in our midst, coming to save his people and his creation, to lead it toward

---

[48]Wright, *Jesus and the Victory of God*, 468.

the destiny for which God always intended it. As Habakkuk might say to us, "[Yahweh] is in his holy temple, let all the earth be silent before him" (Hab 2:20 NIV).

RECOMMENDED READING

France, R. T. *The Gospel of Matthew*. New International Commentary on the New Testament. Grand Rapids, MI: Eerdmans, 2007.

———. *Jesus and the Old Testament: His Application of Old Testament Passages to Himself and to His Mission*. Vancouver, BC: Regent College Publishing, 1988.*

Menken, J. J., and Steve Moyise. *The Minor Prophets in the New Testament*. LNTS 377. London: T&T Clark, 2009.

Wright, N. T. *Jesus and the Victory of God*. Christian Origins and the Question of God 2. London: SPCK, 1996.

Recommended reading marked with a "*" indicates introductory works.

22

The Theology of the Minor Prophets for Today

IF FOR NO OTHER REASON, we ought to retrieve and renew our reading of and listening to the Minor Prophets today because of their importance for understanding *Jesus*. They are indispensable in grasping the magnitude of the Christ event. Precisely as disciples of Jesus, we are pushed to return to the Minor Prophets and listen to all that they have to say as part of Scripture for today. They bring God's word to bear on all of life in their particular contexts, and Jesus is Lord of all of life. Although we are in a different act in the drama of Scripture from them, their discrete witness remains, now enriching and enriched by the fuller and more comprehensive story of which they—and we—are part.

THE GOD WHO SPEAKS

> *The doctrine of the Word of God is at heart nothing else but the doctrine of God as a Person.*
> GERHARD EBELING, *WORD AND FAITH*

Among theologians there is considerable discussion about the validity of referring to God as "personal."[1] In a nuanced fashion Helmut Thielicke rightly defends the use of *personal* to refer to God. Negatively, it is helpful in that, first, it protects us from "the God of the philosophers," that is, a god constructed from human reasoning. Second, it reminds us that God is never just *the answer to the human question*. Indeed, it is inconceivable that the

---

[1] See Hendrikus Berkhof, *Christian Faith: An Introduction to the Study of the Faith*, trans. Sierd Woudstra (Grand Rapids, MI: Eerdmans, 1979), 130-33; Gijsbert van den Brink, *Almighty God: A Study of the Doctrine of Divine Omnipotence*, Studies in Philosophical Theology (Kampen: Kok Pharos, 1993), 116-17.

Minor Prophets would see Yahweh in this way. "Instead, he is the Creator who gives the creature man his own being, and confers on him the destiny of being a counterpart who is capable of decision and can either grasp his destiny or miss it." Positively, speaking of God as personal alerts us "that God freely turns to man and enters into covenant with him, becoming Immanuel and not keeping anything back (in Luther's sense), *finds expression supremely in his speaking*, in his sending forth his word, and his doing this in free sovereignty."[2]

The emphasis on God speaking is so common in the Minor Prophets that it is easy to miss, and yet it is one of the extraordinary characteristics of these books. Amos in particular helps us to see the importance of this theme when he notes that God's judgment will result in a famine, not of food or water "but a famine of hearing the words of the Lord" (Amos 8:11).

As we saw in our chapters on Amos, Amos has a strong doctrine of creation, and we know from Genesis 1–3 that human beings are constituted by their relationship to God. Part of being in the image of God is that humans, like God, are lingual beings, and immediately after they are created in Genesis 1:27 God *speaks to them*. Humans are the only creatures addressed in this way because they are constituted uniquely by their intimate relationship with God. God's speech is their anchor, their compass, the pivot around which they move and find their way amid the creation. Not to hear the speech of God is to be less than fully human, to have the very ground of one's being cut away from one. Hence the enormity of the judgment prophesied by Amos. Jesus shows us the centrality of God's speech for human existence in his temptations in the wilderness. Humans will not—and cannot—live by bread alone but need to be nurtured deeply by the speech of God.

Thielicke notes that by addressing humans, God "makes them responsive. He gives them *responsible* existence."[3] To be human, we might say, is to have *response-ability*. To lose this capacity is to lose one's humanity. The remarkable thing about the Minor Prophets is that even while God's people seem hell-bent on turning away from him, God continues to speak to them, granting them the opportunity to assume responsible existence and to find their way in him to full humanity and blessing.

---

[2] Helmut Thielicke, *The Evangelical Faith*, vol. 2, *The Doctrine of God and of Christ*, trans. Geoffrey W. Bromiley (Grand Rapids, MI: Eerdmans, 1977), 102, 105, emphasis added.
[3] Thielicke, *Evangelical Faith*, 2:105, emphasis original.

There came a time when God ceased speaking and sent his people off to exile. But then, some four hundred years later, John the Baptist appears, *a prophet* in the spirit of Elijah (see Mal 3:23-24 [4:5-6]). He is a voice crying in the wilderness, preparing the way for the one whom John describes as the Logos, the Word of God incarnate. As Hebrews 1:2 reminds us, in these last days, God has spoken to us by his Son. Apart from his constant speech through his creation, every time the gospel is preached, God again turns freely toward his world and its inhabitants, inviting us to become responsive and to assume responsible existence. As with Jesus, he longs to pronounce over us, "This is my beloved."

We should therefore not trivialize statements such as "The word of the Lord . . . ," "This is what the sovereign Lord says . . . ," "declares the Lord," and so on. Such words hold open to us the door to life and are, like Jesus, full of grace and truth. They remind us too of the responsibility of the church, which is missional in its essence, called to carry the word of the Lord in the broken jars of our lives into his world, so that others too may hear his address and his invitation to responsible existence.

Religion as a Tranquilizer

The Enlightenment and the post-Enlightenment eras have subjected religion to ruthless criticism, and especially Christianity.[4] One thinks naturally of the three masters of suspicion, Sigmund Freud, Friedrich Nietzsche, and Karl Marx, but there were also many other figures, such as Ludwig Feuerbach and Arthur Schopenhauer, who remains one of the most widely read philosophers in Germany today.[5] In *The Anti-Christ*, Nietzsche writes:

> The Christian idea of God—God as a god of the sick, God as spider, God as spirit—is one of the most corrupt conceptions of God the world has ever seen; this may even represent a new low in the declining development of the types of god. God having degenerated into a contradiction of life instead of its transfiguration and eternal yes! God as declared aversion to life, to nature, to the will to life! God as the formula for every slander against 'the here and now,' for every lie about the 'beyond'! God as the deification of nothingness, the canonization of the will to nothingness! . . .[6]

---

[4]The heading of this section is taken from Gustavo Gutiérrez, *The Power of the Poor in History*, trans. Robert R. Barr (New York: Orbis, 1983), 123-24.
[5]See Brian D. Ingraffia, *Postmodern Theory and Biblical Theology* (Cambridge: Cambridge University Press, 1995), 19-32.
[6]Friedrich Nietzsche, *The Anti-Christ, Ecce Homo, Twilight of the Idols*, Cambridge Texts in the History of Philosophy (Cambridge: Cambridge University Press, 2005), 15-16.

It cannot and *should not* be denied that strands of Christianity have indeed been world denying. Strands of such thought and escape from the world can be traced from the early centuries of Christianity through the Middle Ages and on into some contemporary evangelicalism. But any reading of the Minor Prophets should show once and for all that this is *not* biblical Christianity.[7] Adrio König, in his discussion of God and history, writes,

> We find here a new perspective on the problems which gave rise to the so-called God-is-dead-theology. On the one hand the questions were asked: Where was God in Hiroshima, in Auschwitz, Biafra? ... By virtue of the structure of the covenant, the questions should rather be: Where is *man*? It is us, the people, who have not discharged our responsibilities, who have not been fully human, i.e. not like Jesus, the real man! Had the gospel been rightly proclaimed and believed in Germany there could have been no Auschwitz. If the rich western lands had rightly proclaimed and believed the gospel, there could have been no starvation in West Africa in 1974.[8]

The Minor Prophets parade before us *an internal critique of religion* that fails to take the world seriously as the theater of the glory of God. Marx was surely right that too much Christianity is the opium of the masses, dulling us into a comfortable euphoria while terrible injustice is rampant before our very eyes. In the process, Christians become instruments of such injustice or at least passive supporters of it. But, once again, this *cannot* be said of the Minor Prophets.

Amos is the bomb that explodes any view of Christianity as world denying or not passionately concerned about injustice and oppression, that is, about *this world*. In his treatment of humankind and sin at the end of his second major point in his discussion of the "Sloth of Man," Karl Barth has a five-page small-print discussion of Amos.[9] Barth is rightly clear in this section as a whole that *inhumanity* is always *the sin* of disobedience, unbelief, and ingratitude: "In short, if I am inhuman, I am also stupid and foolish and godless." The incarnation in particular renders inhumanity totally unacceptable. "He [Jesus] is wholly the Neighbour of us His Neighbours; wholly the Brother of us His brothers; ... in Him, therefore, man is turned not merely to God but to other men."[10]

---

[7] See also Ingraffia's *Postmodern Theory*, trenchant critique of the view of the Bible as world denying.
[8] Adrio König, *Here Am I!* (Grand Rapids, MI: Eerdmans, 1982), 130-31.
[9] *CD* IV/2:445-52.
[10] *CD* IV/2:442, 432.

Barth does not make Jacques Derrida's fatal mistake, in Derrida's reading of Søren Kierkegaard, of collapsing our relationship with God into our relationship with our neighbor, but nor will he separate them: "The relationship of man with his visible fellow-man is not in itself and as such, a relationship with God. But since God is the God of his fellow as well as his God, the latter inexorably includes the former. The former is the horizontal line to which the vertical is related and without which it would not be a vertical." Try as we might, "We cannot, therefore, destroy the fact that others are there as our fellows and neighbours and brothers. We may cause them to wait, and wait in vain, for our corresponding action and attitude."[11] Barth rightly points out, and he should know, living as he did through World War II in Germany and Switzerland, that inhumanity is dangerous, powerful, and terribly infectious, much like the coronavirus.

What the Minor Prophets and Amos in particular understood so acutely is that religion—Christianity—is not exempt from the danger of inhumanity. In his important book on evil, *People of the Lie*, Christian psychiatrist Scott Peck makes the point that evil is particularly attracted to religion because there it can most easily masquerade as the light. Under the cloak of religion, people are far more reluctant to name evil when it keeps presenting itself as holy and good. As noted above, the acquiescence of so many South African Christians to apartheid is a good example. Barth writes, "Not least, the Church itself, the proclamation and hearing of the Word of God, the confession and doctrine and liturgy and order of the Church, and even its theology, offer a vast opportunity for philanthropic activity which is devoid of true humanity."[12] Far from the doctrine of sin being world denying, it alone enables a sufficiently profound diagnosis of what is wrong with the world to be performed. Barth's comment that at bottom every person is inhuman reminds one of G. K. Chesterton's quip, "What's wrong with the world? I am!" Marx's and Freud's analysis of the problem was not nearly *deep enough*. Yes, social alienation is a major problem, and yes, psychic disturbance must be taken into account, but the Minor Prophets insist that at depth inhumanity is caused by a distorted relationship with God.

Barth rightly points out the significance of Amos in this respect. Amos is to a large extent a prophet of one thing: inhumanity. His particular

---

[11] *CD* IV/2:441-42, 433. See Jacques Derrida, *The Gift of Death*, trans. David Willis (Chicago: University of Chicago Press, 1995).
[12] *CD* IV/2:439.

contribution is to insist, to shout from the rooftops, "The affair of God is the affair of man." As Barth perceptively notes, "In other words, he proclaims Yahweh as the God of the fellow-man who has been wronged and humiliated and oppressed by man, and as the Avenger who has been challenged to direct implacable action by what has been done to him." Amid the social changes and the emergence of a monetary economy, the prophet Amos sees to the bottom of things. Terrible injustice is being enacted in Israel, and there is no law to restrain the great and protect the poor, especially when "the gates"—the lawcourts of the day—were themselves corrupt. The problem was *not* one of secularization; "Yahwism" was alive and well, but it was a practice of religion characterized by syncretistic decadence, in which "the evil is masked by the good, the unholy by the holy."[13]

The language of "the war against terrorism" has entered our vocabulary in the West for the foreseeable future. Amos is better characterized in terms of "the war against injustice." Terrorism is a horrible evil—indeed, the Minor Prophets would condemn it unequivocally—and should never be underestimated, but Amos would alert us to make the war against injustice and oppression our first priority, to clean up our own house and to ensure we are not complicit in global structures of oppression before labeling others as evil and thus, by default, ourselves as humane.

The Minor Prophets are of central importance for biblical eschatology. The nations and the whole creation are constantly within their purview. Indeed, it is hard to think of a better place in the Old Testament to find a theology of the kingdom, the rule of Yahweh. Living as we do in between the coming of the King and the final consummation of his kingdom, our situation is different from that of the audience of the Minor Prophets. God's people are scattered among the nations, and while that means our nations are not theocracies like Israel, the ethic of the Old Testament remains valid but has to be appropriated within our new situation. The focus of the Minor Prophets remains as, if not more, relevant in this context. Jesus notes in his Beatitudes that a major characteristic of his people will be that they hunger and thirst for *righteousness*. This righteousness is not just personal but societal and political.

There is a great deal in Western democracies to be celebrated and valued. But it would be absurd to say that all is well. We now live, for example, amid

---
[13] CD IV/2:448, 447, 451.

a global consumer culture that is deeply flawed.[14] In the introductory essay to their very useful *The Consumer Society Reader*, Juliet Schor and Douglas Holt identify three factors causing disquiet about our consumer culture:

1. *The new inequality.* In the United States, the upper 1 percent of households own about 40 percent of all wealth, and the top 20 percent are responsible for half of the country's consumer spending.

2. *The relentless commodification of all areas of life* and the rise of market values. Virtually every aspect of life has been turned into a commodity so that "little remains sacred, and separate from the world of the commodity. As a result people become ever more desperate to sacralise the profane consumer world around them, worshiping celebrities, collections, and brand logos."[15]

3. The *globalization of the world economy* and grassroots resistance to it.

Susan White describes the spirit of our age as follows:

> Sociologists tell us that people interpret their lives through basic narratives, which provide a framework within which to understand the world and to establish goals and values. If there is any overarching metanarrative that purports to explain reality in the late 20th century, it is surely the narrative of the free market economy. In the beginning of this narrative is the self-made, self-sufficient human being. At the end of this narrative is the big house, the big car, and the expensive clothes. In the middle is the struggle for success, the greed, the getting-and-spending in a world in which there is no such thing as a free lunch. Most of us have made this so thoroughly "our story" that we are hardly aware of its influence.[16]

Steven Miles rightly says of consumerism that "the parallel with religion is not an accidental one. Consumerism is ubiquitous and ephemeral. It is arguably *the* religion of the late twentieth century."[17] With the demise of communism—or the triumph of consumerism amid communism, as in China—and the alignment of Western consumerism with democracy, it may

---

[14] We use consumerism as our major example. Many other examples could be used. Amid the mass of literature, see Juliet B. Schor and Douglas B. Holt, eds., *The Consumer Society Reader* (New York: New Press, 2000); Craig G. Bartholomew and Thorsten Moritz, eds., *Christ and Consumerism: A Critical Analysis of the Spirit of the Age* (Carlisle, UK: Paternoster, 2000).

[15] Juliet B. Schor and Douglas B. Holt, "Introduction," in Schor and Holt, *Consumer Society Reader*, vii–xxiii, ix.

[16] Susan White, "A New Story to Live By?," *TransMission* (Spring 1998): 3-4, here 4.

[17] S. Miles, *Consumerism—As a Way of Life* (London: Sage, 1998), 1.

be hard to see why we should be too worried about getting into bed with the spirit of *this* age. However, Roy Harrisville and Walter Sundberg's words are salutary in this respect: "Recently, the left and all its reflection in Marxist structure has collapsed, leaving the entire inhabited world a candidate for free enterprise. But with this change the demonic has not ceased to exist—neither in the world, nor in the church. And who is to say whether or not that evil spirit will bring in to this house swept clean seven other worse than himself?"[18]

The international arms industry is an example of the damage consumerism can cause. In the new democratic South Africa following 1994, the first major ethical crisis to hit South Africa was an arms deal, with Western politicians and corporations involved in the corruption that ensued and is still being suppressed. Globalization has brought many good things, but it has also facilitated an economic apartheid between north and south, with devastating consequences. UNICEF reports,

> *More than 30 per cent of children in* developing *countries—about 600 million— live on less than US $1 a day.*
>
> *Every 3.6 seconds one person dies of starvation. Usually it is a child under the age of 5.*
>
> Poverty hits children hardest. While a severe lack of goods and services hurts every human, it is most threatening to children's rights: survival, health and nutrition, education, participation, and protection from harm and exploitation. It creates an environment that is damaging to children's development in every way—mental, physical, emotional and spiritual.[19]

Thus inequality and injustice are not just a problem in the United States but globally. While every 3.6 seconds a person dies of starvation, in the United States and much of the West and among the elite of the Majority World, we witness "a dazzling display among the nation's newly rich to outdo one another in ostentatious spending." The not-so-rich console ourselves with affordable goods and the endless supply of cheap goods dumped on our cultures, "but all is not well in the kingdom of plastics."[20]

While we are not economists, one thing is clear to us: consumer culture is *not sustainable*, and to a major extent it is *inhumane*, pandering to the

---

[18]Roy Harrisville and Walter Sundberg, *The Bible in Modern Culture* (Grand Rapids, MI: Eerdmans, 1995), 261.
[19]"Goal: Eradicate Extreme Poverty and Hunger," UNICEF, http://www.unicef.org/mdg/poverty.html (accessed December 9, 2022).
[20]Schor and Holt, "Introduction," viii.

worst aspects of human nature. It is not hard to imagine what Amos would have to say to those of us in the Minority World today.

Amos and the Minor Prophets also exhibit a remarkable environmental ethic, and doubtless they would weigh in too on the challenge of climate change, which is threating the very biosphere in which humans—and animals and plants—live. Naomi Klein perceptively notes that we are caught at this critical moment between the forces of global capitalism and the crisis of climate change. She poses the question, "What is really preventing us from putting out the fire that is threatening to burn down our collective house?"[21]

Klein notes that the answer is far simpler than we think; the actions we need to take conflict with deregulated capitalism and are a threat to the minority that controls our economies, our politics, and our major media outlets. She identifies 1988 as a symbolic year; even as the scientific community was making a definitive diagnosis of climate change, global consumerism took off. She notes, "Very little, however, has been written about how market fundamentalism has, from the very first moments, systematically sabotaged our collective response to climate change, a threat that came knocking just as this ideology was reaching its zenith."[22]

A desperate need today is for what Bob Goudzwaard and Harry de Lange describe as "an economy of care": care for the poor and for one another, care for the world of which we are part.[23] Alas, instead we are amid what René Girard describes as "a hurricane of desire." Far too often Christians are fast asleep in the bottom of the boat, just like Jonah, even as the storm gathers momentum around us. And just as with Jonah, it is often non-Christians who are most concerned about the storm even as Western Christians shape numerous models of consumer churches, submerged in the idolatry of our day.

To preach Amos and the Minor Prophets in such a context is no easy challenge. But, as Gerhard von Rad notes, "The biblical texts must be preached—under all circumstances and at any cost. The people for whom we each have a responsibility need them for living (and for dying)."[24] Unless we follow von Rad's advice and interpret and preach the Minor Prophets contextually today, far too much Christianity will continue to function as a

---

[21] Naomi Klein, *This Changes Everything: Capitalism vs. the Climate* (Toronto: Knopf, 2014), 18.
[22] Klein, *This Changes Everything*, 19.
[23] Bob Goudzwaard and Harry de Lange, *Beyond Poverty and Affluence: Toward An Economy of Care* (Grand Rapids, MI: Eerdmans, 1994).
[24] Gerhard von Rad, *Biblical Interpretations in Preaching*, trans. John E. Steely (Nashville: Abingdon, 1977), 11.

tranquilizer, as opium to the masses, with devastating consequences. The Minor Prophets bear solemn testimony to the fact that if we will not submit our practices to prophetic critique, then judgment cannot be far off. In 1999 the World Council of Churches published the following letter, to which we do well to listen.

> *Letter of the Asian Churches to the Churches of the North, Bangkok 1999.*
>
> Next to the pain and suffering in the South, there are the threats in the North. We heard about poverty, coming back in even your richest societies; we received reports about environmental destruction also in your midst, and about alienation, loneliness and the abuse of women and children. And all that, while most of your churches are losing members. And we asked ourselves: is most of that not also related to being rich and desiring to become richer than most of you already are? Is there not in the western view of human beings and society a delusion, which always looks to the future and wants to improve it, even when it implies an increase of suffering in your own societies and in the South? Have you not forgotten the richness which is related to sufficiency? If, according to Ephesians 1, God is preparing in human history to bring everyone and everything under the lordship of Jesus Christ, his shepherd-king—God's own globalization!—shouldn't caring for and sharing with each other be the main characteristic of our lifestyle, instead of giving fully in to the secular trend of a growing consumerism?
>
> We are convinced that the time has come for a return to the fundamental and undiluted teachings of the gospel. It is time for all of us to make a choice: God or mammon, the one true God or the idolatry of wealth. We know that some churches in the North are very active in this regard and we feel strong solidarity with their actions. But the present situation invites us to stand up all together.
>
> We call for concrete acts of solidarity to alleviate the massive suffering in our nations in the North and in the South.[25]

OUR MAKER: THE GOD WITH WHOM WE HAVE TO DO

If Amos is a prophet of one thing, it is only because his life is lived *coram Deo*, before the face of God. The horizontal dimension is so strong in the Minor Prophets *because* the vertical is so utterly overwhelming. König writes,

> A one-sided preaching of the "gospel" without desiring, and where possible giving a full human life to others, has just as little to do with the true gospel

---

[25]Cited in Bob Goudzwaard, "The Principle of Sphere-Sovereignty in a Time of Globalisation," *Koers* 76/2 (2011): 357-71, note 14 (369-70).

as a one-sided humanistic human rights' campaign without the driving force of Jesus Christ. . . . Not only does this lead to great confusion, but it is a betrayal of the gospel, a betrayal of the belief that God made the whole man.[26]

As Amos would remind us, God is our Maker. If we really want to get to the bottom of the malaise of modernity we need far more—far, far more—of our Maker.[27] Years ago a British doctor, Sheila Cassidy, went to serve as a doctor in Chile. She gave medical aid to a government opponent and was arrested, tortured, and eventually released and returned to the UK.[28] Craig heard her speak in Cheltenham, and she made the important point that we need images of God that are *adequate for the journey of life* with all its challenges.

Few things would help us today more than a renewed sense of God and his glory, and the Minor Prophets are there waiting to help us. The Minor Prophets are chock-full of metaphors and images designed to reawaken in us a sense of the wild, dangerous, and oh-so-gracious reality of God, substantial images that are indeed adequate for the journey of life.

In Zephaniah 1:7, for example, Yahweh is depicted as preparing a sacrifice—his own people. In Zephaniah 1:12 he is depicted as searching Jerusalem with a lamp during the dark night for those who think he will not act against their rebellion. Zephaniah also describes God as the "Mighty Warrior," shouting his battle cry as he attacks his own people (Zeph 1:14). Why? The answer is simple: "because they have sinned against Yahweh" (Zeph 1:17) so that the day of Yahweh will be the "day of Yahweh's wrath" (Zeph 1:18).

These are powerful images that drive home to those with ears to listen that Yahweh is *holy* and dwells in unapproachable light, and by his very nature cannot go on and on tolerating sin and rebellion. In a fine monograph on the history of divine wrath as a Christian doctrine, Stephen Murray writes about *Reclaiming Divine Wrath*.[29] He is keenly alert to the abuse of this doctrine but is rightly adamant that we need to recover it. In his final chapter he identifies several misapplications of the doctrine and then positive ways in which it should be reappropriated:[30]

---

[26]König, *Here Am I!*, 117-18.
[27]*The Malaise of Modernity* is the title of Charles Taylor's book.
[28]Sheila Cassidy, *Audacity to Believe: An Autobiography* (London: Collins, 1977).
[29]Stephen B. Murray, *Reclaiming Divine Wrath: A History of a Christian Doctrine and Its Interpretation*, Studies in Theology and Culture 8 (Bern: Peter Lang, 2011).
[30]Murray, *Reclaiming Divine Wrath*, 253-70.

1. The wrath of God affirms that the love of God will not tolerate evil.
2. The wrath of God reminds us that God's character is inherently moral.
3. In the matrix of love, wrath, and justice, God holds us all accountable.
4. The wrath of God reminds us of God's providence.
5. The wrath of God provides an occasion for prayer in times of great difficulty and suffering.

At the same time, and without contradiction, the Minor Prophets portray God as delighting in his people, extraordinarily gracious, patient, and loving. In Hosea 9–14 Yahweh reviews the history of his journey with Israel. His joy at their early love is depicted in rich and evocative imagery. In Hosea 9:10, for example, Yahweh compares his finding of Israel to finding grapes in the desert and seeing early fruit on the fig tree.[31] The precise imagery of Israel as a heifer in Hosea 10:11 is unclear.[32] König suggests that the picture here is that of a willing young heifer who loved to thresh. He argues that it was customary not to yoke such an animal but to grant it free run of the threshing floor, which gave it freedom to eat the corn as well. However we read Hosea 10:11, in Hosea 9–14 we certainly find images portraying Yahweh's sheer delight in his people during their early days (see Hos 11:4). In terms of such anthropomorphisms in Scripture, König perceptively notes that they alert us to the difference between God and humankind.[33] As Yahweh says in Hosea 11:9, "For I am God and not a man—the Holy One among you" (NIV).

Especially in Hosea, we see the tension in Yahweh between his love for Israel and his wrath at their rebellion. The salvation oracles emerge out of this tension. This is graphically evoked in Hosea 11:8-9. Especially among historical critics, there is an attempt to separate these different strands, but, as König rightly says, "Attempts to divide these threats, this inward strife, and these promises into different periods or phrases have always failed, precisely because Hosea is concerned with an actual involvement on God's part in the history of his people—with exactly the opposite of the god-concept of Greek philosophy."[34]

---

[31] See J. Andrew Dearman, "Flora and Fauna Metaphors in Hosea" in *The Book of Hosea*, NICOT (Grand Rapids, MI: Eerdmans, 2010), 356-57.
[32] See Dearman, *Book of Hosea*, 269-71; Francis I. Andersen and David Noel Freedman, *Hosea*, AB (NY: Doubleday, 1980), 566-68.
[33] König, *Here Am I!*, 72-84.
[34] König, *Here Am I!*, 74.

This raises, of course, the challenging issue of the *aseity* of God.[35] Theologians such as Herman Bavinck defend the aseity of God, which does indeed express the independence of God and his sufficiency in himself. However, the sort of biblical portrayal of God we find in the Minor Prophets certainly leads us to see God as emotional in relation to Israel and the nations and as affected by sin and rebellion. It may be that this is one of those places in which Scripture calls for a reform of certain presentations of a doctrine of God shaped too much by Greek philosophy and underinformed by biblical grammar, language, and concepts.[36] König is particularly critical of Bavinck's preference for terms such as *essence* over biblical imagery of God as personal, Father, lover, and so on. König asserts,

> Those who know God as revealed to Jeremiah and Paul [and the Minor Prophets] notice immediately that God defined as "essence" is missing one vital point: his real essence, his true heart. The pain of God which Jeremiah saw, the love in the cross which Paul saw—this is the essence of God, this is the heart of God. Consequently, the "essence" of God presented in classical Trinitarian doctrine may be called an essence without essence. . . . The actual being of God, that which makes him God in the testimony of the biblical writers is precisely what is missing in the traditional discussion of the being of God.[37]

---

[35] On the immutability and pathos of God see König, *Here Am I!*, 84-102; James F. Keating and Thomas J. White, eds., *Divine Impassibility and the Mystery of Human Suffering* (Grand Rapids, MI: Eerdmans, 2009); Isaak A. Dorner, *Divine Immutability: A Critical Reconsideration*, trans. Robert R. Williams and Claude Welch, Fortress Texts in Modern Theology (Minneapolis: Fortress, 1994); Gijsbert van den Brink and Marcel Sarot, eds., *Understanding the Attributes of God*, Contributions to Philosophical Theology 1 (Bern: Peter Lang, 1999).

[36] As Emmanuel Falque notes, "There is no question of not noticing, or not pointing out here, the profound transformations that Christianity brought to Hellenism at the same time as it very directly inherited from this tradition." Falque, *The Metamorphosis of Finitude: An Essay on Birth and Resurrection*, trans. George Hughes (New York: Fordham University Press, 2012) 98. For a more productive view of divine aseity that comports with biblical grammar of divine pathos as we find in the prophets, see Michael Allen, "Divine Attributes," in *Christian Dogmatics: Reformed Theology for the Church Catholic*, ed. Michael Allen and Scott R. Swain (Grand Rapids, MI: Baker Academic, 2016). Allen states: "That is, aseity is not a statement of a monolithic monad but a tripersonal God in himself. The love and life of God is enjoyed among Father, Son, and Spirit not apart from any personal engagement. So aseity as such is defined by triune personal being. . . . While these terms [the attributes] are employed also in natural theology or in certain strands of philosophical theology, they are disciplined by the economy of God as published in the canon of Scripture, that is, by the manifestation of God as eternally triune. Whether aseity, infinity, or otherwise, these terms are defined by the revealed nature of God, not by certain preconceived notions or category assumptions based on creaturely experience. . . . Thus theological definitions of any attribute must be derived from the trinitarian shape of the divine being" (65-66).

[37] König, *Here Am I!*, 200.

In his rich and creative doctrine of God, *Here Am I!*, König identifies four aspects of the essence of God, all of which have strong parallels in the Minor Prophets:[38]

1. God's intolerance of the gods is gracious. God is incomparable and refuses to allow humans any gods besides him. God thus refuses to surrender his people and his world to the gods. Implicit in this but explicit in the Minor Prophets is that God is the gracious and omnipotent Creator.

2. The essence of God is love. "The conviction that God is in his essence love has played only a small part in history, and in Protestant scholasticism virtually no role at all. That God in his external relationships concentrates on people and treats them in love is something unique."[39] König refers to Hosea 11:8-9 as an example of the way in which God's essence as love is revealed in the history of Israel, in which he remains loving in his wrath.

3. God's essence is manifest in his revealing himself in history in which he is really involved. "In contrast to the gods surrounding Israel, the uniqueness of God was repeatedly shown in the fact that he did things, that he kept his promises. He actually does the things appropriate to a God."[40]

4. God's essence is manifest in his character as the God who has power over the future, the faithful God who keeps his promises, who thus opens up life and gives meaning to the present. König notes quite wonderfully that the creation was a beginning and not an end; the new creation in Jesus is not an end but a beginning. "And even the new earth is not an end, but the real beginning, our first opportunity to do our actual work in a completely unhindered and unfettered way: to serve God and to glorify him."[41]

König concludes,

If this is the kind of being God is, and if this is how deity should be described, then one word is also enough: God is *love*. It is a love on which people may count, a love in which he has freely bound himself to achieve this goal, a love

---

[38]König, *Here Am I!*, 201-3.
[39]König, *Here Am I!*, 201.
[40]König, *Here Am I!*, 202.
[41]König, *Here Am I!*, 203.

that means that he does not abandon the work of his hands, a love that enables us to trust him even in the midst of the present terrible spiritual and worldly need of mankind, and a love that allows us to hope confidently that he will remain faithful into all eternity—faithful to himself and therefore faithful to us, to whom he has bound himself, and faithful to our future.[42]

The Minor Prophets thus call us to respond to God, much as Paul does in Romans 12:1-2. "I wished to speak about God in an exclamation, a call. Anyone who learns to know God, learns to call out about him. He is wonderful; he is incomparable; he is love."[43]

Ḥesed and Worship

One simply cannot emerge from such reflections on God without wanting to worship. In churches we often say that God "inhabits the praises of his people." This is just fine, if we understand what it means. The Minor Prophets give us a larger vocabulary for Yahweh's intimate involvement with his people. If the Minor Prophets show us how *not to live*, they also give us a glorious picture of what it means to live *coram Deo*. As we trust and obey God, he delights in us, he enjoys us, even as we glorify him and enjoy him forever. He lifts us like a little child to his cheek, and he bends down to feed us (Hos 11:4). Truly this God is *Immanuel*, God with us. As his covenant people, we are called to unimaginable intimacy with God, a prospect that should transform our worship and our lives. We are caught up as a missional people in his faithful purposes and promises. He is far greater and far more holy and loving than we can imagine, although we have books such as the Minor Prophets to open a window onto his character for us, again and again.

The only adequate and deeply desirable response is to "present our bodies as a living sacrifice, for this is our reasonable worship" (Rom 12:1-2). Paul's use of *bodies* is instructive; the whole of our lives in every dimension is to be placed in the service of this King, and we are called to do this as a community, indicated by the plural *bodies*.

The Minor Prophets are packed with instruction as to what such life looks like, much of which we have explored in earlier chapters. In terms of mission, the Minor Prophets foreground the *centripetal* nature of mission, in which the nations are drawn to Zion for instruction. In the New Testament the *centrifugal* view of mission is central, but the centripetal dimension is never

---

[42]König, *Here Am I!*, 203.
[43]König, *Here Am I!*, 208.

lost sight of. The centripetal dimension alerts us to the inherent *plausibility* of lives lived *coram Deo*, fully human lives passionate about God and his world, lives that draw people to God, like bees to honey.

SPIRITUALITY

The Minor Prophets can and must be preached. But, more than that, they can and must be lived. This will be wonderful but never easy. In Revelation 1:9 (NIV) John describes himself as "your brother and companion in the suffering and kingdom and patient endurance that are ours in Jesus," a rich threefold description of the Christian life. John was living the Minor Prophets, but the result was that he was in exile on Patmos. Exile involves suffering and patient endurance, and so will our lives as exiles as we wait and live in expectation of the consummation of the kingdom.

Israel failed in its calling to be God's people, and so will we unless we develop the sort of spirituality we find among the Minor Prophets. In a letter to Catherine de Hueck Doherty, immersed in service of the poor as she was, Thomas Merton captures the challenge we face:

> Christ is the source and the only source of charity and spiritual life. We can do nothing without Him and His Spirit. . . . That is why the Cross will cast its shadow, still, over your life . . . in that shadow, you will see the Light of Christ, the Light of the Resurrection. He lives in us, and through our poverty He must reign. And I need not tell you how poor He makes us in order to reign in us. If we knew how poor and desolate we would have to be when we begin to follow Him, perhaps we would have fallen back. . . . We have got to be people of hope, and to be so we have to see clearly how true it is that the hopes of a materialistic culture are the worst form of despair. We have to build a new world, and yet resist the world while representing Christ in the midst of it. I have been taken to task for yelling so loud that this is a perverse generation and no doubt I have put a lot of my frustration into the cries: the people of the generation are good, so good, so helpless, some of them: the culture, the generation is perverse and I see little hope for it. Why? Because by its very essence it is against Christ. I hope that I am wrong.[44]

As Jesus told his disciples, apart from him we can do nothing. But with him, all things are possible. To embody the exhilarating vision of a life of *ḥesed*,

---

[44]Thomas Merton, in Robert A. Wild, ed., *Compassionate Fire: The Letters of Thomas Merton and Catherine de Hueck Doherty* (Notre Dame, IN: Ave Maria, 2009), 35-36.

of covenant loyalty to this God, we will need to make spiritual formation a priority. In Genesis we often wonder why, after the promises to Abraham in Genesis 12:1-3, some thirty chapters follow in which we are shown the often foolish and unattractive lives of the patriarchs. The reason is that they had to become formed to be like the promise they carried. In theological vocabulary, they had to undergo *sanctification*. Genesis 12–50, like the Minor Prophets, alerts us to what this might involve. Kingdom, yes; but also suffering and patient endurance.

In our discussions of the Minor Prophets, we have explored their importance for spirituality. Jonah is an important resource in this respect, as he is formed through rebellion and suffering to become like Yahweh, full of compassion for all the creation. Hosea, too, much like Jeremiah, gives us a glimpse into the heart of one who takes seriously the role of carrying the word to the world. As is repeatedly emphasized in the Minor Prophets, we will need to spend much time being still before the Lord, opening ourselves up to his formation, day after day, if we want to become a people in whom he delights, over whom he again and again pronounces with sheer delight, "This is my son!" In a Catholic document titled "Starting Afresh from Christ," it is rightly noted,

> An authentic spiritual life requires that everyone, in all the diverse vocations, regularly dedicate, every day, appropriate times to enter deeply into silent conversation with him by whom they know they are loved, to share their very lives with him and to receive enlightenment to continue on the daily journey. It is an exercise which requires fidelity, because we are constantly bombarded by the estrangements and excesses which come from today's society, especially from the means of communication. At times fidelity to personal and liturgical prayer will require a true effort not to allow oneself to be swallowed up in frenetic activism. Otherwise it will be impossible to bear fruit.[45]

John Paul II reminds us, "Every reality of consecrated life is born and regenerated each day in the unending contemplation of the face of Christ."[46]

Conclusion

Our excitement about the Minor Prophets is palpable. We hope it will be infectious. They are extraordinary books and a treasure in the canon of

---

[45]"Starting Afresh from Christ," 2002.
[46]John Paul II, *Homily*, February 2, 2001; *L'Osservatore Romano*, February 4, 2001.

Scripture. They are multifaceted, rich, sobering beyond belief, full of God, and pregnant with his word, which he wishes to speak to us today. Much work remains to be done to retrieve them for today and to create the space for their riveting message to be heard again and again in our day. Yahweh—the lion, the lover, the king—is in his holy temple. "Let all the earth be silent before him."

RECOMMENDED READING

Bartholomew, Craig G. *The Old Testament and God*. Old Testament Origins and the Question of God 1. Grand Rapids, MI: Baker Academic, 2022. Chapter 8.

Goudzwaard, Bob, and Craig G. Bartholomew. *Beyond the Modern Age: An Archaeology of Contemporary Culture*. Downers Grove, IL: IVP Academic, 2017.

Lewis, C. S. *Mere Christianity*. London: Collins, 1952. Book 4.*

Recommended reading marked with a "" indicates introductory works.*

General Index

allegory, 11-12, 44, 60
Andersen, Francis, 97-99, 106, 117, 121, 123, 313
animals, 3-4, 28, 48, 63, 72-73, 153-55, 157, 170, 194, 208, 210, 258, 272-73, 285, 287, 304-5, 309, 320, 363, 366
apostasy, 42, 209, 301
arrogance, 132, 152, 215, 242, 246
Augustine, 53, 92
Baal, 35, 45, 47-48, 59, 111, 207-9, 270
Balaam, 36, 190, 203
Barth, Karl, 24, 64-65, 107, 110-11, 116, 156-57, 234, 279, 290, 358-60
Bauckham, Richard, 115, 281
blessing(s), 17, 36, 57, 60, 63, 139, 180, 183-84, 188, 268-69, 285, 295, 299, 304, 306, 313, 319, 323-24, 326, 356
Boda, Mark, 74, 286, 304
Branch, 10, 258, 260, 265, 284, 288
brokenness, 54, 83, 141, 188, 192, 219, 226, 234-35, 255, 309, 357
Bruner, Dale, 288, 346
Buber, Martin, 95, 128
Carroll, M. Daniel R., 97, 118-19
chaos, 182, 240, 318, 330
Childs, Brevard, 22, 24, 143, 146-47
comfort, 21, 89, 108, 128, 204-5, 235, 255-56, 319, 324
compassion, 62, 70, 75, 151, 154-55, 157, 159-60, 170, 216, 218-19, 250, 253, 307, 315, 319-20, 325-26, 330, 371
consumerism, 67, 198, 200, 221, 361-64
covenant, 3, 13, 31, 44, 48-49, 51, 55-56, 59-63, 65, 74-75, 79, 81-82, 102-4, 110-11, 113, 118, 121-22, 124, 126-27, 133, 147, 149-50, 156, 159, 163, 175, 183-84, 190-91, 193, 195-97, 207, 211-14, 217, 226, 251, 255, 262, 271, 273, 277-78, 283-84, 294, 295-96, 298-302, 304-8, 310-12, 314-17, 323, 326, 328-29, 333-34, 337, 341, 343, 346, 350, 356, 358, 369, 371

creation, 25, 31, 50, 55-57, 62-63, 66-67, 79, 89, 91, 105, 108, 110, 113, 116-29, 135-36, 155-57, 162-63, 170-71, 184, 185, 207-8, 215, 219, 221, 225-26, 229-30, 233, 237, 251, 261, 271-73, 279, 281, 285, 288-90, 296, 308, 317-24, 329, 333, 346, 351-53, 356-57, 360, 368, 371
  new, 66, 159, 219, 251, 254-55, 272, 290, 332, 334, 368
Creator, 3, 31, 73, 79, 105, 108, 110, 112-13, 116, 119-21, 124-27, 135, 171, 197, 208, 232, 270, 271, 317, 319-24, 356, 368
curse, 230, 262-63, 294, 298, 305, 307, 326
dark night of the soul, 152, 154, 158, 164, 168-69, 365
David, line of, 10, 109, 139-40, 178, 183, 185, 260, 265, 272, 282-85, 287-89, 299-300, 316, 317, 331, 344-48, 352
day of Yahweh, day the Lord, 19, 23, 61, 69-93, 106, 108, 113, 121, 131-37, 207, 209-12, 251, 257, 271-73, 306-8, 310, 324-25, 343, 352-53, 365
Dearman, J. Andrew, 43, 64
Decalogue, 49, 55, 263, 275, 306
deliverance, 17, 41, 139, 147, 163, 169, 182-83, 190-91, 196, 202-4, 225-26, 230, 246, 296, 314
destruction, 31-32, 45, 54, 60, 70-73, 88, 103, 107-9, 138-40, 156, 158-59, 172-73, 175-76, 186, 202, 206, 208, 213, 217, 224-25, 228, 263, 268, 270-71, 292, 295, 302, 326, 364
devotion, 74, 95, 180-81, 192-94, 208, 216, 253, 294, 297, 306
disobedience, 101, 121, 124, 165, 180, 185, 214, 297, 319, 326, 328, 358
divine council, 132, 259-60, 273
doctrine, 2, 51, 65, 157, 232, 279, 355, 359, 365
  of creation, 116, 125-27, 157, 279, 320, 356
  of God, 53, 65, 125, 355, 367-68
Dodd, C. H., 52, 289, 334
economics, economy, 3, 95, 111-12, 114, 198, 200, 221, 321, 360-63

election, 78-79, 104, 183-84, 208, 259, 299-300, 310-11, 318, 338, 350
Ellul, Jacques, 149-51, 158
emotion(s), 40, 53, 195-96, 216, 304, 315, 362, 367
empire(s), 7, 14, 27, 114-15, 130, 202-3, 213, 215-16, 221-22, 224, 264, 293, 302, 313, 320-32, 328
ethics, 102-3, 111-12, 170, 199, 218, 328-29, 334, 360, 362-63
evil, 48, 85, 105, 110, 149, 154, 175-76, 193, 198, 200, 215, 217, 223, 226, 228, 262, 264, 308, 332, 338, 341, 343, 346, 352-53, 359-60, 362, 366
exile, 25, 41-42, 47, 50, 64, 94, 104, 106-9, 130, 140, 143, 149, 158, 178-79, 247, 249-50, 252-53, 255-59, 264, 268, 270-71, 277-79, 282-83, 293-94, 298, 321, 323-24, 327, 330, 351-52, 357, 370
exodus, 46, 59-60, 103-4, 108, 183, 190, 229, 251, 255, 270, 272, 275, 283, 296, 307, 318, 346, 352
faith, 2, 7, 9, 14, 24-25, 67, 80, 128, 147, 182, 188, 199, 221, 223, 227, 230-34, 237-48, 253, 280, 294, 307, 322, 337, 341, 348, 351
faithfulness, 47, 62, 74, 136, 147, 182, 187, 193-96, 213-14, 226-31, 233-35, 237-48, 279, 284, 289, 292, 294-95, 310, 323, 329, 352, 368-69
faithlessness. *See* infidelity
fasting, 36, 70, 72-73, 75, 135, 153, 157, 191, 267-68, 320
fear of God, 150-51, 181, 183, 186, 214, 285, 295, 305-7, 309, 320
fidelity. *See* faithfulness
forgiveness, 75, 156, 172-74, 183-84, 186, 192-93, 200, 299, 330
France, R. T., 343, 345, 347
Freedman, David, 96-99, 106, 117, 121, 123, 313
freedom, divine, 65-66, 75, 238-39, 310-11
Fretheim, Terence, 133, 135-36
Freud, Sigmund, 357, 359
fulfillment, 52-53, 61, 63, 66, 80, 91, 94, 98, 145, 150, 156, 171, 183, 190, 227, 240, 242-43, 245, 250, 254, 262, 265, 269, 275-76, 286-89, 295, 310, 323, 331, 333-35, 340, 343-49, 351
future, 3, 12, 17, 22, 25, 42, 57-58, 61, 63-64, 70, 76, 86, 108, 134, 177-79, 181, 185-88, 215-16, 219-20, 234, 239, 257-58, 260, 269-70, 273, 275-76, 278-79, 293, 296, 298-99, 307, 309-10, 330-31, 344, 360, 364, 368-69
glory, 4, 49, 91, 118, 163, 188, 221, 226, 233-35, 240, 260, 292-93, 295-96, 301-2, 329, 331, 358, 365

Goudzwaard, Bob, 200, 221, 363
grace, 46-47, 65, 74-75, 103, 119, 156-58, 170, 184, 241, 247-48, 256, 272, 311, 318, 325, 334, 346, 357
Gunton, Colin, 65-66, 126
healing, 83, 170, 188, 201, 219, 235, 322, 325, 330, 336-37, 340-41
Heschel, Abraham, 50, 53, 217
holiness, 51, 66, 105, 110, 156, 184, 274, 279, 297-98, 325
hope, 2-3, 17, 21, 25, 31, 43, 46, 52, 58, 60, 64, 75, 90, 108, 137-40, 150, 168, 177, 182, 185-88, 204, 214, 233-35, 237-39, 249, 251, 253, 269, 274, 279-81, 284, 288, 293, 302, 304, 307, 310, 369-371
humility, 87, 132, 181, 186-87, 191, 193-94, 196, 212-14, 216, 222, 289-90, 309, 346
Ibn Ezra, 59, 64
idolatry, 44-48, 50, 55, 58-59, 61, 156, 175, 180, 186, 198, 200, 207-9, 215, 226-29, 264, 270, 272, 323, 325, 327, 341, 363-64
immanence, 105, 108, 110, 118, 120, 124, 126, 255, 260, 271, 279, 322, 324
infidelity, 40, 43-44, 47, 169, 182, 207, 209, 216, 226, 297, 303, 305
injustice, 2, 95, 103-6, 108, 111-13, 140, 148, 175-77, 181-82, 187, 193, 197-98, 200, 204, 215-16, 221, 225-26, 228, 268, 271, 306, 323, 358, 360, 362
See also justice
intertextuality, 18, 25, 39, 48, 52, 54, 60, 69-70, 80-81, 109, 113-14, 121, 140, 150, 154, 160, 178, 192, 220, 228-29, 250, 252-53, 273-78, 280, 284, 287-89, 300-302, 310, 334-50, 352
inwardness, 47, 53-54, 67, 74, 164
Irenaeus, 4, 163, 241
Jerome, 11, 163, 210
joy, 61, 76, 196, 209, 229-30, 233-34, 267-68, 270, 284, 287, 291, 366
judge, 16, 51, 77, 105, 112, 117, 122, 136, 140-41, 182, 186, 190, 202, 227, 239, 242, 247, 252, 323-25
justice, 2-3, 16, 25, 62, 78, 81-82, 85, 92, 103, 105, 110-12, 114, 120, 127, 136, 141, 156, 170, 175-77, 181-82, 184, 186, 187, 189-201, 203, 215, 217-19, 223, 225-26, 229, 232, 234, 239-40, 242, 245, 252, 257, 268, 279, 305-6, 319, 328, 366
See also injustice
Kierkegaard, Søren, 289-90, 359
kindness, 181, 186, 194-97, 201
king(s), 10-11, 17, 25, 31, 33-36, 38, 41, 45, 50, 90, 94-96, 102-3, 108, 139, 142, 144, 148,

General Index

153-54, 157, 173, 175-76, 178-79, 183, 185, 188, 196, 206, 215-16, 220-21, 232-33, 240-42, 261, 264-65, 270, 273, 276-78, 282-92, 299, 302-3, 305, 308, 313, 315-17, 319, 321-22, 327, 332, 334, 340, 342-43, 345-48, 352-53, 360, 369, 372
kingdom(s), 25, 35, 41-42, 45-47, 50, 64, 94-95, 98, 100-101, 103-4, 106, 108-9, 111, 123-24, 140, 142-43, 148-49, 172, 174, 182, 206, 208, 270-71, 278, 314, 321-22, 326-27, 340-41, 362
    of God, 54, 61, 66, 80, 82-83, 84, 86-87, 89, 91-93, 114, 128, 132, 136-37, 139-41, 188, 199-200, 234, 241, 246, 277-78, 280, 282-91, 317-18, 320, 331-32, 335, 339, 341, 343, 347, 351-53, 360, 370-71
knowledge, 49, 62, 67, 144, 209, 225, 232, 280, 329, 337
König, Adrio, 358, 364-69
lament, 30-31, 33-35, 70, 72, 88, 105, 120, 225, 233-34, 255-56, 305, 339
land, 25, 27, 44, 46, 48, 60-61, 63-64, 70-72, 76, 83, 88, 95, 101-3, 109, 111, 120-24, 127, 134-35, 137, 140, 145, 147, 150-52, 168, 173, 175-76, 183, 197-200, 206, 208, 212, 215, 220, 247, 250, 255-58, 260, 263, 268, 270, 272, 282-86, 294, 298, 300, 307, 315, 318-20, 339, 341, 345, 351
law, 13, 38, 48-49, 54-55, 62, 103, 112-13, 118, 122, 190, 230, 240-41, 264, 285, 297, 307, 314, 326, 338, 348, 350, 360
    See also Torah
lawsuit, 16, 42-3, 47-48, 104, 120, 181, 190, 196-97, 263, 314
leader(s), 12, 33, 38, 49-50, 82, 103, 175-77, 182, 187-89, 204, 206-7, 210, 214, 259, 270-71, 294, 327, 341, 345, 347-48
leadership, 11, 38, 49, 103, 173, 176, 187-88, 207, 261, 270, 272, 274, 282, 293, 299, 305, 322, 341, 344
Levenson, Jon, 192, 317
Levites, 249, 274, 306
Lewis, C. S., 53, 312
lion, 37, 50-53, 71-72, 100-101, 104, 109-10, 179-80, 186, 205-6, 325, 372
liturgy, 17, 82, 86, 105, 116-17, 125, 127, 139, 210, 223, 287, 359, 371
love, 2, 43, 46, 50-51, 53, 62, 64-67, 74-75, 127-28, 141, 156, 176, 193-99, 201, 217, 219, 238, 268, 281, 289, 297, 302-5, 308, 337, 346, 366-69
Luther, Martin, 12-13, 240-41, 246, 356
Marx, Karl, 357-59, 362
Mays, James, 60, 94

mercy, 2, 53-54, 62, 74-75, 77, 147, 149, 156, 170, 183, 186-87, 193-94, 199, 217, 219, 253, 255-56, 336-37
Merton, Thomas, 67, 370
Messiah, 9-12, 17, 80, 91, 185, 187, 231, 244, 245-46, 278, 284-85, 289-90, 310, 331, 333, 339-40, 343-49, 351-53
Meyers, Carol, 262, 265-66, 273
Meyers, Eric, 262, 265-66, 273
mission, 7, 54, 143-46, 148-49, 152, 157-60, 201, 256, 273, 280, 295, 331, 338-39, 350, 357, 369
Moses, 32, 37-38, 48, 63, 89, 94, 109, 125, 154, 273, 300-301, 303, 307-8, 325-26, 334, 346
mourning, 36, 72, 75-76, 101, 122-23, 175, 251, 267-68, 271-72, 306, 342, 348
Muilenberg, James, 17, 111
mystery, 227, 229, 232-33
nations, 3, 16, 19, 21-22, 25, 27, 35, 38, 50-52, 70-72, 75, 77-79, 81-82, 89, 96, 99, 101-3, 109-10, 112-13, 122, 124-26, 130-40, 142, 147, 149, 158-59, 172, 174, 177-81, 183-86, 192, 195, 200, 202, 205-7, 211, 213-16, 218, 220-21, 226-27, 238, 246-47, 251, 255-57, 267, 269-73, 284, 286, 288, 296, 298, 302, 305, 308, 312-13, 318-20, 322-23, 329, 331, 342, 348, 353, 360, 362, 364, 367, 369
Newbigin, Lesslie, 66, 290
Nouwen, Henri, 235, 312
obedience, 48, 111, 121, 128, 145, 148, 152-53, 169, 228, 241, 259, 295, 297, 307, 315, 322-23, 326, 346, 369
O'Donovan, Oliver, 197, 322-23
Ollenburger, Ben, 316-17, 319
oppression, 89, 103-4, 108, 112, 128, 135, 141, 179, 187, 193, 196-97, 200, 203-6, 214, 217-19, 221, 227-28, 234, 246, 283, 306, 326, 347, 358, 360
order
    of creation, 91, 120, 125, 135-36, 162, 189, 221, 239, 318-19, 329
    divine, 30, 56, 136, 157, 287, 329
    moral, 135, 237-38, 240
    social, 55-56, 182
patience, 47, 105, 110, 154, 156-57, 170, 204, 217, 233-34, 242, 246, 252-53, 323, 328, 366, 370-71
peace, 3, 63, 67, 78, 85-86, 88, 95, 109, 141, 164, 177, 188, 195, 204-5, 214, 233, 250, 253, 255, 260, 264, 268, 270, 273-74, 284, 286, 288-89, 297, 314, 342, 344, 346
Peck, Scott, 110, 359
perseverance, 231, 235, 242, 245, 246, 253

personal God, 53, 110-11, 126, 156, 312, 355-56, 367
pilgrimage, 177, 185-86, 204-5, 209, 230, 273
politics, 2-3, 50, 103, 106, 110-11, 114, 127-28, 141, 189, 200, 216, 255, 273, 313, 316, 321-23, 327, 360, 362-63
poverty, 103, 105, 107, 112, 128, 132, 197-200, 203, 212, 221, 290, 326, 360, 362-64, 370
prayer, 9, 17, 53, 67, 70, 73, 75, 86, 111, 114, 145-48, 150-52, 154, 166-69, 171, 182-83, 185, 191, 223-25, 229, 233-34, 319, 329, 366, 371
presence, divine, 1, 67, 82, 126, 149, 164, 167, 177, 189, 219-20, 232, 258, 260-61, 264, 272, 295-96, 299, 306, 316-17, 319, 323
pride, 132, 138, 193, 211, 213-14, 228, 233, 240-42, 342, 349
priest(s), 10, 29, 38, 49, 72, 82, 89, 94, 96, 107, 142, 158, 165, 170, 177, 209-10, 214, 249-51, 258-62, 265, 267, 279, 289, 294, 297-98, 304-5, 309, 313, 334-37
protection, 30-31, 157, 178, 190, 196-97, 218, 257-58, 269, 355, 360, 362
punishment, 16, 36, 41, 45, 47-48, 54-55, 60, 64, 74-75, 81, 86-87, 133-36, 138, 210, 215, 226, 229, 240, 242, 262, 271, 313, 321-23, 342-43
purification, 75, 79, 91, 175, 185, 225, 259-60, 262, 264, 274, 308, 331, 341, 353
rebellion, 48, 51, 58, 65, 94, 101, 103, 124, 136, 140, 145, 147-49, 152, 155-57, 174, 207, 214, 289, 309, 323-24, 365-67, 371
reconciliation, 53, 78, 199, 252, 309
redemption, 3, 12, 25, 51, 85, 109-10, 122, 152, 160, 163, 179, 185, 215, 234, 251, 269, 310, 317, 319-20, 323, 350
reign of God, (rule) 3, 25, 79, 82-83, 85-90, 137, 140-41, 158, 178, 199, 205, 209, 215-16, 220, 221, 229, 240, 278, 285-86, 288-89, 308, 319, 332, 370
　See also sovereignty
rejoicing. *See* joy
relationship, 1, 42-44, 47-49, 53-55, 59-64, 67, 91, 97, 102, 104-5, 110-13, 121, 136-37, 160, 167, 171, 175, 191-92, 194-97, 211-13, 216-17, 219-20, 223, 255-56, 261, 274, 284, 286, 301, 304-6, 308-10, 313-16, 323, 326, 329-31, 334-35, 341, 344, 356, 359, 368
religion, 2-3, 14-15, 24, 30-32, 47, 50, 53, 63, 95, 103-6, 108, 110-11, 127, 153, 163, 172, 181, 189, 271, 316, 321, 326-27, 329, 337, 341, 352, 357-61
remembrance, 72, 152, 166, 168, 229, 247, 279, 296, 305, 307-8, 326, 328

remnant, 76, 108-9, 131, 134, 137, 140, 172-74, 176, 178-80, 183-84, 208, 214, 216, 220, 228, 247, 269, 272, 295, 297, 325, 330
renewal, 31, 43, 60-63, 67, 79, 81, 83, 87, 91, 109, 140, 180, 215, 220, 273, 277-79, 298, 309, 351, 355, 365
repentance, 46, 58, 64, 70, 72, 74, 77, 80-82, 94, 105, 128, 135, 139, 144, 148, 152-54, 156-57, 169, 186, 207, 211-12, 246, 252, 279, 320, 325-26, 337, 341, 353
restoration, 17, 19-20, 25, 47, 61, 63-64, 70-71, 75-77, 79, 83, 86-87, 109, 130-32, 135, 137, 139-40, 142, 154, 156, 173, 177-78, 183, 185, 192, 205, 207-8, 211, 213, 215-16, 220, 247, 251, 256-58, 260, 265, 267-68, 270, 275, 283-84, 292-93, 296-99, 306, 309, 327, 330, 341, 352
resurrection, 9, 80, 92, 102, 159, 168, 200, 221, 228, 235, 244-45, 247, 290, 370
retribution, 78, 133, 135, 296
return, 19-20, 60, 73-74, 105, 133, 135, 178, 185, 188, 247, 249-55, 257-59, 264, 268, 271-72, 277-79, 282, 286-87, 290, 298, 303, 306, 309, 322, 324, 330-35, 346, 351-53, 355, 364-65
Rieff, Phillip, 55-56, 279
righteousness, 16, 62, 78, 81, 85-87, 89, 91, 105, 111-12, 114, 132, 136, 140, 190, 195, 199, 212-14, 225, 227-28, 230-31, 238-40, 242-47, 270, 284-85, 289, 326, 336-38, 360
sacrifice, 48, 54, 66, 72, 75-76, 149, 152, 166, 181, 190-95, 210, 226, 269, 274, 297-98, 304-6, 309-10, 335-38, 351, 365, 369
salvation, 9, 17, 19, 38, 50-51, 61, 67, 70, 78, 80-81, 83, 85-89, 91-93, 127, 136, 139, 147, 151, 158, 163, 166-67, 175, 178-79, 182-83, 185-87, 190, 205, 211, 217, 219, 221, 229-33, 235, 239, 242, 246-47, 257-58, 269-70, 272-74, 285-86, 297, 306, 308, 310, 318, 320, 322, 330-31, 344, 348, 351-52, 366
sanctuary, 31, 108, 261, 305, 313, 342
　See also shrine(s), temple
security, 48, 132, 177, 180-81, 211, 215, 221, 237-38, 270, 316, 319
shalom. *See* peace
shame, 70, 76, 177, 183, 196, 206, 214-15, 218, 221, 228-29, 235, 240
shepherd, 38, 96-97, 101, 176, 179, 183, 185, 188, 251, 265, 270-72, 278, 282, 341-48, 353, 364
shrine(s), 31, 33-35, 48, 104, 174-75
　See also sanctuary, temple
sin, 3-4, 43, 49, 60, 64, 66, 73-74, 81, 88, 102, 110-11, 126, 128, 132, 136, 141, 156, 172-73, 175, 177, 181-87, 189, 190-93, 200, 204, 210-11,

General Index

213-15, 220-21, 224, 226, 228-29, 234, 247, 251, 259-60, 272, 299, 301, 306, 308, 310, 325-27, 346, 348, 352, 358-59, 365, 367
Sinai, 48, 59-60, 63, 65, 111, 121, 125, 299-301, 307, 314, 325, 334
social injustice. *See* injustice
social justice. *See* justice
Son of Man, 91, 159, 333, 336, 340, 349
sovereignty, 75, 89, 97, 156, 159, 178, 185, 202, 255, 257-58, 270, 273, 279, 289, 317-18, 328-29, 356-57
Spirit of God 2-3, 9, 38, 71, 76-77, 80, 82, 90-91, 171, 177, 261, 264, 268, 272, 296, 331, 348, 351, 370
spiritual formation, 54-55, 161-71, 232, 235, 329, 371
spirituality, 67, 157, 164, 232-33, 319, 329, 334, 370-71
Stuart, Douglas, 119, 124, 144
suffering, 31, 52, 54, 72, 112, 130, 134, 140-41, 158, 187, 189, 200, 221, 223, 231, 233, 235, 244, 253, 259, 277, 281, 290-91, 328-29, 334, 347, 364, 366, 370-71
Sweeney, Marvin, 20, 202, 250, 254-56, 258, 262, 264-65, 267-68, 293, 298
temple, 32-35, 44, 72, 82, 100, 107, 118, 149, 152, 166, 168-69, 174, 190, 208-9, 229, 232, 240, 250-52, 254-55, 257-58, 260-65, 267-29, 271-72, 274, 277-79, 283-84, 287-88, 290, 292-99, 309, 315, 317-20, 326, 336, 338, 349, 353-54, 372

See also sanctuary, shrine(s)
theophany, 85, 96, 123
Torah, 48-49, 103, 125, 155, 191, 240, 245, 262, 273, 306, 308, 323
transcendence, 53, 105, 110, 118, 125-27, 156, 232, 271, 279, 308, 322, 324, 331
transformation, 25, 72, 75-76, 89-91, 158, 164, 168-69, 219-20, 281, 295, 331, 345, 369

Trible, Phyllis, 145-6, 167
trust, 25, 81, 141, 180, 186, 211, 214, 227, 230-32, 239-40, 242-48, 308, 322, 342, 369
unfaithfulness. *See* infidelity
vengeance, 45, 139, 141, 180, 203-4, 217, 219
vindication, 73, 86-87, 89, 91, 183, 215, 239-40, 242, 244, 246-47, 309
violence, 128, 133, 177, 181, 193, 203, 216-19, 221, 225-28
von Rad, Gerhard, 317, 363
war, 3, 32, 34, 63, 77, 85, 95, 102-3, 133, 136, 177, 186, 205, 211, 229, 270, 273, 285, 286, 289, 359-60
wealth, 38, 95, 97, 106, 132, 181, 197-200, 205, 210-11, 271-72, 278, 290, 294, 296, 358, 361-62, 364
wickedness, 3, 48, 81, 86-87, 89, 91, 132, 136, 149, 177, 181-82, 184, 200, 202, 219-20, 225-26, 229, 239, 242, 245, 263-64, 307, 340
wilderness, 58-59, 67, 135, 164, 247, 273, 340, 356-57
wisdom, 17, 25, 36, 51, 98, 133, 136, 138, 181, 189, 276, 285, 289, 314, 320, 326, 333-34
woe oracles, 17, 99-100, 105-6, 175, 227-29
worship, 30, 47-48, 61, 72, 82, 100, 105, 118, 150-51, 165, 174, 181, 190-94, 197, 204-5, 207-10, 212, 264, 273, 317-18, 320, 323, 327-29, 361, 369
wrath, 50, 53, 80, 100, 110-11, 131, 134-36, 141, 180, 203, 209, 211-12, 219, 229, 242, 252, 319, 325, 365-66, 368
Wright, N. T., 88, 276-77, 287, 289, 333-34, 338-42, 350-53
Zion, 70-73, 78-79, 81-83, 88, 100, 106, 110, 113, 116, 134-35, 176-80, 182-83, 185-86, 204-5, 207-8, 213-16, 220, 229, 240, 247, 256, 258, 260, 262, 268, 270, 272, 274, 284, 286-87, 300-301, 314-20, 322-25, 330, 334, 346, 352, 369

Scripture Index

Old Testament references are listed according to Hebrew versification.

OLD TESTAMENT

Genesis
1, *48, 63, 121, 124*
1–2, *55, 119, 320*
1–3, *119, 314, 356*
1:1–2:3, *162*
1:2, *261*
1:20-28, *208*
1:24-26, *259*
1:26-27, *237*
1:27, *356*
1:28, *162, 232*
2, *271*
2–3, *150*
2:4-5, *124*
2:24, *40*
6–9, *121, 225*
6:11, *225*
6:13, *225*
9:8-10, *62*
9:9, *63*
12–50, *158, 371*
12:1-3, *63, 109, 158, 180, 183, 371*
12:1-4, *269*
15:18-21, *286*
20:7, *37*
22, *164*
22:17, *47*
25–26, *130*
25–36, *133, 302*
25:24-26, *102*
34:3, *60*
42:17, *151*
49:11, *285*

Exodus
1–24, *59*
2:23, *72*
3, *121*
3:12, *295*
4:22, *304*
6, *19, 70, 84, 121*
6:1, *303*
7:1, *37*
10, *70*
10:12, *71*
12:22, *124*
12:46, *348*
14:12, *154*
15, *229, 317*
15:1-11, *184*
15:3, *229*
15:5, *254*
15:7, *213*
15:17, *109*
15:18, *315*
15:20, *37*
15:20-21, *38*
15:21, *61*
19–24, *48, 60, 104*
19:4, *51, 60*
19:4-6, *158, 295, 296*
19:5, *295*
20–24, *296*
20:1-2, *302*
20:3, *49*
20:5-6, *204*
20:7, *49*
20:12, *304*
20:13, *49*
20:14, *49, 306*
20:15, *49*
20:16, *49, 306*
20:17, *49, 175*
20:26, *124*
21:16, *49, 102*
21:32, *347*
22:29, *192*
23:20, *339*
23:31, *286*
24:3-8, *60*
24:8, *283*
25–27, *275*
25:31-40, *261*
27:2, *256*
28:36, *273*
28:36-38, *259*
29, *259*
29:23, *264*
31:2-3, *296*
34, *19, 70, 75, 84*
34:6, *154*
34:6-7, *19, 74, 75, 154, 183, 184, 204, 325*
34:7, *154*
35:30-31, *296*
37:17-24, *261*

Leviticus
1:4, *191*
5:15, *191*
5:18, *191*
6:3, *263*
6:6, *191*
7:18, *191*
8–9, *259*
8:21, *191*
9:2, *191*
9:3, *191*
9:4, *191*
11:44-45, *297*
18:2, *297*
18:4, *297*
19:2, *297*
19:7, *191*
19:12, *263*
20:7, *297*
20:26, *297*
21:8, *297*
22:17-33, *304*
22:23, *191*
22:25, *191*
22:27, *191*
23:20, *273*
23:40, *254*
23:42, *273*
26:19-20, *294*
26:25, *203*
27:30, *273, 306*
27:32, *273*

Numbers
6:14, *191*
6:17, *191*
10, *48*
12:6, *37*
14:18, *154*
14:21, *228*
14:44, *241*
19, *298*
20:14-21, *102, 302*
23–24, *190*
25:1-11, *59*
28:9-10, *336*
34, *286*

Scripture Index

Deuteronomy
2:4, *102*
2:4-5, *304*
4:3-4, *59*
4:20, *183*
4:29, *212*
4:32-34, *304*
4:37, *304*
5:1-4, *307*
5:9-10, *204*
5:10, *302*
5:16, *304*
5:18, *306*
5:20, *306*
6, *273*
6:5, *302*
7:8-9, *304*
7:13, *302*
9:26, *183*
9:29, *183*
10:12, *194, 304*
10:12-13, *194, 195*
10:14-15, *304*
10:18-19, *304*
11:1, *304*
11:12, *304*
11:22, *194, 304*
11:25, *286*
13, *304*
13:1-5, *37*
13:3, *304*
14:22-29, *306*
15:18, *306*
17:18-20, *285*
18:1-8, *72*
18:12, *305*
18:15, *94*
18:15-22, *37*
19:9, *194, 304*
21:15, *304*
23:5, *304*
23:7, *102*
24:17-22, *306*
25:16, *305*
26:12-13, *306*
26:12-15, *306*
28, *70*
28:23-24, *294*
28:30, *60, 294*
28:38-40, *294*
28:39, *60*
28:48, *294*
29:23, *50*
30:1-10, *307*
30:16, *194, 304*
32:13, *119*
32:39, *116*
33:29, *285*
34:10, *37*

Joshua
1:5, *295*
1:6, *296*
1:8-9, *82*
1:9, *295, 296*
1:18, *296*
2:18, *60*
2:21, *60*
6:19, *273*
7:24-26, *60*
22:5, *194*
24:19, *204*

Judges
4:4, *37, 38*
5:4, *96*
19:3, *60*

Ruth
1:8, *62*
2:13, *60*
3:10, *62*

1 Samuel
2:6-8, *116*
3:20, *37*
5:6, *241*
9:9, *37*
16:1, *345*
17:12, *179*
20:2, *313*
21:2-7, *336*
22:5, *37*
28:6, *37*
28:15, *37*

2 Samuel
2:25, *124*
5:2, *179, 345*
5:7, *178, 315*
6–7, *315*
6:6, *123*
7, *275, 315*
7:12-14, *299*
8:12-14, *130*
8:15, *176*
22:8, *96*
23:3-4, *285*

1 Kings
3:3, *194*
3:4, *191*
3:6, *194*
8, *70*
8:3, *194*
8:65-66, *254*
10:9, *176*
10:19-20, *124*
11:14-22, *130*
12, *104*
12:32, *254*
17:21, *151*
19:4, *154*
19:11-12, *96*
21, *182*
22, *259*

2 Kings
3:4, *96*
8:20-22, *130*
9:13, *124*
9:36, *303*
10:30, *45*
14, *142*
14:23-27, *41*
14:23-29, *95*
14:25, *142*
17:13, *303*
20:8, *151*
22–23, *208*
22:3–23:23, *207*
22:13, *209*
22:14, *38*

1 Chronicles
3:17-19, *299*
3:19, *294*
29:21, *191*

2 Chronicles
7:6, *223*
8:14, *223*
24:20-22, *278*
35:2, *223*
36:15-16, *292, 293*

Ezra
2, *293*
2:2, *294*
3:1-7, *254*
3:2, *294*
3:8, *294*
4:2-3, *294*
5:1, *249, 250*
5:2, *294*
5:11–6:13, *293*
6:14, *249, 250, 297*
10:18, *294*

Nehemiah
2–6, *257*
3:15, *124*
3:26, *241*
7, *293*
7:7, *294*
8:15, *254*
9:17, *155*
12:1, *294*
12:4, *249*
12:16, *249*
12:26, *294*
12:47, *294*
13:30, *223*

Job
1, *259*
1:1-5, *133*
9:10, *121*
38:31, *121*

Psalms
1, *122, 323*
1–2, *323*
1:1, *323*
2, *122, 323*
2:12, *323*
4:2-4, *73*
7:1, *223*
10:16, *305*
11:4, *229*
14:1, *110*
15, *240*
17:6, *73*
18:7, *73*
19, *122*
19:1-6, *122*
19:7-14, *122*
22:29, *137*
24:8, *305*
24:8-10, *316*
24:10, *305*

25:9, *196*
29, *96*
29:10, *305*
33:16, *285*
34:2, *196*
34:13, *181*
34:16-17, *166*
34:21, *348*
41:6, *181*
46, *96, 316, 318*
46:7, *123*
47:2, *305*
48, *316*
65, *318*
65:6, *119*
68, *316*
72, *176*
72:8, *284, 286*
75:4, *123*
75:9, *134*
76, *316, 318*
84:3, *305*
85:10-11, *289*
87, *318*
89:3, *300*
89:26, *286*
93:1, *305*
95:2, *191*
95:3, *305*
96:10, *305*
97:1, *305*
98:6, *305*
99:1, *305*
103:19, *305*
109:2, *181*
120:2-3, *181*
120–134, *273*
130:1, *72*
132, *316, 318*
132:13, *318*
137, *50, 137, 139, 141*
137:7-8, *130, 139*
138:4-5, *139*
140:12, *197*
145:14, *191*
146:7, *197*
146:8, *191*
149:4, *196*

Proverbs
1:7, *320*
3:34, *196*
5:18, *305*
8:25, *119*
10:11, *272*
11:2, *196*
13:14, *272*
13:24, *217*
14:25, *181*
18:10, *237, 239*
19:1, *181*
21:3, *195*
22:15, *217*
23:13, *217*
24:3, *228*
29:15, *217*
30:8, *181*

Ecclesiastes
10:19, *64*
12:1, *168*
12:13, *307*

Isaiah
1:1, *40*
1:10-17, *268*
1:17, *193, 197*
1:24, *203*
2:1-4, *177*
2:2-4, *172, 260*
2:3, *273*
2:4, *70, 78*
2:6-21, *172*
3:22, *259*
5:8-10, *172*
5:20, *193*
6, *259*
6:5, *305*
6:11, *255*
7:4, *259, 296*
8, *38*
8:1-4, *250*
8:3, *38*
10, *226, 242*
10:5-15, *242*
10:12-15, *242*
10:19-22, *137*
11, *260*
11:2, *177*
11:9, *228*
11:11-16, *137*
12–14, *275*
13:2, *72*
13:6, *70*
13:10-13, *73*
17:12-14, *172*
20:2, *303*
30:8, *237*
30:18, *195*
30:31, *181*
32:1, *176*
32:14, *241*
33:15-16, *240*
33:22, *305*
34:14, *302*
35:4, *296*
40–55, *275, 277*
40:1, *255*
40:9, *296*
40:11, *179*
40:12, *119*
41:10, *296*
41:13, *296*
41:19, *254*
42:1, *76*
43:7, *119*
43:15, *305*
44:3-4, *76*
44:6, *305*
44:26, *292, 293*
44:27, *254*
45:5, *213*
45:5-6, *76*
45:7, *119*
45:18, *119*
46:3, *137*
51:1, *212*
52, *253*
52:7, *205, 220, 286*
52:7-10, *286*
54, *253, 275*
55:1-5, *284*
55:13, *254, 255*
56:1, *240*
58:5, *191*
58:6, *124*
58:14, *119*
59:3, *77*
59:13, *77*
59:21, *76, 82*
60, *142, 296*
60:7, *296*
60:8, *142*
60:9, *142*
62:11, *287*
63:1-6, *131*

Jeremiah
1:1, *40, 97*
1:14, *258*
2:2-3, *59*
2:13, *272*
2:18, *203*
2:36, *203*
3:15, *179*
4:6, *258*
5:9, *203*
5:14-17, *226*
6:14, *314*
7, *268*
7:18, *264*
9:24, *197*
10:22, *258*
13:9, *213*
15:18, *175*
17:13, *272*
19:1-13, *347*
19:9, *176*
21:12, *197*
22:14, *294*
22:15, *176*
23, *269*
23:2, *179*
23:5, *285*
23:5-6, *260*
25:11, *255*
29:10, *255*
29:13, *212*
30–33, *275*
30:12, *175*
31:38-39, *257*
33:14-26, *260*
44:19, *264*
48–51, *275*
49, *137, 138, 139*
49:7, *133*
49:7-22, *130, 137, 139, 141*
49:12-13, *302*
49:17, *302*
51:34, *164*
51:44, *164*
51:58, *228*

Lamentations
2, *275*
2:20, *176*
3:1, *181*
4:10, *176*

Scripture Index

4:21-22, *130*
5:6, *203*

Ezekiel
11:3, *176*
11:7, *176*
11:11, *176*
16:56, *213*
24:1-14, *176*
24:8, *203*
25:13, *302*
32:7-8, *73*
32:12, *213*
32:29, *302*
35, *137, 139*
35:3-4, *302*
35:7, *302*
35:9, *302*
35:10-14, *139*
35:14-15, *302*
36:27, *76, 77, 82*
36:33-36, *302*
37:14, *76*
37:27, *82*
38–39, *275*
39:29, *76*
40–48, *275*
47, *79*

Daniel
6:10, *151*
7, *91, 159, 277*
8:19, *238*
11:27, *238*
11:29, *238*
11:35, *238*

Hosea
1, *21, 42*
1–2, *52*
1–3, *42, 43*
1–11, *52*
1:1, *40, 41, 42, 43, 44, 45, 97, 174*
1:2, *43, 44*
1:2-9, *43*
1:2-11, *43*
1:2–3:5, *43*
1:4, *45*
1:4-5, *45*
1:4-8, *44*
1:6, *19*

1:7, *46*
1:8, *58*
1:8-9, *46*
1:9, *52*
1:10–2:1, *17*
1:11, *46*
2, *19, 43, 46, 57, 58, 66*
2:1-2, *46*
2:2-13, *57*
2:4, *46*
2:4-15, *57*
2:4-17, *57*
2:4-23, *47*
2:5, *59*
2:7-9, *16*
2:8, *48, 57*
2:8-15, *57*
2:10, *60*
2:10-11, *60*
2:11, *47, 57*
2:14, *325*
2:15, *16*
2:16, *46, 57, 59, 61, 325*
2:16-17, *59*
2:16-25, *57, 58, 59*
2:17, *59, 61, 64*
2:18, *48, 61, 314*
2:18-25, *61*
2:19, *61*
2:20, *55, 61, 62, 63*
2:20-25, *25*
2:21, *62*
2:21-22, *61, 67*
2:22, *49, 62*
2:23-24, *325*
2:23-25, *61*
2:23-26, *64*
2:25, *63, 64*
3, *21, 43, 47*
3:5, *17, 177, 212*
4, *16, 49, 268*
4–13, *47*
4–14, *42, 43*
4:1, *47*
4:1–14:9, *43*
4:2, *49*
4:3, *48*
4:6, *49*
4:12, *47*
4:13, *47, 48*
4:14, *48, 55*

4:15, *48*
4:16, *179*
4:17, *47*
5:1, *49*
5:5, *213*
5:10, *48, 49*
5:11, *47*
5:13, *322*
5:13–6:3, *325*
5:14, *100, 325*
5:14-15, *51*
5:15, *325*
6, *337*
6:1-2, *228*
6:2, *247*
6:3, *325*
6:4, *337*
6:4-10, *337*
6:5, *328*
6:6, *53, 336, 337, 338*
6:7, *48, 314*
6:7-9, *49*
7, *49, 50*
7:1, *325*
7:7, *50*
7:8, *50*
7:10, *213*
7:11, *50, 203, 321, 322*
7:13, *17*
7:14, *47*
8:1, *48, 316*
8:4, *41, 50*
8:5, *47*
8:6, *47*
8:7, *51*
8:9, *321, 322*
8:14, *326*
9–14, *366*
9:3, *48, 321*
9:5, *19*
9:7-8, *314*
9:10, *47, 48, 59, 326, 366*
9:15, *48, 316*
10, *342, 343*
10:5, *47*
10:6, *321, 322*
10:8, *47, 342, 352*
10:11, *366*
11, *20, 43, 52, 346*
11:1, *48, 52, 304, 315, 326, 343, 344, 346, 352*

11:3, *325*
11:4, *304, 325, 366, 369*
11:5, *203, 321, 322*
11:7, *47*
11:8, *50, 53, 65, 315*
11:8-9, *366, 368*
11:8-11, *50*
11:9, *51, 323, 366*
11:10, *100, 325*
11:10-11, *51*
11:11, *203, 321, 322*
11:12, *323*
12, *48*
12:1, *203*
12:2, *48, 50, 321*
12:6, *242*
12:10, *314, 348*
12:11, *313*
13:1, *47*
13:2, *47*
13:7, *51, 100*
13:7-9, *325*
13:8, *51*
13:16, *50*
14, *43*
14:1, *50*
14:2, *21, 325*
14:4-8, *46*
14:5, *304*
14:9, *51, 320, 326*
14:10, *25, 42, 43*

Joel
1, *72, 82*
1–2, *17, 76, 77, 81, 82*
1:1, *70, 71, 97*
1:1-7, *70, 71*
1:1–2:17, *70*
1:1–3:5, *82*
1:2, *71*
1:2-3, *72*
1:2-5, *107*
1:3, *71*
1:3-14, *71*
1:3–2:17, *76*
1:4, *71, 76, 206*
1:5, *72, 76*
1:6, *71, 72, 76, 205*
1:6-20, *71*
1:8, *70, 72*
1:8-19, *72*

1:9, *72, 76*
1:9-12, *70*
1:10, *76*
1:10-20, *70*
1:11-12, *76*
1:12, *72*
1:12-14, *76*
1:13, *72, 76*
1:13-14, *70, 72*
1:14, *72*
1:15, *69, 71, 72, 86, 211*
1:15-16, *72, 73*
1:15-18, *70, 72*
1:16, *72*
1:16-17, *76*
1:17, *72*
1:18, *25, 72, 76, 320*
1:19, *73*
1:19-20, *75*
1:20, *73, 76, 320*
2, *76, 79, 275, 351*
2:1, *73*
2:1-2, *86*
2:1-11, *70, 73*
2:2, *73, 80, 86, 211*
2:3, *320*
2:10, *73, 80, 86*
2:11, *73, 80, 81, 82, 86*
2:12, *16, 21, 73*
2:12-13, *306*
2:12-14, *73, 74, 325*
2:12-17, *73, 75*
2:13, *19, 70, 74, 75, 154, 155, 325*
2:13-14, *70*
2:14, *70, 75, 76, 154*
2:15, *73*
2:15-17, *70, 327*
2:18, *75*
2:18-20, *70*
2:18-27, *75, 76*
2:18–4:21, *70*
2:19, *75, 76*
2:20, *72, 76, 82*
2:21, *76*
2:21-22, *17, 296*
2:21-24, *70*
2:22, *76*
2:23, *76*
2:24, *76*
2:25, *72*
2:25-26, *70, 76*

2:26, *76*
2:27, *76, 87*
2:28, *3*
2:28-29, *38*
3, *82*
3–4, *76*
3:1, *76, 77, 80, 86*
3:1-2, *76, 77*
3:1-5, *71, 75, 76, 77, 80, 82, 86*
3:2, *77, 320*
3:3-4, *86*
3:4, *19, 80*
3:5, *69, 79, 81, 83, 86, 87, 134, 137*
3:16, *100*
4, *77, 82, 83, 89*
4:1, *20, 83, 86*
4:1-3, *71, 87*
4:1-13, *77*
4:1-21, *81*
4:2, *77, 82*
4:4, *20, 82, 133*
4:4-8, *16, 71, 78, 84, 296*
4:5, *296*
4:7, *20, 133*
4:9-13, *71, 78*
4:10, *70, 78*
4:12, *77, 78, 83*
4:13, *78, 81*
4:14, *72, 78, 83*
4:14-16, *71*
4:14-21, *78*
4:15-16, *83*
4:15-17, *79*
4:16, *21, 69, 325*
4:16-18, *83, 87*
4:16-21, *79*
4:17, *71, 78, 83, 87*
4:17-18, *83*
4:18, *69, 79, 83*
4:18-21, *71, 79, 82*
4:19, *82, 83*
4:20, *83*
4:21, *78, 83*

Amos
1–2, *16, 99, 213, 329*
1–6, *99*
1:1, *40, 95, 96, 97, 98, 99, 100, 174*

1:1–2:3, *112*
1:2, *21, 69, 99, 100, 101, 104, 325*
1:2–3:8, *99*
1:2–4:13, *100*
1:3, *16, 101, 313*
1:3-5, *101*
1:3-16, *99*
1:3–2:3, *103, 112*
1:3–2:16, *101, 320*
1:3–4:13, *100*
1:4, *103*
1:5, *101, 103*
1:5-6, *16*
1:6-8, *102*
1:7, *103*
1:8, *103*
1:8-9, *16*
1:9-10, *102*
1:10, *103*
1:11, *16, 302*
1:11-12, *102, 109*
1:12, *103*
1:13, *16*
1:13-15, *102*
1:14, *103*
1:15, *16, 103*
2, *98*
2:1, *16*
2:1-3, *102*
2:2, *103*
2:3, *103*
2:3-4, *16*
2:4-5, *103*
2:5, *103*
2:6, *16, 99*
2:6-16, *98, 103*
2:9-12, *103*
2:10, *103*
2:11, *16*
2:12, *103*
2:13, *104*
2:13-16, *103*
2:16, *16*
3–4, *99, 104*
3:1, *104, 314*
3:1-2, *104*
3:1–4:13, *103*
3:2, *313*
3:3, *104*
3:3-8, *313*
3:4, *100, 104, 205, 325*
3:4-6, *104*

3:7, *37, 97, 105, 118, 313*
3:7-8, *97*
3:8, *37, 97, 99, 100, 104, 125, 313*
3:9, *104*
3:9-10, *104*
3:9–6:14, *99*
3:10, *16, 104*
3:11-12, *16*
3:11-14, *104*
3:13, *104*
3:13-15, *96*
3:15, *16*
4, *25*
4:1, *104*
4:1-2, *16*
4:1-12, *104*
4:2, *104, 106*
4:2-3, *104*
4:3, *16*
4:4-5, *95, 100, 104*
4:6, *16, 105*
4:6-11, *105, 117*
4:8, *16, 105*
4:9, *105*
4:9-11, *16*
4:10, *105*
4:11, *96, 105, 259*
4:12, *99, 105, 120*
4:13, *100, 105, 116, 117, 120, 121, 122, 123, 126, 320, 324*
5, *268*
5–6, *99*
5:1-17, *121*
5:1–6:14, *100, 105*
5:1–9:6, *99*
5:2, *105, 120*
5:3-4, *16*
5:3-17, *105*
5:4, *105, 240*
5:4-15, *120*
5:5, *105*
5:6, *105*
5:7, *105, 120*
5:8, *100, 116, 120, 121, 122, 123, 124, 320*
5:8-9, *121*
5:9, *122*
5:10, *105*
5:11, *105*

Scripture Index

5:12, *105*, *326*
5:14, *105*, *193*
5:14-15, *193*
5:15, *105*, *137*, *193*, *197*
5:16, *120*
5:16-17, *16*
5:17, *120*
5:18, *106*, *121*, *211*
5:18-20, *19*
5:18-27, *106*
5:20, *106*, *211*
5:21-26, *327*
5:22-23, *105*
5:24, *2*, *3*, *105*, *189*
5:25-26, *105*
5:27, *16*, *106*
6:1, *106*
6:1-7, *17*, *106*
6:2, *106*
6:3, *106*
6:4, *106*
6:5, *106*
6:6, *106*
6:7, *106*
6:8, *106*, *213*
6:8-11, *106*
6:10, *106*
6:11, *106*
6:12, *105*
6:14, *106*
7–9, *99*
7:1-3, *107*
7:1-7, *103*
7:1–9:6, *97*, *99*, *100*, *107*, *122*
7:1–9:15, *99*
7:4, *113*
7:4-6, *107*
7:7, *107*
7:7-8, *107*
7:7-9, *257*
7:8, *107*
7:10-17, *21*, *99*, *113*, *142*, *313*, *327*
7:11, *107*
7:12, *113*
7:14, *96*, *97*, *98*, *272*
7:14-15, *96*
7:14-17, *16*
7:15, *97*
7:16, *314*
7:17, *16*, *107*

8:1-2, *107*, *108*
8:2, *108*
8:3-14, *107*
8:4-6, *326*
8:5, *108*
8:7, *106*
8:8, *95*, *96*, *123*
8:9, *113*, *119*, *121*
8:11, *356*
8:11-12, *108*
9, *114*, *139*, *140*
9:1, *96*
9:1-4, *107*, *108*
9:1-5, *96*
9:3, *101*
9:5, *123*
9:5-6, *100*, *108*, *116*, *122*, *320*
9:6, *108*, *121*
9:7, *108*, *109*, *124*, *125*, *157*
9:7-8, *16*
9:7-10, *108*
9:7-15, *99*, *100*
9:8, *108*
9:8-10, *108*
9:9, *109*
9:10, *108*
9:11, *20*, *109*, *114*
9:11-12, *109*, *113*, *114*
9:11-15, *109*, *114*
9:12, *21*, *109*, *113*, *124*, *126*, *173*, *352*
9:13, *16*, *69*, *123*
9:13-14, *109*
9:14-15, *109*
9:15, *16*, *109*

Obadiah
1, *16*, *21*, *131*, *132*
1-15, *131*, *132*
1:15, *20*
2, *133*
2-4, *131*, *132*, *136*
2-15, *132*
3, *132*
4, *16*, *132*
5-6, *132*
5-7, *132*
5-14, *131*
6, *133*
7, *133*, *302*

7-8, *133*
7:10, *302*
7:12, *302*
8, *133*, *136*
9, *133*
10, *133*
10-14, *132*, *133*, *136*
11, *133*
12, *133*
12-14, *137*
13, *133*
14, *133*
15, *19*, *72*, *130*, *131*, *133*, *134*, *136*, *137*
15-16, *136*, *140*
16, *131*, *134*, *136*
16-20, *132*
16-21, *131*, *134*
17, *69*, *133*, *134*
17-18, *131*
17-21, *17*
18, *133*, *134*, *135*
19, *21*, *133*
19-21, *131*
21, *3*, *132*, *133*, *135*, *137*, *140*, *141*, *320*

Jonah
1, *162*
1–2, *145*, *147*, *148*
1:1, *142*, *145*, *146*, *148*, *162*
1:1-3, *147*, *148*
1:1-4, *148*
1:2, *146*, *149*, *153*
1:3, *146*, *149*, *153*, *155*
1:4, *146*, *148*, *349*
1:4-6, *147*, *149*
1:5, *146*, *149*, *150*, *151*
1:6, *146*, *151*
1:7-15, *146*
1:7–2:1, *147*, *150*
1:8, *154*
1:9, *149*, *150*, *320*
1:10, *151*, *349*
1:12, *151*
1:13, *151*
1:15, *151*
1:16, *146*, *151*, *152*
2, *145*, *146*, *147*, *157*, *161*, *165*, *166*, *343*
2:1, *148*, *151*, *340*

2:1-11, *146*
2:2, *150*, *151*, *165*, *167*
2:2-3, *151*
2:2-11, *146*, *147*, *151*
2:3, *165*, *167*, *169*
2:4, *149*, *167*, *168*, *169*, *254*, *316*
2:4-5, *167*
2:5, *152*, *167*, *168*, *169*
2:6, *154*, *168*, *169*
2:6-7, *152*, *168*
2:7, *149*, *152*, *168*, *169*, *316*
2:8, *147*, *152*, *168*, *169*
2:9, *168*, *169*
2:10, *152*, *167*, *169*
2:11, *152*, *168*
3–4, *145*, *152*, *169*
3:1, *145*, *146*, *148*
3:1-2, *152*
3:1-4, *148*, *152*
3:2, *146*, *153*
3:3, *152*, *153*
3:3-4, *146*
3:4, *142*, *146*, *153*
3:5, *146*
3:5-10, *148*, *153*
3:6-7, *144*
3:6-9, *146*
3:7-9, *320*
3:9, *19*, *70*
3:10, *74*, *75*, *146*, *154*
4, *145*, *146*, *147*, *155*, *168*
4:1, *146*, *154*
4:1-4, *145*, *148*, *154*
4:1-11, *145*
4:2, *21*, *70*, *74*, *75*, *77*, *147*, *155*, *325*
4:2-11, *146*
4:4, *145*, *155*
4:5-7, *145*, *148*, *155*
4:5-11, *145*
4:8, *154*
4:8-11, *145*, *148*, *155*
4:9, *145*, *154*, *155*
4:11, *3*, *73*, *153*, *154*, *155*, *158*, *160*

Micah
1, *172*
1–2, *174*

1–3, *173*, *187*
1:1, *40*, *172*, *174*
1:2, *174*
1:2-7, *16*, *174*
1:2–2:11, *173*
1:2–3:12, *173*
1:3, *118*, *119*, *174*
1:4, *174*
1:5, *173*, *174*, *175*
1:5-7, *186*
1:7, *175*
1:8, *175*
1:9, *175*
1:10, *193*
1:10-15, *175*
1:12, *184*
1:13, *173*
2, *175*
2–3, *181*, *189*
2:1, *17*, *175*
2:1-2, *186*, *200*
2:1-4, *16*
2:1-5, *175*, *176*, *198*, *201*
2:2, *172*, *175*
2:3, *16*
2:3-4, *175*
2:4, *19*, *176*
2:6, *176*, *314*
2:6-11, *175*
2:7, *176*
2:8, *176*
2:8-9, *186*
2:9, *176*
2:9-12, *16*
2:10, *176*
2:11, *314*
2:12, *173*, *174*, *176*, *179*, *183*
2:12-13, *17*, *173*, *174*, *175*, *176*
2:13, *17*, *176*
3, *177*, *327*
3:1, *176*, *177*
3:1-2, *176*
3:1-3, *175*, *176*, *186*
3:1-4, *16*, *176*
3:1-12, *173*
3:1–4:8, *176*
3:2, *193*
3:2-3, *176*
3:3, *187*

3:4, *176*
3:5, *16*, *176*, *177*, *314*
3:5-8, *176*
3:6, *177*
3:7, *177*
3:8, *177*, *186*, *193*
3:9, *176*, *177*
3:9-12, *173*, *175*, *176*, *186*
3:10, *176*, *177*, *204*, *228*
3:10-11, *190*
3:11, *176*, *177*
3:12, *177*
4, *180*
4–5, *173*, *185*, *188*
4:1, *177*, *185*
4:1-2, *130*, *177*
4:1-3, *172*, *318*
4:1-5, *3*, *17*, *185*
4:1-6, *180*, *183*
4:1-8, *173*, *174*, *177*
4:1-4, *177*
4:1–5:14, *173*
4:2, *180*, *273*
4:2-3, *178*, *352*
4:3, *70*, *78*, *178*
4:4, *178*, *260*
4:5, *178*
4:6, *16*, *178*, *180*, *185*
4:6-7, *178*
4:7, *173*, *174*, *178*, *179*
4:7-8, *178*
4:8, *20*, *178*
4:9, *178*, *185*
4:9-14, *173*
4:9–5:14, *178*
4:10, *179*, *321*
4:10–5:14, *179*
4:11, *179*, *185*
4:11-13, *172*
4:12, *179*
4:13, *179*
4:14, *185*
4:14–5:5, *179*, *344*
5, *180*, *185*
5:1, *10*, *179*, *187*, *343*, *344*, *345*, *346*, *349*
5:1-4, *185*
5:1-5, *183*
5:1-8, *17*
5:1-14, *173*, *174*

5:2, *178*
5:3, *20*, *179*, *185*, *188*, *344*, *345*
5:4, *188*, *345*
5:6, *180*
5:6-7, *174*, *179*, *180*
5:7, *180*, *205*
5:7-8, *173*
5:8, *180*, *325*
5:9, *16*, *180*, *185*
5:9-11, *181*
5:9-13, *172*
5:9-14, *180*
5:10, *180*
5:11, *180*
5:12, *180*
5:13, *180*
5:14, *180*
6, *175*, *189*, *194*, *326*, *339*
6–7, *181*
6:1, *181*
6:1-5, *190*
6:1-8, *181*, *189*, *197*
6:1–7:6, *173*
6:1–7:7, *173*, *189*
6:1–7:20, *173*
6:2, *190*, *326*
6:3, *190*
6:3-5, *196*
6:4, *314*
6:4-5, *190*, *196*, *197*
6:5, *190*
6:6, *191*, *193*, *194*
6:6-7, *190*, *193*, *194*, *197*
6:6-8, *17*, *189*, *197*, *268*
6:7, *192*, *193*
6:8, *2*, *3*, *186*, *187*, *192*, *193*, *194*, *195*, *197*, *198*, *240*, *268*
6:9, *181*, *186*, *320*
6:9-16, *16*, *173*, *175*, *186*, *198*
6:10, *181*
6:10-12, *182*
6:10-16, *181*
6:11, *181*
6:12, *181*
6:13, *181*
6:14, *181*, *182*
6:14-15, *181*

6:15, *182*
6:16, *182*
7, *182*, *185*, *187*, *339*
7:1-6, *182*
7:2-3, *186*
7:6, *187*, *338*, *339*, *350*
7:7, *182*, *186*, *242*
7:7-20, *174*
7:8, *183*
7:8-10, *182*, *183*
7:9, *183*
7:10, *183*
7:11-13, *183*
7:14, *183*, *185*
7:15, *183*
7:15-17, *183*
7:16-17, *183*
7:17, *183*
7:18, *173*, *174*, *184*, *325*
7:18-19, *21*, *183*
7:18-20, *19*, *74*, *75*, *186*
7:19, *184*, *254*
7:20, *183*

Nahum
1, *17*, *202*, *203*
1:1, *16*, *21*, *202*, *203*, *303*
1:2, *203*
1:2-3, *19*, *21*, *74*, *217*
1:2-8, *203*, *204*, *216*
1:2-10, *203*
1:2–2:1, *203*
1:3, *74*, *75*, *155*, *204*
1:5, *123*
1:6, *81*, *204*
1:7, *204*
1:11, *215*
1:12, *16*
1:12-13, *215*
1:12-15, *17*, *204*
1:14, *215*, *313*
1:15, *216*
2:1, *204*, *205*, *220*
2:1-13, *205*
2:2, *205*, *216*
2:2–3:19, *203*
2:3, *20*, *205*
2:4-7, *205*

Scripture Index   385

2:4-14, *205*
2:7, *205*
2:8-14, *205*
2:9-11, *205*
2:10, *205*
2:11, *205*
2:12-13, *205*
2:14, *205, 206*
3:1, *204, 215*
3:1-7, *202*
3:1-19, *206*
3:4, *215, 220, 221*
3:5, *206, 313*
3:5-6, *206*
3:8-9, *206*
3:8-10, *202*
3:15-17, *206*
3:18, *202, 206*
3:18-19, *202*
3:19, *206*

Habakkuk
1:1, *16, 21, 223, 224, 303*
1:1–2:1, *225*
1:2, *225, 226, 323*
1:2-4, *225, 230*
1:2-41, *224*
1:2–2:3, *233*
1:3, *225*
1:4, *225, 226*
1:5, *226, 229*
1:5-11, *202, 225, 226, 227*
1:5-111, *224*
1:6, *226*
1:7, *226*
1:9, *226*
1:12, *226, 246, 323*
1:12-14, *226*
1:12-17, *224, 226, 237, 238, 239*
1:12–2:1, *225*
1:14, *232, 237*
1:15-17, *226*
1:16-17, *228*
1:17, *226*
2, *227, 228, 239*
2:1, *17, 223, 227*
2:1-2, *247*
2:2, *227, 231, 236, 237, 239, 240, 313*

2:2-3, *239, 240, 242, 243, 244, 246, 247*
2:2-4, *89, 231, 246*
2:2-5, *227, 237*
2:2-19, *229*
2:2-20, *225, 226, 227*
2:2-202, *224*
2:3, *227, 238, 240, 243, 244*
2:3-4, *243, 248*
2:3-5, *231*
2:4, *227, 228, 230, 231, 239, 240, 241, 242, 243, 244, 245, 246, 247, 248*
2:4-5, *239*
2:4-20, *239*
2:4–3:19, *233*
2:5-19, *240*
2:5-20, *240, 242*
2:6-8, *228*
2:6-17, *228*
2:6-20, *3, 17, 227, 237, 239*
2:8, *229*
2:9-11, *228*
2:12, *224, 228*
2:12-14, *228*
2:13, *228*
2:14, *228, 329*
2:15-17, *229*
2:17, *228, 229*
2:18-19, *228*
2:18-20, *229*
2:20, *21, 106, 209, 227, 229, 240, 258, 329, 354*
3, *17, 202, 225, 233, 234, 239*
3:1, *223, 224, 229*
3:1-19, *229*
3:2, *224, 229*
3:3, *323*
3:3-15, *224, 229*
3:13, *17, 229*
3:16, *19, 232, 242*
3:16-19, *224*
3:17, *233*
3:18, *229, 233*
3:19, *224, 229, 230*

Zephaniah
1:1, *40, 207, 208*
1:2-3, *16, 207, 208*
1:2-17, *210*
1:2-18, *207, 216*
1:2–2:3, *208*
1:3, *211*
1:4, *207, 208, 209*
1:4-6, *208, 209*
1:4-13, *207*
1:5, *207, 209*
1:5-6, *209*
1:6, *209*
1:7, *21, 72, 209, 210, 215, 258, 329, 365*
1:7-8, *210*
1:7-16, *19*
1:8, *207*
1:10, *16, 211*
1:10-13, *210*
1:11, *207*
1:12, *210, 365*
1:14, *72, 211, 365*
1:14-18, *207, 210*
1:15, *73, 211*
1:15-16, *211*
1:16, *211*
1:17, *211, 365*
1:18, *211, 365*
2, *207*
2:1, *211, 212*
2:1-2, *211, 212*
2:1-3, *207, 211*
2:1-316, *207*
2:2, *211*
2:2-3, *207*
2:3, *196, 207, 212, 213, 214*
2:4, *213*
2:4-7, *207, 213*
2:4-15, *207, 213, 214, 216*
2:7, *20*
2:7-9, *173*
2:8-9, *213*
2:8-11, *16, 207, 213*
2:9, *213*
2:10, *20, 213*
2:12, *207, 213*
2:12-15, *213*
2:13, *202*
2:13-15, *207, 213*

2:15, *213, 214*
3, *25, 213*
3:1, *17*
3:1-2, *214*
3:1-5, *213*
3:1-8, *213*
3:1-20, *207, 213*
3:2, *214*
3:3, *205, 207, 214*
3:3-5, *214*
3:4, *207, 214, 314*
3:5, *214*
3:7, *214*
3:8, *16, 242*
3:9, *214, 216, 220*
3:9-13, *216*
3:9-20, *208, 213*
3:11, *214*
3:12, *214, 216, 222*
3:13, *214, 215, 216, 220, 349*
3:14, *215, 284*
3:14-20, *17, 215, 220*
3:15, *17, 215, 216, 220*
3:16, *296*
3:17, *220*
3:18, *215*
3:20, *20*

Haggai
1–2, *299*
1–9, *295*
1:1, *259, 292, 293, 294*
1:1-11, *16, 293, 294*
1:2, *16, 294*
1:2-4, *299*
1:4, *294*
1:5, *16, 294*
1:5-11, *319*
1:6, *294*
1:7, *16, 294*
1:8, *294, 299*
1:9, *294, 299*
1:10, *294*
1:12, *259, 295*
1:12-13, *295*
1:12-14, *173*
1:12-15, *293, 295*
1:13, *16, 292, 293, 295*
1:14, *259, 295, 299*
1:15, *292, 293, 295, 297*
2, *295*

2:1, *292, 293, 295, 297*
2:1-9, *293, 295*
2:2, *173, 259*
2:3, *295*
2:4, *16, 259, 296*
2:4-5, *296*
2:4-8, *17*
2:5, *296, 314, 331*
2:6, *16, 300*
2:6-7, *296*
2:6-8, *299*
2:6-9, *296*
2:7, *302, 322*
2:8, *296*
2:9, *292, 293, 297*
2:10, *292, 293, 297*
2:10-19, *293, 297, 299*
2:11, *16*
2:11-12, *298*
2:11-13, *17*
2:12, *295*
2:13, *295*
2:13-14, *298*
2:14, *16, 298, 299*
2:15, *298*
2:17, *16*
2:18, *292, 293, 298*
2:19, *295, 299*
2:20, *292, 293*
2:20-23, *17, 293, 298, 300*
2:21, *299, 300*
2:21-22, *130*
2:22, *302*
2:23, *16, 19*

Zechariah
1–6, *250, 253, 265, 267, 268, 279, 283*
1–8, *21, 22, 249, 250, 253, 254, 257, 258, 260, 262, 263, 265, 274, 275, 276, 284, 285, 297, 303*
1:1, *249, 250, 251, 266, 267*
1:1-6, *250, 251, 253, 255, 266, 279*
1:2, *251, 252*
1:2-6, *252*
1:3, *252, 253, 276, 306*
1:3-4, *16*
1:4, *16, 252*

1:4-5, *252*
1:6, *252, 253*
1:7, *249, 250, 253, 266, 267*
1:7-17, *250, 253, 264*
1:7–6:15, *250, 253, 266*
1:8, *253, 254*
1:9, *256*
1:10, *255*
1:12, *278*
1:14, *16, 255, 258, 268*
1:16, *254, 255, 257, 268*
1:16-17, *16*
1:17, *255*
2, *275*
2:1-4, *256*
2:3, *257*
2:5, *257, 278*
2:5-6, *257*
2:5-17, *251, 257*
2:7, *257*
2:8, *258*
2:9, *16*
2:10, *256, 258, 264*
2:11, *352*
2:12, *16*
2:12-13, *257*
2:14, *257, 274, 284*
2:15, *257*
2:16, *259*
2:17, *257, 329*
3, *273*
3–4, *294*
3:1, *258, 278*
3:1-2, *259*
3:1-10, *251, 258*
3:2, *259*
3:3-5, *259*
3:4, *269*
3:5, *259, 274*
3:6-7, *259*
3:6-10, *259*
3:7, *260*
3:8, *259, 260*
3:8-9, *260*
3:9, *259, 260*
3:10, *260*
4–5, *275*
4:1, *253*
4:1-14, *251, 261*
4:2, *259, 260, 278*
4:4, *261*

4:6, *331*
4:7, *261*
4:10, *259, 260, 263, 278*
4:11-12, *261, 278*
4:14, *261, 262*
5:1-3, *280*
5:1-4, *251, 262, 326*
5:3, *262*
5:4, *263*
5:5-6, *263*
5:5-11, *251, 263*
5:6, *263*
5:8, *263*
6, *331*
6:1, *256*
6:1-8, *264*
6:1-15, *251, 264*
6:5, *256, 278*
6:8, *264*
6:9-15, *264, 294*
6:10, *264*
6:11, *259*
6:12, *10, 265, 277, 288*
7, *303*
7–8, *267*
7–14, *251, 265*
7:1, *250, 266, 267*
7:1–8:23, *251*
7:1–14:21, *266, 267*
7:2, *267*
7:3, *268*
7:4, *266, 268*
7:4-7, *268*
7:7, *268*
7:8, *266, 267*
7:8-14, *16, 268*
7:8–14:21, *268*
7:9, *268*
7:12, *268*
8:1, *266, 267*
8:1-23, *268*
8:2, *268*
8:4, *268*
8:5, *269*
8:6-12, *173*
8:9, *268*
8:11-12, *137*
8:12, *269*
8:13, *268, 269*
8:14-15, *268*
8:16, *268*
8:17, *263*

8:18, *266*
8:19, *268*
8:20-23, *17, 269*
8:22-23, *352*
8:286, *262*
9, *269, 282, 284, 289, 346*
9–11, *251, 267, 269, 282*
9–14, *225, 251, 265, 266, 267, 269, 270, 272, 273, 274, 276, 279, 282, 283, 284, 285, 286, 291, 303*
9:1, *16, 269, 282, 283*
9:1-6, *269*
9:1-7, *284*
9:1-8, *251, 269, 282, 283*
9:6, *213*
9:6-7, *274*
9:7, *269*
9:7-8, *284*
9:8, *283*
9:9, *17, 265, 270, 274, 276, 277, 284, 285, 287, 288, 289, 290, 343, 346, 352*
9:9-10, *282, 283, 284, 286, 287, 288*
9:9-13, *265, 352*
9:9-17, *17, 251, 269*
9:10, *270, 285, 286*
9:11, *269*
9:11-17, *283*
9:12, *249, 269*
9:13, *270*
9:14, *283*
9:14-16, *283*
9:14-17, *270*
9:15, *270*
9:16, *265, 282*
9:17, *282*
10, *282*
10:1, *270, 271, 279, 282*
10:1-12, *251, 270*
10:2, *270*
10:3, *270, 271, 272, 282*
10:3-6, *270*
10:4, *265*
10:5, *270*
10:7-12, *270*

Scripture Index

10:9, *247*
10:10, *270, 271*
10:11, *203, 213, 254, 270*
10:12, *270*
11, *272*
11:1-3, *271*
11:1-17, *251, 271*
11:3, *205*
11:4, *271*
11:4-5, *271*
11:4-17, *269, 276, 347*
11:7-8, *271*
11:12-13, *276, 347*
11:13, *343, 347*
11:17, *17, 271*
12, *269, 271, 320, 348*
12–14, *251, 267*
12:1, *16, 269, 271, 279*
12:1-14, *251*
12:2, *271, 280*
12:3, *271*
12:6, *271*
12:8, *272*
12:9, *271*
12:10, *265, 290, 331, 348*
12:10-14, *272, 348*
13, *278, 314, 341, 342*
13:1, *274*
13:1-6, *251, 272*
13:2-6, *272, 341*
13:2-9, *341*
13:5, *272*
13:7, *278, 341*
13:7-9, *251, 272*
13:8, *341*
13:9, *341*
14, *265, 269, 272, 278*
14:1, *272*
14:1-21, *251*
14:2, *272*
14:3-4, *273*
14:4, *272, 287*
14:5, *95, 273, 323*
14:5-11, *332*
14:6, *272*
14:6-11, *273*
14:7, *272, 278*
14:8, *265, 272, 348, 349*
14:9, *17, 272, 273, 277, 278*

14:12-15, *272*
14:13, *272*
14:15, *272*
14:16-20, *265*
14:16-21, *274*
14:17, *17*
14:20, *272*
14:20-21, *273, 277*
14:21, *272, 274, 278, 349*

Malachi
1, *25*
1–2, *305*
1:1, *16, 303*
1:2, *16, 303*
1:2-3, *304, 310*
1:2-5, *303, 308*
1:4, *16*
1:6, *304, 305, 307*
1:6-8, *309*
1:6-9, *304*
1:6-13, *309*
1:6-14, *308*
1:6–2:9, *303, 304*
1:7, *304, 309, 310*
1:8, *304*
1:9, *74*
1:10, *304*
1:10-14, *304*
1:11, *130, 307*
1:12, *309, 310*
1:14, *305, 307, 308*
2, *349*
2:1-9, *304, 305*
2:3, *305*
2:5, *307*
2:7, *209*
2:9, *305*
2:10, *349*
2:10-17, *303, 305, 309*
2:11, *305*
2:11-17, *305*
2:13, *305*
2:14, *305*
2:14-16, *305*
2:15, *305*
2:17, *305, 308*
3:1, *301, 306, 309, 339, 340, 349, 353*
3:1-7, *302, 303, 306*
3:2, *306*

3:2-4, *306, 309*
3:4, *306*
3:5, *306*
3:6-7, *306*
3:7, *20, 309*
3:8-12, *302, 303, 306*
3:10, *306*
3:13-21, *303, 306*
3:14, *306*
3:14-16, *309*
3:16, *307*
3:17, *307*
3:17-18, *309*
3:19, *307*
3:20, *307*
3:21, *307*
3:22, *307*
3:22-23, *339*
3:22-24, *303, 307*
3:23, *73, 310, 340, 349*
3:23-24, *307, 357*
4:1, *19*
4:4, *326*

APOCRYPHA

Sirach
49:10, *21*

NEW TESTAMENT

Matthew
1, *345*
1:1-17, *344*
1:18, *344*
1:18–2:23, *344*
1:22, *343, 344*
2, *344*
2:1, *345*
2:5, *345*
2:5-6, *343*
2:6, *187, 335, 344, 345*
2:13-23, *346*
2:15, *52, 335, 343, 344, 346*
2:17, *343*
2:23, *343*
3:11, *113*
4:14, *343*
5–7, *329*
5:6, *114*
5:45, *270*

6:10, *86, 114, 234*
6:13, *86*
8:17, *343*
9, *336, 337, 338*
9:9-13, *337*
9:13, *54, 335, 336*
10, *338, 339, 350*
10:5-6, *350*
10:7, *339*
10:35-36, *187, 335, 338, 350*
11:10, *309, 335, 339*
11:14, *310, 340*
12, *338*
12:6, *338*
12:7, *54, 335, 336*
12:8, *338*
12:17, *343*
12:22-23, *340*
12:25-37, *340*
12:38, *159*
12:38-42, *159*
12:40, *335, 340*
12:41, *341*
13:35, *343*
14–28, *287*
16:4, *159*
16:24-25, *248*
17:10-12, *310*
21, *287, 288, 289*
21:1, *287*
21:1-11, *352*
21:1-22, *277, 287*
21:2, *287*
21:4, *343*
21:5, *277, 287, 288, 335, 344, 346*
21:10, *289*
21:11, *289*
21:43, *199*
23:35, *278*
24:29-31, *91*
26:3, *335*
26:15, *276*
26:31, *277, 335, 341, 342*
27:9, *343*
27:9-10, *276, 335, 344, 347*
27:45, *113*
27:51, *290*
28:18, *346*

Mark
1:2, *309, 310, 339*
4:35-41, *349*
9:11-13, *310, 339*
10:45, *342*
11:1-11, *352*
11:1-25, *277, 287*
11:16, *277*
12:35-37, *352*
13:27, *352*
14:27, *341*
15:33, *113*

Luke
1:16-17, *310*
1:17, *310*
7:24-30, *339*
7:27, *309*
9:23, *235*
10:27, *195*
11:29-32, *159, 340*
12:53, *187*
13:31, *113*
17, *91*
17:22-26, *91*
18:1-8, *225*
19:28-48, *277, 287*
19:42, *342*
23:30, *342*
23:31, *342*
23:44, *113*
24:50-51, *287*

John
1:21, *349*
1:47, *349*
2:13-17, *277*
2:16, *349*
3:28, *349*
7:38, *348, 349*
7:42, *349*
8:41, *349*
12, *346*
12:12-19, *277, 287*
12:15, *346*

12:32, *290*
15:15, *1*
17:3, *66*
19:37, *348*

Acts
1:11-12, *287*
2, *80, 91, 351*
2:17, *80*
2:17-21, *80*
15, *115*
15:16-17, *113*
15:16-18, *109*
15:17-18, *113*
16:20, *113*
17:31, *91*

Romans
1:16, *231*
1:16-17, *231*
1:17, *230, 231, 240, 244*
1:28, *50*
5:2-4, *233*
9, *52*
9:4, *118*
9:13, *310*
10:15, *220*
12:1-2, *369*
12:12, *233*
12:19, *141*

1 Corinthians
1:2, *79*
1:8, *90*
10:21, *310*
15:3-5, *9*

2 Corinthians
1:4-5, *235*
4:7, *234*
4:17, *233*
5:19-21, *52*

Galatians
2:19-20, *248*
2:20, *230*

3, *230*
3:11, *230, 232, 240*

Ephesians
1, *364*
2:19, *199*

Philippians
1:10, *90*
2:16, *90*
3:10, *233*
3:20-21, *91*

Colossians
1:15-20, *199*
1:24, *233*

1 Thessalonians
1:10, *91*
5:2, *90*

2 Timothy
1:12, *233*
2, *91*
4:1, *91*

Hebrews
1:2, *357*
1:3, *157*
10:37, *231*
10:38, *231*
12, *300*
12:18-21, *300*
12:18-25, *301*
12:22-25, *300*
12:24, *301*
12:25, *300, 301*
12:25-29, *300*
12:26, *300, 301*

James
1:2, *233*
4:8, *276*
5:7-10, *233*

1 Peter
1:6-9, *233*
2:10, *52*
3:8-22, *233*
3:15, *157*
4:1-19, *233*

2 Peter
3, *91*
3:10, *90*

1 John
4:8, *65*

Revelation
1:7, *348*
1:12, *278*
2:4, *67*
3:3, *90*
4:5, *278*
5:6, *278*
6, *81*
6:10, *278*
6:12, *80*
6:12-17, *80*
6:16, *80*
6:17, *81*
7:1, *278*
9, *81*
9:7-9, *81*
11:1, *278*
11:4, *278*
11:15, *140, 320*
12:10, *278*
14:4, *81*
14:5, *220*
14:14-20, *81*
16:15, *90*
17:2, *220*
21:5, *352*
21:15, *278*
21:25, *278*
22:20, *234*

A Theological Introduction series

Old Testament Wisdom Literature
978-0-8308-5218-5

Finding the Textbook You Need

The IVP Academic Textbook Selector
is an online tool for instantly finding the IVP books
suitable for over 250 courses across 24 disciplines.

ivpacademic.com